Macroeconomic Policies in an Interdependent World

Edited by

Ralph C. Bryant
David A. Currie
Jacob A. Frenkel
Paul R. Masson
Richard Portes

 The Brookings Institution

 Centre for Economic Policy Research

 International Monetary Fund

Library of Congress Cataloging-in-Publication Data

Macroeconomic policies in an interdependent world / edited by Ralph C. Bryant . . . [et al.].
    p. cm.
    Papers from a conference held at the Brookings Institution in Dec. 1988, sponsored by the institution, the International Monetary Fund, and the Centre for Economic Policy Research.
    ISBN 1-55775-111-0 (Centre for Economic Policy Research)
    1. International economic relations—Congresses. 2. Economic policy—Congresses. 3. Macroeconomics—Congresses. I. Bryant, Ralph C., 1938–
II. Brookings Institution. III. International Monetary Fund. IV. Centre for Economic Policy Research (Great Britain)
HF 1352.M34   1989
339.5—dc20   89-24417
                                                           CIP

Price: US$17.50

Contents

Preface

This collection of essays is a joint publication of the International Monetary Fund, The Brookings Institution, and the Centre for Economic Policy Research (CEPR). Each essay focuses on some aspect of international economic interdependence, and the book itself is the result of an international collaboration in the production and dissemination of economic research.

During the four and a half decades since the establishment of the International Monetary Fund, its staff has been a leading contributor to the development of knowledge about the functioning of the world economy and about the effects of national economic policies. In recent years, the Fund staff has been actively cooperating with a variety of individuals and institutions in member countries to present and evaluate international macroeconomic research. Since its establishment in 1983, the Centre for Economic Policy Research has promoted the independent analysis and public discussion of open economies and the relations among them. And The Brookings Institution, as an integral part of its effort to aid in the development of sound public policies and to promote public understanding of important policy issues, has a long-standing commitment to research in international economics.

Beginning in 1985, CEPR and Brookings launched a three-year joint research program to further the study of macroeconomic interactions and policy design in interdependent economies. Financial support for this research was generously provided by the Ford Foundation and the Alfred P. Sloan Foundation. To conclude the joint CEPR/Brookings program, policymakers and academic researchers were gathered to assess the major issues of international macroeconomic interdependence and policy design. Given the research activities of the Fund staff, the Fund was asked to join forces with Brookings and CEPR in organizing a conference to foster this assessment. These collaborations resulted in the conference on macroeconomic policies held at The Brookings Institution in December 1988. The essays and discussant comments contained in this volume are revised and edited versions of the papers and comments presented at that conference.

The editors were jointly responsible for organizing the December 1988 conference and for overseeing the preparation of this volume. Ralph C. Bryant is a Senior Fellow in the Economic Studies program at Brookings. David Currie is Professor of Economics at the London Business School and was Co-Director of CEPR's International Macroeconomics Programme during 1985–88. Jacob A. Frenkel is the Economic Counsellor and Director of the Research Department at the International Monetary Fund. Paul R. Masson is an Advisor in the Fund's Research Department. Richard Portes is the Director of the Centre for Economic Policy Research and Professor of Economics at Birkbeck College, London.

Numerous individuals provided crucial assistance in the organization of the conference and the preparation of this book. Special acknowledgment is due David M. Cheney of the External Relations Department of the International Monetary Fund, who ably supervised and coordinated the many tasks of editing and production. We would also like to thank Hernan Puentes, also of the IMF External Relations Department, for helping with the organization of the conference. Evelyn M. E. Taylor, Boban Mathew, and Kenneth P. Pucker provided administrative and research assistance at The Brookings Institution. Support at the Centre for Economic Policy Research was coordinated by Stephen Yeo.

Ralph C. Bryant
David A. Currie
Jacob A. Frenkel
Paul R. Masson
Richard Portes
August 1989

Introduction

Ralph C. Bryant, David A. Currie, Jacob A. Frenkel,
Paul R. Masson, and Richard Portes

International macroeconomic policy coordination is high on the agenda for debate among policymakers and academic economists. Since 1985, officials of the Group of Seven industrial countries have met periodically to examine world macroeconomic developments and to coordinate their policies. Particularly marked has been the cooperation between Group of Seven central banks on exchange-market intervention. Starting with the Plaza Agreement of September 1985, followed by the Tokyo Summit of May 1986, the Louvre Accord of February 1987, and in more recent meetings, finance ministers have been increasingly concerned with developing a framework for coordination. This has led to a focus, during multilateral discussions, on a series of economic indicators that provide appropriate signals for the conduct of monetary, exchange rate, and fiscal policies. The International Monetary Fund has been actively involved in this process, both through the participation of the Managing Director of the IMF in Group of Seven meetings and through its use of indicators in bilateral and multilateral surveillance over the policies of industrial countries.

The heightened attention paid by policymakers to international policy coordination was anticipated in large degree by the academic research community. Consequently, policymakers had a considerable body of research to draw on. The early analytical work of Koichi Hamada and Richard Cooper began the theoretical literature, and in the 1980s, this work was extended to the area of policy coordination in dynamic economic models. Empirical evidence for the need for coordination—which arises because of economic interdependence—has also been extended.

Some major theoretical advances were presented at a conference held in 1984 by the Centre for Economic Policy Research and the National Bureau of Economic Research on the subject of *International Economic Policy Coordination* (published in 1985 in a book by that name, edited by Willem Buiter and Richard Marston). Further progress was made in a Centre for Economic Policy Research conference volume, *Global Macroeconomics* (edited by Ralph Bryant and Richard Portes, 1988). Evidence from empirical multicountry models was the topic of a conference sponsored by The Brookings Institution in 1986, whose proceedings were published as *Empirical Macroeconomics for Independent Economies* (edited by Ralph Bryant and others, 1988). Other research in this area has also been sponsored by Brookings and the CEPR, as well as by the IMF, which has continued to conduct research on international interdependence (including the construction of a multiregion model, MULTI-

MOD) and on policy coordination.

Recent theoretical and empirical research has covered several areas. *First*, studies have examined the nature of spillover effects among different regions of the world economy, concentrating on linkages between the Group of Seven countries. (Linkages between the developed and less developed regions of the world economy have received far less attention.) *Second*, there have been evaluations of different economic policies (whether coordinated or not) in the context of empirical models that take account of the interdependencies among different regions of the global economy. An important aspect of this research has been concerned with the performance of different exchange rate regimes. *Third*, there has been a growing literature on the welfare implications of policy coordination and on the difficulties involved in coordinating macroeconomic policies, resulting from imperfect information and incomplete credibility. Attention has also been directed to the practical and institutional problems of policy coordination, including the experience of exchange rate systems such as the European Monetary System (EMS), and the role that international institutions could play in the implementation and surveillance of policy coordination.

Against this background, the International Monetary Fund joined forces with The Brookings Institution and the Centre for Economic Policy Research to organize an international conference among policymakers and academic researchers to assess where we stand on questions of international macroeconomic interdependence and policy. The conference on "Macroeconomic Policies in an Interdependent World" was held at The Brookings Institution, Washington, D.C., on December 12–13, 1988.

The papers in this volume cover a range of issues concerned with macroeconomic interdependence and policymaking. The volume begins with two broad surveys: the first gives an overview of the issues involved in international coordination of economic policies and considers the benefits to be gained from coordination; the second surveys empirical evidence on macroeconomic interactions in the world economy. These are followed by a group of papers that evaluate alternative rules or regimes for the international macroeconomy, using empirical multicountry macromodels. The volume then turns to studies concerned with more specific policy issues: the target zone proposal; the European Monetary System as a possible example for the international economy; and plans for a European central bank. A subsequent paper examines more general institutional questions concerned with policy coordination and the role of international organizations in the process. And the final paper takes up a neglected but important issue: macroeconomic interdependence between industrial and developing countries, and the implications of these interactions for international policy coordination.

In the paragraphs that follow, we briefly identify some main points made in each of the papers and indicate some reactions contained in the discussants' comments.

Issues of Interdependence and Coordination

The first paper of the volume is "The Theory and Practice of International Policy Coordination: Does Coordination Pay?", by David A. Currie, Gerald Holtham, and Andrew Hughes Hallett. It provides a broad overview of the issues pertinent to policy coordination, many of which are considered in more detail later in the volume. The authors' account of the recent historical experience of policy coordination distinguishes between absolute and relative policy coordination. The former is directed toward the overall stance of policy in all the main industrial countries; it would try to counteract shocks to the world economy as a whole. Relative policy coordination, in contrast, is concerned with the interactions between countries and tends to focus on exchange rates and balances of payments. Messrs. Currie, Holtham, and Hughes Hallett argue that relative coordination was the chief concern during the Bretton Woods era, except insofar as the adequacy of aggregate world liquidity was addressed. Furthermore, the recent resurgence in policymakers' interest in policy coordination appears to have been motivated by a perceived need for relative coordination following the U.S. fiscal expansion in the early 1980s and the large current account imbalances that resulted.

Currie, Holtham, and Hughes Hallett describe the conclusions of economic analysis on the potential payoffs from coordination. They outline a number of possible levels of intergovernmental cooperation, ranging from information exchange to full policy coordination across all policy targets and instruments. The gains to be achieved depend on the degree of cooperation adopted; they accrue from a number of different sources and not solely from coordination proper. Even limited cooperation in terms of information exchanges may bring substantial gains in terms of more efficient "noncooperative" policies. Additional gains may derive from the use of "shared targets," such as the exchange rate or other intermediate targets, and of common simple policy rules. Such gains may not be realized, however, if cooperative policies encounter problems of unsustainability, lack of credibility, imperfect information, and uncertainty over objectives and the functioning of the economy. Three of the authors' conclusions merit special attention. First, information exchange is an important part of the process of intergovernmental cooperation insofar as it improves the quality of "noncooperative" outcomes (outcomes reached without coordination proper). Second, the adoption of a rule-based system of coordination may lead to benefits in terms of credibility and reputation, especially if it is based on simple and robust rules. Third, exchange rate agreements may be an important vehicle for policy cooperation because they may prevent inappropriate monetary and fiscal policies.

Vito Tanzi's discussion points out that the gap between the rhetoric and practice of policy coordination may have been narrowed because officials have aimed at the less demanding goal of "relative" coordination. Global demand management, in Tanzi's view, is not a realistic aim. Tanzi does not believe that reneging on agreements is a problem. Sustainability is more likely to be impaired by policymakers' inability to achieve total control over their policy targets and by a lack of political continuity. He sees precommitment to fiscal policy as more difficult than agreements on monetary policy and intervention in exchange markets. Tanzi points out that coordination is impaired by the unreliability of forecasts, especially if policies take a long time to implement.

Jeffrey Frankel's comments stress uncertainty as the main obstacle to coordination. Each country considering participation in a coordination agreement must believe that it stands to gain, ex post, in most states of the world. Commitment to an intermediate target may be bad, ex post, because of the different shocks impinging on the system. But in Frankel's view, adopting an intermediate target may be advantageous for policymakers in helping them gain reputation. A policy rule involving an intermediate target should be robust across a whole range of possible shocks, and Frankel disagrees with the authors' contention that the exchange rate is a good target, arguing instead that the main candidate should be nominal gross domestic product.

The second paper of the volume, entitled "Domestic and Cross-Border Consequences of U.S. Macroeconomic Policies," by Ralph C. Bryant, John F. Helliwell, and Peter Hooper, provides an overview of the available empirical evidence about macroeconomic interactions between the United States and the rest of the world. The authors present evidence from simulations generated by a number of global macroeconometric models to yield evidence on the effects of changes in fiscal and monetary policy in the United States. They calculate averages and standard deviations of the effects obtained with the various models. Though the effects predicted by different models for particular U.S. fiscal and monetary actions differ considerably, the authors argue that careful use of the model-average effects and their standard deviations can prove useful as guides to policy. They reach a number of conclusions. First, an unanticipated cut in U.S. government expenditure would have a substantial negative impact on U.S. output, prices, interest rates, and the exchange value of the dollar; such a cut would also reduce the U.S. trade deficit, over a six-year horizon (although output would be recovering by the end of this six-year period). Second, if it were judged desirable, a temporary expansion in U.S. monetary policy could offset some of the negative effect on U.S. output caused by the fiscal contraction; U.S. monetary expansion, however, would not offset any negative impact on foreign output. Third, if a U.S. fiscal contraction were anticipated and credible, it could bring forward the decline in interest rates and the U.S. dollar, offsetting some of the output reduction that would occur from an unanticipated fiscal contraction. Fourth, alternative types of fiscal actions that have equivalent effects on the fiscal deficit have different effects on major macroeconomic variables, depending on the specific fiscal action chosen: for example, increases in excise and corporate taxes could have a more damaging long-run effect on output than increases of equivalent size in personal taxes or comparable reductions in transfers. In their policy conclusions, the authors favor the announcement of a gradual and credible U.S. fiscal retrenchment incorporating personal tax increases or transfer decreases.

Haruhiko Kuroda argues in his comment that a U.S. fiscal deflation might, by reducing the U.S. current account deficit and increasing confidence in the U.S. economy, actually lead to an appreciation of the dollar by attracting foreign capital. He also constructs, using the model-average estimates presented by Bryant and others, a U.S. fiscal package composed of expenditure cuts and increases in transfers that, taken literally, could reduce the U.S. budget and current account deficits without any output loss—in fact, he argues, U.S. output would be higher! Kuroda's use of the illustrative estimates in the paper underlines the need for caution in translating such estimates directly into policy prescriptions.

David Begg points out that the authors do not deal with issues of policy coordination, but only with specific U.S. policies. Ignoring policy interactions among countries, he argues, may bias the results. Begg also notes that the horizon over which the models were simulated (five to six years) was longer than the typical political horizon, which might be inconsistent with the importance of credibility in the analysis. Finally, Begg suggests that, in evaluating the output effects of different taxation policies, policymakers may be just as interested in the composition of output as in the total.

Evaluating Alternative Policy Rules and Regimes

The next three papers use a specific international macromodel to evaluate alternative rules or regimes for the international economy.

"Policy Analysis with a Multicountry Model," by John B. Taylor, examines the properties of alternative monetary policy rules under different exchange rate regimes. Using the estimated multicountry model that he has constructed, Taylor assesses alternative choices of targets for simple feedback interest rate rules. He assumes nominal wages to be sticky and to adjust according to a standard contracts model. Output in each region converges in the long run to the exogenous level of potential output; fiscal policy is also exogenous, so monetary policy is the only effective instrument of stabilization policy. The model features time-varying risk premia in both the uncovered interest parity condition and the long-short interest rate differential, with forward-looking behavior in many behavioral relationships.

Taylor conducts his policy evaluations in the light of the actual shocks to the world economy during 1972–86. Given the statistical properties of the shocks experienced in the past, he uses stochastic simulation techniques to examine the possible behavior of future outcomes under similar patterns for the shocks. Taylor concludes that a flexible exchange rate system performs better than a fixed exchange rate system in terms of stabilizing domestic price and output levels in the Group of Three countries. This result holds even with the imposition of Taylor's assumption that a fixed exchange rate regime will have beneficial effects in eliminating the risk premia in the model's exchange rate equations. The simulations also suggest that a "mixed" price-real output rule for monetary policy is generally more effective in stabilizing Group of Three prices and output than a "pure" rule based on either price or nominal gross national product (GNP).

Manfred Neumann's comment expresses concern that Taylor's conclusions depend initially on his working analytical assumption that future exogenous shocks to the world economy will follow the same statistical distribution as in the turbulent period of the 1970s and early 1980s. Furthermore, suggests Neumann, the export and import functions, which were estimated over a period of flexible exchange rates, might be different under a fixed rate regime. In the discussion that followed his presentation, Taylor acknowledged the problem of assessing the performance of fixed exchange rates using data from a period of flexible exchange rates. On the other hand, Taylor pointed out that the distribution of shocks and the degree of economic integration via trade would be unlikely to change immediately upon the adoption of a fixed rate system; his result that macroeconomic performance would deteriorate in the short run, he believes, is thus still plausible. Ralph Tryon, in his comment, suggests that data from earlier periods of fixed rates may be used to assess the significance of this problem. He points out that Taylor's results seem to conflict with those of other researchers, who do not so clearly find flexible rates to be superior to fixed rates. Taylor's conclusions, suggests Tryon, may be very sensitive to the properties of his trade equations.

The next paper, on "Implications of Policy Rules for the World Economy: Results from the MSG2 Model," is by Warwick McKibbin and Jeffrey Sachs. Using their MSG2 econometric model of the world economy, the authors investigate what policies could solve the current trade imbalances in the world economy, and what policy rules could be adopted to avoid the recurrence of such problems. One of the features of their model is that fiscal and current account imbalances affect asset stocks, so full stock equilibrium is required in the long run. The model also incorporates rational expectations in asset markets and (partially) in the behavior of households and firms. It has "Keynesian" short-run properties, however, because it assumes slow adjustment in nominal wages in most regions; in keeping with existing empirical evidence, the degree of stickiness varies considerably among regions.

The analysis by McKibbin and Sachs suggests that a reduction in the U.S. fiscal deficit might not be as deflationary as some observers predict, since it would be offset by lower long-term interest rates in the United States and elsewhere after the announcement of fiscal contraction. But a small cut in the fiscal deficit may not by itself be sufficient to close the U.S. trade deficit by 1993. The authors also examine the properties of a number of different policy "regimes"—sets of rules governing the domestic monetary and fiscal policies of the Group of Three countries. They find some instability associated with the "blueprint" proposal advanced by Williamson and Miller (targeting real exchange rates using monetary policy, with fiscal policy used to target domestic demand). This instability may arise from fixing the target real exchange rate once and for all in the model simulation, and from the fact that the MSG2 model allows for debt accumulation, which would tend to change the real exchange rate, ceteris paribus.

In his comment, Patrick Minford points out that, although the model relies on intertemporal maximization for much of its structure, this seems difficult to reconcile with the assumptions of a high degree of wage stickiness in some regions and the presence of hysteresis effects. Minford also doubts the result that the recessionary effects of U.S. fiscal contraction could be easily offset by monetary expansion in the Group of Three countries; he questions the positive transmission effects for monetary policy in McKibbin and Sachs' model, which occur even when fully anticipated by the private sector. David Currie suggests that the instability properties of the blueprint proposal as implemented in the MSG2 model may result from trying to hit targets too precisely (fine-tuning), and that the McKibbin-Sachs implementation differs from that advocated by Williamson and Miller, who argue for the use of policy in a "coarse-tuning" way. Currie also points out that one cannot fix the real exchange rate once and for all if asset stocks change.

The final paper in the group of model-based evaluations of rules or regimes is by Jacob A. Frenkel, Morris Goldstein, and Paul R. Masson, entitled "Simulating the Effects of Some Simple Coordinated Versus Uncoordinated Policy Rules." The authors evaluate how different simple monetary and fiscal rules perform in the International Monetary Fund's MULTIMOD. This model includes forward-looking expectations and is a fully closed model of the world economy, in contrast to many other multicountry models. The authors consider both uncoordinated policies—which include policy rules under which each country independently targets monetary policy on either the monetary base or nominal GNP—and "coordinated policies," in which monetary policy is targeted to real or nominal exchange rates, or where monetary and fiscal policy target both real exchange rates (or the current account) and nominal domestic demand. Rather than running historical simulations with different policy rules, Frenkel and others simulate the model for a future period by applying to the baseline of the model shocks drawn from the actual historical distribution of disturbances. They then examine how successful each rule is at minimizing the deviations of the target variables from the baseline. This procedure, which is similar to the stochastic simulation techniques used in Taylor's paper, allows multiple simulations to be carried out by selecting a new set of shocks from the distribution of past shocks. In contrast to the Taylor paper, Frenkel and others do not find a clear ranking of different policy rules. For instance, the choice is not clear cut among the two uncoordinated rules (money supply and nominal GNP targets, each of which entails flexible exchange rates) and a fixed exchange rate rule. Second, although the Williamson-Miller blueprint proposal tends to work well in stabilizing key target variables, the authors are skeptical about the flexible use of fiscal policy that it implies. Third, pursuing target zones by using monetary policy alone—or making the response of fiscal policy less flexible—tends to produce instability, probably because of the relatively weaker effect of systematic monetary policy in affecting real magnitudes, compared with fiscal policy, in the model.

Jeffrey Shafer suggests that the authors found it difficult to discriminate among the performances of different rules because they all performed reasonably well. In actual practice, policies do not work quite as well, however, so perhaps the authors' methods of assessing different rules may be optimistic. Shafer also proposes considering the effects of model uncertainty on the results. Stanley Fischer, in commenting on the paper, suggests that one way of overcoming instrument instability is by setting a loss function that penalizes extreme policy settings. He also points out that the paper concentrates on policy rules for the interest rate, even though monetary policy appears less effective than fiscal policy in influencing real variables such as output and net exports.

Target Zone Proposal

The next paper in the volume, "The Stabilizing Properties of Target Zones," by Marcus Miller, Paul Weller, and John Williamson, considers a specific blueprint for policy coordination, namely the target zone proposal. The authors examine how target zones might cope with shocks originating from the private sector in exchange markets in the presence of two types of inefficiencies: Blanchard "bubbles" and currency "fads." In an analytical model in which the authorities choose the target zone to encompass the equilibrium exchange rate, the authors show that target zones can have a deterrent effect where bubbles are present. In the presence of "fads," the adoption of a target zone may encourage smart money to play a stabilizing role in exchange markets. The authors question whether the simulations of empirical multicountry models in the papers by Taylor, McKibbin-Sachs, and Frenkel-Goldstein-Masson—even though the simulations remove noise in exchange markets when simulating fixed exchange rates—do justice to the target zone proposal.

Michael Mussa argues that if the authors see target zones as a deterrent for Blanchard bubbles, there is no reason to propose a narrow target zone, as any announced limit on exchange rate fluctuations will do. Furthermore, Mussa doubts whether the presence of fads could explain the behavior of the dollar during the early 1980s, as the authors suggest; in the authors' model, a high dollar would have had to coincide with a high interest rate and with an economy in recession; yet this did not occur in practice. As a result, the model yielded some rather perverse policy prescriptions. James M. Boughton points out that the policymaker would have to distinguish to what extent currency fluctuations owed to fundamentals and to what extent "bandwagon effects" were important. Boughton also questions the assignment of monetary policy to external balance; one would expect that fiscal policy would be more effective in hitting current account targets.

Policy Coordination and Integration in Europe

Some argue that developments in Europe offer a possible model for more general moves toward policy coordination at the world level. "The Exchange Rate Question in Europe," by Francesco Giavazzi, examines the possible evolution of the European Monetary System beyond its present form of fixed but adjustable parities. Many believe that the abolition of capital controls will put pressure on the EMS that will force it back toward greater exchange rate flexibility or toward permanently fixed parities (European Monetary Union, or EMU). Giavazzi examines the arguments for and against such monetary unification. Permanently fixed rates would eliminate the incentive to use "beggar-thy-neighbor" policies, but it may be desirable to retain the ability to realign EMS parities even when all countries face common shocks but retain structural asymmetries. Moreover, in a fixed rate system, if monetary policy is set by one of the countries—presumably the least inflation-prone member of the group—other countries tend to lose monetary sovereignty. This may pose problems for countries whose fiscal structures involve a large ratio of money financing to tax revenues.

William H. Branson emphasizes that a move toward permanently fixed rates would require detecting the appropriate rates on which to fix. This is particularly important in the European context, with the present large and growing German current account surplus. Branson also highlights the difficulty of instituting fiscal transfers among regions in the absence of a fully integrated European fiscal system. Moreover, the development of an integrated financial system will have important implications for small firms in each region, which do not have access to centralized bond markets for finance. Mario Draghi argues that the current system would survive under perfect capital mobility, so long as individual regions did not attempt to carry out independent monetary policies. He points out that problems may arise during periods of increased competition in financial services—as envisaged in the move to a single European market in 1992—if countries' banking systems continue to have different reserve requirements; those with higher required reserves would be placed at a competitive disadvantage.

The second paper on European issues, "The European Monetary Union: An Agnostic Evaluation," by Daniel Cohen and Charles Wyplosz, also assesses arguments for and against the EMU. "Nonstrategic" considerations include the need for seigniorage by countries with inefficient tax systems, the desire of countries with large public debts to use surprise inflation to erode the public debt, and the possibility that the European currency unit (ECU) would become an important asset held in official international reserves. Cohen and

Wyplosz conclude that these considerations do not yield a decisive verdict on the EMU. They then examine the strategic issues underlying the arguments for fixed rates. Although an inflation externality points toward the efficiency of the EMU, the authors argue that in the presence of other externalities—for example, the collective determination of the zone's balance of trade—the EMU might yield a suboptimal outcome.

Massimo Russo points out that the EMU should be considered in part as the result of political moves. Furthermore, seigniorage should be viewed as a second-order effect, as the reduction of exchange rate risk would probably compensate high-debt countries for their loss of seigniorage. Alberto Giovannini agrees that seigniorage is probably a second-order issue but he emphasizes that convergence to a common inflation rate in the 1980s has produced interest rate increases and cyclical falls in taxation revenues, thus worsening the fiscal problem for some countries. He also stresses serious identification problems in Cohen and Wyplosz's empirical analysis of symmetric and asymmetric shocks.

Institutional Issues

The next paper, on "The Role of International Institutions in Surveillance and Policy Coordination," by Andrew Crockett, turns to more institutional considerations of policy coordination. The usual arguments in favor of coordination are that it eliminates the externality caused by spillover effects and supplies the public good of worldwide economic stability. Against the background of these arguments, Crockett describes the development of efforts to underpin international economic cooperation. Under the Bretton Woods system, Working Party 3 of the Organization for Economic Cooperation and Development (OECD) established procedures whereby countries exchanged information on balance of payments aims and forecasts. A Working Party 3 report proposed the use of indicators to diagnose the emergence of imbalances and a set of guidelines for appropriate policy reactions.

Crockett examines the working of policy cooperation under the initial years of floating exchange rates in the 1970s and early 1980s. The "rules of the game" seemed imprecise, partly because of the difficulty in making clear prescriptions in a floating rate regime, and partly because of the demise of the "Keynesian consensus" on the operation of macroeconomic policy. Thus, a greater weight was placed on surveillance, another component of cooperation. This failed to prevent the emergence of the debt crisis in 1982 and the excessive dollar appreciation up to 1985. The period after 1985 has seen the strengthening of cooperation, partly through the regular meetings of the Group of Seven and the undertaking to strengthen surveillance in conjunction with the Fund. Finally, Crockett analyzes steps that could be taken to make the policy coordination process systematic rather than episodic and argues that the role of the Fund will probably have to remain central.

Sylvia Ostry suggests that Crockett's analysis of the process of coordination is optimistic. She stresses that there may be sharp differences in individual countries' views of the underlying model and the appropriate policy targets. Such differences can only be resolved through political processes. Ostry points out that Crockett's account omits a discussion of trade issues and the General Agreement on Tariffs and Trade, despite their importance: it is arguable that the moves in 1985 by the major countries toward coordination were triggered by fears of increased protectionism. In his comment, Jacques Polak points out that there are limits to the feasible number of parties in the management of exchange rates, which is probably best conducted within the confines of the Group of Five or Group of Seven. There are other aspects to policy coordination, however, since exchange rate management has to be underpinned by fiscal and monetary policies. Furthermore, Polak argues that countries should recognize the danger of any coordinated approach: it can lead to a struggle to determine each country's share of the burden of adjustment.

North-South Interdependence

The final paper in the volume addresses an issue that is largely neglected in earlier papers, but may well be of great importance, the interdependence between industrial countries (the "North") and developing countries (the "South"). In their paper on "Macroeconomic Interactions Between the North and South," David Vines and Anton Muscatelli argue that spillover effects between North and South should be taken into account when discussing Northern policy proposals. Muscatelli and Vines analyze the main channels of North-South economic interdependence using a theory-based simulation model. They emphasize the linkages that relate to the demand-side effects of Northern policies, which may feed back on commodity prices and affect the North's own supply sector. Furthermore, any effect of Northern policies on Southern capital accumulation will have a long-run effect on commodity prices. The authors emphasize that the determinants of investment in the South and the determinants of financing flows from the North to the South warrant specific empirical investigation. They argue for a coordinated policy package that would involve maintenance of a satisfactory policy environment in the Group of Seven countries; implementation of satisfactory adjustment policies in the South—including increased investment expenditure—and resumption of new financing flows to the South.

Michael Dooley points out that Muscatelli and Vines assume that additional finance is readily available to the South at an interest rate that incorporates a risk premium, while in MULTIMOD no more finance is available to countries that do not satisfy a solvency criterion. Dooley finds the MULTIMOD approach more realistic; in actual practice, the flow of new finance to the South seems to have dried up, and as a result the large market discounts on the debt of some developing countries probably do not affect the level of

Southern investment. Pierre Defraigne agrees with the authors that the South is an important "missing link" in the modeling of economic interdependence, but proposes adding two features to the model. First, he argues that the authors should recognize that the share of manufactures in Southern exports had risen to 52 percent by 1982; the authors neglect the possible erection of trade barriers on these exports in their discussion of policy cooperation. Second, in empirical work, the building of a multiregional model should recognize the strong bilateral links between particular Northern and Southern regions (for example, between Japan and the Asian newly industrialized economies, or NIEs).

Directions for Further Research

The papers in this volume are evidence of the advances in economic knowledge that have been made in recent years and of the renewed interest in economic interdependence and international policy coordination. The volume, however, should not be viewed as a definitive study, but rather as a signpost for future research. It is important to push forward in our attempts to understand and model the intricacies of the policy coordination process. The themes taken up in this book will undoubtedly be pursued in subsequent research, and indeed represent a major research agenda.

In this book, we have focused on issues of coordination between the policymakers of different countries. But the issue of coordination has further dimensions: the various arms of government need to be coordinated within a country (for example, the central bank and the finance ministry); while coordination between countries may first take the form of coordination within regional groups (such as the European Community group) and then among these regional groups. These issues of internal and hierarchical coordination are touched upon in the book, but they deserve more thorough study. Moreover, coordination need not, and indeed cannot, be complete: coordination in practice will be partial, taking the form of agreement over some aspects of policy, while leaving other dimensions of policy free to be determined by countries individually. Which aspects of policy are most in need of coordination is a key unresolved question.

These aspects of the coordination process can be illuminated by studying the most obvious example of coordination in practice, namely, the European Monetary System. The dominant interpretation of the evidence is that the EMS operates in an asymmetrical manner, with German monetary policy providing an absolute inflation anchor, while the monetary policy of other member countries is directed toward an exchange rate target relative to the deutsche mark. Moves in the direction of a European central bank may be interpreted as introducing greater symmetry in the process of macroeconomic coordination, with potential benefits and costs that need to be assessed, along with their distribution across countries. The Delors Committee report on the European Monetary System has also highlighted the issue of whether greater monetary integration requires greater fiscal coordination; the answer depends partly on how financial markets will treat borrowing by countries joined in a monetary union.

At the global level, research is needed to help establish how macroeconomic indicators of developments in the world economy can be used to guide the conduct of policy, so as to achieve what has been termed "absolute coordination." There is also the question of how best to conduct policy to adjust, and subsequently avoid, undue imbalances between the major Group of Seven countries. We still have unanswered questions about the role of the exchange rate as a "pivot" for policy coordination and, to the extent that this is judged desirable, how exchange rates should best be managed.

Underlying all these questions is the issue of how to establish and maintain credibility of policy. Modern techniques of policy design allow us to investigate these questions in powerful ways, using ideas of sustainability and incentive compatibility. But the manner in which a hierarchical structure of policymaking, partial coordination, or complexity of policy design affects questions of credibility has not yet been properly investigated. This represents an important and potentially fruitful area of research.

These and other issues need a better grounding in empirical research. The areas mapped out by the papers in this volume should be further explored. Macroeconomic models can be used to evaluate a wider range of policy rules, and to attempt to discover simple but robust frameworks for coordination. Moreover, these models should be extended and refined. A major need in this regard is the development of better methods of modeling North-South interactions through commodity prices, financing flows, and other channels.

The list of relevant research topics is long. Though the research agenda is daunting, it should not detract from the substantial contributions made by the papers in this volume to our knowledge in the important area of economic policymaking.

1

The Theory and Practice of International Policy Coordination: Does Coordination Pay?

David A. Currie, Gerald Holtham, and Andrew Hughes Hallett

I. Introduction

This paper reviews the theory and practice of economic policy coordination. It follows the taxonomy of Horne and Masson (1988) in interpreting coordination to mean the joint planning or setting of at least some macroeconomic policies.[1] This may be distinguished from a more general interchange of information and opinion on economic affairs and from agreements on "rules of the game" outside the macroeconomic sphere, as under the General Agreement on Tariffs and Trade (GATT). These broader forms of interaction may be styled policy cooperation. For our purposes, the establishment of agreed rules of the game in the macroeconomic sphere that constrain, or determine, at least some instruments of macroeconomic policy is to be regarded as a form of policy coordination.

The paper is in three sections. Section I reviews the historical experience of macroeconomic policy cooperation in the postwar era. Section II surveys the literature on policy coordination, emphasizing the attempts to quantify coordination gains. And the concluding section summarizes the state of the current debate on coordination and offers some conclusions.

In reviewing the history of policy cooperation, it is evident that such economic coordination as has occurred has been a looser and more partial affair than the situations analyzed in the theoretical literature. In considering the historical experience, a useful distinction, not found in the theoretical literature, is that between relative and absolute coordination.[2] Absolute coor-

---

[1] Bryant (1987) and Cooper (1985) have proposed similar taxonomies.

[2] Although implicit in the early discussion of policy coordination, this distinction was stated most explicitly by the Group of 30 Study Group on International Macroeconomic Policy Coordination (Group of 30, 1988).

dination covers the overall stance of policy in the leading industrial countries and seeks to ensure that, in pursuing separately their own interests, countries do not, in the aggregate, adopt excessively loose or tight policies for the world as a whole. Relative coordination, on the other hand, is concerned with the relative positions of countries and therefore tends to focus on exchange rates and balances of payments.

Clearly, this is not a watertight distinction. Absolute coordination has relative consequences and vice versa. A lack of mutual exclusivity in the definitions may explain why the distinction has not been used in academic discussion. Its interest, in our view, derives from a clear revealed preference on the part of policymakers for relative coordination as opposed to absolute coordination or to none at all.

Theory would suggest that the gains to coordination are greatest at a time of a large common shock, when countries acting in isolation might indulge in beggar-thy-neighbor attempts to manipulate exchange rates. In practice such periods (the 1930s or the early 1980s) have generally seen the decline, rather than the intensification, of economic cooperation. Coordination has generally not followed at all quickly upon systematic underperformance of the world economy. Most recently it has been triggered by episodes of imbalances among the major industrial countries when current account deficits grew and/or exchange rates became unstable, and it has always concerned itself with such developments.

Our conclusions are frankly opinionated. We do not pretend that the academic literature is anything other than inconclusive as to whether there are substantial gains to coordination or what is the best means to achieve them. A review of experience provides some guide but no more. A lot of judgments are necessary on both issues. In considering the best way forward, we have certainly been influenced by the revealed preference of policymakers, as noted above.

II. The Experience of International Coordination

International coordination on matters of economic policy goes back at least to the interwar period. In a number of areas—such as rules governing trade and double taxation agreements—cooperation has been continuous, if of variable intensity. In this section, we give a short overview and interpretation of trends and developments in coordination in the macroeconomic sphere since World War II, focusing mainly on the post-1973 period. It is convenient to divide the postwar era into five periods: the immediate postwar period, 1945–58, of fixed exchange rates and limited capital mobility; the 1959–73 period when capital mobility progressively increased and the Bretton Woods system came under increasing pressure; the 1974–79 period of generalized floating and attempts at discretionary coordination; the 1980–85 period of "monetarist" thinking; and the period since 1985 during which interest in policy coordination has revived.

The period immediately following the establishment of the Bretton Woods system in *1945–58* was one of fixed exchange rates, extensive exchange and capital controls, and a prevalence of bilateral payments mechanisms for settling accounts among nations. It was also a period of the most clear hegemony or economic dominance by one country, the United States, as revealed in a "dollar shortage."

The period *1959–73* was the "Golden Age" of the Bretton Woods system. A multilateral payments system was established among the leading industrial countries. Exchange rates were managed according to an adjustable peg system, with fluctuations restricted to 1 percent on either side of an agreed central parity. Exchange controls continued, but the growth of international capital flows and banking transactions made controls progressively less effective. The economic dominance of the United States continued, though it became progressively less overwhelming. These tendencies, combined with certain inflationary developments in the world economy, led to the collapse of the system. Its final two years are the story of vain attempts to shore it up.

The period immediately after the end of Bretton Woods, *1974–79*, was characterized by a generalized floating of exchange rates in a context of high and differing inflation rates. The institution of annual economic summit meetings dates from this period. The summits epitomized the then dominant approach of trying to develop essentially discretionary forms of economic coordination to replace the more routine, rule-bound procedures of Bretton Woods. The dominant framework for thinking about economic policy during this period was Keynesian: policymakers regarded themselves as responsible for demand management, seeking to stabilize both real activity and inflation. The high-water mark of this period was the Bonn Economic Summit of 1978.

The period *1980–85* was when the leading ideology of economic management changed to one loosely called "monetarism." Countries came to regard control of inflation as the top priority; indeed many denied that the government could have any durable or worthwhile influence on the level of real economic activity with the conventional tools of macroeconomic policy. It followed from such an intellectual position that macroeconomic policy coordination was irrelevant; if governments have only one legitimate policy objective, they have instruments enough to achieve it. The theoretical case for coordination disappears. It was argued that the best service governments could render their own people and other countries was to "get their house in order," that is, eliminate inflation through strict control of monetary policy. International coordination was restricted to mutual exhortations, whereby treasuries and ministries of finance bolstered each other against competing interests in each other's countries. This was therefore a period of convergence in monetary policy, though not in fiscal policy—without policy coordination.

The period *1985–present* has seen a reawakening of interest in policy coordination, with a form of loose coordination of monetary policy and foreign exchange market intervention. The trigger for this renewed interest in coordination was the emergence of large external imbalances among the leading industrial countries, coupled with exchange rate movements that seemed likely to worsen, rather than reduce, the imbalances. Whether ascribed to "incompatible" fiscal policies, or a myopia of the foreign exchange markets, these developments required coordinated action to prevent a severe breakdown of liberal multilateral trade.

The response has been an intensification of the sort of discretionary consultation characterizing 1973–79. This time, however, the objectives have been more limited, namely the stabilization of important exchange rates around agreed levels. In setting, or at least altering, those levels, policymakers have been driven by the market, rather than proceeding on the basis of their own perception of fundamentals.

In considering these episodes further, it is useful to make the distinction, noted above, between absolute and relative coordination.

The Bretton Woods era was one in which international coordination took the relative form. The obligation, which countries undertook, to maintain fixed exchange rates meant that their domestic policies relative to those of other countries were constrained by the balance of payments and their finite reserves.

Countries could borrow from the International Monetary Fund, and, after 1962, ten of the leading industrial countries borrowed under the General Arrangements to Borrow. A corollary of this facility was a system of mutual surveillance carried out by the Group of Ten and Working Party 3 of the Organization for Economic Cooperation and Development (OECD), which focused heavily on balance of payments positions. These facilities enabled countries to withstand speculation against their currencies provided that other countries were persuaded that their economic policies were sound, that is, consistent with everyone else's.

It has been argued that the United States enjoyed a special position by virtue of the general acceptability of its currency as a means of payment, and that this removed external discipline in its case. Though the United States enjoyed some seigniorage, it did not escape all discipline while the dollar remained convertible into gold on demand. There were periods when the United States ran a balance of payments deficit and the dollar suffered a loss of confidence, leading to speculative surges in the demand for gold, such as occurred in 1960–61 (Tew, 1967). The U.S. attempt to evade such pressures by ending the dollar's convertibility into gold helped to undermine the system.

There seems to have been relatively little cooperative consideration of the overall stance of policy worldwide as such. The issue was in fact discussed but took the form of a debate about the adequacy of world liquidity to finance the continued growth of world trade. In the 1960s there were concerns that the financing of world trade depended on an expanding supply of dollars; yet such an expansion implied a U.S. payments deficit that threatened confidence (Triffin, 1961).

During the Bretton Woods period the proportion of dollars in world reserves rose steadily. Issues of absolute coordination became confused with those of relative coordination. It was in the countries with chronic tendencies to balance of payments deficits (the United States and the United Kingdom) that the shortage of world liquidity was perceived. In surplus countries (the Federal Republic of Germany, Italy, and the Netherlands), there was suspicion that deficit countries were prepared to countenance world inflation (Boffi, 1969). Nonetheless, in 1967 in Rio de Janeiro, an agreement was achieved to create a new reserve asset, the special drawing right (SDR). Creation of liquidity in this form was discretionary and required an 85 percent majority vote of the IMF Board of Governors. In fact, world trade growth was not noticeably impeded by reserve shortages when the United States ran conservative policies; but the system was put under insupportable strain when the United States followed policies after 1967 that greatly increased the supply of dollars and necessitated devaluations. The expansionary policies of the United States and the inflationary finance of the Vietnam War are now generally credited with undermining the system.

The subsequent 1974–79 period of discretionary cooperation was concerned with both relative and absolute coordination.

The response of many governments to the oil price rise of 1973 was to cut taxes in order to maintain the level of demand. Governments did this to differing extents, and the industries of different countries also showed differing abilities to adapt to a new pattern of demand in world trade, following the rise of the Organization of the Petroleum Exporting Countries (OPEC). The combination led to large current account imbalances and, in particular, a weakness of the dollar.

Despite these policies, unemployment rose generally, largely because profits bore the brunt of the adverse terms of trade shock, while wages did not adjust. Unemployment was regarded as a serious problem, while the view that potential growth (as opposed to the potential level of output) had been permanently reduced was not yet general. Meanwhile, inflation, though subsiding from its 1974 peak, remained high in many countries.

Several years of discussion in this climate led to the Bonn Summit agreement of 1978, which epitomized the period. There were long discussions, careful staffwork, and finally a wide-ranging agreement that embraced, but went beyond, macroeconomic policy. In an effort to offset what was seen as flagging growth while contributing to better-balanced international payments, Japan and Germany took stimulative fiscal policy actions. The United States agreed to liberalize energy prices in the United States so that these rose to world levels. The U.S. slowdown, by dampening U.S. energy demand, was expected to reduce prices for all oil importers.

The agreement has been extensively mythologized. It has been viewed as the imposition of American power, pressuring the hapless Germans and Japanese to inflationary policies in order to help out the United States. It has also been castigated as an example of inappropriate procyclical fine-tuning of aggregate demand.

In fact, the Bonn summit helped substantial groups in each country to interact to achieve domestic policies that they favored in any case (Putnam and Henning, 1989). The summit may have been necessary to bring about the policies at the time they were implemented, but dominant groups in each country favored them anyway. Altruistic policies were not imposed on reluctant governments.

Moreover, given the priorities of the policymakers at the time, the summit measures were not even mistaken. However, soon afterwards policy preferences changed substantially. In 1978, the German Government wanted faster growth when faced with forecasts of 3½ percent real growth and 3½ percent inflation when unemployment was 4 percent. A strong temporary surge of inflation, caused by the second oil shock, together with the replacement of Democratic and Social Democratic governments in the United States and Germany by Republican and Christian Democratic administrations, led to a substantial reordering of priorities (Holtham, 1989). It is politically convenient to describe new priorities as the result of superior wisdom and of learning from the errors of the past; such a political redescription is what took place.

The fiscal policy measures in Germany and Japan were modest; in Germany, they barely offset fiscal drag and they were accompanied by a tightening of monetary policy. The summit agreement did not cover monetary policy, though it made clear that the German expansion would be bond-financed. The fiscal measures had a negligible impact on inflation and a very small effect on the current account, being swamped by the effects of the second oil shock. The main enduring effect of the summit was the deregulation of American oil prices—which everyone agrees to have been beneficial.

Moreover, unlike the first oil shock, it is implausible to ascribe the second oil shock to monetary expansion in the industrial countries. It was triggered by the fall of the Shah of Iran. Although this did not lead to a substantial reduction in oil supplies, it caused a surge of speculative buying that drove up the oil price.

Nonetheless by 1980, popular tolerance of inflation was exhausted, and the threat that a new surge in inflation could again ratchet up the underlying rate made for considerable uniformity of view in all countries. This was reflected in several changes of government. It was also reflected in a lack of interest in policy coordination and an emphasis in each country on putting its own house in order.

There was general agreement on the need to reduce inflation and a much greater readiness than formerly to bear the costs in unemployment and recession of doing so—a readiness that had democratic endorsement. To a large extent this readiness was disguised behind the assertion that there were no lasting output or unemployment costs of eliminating inflation. Indeed, some even asserted there would be no costs at all so long as the authorities carried conviction because the private sector would adjust its expectations to the new policy regime.

The harmonization on tighter monetary policies that followed led to sharply higher interest rates in all countries. A recession followed of comparable depth to that of 1975, though it lasted longer. A recovery was expected in early 1982 but failed to appear, partly because exports to the non-OECD area were much weaker than expected. That, in turn, was due to an underestimate of, or more accurately obliviousness to, the effect of a synchronized OECD slump on economic activity in the rest of the world.

Eventual recovery was expedited by a discretionary policy shift by the U.S. Federal Reserve in the autumn of 1982, in response to strains that high interest rates were creating in the U.S. financial system and in the economy of Mexico. The subsequent recovery in the level of activity was probably facilitated by discretionary tax cuts enacted in the 1981 budget, which raised the disposable income of those households unfamiliar with the works of David Ricardo and Robert Barro. The United States led the rest of the OECD out of recession at the cost of a progressively deteriorating current account.

In the early to mid-1980s, none debated the need to give priority to reducing or eliminating inflation. After the fact of recession, it was also widely discovered that recession had been a necessary cost. Some noticed that the recession had been deeper and longer than expected, and a few argued that it was because countries had ignored the cumulative effects of synchronized policy. It was argued by some that had each country set policy in the light of the policy actions of others, the overall degree of deflation would have been less. In other words, absolute coordination had been lacking in the early 1980s.

This argument, however, won few converts to the cause of coordination. Subsequent elections confirmed the popularity of reducing inflation, even at a cost of considerable employment. Less recession could well have meant more residual inflation. Moreover, there was still, at that time, a general belief in the concept of a stable natural rate of unemployment, or NAIRU. The unemployment costs of disinflation, while greater and more persistent than expected in 1979, were still thought to be temporary. The experience of recession was not in itself sufficient to reawaken interest in coordination.

The reawakening, when it came, sprang from the requirements of relative coordination, not from a perceived need for absolute coordination. While U.S. fiscal policy had become expansionary, that in Germany and Japan became contractionary after 1981, aimed at reducing the public sector deficit and stabilizing public debt. The latter became a more salient objective as real interest rates rose. The U.S. current account widened while the dollar rose strongly. The precise contribution of relative monetary and fiscal policy remains controversial. In 1984, interest rate differentials between the United States and other countries narrowed, yet still the dollar rose in what was increasingly seen as a speculative bubble. (The nonconcave, indeed nonmonotonic, path of the dollar, however, indicated that if this were a bubble, it was not of the "rational" type acceptable to theorists.)

Other countries, while complaining to the United States about the inflationary consequences for them of the dollar's rise, were quite happy to accept the favorable effects on their export industries. The more thoughtful became increasingly concerned, however, that the situation was not sustainable (despite much talk of a "supply-side miracle," induced by the tax reductions), and some bureaucrats feared that investments currently being made in their countries on the basis of a high dollar were unlikely to be viable given a sustainable one. As the conviction grew that the dollar was at unsustainable levels, policymakers became interested in securing an orderly decline to avoid the risk of a later "hard landing" with financial crisis and recession. Matters were brought to a head by the growing protectionist sentiment in the U.S. Congress. This forced the administrations of the three largest countries to begin intervention and jawboning with a view to driving down the dollar—which was already some way below its peak.

This phase since 1985 saw some de facto coordination of monetary policy—Japan, for example, raised interest rates. And large-scale interventions were not entirely sterilized in their effect on domestic monetary conditions. This coordination was necessary to ensure a controlled depreciation of the dollar, and the key issue was how far and how fast the dollar should fall. After about a year, the consensus that the dollar should go lower gave out. Murmurings were made that stability was needed. When these had little effect and the dollar fell further, the world entered the current phase of the Louvre Agreement (in February 1987).

The current regime seems to consist of attempts to preserve stability among the more important exchange rates on the more or less explicit assumption that these can move in ways at variance with "fundamentals" for significant periods of time—the corrective forces seem weak. Most parties recognize the relevance of relative fiscal policies to this effort and there has been a sustained verbal offensive by each of the larger countries on the others to adapt their policy. The United States has been urging fiscal expansion on Japan and Germany while the latter have urged fiscal restraint on the United States. These urgings have had some effect, though it is difficult to say how much since domestic forces have often operated in the same direction.

The United States curtailed the growth of spending on armaments and enacted the Gramm-Rudman-Hollings law. Japan, while continuing to restrict recurrent government expenditure, boosted public sector investment substantially in 1986 and 1987. Germany did the least, implementing a series of direct tax reductions in 1986, 1988, and 1990, calculated to offset fiscal drag. Responding to pressure, it increased the scope of the 1988 tax cuts only to announce offsetting increases in indirect taxes for 1989. Neither the United States nor Germany was content with the policies of the other; Japan largely escaped criticism.

Much of the burden of ensuring exchange rate stability in the short term thus fell on monetary policy. However, a paradox emerged in 1987. Once the larger industrial countries had made plain their desire to have stable exchange rates, the market came to believe them. The view became widespread that exchange rates would be stable for some time. There was less consensus about how long the stability would persist. Given the short-run expectation, the higher interest-rate currencies, in particular the dollar, began to appreciate.

The absence of any official reaction was interpreted by the markets as an official desire for a higher dollar, and the appreciation proceeded through the summer of 1987. Something similar was to happen in the summer of 1988. In 1987, the dollar appreciation exposed differences in matters of relative coordination. The Deutsche Bundesbank, having a greater fear of inflation than the U.S. administration, began to raise interest rates; while this was consistent with the Louvre Agreement, it raised the ire of the U.S. treasury secretary. The subsequent public recrimination has been blamed, no doubt wrongly, for the global stock market slide that followed.

Certainly governments in the larger countries are aware that attempting to manage a quasi-fixed exchange rate system raises the "n-1 problem" of what determines monetary policy in the nth country or in the system as a whole. Disagreements about the overall thrust of policy can break agreements on relative policy stance and lead to a collapse into unmanaged floating, which they wish to avoid. The U.S. answer to this has been to propose the use of "indicators" as to the state of the whole system, including variables like commodity prices. No country has disputed the usefulness of "indicators," but all have been at pains to emphasize that these are for information only and should not be the focus of any policy precommitment or introduce any automaticity into policy.

The present situation is therefore one that satisfies no one. The impetus on the part of policymakers to coordinate seems to be based substantially on a belief in the irrationality of the foreign exchange market, or at least a belief that, given the prevailing uncertainty, the constraints imposed by fundamentals on short-run exchange rate movements are extremely weak. Many economists, lacking a theory of the exchange rate in the presence of comprehensive uncertainty, find the belief of policymakers paradoxical and hard to deal with. Those economists who favor fixing exchange rates do so generally because they believe it could improve the discipline on policymakers. The latter, while apparently ready to accept some constraint on their monetary policy autonomy, show little readiness to accept the same constraint on fiscal policy.

Moreover, while distrusting the foreign exchange market, policymakers are not prepared to accept macroeconomic analysis either as a means of determining the "appropriate" exchange rate. Thus, no officially sanctioned studies of the equilibrium exchange rate are published, and no target zones—hard or soft—are announced. This leads to the spectacle of countries solemnly declaring that current exchange rates are "appropriate," without offering any supporting evidence, apart from the fact that those rates are what they are. Should the market then misinterpret the statements or interventions of policy-makers and drive exchange rates somewhere else, the authorities can be relied upon to announce that the new levels are appropriate too. In effect, policy-makers' countries appear to be asserting that "stability" of exchange rates is all that matters, though they do not have any opinions as to the level of exchange rates at which stability should be achieved. We return to this set of questions in Section V, having first reviewed the lessons to be learned from the academic literature on coordination.

III. What Are the Payoffs?

Academic research has produced an expanding literature on policy coordination. Much of the work, however, has been theoretical and based on highly simplified models. As these have abstracted from some of the difficulties of which policymakers are most vividly aware, the literature may have a flavor of unreality to practical men. The impetus to cooperation has come from experience, not from theoretical demonstrations of the benefits. Bringing theory to bear on current concerns is unfinished business.

The Research Agenda

The benefits of coordinating the policies of interdependent, but politically sovereign, policymakers have nearly always been stated in "efficiency" terms: a cooperative policy bargain can be made that leaves some countries better off, without others being worse off. By cooperating to coordinate policies to take account of spillovers, each country may better achieve its specific objectives relative to the alternative of determining policy. Independent policymaking is generally suboptimal.

This is an argument that is well established in theory and that has been demonstrated in a range of analytic and empirical models (Hamada, 1974, 1976; Canzoneri and Gray, 1985). Since then the academic literature has focused on the following more specific issues:

- How large are the potential gains from policy coordination in practice, and how are they likely to be distributed among participating countries? To what extent does policy interdependence limit the ability of policymakers to control their own economies?

- What are the key determinants of the size and distribution of the payoffs? In which variables do the gains appear; are the targets reached earlier; and are the outcomes more stable than their noncooperative counterparts?

- Are the policies of a coordinated policy bargain sustainable? The problem is that once a country is persuaded to adopt policies different from those that are optimal in a noncooperative sense, the other countries have an incentive to reoptimize conditional on that information. Hijacking an agreement might occur instantaneously (cheating against those who hold to their part of the bargain), or over time (time-inconsistent policies directed against agents thought to be "locked in"). This has led to a search for means of establishing credibility or reputation.

- What are the obstacles to coordination? There may be political and institutional reasons why it is more difficult to secure agreement on certain policy variables, but easier on others. Hence, what scope is there for limited cooperative agreements by means of simple policy rules, particular policy assignments, or intermediate targeting schemes?

- To what extent are coordinated policies sensitive to errors or disagreements over the assumed policy responses or priorities?

Levels of Policy Cooperation and Coordination

The potential benefits and costs of policy coordination will depend on the degree of cooperation among the policymakers of different countries. Following Cooper (1987) and Horne and Masson (1988), we can distinguish a hierarchy of degrees of cooperation:

Information exchanges. Here, countries would freely exchange information about their targets, priorities, information sets, and how they think those targets would respond to domestic (or foreign) policy changes, but they would continue to make decisions in a decentralized, autonomous way. By coordinating their information, countries could make gains by eliminating incomplete or faulty information over objectives, expectations, and assumed policy responses. On the other hand, by sharing faulty information about policy responses, for example, they could spread those errors around the whole system.

Crisis management. Here, coordination would arise in response to episodes of particular difficulty in the international economy, involving policy changes that are particular to that episode. It might involve ad hoc policy adjustments, or "coarse-tuning" for difficult periods, when maladjustments and current policies interact to give a crisis (for example, the problem of international debt).

Avoiding conflicts over shared targets. Shared targets arise where countries actually target the same variable (for example, a mutual exchange rate), or where they target variables that are directly linked by an identity that is not capable of relaxation via policy interventions (for example, the "n-1 problem" in a set of current accounts). In this case, coordination could generate gains by means of agreements that prevent countries from setting incompatible targets for the same variable or by preventing countries attempting competitive policy changes that cannot all be achieved simultaneously. In either case, countries could save policy effort as they would be prevented from pushing in vain against each other.

Cooperative intermediate targeting. A limited degree of coordination may be achieved when countries jointly control the variables that form the main links between their economies, or that cause the main spillovers from one to another. In that case, the link/spillover variables are treated as intermediate targets, being instrumental in obtaining better results for the other targets but without significance in themselves. Intermediate targeting therefore implies that some variable is used as a surrogate for the targets that policymakers really care about or to reduce strong, adverse spillovers. Intermediate targets may or may not be shared targets, although the scope for fruitless competition over shared targets makes them the most obvious candidates. Examples of that type are the Williamson-Miller (1987) proposal for exchange rate target zones and Boughton's (1988) current balance targeting proposal, or McKinnon's (1984) suggestion for targeting fixed exchange rates in the context of world monetary growth rule. But intermediate monetary targeting could be an example of the other type.

Partial coordination. Countries cooperate in achieving certain targets but may aim at other targets uncooperatively or according to some preassigned (national) rules. It is often suggested that countries should coordinate their monetary policy, leaving fiscal policy (which is hard to manipulate in the short term) for domestic targets. However, one may also argue that fiscal policy needs to be sustainable so that a minimal degree of fiscal coordination is required to set the background for effective monetary coordination. Another form of partial coordination involves agreeing on policy assignments, for example, fiscal policy for achieving the internal targets, and monetary policy for controlling the external or link targets (Williamson and Miller, 1987) or vice versa (Boughton, 1988).

Full coordination. Here, countries adopt a certain bargain across all targets and fiscal, monetary, and exchange rate instruments. This would aim to maximize the gains over the noncooperative policy settings, subject to a reasonable distribution of those gains.

Estimating the Gains from Coordination

The Benefits of Full Coordination

Studies that set out to evaluate empirically the potential gains from policy coordination have generally found the benefits to be valuable but relatively small. In their pioneering study, Oudiz and Sachs (1984) estimated that the gains among the Group of Three countries in the mid-1970s would be worth no more that ½ of 1 percent of gross national product (GNP) to each country, compared with the best noncooperative outcomes. It may, of course, be debated whether ½ of 1 percent of GNP is only a "small" gain. It would represent a significant amount of extra productive capacity if fully invested, but it is not large compared with annual growth rates. Moreover, gains of this size are not much bigger than the forecast standard of errors of the target variables: if the expected gains are small relative to the imprecision with which policies can be implemented, those gains may be hard to realize in practice. This points to the question of the robustness of these gains from coordination.

Later studies have confirmed that the gains from coordination among the OECD economies are likely to be small.[3] In a more general analysis that allowed for dynamic decision making, Hughes Hallett (1986a,b; 1987a) found the gains became slightly larger—between ½ of 1 percent and 1½ percent of GNP for the United States, the European Community (EC), and Japan. More recently Canzoneri and Minford (1986), Minford and Canzoneri (1987), and Currie, Levine, and Vidalis (1987) have also suggested relatively small gains in the absence of major shocks, based on calculations from versions of the Liverpool and OECD models for the United States and the EC or OECD, respectively. However, those results turn out to vary significantly with the size and persistence of external shocks and the perceived reputations of the governments concerned. Persistent shocks and the existence of "reputation" appreciably increase the relative value of coordination (Currie, Levine, and Vidalis, 1987).

Little work has been done on the likely distribution of cooperation gains among countries. Oudiz and Sachs (1984) found gains distributed roughly 2:1 in favor of Germany, relative to the United States, for two different econometric models. Hughes Hallett's (1986b) study of the United States and EC in the mid-1970s suggests gains distributed 2:1 in favor of the EC using a wide range of bargaining models, corroborating this finding. Later work showed this result to be somewhat sensitive to alternative types of exogenous shocks (Hughes Hallett, 1987b), although in no case was the position of the EC as main gainer overturned. Hughes Hallett, Holtham, and Hutson (1989) also find the gains to be asymmetrically distributed among the Group of Five countries in the late 1980s, and that it is extremely difficult to find ways of improving the lot of those countries that benefit least from coordination. These are important but awkward results because they suggest that, whatever the overall gains, (1) it will be hard to secure *and maintain* a coordination

---

[3] The gains from coordinating policies among the OECD countries and the developing countries may be rather larger (Currie and Vines, 1988), or when the free trade assumption is abandoned (Helkie and others, 1989).

agreement in the face of significant uncertainties, and (2) if those who make the gains and those who shoulder the burden of adjustment are different sets of people, securing any agreement will be politically difficult. However, it may well be that these distributional problems can be reduced by a hierarchical approach to coordination, focusing first on coordination among the Group of Three countries and subsequently on coordination within regional groupings.

These results have been drawn from empirical macromodels. Some of the literature has sought to examine these findings from a theoretical vantage point, using small demonstration models in which each economy is represented by a few simplified equations. Typically those equations restrict us to a world of two identically symmetric economies with either no dynamics or steady-state dynamics, where the policy responses are known with certainty and there are no information innovations. These limitations reduce the interest of the resulting research findings. Nevertheless, these simplified models also suggest that the gains from coordination are likely to be fairly small, but not insignificant; see, for example, Carlozzi and Taylor (1985), Oudiz and Sachs (1985), Currie and Levine (1985), Levine and Currie (1987), Miller and Salmon (1985), or Taylor (1985).

Cooperation Through Information Exchange

The gains from coordination relative to noncoordination may well be substantially smaller than those of efficient noncooperative policies over strategies that ignore predictable policy changes abroad. Thus, coordination in the sense of *information exchanges*, rather than detailed coordination across all variables, may supply the major part of the improvements available from policy coordination. If this is so, an important function of international forums for policy discussion is the exchange of information among policymakers concerning their policies and the state of their economies. Interestingly, this conclusion can hold even when the information exchanged is found to contain prediction errors (Hughes Hallett, 1987b). It has also been confirmed in a series of experiments carried out by Minford and Canzoneri (1987), using a different model of the Group of Seven countries over three different episodes in the 1980s.

Thus, information exchanges do appear to be a key part of the coordination process, irrespective of the model or time period. One might suppose that the wider the range of policies reviewed, the greater the benefits of information exchange to the decisions subsequently made (Bryant, 1987). Certainly prior consultation would alert policymakers to potential and self-defeating conflicts, such as incompatible exchange rate or trade balance targets that would lead to competitive appreciations or depreciations, or inconsistent fiscal and monetary programs. Prior consultation could also help policymakers avoid any losses attributable to conditioning their own decisions on erroneous information about other policymakers' intentions (for example, what priorities they have, what target paths they aim at, what model they use for policy selection, and so forth). Whatever the difficulty of predicting the true state of the world, errors owing to mistakes made about the information base being used by other decision makers should be avoidable, and there is no point in adding them to unavoidable (or genuinely random) errors. Information exchanges that take place through regular consultation may be routine, but we should not be surprised if they make significant contributions to improving policy choice.

Avoiding Conflicts over Shared or Linked Targets

None of these studies of policy coordination considered exchange rates to be a target of policy, either in their own right or as a surrogate target. Yet much of the recent policy debate has been concerned with exchange rate management, with the aim of either stabilizing exchange rates or of making controlled realignments. This may serve as a means of improving relative coordination among countries. The Holtham, Hughes Hallett (1987) study points out that, although exchange rates will then be included among the targets during policy selection, they can either be included in the associated objective function evaluations (in which case exchange rate stability is a target in its own right) or excluded from those evaluations (in which case exchange rates are just an intermediate target, instrumental in securing improvements elsewhere). If the former holds, the gains from coordination appear larger than before, about 3–6 percent of GNP as estimated across seven multicountry models. If exchange rates are treated merely as intermediate targets, the gains are significantly smaller, much the same as in the earlier literature cited above. Later work that looked at the exchange rate targeting issue in more detail for the Group of Five countries (Hughes Hallett and others, 1989) generated the same findings: gains at 0.7 percent to 1.7 percent of GNP, inclusive of exchange rate stability, were larger than others had estimated, but those figures were reduced by 0.3 percent for each country when exchange rates were just taken as intermediate targets.

The point here is that an exchange rate is a shared variable whose domestic impact is the same whether exchange rate changes originate at home or abroad. By contrast, most other variables exert impacts that are significantly smaller internationally than domestically. The need to limit exchange rate spillovers is therefore greater than for other linkage variables, and the potential gains for coordination appear correspondingly larger when that is done. In fact, coordination itself appears to generate extra stability in the targets and more continuity in the policy interventions—a characteristic that had already been noted in nonexchange rate exercises (Hughes Hallett, 1986a). The explanation, according to Cooper (1969), is that ignoring independence within or among economies leads to oscillation and overshooting because the implied assignments (country by country) ignore the international side-effects of decisions made in the domestic interest until after they have appeared. Corrections have then to be applied. These are the costs of imposing policy assignments in a dynamic, interdependent system, in this case national assignments rather than instruments to targets on a one-to-one basis, as proposed in some of the target zone literature. Target stability and policy continuity are thus particularly sensitive to the coordinating effects of exchange rate management.

Success with shared targets, whether treated as intermediate or not, requires a measure of coordination of how they are controlled, and also some consensus about the target path that they should pursue. If this is missing, countries will inevitably waste policy power pushing against each other in a vain attempt to achieve the impossible. This follows from the n-1 problem: there are one fewer independent exchange rates (or current accounts) than independent policymakers. However, it does not follow that any agreed target path is better than none. Hughes Hallett, Holtham, and Hutson (1989) find that, among the Group of Five countries, jointly specifying exchange rate target paths independently of other objectives is frequently more damaging than moderate disagreement about what that target path should be so long as the suggested targets are not inconsistent with the other objectives. Hence, the problem appears to be one of choosing an appropriate set of target paths, not of securing precise agreement on some path. Whether this conclusion is true of other shared variables, such as the current account, is an open question.

Intermediate Targeting

An important argument for targeting exchange rates is that it will replicate many of the gains from coordination of policies among countries (Oudiz and Sachs, 1984). This suggests the need for the management of exchange rates, as in the target zone proposals. The point is that countries always face a temptation to move an exchange rate selfishly in order to improve a trade balance, the rate of growth, or to reduce inflation. But if two countries attempt this simultaneously, it will be self-defeating and lead to excessive inflation or deflation (depending on whether the policies employed promote competitive depreciations or appreciations), rather than output growth. Targeting exchange rates, on the other hand, would restrict the policy interventions and, hence, it is argued, the losses from this fruitless competition.

Put differently, exchange rate targets may serve not just to promote relative coordination among economies, but may also be conducive to absolute coordination. This is an important part of the rationale for exchange rate targeting regimes. Important though this argument is, it cannot be accepted without qualification. Hughes Hallett, Holtham, and Hutson (1989) compare exchange rate targeting with noncooperative no-targeting policies, using the U.S. Federal Reserve Board's multicountry (MCM) model. They find the gains to targeting to be small, hard to achieve, and badly distributed across countries. It is not just that some countries do better than others; some actually lose compared with the no-targeting case. Moreover, the target paths had to be very carefully chosen to achieve any gains. These results suggest that losses attributable to attempts at competitive appreciation or depreciation are small in general, but may become significant during particular historical episodes, such as the early 1980s, when countries have uniform objectives and attach great weight to one, high-priority, objective. At other times, the gains to eliminating such competition are easily outweighed by the losses attendant on attempting to achieve an extra (and possibly, inappropriate) exchange rate target. The essential point here is that it is necessary to choose the appropriate exchange rate targets carefully. Moreover, the issue of the distribution of benefits points to the possible advantages of a hierarchical structure for coordination. Thus, it will be easier to choose appropriate and sustainable targets for the Group of Three than for the larger Group of Seven.

The lessons for the target zone proposal are that it is more important to choose the target paths (parities) correctly than to determine the best zone width. Similarly, it is more important to choose those parities carefully than to insist on precise agreement on the policies needed to support them. And even if the target zone proposal looks simple on a bilateral basis, its operation for many countries will be considerably more complex. The advantages of a hierarchical coordination structure for the target zone proposal may be appreciable.

Exchange rate targeting has also been investigated empirically by Edison and others (1987) using the MCM model, and by Currie and Wren-Lewis (1988, 1989) using the London Business School-National Institute Global Econometric Model (GEM). Both conclude that exchange rate targeting—possibly in the form of target zones—could make an important contribution to the coordination of economic policies, at least relative to the historical choices. Both also stress that such a proposal should only be part of a package of measures, where both monetary and fiscal policy are used to attain internal and external objectives.

In assessing this literature, it is important to appreciate that these studies may overlook one important advantage in targeting exchange rates. If fads, bubbles, and volatility are a common feature of foreign exchange markets, then policymakers would take exchange rate stability to be an important goal in its own right. Large departures from equilibrium would mean trade distortions, and consequent hysteresis effects, which are expensive to put right again when markets do return to their fundamentals. Large misalignments, therefore, tend to entail large welfare costs, while the costs of smaller misalignments are negligible. Perhaps the main contribution of exchange rate targeting will be in preserving stability and preventing major misalignments.

Simple Rules

Throughout this literature there has been concern that policy coordination involves extremely complex policy adjustments, and, worse, that the expected outcomes are likely to be error prone or hard to sustain. It is often argued that policy needs to follow rules that are easily monitored, easily implemented, and whose advantages are readily seen, if they are to be acceptable to policymakers. It may well be that well-designed, simple rules will increase the credibility of policy commitments in the eyes of the private sector and foreign governments. In that case, how far can simple policy rules be designed to replicate the gains from full coordination?

This raises the issue of what is meant by simple policy rules. One aspect of simplicity is to ensure that the rules have a simple, dynamic structure. A second aspect is to restrict the range of variables or information to which policy instruments respond. If this goes together with a specialization whereby different instruments respond to distinct subsets of variables, then one arrives at assignment rules, which represent a specific form of simplification.

One system of simplified rules that has been proposed is the Williamson-Miller (1987) extended target zone proposal, which blends each of these elements of simplicity. They propose that fiscal policy should be used to manage internal nominal demand growth, while monetary policy is aimed at maintaining external balance by holding exchange rates within wide bands around equilibrium (FEER) levels. In addition, the absolute level of world interest rates is used to steer world nominal income growth. Objections to this policy are that monetary policy has a rather limited effect on the current account, so that the scheme may be rather poor at dampening current account imbalances, and that fiscal policy is too inflexible for successful management of internal demand. An alternative scheme, proposed by Boughton (1988), suggests that fiscal policy should instead be assigned to achieving external current account balance in the medium term, while monetary policy steers internal demand growth.

Empirical testing of these simple policy rules is still fairly sparse. Some examples appear in the papers by Frenkel and others and by Taylor in this volume. Currie and Wren-Lewis (1988, 1989), using the GEM model, find that the extended target zone scheme could well have improved on historical performance over the past decade, and that this conclusion is fairly robust with respect to changes in the objective function (including the implied flexibility of fiscal policy). Moreover, the extended target zone proposal is found to outperform the alternative scheme proposed by Boughton. These findings are for the Group of Three countries alone, supporting a hierarchical structure of coordination: it is not clear whether they would generalize to a larger group of countries adopting the target zone proposal in a nonhierarchical way. However, these comparisons are based on historical outcomes only. Further work is required to show whether or not these schemes genuinely outperform noncooperative decision making and, therefore, help to contain the potential inefficiencies of noncooperative decision making. The results in Hughes Hallett, Holtham, and Hutson (1989) suggest that they do if exchange rate stability is an objective in itself, because of the costs of resource reallocation among sectors as a consequence of exchange rate misalignments; but that they do not if exchange rates are merely being used as an intermediate targeting scheme. Levine, Currie, and Gaines (1988) find that agreement on the form of simple rules, together with noncooperative decision making over the parameters of these rules, can be helpful in coordinating policies.

IV. The Dangers of Coordination

The evidence is that, while the efficiency gains of policy coordination may be worthwhile, they may not be large relative to the gains that can be made by designing policies in a noncooperative framework with improved information exchanges. Because the gains may not be large, obstacles to coordination may easily arise. Policymakers may prefer not to cooperate if they feel that other countries will not stick to their part of the bargain; or if they think there are potential errors in the exogenous information or external shocks that would invalidate their calculations about their gains from coordination; or if they think they may have misestimated the priorities of other policymakers; or if there is a serious possibility that policymakers differ in their views of how the world economy works, or that the models they use to evaluate the bargains contain errors. Any of these may mean that the expected gains are eliminated. Feldstein (1983), among others, has argued that that is precisely why the industrial nations should not attempt to coordinate their policies.

In this section, we examine four potential obstacles to coordination: the issue of sustainability, or the incentive to renege; exogenous shocks; uncertainty over objectives and priorities; and model uncertainty and disagreement.

Sustainability

The issue here is whether policymakers will stick to their part of the bargain or cheat by redesigning their future policies once they have gotten the other participants into position. The first question involves breaking a bargain, with one party finding it advantageous to deviate from what was agreed once the other participants have taken up their (agreed) positions; that is, governments cheat each other. The second is the usual time-inconsistency or credibility problem discussed in the reputation literature, that is, governments cheating against the private sector. It does not involve a bargain as such but represents an internal inconsistency in one of the policy sequences. A standard example is due to Rogoff (1985), who points out that international policy coordination may actually be welfare-decreasing, if the coordination process eases the constraints on governments engaging in inflationary monetary expansions.[4] The reason is that there is really more than one set of actors per economy (the government and a private sector, whose forward-looking expectations affect the exchange rate and, hence, policy success) so that coordination among governments may represent a coalition against the private sectors, not full coordination. Although the example is specific, it is a general point

---

[4] Miller and Salmon (1985) offer another example.

that coordination without reputation may be counterproductive (see Miller and Salmon, 1985; Levine and Currie, 1987; and Currie, Levine, and Vidalis, 1987). On the other hand, it may not always be counterproductive. Carraro and Giavazzi (1988) produce a different model of policy cooperation with three sectors per economy (government, firms, and trade unions) and show that under *no* circumstances will cooperation be welfare-decreasing.

With such conflicting results from simplified models (and no empirical evidence on the issue), it is hard to make any definitive judgment on the importance of reputation. But it is clearly important to ensure that all actors and expectations are correctly modeled. It could also be that, in the absence of cooperation, reputations are undesirable. Currie, Levine, and Vidalis (1987) argue that noncooperative, nonreputational policy is prone to instability, because governments are tempted to engage in self-defeating competitive appreciations of their exchange rates to combat inflation, coupled with fiscal expansion to avoid undue consequences for output. The nonreputational policies are also prone to excessive inflation. Thus, to the extent that reputations exist, coordination becomes important because of the governments' ability to influence expectations.

The question of the sustainability of policy bargains has received somewhat less attention. The argument here is that coordinated policies will be sustainable against cheating if the losses that a country would suffer under retaliation or preemptive cheating by the opponent significantly outweigh the gains that the other opponent might make by cheating. Hughes Hallett (1986b) finds that this condition is easily satisfied in a reflation game between the United States and the EC; Currie, Levine, and Vidalis (1987) find that there is no incentive to renege on bargains struck among policymakers.

Exogenous Shocks

There is some evidence that forecasting errors or exogenous shocks can cause significant disturbances and affect incentives to coordinate. But those shocks have to be both large and persistent. Canzoneri and Minford (1986), in a static analysis with the Liverpool model, show that the mix of shocks can certainly affect the gains from coordination. Currie and others (1987), in a dynamic analysis of a reduced version of the OECD model, find the benefits of coordination to be small in the face of temporary disturbances. But the benefits rise steeply as the persistence of the disturbance increases.

These results, and the fact that it is not obvious why noncoordinated policies should be disturbed less than coordinated policies, suggest that coordination may actually *increase* policy robustness. In fact, coordination may reduce policy errors because decision makers try to share the risks rather than offload them onto their rivals. Performance indicators are generally taken to be aggregations of national targets that are affected in different (and often conflicting) ways by external shocks, while coordinated policies follow by aggregating those national indicators into some global performance index.

Coordinated policies will therefore normally be more robust than noncooperative policies, which lack that extra aggregation stage and, hence, the added ability to cancel error disturbances.

Brandsma and others (1987) look at these robustness arguments explicitly using an example of U.S.-EC coordination for the 1974–78 recession, and secondly a model of U.S.-EC-Japan coordination for the 1979–81 recession, subject to a range of "favorable" and "unfavorable" shocks to each of the target variables. They found that while coordination almost always produced better outcomes, it was not always the more robust strategy for *open* loop calculations. However, policymakers would certainly wish to revise their calculations in the light of past shocks and errors. If they do so, coordination quite clearly yielded the more robust policies and, probably more important, the degree of that robustness *increased* with the size of shock. This will be an important property of coordination, though its generality remains to be established.

Uncertainty over Objectives and Priorities

Misspecification of policy objectives and priorities, especially those specified for "foreign" policymakers, could introduce serious errors into policy calculations. Policymakers understandably fear that the errors caused by misestimating the preferences and intentions of others would destroy the potential gains from coordination.

The simplest way to approach this difficulty is to conduct a sensitivity analysis of the different policies and their performances to reasonable variations in the parameters, ideal values, and even the list of arguments of the objective functions concerned. Very few studies of this type have been undertaken. A little evidence can be obtained from Taylor (1985) and Hughes Hallett (1987a); both show that policies, and, hence, the incentives to coordinate, are not sensitive to quite large variations in the relative priorities. A more detailed study (Hughes Hallett, 1987c) shows the same thing for all variables except the shared exchange rate target. These are results obtained from three quite different models and time periods, covering a range of problems from the United States versus OECD to games among the Group of Seven countries, but no general principle has been established.

Another (and possibly more serious) manifestation of this difficulty is where policymakers try to mislead their rivals about their priorities. For example, officials in Country A say they are concerned about inflation, when they are really most worried about their trade imbalance, because they think that this deception will lead Country B to take actions that will make it easier for Country A to correct that trade imbalance. But Country B will suffer losses relative to what it could have achieved with the correct information. Country B may or may not be aware of this possibility; but, if it is, uncertainty about Country A's *true* preferences will surely dampen the chances of coordinating policies. The difficulty here is that in an international policy context it is hardly politically possible, let alone technically feasible, to set up "truth-revelation" exercises to force policymakers to be honest about their intentions. The fact that we need, in principle, to go in for truth-revelation exercises shows that this is really a reputational matter. We may fear errors in our assessment of our rivals' priorities, but if we fear misrepresentation, the associated policies will not be sustained. The best we can do is conduct sensitivity exercises of how much a country might expect to lose by wrongly estimating its rivals' preferences. If those losses, and the rivals' gains, are small, there is no problem. But if they are large, some form of robust policy rule will be needed. Hughes Hallett (1987c) looks at those gains and losses using the MCM model on a United States versus OECD exercise and finds that neither player has any real incentive to misrepresent its preferences on any but the shared exchange rate target. Moreover, coordination reduces the dangers of such deceptions or specification errors. These findings appear to support the common presumption that policymakers will not deliberately mislead each other.

Model Uncertainty and Model Disagreement

Another source of error that is likely to damage policy calculations and thus reduce the incentives and willingness to coordinate is modeling errors. On top of this, policymakers may (and often do) disagree about which model to use. Frankel and Rockett (1988) examine the consequences of the assumption that governments differ about their view of the world. Using ten of the international models participating in the recent Brookings model comparison exercise (Bryant and others, 1988), they examine all 1,000 possible combinations where the two governments (the United States and the rest of the world) can subscribe to any of the ten models, and the true state of the world can in turn be any of the ten models. Coordination yields benefits in just over 60 percent of the combinations; in more than one third of the combinations, cooperation makes matters worse for at least one of the countries. However, this rather pessimistic view of the benefits to be expected from international policy coordination has been questioned by more recent work. It depends on the assumption that policymakers take no account of the presence of different views about the probabilities to be assigned to each model being correct when computing the expected outcomes under each bargain. To be fair, Frankel (1987) does show that use of a compromise model in cases of disagreement can increase the probability of benefits from coordination, although this result must depend on the choice of models and probabilities used to construct that compromise. If policymakers disagreed with that choice of models or probabilities, they would not be convinced. For this reason Holtham and Hughes Hallett (1987) have shown that ruling out "weak" bargains, in which either one party or the other expects his rival to be made worse off by the bargain, greatly improves the success rate of coordination when it occurs. They argue that governments would wish to rule out such bargains because they will be liable to reneging and could jeopardize future coordination attempts. In other words, governments would need to expect gains ex post, as well as ex ante, before entering a bargain. Ghosh and Masson (1988a,b) similarly show that the presence of model uncertainty may appreciably raise the expected benefits of coordination if governments design their policies with explicit regard to the presence of model uncertainty.

Once again the importance of information exchanges comes to the fore: stubbornness by policymakers points more to the need to educate policymakers by exposing them to alternative views of the world than to avoiding international coordination altogether. Governments aware of the adverse consequences of model disagreement would certainly take those consequences into account when choosing their policies, models, and degree of coordination, greatly reducing the force of this objection to policy coordination.

A more specific aspect of model uncertainty arises in the target zone proposal in the choice of the target equilibrium exchange rates (or FEERs). Disagreements over the choice of FEERs will clearly arise if there is disagreement over model structure. If different policymakers aim for inconsistent FEERs, the result clearly may be destabilizing (Hughes Hallett, 1989). Once again, the answer is that model uncertainty should be explicitly acknowledged by policymakers and compromise FEERs agreed on. Taking explicit account of uncertainty will do much to mitigate the conflicts that might otherwise arise.

V. The Forms of Coordination

What lessons may be drawn from the extended body of research now available on the international coordination of macroeconomic policy, and what guidance does it offer for the practice of coordination?

One conclusion highlighted by our previous discussion is the benefit of information exchange among international policymakers. Thus, an appreciable part of the benefits that derive from discussions among policymakers from different countries derives not from the explicit coordination of policies, but rather from making policymakers aware of the consequences of their actions on other countries and of the impact of foreign policy changes on them. Information exchange improves the quality and efficiency of the non-coordinated outcome, even if coordination over actual policy actions is not forthcoming.

It is sometimes suggested that the efficient exchange of information among the policymakers of different governments can be taken for granted, given the range and frequency of meetings of international policymakers. But it is important to distinguish different levels of information exchange. Routine forecasts may be readily transmitted, but other critical information (for example, on the quality of, and confidence in, these forecasts) may be communicated only in small group interactions of a less routine kind. Moreover, the range of relevant information includes that about potential policy responses to the policy actions of others (which in the academic literature are labeled, somewhat misleadingly, as "threats"), information about which will be exchanged only in rather special circumstances. Since knowledge of the potential policy reactions of others may be crucial in ensuring the attainment of efficient outcomes, it is a mistake to take for granted that information is efficiently exchanged. In general, national representations at international meetings show a marked reluctance to discuss hypothetical questions or to make conditional undertakings.

It is of interest in this regard to note the possible consequences of increasing the role of the Group of Three countries as the focus for policy coordination. By excluding less important participants, this may have acted to enhance the effective exchange of information among the Group of Three countries themselves, with potential efficiency gains. However, the exclusion of other Group of Seven members, and the absence of a voice from other interests, may also have reduced the quality of information exchange outside the Group of Three. An important issue for policy coordination is to consider how this possible deficiency may be repaired, perhaps by means of a more explicit hierarchy in the exchange of information.

A further conclusion that emerges from the literature concerns the benefits to be derived from a rule-based system of coordination. These benefits accrue from the advantages of reputation and credibility in policymaking, on which policymakers are rightly placing greater weight. The advantage of reputation is that it may be used to avoid the inefficiencies that otherwise arise from an overemphasis on the short term in policymaking. However, as discussed above, the literature on coordination suggests that these benefits may not accrue if national policymakers pursue reputational policies independently of one another; indeed, the pursuit of independent reputational policies may generate a highly undesirable outcome.

Explicit rules for the international macroeconomy may also act as an important discipline on the actions of government. While democratic governments should, and do, have appreciable freedom of action, the public choice literature, springing from the work of Buchanan and others, emphasizes that pressure groups and sectional interests may exert undue influence on government policy, leading to severely inefficient outcomes for government fiscal, monetary, and other policies. There may be scope for constraining government action to more efficient outcomes by means of appropriate rules. Such rules may be internal, as in the separation of fiscal and monetary powers in some countries or limits on final action. But the diversity of political structure and constitution across countries means that reliance on internal rules alone will generate rather uneven outcomes across countries, making for imbalances in the international system. This suggests a need for international agreements concerning rules that act as a further constraint on governments' policy actions.

We have also argued that policy rules should be simple in design, not least to avoid opaqueness in the conduct of policy. It would be difficult, if not impossible, for policymakers to explain the rationale for their actions, save by appeal to a technical box of tricks that neither they nor the public understand. The simplest forms of rules are, of course, fixed open-loop rules where the key policy variables are set on a fixed trajectory, independently of economic developments. Examples would be Friedman's k% rule for the money supply, a fiscal policy of balancing the budget at all times, and a system of irrevocably fixed exchange rates. Such rules combine the virtue of total simplicity with the possibility that they may be enshrined in law or constitution if that is felt to be appropriate. Moreover, certain forms of these rules have the advantage that they obviate the possibility of international coordination. Thus, monetary targets and budget balance are wholly consistent with each country "putting its own house in order" and entail operating independently of policy actions elsewhere. (Exchange rate targeting, by contrast, requires agreement as to where the responsibility for stabilizing foreign exchange markets lies, and coordination among the authorities of different countries if this responsibility is shared.)

A common objection to fixed rules of this kind is that they perform rather poorly in terms of short-run stabilization policy. However, this argument has limited force since it relies too heavily on a detailed knowledge of the short-run dynamic behavior of the system, which is not at hand. The more serious objection is that they perform satisfactorily only in a world characterized in the long run by a unique, non-path-dependent equilibrium. Path dependency may arise from a variety of forms of hysteresis in the labor and goods markets, including external trade. Those who argue for policy coordination rest their case most readily on the presence of such effects. Not surprisingly, those who adhere to belief in a unique NAIRU are unconvinced of the benefits of coordination.

The presence of path dependencies points to the need for flexible policy rules. But we have already suggested that such rules should be simple. A set of rules or a blueprint that conforms to these requirements of flexibility and simplicity includes the Williamson-Miller extended target zone scheme (Williamson and Miller, 1987). However, the systematic evaluation of such schemes (reviewed above) is still in progress. What is required is to find blueprints that are robust in their performance, that is, that perform well in a wide variety of circumstances. The academic literature on the design of simple rules that are robust is a rapidly growing one, and one that is likely to yield appreciable insights. One helpful insight is that it may not be necessary to seek agreement in all aspects of policy to obtain the benefits of coordination. Levine, Currie, and Gaines (1988) show how agreement over the *form* of rule may be sufficient, leaving governments to determine in an independent, noncooperative manner the degree of response built into the rule. Thus, the benefits of coordination can be derived from international agreements that cover only certain dimensions of international macropolicy, though this may depend on the choice of variables included in such agreements.

If such rules are to offer the benefits of greater credibility in policy, as we have argued they should, it is important that they be well understood. This requires greater transparency in public policymaking than we have been accustomed to. It also requires that the rules and targets be publicly announced.

Exchange rates have provided the principal focus for policy coordination over the past few years, and there are sound reasons why this should be so. Commitment to an international agreement on exchange rates may do much to limit divergencies in underlying policy stances among countries. (Thus, it may be argued that, although the European Monetary System (EMS) has not led to marked convergence on fiscal policy between member countries, it has avoided excessive divergence of the kind that has been observed outside the EMS.) In addition to this role in *relative* coordination, such agreements may also be failures of coordination. Thus, by limiting the scope for individual policymakers to bring down domestic inflation by an over-appreciated exchange rate, such agreements may reduce the scope for excessive mismatches between monetary and fiscal policy at the global level. As important, perhaps, is the fact that exchange rates are readily monitored in an objective manner, making them a ready vehicle for international agreements. Sensibly designed agreements can avoid undue exchange rate volatility and longer-term misalignments. While short-run volatility probably imposes rather low costs, the costs of prolonged misalignments may well be appreciable.

International agreements on exchange rates need to be based on some view of what constitutes a sustainable or equilibrium set of exchange rates. These FEERs will, of course, change over time; thus, real FEERs will change because of movements in underlying real determinants, and nominal FEERs will change in addition, to reflect inflation differentials. It is important, therefore, that agreements are able to incorporate trends in equilibrium rates. This suggests that agreements that seek simply to fix nominal rates will prove rather vulnerable.

Some critics of exchange rate agreements argue that there is no reason to suppose that policymakers can take a better long-run view of exchange rates than the market. The difficulty with this view is that the foreign exchange market is dominated by short-run speculation, including beliefs about what monetary authorities will do next. This short-run focus is due partly to the fact that, in a world of volatile exchange rates, the premium is in assessing short-run market developments, not longer-run trends. But it is also because institutional fund managers are remunerated in such a way that emphasizes short-run gains. Frequently, to take a correct long view merely bequeaths higher bonuses to one's successor. Moreover, most market participants are skilled in gathering information about the positions of other market participants and in guessing what they will do. This, rather than economic analysis of fundamentals, is their stock in trade. Of course they can, and do, hire economists to describe fundamentals, but these are usually less regarded in making trading decisions than the views of traders themselves. This situation would not persist if the economic fundamentals rapidly and decisively determined exchange rates, but that is not the case. Given that large and volatile funds are driven by expectations, fundamentals work slowly and feebly. Moreover, they can be changed by the actual path of the exchange rate, which can influence, for example, real investment decisions. For these reasons, the authorities can helpfully guide the market concerning medium-term trends. If the authorities make credible commitments to guide exchange rates toward equilibrium levels, the market will give greater weight to such considerations, so that policy will go with the grain of the market. The role of exchange market intervention consists in the authorities demonstrating to the market that they are ready to bet on their own views, thus influencing market expectations in a climate of uncertainty.

It may be argued that the calculation of equilibrium exchange rates is fraught with difficulties and uncertainties. We may put to one side McKinnon's purchasing-power-parity view of equilibrium rates, fatally flawed as it is by problems of index numbers. Part of this uncertainty reflects uncertainties and divergencies in our models of the international economy (see Bryant and others, 1988). A particularly vulnerable aspect of such models, important to the calculations of FEERs, is the modeling of the medium-term capital account, reflecting international investment and location decisions together with savings behavior. This is a much under-researched area that may well yield substantial return. It is perhaps unfortunate, from a policy perspective, that so much research effort has been diverted toward the modeling of short-run exchange rate behavior—dominated as it is by speculative behavior that is hard to model—and relatively little on underlying capital flows.

It is, however, important to appreciate the link between FEERs and the underlying stance of monetary and fiscal policies. In calculating FEERs, it is necessary to make assumptions about the medium- to longer-run stance of fiscal and monetary policy. It thus does not make sense to calculate FEERs and then, as a second stage, to calculate the medium- to longer-run policy stance required to sustain those FEERs; rather the calculations are simultaneous. What is required is the simultaneous assessment of sustainable monetary and fiscal policies and of sustainable exchange rates. One technique for doing this is put forward in Hughes Hallett, Holtham, and Hutson (1989).

Thinking about the issue in this way helps to narrow the gap between those who emphasize the link between current accounts and savings-investment positions (see Frenkel and Goldstein, 1986; Boughton, 1988; and the target zone approach of Williamson and Miller, 1987). The target zone proposal may be thought of as setting sustainable medium-term policies, coupled with shorter-run management of exchange rates within wide bands around their sustainable levels. It is consistent with this that monetary policy should be used primarily with a high frequency response to ensure exchange rate stability, while fiscal policy is adjusted more gradually to ensure internal balance and to avoid longer-run problems of sustainability.

Within this approach, a system of bands should be capable of coping with the uncertainties and divergencies of view over equilibrium exchange rates. Such bands may be wide at the outset, but success and growing confidence in the system and greater certainty about the long-run tendencies of the system should permit a narrowing over time. In addition, the central target may be publicly announced, but the edges of the zone may be left vague; this gives added freedom for maneuver to authorities without undermining the credibility of their commitment to stabilize exchange rates. Over time, confidence in the system may allow the authorities to define the limits of the zone more precisely. A further possibility is that the width of bands is set to reflect the degree of agreement among countries. Such an arrangement would recognize explicitly the continuum of possibilities between the extremes of full cooperation and noncooperation.

A system of explicit target bands would compel discussion on the overall thrust of policy and the appropriateness of policy stance in different countries. As such, it would provide a fertile ground for disagreement and friction. However, it is a matter of historical record that free floating did not abolish such friction.

In any event, the development of indicators and forecasts to guide the overall policy stance must appear necessary to all except those policymakers or economists who continue to believe the following: either that governments need only concern themselves with inflation because the costs of any disinflationary policy—no matter how draconian—are small and evanescent, or alternatively that while it does matter to gauge macroeconomic policy correctly, the monetary aggregates, for example, provide an infallible means of doing so. If neither of these holds, any government, whatever the weights in its objective function, must set policy with the awareness of potential trade-offs and with regard to the likely consequences.

That said, recent experience does not encourage confidence in our ability to forecast accurately. In 1988, demand and output were much stronger than expected, whether owing to monetary ease in late 1987 or, more probably, the delayed effects of terms-of-trade gains in 1986 and capital scrapping providing a "Hicksian floor" to a period of slow growth. Recent experience provides evidence against activist "demand management" and in favor of cautious policy responses. But that is not evidence for complete immobility or against a firmer framework of international cooperation. Indeed, the experience of the past decade has made international cooperation appear not only desirable, but inevitable.

VI. Conclusions

In this paper, we have reviewed the theory and practice of international macroeconomic policy coordination. We have argued that policymakers have revealed in practice a preference for coordination based around the targeting of exchange rates. We have also argued that there is an economic rationale for exchange rate targeting, contrary to much of the academic literature. This is partly because exchange rate stability matters in its own right, and exchange rate targeting can help to dampen fads and speculative bubbles in foreign exchange markets. It is also because a regime of exchange rate targeting acts as a discipline on the monetary and fiscal policies of the participating countries. In so doing, exchange rate targets help what we have termed absolute coordination as well as relative coordination.

Recent Group of Seven coordination exercises have made a start at establishing a system of macroeconomic coordination based on exchange rates. The question now is how this system can be developed further and strengthened. One significant development would be for governments to commit to publicly announced exchange rate objectives, which could serve as the basis for private sector expectations and consistent policies. The current arrangement of unannounced targets weakens the efficacy of such targets in providing an anchor for expectations, preventing fads and bubbles. However, although the central rates should be announced, it may be advantageous to have soft shoulders to the target zones, so that the edges of the zones are uncertain. The process of setting target zones collaboratively is also a possible basis for determining a coherent set of fiscal policies. Complete coordination of fiscal policy is neither practical nor necessary as there is no reason to suppose that there is a unique fiscal policy consistent with equilibrium in each country. Yet it would be necessary in settling on target zones to decide whether current and planned fiscal policies are broadly compatible and sustainable. Establishing well-defined target zones requires the elimination of the grossest forms of fiscal excess and inconsistency among countries' policies.

Against the background of fiscal stances that are mutually consistent in the medium term, the onus of coordination would fall primarily on monetary policy. Monetary policy could be directed to maintaining exchange rates within the target zone and to ensuring that the growth of world nominal income proceeds at a moderate, controlled rate. Setting monetary policy in that way entails either continuous cooperation among all central banks or, more plausibly, a hierarchy in which the Group of Three countries set monetary policy according to global indicators and other countries manage monetary policy consistently while keeping exchange rates within the designated target zones.

Zones may need to be revised explicitly in the light of persistent market-driven movements of exchange rates, policy disagreements on the rate of nominal income growth, or large shocks to the system. Zone widths should be large enough to reflect the uncertainties involved and to make realignments rare.

Such a program does not appear to be politically infeasible. Indeed, we would argue that it represents a modest, but helpful, advance from the current position. It would differ from Bretton Woods in giving much greater freedom for exchange rates to move moderately in response to supply and demand in the foreign exchange market, and in being buttressed by a more explicit focus and coordination on the issue of "world" monetary policy. It would not encourage or require coordinated fine-tuning of demand.

Although we are positive about a development along these lines, we are not necessarily optimistic about it coming about quickly or readily. It is unlikely that such developments as these will be undertaken without the goad of further alarms, or even crises, in world monetary affairs. On the other hand, under the current dispensation, such alarms can be expected to occur.

References

Boffi, Paolo, "Comments on International Liquidity, Paper by Professor Scitovsky," in *International Economic Relations,* ed. by Paul Sammelton (London: Macmillan, 1969).

Boughton, James, "Policy Coordination with Somewhat Flexible Exchange Rates," in *Blueprints for Exchange Rate Management,* ed. by Barry Eichengreen, Marcus Miller, and Richard Portes (London: Macmillan, 1988).

Brandsma, Andries S., Andrew Hughes Hallett, and Joop Swank, "The Robustness of Economic Policy Selections and the Incentive to Cooperate," *Journal of Economic Dynamics and Control,* No. 11 (Amsterdam: 1987).

Bryant, Ralph, "Intergovernmental Coordination of Economic Policies: An Interim Stocktaking," in *International Monetary Cooperation Essays in Honor of Henry C. Wallich, Princeton Essays in International Finance, No. 169* (Princeton, New Jersey: Princeton University Press, 1987).

————, and others, eds., *Empirical Macroeconomics for Interdependent Economics* (Washington: The Brookings Institution, 1988).

Canzoneri, Matthew, and JoAnna Gray, "Monetary Policy Games and the Consequences of Non-Cooperative Behavior," *International Economic Review* (Philadelphia, Pennsylvania: Wharton School of Finance and Commerce, 1985).

Canzoneri, Matthew, and Patrick Minford, "When Policy Coordination Matters: An Empirical Analysis," Centre for Economic Policy Research Discussion Paper No. 119 (London: CEPR, July 1986).

Carlozzi, Nicholas, and John Taylor, "International Capital Mobility and the Coordination of Monetary Rules," in *Exchange Rate Management under Uncertainty,* ed. by J. Bhandari (Cambridge, Massachusetts: MIT Press, 1985).

Carraro, Carlo, and Francesco Giavazzi, "Can International Policy Coordination Really be Counterproductive?" Centre for Economic Policy Research Discussion Paper No. 258 (London: CEPR, August 1988), pp. 1–23.

Cooper. Richard N., "Macroeconomic Policy Adjustment in Interdependent Economies," *Quarterly Journal of Economics*, Vol. 83 (New York: February 1969).

―――, "Economic Interdependence and Coordination of Economic Policies," in *Handbook of International Economics*, ed. by R. W. Jones and P. B. Kenen, Vol. 2 (Amsterdam: North-Holland, 1985).

―――, "International Economic Cooperation: Overview and a Climate of the Future in OECD, Interdependence and Cooperation in Tomorrow's World" (Paris: Organization for Economic Cooperation and Development, 1987).

Currie, David A., and Paul Levine, "Macroeconomic Policy Design in an Interdependent World," in W. H. Buiter and R. C. Marston, eds., *International Economic Policy Coordination* (Cambridge and New York: Cambridge University Press, 1985).

Currie, David A., Paul Levine, and Nic Vidalis, "Cooperative and Noncooperative Rules for Monetary and Fiscal Policy in an Empirical Two-Bloc Model," in Ralph Bryant and Richard Portes, eds., *Global Macroeconomics: Policy Conflict and Cooperation* (London: Macmillan, 1987).

Currie, David A., and David Vines, *Macroeconomic Interactions between North and South* (Cambridge: Cambridge University Press, 1988).

Currie, David A., and Simon Wren-Lewis, "Evaluating the Extended Target Zone Proposal for the G3," Centre for Economic Policy Research Discussion Paper No. 221 (London: CEPR, January 1988).

―――, "Evaluating Blueprints for the Conduct of International Macropolicy," *American Economic Review*, Vol. 79, No. 2 (Nashville, Tennessee: 1989).

Edison, Hali, Marcus Miller, and John Williamson, "On Evaluating and Extending the Target Zone Proposal," *Journal of Policy Modelling*, No. 9 (New York: 1987).

Feldstein, Martin, "The World Economy Today," *The Economist* (London), June 11, 1983.

Frankel, Jeffrey A., "Obstacles to International Macroeconomic Policy Coordination," International Monetary Fund Working Paper No. 87/28 (Washington: IMF, 1987).

―――, and Katherine E. Rockett, "International Macroeconomic Policy Coordination When Policy Makers Do Not Agree on the True Model," *American Economic Review*, Vol. 78 (Nashville, Tennessee: 1988).

Frenkel, Jacob A., and Morris Goldstein, "A Guide to Target Zones," International Monetary Fund, *Staff Papers*, Vol. 33 (Washington: IMF, 1986).

Ghosh, Atish R., and Paul R. Masson (1988a), "International Policy Coordination in a World with Model Uncertainty," International Monetary Fund, *Staff Papers*, Vol. 35 (Washington: IMF, 1988).

―――― (1988b), "Model Uncertainty, Learning and the Gains from Coordination," International Monetary Fund Working Paper (Washington: IMF, December 1988).

Hamada, Koichi, "Alternative Exchange Rate Systems and the Interdependence of Monetary Policies," in R. Z. Aliber, ed., *National Monetary Policies and the International Financial System* (Chicago: University of Chicago Press, 1974).

————, "A Strategic Analysis of Monetary Interdependence," *Journal of Political Economy*, Vol. 83 (Chicago: 1976), pp. 677–700.

Helkie, William, and others, "Protectionism and the U.S. Trade Deficit: An Empirical Analysis," Centre for Economic Policy Research Discussion Paper No. 286 (London: CEPR, 1989).

Holtham, Gerald, "German Macroeconomic Policy and the 1978 Bonn Summit," in *Can Nations Agree?*, ed. by Ralph Bryant and E. Hodgkinson (Washington: The Brookings Institution, 1989).

————, and Andrew Hughes Hallett, "International Policy Cooperation and Model Uncertainty," in Ralph Bryant and Richard Portes, eds., *Global Macroeconomics: Policy Conflict and Cooperation* (London: Macmillan, 1987); an extended version in Centre for Economic Policy Research Discussion Paper No. 190 (London: CEPR, 1989).

Horne, Jocelyn, and Paul R. Masson, "Scope and Limits of International Economic Cooperation and Policy Coordination," International Monetary Fund, *Staff Papers* Vol. 35 (Washington: IMF, 1988).

Hughes Hallett, Andrew (1986a), "Autonomy and the Choice of Policy in Asymmetrically Dependent Economies," *Oxford Economic Papers*, Vol. 38 (Oxford, England: 1986).

———— (1986b), "International Policy Design and the Sustainability of Policy Bargains," *Journal of Economic Dynamics and Control*, Vol. 10 (Amsterdam: 1986).

———— (1987a), "The Impact of Interdependence on Economic Policy Design: The Case of the US, EEC and Japan," *Economic Modelling*, No. 4 (London: Butterworth, 1987).

———— (1987b), "Robust Policy Regimes for Interdependent Economies: A New Argument for Coordinating Economic Policies," Centre for Economic Policy Research Discussion Paper No. 151 (London); forthcoming in *Economic Modelling* (1989).

———— (1987c), "How Robust Are the Gains to Policy Coordination to Variations in the Model and Objectives?" *Ricerche Economiche* (special issue on Game Theory and Economics), No. 41, 1987.

————, "What Are the Risks in International Policy Coordination?" in R. MacDonald and M. Taylor, eds., *Exchange Rates and Open Economy Macroeconomics* (Oxford: Blackwell and Co., 1989).

————, Gerald Holtham, and Gary Hutson, "Exchange Rate Targetting as a Surrogate for International Policy Coordination," in Barry Eichengreen, Marcus Miller, and Richard Portes, eds., *Blueprints for Exchange Rate Management* (London and New York: Academic Press, 1989).

Levine, Paul, and David A. Currie, "Does International Policy Coordination Pay and Is It Sustainable? A Two Country Analysis," *Oxford Economic Papers*, Vol. 39 (Oxford, England: 1987).

Levine, Paul, David A. Currie, and Jessica Gaines, "The Use of Simple Rules for International Policy Agreements," in Barry Eichengreen, Marcus Miller, and Richard Portes, eds., *Blueprints for Exchange Rate Management* (London and New York: Academic Press, 1989).

McKinnon, Ronald, "An International Standard for Monetary Stabilization," Institute for International Economics, *Policy Analyses in International Economics*, No. 8 (Washington: IIE, 1984).

Miller, Marcus H., and Mark H. Salmon, "Policy Coordination and Dynamic Games," in W. M. Buiter and R. C. Marston, eds., *International Economic Policy Coordination* (Cambridge: Cambridge University Press, 1985).

Miller, Marcus H., and John Williamson, "The International Monetary System: An Analysis of Alternative Regimes," *European Economic Review*, Vol. 32 (Amsterdam: 1988).

Minford, Patrick, and Matthew Canzoneri, "Policy Interdependence: Does Strategic Behaviour Pay?", Centre for Economic Policy Research Discussion Paper 201 (London: CEPR, 1987).

Oudiz, Gilles, and Jeffrey Sachs, "Macroeconomic Policy Coordination Among the Industrial Economies," *Brookings Papers on Economic Activity: 1* (Washington: The Brookings Institution, 1984).

_____,"International Policy Coordination in Dynamic Macroeconomic Models," in W. H. Buiter and R. C. Marston, eds., *International Economic Policy Coordination* (Cambridge and New York: Cambridge University Press, 1985).

Putnam, Robert D., and C. Randall Henning, "The Bonn Summit of 1978: A Case Study in Coordination," in *Can Nations Agree?*, ed. by Ralph Bryant and E. Hodgkinson (Washington: The Brookings Institution, 1989).

Rogoff, Kenneth, "Can International Monetary Policy Coordination Be Counterproductive?" *Journal of International Economics*, Vol. 18 (Amsterdam: May 1985).

Taylor, John B., "International Coordination in the Design of Macroeconomic Policy Rules," *European Economic Review*, Vol. 28 (Amsterdam: June-July 1985).

Tew, Brian, *International Monetary Cooperation 1945–67* (London: Harkinson, 1967).

Triffin, Robert, *Gold and the Dollar Crisis* (New Haven, Connecticut: Yale University Press, 1961).

Williamson, John, and Marcus H. Miller, *Targets and Indicators: A Blueprint for the International Coordination of Economic Policy* (Washington: Institute for International Economics, 1987).

Comments

Vito Tanzi

The title of the paper by Currie and others refers to the theory *and* practice of coordination. Jeffrey Frankel is more qualified than I am to address the theoretical aspects. I shall, therefore, focus on the practical aspects—emphasizing difficulties that are likely to be encountered in the process of coordinating fiscal policies, an area where, perhaps, I have a comparative advantage.

The paper begins with a useful description of the experience of international *cooperation*. I assume that the choice of the word—cooperation rather than coordination—is intentional. Perhaps the literature on coordination has agreed on precise meanings for these two words, so that it was not necessary for the authors to spell out the differences. However, the paper keeps shifting back and forth in the use of these two terms and I sometimes had difficulty in understanding the difference.

The authors identify five periods: (a) a U.S. dollar shortage period, from 1945 to 1958; (b) the "Golden Age" for the Bretton Woods System, from 1959 to 1973; (c) a period of generalized floating, from 1974 to 1979; (d) a period dominated by the ideology of monetarism, between 1980 and 1985; and (e) the most recent period in which a "form of loose coordination of monetary policy and foreign exchange market intervention is practiced." For the 1980–85 period, the authors tell us we had convergence but not coordination! Considering how divergent American fiscal *and* tax policies were from those of other large industrial countries, I have some difficulty in seeing this convergence. Indeed, it would be hard to find another period when economic policies (and not just macroeconomic policies) were more misaligned.

The paper distinguishes between *absolute* and *relative* coordination. Here the authors do give us definitions. The first ". . . covers the overall stance of policy in the leading industrial countries and seeks to avoid aggregate errors such as excessively loose or tight policies for the world as a whole." The second ". . . is concerned with the interactions between countries and, therefore, tends to focus on exchange rates and balance of payments positions." Absolute coordination is far more demanding in terms of commitments by policymakers than relative coordination. It is also more demanding on intellectual grounds, so that some who may favor relative coordination may feel uncomfortable with absolute coordination. To me, the latter smells of demand management or even fine-tuning on a world scale!

The authors remark that absolute and relative coordination have often been confused. The coordination that we have had since 1985 is much closer to relative than absolute. One has to wonder whether it would have made much sense to attempt a policy of absolute coordination given the many obstacles to it. Thus, perhaps, the gap between the rhetoric and the practice of coordination has been reduced by aiming at the more modest and realistic objective of relative coordination.

The paper reviews studies that have attempted to answer the question of whether coordination pays. It recognizes that much theoretical work has proceeded in the context of "highly simplified models" and comments that "the literature has an unusually strong flavor of unreality to practical men." I could not tell whether this was intended to be a comment on the practical men or on the literature.

The authors summarize the results of several studies on the potential gains from *full* policy coordination. (Does full mean absolute?) These studies have concluded that (a) the gains from full coordination are likely to be small; and (b) it is not clear how these gains are distributed across countries. In other words, it is likely that some of the participating countries will get nothing from the exercise. If these conclusions are correct, this may be one reason why it is difficult to secure and maintain coordination agreements. After all, policymakers' time is valuable and policy actions necessitated by coordination have domestic political costs. Furthermore, pressures on the policymakers of some countries to induce them to take policy actions that—because of their high domestic political costs—they do not like, may become very intense at coordinating meetings. Coordination is joint policymaking with differential political leverage. Here one may run into a problem that, elsewhere, I have referred to as the fox-without-the-tail syndrome.[1] As in Aesop's tale, where the fox that lost its tail went around trying to convince the other foxes to get rid of theirs, the politically more powerful countries may find it convenient to push other countries to take actions that would reduce the pressures on the former to put their houses in order.

Another important conclusion seems to be that the gains from coordination (or is it cooperation?) come mostly from the exchange of information among countries. I would strongly agree with this conclusion. In this connection, the important role played by some of the activities of the international institutions (Article IV consultations in the Fund, the World Economic Outlook exercise and discussion, meetings of the Organization for Economic Cooperation and Development, etc.) cannot be overemphasized. These are often the main vehicles for spreading information. However, the authors believe that meetings on policy coordination may provide a vehicle to pass on useful confidential, or nonpublic, information. This is a romantic view of coordination meetings. I would be far less sanguine about the value of this nonpublic information. Outside of foreign market intervention, it is difficult to

---

[1] See Vito Tanzi, "International Coordination of Fiscal Policies: A Review of Some Major Issues," forthcoming in *Fiscal Policy, Economic Adjustment and Financial Markets*, edited by Mario Monti (Washington: International Monetary Fund, 1989). This paper was presented at a conference organized by the IMF and the Università Bocconi in Milan, and held January 27–30, 1988.

think of other areas where this secret information would be passed on or would be useful.

The authors argue that the realization of the (small) gains from (full) coordination *depends on everything going according to plan*. But, of course, things rarely go fully according to plan. They identify four potential dangers: sustainability, exogenous shocks, uncertainty over objectives and priorities, and model disagreement or modeling errors. These have been discussed in several papers so I will limit my comments to some aspects of sustainability and exogenous shocks that have not attracted the attention that they deserve.

Sustainability. The authors ask the following question: Will coordinating policymakers stick to their part of the bargain or will they cheat by redesigning their future policies once they have the desired commitments from other participants? Though pertinent, this is really not the key question. The main danger is not likely to be one associated with the likelihood of cheating by policymakers of other countries. Policymakers are, one would hope, honorable men or women. Rather, there are two other questions that are more central. First, coordination must obviously be based on commitments for *future policy* actions. Can policymakers make such commitments with the assurance that they will be able to carry them out? Second, and not unrelated to the first, how much control do these policymakers have over the instruments of economic policy that need to be changed to make the agreements stick?

Although in theory coordinating agreements are made by governments, in practice they reflect the roles of specific men. For example, on December 9, 1988 the news agencies reported the resignation of the Japanese Finance Minister Kiichi Miyazawa. They also reported an announcement by a senior Japanese Finance Ministry official to the effect that ". . . Miyazawa's departure is unlikely to affect cooperation among [Group of Seven] countries on policy coordination and exchange rate stability" (IMF *Morning Press*, December 9, 1988). If one recalls the changes (for example vis-à-vis intervention in the foreign exchange market) that accompanied the replacement of Donald Regan with James Baker at the U.S. Treasury, one immediately sees the need for the Japanese reassurance. That replacement could well have been accompanied by a statement by a senior U.S. Treasury official to the effect that Mr. Regan's departure was likely to affect cooperation among Group of Seven countries on policy coordination and exchange rate stability. Of course if the change is not limited to specific individuals but extends to governments, the probability that a country will stick to a commitment is likely to be even smaller. The longer the period for which the commitment is made, the greater the probability that these changes will occur.

This issue of sustainability is particularly important for policies that require time to implement. Coordinating policymakers have tenuous control over the instruments relevant to such policies. Unlike monetary policy or foreign exchange intervention, which can be carried out in a relatively short period of time and by a few individuals, control over fiscal policy in many countries is very limited and diffused. In such cases, it may be more difficult to agree on policy action within a country than across countries. Therefore, a commitment to a given fiscal policy may often have limited value. Even when that commitment takes the force of law, as, for example, with Gramm-Rudman-Hollings, it may be much less firm than one might assume. As Rudy Penner, former Director of the U.S. Congressional Budget Office, has, somewhat cynically, recently put it:

> Gramm-Rudman-Hollings is a wonderful law. All you have to do is forecast that you'll meet the targets. You don't have to actually meet them. One hundred billion dollars is within cheating distance—otherwise they'll amend the targets. (*Tax Notes*, December 5, 1988, pp. 1008–1009.)

It is no accident that coordination has been most successful in those areas (exchange rate intervention and monetary policy) where a few individuals who know each other well have, in many cases, the power to take the necessary actions. Furthermore, as in the case of foreign market intervention or changes in discount rates, these actions can be taken within a short time.

Exogenous shocks. The authors state that there is evidence that information errors and exogenous shocks can cause significant disturbances and affect incentives to cooperate, especially if the shocks are large and persistent. Forecasting errors would, of course, be a most serious example of information error. It is thus surprising that the section on dangers does not explicitly raise the issue of the reliability of forecasts even though the authors concede that ". . . recent experience does not encourage confidence in our ability to forecast very accurately." In view of the 1988 experience, that conclusion could establish a good claim to be the understatement of the year. As a recent article has stated, "The year 1988 is one economic forecasters will prefer to forget." (See Rodney Lord, "Forecasting the Future Yet Ignorant of Today," *The Times* (London), December 28, 1988, p. 23.)

In October 1987 the growth rate of the industrial countries for 1988 was generally projected at about 2.5 percent. In April 1988, the forecast was raised to almost 3 percent. It is now estimated that actual growth for 1988 is likely to have exceeded 4.25 percent. A forecasting error of 70 percent is just too large. Should countries change policies that require a long time to implement (such as fiscal policy) away from their medium-term objectives on the basis of forecasts that can be so wrong? Or, putting it differently, should countries attempt *absolute* coordination even if they can control the relevant instruments? But, of course, as argued earlier, some of the relevant instruments are not controllable. It would seem that realism would argue in favor of relative rather than absolute coordination.

Jeffrey A. Frankel

The paper by Currie, Holtham, and Hughes Hallett provides a nice review of the history of international macroeconomic policymaking since 1945 and a good review of the recent empirical literature on the subject, much of it produced in Great Britain. In my view all the twists and turns of the historical recounting are right on track.[1] But I will direct most of my comments to the discussion of the empirical literature.

The authors discuss a variety of issues with which international policy coordination is forced to deal. These issues seem to me to fall into three categories: (1) the sustainability of an agreement, (2) uncertainty, in its various forms, and (3) the time-inconsistency of inflation-fighting.

Sustainability

The starting point in the coordination literature is the proposition that an agreed-upon package of policy changes necessarily raises the economic welfare of each country participating (at least ex ante)—otherwise the country would not have agreed to it—but that each country has an incentive to reap further gain in the short run by deviating from the agreement and leaving its partners to carry the burden alone. It has been suggested that economists often over-emphasize the problems of enforcement, what Currie and others call the problem of sustainability.[2] Countries are unlikely in practice to "cheat," provided that the agreement specifies clearly what is expected of them. My own conjecture is that two requirements are necessary for an agreement to be sustainable, that is, for each of the members to decide in each period that the long-run gains of continuing to abide by the agreement outweigh any short-run gains to be had from unilaterally abrogating the agreement. The two requirements are as follows:

(1) The members must be able to monitor each other's compliance. This leads to a preference for "intermediate targeting" schemes, in which the members commit to specific observable targets, which we might call "performance criteria" by analogy with International Monetary Fund country programs. As Currie and others point out, these intermediate targeting schemes are more likely to be sustainable if they are simple. They are also more likely to hold up if the targets are publicly announced, rather than kept secret, as in the Group of Seven meetings of recent years. When a member questions another's compliance with an agreement, there is not much that can

---

[1] I particularly like some of the phrasing, such as the description of how the 1981 U.S. tax cut raised "the disposable income of those households unfamiliar with the works of David Ricardo or Robert Barro."

[2] Bryant (1987), Kenen (1987), and Holtham and Hughes Hallett (1987) have each suggested that economists may have exaggerated the problems of enforcement.

be done if the agreement was not explicit and public to begin with.

(2) Each party must believe that it gains, not just in an ex ante sense, but also ex post, under most realized states of the world. Otherwise, when a situation develops under which the agreement turns out to have been bad for a particular country in a particular period, that country's residents will consider the agreement "unfair," and strong political pressure will build to abrogate it.

If both of these conditions for sustainability of an agreement are met, it is probably less important in practice that any party could in theory gain still more by unilateral cheating (for the short time before the others retaliate). Notions of "fairness" and "honor," or—in terms that more easily lend themselves to economic modeling—the existence of reputations, are probably sufficient to enforce an agreement under these two conditions. But the two conditions may be difficult to satisfy in practice, due to the existence of the second set of issues that Currie and others discuss, those dealing with uncertainty.

Uncertainty

Currie and others discuss uncertainty of several kinds. There is uncertainty over (a) the status of the economy (what they call information errors and exogenous shocks), (b) the proper goals, and (c) the model. All three kinds of uncertainty can mean that one country or the other may lose ex post from an agreement even though it gains ex ante. Some of the presenting authors and I have each illustrated in some detail the last type of uncertainty, that regarding the correct policy multipliers. Coordination in the presence of model uncertainty can leave countries worse off ex post as easily as better off.[3] This conclusion holds even if policymakers recognize that they do not know the correct model with certainty.[4]

A classic example discussed in the paper by Currie and others is the Bonn Summit of 1978. In line with the famous "locomotive theory," the Federal Republic of Germany and Japan agreed to expand their economies to help the United States pull the world out of recession. In retrospect, the Germans consider this experiment to have been a clear failure, even though at the time they presumably thought that the package they agreed to was in their interest. The prevailing view by 1980 had become that inflation was the major threat, and that discipline, rather than expansion, was called for. This episode can be

---

[3] Holtham and Hughes Hallett (1987), Frankel and Rockett (1988), and Frankel (1988).

[4] In their paper, Currie and others erroneously state, as have a number of others, that the policymakers in my experiments ignore the existence of uncertainty despite the fact that they live in a world of competing models. This inaccuracy is easily understood, as the first draft of the Frankel and Rockett paper did indeed represent policymakers as stubbornly set on their own models. But in 1986, I performed the experiment where the policymakers place equal weight on each of the ten models being the correct one, and then maximize their expected welfare. (The conclusions change little.) The published versions of my papers (cited in the previous footnote) report these results, and I would now like to point this out.

used to illustrate any of the three kinds of uncertainty mentioned above. Illustrating the first type of uncertainty is the fact that because of the Iranian crisis of 1979 and the consequent second oil price shock, the world economy proved to be more inflationary than had been anticipated in the baseline forecast in 1978, so that in retrospect expansion was not called for. A second interpretation—illustrating uncertainty over policy goals—is that, after the more conservative Christian Democrats came to power in Bonn—with the Republicans in Washington at about the same time—the prevailing view assigned more weight to the inflation-fighting objective, relative to their predecessors who had assigned more weight to the growth objective. I would add a third possible interpretation, concerning model uncertainty: that the slope of the German aggregate supply function turned out to be higher, in other words, that the monetary expansion showed up more in the form of higher wages and prices and less in the form of higher output—at least in the view of the Germans—than had been anticipated in 1978. Any of these three interpretations is sufficient to illustrate the point that coordination, in the presence of uncertainty, can turn out to reduce economic welfare as easily as enhance it.

It follows that uncertainty can make it difficult to satisfy the requirement that each party see a gain in order for an agreement to be sustainable. The intermediate target variable must be chosen carefully. Our first lesson is that the intermediate target must be related relatively directly to the target variables that the countries ultimately care about—which include real growth and inflation. This makes the money supply, in particular, a bad choice. Large shifts in money demand (for example, the shifts in the U.S. money demand, downward in the 1970s and upward in the 1980s) could, ex post, render disastrous a money target that, ex ante, appeared desirable. Or, to return to the point about the conflicting results from the econometric models, the U.S. Treasury could ask Germany and Japan to adopt more expansionary monetary policies, because it believes the results from the models of the European Economic Community (EEC), McKibbin-Sachs Global (MSG), and the Organization for Economic Cooperation and Development (OECD), which suggest that this will have a positive effect on the U.S. current account and income—and yet the effect of such expansion may turn out to be negative as in the Multi-Country Model (MCM), MINIMOD (developed by Richard Haas and Paul Masson at the IMF), and Taylor models. (It depends whether the effect of a depreciation of the deutsche mark and Japanese yen on the trade balance outweighs the effect of higher German and Japanese income on U.S. exports.) If Americans think that they are losing from an international agreement, not just relative to the alternative of unilaterally violating the agreement *but also relative to not having entered into it to begin with*, they are likely to abrogate it.

Uncertainty can also make the requirement for mutual monitoring for sustainability difficult to satisfy. If the intermediate target or performance criterion is the overall inflation rate or the real growth rate, then an unexpected aggregate supply or aggregate demand shock can put a country out of compliance through no fault of its own. (Or, at least, the country can claim that this is what has happened, with some plausibility. This problem is, of course, familiar to Fund staff conducting surveillance of member countries.) Thus, our second lesson is that the variable chosen for the intermediate target must not be too far outside the control of the government authorities who are entering into the agreement. In my view (and here I think I part company with Currie and others, not to mention with Miller and Williamson, 1987), the exchange rate fails this requirement. I am sympathetic to the claim that some portion of exchange rate volatility is noise, unrelated to economic fundamentals. But even if a regime switch to an exchange rate target zone magically eliminated the worst of speculative bubbles, I doubt that countries would again be able to control the exchange rate as closely as they once could. In any case, we can all agree that the price of gold violates both of the requirements I have laid down for sustainability: it is simultaneously too far outside the control of the authorities and too distantly related to the target variables that we ultimately care about. My own choice for the best target is nominal gross national product (GNP), or nominal demand, because it is neither too distantly related to inflation and output, nor too far outside the control of the monetary authorities.

Robustness and Ruling Out "Weak" Bargains

I do not believe that the requirements for sustainability are well-stated as ruling out what Currie and others call "weak" bargains, those in which one party or the other expects its partner to be made worse off, ex post, by the bargain, and therefore to renege. The logic of the coordination experiments is that an admissible bargain is any in which each party expects, in the light of its own beliefs, that the bargain will, ex ante, leave it better off. It is not up to a country to be "its brother's keeper," to say in effect, "I know you would like to make this bargain, but I am going to protect you against your own foolishness by refusing to do it; you will thank me tomorrow."

Currie and others would argue that the country is merely operating in its own interest, because it knows that the partner will not abide by the agreement in the subsequent period when the truth is revealed. But certainly the partner will not accuse the first of failing to comply with the agreement; if it delivered the money supply or whatever other target that it promised, it cannot be blamed for the outcome being different from what the partner was expecting. So Currie and others must have something else in mind, such as my second requirement above: if the partner turns out badly off under the agreement, it will want to renege even if it has no grounds for questioning the good faith of the first country. I agree that a proper accounting for uncertainty means that it is useful to check for robustness of coordination schemes. But it seems a poor check on robustness to rule out only those cases where a particular model says that the other party will lose in the absence of any surprises.

A rational Bayesian would not interpret most of his prediction errors as grounds to abandon his preferred model; the exogenous shocks are certainly capable of explaining most prediction errors. The truth will not, in fact, be revealed in the next period. Thus, a country should not be overly concerned if it thinks in expected value terms that the proposed bargain will leave its partner slightly worse off. If the expected value indeed occurs, the partner will probably attribute it to an exogenous shock rather than switching over to the first country's model, and it will make the same bargain again. If the outcome is likely to leave the partner *much* worse off, then I agree that the bargain is likely to break down. But I think that the "weak" bargain criterion is not the best way of getting at this issue.

Having said that, I have nothing against doing some easy checks for robustness, until proper tests are completed.[5] Such easy tests include not only ruling out the cases of "weak" bargains, but also selecting the subset of cases where the two countries agree on the model. Another possibility is to select the subset of cases where a large proportion of the models say that the bargain will be beneficial for both. At this stage, I read the results as saying that restricting in this way the set of circumstances under which coordination is allowed to take place does not much improve the odds.[6]

Lest I sound too pessimistic regarding the potential benefits of cooperation more broadly defined, let me state that I agree with the position of Currie and others in favor of the gains from exchanging information, the gains from "exposing [policymakers] to alternative views of the world . . . and the consequences of their actions on other countries and of policy actions elsewhere on their own country." Furthermore, I agree with their emphasis on searching for alternative "forms of coordination" that could make cooperative bargains more likely to work. My pessimism attaches most to bargains that

---

[5] Hughes Hallett has been testing for robustness in a series of papers.

[6] One point is that restricting the set in such ways leads immediately to the conclusion that coordination simply will not be able to take place most of the time. But there is still interest in seeing how often coordination improves welfare within the restricted subset. Frankel and Rockett (1988), p. 330, find that restricting coordination to those cases where both countries agreed on the (not necessarily correct) model improved the odds slightly for the United States (from 55 percent gains up to 65 percent gains) and for Europe (from 54 percent gains to only 59 percent gains), findings similar to those of Holtham and Hughes Hallett (1987), p. 25. We did not report the results of eliminating the "weak" bargains as Currie and others would like. But one can count up in the 4x4x4 tables. The odds improve again a little (to 75 percent for the United States, and to 69 percent for the rest of the world). I hope to have the results for the complete 10x10x10 set in the future. But my sense at this point is that these counts may be close to random draws around 50 percent, except to the extent that the cases where a country has precisely the correct model show up in the totals. (Excluding such cases lowers the odds for coordination; for the experiment that eliminates the "weak" cases, the odds are 71 percent for the United States and 55 percent for the rest of the world.)

specify money supplies and fiscal policies as the variables to be agreed upon. I will explain shortly the form of coordination that I personally think stands the best chance of overcoming the formidable obstacles to coordination that we are discussing.

Time-Inconsistency of Inflation-Fighting

The third set of issues in the modern monetary policy literature most often goes under the name of "time inconsistency." Currie and others raise it in two ways, both of them associated with Ken Rogoff (among others). First is the point—which holds equally well in a closed economy as in the international context—that the optimal monetary regime has the authorities pre-committing to some degree to an intermediate target, whether that target is the money supply, price level or something else.[7] Many have argued in the domestic context that nominal GNP makes a superior intermediate target, on the same grounds as I have cited above.

The other point is that of Rogoff (1985b), that if coordination on a period-by-period basis entails greater joint expansion (as in the 1978 and 1986–87 examples), it will raise expectations of inflation and result in long-run equilibrium with a higher level of inflation for any given level of output. Renouncing the institutions of coordination is a way that central banks can pre-commit in a time-consistent way to lower levels of inflation. But this seems to me to be an argument not against coordination per se, but only against coordination with complete period-by-period discretion. The answer is some degree of *cooperative* commitment to a nominal target. (Currie and others cite the findings of Currie, Levine, and Vidalis in favor of coordination *with reputations*.) Currie, Holtham, and Hughes Hallett give the familiar examples of the intermediate nominal targets toward which countries might cooperatively commit: Friedman's money growth rule, fixed exchange rates, and so forth. They also state the problem: "What is required is to find blueprints that are robust in their performance, that is, that perform well in a wide variety of circumstances." The money rule, a gold standard, and exchange rate target zones are each not robust to shifts in demand (shifts in demand, respectively, for money, gold, and foreign exchange). Nor are any of the other eight variables on the Group of Seven's list of "indicators" any better.

My own choice for monetary policy cooperatively to target nominal GNP

---

[7] The argument is that complete period-by-period discretion will result in a greater degree of expansion. By pre-committing, the monetary authorities reduce expected inflation and thereby in long-run equilibrium attain a lower level of inflation for any given level of output (see Rogoff, 1985a). Currie and others follow Rogoff in describing pre-commitment as a way to "generate some of the gains of full coordination between agents"; this language is useful to the theorist, but could be confusing to the general reader who may wonder what the connection is with international coordination.

(or, better yet, nominal demand[8]) has been laid out elsewhere.[9] My INT (International Nominal Targeting) proposal is simple. At each Group of Seven meeting, the national authorities would:

- commit themselves, without any obsessive degree of firmness, to target rates of growth, or ranges, for their countries' levels of nominal demand for five years into the future, and
- commit themselves, with somewhat greater firmness, to targets for the coming year.

A more stylized version of this proposal would simply have the national authorities bargain over levels of national demand instead of bargaining over money supplies and government spending. I have not yet tried out this form of coordination on the existing econometric models, the way that Hughes Hallett and I have each tried out the standard forms of coordination that focus on money supplies and government spending. But I think this should be a priority for future research.

References

Bryant, Ralph, "Intragovernmental Coordination of Economic Policies: An Interim Stocktaking," in *International Monetary Cooperation: Essays in Honor of Henry C. Wallich*, Essays in International Finance No. 169 (Princeton, New Jersey: International Finance Section, Department of Economics, Princeton University, 1987).

Currie, David, Gerald Holtham, and Andrew Hughes Hallett, "The Theory and Practice of International Policy Coordination: Does Coordination Pay?" (1988).

Currie, David, Paul Levine, and Nicholas Vidalis, "Cooperative and Non-Cooperative Rules for Monetary and Fiscal Policy in an Empirical Two-Bloc Model," in *Global Macroeconomics: Policy Conflict and Cooperation*, ed. by Richard Bryant and Richard Portes (London: Macmillan, 1987).

Frankel, Jeffrey, *Obstacles to International Macroeconomic Policy Coordination*, International Monetary Fund Working Paper 87/28 (Washington: International Monetary Fund, 1988), and *Studies in International Finance* No. 64 (Princeton, New Jersey: International Finance Section, Department of Economics, Princeton University, December 1988).

————, "An Analysis of the Proposal for International Nominal Targeting (INT)," National Bureau of Economic Research Working Paper No. 2849, in *International Policy Coordination and Exchange Rate Fluctuations*, ed. by William Branson and others (forthcoming, Chicago: University of Chicago Press, February 1989).

---

[8] There is a reason for choosing nominal demand (defined as GNP minus the balance on goods and services) as the target variable in place of nominal GNP, even though the latter is a more familiar concept. In the event of a recession, countries need to be discouraged from the temptation to accomplish their expansion of output through net foreign demand—for example, through protectionist trade measures—as opposed to domestic demand.

[9] Frankel (1989).

————, and Katharine Rockett, "International Macroeconomic Policy Coordination When Policymakers Do Not Agree on the True Model," *American Economic Review* (Nashville, Tennessee), Vol. 78 (June 1988), pp. 318–40.

Holtham, Gerald, and Andrew Hughes Hallett, "International Policy Coordination and Model Uncertainty," in *Global Macroeconomics: Policy Conflict and Cooperation*, ed. by Richard Bryant and Richard Portes (London: Macmillan, 1987).

Kenen, Peter, "Exchange Rates and Policy Coordination," Brookings Discussion Paper No. 61 (Washington: The Brookings Institution, October 1987).

Miller, Marcus, and John Williamson, "Targets and Indicators: A Blueprint for the International Coordination of Economic Policy," *Policy Analyses in International Economics*, No. 22 (Washington: Institute for International Economics, September 1987).

Rogoff, Kenneth (1985a), "Can International Monetary Policy Coordination Be Counterproductive?", *Journal of International Economics*, Vol. 18 (Amsterdam: 1985), pp. 199–217.

————(1985b), "The Optimal Degree of Commitment to an Intermediate Monetary Target," *Quarterly Journal of Economics*, Vol. 100 (New York: November 1985), pp. 1169–89.

2

Domestic and Cross-Border Consequences of U.S. Macroeconomic Policies

*Ralph C. Bryant, John F. Helliwell, and Peter Hooper**

I. Introduction

S ound decisions about economic policies by national governments—and, even more so, efforts to coordinate policies internationally—must rest on a foundation of empirical knowledge about the macroeconomic behavior of the world economy. It is important to provide better quantitative estimates of interactions among the largest national economies and to encourage a better use of those estimates in national policymaking. This is especially so at present, as the new U.S. administration and Congress are facing important choices about the future course of U.S. fiscal policy.

Our paper, motivated by these needs, has two purposes. One is to review the empirical evidence about the effects of changes in U.S. fiscal and monetary policies in a series of collaborative research projects. This research effort has

* Our biggest debt is to the numerous modeling groups that have collaborated in this research to provide results for a consistently defined set of experiments. We also wish to thank those who have generously given of their time to conduct new experiments for inclusion in this paper, especially Flint Brayton of the MPS modeling group at the U.S. Federal Reserve Board, Nigel Gault of the DRI modeling group, Jaime Marquez of the MCM group at the U.S. Federal Reserve Board, and Guy Meredith and Phil Bagnoli of the INTERMOD group. Gary Burtless, Robert Lafrance, Paul Masson, Guy Meredith, and Ted Truman gave us helpful suggestions on early drafts. Kathy Larin, Carolyn Litynski, Boban Mathew, and Alan Chung have provided able research assistance. The views expressed in this paper are the authors' alone, and should not be taken as representing the views of the institutions with which the authors are associated or the views of the authors' many collaborators in the construction and evaluation of multicountry empirical models. An unabridged version of this paper appears as a Brookings Discussion Paper in International Economics and an International Finance Discussion Paper of the U.S. Federal Reserve Board (Bryant, Helliwell, and Hooper, 1989).

focused primarily on comparative policy simulations generated by a variety of global macroeconometric models.[1]

Our second objective is to use the accumulated evidence, as well as some new empirical estimates prepared for this paper, to illuminate the macroeconomic policy choices now facing the U.S. government. We analyze, in particular, the likely consequences for key U.S. and foreign economic variables of a substantial U.S. fiscal contraction. Our time horizon is the next five to six years, a period lengthy enough to capture medium- as well as shorter-run effects (but not effects that manifest themselves only over the very long run). We pay special attention to the consequences of alternative types of fiscal action on the "twin" deficits—the U.S. fiscal deficit and the external (current account) deficit.

In Section II, we review the evidence on the domestic and international effects of U.S. fiscal policy, typified by reductions in U.S. government purchases of goods and services. Section III reviews the evidence on the effects of changes in U.S. monetary policy, calibrated as expansions in the U.S. money supply. Our objective in Sections II and III is to summarize, for U.S. macroeconomic policies, the main generalizations that can be extracted from the recent empirical research. An appendix briefly outlines the sources and main features of that research.

To present the evidence in accessible form, we have prepared averages and standard deviations for two substantial samples of the model simulations. Our full sample includes an almost complete set of model results—typically 20 simulated time series per variable. The smaller sample, a subset of the full sample, typically contains 12 simulated series per variable. The two samples are similar for most variables. The main differences are the smaller standard deviations for the 12-series sample. We put more emphasis on the partial sample than on the full sample; the former eliminates some of the model results that seem to us most problematic.[2]

In Section IV, we focus on the ways in which the estimated results of policy actions are influenced by a model's treatment of expectations. In particular, we distinguish between adaptive and rational (or model-consistent) expectations. Most of the simulations reviewed in Sections II and III were generated by models that treat expectations adaptively. Under model-consistent expectations, it can make a substantial difference whether policy

---

[1] The initiative for the projects was taken by a group of researchers sponsored by the Brookings Institution, in cooperation with the Centre for Economic Policy Research in London, with organizing support from a variety of other institutions, in particular the staffs of the Japanese Economic Planning Agency and the U.S. Federal Reserve Board. Support for the research was provided by the Ford Foundation and, beginning in 1987, the Tokyo Club Foundation for Global Studies.
    [2] The appendix gives more information about the model simulations included in the samples. Readers interested in further details of our survey should consult the unabridged discussion-paper version of the study.

actions are a surprise when they occur or, alternatively, whether they are anticipated prior to implementation. We thus also report some evidence bearing on this distinction between unanticipated and anticipated policy actions.

Section V presents additional evidence—prepared by modeling groups responsible for three well-known macroeconometric models—contrasting the macroeconomic effects of cuts in government purchases with the effects of changes in various taxes or transfer payments. These estimates of alternative kinds of fiscal actions are preliminary and must be corroborated by further research. Nevertheless, they suggest that different fiscal actions may imply significantly different trade-offs between the gains from reductions in U.S. budget and external deficits and the losses from reduced output at home and abroad.

Our analysis in Section VI illustrates how the empirical evidence reviewed in Sections II through V can be used to assess the consequences of alternative U.S. macroeconomic policies in the circumstances facing the President and Congress at the beginning of 1989. Our examples focus on fiscal contractions that are phased in over a four-year period. We consider alternative assumptions about the specific spending, tax, and transfer actions that might be involved. We also illustrate the possible consequences of forward-looking expectations and of combining some monetary expansion with the fiscal retrenchment.

Section VII gives concluding remarks, including a summary assessment of the empirical evidence.

II. Effects of Changes in U.S. Government Spending

The standardized change in fiscal policy considered here is a reduction in real U.S. government purchases of goods and services equivalent to 1 percent of baseline U.S. real gross national product (GNP), maintained throughout a six-year simulation period.[3] For the accompanying monetary policy, the modeling groups held the level of a key monetary aggregate unchanged along its baseline path.[4]

Chart 1 summarizes the macroeconomic consequences of this reduction of government spending. All results are reported as deviations of the "shock"

---

[3] Those models incorporating forward-looking, model-consistent expectations assumed that the change in government purchases (from baseline) was gradually phased out after the completion of the six-year simulation period, or else altered tax rates (sometime after the end of the six-year period), so as to restore long-term fiscal balance.

[4] The simulation results contain elements of noncomparability in the models' treatments of monetary policy. See the appendix to the unabridged version (Bryant, Helliwell, and Hooper, 1989).

simulation from a "baseline" simulation.[5] The panels for most variables, here and later, show results as percent deviations from the baseline. Variables such as interest rates are reported as absolute deviations from the baseline in percentage points, while deviations in current accounts and government deficits are measured as percents of baseline nominal GNP.

The six panels on the first page of Chart 1 show domestic and external-sector effects. The top pair of panels plots the responses of real GNP and the price level.[6] The middle panels show the changes in the U.S. budget position and in the U.S. current account balance. The bottom panels illustrate the effects on the U.S. short-term interest rate and the exchange value of the U.S. dollar.[7] Each panel in Chart 1 (and in the analogous chart in Section III) plots two averages: the 12-series average with a heavier solid line, and the 20-series average with a less prominent solid line. As a rough measure of the variability of the models' responses, each panel also shows, with dashed lines, the interval defined by plus and minus one standard deviation around the mean. The interval around the 12-series mean is shown with the heavier dashed lines, the 20-series interval less prominently.

In the initial year of the simulations, U.S. output falls relative to baseline by somewhat more than the decrease in government spending. After the second year, the models exhibit "crowding-in" behavior, as the negative income effects of the government-spending reduction begin to be offset by increases in other spending on domestic output induced by lower interest rates, lower prices, and a depreciation of the dollar.[8] The amount and timing of these offsetting effects vary across the models, as is evident from the standard-deviation intervals. Nevertheless, by the sixth year of the simulation, both the smaller and larger sample averages suggest that output will have returned most of the way back to its baseline path. The effects on the U.S. price level tend to cumulate throughout the six-year simulation period.

The models all predict reductions in the U.S. government budget deficit stemming from the fiscal contraction, but with sizable differences in magnitude across the models. In the third year, the average reduction in the fiscal deficit is about 85 percent as large as the initial reduction in spending (with a standard deviation equal to about one fifth of the initial change in spending).

---

[5] The baseline (sometimes referred to as "control") simulation is a benchmark set of commonly defined paths for important macroeconomic variables appearing in the model. The shock simulations are prepared by changing an exogenous fiscal (in Section III, an exogenous monetary) variable by a specified amount from its baseline path and using the models to calculate the alterations in the paths of endogenous variables caused by the shock.

[6] Where available, an index of consumer prices is used to represent the price level. If the consumer price index is not available, a general index for absorption prices is used. In the absence of either index for spending prices, the GNP deflator is used.

[7] A minus value for the exchange value indicates a depreciation of the dollar against a trade-weighted average of foreign currencies, measured as a percent of the baseline value.

[8] This crowding-in behavior is discussed in more detail in Section V.

The direction of movement of the exchange value of a country's currency after a fiscal action is ambiguous in expository theoretical models. Among other things, it depends on the assumed degree of substitutability between assets denominated in the home currency and in foreign currencies. In simplified expositions of the theory, the direction of movement of the exchange rate depends on the relative slopes of the "BP" and "LM" curves (representing, respectively, equilibrium in the external sector and the money market). The greater the degree of substitutability between home-currency and foreign-currency assets, the flatter will be the slope of the BP curve. A slope that is flatter (steeper) for the BP curve than for the LM curve implies that a contractionary fiscal action will depreciate (appreciate) the home currency.[9]

The ambiguity in theoretical models is largely absent in the simulations discussed here. The prevailing result in multicountry empirical models is that the home currency depreciates in the initial years following a fiscal contraction. The empirical models tend to embody either perfect or near-perfect substitutability of assets denominated in different currencies (relatively flat BP curves). Exchange rates are determined for the most part in asset-market equations, either in the form of real-interest-parity conditions or in portfolio-balance sectors in which asset demands are interest-elastic and exchange rate expectations are directly affected by relative price movements (or purchasing-power-parity considerations). Hence, nominal exchange rates move in response to changes in nominal interest-rate differentials, expected inflation differentials, current and expected relative price levels, and, in a few cases, factors that may influence equilibrium real exchange rates in the long run, such as the wealth of national residents and the stocks of governments' debts.

Under the 1 percent U.S. fiscal contraction, the average decrease in the nominal value of the dollar is about 2 percent. There is substantial variation among the models in their estimates of the size and persistence of the extent of the depreciation, as evidenced by a standard deviation almost as large as the mean estimate of the change.

With the domestic economy weaker and the dollar tending to depreciate, the U.S. current account improves. Expenditure-reducing and expenditure-switching effects both work in the same direction to contribute to this improvement. The size of the effects varies considerably across the models, especially

---

[9] In the textbook theoretical framework, the exchange rate responds to interest rates (via capital flows) and to income/absorption (through import effects on the trade balance). A fiscal contraction tends to lower the home interest rate (putting pressure on the home currency to depreciate) and to reduce home income (putting pressure on the currency to appreciate by improving the trade balance). The flatter the BP curve relative to the LM curve, the more the interest-rate effects on the exchange rate dominate the effects working through income and the trade balance. See, for example, Ethier (1983, pp. 338–42, 390–92). In more complicated theoretical models, the home currency's exchange value may follow a complex dynamic pattern —for example, depreciating temporarily after a fiscal contraction but eventually appreciating to an inflation-adjusted value significantly above its original level.

Chart 1. Averages of Simulated Effects of U.S. Fiscal Contraction[1]

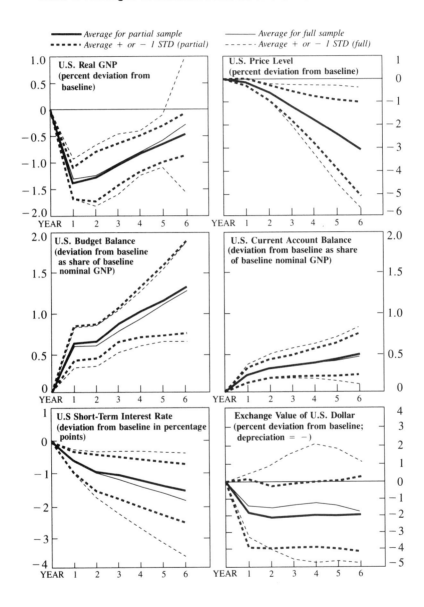

Chart 1 *(concluded).*

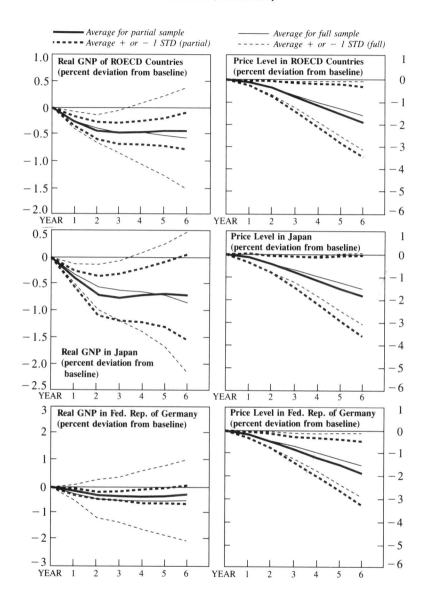

¹ Reduction below baseline in real U.S. Government purchases of goods and services equal to 1 percent of baseline real GNP, maintained throughout the six years of the simulation period.

in the later years of the simulation. Measured in current dollars, the range of sixth-year improvements in the U.S. current account runs from nearly zero to more than $70 billion. For the 12-series average, each $100 billion reduction in U.S. government spending would lead, in the third year, to a reduction of $35 billion (with a standard deviation of $15 billion) in the current account deficit, some two fifths as large as the average net reduction of $85 billion in the fiscal deficit.

To what extent is the improvement in the current account due to the induced change in the nominal exchange rate? Experiments conducted for the 1988 symposium of the Japanese Economic Planning Agency (EPA), discussed in Helliwell (1988b), ran government expenditure changes (assuming unchanged money growth) under both fixed and flexible exchange rates to answer this question. The results suggested that by far the largest part of the net improvement in the current account comes from the changes in domestic spending, prices, and interest rates, with relatively little from the small change in the nominal exchange rate. Of course, changes in the nominal exchange rate would play a greater role in the net effects on the current account if the fiscal contraction took place in the context of an easier U.S. monetary policy, in which case the dollar would fall more and domestic demand less, as we will discuss further in Section VI.

It is noteworthy that the "full-model" effects on the external deficit of an exogenous nominal depreciation of the dollar are considerably smaller than the effects predicted by partial-equilibrium models of the current account. For the three models assessed in the 1988 EPA symposium, a 10 percent exogenous depreciation of the dollar improved the U.S. current account by about $35 billion in the third year, according to the partial simulations, compared with only about $10 billion in the full-model simulations.[10] This evidence indicates how important it is, when evaluating the effects of exchange rate changes, to take account of the induced changes in domestic incomes and prices, as is done in the full model but not the partial simulations.

What about the spillover effects of the U.S. fiscal contraction on other countries? Changes in actual and expected exchange rates, and in the prices and volumes of trade flows, are the main channels through which fiscal actions are transmitted to the rest of the world.

Chart 1 also shows the estimated effects of the U.S. expenditure reduction on the real output and the domestic price level of the aggregate region of the rest of the Organization for Economic Cooperation and Development (ROECD), of Japan, and of the Federal Republic of Germany. All of the models show reductions in foreign real gross domestic product (GDP), although there is substantial diversity in the estimates, especially for the later years. The reductions in foreign GDP lag behind those in the United States, and show, on average, their largest magnitude in the third year of the U.S.

---

[10] See Helliwell (1988b), especially Chart 12.

fiscal contraction (0.4 percent of GDP), while the U.S. real GDP effects peak in the second year. On average, the foreign GDP effects are about one quarter as large as those in the United States, where both effects are measured as percentages of that country's GDP. The effects on Japan are estimated to be, on average across the models, about twice as large as those in Germany and the aggregate of the ROECD countries, reflecting Japan's proportionately greater reliance on export sales to U.S. markets.

All of the models predict that a U.S. fiscal contraction will lower the price level abroad relative to the baseline—and by growing amounts over the first four years.[11] Interest rates abroad tend to fall, but by only a fraction of the fall in interest rates in the United States. In keeping with the overall depreciation in the dollar's exchange value, currencies such as the Japanese yen and the deutsche mark strengthen against the dollar.

III. Effects of Changes in U.S. Monetary Policy

For the fiscal policy simulations discussed in the preceding section, the models assumed that a key U.S. monetary aggregate (either M1 or M2) was held unchanged from its baseline path. In this section we review the evidence on the effects of raising the U.S. monetary aggregate above baseline by 1 percent throughout the simulation period. Targeted monetary aggregates in other countries were assumed to be held unchanged from the baseline in the face of the U.S. monetary expansion.[12]

The own-country effects of the U.S. monetary expansion are summarized on the first part of Chart 2, which also shows induced effects on real output and prices in the ROECD, Japan, and Germany.

Theoretical models predict that a home-country monetary expansion will result, at least over the short run, in a fall in home interest rates and increases in both the home output and price levels. The own-country simulated effects of a U.S. monetary expansion in these empirical models accord with theoretical presumptions. Interest rates tend to fall sharply immediately after the monetary expansion. The decline during the first year averages some 80 basis points, with a considerable range across models, generally reflecting differences in their estimates of the interest elasticity of money demand. On average, the nominal interest rates then gradually rise back toward their baseline values over the six-year simulation horizon.

---

[11] The size of this price transmission is small in models such as GEM and OECD, and only modest in models such as MCM and TAYLOR. The largest effects, as for the own-country price effects in the United States, are predicted by MULTIMOD and INTERMOD. (See appendix for background on models discussed in this paper.)

[12] See the appendix to the unabridged version for further discussion. We also consider in the unabridged version the differing implications of holding either M1 or M2 exogenous for simulations of monetary shocks, based on experiments with two of the three models used to prepare the simulations reported in Section V.

Chart 2. Averages of Simulated Effects of U.S. Monetary Expansion[1]

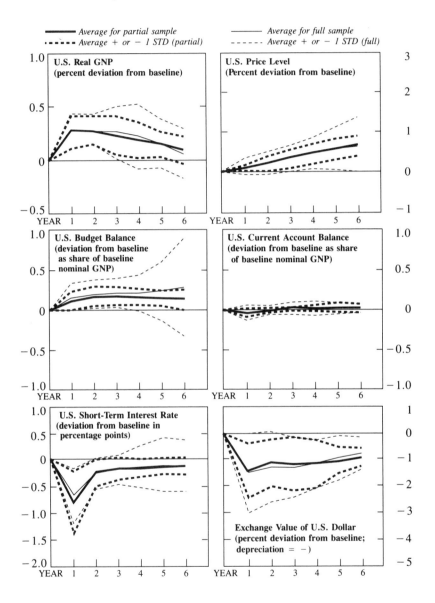

Chart 2 *(concluded).*

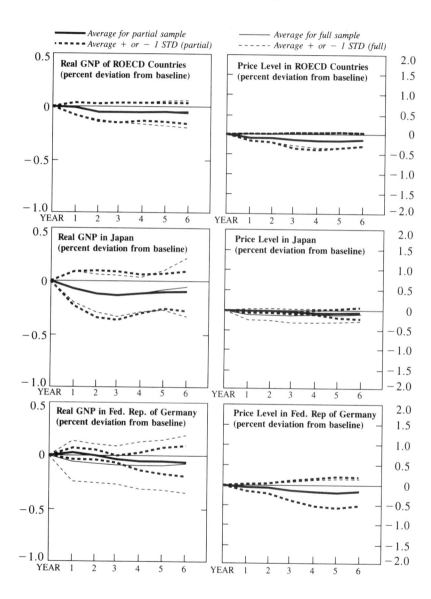

[1] Increase of money stock above baseline by 1 percent, maintained throughout the six years of the simulation period.

In the first year U.S. real GNP rises above the baseline by an average of ¼ of 1 percent. This average increases slightly in the second year and gradually tends back toward zero over the following four years. The reversal starts earlier (after the first year) for models such as OECD, TAYLOR, and GEM, and later for the MCM (in the fourth year). The return of real GNP toward the baseline in later years generally accords with the "long-run neutrality of money" assumption of many theoretical models. Most models have U.S. prices rising continuously throughout the simulation period. All of the models, as expected, simulate a depreciation in the nominal exchange value of the dollar in response to U.S. monetary expansion. They tend to exhibit overshooting, with the dollar dropping by an average of about 1.5 percent in the first year, and then climbing back toward the expected long-run value about 1 percent below the baseline value, commensurate with the 1 percent increase in the money stock.

Expository theoretical models cannot predict unambiguously the effects on the own-country's current balance. The higher home incomes and output tend to pull in more imports; thus, the income-absorption effects of the monetary expansion work to worsen the trade and current account balances. The expenditure-switching effects associated with the depreciation of the currency, in contrast, tend to improve the trade and current account balances.[13] The empirical results in Chart 2 broadly confirm that the net effects of a U.S. monetary expansion on the U.S. nominal current account are small.

Spillover effects on foreign output also tend to be small. In about half the models, the foreign real income effects are negative, exhibiting the "beggar-thy-neighbor" property of monetary expansion in the Mundell-Fleming model with perfect capital mobility and static exchange rate expectations. Other models show some small positive effects, which can arise in more general models. Averaged across the models, the effects on foreign income are slightly negative.[14]

An unexpected U.S. monetary expansion would have adverse effects on the long-run value of foreigners' wealth. The long-run increase in the U.S. price level and the long-run drop in the nominal foreign exchange value of the

---

[13] In the initial versions of the standard Mundell-Fleming theoretical model, the second of these effects necessarily had to dominate the first, leading to an improvement in the current account balance. When expository theoretical models are enriched with additional behavioral assumptions (for example, allowing for nonstatic expectations of exchange rates), however, the models can generate either a net capital inflow or outflow (and, hence, either an improvement or deterioration in the current balance). See Frankel (1988).

[14] Jeffrey Frankel has cited (in, for example, Frankel and Rockett, 1988) the uncertain sign of the effects of monetary policy on the current account, and on foreign output, to buttress his view that model uncertainty is a major obstacle to international policy coordination. As can be seen in Chart 2 (and also in Figure A-4 and Table A-4 in the appendix to the unabridged, discussion-paper version), the variation in sign of the net effects is less noteworthy than the fact that the absolute sizes of the net effects, whatever the sign, tend to be small.

dollar would combine to impose a capital loss (valued in foreign currencies) on that portion of foreigners' net wealth held in the form of dollar-denominated bonds. The offsetting gains would accrue to those who are net debtors in U.S. dollars.[15]

IV. Alternative Treatments of Expectations

In the preceding sections, we did not distinguish between the results using models with adaptive and those with model-consistent expectations. In this section, we include some evidence about the extent to which alternative ways of modeling expectations influence the size and timing of the estimated responses to changes in fiscal and monetary policies. Two issues are of primary concern: the extent to which model results are influenced by the use of model-consistent rather than adaptive expectations, and the extent to which the consequences of future policy actions are altered when the policy changes are credibly announced and correctly anticipated.

Expectations that are forward-looking and model-consistent—in contrast to adaptive expectations—take into account the future effects of policy changes. Forward-looking expectations thereby tend to reduce the impacts of temporary policies and to accelerate the responses to sustained policy changes. If policy changes are announced in advance, *and* if the announcements are treated as firm commitments, anticipated future policies can influence current market prices and current spending, in a way not captured by models without explicit forward-looking expectations. Such anticipatory effects may have the opposite sign to the direct effects of the policy when it is finally implemented. For example, the multiplier effects of tax increases or cuts in government spending do not generally show up until the expenditure change is actually implemented; in contrast, the expenditure-increasing effects of exchange rate depreciation, lower interest rates, and anticipated lower prices—which occur immediately after a credible announcement—feed back to induce additional expenditures before the tax or government spending changes are implemented.

To illustrate the nature and possible size of these effects, Chart 3 shows the consequences of a reduction in U.S. government purchases of goods and services of the same size as that analyzed in Section II. Each panel of Chart 3 shows three simulated results, based on three different runs of INTERMOD. By means of these experiments—which corroborate the earlier MINIMOD results of Haas and Masson (1986)—we can illustrate (in the context of this specific model) the differences between adaptive and model-consistent treatments of expectations. To show the potential importance of anticipatory effects, we use two different expectational assumptions in the consistent-

---

[15] Such valuation effects are absent in most of the existing empirical models. In the shorter run, foreign holders of dollar-denominated bonds could experience capital gains resulting from lower interest rates on dollar assets. The net short-run effects on the foreign-currency valuation of foreigners' wealth are uncertain.

Chart 3. Simulated Effects of U.S. Fiscal Contraction with Alternative Treatments of Expectations

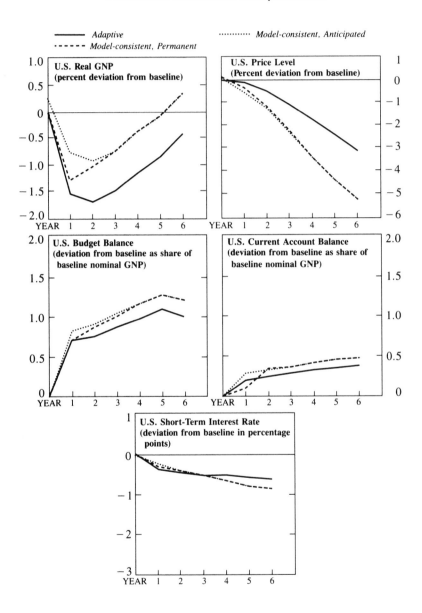

Chart 3 *(concluded).*

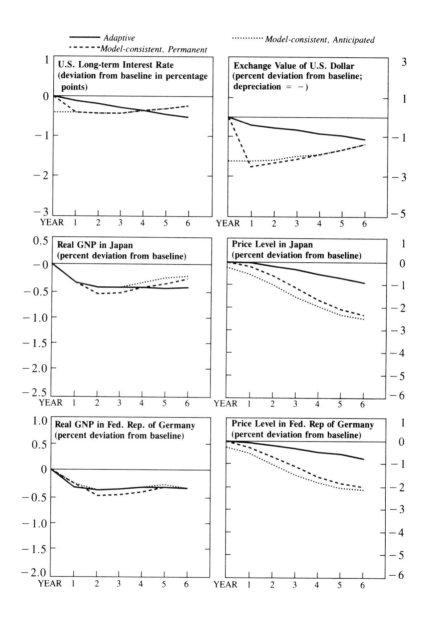

expectations version of the model. These alternative assumptions relate to whether the policy change is anticipated before the spending change actually takes place. In all cases, the spending cut, once implemented, is taken to be permanent, and to influence private-sector expectations about the long-run share of government spending in the economy, and, hence, the long-run expected tax rate.[16]

In all three simulations, U.S. government spending is reduced (by an amount equal to 1 percent of real GNP) in year 1, and maintained lower on a permanent basis. In the adaptive-expectations simulation (shown in the chart with a solid line), no change is made to the long-run expected share of government spending as a share of GNP. In the other two cases this ratio is reduced by 1 percent. In one of the consistent-expectations cases (shown with a dashed line and labeled "permanent"), the spending change is announced and implemented in year 1 (1989 in the simulations). In the other consistent-expectations case (shown with a dotted line and labeled "anticipated"), the change is implemented in year 1, but announced a year earlier, and thus can influence year 0 prices, interest rates, exchange rates, and activity levels.

As with most other consistent-expectations models with high international mobility of capital, INTERMOD shows an immediate "jump" depreciation of the dollar in response to a government expenditure cut, as soon as the cut is announced. The adaptive-expectations simulation also shows depreciation, but the process is slow starting and gradual. The consistent-expectations simulations, by contrast, show sharp movements that are subsequently reversed to ensure the expected future maintenance of the interest parity condition.

There is a parallel difference between the adaptive- and consistent-expectations simulations with respect to long-term interest rates. In the adaptive simulation, changes in long-term interest rates—which provide the key link between monetary conditions and real spending—lag behind changes in short-term interest rates. In the consistent-expectations simulations, by contrast, long-term rates move down immediately, falling in the first year by several times as much as in the adaptive-expectations version, thus accelerating the crowding-in of private investment and consumption spending.

The sharp jumps in long-term interest rates and exchange rates in the consistent-expectations simulations stimulate real demand for domestic output, and, hence, lower the fiscal multiplier. The peak multiplier appears in the second year in the adaptive results; it is about 30 percent greater than the earlier-appearing peak multiplier for the unanticipated permanent expenditure cut with consistent expectations.

Another important feature of these INTERMOD simulations, which confirms the earlier work of Masson and Blundell-Wignall (1985) and of Haas and Masson (1986), relates to the difference between the consistent-expecta-

---

[16] In INTERMOD, tax rates are endogenous in the long run, moving so as to achieve an exogenously determined target ratio of nominal government debt to nominal GNP.

tions results for anticipated and unanticipated expenditure changes. In year 0, before the policy action is implemented, the anticipated future spending cut lowers the value of the dollar and leads to an increase in real GNP. Lagged effects of the anticipatory crowding-in of spending spill over into years 1 and 2. Thus, the peak multiplier effect is one year later (appearing in year 2) and one third smaller in the anticipated case than in the unanticipated case.

The importance of this result is that a series of credibly announced fiscal actions can achieve reductions in the budget deficit with a considerably smaller loss of real output than would be estimated with adaptive expectations, or even with consistent expectations in the absence of the anticipatory effects. For example, under adaptive expectations, the spending cut is estimated to reduce real GNP by an average of 1 percent over the seven years (year 0 through year 6), three times the average reduction in GNP (⅓ of 1 percent) when the cut is announced in year 0 and correctly anticipated to be permanent. The cumulative reduction in U.S. government debt, at the end of year 6, is some $320 billion with adaptive expectations and $375 billion in the anticipated case. In terms of cumulative output loss per dollar of debt reduction, during 1989–94, the anticipated case is thus less than one third as painful as the adaptive case.[17]

These INTERMOD results for the adaptive and consistent cases support the conjecture made on the basis of the earlier *EMIE* comparisons (Bryant and others, 1988), where models with consistent expectations had, on average, lower fiscal multipliers than did models with adaptive expectations.[18]

---

[17] The simulation results summarized in the text were prepared with the same version of INTERMOD for which results were reported in Sections II and III. The use of monetary-policy reaction functions, combined with the high coefficients on the lagged dependent variables in the INTERMOD and MULTIMOD demand-for-money equations, gives those models unusually small interest-rate responses to expenditure shocks (as shown in the tables of the appendix to the unabridged, discussion-paper version of the study). The INTERMOD modeling group has since estimated a U.S. monetary sector with more conventional properties, having short-run and long-run increases of 72 and 53 basis points in response to a 1 percent increase in GNP, about the middle of the range of the LM curve properties surveyed by Helliwell, Cockerline, and Lafrance (1988, Table 3.1). When this alternative version of the financial sector is incorporated in the U.S. block of INTERMOD, the simulated money supply is held close to the baseline path, thereby leading to larger interest-rate decreases in response to cuts in expenditures. The alternative version of INTERMOD thus exhibits more crowding-in for both the adaptive and the model-consistent treatments of expectations.

[18] However, as Dungan and Wilson (1988) point out, the lower multipliers observed in these models may reflect other differences in model structure, not just their treatment of expectations. Dungan and Wilson find higher fiscal multipliers under model-consistent than under adaptive expectations. The most likely reason for this lies in the fact that their FOCUS model shows an appreciation of the domestic currency in response to fiscal contraction, while the other models— with flatter BP curves—show depreciation. The application of consistent expectations brings forward the induced effects of these exchange rate changes, thus raising the multiplier effects for Dungan and Wilson and lowering them in other models. Most of the multicountry empirical models embody specifications or assumptions leading to relatively mobile capital, and are thus likely to fall into this latter category.

Consistent-expectations models differ with respect to which variables are treated as explicitly forward-looking in model simulations. In most of these models, economic agents are assumed to form explicit expectations about future values of inflation, the term structure of interest rates, and exchange rates. In addition, the TAYLOR model incorporates explicit forward-looking expectations of income in its investment, consumption, and wage equations. The MULTIMOD/INTERMOD consumption function is forward-looking, but permanent wealth is currently not varied when simulations are run.

Thus, the INTERMOD results about the effects of different treatments of expectations illustrated in Chart 3 would not necessarily be replicated by other models with consistent expectations, and should be subjected to further tests with alternative model structures.

There is evidence from a number of other models about the effects of anticipated future policy changes. Taylor (1988) reports the results of anticipated monetary expansions in four rational-expectations models, all of which show positive income and price effects after the policy is announced but prior to its implementation. Anticipatory effects of fiscal policies, by contrast, tend to have income effects that are of opposite sign to the effects that arise when the actual policy change is implemented. Such effects can be substantial, as shown in Chart 3. Masson and Blundell-Wignall (1985, p. 23) also show own-country real GNP effects—in the anticipatory year 0—that are about one third as large as (and of the opposite sign to) the effects in year 1. McKibbin (1988) reports recent experiments from the MSG2 model showing that real output effects in the year of expenditure-policy anticipation can be one half or more as large as the effects in the first year when the spending change is implemented. These fiscal policy results suggest that the anticipation of future expenditure cuts helps to reduce the income losses that are entailed as the economy adjusts to a lower level of government spending.

V. Alternative U.S. Fiscal Actions

The simulations of fiscal actions analyzed in earlier model-comparison exercises and reviewed in Sections II and IV involve changes in government purchases. In this section we present evidence on a broader range of fiscal actions, including not only changes in federal purchases but also transfers, personal taxes, corporate taxes, and federal sales (or excise) taxes.[19]

---

[19] Surprisingly little empirical analysis of the comparative macroeconomic effects of these alternative fiscal actions exists in the literature. Coen and Hickman (1984) consider the effects of alternative tax policies in simulations with the Hickman-Coen model; Fair (1984) presents simulations of a number of different fiscal policy measures with the Fair model; Hickman, Huntington, and Sweeney (1987) surveyed a number of U.S. models to assess the effects of alternative tax policies in the face of an oil price shock; and both Christ (1975) and Fromm and Klein (1973) provide evidence on the comparative effects of change in government expenditures

Our analysis is based on simulations carried out with the DRI, MPS, and MCM models. These models contain sufficiently detailed specifications of the U.S. economy to permit them to distinguish, at least to some degree, among the alternative fiscal policy shocks.[20]

All three models have basic Keynesian (IS-LM) structures, and also contain significant supply-side linkages. Changes in taxes and transfers directly affect household and corporate incomes and spending. Shifts in corporate and personal tax rates also affect the user costs of capital for both business investment and housing. Labor supply is a function of the after-tax real wage in the DRI model (although with a small coefficient), but not in the MPS or MCM models.[21] The DRI and MPS models distinguish between households and corporations, and between federal and state and local governments. The MCM model does not make these distinctions within the private and government sectors, treating each as a composite sector. All three models treat expectations adaptively.

The simulations of the five types of fiscal actions were run over a six-year horizon, beginning in the first quarter of 1988 and ending in the fourth quarter of 1993, and making use of reasonably comparable baseline assumptions.[22] The simulations were standardized to produce an initial impact on the budget deficit (that is, before taking into account endogenous feedbacks to revenues, interest payments, and other transfers) equal to 1 percent of baseline nominal GNP in the first quarter of 1988, or $47 billion (at an annual rate). In each of

---

and personal taxes, based on simulations with a group of U.S. models. More recently, in a report to the National Economic Commission, the U.S. Congressional Budget Office (1988) surveyed what three U.S. models (the DRI model, the Fair model, and the Washington University model) had to say about the effects of deficit reduction packages that contained different mixes of cuts in purchases and transfers and increases in taxes.

[20] The DRI and MPS models are large U.S. models that also contain reduced-form relationships for key foreign macroeconomic variables. (The DRI U.S. model used here is essentially the same as the U.S. sector in DRI's international model that was used in the *EMIE* exercises.) The MCM is a "global" model that contains medium-sized models of the U.S. economy and four other major countries, plus reduced-form relationships for the rest of the world.

[21] This omission in the MCM and MPS models may not be significant, given that a reduction in after-tax wage rates and income associated with an increase in personal taxes will have offsetting effects on labor supply: on the one hand, a "substitution effect"—reduced willingness to work for lower after-tax income—and, on the other hand, an "income effect"—an increase in work effort in order to maintain income levels. A substantial body of empirical evidence on this question suggests that while both effects may be significant, neither is dominant, and that the net effect is probably small; see Burtless (1987).

[22] The MPS simulations were run over the period from the first quarter of 1988 to the fourth quarter of 1992. The key features of the baseline solution are (a) U.S. real GNP grows at an average annual rate of 2.5 percent during 1988–93, (b) unemployment stays about unchanged from its average level in the first half of 1988, (c) inflation remains about 4 percent, (d) real federal expenditures grow at 1 to 2 percent a year, (e) interest rates remain about unchanged from their levels in the first half of 1988, and (f) the U.S. dollar remains little changed but falls moderately over the baseline period.

the simulations, the shock to expenditures or revenues was essentially tied to nominal GNP, so that the dollar amount of the shock increased gradually over time.[23]

For each of the five simulations, the modeling groups kept the U.S. money supply (either M1 or M2) unchanged from its baseline path. The DRI results were reported with M1 held exogenous and the MCM and MPS results, with M2 exogenous. Alternative choices for the definition of unchanged monetary policy have important implications for the simulation results, as discussed in more detail later on. In the DRI and MPS models, changes in foreign interest rates were tied to changes in U.S. interest rates. In the MCM model, key foreign monetary aggregates were held exogenous (except in the case of Canada, where interest rates were tied to U.S. interest rates).

The specific simulations were as follows:
- Real federal purchases of goods and services were reduced below their baseline path throughout the six-year simulation period by an amount equal to 1 percent of baseline real GNP (equivalent to a 12.0 percent reduction in real federal purchases of goods and services in the first quarter of 1988).
- Real federal transfer payments to persons (social security, and so forth) were reduced below their baseline path for all six years by an amount equal to 1 percent of baseline real GNP, or 11.2 percent of real federal transfers to persons in the first quarter of 1988.
- The average federal personal income tax rate was raised by enough to increase revenues exogenously by 1 percent of baseline nominal GNP (or 11.9 percent of personal income tax revenues) in the first quarter of 1988. The tax rate was then kept at that higher level for the entire simulation period.[24]
- The average federal corporate profits tax rate was raised by enough to increase revenues by 1 percent of the baseline nominal GNP (or 44

---

[23] For the purchases and transfer shocks, the "exogenous" increase in constant-dollar expenditures over time was tied to the baseline level of constant-dollar GNP; in the tax-rate shocks, the "exogenous" increase in nominal revenues over time was tied to the simulated level of nominal GNP. While the shocks were designed to be equivalent in the absence of feedbacks to GNP (assuming that revenues and expenditures use the same price deflator), they are not strictly equivalent when simulated real GNP deviates from its baseline path. The magnitude of this discrepancy is small, however, as real GNP generally falls only temporarily, and at most by only about 2 percent below baseline (implying that the tax shocks are at most 2 percent "smaller" than the spending shocks). Some shocks were run on a smaller scale (to produce 0.5 percent of GNP), with the results doubled for reporting here.

[24] The DRI and MPS models include a total federal personal tax revenue equation, with an average personal tax rate that was shifted by enough to achieve the required increase in revenues at the baseline levels of personal income. The MCM identifies total personal tax revenues (federal plus state and local) as a function of an average personal tax parameter times nominal GNP; that parameter was shifted sufficiently to achieve the requisite increase in baseline revenues.

percent of corporate tax revenues) in the first quarter of 1988, and then maintained unchanged thereafter.[25]

- The federal sales tax rate (that is, indirect business tax or excise tax on domestic consumption expenditures, including liquor, tobacco, and so forth) was raised sufficiently to increase revenues exogenously by 1 percent of baseline nominal GNP (146 percent of excise tax revenues) in the first quarter of 1988.[26]

Chart 4 shows the simulated impacts of the five types of fiscal actions on the levels of U.S. real GNP, consumer prices, personal consumption expenditures, business fixed investment, short-term interest rates, and the budget balance as a share of baseline nominal GNP. Each panel of Chart 4 reports an average of the effects across the three models.[27] The results are presented in terms of deviations from baseline paths.

The three-model average results for real GNP indicate that all of the fiscal actions produce the familiar pattern of initial decline for about two years, followed by a rebound as domestic expenditures and net exports are "crowded in," owing to lower interest rates, domestic prices, and (in most cases) dollar depreciation.[28] For each of these actions output returns toward, and, in four out of five cases, rises above its baseline level, reflecting a tendency of the models to cycle about the baseline path in the longer run.[29] Nevertheless, significant

---

[25] This tax refers to the tax on corporate profits excluding federal reserve banks. The shock was implemented by shifting average corporate tax rate parameters in the models, much the same as in the personal tax simulation. These parameters also enter directly into the determination of the user cost of capital in all three models.

[26] This shock was implemented in the DRI and MPS models by raising the indirect business tax (or excise tax) parameter in the federal revenue sector. In addition, in the DRI model the residuals in all personal consumption deflator equations were raised by 1 percent of the dependent variable multiplied by the ratio of baseline GNP to total personal consumption expenditures. (In the MPS model a shift in the federal excise tax rate is passed through directly into higher consumption deflators.) In the MCM, the tax was treated as a combination of a lump-sum increase in tax revenues equivalent to 1 percent of baseline GNP, and an increase in the residual in the equation for the total domestic expenditure deflator enough to raise the deflator by 1 percent. Thus, in all three cases, the tax was assumed to be passed through fully and immediately to consumers.

[27] The average results presented here mask some significant differences among the three models. The individual model results are documented and compared in the unabridged version of the paper.

[28] This pattern of crowding in depends crucially on the assumption that money growth is held unchanged. In the unabridged version, we consider the effects of alternative monetary policy assumptions, including holding interest rates unchanged. The results can differ dramatically under the alternative assumptions.

[29] Cycling of output arises because interest rates respond quickly to changes in money demand, whereas output (which, in turn, affects money demand) responds slowly to changes in interest rates. This cycling behavior is discussed by Anderson and Enzler (1987), Brayton and Mauskopf (1985), and Enzler and Johnson (1981).

Chart 4. Effects of Alternative U.S. Fiscal Policies on Key U.S. Variables: Based on Averages of DRI, MCM, and MPS Simulations

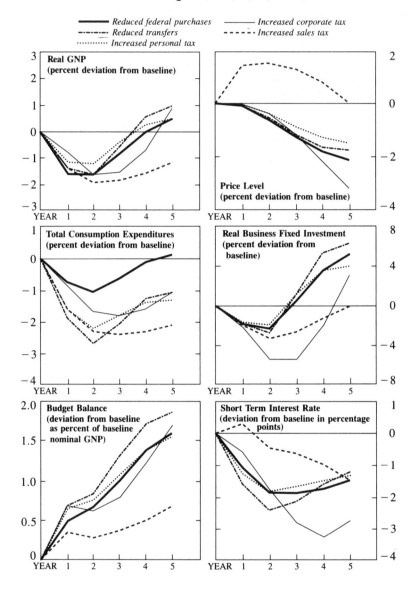

differences in the effects of the various shocks are evident.

The shift in government purchases has a somewhat greater initial negative impact on real GNP than shifts in taxes and transfers, consistent with the predictions of standard textbook multiplier analysis. A change in corporate taxes has smaller initial impacts than a change in either personal income taxes or sales taxes, and about one half the first-year impact of a comparably scaled shift in federal purchases. The marginal propensity of the private sector to spend corporate profits is smaller and has longer lags than the marginal propensity to spend labor income or transfers.

By major domestic expenditure category, personal disposable income and consumption are initially more than twice as sensitive to transfers and personal taxes as they are to federal purchases and corporate taxes, while their sensitivity to a sales tax is intermediate. The range of initial impacts on business fixed investment is somewhat narrower in the near term, with corporate taxes having the largest negative impact and personal taxes the smallest.

Beyond the first year, the increases in sales taxes and corporate taxes result in larger average losses in output over the simulation period than the other fiscal actions. The increase in the sales tax results in much less crowding in of domestic expenditures and net exports than the other simulations in the longer run. This is because it has direct positive impacts on the level of domestic prices and money demand, and, hence, on interest rates and the dollar's exchange rate.[30] The increase in the corporate income tax rate has a more prolonged negative impact on output (and especially on investment) than the personal tax increase or either of the expenditure cuts, because it raises the user cost of capital considerably more (or reduces it much less) than these other measures do. "Supply-side" effects are thus more significant in the corporate tax case; the greater reduction in business fixed investment results in greater reductions in the capital stock and potential output.[31]

The cut in transfers and the increase in personal taxes—both of which have relatively large negative effects on consumption and relatively small negative effects on investment—result in smaller average losses in total output than the other measures.[32] Negative supply-side effects are apparently less important in these cases. The cut in federal purchases results in a greater loss in output than the increase in personal taxes over much of the simulation

---

[30] A Congressional Budget Office report (CBO, 1988) also found that in two out of the three models they surveyed (including the DRI model), excise taxes had relatively strong contractionary effects.

[31] The finding that corporate taxes tend to depress output more than personal taxes (because of their relatively greater negative "supply-side" effects) is consistent with the results of Coen and Hickman (1984), as well as with the implications of a substantial body of empirical analysis in public finance. (See Boskin, 1988, for a recent survey of some of this literature.)

[32] The CBO (1988) report also found that cuts in transfers involved smaller negative impacts on output than cuts in federal purchases.

period, consistent with the predictions of static multiplier analysis.[33]

The different fiscal measures show qualitatively similar patterns of change in the federal budget over time (see Chart 4), but they have different implications for the absolute magnitude of reduction in the budget deficit. Most of the simulations show an initial fall in the deficit in the first year, followed by a partial reversal in the second year as lower income temporarily reduces tax revenue and raises transfer payments; the deficit then falls further over the longer run, as income shifts and begins rising.[34] Throughout the simulations, the ex-post effects on the budget of shifts in transfers are somewhat larger than for the other fiscal actions. The deficit-reducing effects of higher sales taxes are generally less than half as large as for the other actions.

The relative magnitudes of the effects of these actions on the budget balance can be traced to their impact on real GNP, interest rates, and prices. The sales tax reduces the budget deficit by a smaller amount than the other actions, for example, because it produces the largest decline in real income (which depresses revenues and raises transfer payments); the smallest decline in interest rates (which reduces interest payments on the national debt); and the largest increase in prices (which raises the absolute level of nominal expenditures more than it does the absolute level of revenues).[35]

Chart 5 shows the three-model average effects for the U.S. current account balance, for the exchange value of the U.S. dollar against the currencies of other industrial countries (in terms of foreign currency per dollar), and for the real output, consumer prices, and interest rates of a weighted average of other industrial countries.

The U.S. current account improves in all cases, although the magnitude of improvement varies widely across the alternative fiscal actions, and is generally much smaller than the improvement in the federal budget balance.

---

[33] The comparison of the results for reduced purchases and increased personal taxes actually indicates a balanced-budget multiplier somewhat less than the 1.0 predicted by simple Keynesian multiplier analysis. (A balanced-budget multiplier of 1.0, at least in the near term, appears to have been supported by simulations with the DRI, MPS, and several other models, in an earlier model comparison exercise; see Fromm and Klein, 1973.) The balanced-budget multiplier will be less than unity, and will decline over time, to the extent that the tax and spending shocks induce comparable crowding-in effects through lower interest rates, prices, and exchange rates, as well as to the extent that the tax increase depresses labor participation rates (which it does, to a small extent in the DRI results). The crowding-in effects of the DRI and MPS models appear to be more pronounced than they were in the earlier model-comparison exercises. See Fromm and Klein (1973), Christ (1975), Hickman and Huntington (1987), and Blinder (1984).

[34] In addition, because of the way the simulations were designed, the "exogenous" component of the improvement in the budget deficit increases over time, essentially in proportion to increases in the level of the baseline nominal GNP.

[35] The effects of price increases follow from the fact that expenditures exceed revenues by a substantial margin in the baseline, and from the assumption in the simulations that the exogenous component of expenditures is held fixed in real terms.

Chart 5: Effects of Alternative U.S. Fiscal Policies on Key International Variables: Based on Averages of DRI, MCM, and MPS Simulations

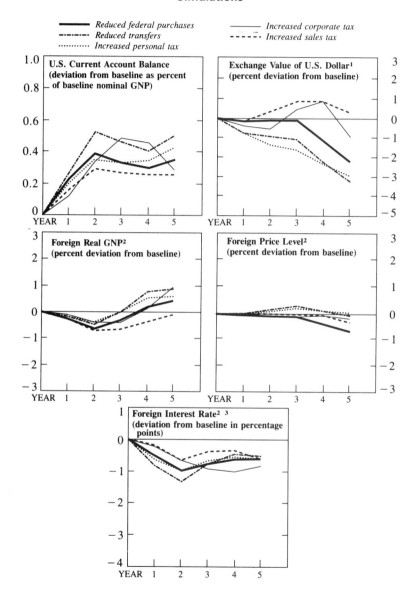

---
[1] Foreign currency units per U.S. dollar.
[2] Weighted average for major industrial countries.

Elements that tend to improve the current account balance include reduced income (hence, lower demand for imports); reduced interest rates (hence, lower investment income payments to foreigners); and, in several cases, a lower dollar and lower domestic prices (hence, increased U.S. price competitiveness). The relative ordering of the current account effects across the fiscal actions can be traced primarily to movements in real exchange rates and interest rates. The personal tax and transfer shifts produce greater real depreciations of the dollar and greater improvements in the current account balance, while the sales tax results in a real appreciation of the dollar (for reasons discussed below), little decline in interest rates, and a smaller improvement in the current account. The ordering of the current account impacts cannot be attributed to movements in U.S. real GNP. (Relatively low output and import demand in the case of the sales tax, for example, is not associated with a larger improvement in the current account, as might be expected, but rather with smaller improvement.) Apparently the effects of changes in U.S. income are being offset in part by similar movements in foreign income.

The dollar depreciates in response to three out of the five fiscal actions (see Chart 5). The actions that produce relatively larger declines in U.S. interest rates (purchases, transfers, and corporate taxes) also show declines in the dollar. The magnitude of depreciation is fairly small, however, because declines in foreign interest rates offset much of the fall in U.S. rates.[36]

The relative magnitudes of the effects of the fiscal actions on foreign output mirror their effects on U.S. output, although the sizes of the effects are smaller and less negative overall.[37] Foreign output falls initially in all cases as U.S. output declines and reduces demand for imports from abroad. Foreign output then returns to (and often rises above) the baseline as U.S. output recovers, and as declines in foreign interest rates stimulate domestic expenditures abroad. Reduced aggregate demand and local-currency appreciations result in lower own prices and interest rates. For the three-model averages, output abroad shows the greatest net loss (or smallest net gain) for the U.S. fiscal contractions involving reduced purchases or increased sales taxes.

---

[36] Foreign interest rates fall by construction in the DRI and MPS models, because in those models they are tied directly to U.S. rates (with long-run coefficients of, respectively, 0.5 and 0.94). Nevertheless, foreign rates also fall by comparable amounts in the MCM model (in those countries in which money is held exogenous), as reductions in own-nominal GNP reduce money demand. In addition, in the MPS model, assets denominated in different currencies are assumed to be imperfect substitutes, so that an improvement in the U.S. current account (which reduces the rate of foreign accumulation of net claims on the United States) leads to a rise in the dollar as a result of portfolio rebalancing. For the DRI and MCM models (both of which assume perfect substitutability of assets denominated in different currencies), the dollar depreciates in response to all types of fiscal action. It is sizable appreciations of the dollar in the MPS model that cause the three-model average to show small appreciations for the cases of the sales-tax and corporate-profit tax actions (although in the latter case the dollar depreciates in real terms).

[37] In the DRI model, this outcome occurs largely because the model links foreign activity directly to U.S. real GNP.

The evidence presented in this section suggests several broader inferences. First, the effects on U.S. real GNP across the five types of fiscal actions
differ quantitatively, but for the first two to three years are generally within the
range of estimates discussed in Section II. As a first approximation, therefore,
analysts can probably infer at least the qualitative pattern of short-run effects
of all types of fiscal actions by using the estimates for cuts in purchases
summarized in Section II.

The differences among various types of fiscal actions become more
important over longer horizons. To judge from the average-model results
presented here, two out of the three types of contractionary fiscal policies that
would directly restrict private consumption (that is, increases in personal taxes
and reductions in transfers) could have somewhat less negative implications
for U.S. and foreign output and somewhat more positive implications for both
the budget deficit and the current account deficit than a comparably scaled cut
in federal purchases. The other policy that would restrict private consumption
directly—increases in sales taxes—would yield by far the worst trade-off of all
the fiscal measures considered: it would register the largest losses in U.S. and
foreign output, and yet would yield the smallest amounts of progress in
reducing the U.S. budget and current account deficits.[38]

Finally, the corporate profits tax appears to be "second worst" in terms of
the GNP/budget-current account deficit trade-off, because of its supply-side
effects (raising the cost of capital and depressing investment).

We conclude this section with three important caveats. *First*, some of the
effects of the alternative fiscal policies on output could, in principle, be offset
by a more or less expansionary monetary policy. In that case, the differences
would show up as differences in impact on the price level. An excise tax would
result in a significantly greater increase in prices—with output held unchanged
—than the other policies. *Second*, the results for alternative types of fiscal
actions reported here are from only three models. The simulated effects of
fiscal actions differ in some major ways across those models, partly because of
difficulties in conducting the simulations on a fully comparable basis, but also
because of fundamental differences in model specification. We do not have
space here to dwell on these differences. *Third*, the three models used in this
section all treat expectations adaptively; models with forward-looking expectations could yield quite different results. In particular, to the extent that agents

---

[38] The adverse macroeconomic effects of increases in sales taxes may well depend on the
assumption of unchanged money growth and hence considerable flexibility of interest rates. Under
the unlikely possibility that interest rates were held unchanged, a sales-tax increase could well
produce the smallest decline in GNP of all the policies considered. Moreover, the longer-run
negative effects of a sales tax could be reduced somewhat if the tax were less than fully passed
through to higher prices (contrary to the full pass-through assumptions used in preparing the
simulations reported here). In this case, the results might resemble those of a corporate profits tax,
since profits would be squeezed to the extent that businesses absorbed the sales tax.

with forward-looking expectations tend to "see beyond" the transitory inflationary effects of a sales-tax increase, that policy change could yield a more favorable trade-off between output loss and deficit reduction than the results described here.

Until further research can refine the new evidence reported in this section and place the preceding caveats in appropriate perspective, readers should use the results with caution.

VI. Illustrative Use of Empirical Estimates in Policy Analysis

Although the evidence reviewed in preceding sections about the quantitative effects of U.S. fiscal and monetary actions is far from definitive, policymakers and their analysts have, for the time being, little else to go on when choosing among alternative policies. In this section, therefore, we illustrate the potential applications of the existing evidence to the current macroeconomic difficulties facing the U.S. President and Congress. Our limited purpose is to consider what the possible macroeconomic consequences would be if the United States succeeded in substantially reducing the federal budget deficit over the next four years; we do not try to deal with the political dimensions of this issue.

Baseline Economic Outlook. As an illustrative baseline for our analysis, we find it convenient to adopt the projections in the *World Economic Outlook* of the International Monetary Fund (IMF, 1988). As of October 1988, the IMF staff foresaw a continuation through 1989 of expansion in real activity for all of the major industrial countries.[39] It noted concerns for some countries that output might be approaching capacity limits and that inflation could increase somewhat.

For the United States, the budget deficit was expected to remain very high, with only modest further progress toward reduction; the Fund staff's "working assumption" was that the deficit would still remain above $120 billion in the years 1990–92.[40] Total domestic demand in the United States was expected to increase slightly less rapidly than growth in output, resulting in a further small reduction in the U.S. current account deficit. By 1989, however, this improvement in the external deficit was projected to be minor (virtually no change between the calendar 1988 and 1989 current account deficits, each of

---

[39] For example, output for the industrial countries as a whole was projected to increase 3.9 percent for calendar 1988 (year over year) and 2.8 percent in 1989. The corresponding figures for Japan were 5.8 percent and 4.2 percent; for Germany, 2.9 percent and 1.9 percent; and for the United States, 4.0 percent and 2.8 percent. (By the end of 1988 it appeared that these projected growth rates for 1988 were somewhat below the 1988 growth rates actually realized.)

[40] *World Economic Outlook, October 1988*, p. 20. This projection of the budget deficit implies that the targets embodied in the Gramm-Rudman-Hollings legislation would not be met (and hence, implicitly, that the legislation as currently written would not be enforced).

which was projected at $129 billion).[41]

The Fund's baseline outlook thus has several unsettling features. While it does not entail a worldwide recession in real economic activity, nor a resumption of strong inflationary pressures, it projects external imbalances continuing at unacceptably high rates. Moreover, it points to risks that those imbalances could lead to significant tensions among the major countries.[42]

What adjustments in macroeconomic policies could improve this outlook? Most analysts, inside and outside the United States, focus first on the large budgetary imbalance in the United States. A thorough treatment would have to discuss policies in all of the industrial countries, not merely in the United States. But we too believe that U.S. fiscal retrenchment is a necessary condition for improvement in the U.S. and the world economic outlook. Therefore, our illustrations of policy modifications concentrate on U.S. fiscal policies.

A Phased-in Package of Expenditure Cuts. We focus mainly on expenditure reductions, because we have more model-based evidence on the effects of spending changes. We emphasize phased reductions in part because our results (from Section IV, especially) suggest that a series of expenditure reductions implemented over several years is likely to be less economically painful than a single, large, unannounced reduction. Our illustrative package involves successive incremental expenditure reductions of ½ of 1 percent of GNP in each of the four years 1989–92, with government spending in real terms in and after 1992 below that in the baseline by an amount equal to 2 percent of real GNP. The ultimate size of the package of cuts is thus twice the size of the standardized expenditure reduction analyzed in Section II.

What macroeconomic consequences would ensue from this phased-in package of expenditure cuts ("package A")? Two illustrative projections are shown in each panel of Chart 6. The solid curves show estimated effects derived from the 12-series sample averages in Section II. The curves with dashes, shown less prominently, plot the effects using the three-model averages discussed in Section V. All panels of Chart 6 show the effects measured as deviations from the baseline outlook. The baseline paths themselves are not

---

[41] Other analysts have suggested that the short-run prospects for further reductions in the U.S. external deficit in 1989 and even 1990 could be somewhat brighter than envisaged by the IMF staff (see, for example, Hooper, 1988). Nonetheless, given exchange rates similar to those prevailing in the fall of 1988 and roughly similar rates of growth in the United States and other industrial countries, it is difficult to imagine enough improvement in the U.S. external imbalance to bring the deficit down to a range regarded as acceptable and indefinitely sustainable. For further discussion of the prospects for the U.S. external deficit, see Bryant, Holtham, and Hooper (1988), Hooper and Mann (1989a, 1989b), and Bryant (1988).

[42] The IMF's *World Economic Outlook* of October 1988 does not make explicit projections for years beyond 1989. In thinking of an illustrative baseline against which to evaluate the calculations in this section, the reader could (for example) roughly extrapolate to 1990–94 the broad trends envisaged by the IMF for late 1988 and 1989.

Chart 6. Estimated Effects of a Phased-In Package of Expenditure Cuts

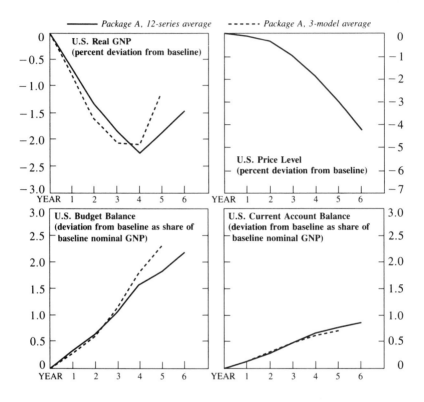

plotted, but rather the *changes* resulting from the assumed modification in fiscal policy. (In effect, the baseline paths are the horizontal lines beginning at the zero points on the vertical scales.)[43]

---

[43] Tables with the data plotted in the chart are in the appendix to the unabridged version of the paper. Our approach in preparing the calculations in this section follows the analytical procedures explained in Bryant, Henderson, and Symansky (1988). The procedures use particular simulation results to derive standardized estimates of the consequences of policy actions (in effect, final-form coefficients from the relevant model), which can then be used as shortcut "ready reckoners" to assess hypothetical policy actions, including combinations of actions in policy "packages." In the calculations underlying the illustrations in Chart 6 and elsewhere in this section, we applied these procedures not only to the simulations from individual models but also to the model-average simulation results reported in Sections II and III. For reasons discussed in Bryant, Henderson, and Symansky (1988, pp. 69–71), the procedures for deriving and using final-form coefficients cannot legitimately be applied to simulation results from individual models with a rational, forward-looking treatment of expectations. For such a model, there seems to be no

Chart 6 *(concluded).*

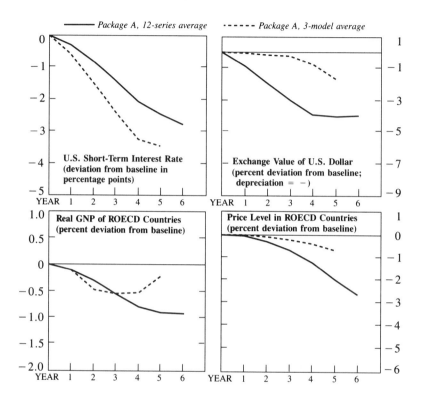

These estimates suggest that the expenditure cuts would sharply diminish the twin-deficit problem. The package would produce a large decline in the budget deficit, building up gradually over each of the six years 1989–94; by the fifth year, the deficit would fall by at least 1¾ percent (perhaps more than 2 percent) of baseline nominal GNP (some $120–150 billion). The package would also gradually reduce the external deficit, but by smaller amounts—in the fifth year, for example, by about ¾ of 1 percent of nominal baseline GNP (roughly $45–50 billion).

Output would fall substantially below baseline (top left panel in Chart 6)—according to these estimates, more than 1⅓ percent of real GNP by the second year and perhaps by some 2 percent by the third and fourth years. The U.S. price level would also fall below baseline, by increasing amounts with

---

shortcut substitute for a hands-on use of the model itself. The results reported in Chart 8 below for the version of INTERMOD using forward-looking expectations were obtained from direct simulations of the personal computer version of that model.

each year. Because the U.S. Federal Reserve is assumed to keep a key monetary aggregate unchanged from its baseline path, interest rates in the United States would fall below the baseline by progressively larger amounts. And the dollar would depreciate modestly in exchange markets. These movements in prices, interest rates, and exchange rates would induce, with a lag, a turnaround ("crowding in") of the deviations of output from baseline.[44]

Packages with Tax and Transfer Changes. A realistic budget compromise is unlikely to place the entire burden of fiscal contraction on reductions in government expenditures. "Revenue enhancements" of one sort or another, and perhaps reductions in transfer payments, will also have to play a role. It is therefore useful to illustrate how much difference it might make, for macroeconomic consequences, if packages were structured in alternative ways.

For comparison with package A's exclusive use of expenditure cuts, consider two other polar cases: one composed entirely of reductions in transfer payments and increases in personal taxes ("package B"), and the other composed entirely of increases in corporate taxes and in excise/sales taxes ("package C"). Packages dominated by reductions in transfer payments or personal tax increases initially would affect personal disposable income and private consumption especially strongly, but would have relatively little impact on investment and potential output. Packages dominated by corporate and excise taxes would curtail private capital formation more strongly than other actions.

We have designed packages B and C to have the same overall size as package A, namely, a total of fiscal actions measured in constant dollars equivalent to ½, 1, 1½, 2, 2, and 2 percent of baseline real GNP, respectively, in the six years beginning in 1989. Roughly one half of package B takes the form of cuts in transfer payments. The other half comes from increases in personal taxes.[45] Package C is composed half of increases in corporate taxes and half of increases in sales or excise taxes.[46]

The effects of the three packages are compared in Chart 7. The three prominent curves plot the estimated effects using the three-model averages

---

[44] The crowding-in effects here are delayed relative to those shown in Sections II and V because the fiscal contraction is phased in over time. Crowding-in effects appear much sooner when allowance is made for forward-looking expectations, as we show below.

[45] For the cuts in transfer payments, the assumed amounts for the six years 1989–94 in constant dollars are, respectively, ¼, ½, ¾, 1, 1, and 1 percent of real baseline GNP. For the increases in personal taxes, the (average) personal tax rate is assumed to be raised in 1989 by an amount necessary to generate additional revenue equivalent to ¼ percent of nominal baseline GNP; the rate is raised in each of the next three years by an additional step, each time so as to raise incremental revenue equivalent to another ¼ percent of nominal baseline GNP in that year; from the fifth year (1993) on, the tax rate remains unchanged at the higher level attained in 1992.

[46] For each type of tax, as for the personal tax increase in package B, the (average) tax rate is assumed to rise in four annual increments during 1989–92, and to remain unchanged thereafter. Each annual increment in the rate, for corporate taxes and sales taxes, is calculated to raise additional revenues in that year by an amount equal to ¼ percent of baseline nominal GNP.

developed in Section V; package A is shown with a solid line (repeated from Chart 6), package B with dots, and package C with short dashes. For comparison, the panels also show in the background the effects from the 12-series sample average (repeated from Chart 6).[47]

The estimates in Chart 7 suggest that it could make a significant difference to key macroeconomic variables over the medium and long runs if tax increases and transfer payments were used in addition to expenditure reductions in a budget package. Packages including changes in personal taxes or transfers appear, from the three-model results, to offer more leverage on the twin deficits per dollar of cost paid in reduced output. The worst trade-offs for macroeconomic variables per dollar of fiscal action would result from increases in sales taxes and, less clearly, from increases in corporate taxes.

For example, U.S. real GNP by the third and fourth years might fall below the baseline by, respectively, as much as 2.3 and 2.9 percent for package C, but only by some 1.6 and 1.4 percent for package B. Yet the medium-run reduction in the budget deficit in package C might be only one half the reduction stemming from package B. The current account deficit would also fall slightly less under package C than under B.

The politics of obtaining agreement on increased sales and excise taxes —for example, on gasoline, liquor, and tobacco ("promote energy conservation, reduce dependence on imported oil, discourage sin")—and on raising the burden of corporate taxation ("the corporations are wealthy and can readily absorb increased taxes") might well be less difficult than the politics of obtaining agreement on personal tax increases or curtailments in entitlement programs. If so, however, it ought to be recognized that the easier political solution could be less efficient in redressing the macroeconomic problems that require a budget compromise in the first place.

Expectations of Phased-in Fiscal Packages. We emphasized in Section IV that a phased-in package of fiscal actions could have important anticipatory effects not captured in models that treat expectations adaptively. In principle, the more credible the initial announcement of a multiyear sequence of actions, the greater the degree to which favorable crowding-in effects would be accelerated, and the less would be the output loss throughout the adjustment process. The estimated consequences of U.S. fiscal packages shown in Charts 6 and 7 do not allow for such expectational effects.[48]

---

[47] Chart 6 does not plot sixth-year (1994) estimates for the three-model averages because here, as in Section V, we did not have the required sixth-year simulation results for all three models.

[48] The DRI, MCM, and MPS models (used in the three-model averages of Section V) all treat expectations adaptively. The procedures used for extracting final-form coefficients from the 12-series sample of Sections II and III implicitly assume that the "composite model" treats expectations adaptively.

**Chart 7. Estimated Effects of Alternative Packages of Phased-In
Fiscal Contraction**

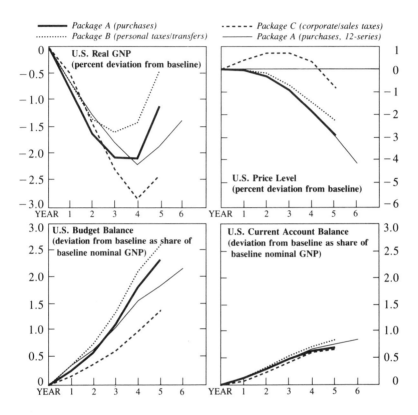

To illustrate the potential importance of forward-looking expectations, Chart 8 reports some additional simulation results generated with INTER-MOD. One of the two prominent curves in that figure shows the simulated results for package A (phased-in expenditure cuts) when INTERMOD treats expectations adaptively. The other prominent curve plots the estimated effects of package A when INTERMOD is in consistent-expectations mode; for the purpose of that simulation, it was assumed that none of the package was anticipated prior to its announcement and first-part implementation at the beginning of year 1 (1989), but that all subsequent changes were correctly anticipated.[49]

---

[49] As a benchmark for comparison, Chart 8 also repeats—less prominently in the background —the estimated effects of package A using the 12-sample model average (which makes no allowance for anticipatory effects).

Chart 7 *(concluded).*

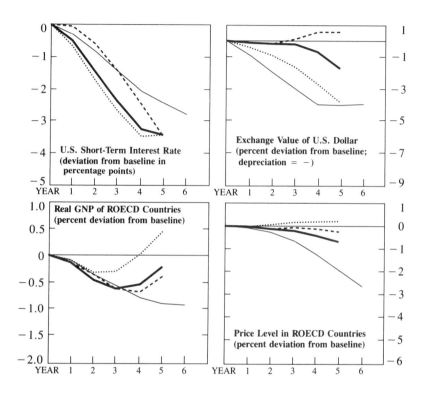

The differences between the adaptive- and consistent-expectations simulations in Chart 8 are noteworthy. For the consistent-expectations simulation, anticipations in 1989 of the further phased-in cuts to be implemented in the subsequent years 1990–92 reduce interest rates and price expectations immediately, and thus lead to increases in private spending that cushion the output loss from the drop in public spending. As a consequence, U.S. real GNP falls significantly less when INTERMOD is simulated with model-consistent than with adaptive expectations. For example, package A is estimated to push real GNP below baseline by 1.4 percent in the second year (1.9 and 2.3 percent in the third and fourth years) when INTERMOD is run with adaptive expectations; the fall below baseline with expectations treated as model-consistent is only 0.4 percent in the second year (1.0 and 1.6 percent in the third and fourth years). When expectations are model-consistent, the exchange value of the dollar and long-term interest rates (not shown in the chart) fall much more sharply in the initial year, and the U.S. price level falls more. Moreover, the

Chart 8. Estimated Effects of Phased-In Expenditure Cuts Under Alternative Expectations Assumptions

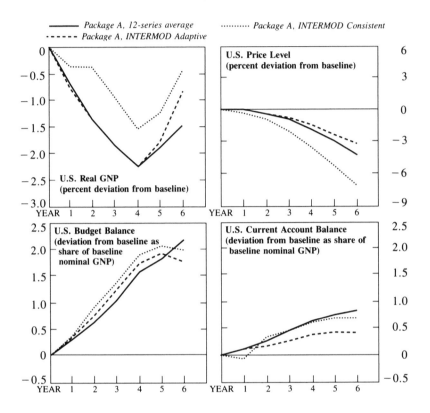

reductions in the budget and the current account deficits are larger than with adaptive expectations, even though the reductions in real GNP are markedly less. Hence, the trade-off is much better: if private agents regard the announced fiscal package as credible and, therefore, anticipate the effects of the expenditure cuts that will be implemented in future years, the initial cost in lost output per dollar of reduction in the twin deficits is significantly smaller.[50]

---

[50] The results reported in Chart 8 employ the published version of INTERMOD, in which money supply and money demand behave in ways that give small reductions in interest rates in response to expenditure reductions. When a more typical specification is used for the money-demand equation, as reported in a footnote in Section IV, interest rates fall further, and the crowding-in effects are correspondingly stronger. For example, when the revised money supply and demand equations are in effect in INTERMOD and when the model treats expectations as model-consistent, real GNP in the package-A simulation falls below control by a maximum of 0.8 percent (in year 4); is below control by 0.2 percent on average over the six years of the simulation; and is above control by the end of the period.

Chart 8 *(concluded).*

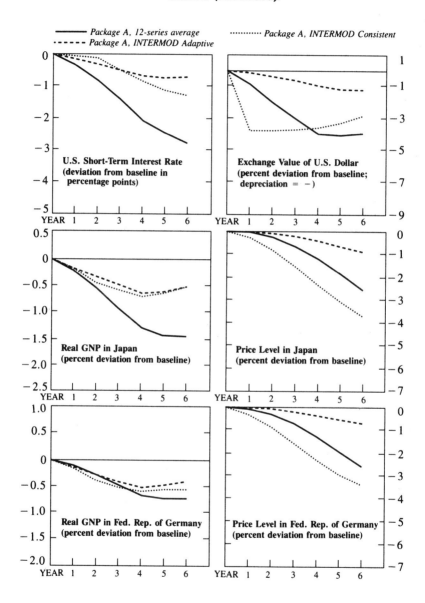

The consistent-expectations simulation shown in Chart 8 assumes that the phased-in fiscal package has complete credibility once it has been announced. Those estimates, and the differences between them and the results shown in Charts 6 and 7, do not illuminate cases in which private agents would distrust the announcement of a multiyear fiscal program and thus would doubt that the subsequent years of the program would actually be implemented as announced.[51]

Combinations of Fiscal Contraction and Some Monetary Offset. Would macroeconomic consequences such as those projected in Charts 6–8 be welcome? Judgments about the degree of welfare loss associated with the fall of output below the baseline would of course depend on the details of the baseline outlook. Because phased-in budget compromises of the size of packages A, B, and C could cause U.S. output to fall further than might be judged appropriate, we include here some results for a further illustrative package of policies. For our example, we suppose that the U.S. Federal Reserve goes beyond allowing interest rates to fall as a consequence of its maintenance of the money stock on the baseline path and instead for a period of three years gradually raises the money supply above baseline, facilitating even larger declines in interest rates.

To acknowledge that a permanent monetary expansion could have undesired long-run consequences for the price level, we suppose that the U.S. Federal Reserve's monetary expansion is gradually reversed beginning in the sixth year of the simulation period. This change in the policy "mix"— a fiscal contraction taking the form of expenditure cuts combined with a partially offsetting monetary expansion—we label as "package D."[52] The estimated effects of this combination of fiscal and monetary policies are reported in Chart 9 with heavy dashed curves. For ease of comparison, the figure once again repeats the package-A results (solid curves) for fiscal contraction alone.

The differences in Chart 9 between the consequences of packages D and A are of concern here. Interest rates in the United States would fall significantly further under package D, and the exchange value of the dollar would

---

[51] The effects of a multiyear phased-in package that was regarded as partially credible might fall somewhere in the range between the two simulations highlighted in Chart 8.

[52] The size and timing of the expenditure cuts in package D is identical to that assumed for package A. The detailed assumption about monetary policy is that the Federal Reserve raises the level of its key monetary aggregate above the baseline by 2 percent in year 1, 3 percent in year 2, 4 percent in each of years 3, 4, and 5, 3 percent in year 6, 2 percent in year 7 (which is beyond the actual simulation period), 1 percent in year 8, with money back on its baseline path in year 9, and thereafter. Not enough information is available from the newly generated evidence discussed in Section V to permit the calculation of illustrative packages that combine monetary actions with the use of changes in transfers or taxes on the fiscal side. Hence, our illustration of a change in the policy mix uses a combination of expenditure cutting and some monetary action. By using the information in Chart 7, readers interested in estimates incorporating transfers or taxes in a fiscal package can make rough adjustments to the results shown in Chart 9.

depreciate more. Because the monetary expansion would partially offset the effects of the fiscal contraction, the fall in U.S. real GNP would be markedly less with package D; according to these estimates, for example, the second and third year reductions below the baseline would be only 0.5 and 0.8 percent, respectively, whereas under package A the comparable shortfalls would be 1.3 and 1.9 percent. The U.S. price level under package D would be little changed from the baseline in the first and second years and then would begin to fall below the baseline, but by smaller amounts than the declines under package A. As expected (see Sections II and III), the estimated improvement in the external imbalance is roughly the same for both packages. For package D, however, the expenditure-switching effects of a lower dollar (lower because of both fiscal contraction and monetary expansion) would account for considerably more of the net effects on the external deficit.[53] For the budget imbalance, in contrast, the two packages would produce significantly different results. Because of the additional decline in interest rates in package D, the budget deficit would have fallen by the fourth year by as much as 2.3 percent of baseline nominal GNP (some $140 billion), compared with 1.6 percent of GNP ($95 billion) in package A.

As with the effects shown in Charts 6 and 7, the estimates in Chart 9 ignore forward-looking expectations. The estimates could, therefore, give a misleading impression for cases where a phased-in combination of fiscal and monetary actions was announced and believed to be credible. As seen in Chart 8, if the fiscal package could be designed to be fully credible, the need for a temporary, offsetting monetary expansion would not be as large, and its consequences would be less advantageous.

Spillover Effects on Other Countries. The panels on the second page of Chart 9 show the estimated effects of packages A and D on the real GNPs and price levels of Japan, Germany, and the aggregate of the ROECD countries. Other countries would experience moderate but nontrivial declines (below baseline) in output and prices. Most of the spillover effects would come from U.S. fiscal actions, with U.S. fiscal contraction reducing foreign income and prices. The temporary monetary expansion, which would help to cushion U.S. output, would achieve its gains for the United States partially at the expense of other countries, whose real GNP might be somewhat lower with package D than with package A. In addition, the lower value of the dollar and higher U.S. price level (in package D, compared with package A) would reduce the real wealth of foreigners holding net claims in U.S. dollars.

For Germany, the estimated fall below baseline in real GNP from the package-A fiscal contraction by the United States builds up to about ¾ of 1 percent by the fourth year. Because U.S. monetary policy seems to have

---

[53] The income-raising effects of the monetary expansion on the external balance would work to offset the income-reducing effects of the fiscal contraction.

Chart 9. Estimated Effects of Phased-In Fiscal Contraction
Combined with Monetary Expansion

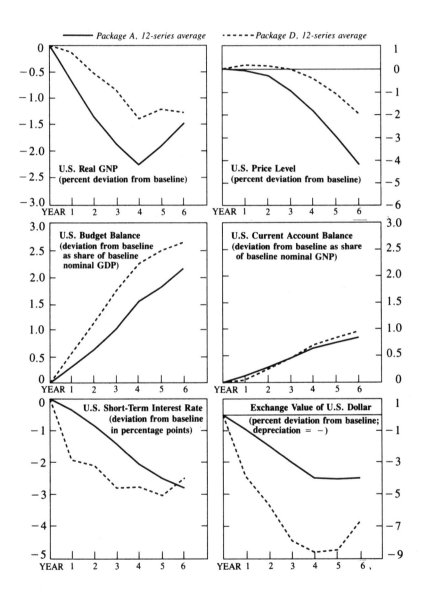

Chart 9 *(concluded).*

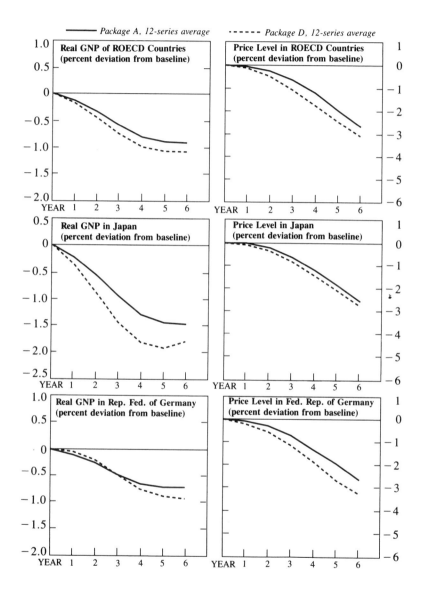

such small net effects on German output, the effects of package D would be little different from those of package A. The effects of U.S. policy actions on Japan would be somewhat larger. Japanese real GNP by the fourth year would fall below baseline by some 1⅓ percent under package A; the decline under package D, according to these estimates, could be as large as 1¾ percent. The relative size of effects on real GNP for the ROECD as a whole would probably be intermediate between those for Germany and Japan.

The extent of appropriate adjustments in the macroeconomic policies of individual foreign governments in response to U.S. policy actions would depend on details of the baseline outlook for their economies. If aggregate demand in the baseline outlook for a foreign country were judged to be excessively buoyant, the government of that country might welcome the moderate contractionary effects on its output and prices of a U.S. fiscal retrenchment. In the IMF's October 1988 *World Economic Outlook*, however, a number of foreign countries were not expected to face that situation. Under those circumstances, it probably would be appropriate for some foreign governments to shift gradually in the direction of more expansionary macro-economic policies than they would choose in the absence of U.S. policy changes.

VII. Conclusions

In this paper we have summarized a substantial body of evidence about the effects of U.S. fiscal and monetary policies and presented some new evidence on the effects of alternative treatments of expectations and of alternative types of U.S. fiscal actions. We have also illustrated the possible consequences, in the current circumstances facing the United States, of some policy packages involving phased-in actions.

Predicted effects from individual models vary considerably. Nonetheless, the extended process of collaborative research underlying our model averages and standard deviations in Sections II and III has generated estimates that we believe are useful for attaching rough magnitudes to the domestic and foreign effects of macroeconomic policies.

We likewise believe that the new results in Sections IV and V provide useful, rough insights for the analysis of policy decisions. These results, however, are tentative. Much research remains to be done in analyzing the possible linkages between macroeconomic policies and macroeconomic per-formance. This need is especially great for the analysis of international repercussions of national policies, which often depend on the net effects of offsetting tendencies and on the operation of internationally integrated markets that are strongly influenced by expectations of future events and policies.

Provided that analysts consider simulations generated by a variety of existing models, the predictions of any one model can be placed in a broader perspective. Results that are clear outliers or otherwise implausible can be weeded out. Averaging across the remaining results provides a mean outcome, and a quantifiable range of plausible outcomes around that mean.

Our average results, derived mainly from models with adaptive expectations, suggest that an unanticipated cut in U.S. federal purchases could have a substantial negative impact on the level of U.S. real output for up to several years, as well as on prices, interest rates, the exchange value of the dollar, and, to a lesser but still significant extent, on output outside the United States. Nonetheless, the declines in U.S. prices, interest rates, and the dollar would eventually stimulate domestic demand and net exports enough to reverse most of the decline in output within five to six years. The external deficit would fall, although generally by only one third to one half as much as the budget deficit (a reminder that there is not a "one-for-one" relationship between the two deficits). A fiscal contraction has beneficial effects on the external deficit in large part by reducing total domestic expenditures and prices and to a lesser extent by lowering interest rates and the dollar.

With respect to the effects of monetary policy, the model simulations suggest that initial declines in U.S. output stemming from fiscal contraction could be diminished by a temporary addition to the U.S. money stock. This offset to output in the United States would not, however, be matched by any analogous offset to output declines abroad; indeed, taken literally, the model-average results suggest that the addition of U.S. monetary expansion could even augment the losses in foreign output that would arise from the U.S. fiscal contraction without monetary expansion. A U.S. monetary expansion would cause further dollar depreciation. And, especially in the absence of credible prospects for a fiscal contraction, a monetary expansion might lead to counter-productive reactions in domestic financial markets.

In any event, simulations with forward-looking model-consistent expectations (discussed in Section IV) suggest that—even in the absence of a monetary expansion—the initial depressing effects of a fiscal contraction on U.S. output could be substantially mitigated if the fiscal contraction were anticipated prior to implementation. With anticipation, the beneficial crowding-in effects—induced by more rapid initial declines in long-term interest rates and the dollar—would arrive sooner, in time to offset much of the output reduction that would occur when the fiscal contraction was actually implemented. Such beneficial effects of anticipated future actions, of course, could only occur if an announced fiscal program were widely thought to be credible. In turn, a credible program would be likely to require substantial up-front action if promises of future actions were to be regarded as genuine commitments.

Our tentative analysis of alternative fiscal policies suggests that different types of commensurately sized fiscal actions would have effects on output, as well as on the twin deficits, that were quantitatively different but qualitatively similar in the first year or two. Over a longer horizon of three to five years, actions involving higher sales or corporate taxes would induce, relative to a cut in government purchases, a greater loss of actual and potential output for any given reduction in either the fiscal or the external deficit. The trade-off (loss in output per unit of gain in reducing one or the other of the deficits) for increased personal taxes or reduced transfers could be somewhat more favorable than that for a cut in purchases. Fiscal actions such as hikes in excise taxes or increases in the burden of corporate taxation might prove to be politically less difficult to negotiate than others, for example, increases in personal taxes or cuts in transfers. Changes in excise or corporate taxes, however, cannot be recommended on macroeconomic grounds as the most efficient ways of reducing the domestic and external deficits.

If macroeconomic considerations were to be given paramount attention, our analysis suggests that a U.S. fiscal retrenchment should be phased in gradually, with announcement of the program embodying credible precommitments for the whole sequence of actions. Gradual, predictable programs would be most efficient—again, in the sense of keeping output losses to the smallest possible size for any given targeted reduction in either the fiscal or the external deficit. Reduced government spending will undoubtedly play an important role in any politically agreed compromise. On macroeconomic grounds, our results point also to the inclusion of personal tax increases or transfer decreases. Either of those measures would appear to restrain private consumption and the fiscal deficit more, and discourage investment and total output less. Furthermore, fiscal packages embodying current and future phased-in increases in taxes would probably be more believable than packages promising only current and future cuts in government spending. And announced plans for future spending cuts, especially if unaccompanied by tax increases or transfer reductions, would likely be regarded with skepticism unless a considerable amount of spending reduction were implemented at the outset of the process.

Appendix

The bulk of the empirical research reviewed in this study stems from a series of projects initiated in 1983. This research gathered momentum in succeeding years and, through the cooperation of numerous institutions and individuals in a variety of countries, has evolved into an international collaborative effort.

Planning among modeling groups for the first of a series of workshops and conferences began in the fall of 1984. Preliminary results of commonly specified simulations for U.S. monetary and fiscal policy actions, and for alternative policy responses abroad, were compared and evaluated at a workshop held at the Brookings Institution in October 1985. Revised simulations were then prepared for a two-day conference at Brookings in March 1986. After further revisions and preparation of supplementary material, a two-volume publication about the project—*Empirical Macroeconomics for Interdependent Economies,* referred to in this paper as *EMIE*—appeared in early 1988.[54] The models participating in the *EMIE* project included the international model developed by Data Resources, Inc. (DRI; Brinner, 1985),[55] the COMPACT model of the staff of the Commission of the European Communities (EEC; Dramais, 1986), the world econometric model of the Japanese Economic Planning Agency (EPA; Japanese Economic Planning Agency, 1986), the Project LINK system of linked individual country models (LINK; Hickman, 1989), the model developed at the University of Liverpool (LIVERPOOL; Minford, 1984), the Multi-Country Model developed by the staff of the U.S. Federal Reserve Board (MCM; Edison, Marquez, and Tryon, 1987), a simulation model developed by Richard Haas and Paul Masson at the International Monetary Fund (MINIMOD; Haas and Masson, 1986), the global simulation model of Warwick McKibbin and Jeffrey Sachs (MSG; McKibbin and Sachs, 1986), the INTERLINK model of the Organization for Economic Cooperation and Development (OECD; Richardson, 1988), the multicountry model developed by John Taylor at Stanford University (TAYLOR; Taylor, 1988), a world vector autoregression model developed by Christopher Sims and Robert Litterman (VAR; Sims, 1988), and the world model of Wharton Econometric Forecasting Associates (WHARTON; Green and Howe, 1987).

The *EMIE* evidence pertained to full-model simulations. In January 1987, another workshop was held at Brookings that focused on the U.S. current account imbalance, using primarily partial-model simulations that disengaged the U.S. current account sectors from the rest of the models. Results from this project were published in *External Deficits and the Dollar: The Pit and the Pendulum.*[56]

Further joint efforts to generate empirical evidence from multicountry models were planned during 1987 and implemented in the first half of 1988. The Japanese Economic Planning Agency devoted a substantial part of its biennial symposium to evaluating new simulations from three large multicountry models (EPA, MCM, and OECD). These simulations focused on the Japanese and U.S. economies and the global and domestic policy implications of correcting the large external imbalances of those two countries.[57]

---

[54] Bryant and others (1988).

[55] For each model, we give in parentheses the mnemonic used to describe it and (after the semicolon) a single bibliographical reference. Brief descriptions of the models and additional bibliographical references are provided in the unabridged version of the paper.

[56] Bryant, Holtham, and Hooper (1988). For subsequent updates and elaborations, see Hooper and Mann (1989a and 1989b), Bryant (1988), and Hooper (1988).

[57] The volume of papers prepared for this symposium includes, among others, Helliwell (1988b), and Edison and others (1988).

In May 1988, the U.S. Federal Reserve Board sponsored a conference on monetary aggregates and financial-sector behavior in interdependent economies. The papers at that conference focused on financial modeling for the United States and other major countries, with one session devoted to new simulation evidence, paying particular attention to Japan, Germany, and the United States. Models for which simulations were prepared included several —EPA, LINK, MCM, OECD, TAYLOR—that had participated in earlier projects plus the global economic model of the National Institute of Economic and Social Research in London (GEM; Wren-Lewis and Barrell, 1988) and the main domestic-economy model of the Federal Reserve Board staff (MPS; Brayton and Mauskopf, 1987).[58]

Finally, an additional source of evidence became available in 1988 as a result of modeling efforts at the International Monetary Fund and the Canadian Department of Finance. Members of the IMF staff, extending earlier work with the two-region MINIMOD, constructed a seven-region rational expectations model of the world economy known as MULTIMOD. The focus of that model is on the transmission of policy effects. In its summer 1988 version, MULTIMOD contained separate sub-models for the United States, Japan, and Germany but treated the remaining four members of the Group of Seven as a single aggregated region. A team of researchers at the Canadian Department of Finance, collaborating with the IMF modeling group, has disaggregated that four-country region into four additional sub-models, one each for Canada, France, Italy, and the United Kingdom. Their resulting multicountry model is known as INTERMOD. A significant feature of INTERMOD, and of the predecessor MINIMOD, is the ability to treat expectations either adaptively or in a forward-looking, model-consistent manner. MULTIMOD and INTER-MOD share a common modeling strategy and have similar properties.[59]

The unabridged discussion-paper version of this paper, especially its appendix, provides more detailed information about the modeling groups identified above, about their collaborative preparation of the data underlying this paper, and about several adjustments to the simulations that were required to make them as comparable as possible.[60]

---

[58] A volume based on the papers and discussion at the May 1988 conference is scheduled for publication in 1989. See in particular the contributions of Brayton and Marquez (1988) and Helliwell, Cockerline, and Lafrance (1988), which deal especially with the features and properties of the linkage models discussed in that conference.

[59] MULTIMOD is described in Masson and others (1988). For a description of INTERMOD and examples of its simulation properties, including a comparison with the properties of MULTI-MOD, see Helliwell and others (1988).

[60] In addition to the information about the participating models in the appendix to the unabridged discussion-paper version of this study, readers may also consult the *EMIE* volumes. For the main differences among the models, see especially "Contrasts Among the Participating Models," Bryant and others (1988, main volume, pp. 27–29). Additional bibliographic references for many of the models are given in the *EMIE* supplementary volume, pp. 341–47.

For our full sample of the available results, we typically used 20 time series for a U.S. fiscal contraction and 19 time series for a U.S. monetary expansion. Slightly fewer time series were available for some of the foreign-spillover variables. The full sample statistics, as well as illustrative tables of the simulation results, are included in the unabridged version.

The data for the simulation results exhibit considerable diversity. Much of this diversity reflects fundamental uncertainty that can be diminished only by further empirical research. In the case of some particular models, however, outlier simulations can be traced to unusual properties that are, on the basis of already existing knowledge, suspected of being problematic. Analysts and policymakers seldom wish to give equal weight to every piece of information bearing on an analytical issue. Much of our analysis, therefore, focuses on a partial sample that eliminates results that were judged to be problematic in one respect or another.

Our partial sample is a subset of 12 of the 20 time series included in the full sample (12 out of the 19 for U.S. monetary expansion). The series in the partial sample are DRI (*EMIE*); EEC (*EMIE*); INTERMOD adaptive; INTER-MOD model-consistent; MCM (*EMIE*); MCM (1988 FR); MINIMOD (*EMIE*); MULTIMOD; OECD (*EMIE*); OECD (1988 FR); TAYLOR (*EMIE*); and TAYLOR (1988 FR).[61]

For the partial sample, Table 1 (U.S. fiscal contraction) and Table 2 (U.S. monetary expansion) present means, standard deviations, and ranges (maximum value less minimum value) for key macroeconomic variables.[62]

To give readers additional perspective on the data, the unabridged version of the paper includes several additional charts emphasizing the diversity of the results across models. Those charts plot not only the sample means and intervals for plus and minus one standard deviation, but also the data for the individual simulation results.

The unabridged version also supplies the actual data used in preparing the charts in Sections IV through VI of this paper.

---

[61] The identification in parentheses indicates whether the result comes from the *EMIE* volume or from the May 1988 conference held at the U.S. Federal Reserve.

[62] These two tables correspond to Tables 7 and 8 in the unabridged, discussion-paper version of the study.

Table 1. Partial Sample:
Averages, Standard Deviations, and Ranges for Simulated Effects
of a U.S. Fiscal Contraction*

	Year 1	Year 2	Year 3	Year 4	Year 5	Year 6
U.S. Real GNP (percent deviation from baseline)						
Mean	-1.397	-1.281	-1.032	-0.830	-0.642	-0.464
Standard Deviation	0.307	0.478	0.400	0.334	0.345	0.399
Range	1.037	1.536	1.032	1.126	1.219	1.255
U.S. Price Level (percent deviation from baseline)						
Mean	-0.153	-0.604	-1.166	-1.791	-2.428	-3.069
Standard Deviation	0.139	0.323	0.613	1.021	1.521	2.056
Range	0.496	1.111	1.988	3.346	4.918	6.528
U.S. Short-Term Interest Rate (deviation from baseline in percentage points)						
Mean	-0.675	-1.024	-1.140	-1.297	-1.484	-1.661
Standard Deviation	0.331	0.571	0.613	0.692	0.806	0.907
Range	0.936	1.478	1.660	1.808	2.163	2.587
U.S. Long-Term Interest Rate (deviation from baseline in percentage points)						
Mean	-0.367	-0.645	-0.816	-0.938	-1.060	-1.186
Standard Deviation	0.217	0.313	0.449	0.564	0.683	0.807
Range	0.729	0.995	1.270	1.562	1.741	2.018
U.S. Government Budget Balance (deviation from baseline as percent of baseline nominal GNP)						
Mean	0.615	0.644	0.850	1.013	1.161	1.321
Standard Deviation	0.212	0.210	0.210	0.316	0.443	0.568
Range	0.614	0.560	0.653	1.009	1.575	2.079

Weighted Average Exchange Value of U.S. Dollar (percent deviation from baseline)

Mean	-1.864	-2.097	-2.043	-1.949	-1.939	-1.911
Standard Deviation	2.000	1.820	1.846	1.899	2.012	2.199
Range	6.620	6.500	6.457	6.409	6.379	7.304

U.S. Current Account Balance (deviation from baseline as percent of baseline nominal GNP)

Mean	0.238	0.320	0.354	0.396	0.442	0.501
Standard Deviation	0.095	0.121	0.141	0.167	0.211	0.264
Range	0.281	0.460	0.496	0.639	0.806	0.986

Japanese Real GNP (percent deviation from baseline)

Mean	-0.392	-0.717	-0.772	-0.711	-0.690	-0.742
Standard Deviation	0.149	0.351	0.451	0.510	0.613	0.802
Range	0.407	0.995	1.157	1.441	1.695	2.538

Japanese Price Level (percent deviation from baseline)

Mean	-0.107	-0.378	-0.746	-1.119	-1.461	-1.765
Standard Deviation	0.141	0.359	0.650	1.018	1.415	1.771
Range	0.461	1.082	1.758	2.686	3.791	4.800

Japanese Short-Term Interest Rate (deviation from baseline in percentage points)

Mean	-0.157	-0.392	-0.491	-0.514	-0.536	-0.576
Standard Deviation	0.113	0.233	0.246	0.210	0.220	0.261
Range	0.415	0.628	0.750	0.625	0.660	0.787

German Real GNP (percent deviation from baseline)

Mean	-0.224	-0.342	-0.380	-0.387	-0.357	-0.312
Standard Deviation	0.106	0.108	0.172	0.260	0.292	0.337
Range	0.288	0.351	0.528	0.704	0.804	1.053

Table 1 (*concluded*).

	Year 1	Year 2	Year 3	Year 4	Year 5	Year 6
German Price Level (percent deviation from baseline)						
Mean	-0.155	-0.467	-0.821	-1.158	-1.495	-1.826
Standard Deviation	0.131	0.310	0.561	0.865	1.161	1.404
Range	0.332	0.829	1.505	2.353	3.208	3.999
German Short-Term Interest Rate (deviation from baseline in percentage points)						
Mean	-0.249	-0.409	-0.455	-0.502	-0.600	-0.686
Standard Deviation	0.233	0.334	0.261	0.218	0.259	0.319
Range	0.797	1.105	0.900	0.760	0.680	0.864
ROECD Real GNP (percent deviation from baseline)						
Mean	-0.244	-0.428	-0.478	-0.459	-0.444	-0.440
Standard Deviation	0.093	0.163	0.193	0.222	0.257	0.355
Range	0.277	0.449	0.590	0.711	0.852	1.070
ROECD Price Level (percent deviation from baseline)						
Mean	-0.137	-0.423	-0.793	-1.161	-1.533	-1.881
Standard Deviation	0.121	0.325	0.604	0.937	1.262	1.540
Range	0.370	0.961	1.773	2.655	3.498	4.215
ROECD Short-Term Interest Rate (deviation from baseline in percentage points)						
Mean	-0.155	-0.316	-0.417	-0.500	-0.591	-0.688
Standard Deviation	0.115	0.208	0.229	0.244	0.270	0.295
Range	0.335	0.630	0.715	0.800	0.895	0.945

*Reduction below baseline in real U.S. government purchases of goods and services equal to 1 percent of baseline U.S. real GNP, maintained throughout the six years of simulation period.

Table 2. Partial Sample:
Averages, Standard Deviations, and Ranges for Simulated Effects
of a U.S. Monetary Expansion*

	Year 1	Year 2	Year 3	Year 4	Year 5	Year 6
U.S. Real GNP (percent deviation from baseline)						
Mean	0.268	0.278	0.233	0.188	0.143	0.086
Standard Deviation	0.155	0.127	0.186	0.171	0.116	0.129
Range	0.480	0.380	0.554	0.552	0.356	0.464
U.S. Price Level (percent deviation from baseline)						
Mean	0.089	0.199	0.331	0.452	0.562	0.645
Standard Deviation	0.076	0.173	0.234	0.260	0.271	0.263
Range	0.236	0.622	0.861	0.988	1.053	0.991
U.S. Short-Term Interest Rate (deviation from baseline in percentage points)						
Mean	−0.798	−0.234	−0.174	−0.154	−0.121	−0.107
Standard Deviation	0.590	0.248	0.201	0.169	0.155	0.164
Range	1.731	0.776	0.735	0.623	0.541	0.541
U.S. Long-Term Interest Rate (deviation from baseline in percentage points)						
Mean	−0.241	−0.172	−0.150	−0.126	−0.094	−0.079
Standard Deviation	0.207	0.181	0.159	0.142	0.109	0.116
Range	0.706	0.562	0.527	0.527	0.357	0.362
U.S. Government Budget Balance (deviation from baseline as percent of baseline nominal GNP)						
Mean	0.124	0.184	0.191	0.172	0.157	0.144
Standard Deviation	0.118	0.118	0.114	0.103	0.101	0.124
Range	0.366	0.291	0.308	0.271	0.281	0.362

Table 2 (*concluded*).

	Year 1	Year 2	Year 3	Year 4	Year 5	Year 6
Weighted Average Exchange Value of U.S. Dollar (percent deviation from baseline)						
Mean	-1.465	-1.126	-1.188	-1.176	-1.059	-0.939
Standard Deviation	1.045	0.876	1.035	0.905	0.486	0.332
Range	3.268	3.396	3.985	3.510	1.825	1.289
U.S. Current Account Balance (deviation from baseline as percent of baseline nominal GNP)						
Mean	-0.039	-0.002	0.015	0.020	0.023	0.021
Standard Deviation	0.053	0.028	0.022	0.033	0.046	0.042
Range	0.149	0.091	0.065	0.105	0.160	0.133
Japanese Real GNP (percent deviation from baseline)						
Mean	-0.076	-0.128	-0.145	-0.126	-0.103	-0.099
Standard Deviation	0.152	0.219	0.228	0.184	0.164	0.186
Range	0.502	0.707	0.727	0.562	0.418	0.486
Japanese Price Level (percent deviation from baseline)						
Mean	-0.028	-0.039	-0.056	-0.068	-0.070	-0.062
Standard Deviation	0.035	0.026	0.050	0.073	0.107	0.146
Range	0.114	0.090	0.140	0.252	0.354	0.531
Japanese Short-Term Interest Rate (deviation from baseline in percentage points)						
Mean	-0.055	-0.051	-0.055	-0.052	-0.038	-0.019
Standard Deviation	0.125	0.126	0.115	0.080	0.042	0.043
Range	0.433	0.470	0.419	0.272	0.131	0.157

German Real GNP (percent deviation from baseline)

Mean	0.027	0.013	-0.022	-0.044	-0.046	-0.048
Standard Deviation	0.052	0.049	0.030	0.079	0.124	0.145
Range	0.178	0.154	0.095	0.231	0.400	0.476

German Price Level (percent deviation from baseline)

Mean	-0.056	-0.089	-0.137	-0.179	-0.192	-0.165
Standard Deviation	0.077	0.120	0.240	0.350	0.395	0.339
Range	0.232	0.369	0.789	1.168	1.357	1.207

German Short-Term Interest Rate (deviation from baseline in percentage points)

Mean	-0.029	-0.023	-0.052	-0.095	-0.095	-0.075
Standard Deviation	0.174	0.062	0.075	b0.148	0.187	0.181
Range	0.600	0.229	0.233	0.484	0.620	0.658

ROECD Real GNP (percent deviation from baseline)

Mean	-0.017	-0.046	-0.050	-0.042	-0.043	-0.052
Standard Deviation	0.059	0.083	0.089	0.086	0.089	0.102
Range	0.192	0.237	0.306	0.316	0.315	0.329

ROECD Price Level (percent deviation from baseline)

Mean	-0.059	-0.081	-0.119	-0.137	-0.126	-0.094
Standard Deviation	0.064	0.105	0.182	0.207	0.172	0.136
Range	0.183	0.327	0.572	0.650	0.549	0.376

ROECD Short-Term Interest Rate (deviation from baseline in percentage points)

Mean	-0.070	-0.064	-0.073	-0.078	-0.073	-0.064
Standard Deviation	0.077	0.092	0.106	0.108	0.091	0.074
Range	0.185	0.272	0.323	0.331	0.272	0.198

*Increase of money stock above baseline by 1 percent, maintained throughout the six years of simulation period.

References

Anderson, Robert, and Jared Enzler, "Toward Realistic Policy Design: Policy Reaction Functions That Rely on Economic Forecasts," in *Macroeconomics and Finance: Essays in Honor of Franco Modigliani*, ed. by Rudiger Dornbusch and others (Cambridge, Massachusetts: MIT Press, 1987).

Blinder, Alan S., "Reaganomics and Growth: The Message in the Models," in *The Legacy of Reaganomics: Prospects for Long-Term Growth*, ed. by Charles R. Hulten and Isabel V. Sawhill (Washington: Urban Institute Press, 1984).

Boskin, Michael J., "Tax Policy and Economic Growth: Lessons From the 1980s," *Journal of Economic Perspectives*, Vol. 2, No. 4 (Nashville, Tennessee: Fall 1988).

Brayton, Flint, and Jaime Marquez, "The Behavior of Monetary Sectors and Monetary Policy: Evidence from Multicountry Models," presented at the May 1988 Federal Reserve Board conference, forthcoming in *Financial Sectors in Open Economies: Empirical Analysis and Policy Issues*, ed. by Peter Hooper and others (Washington: Board of Governors of the Federal Reserve System, 1988).

Brayton, Flint, and Eileen Mauskopf, "The Federal Reserve Board MPS Quarterly Econometric Model of the U.S. Economy," *Economic Modelling*, Vol. 2, No. 3 (London: Butterworth Scientific Ltd., 1985), pp. 170–292.

————, "Structure and Uses of the MPS Quarterly Econometric Model of the United States," *Federal Reserve Bulletin* (Washington: February 1987), pp. 93–109.

Brinner, Roger, "The 1985 DRI Model: An Overview," in *Data Resources Review of the U.S. Economy* (Lexington, Massachusetts: Data Resources/McGraw-Hill, September 1985).

Bryant, Ralph C., "The U.S. External Deficit: An Update," Brookings Discussion Paper in International Economics No. 63 (Washington: The Brookings Institution, January 1988). Published version without appendix in *Tokyo Club Papers No. 1, 1988* (Tokyo: Tokyo Club Foundation for Global Studies, Nomura Research Institute, 1988).

————, Dale W. Henderson, and Steven A. Symansky, "Estimates of the Consequences of Policy Actions Derived from Model Simulations," Chapter 4 in Bryant and others (1988).

Bryant, Ralph C., Gerald Holtham, and Peter Hooper, *External Deficits and the Dollar: The Pit and the Pendulum* (Washington: The Brookings Institution, 1988).

Bryant, Ralph C., John F. Helliwell, and Peter Hooper, "Domestic and Cross-Border Consequences of U.S. Macroeconomic Policies" (unabridged version of present paper); Brookings Discussion Paper in International Economics No. 68 (Washington: The Brookings Institution, January 1989); also circulated as a Federal Reserve Board Discussion Paper in International Finance (Washington: February 1989).

Bryant, Ralph C., and others, eds., *Empirical Macroeconomics for Interdependent Economies* (Washington: The Brookings Institution, 1988).

Burtless, Gary, "The Work Response to a Guaranteed Income: A Survey of Experimental Evidence," in *The Income Maintenance Experiments: Lessons for Welfare Reform,* ed. by Alicia Munnell (Boston: Federal Reserve Bank of Boston, 1987).

Christ, Carl F., "Judging the Performance of Econometric Models of the U.S. Economy," *International Economic Review,* Vol. 16, No. 1 (Osaka: February 1975).

Coen, Robert M., and Bert Hickman, "Tax Policy, Federal Deficits and U.S. Growth in the 1980s," *National Tax Journal,* Vol. 37, No. 1 (Columbus, Ohio: March 1984).

Congressional Budget Office, "Economic Effects of Deficit Reduction in Commercial Econometric Models," A Report to the National Economic Commission (Washington: Congressional Budget Office, December 7, 1988).

Dramais, Andre, "COMPACT: Prototype of a Macro Model for the European Community in the World Economy," Discussion Paper 27, Commission of the European Communities, Directorate-General for Economic and Financial Affairs (Brussels: March 1986).

Dungan, Peter D., and T.A. Wilson, "Modelling Anticipated and Temporary Fiscal Policy Shocks in a Macro-econometric Model of Canada," *Canadian Journal of Economics,* Vol. 21 (Toronto: February 1988).

Edison, Hali J., Jaime R. Marquez, and Ralph W. Tryon, "The Structure and Properties of the Federal Reserve Board Multicountry Model," *Economic Modelling,* Vol. 4 (London: Butterworth Scientific Ltd., April 1987).

Edison, Hali J., and others, "Monetary Policy Effects on Income, Prices and the External Balance: A Comparative Analysis of Simulations of Three Multi-country Models," in *Global and Domestic Policy Implications of Correcting External Imbalances,* papers of the Fourth EPA International Symposium (Tokyo: Economic Planning Agency, 1988).

Enzler, Jared, and Lewis Johnson, "Cycles Resulting from Money Stock Targeting," in Board of Governors of the Federal Reserve System, *New Monetary Control Procedures,* Vol. 1 (Washington: February 1981).

Ethier, Wilfred, *Modern International Economics* (New York: Norton, 1st ed., 1983).

Fair, Ray C., *Specification, Estimation, and Analysis of Macroeconometric Models* (Cambridge, Massachusetts: Harvard University Press, 1984).

Frankel, Jeffrey A., "Ambiguous Policy Multipliers in Theory and in Empirical Models," Chapter 2 in Bryant and others (1988).

————, and Katherine Rockett, "International Macroeconomic Policy Coordination When Policymakers Do Not Agree on the True Model," *American Economic Review,* Vol. 78 (Nashville, Tennessee: June 1988).

Fromm, Gary, and Lawrence R. Klein, "A Comparison of Eleven Econometric Models of the United States," *American Economic Review, Papers and Proceedings,* Vol. 63 (Nashville, Tennessee: May 1973).

Green, John, and Howard Howe, "Results from the WEFA World Model," Brookings Discussion Paper in International Economics No. 59-B (Washington: The Brookings Institution, March 1987).

Haas, Richard, and Paul R. Masson, "MINIMOD: Specification and Simulation Results," *Staff Papers,* Vol. 33 (Washington: International Monetary Fund, December 1986).

Helliwell, John F. (1988a), "Empirical Macroeconomics for Interdependent Economies: What Next?" Chapter 6 in Bryant and others (1988).

———— (1988b), "The Effects of Fiscal Policy on International Imbalances: Japan and the United States," in *Global and Domestic Policy Implications of Correcting External Imbalances,* papers of the Fourth EPA International Symposium (Tokyo: Economic Planning Agency, 1988). Also available as NBER Working Paper 2650 (Cambridge, Massachusetts: National Bureau of Economic Research, July 1988).

————, Jon Cockerline, and Robert Lafrance, "Multicountry Modelling of Financial Markets," presented at the May 1988 Federal Reserve Board conference, forthcoming in *Financial Sectors in Open Economies: Empirical Analysis and Policy Issues,* ed. by Peter Hooper and others (Washington: Board of Governors of the Federal Reserve System, 1988).

Helliwell, John F., and others, "INTERMOD 1.1: A G-7 Version of the IMF's MULTIMOD," Working Paper 88-7 (Ottawa: Working Group on International Macroeconomics, Department of Finance, 1988).

Hickman, Bert G., "Project LINK and Multicountry Modeling," in *A History of Macro-Econometric Model-Building,* ed. by R.G. Bodkin, L.R. Klein, and K. Marwah, forthcoming.

————, and Hillard G. Huntington, eds., *The Macroeconomic Impacts of Energy Shocks: Contributions from Participating Modelers,* EMF Report No. 7, Vol. 3 (Stanford: Energy Modeling Forum, Stanford University, December 1987).

————, and James L. Sweeney, eds., *Macroeconomic Impacts of Energy Shocks* (Amsterdam: North-Holland, 1987).

Hooper, Peter, "Exchange Rates and U.S. External Adjustment in the Short Run and the Long Run," Brookings Discussion Paper in International Economics No. 65 (Washington: The Brookings Institution, October 1988).

————, and Catherine Mann (1989a), "The U.S. External Deficit: Its Causes and Persistence," in *The U.S. Trade Deficit: Causes, Consequences and Cures,* ed. by Albert E. Burger, 12th Annual Economic Policy Proceedings, Federal Reserve Bank of St. Louis (Boston: Kluwer Academic Publishing, 1989).

———— (1989b), *The Emergence and Persistence of the U.S. External Imbalance: 1980–87,* Princeton Studies in International Finance (Princeton, New Jersey: International Finance Section, Princeton University, 1989).

International Monetary Fund, *World Economic Outlook, October 1988: Revised Projections by the Staff of the International Monetary Fund,* World Economic and Financial Surveys (Washington: IMF, October 1988).

Japanese Economic Planning Agency, World Economic Planning Group, "The EPA World Economic Model: An Overview," Discussion Paper 37 (Tokyo: Economic Planning Agency, Economic Research Institute, February 1986).

Masson, Paul R., and A. Blundell-Wignall, "Fiscal Policy and the Exchange Rate in the Big Seven: Transmission of U.S. Government Spending Shocks," *European Economic Review,* Vol. 28 (Amsterdam: May 1985), pp. 11–42.

Masson, Paul R., and others, "MULTIMOD: A Multi-Region Econometric Model," in *Staff Studies for the World Economic Outlook* (Washington: International Monetary Fund, July 1988), pp. 50–104.

McKibbin, Warwick J., "The World Economy from 1979 to 1988: Results from the MSG2 Model," mimeographed, Sydney: Reserve Bank of Australia, 1988.

_____, and Jeffrey D. Sachs, "Comparing the Global Performance of Alternative Exchange Arrangements," Brookings Discussion Paper in International Economics No. 49 (Washington: The Brookings Institution, August 1986).

Minford, Patrick, "The Effects of American Policies—A New Classical Interpretation," in Willem H. Buiter and Richard C. Marston, eds., *International Economic Policy Coordination* (Cambridge, England: Cambridge University Press for the Centre for Economic Policy Research, 1985).

Richardson, Pete, "The Structure and Simulation Properties of OECD's Interlink Model," *OECD Economic Studies,* No. 10 (Paris: Organization for Economic Cooperation and Development, Spring 1988).

Sims, Christopher A., "Identifying Policy Effects," Annex A in Bryant and others (1988).

Taylor, John B., "The Treatment of Expectations in Large Multicountry Econometric Models," Chapter 7 in Bryant and others (1988).

Wren-Lewis, Simon, and Ray Barrell, "GEM Model Manual: A Description and Equation Listing of the National Institute's Global Econometric Model," preliminary mimeograph version (London: National Institute for Economic and Social Research, January 1988).

Comments

Haruhiko Kuroda

As pointed out by many economists, most notably by Jeffrey Frankel,[1] we must have a reasonable degree of agreement on the impacts of our economic policies on our economies if international policy coordination is to succeed. And yet it is notoriously difficult for us to agree on the probable magnitude—or even the direction—of macroeconomic policy effects. I can recall when the U.S. administration insisted that there was no causal relationship between the U.S. budget deficit and the trade deficit, despite the strong counter-arguments put forward by other governments.

The paper by Messrs. Bryant, Helliwell, and Hooper intends to help us by providing averages and standard deviations of domestic and cross-border effects for U.S. macroeconomic policies simulated on 20 global econometric models. The results are illuminating as well as fascinating.

Of course, you may argue that collective wisdom is not necessarily better than individual wisdom, partly because there is no guarantee of internal consistency for averaged figures. To this, I can say that by carefully studying the differences and similarities in simulated results, we can acquire the "feeling" or "sense" of effects of economic policies. As a Japanese, who tends to make decisions on the basis of compromise and consensus, I warmly welcome the intention of the paper.

Turning to the substance of the paper, I will offer some comments on the effects of U.S. fiscal and monetary policy, and on policy prescriptions for the new U.S. administration.

On fiscal policy issues, I can generally agree with the paper. That a U.S. fiscal contraction brings about a fall in output, a lower price level, and improvements in budget and external balances in the United States is "common sense," and is verified by all simulations presented in the paper. The spillover effects on foreign real gross national product (GNP) are small, compared with the effects on U.S. real GNP, but they are still sizable, especially in the case of Japan. Since the spillover effects of Japanese or German fiscal policy on U.S. real GNP are known to be minimal, important asymmetry exists, as pointed out by Masaru Yoshitomi.[2]

I appreciate that the paper stresses the need for the United States to reduce its budget deficit in order to rectify its current account imbalance, which is so large and unsustainable. In this connection, I noted with interest that according to the authors, "the results suggested that by far the largest part of the net improvement in the [U.S.] current account comes from the changes in domes-

---

[1] See Frankel (1988) and Frankel and Rockett (1988).
[2] See Yoshitomi (1986 and 1988).

tic spending, prices and interest rates, and relatively little from the small change in the nominal exchange rate."

One related question I have is why is it that most simulations show the U.S. fiscal contraction leading to a small depreciation of the U.S. dollar? Although in these models a reduction in the budget deficit decreases the interest rate and, hence, depreciates the dollar, in the real world it could increase the value of the dollar because it would improve the U.S. current account balance and also might enhance confidence in the U.S. economy.

On monetary policy, I have no difficulties in understanding the simulation results. As expected, a U.S. monetary expansion tends to reduce home interest rates and the value of the dollar, and to increase home output and the domestic price level. Spillover effects on foreign output are again small, but are negative in about half the models. What is most interesting is that the experiments have produced an unusually skewed distribution of U.S. current account balances around zero deviation from the baseline. This fact would not be left unnoticed for long by policymakers.

Policy Prescriptions

On the issue of policy prescriptions, unfortunately, I have some doubts about the analysis presented in the paper. The authors present three fiscal contraction packages: A (expenditure cuts), B (transfer payments reduction and personal tax increase), and C (corporate tax and sales tax increase), as well as a fiscal-monetary policy mix D (expenditure cuts and monetary expansion). Since A, C, and even B do involve a significant output loss, D is recommended by the authors, although D would reduce foreign output most. But even based on their simulations, this judgment does not seem to be correct, as the rough calculation in the table (which assumes virtual linearity) shows.

Fourth-Year Effects
(Percent of GNP)

	GNP	Budget Balance	Current Balance
A	−2	1½	¾
B	−1½	2	¾
C	−3	1¼	¾
D	−1¼	2¼	¾
B-A	½	½	0
A-C	1	¼	0
2B-C	0	2¾	¾

Utilizing the differential effects between A and B, we can improve the budget balance and increase output at the same time if we adopt B with reversed A (expenditure increase)—pointing to the "catalytic effect" of the tax increase, as named by Michio Morishima.[3] Combining A with reversed C (tax reduction), we can further improve the outcome, since C is assumed to be so bad! If we combine twice of B with reversed C, the budget balance and current balance will be improved without any output loss. In general, you can attain three objectives (GNP increase, budget balance, current account balance) with three instruments (A,B,C)—a simple application of the Tinbergen Principle.[4]

Of course, I do not mean that implementing such policy prescriptions is politically easy, or even possible. I only wish to say that we have to be careful when we prescribe economic policies on purely macroeconomic grounds.

Finally, if you allow me to touch on a possible strategy for economic policies for the United States, I personally recommend the following one: The U.S. Congress must try to reduce the budget deficit as much as possible through expenditure cuts and "revenue enhancement," both of which are necessary for a credible deficit reduction, as suggested by the paper. Then the U.S. Federal Reserve Board, in deciding on its monetary policy, and partner countries, in managing their economic policy, should take account of the progress made in the U.S. Congress. Since the U.S. Congress is powerful, makes unilateral decisions paying little regard to economic policies taken by others, and takes a long time to decide important policies, the best strategy for others seems to be to adjust their policies flexibly and in a timely fashion based on what the U.S. Congress decides.

References

Frankel, Jeffrey A., "Ambiguous Policy Multipliers in Theory and in Twelve Econometric Models," in *Empirical Macroeconomics for Interdependent Economies*, ed. by Ralph C. Bryant and others (Washington: The Brookings Institution, 1988).

_____, and Katherine Rockett, "International Macroeconomic Policy Coordination When Policymakers Do Not Agree on the True Model," *American Economic Review*, Vol. 78 (Nashville, Tennessee: June 1988).

Morishima, Michio, *Economic Theory and Modern Society* (Cambridge: Cambridge University Press, 1976).

Tinbergen, Jan, *On the Theory of Economic Policy* (Amsterdam:North-Holland, 1952).

---

[3] This is an extension of Haavelmo's "balanced budget multiplier." See Morishima (1976).

[4] See Tinbergen (1952).

Yoshitomi, Masaru, "Growth Gaps, Exchange Rates and Asymmetry: Is It Possible to Unwind Current Account Imbalances Without Fiscal Expansion in Japan?" in *Japan and the United States Today*, ed. by Hugh Patrick and Ryuichiro Tachi (New York: Columbia University Press, 1986).

————, "Domestic and Global Policy Implications of Correcting International Imbalances," in *Papers and Proceedings of the Fourth EPA International Symposium*, ed. by Minoru Ikeda and others (Tokyo: Economic Planning Agency, 1988).

David Begg

The paper by Bryant, Helliwell, and Hooper offers a clear, comprehensive, and useful comparison of simulation results in different econometric models. The paper is not, however, strictly about policy coordination, as foreign policy variables are held constant in alternative simulations of U.S. policy. I shall return to this point later. Nor, unlike much of this conference, is the paper about the systemic properties of simple policy rules, whether within a deterministic or a stochastic environment. Rather, the authors focus on the choices facing U.S. policymakers and what they could usefully learn from the consensus of empirical research.

The authors do not blindly follow the arithmetic of computer simulations; they are prepared to make judgments, and I like their use of discretion. I also like their attempt to puzzle out why different models yield different results, and their discussion of the significance of the policy mix on the one hand, and of the role of expectations on the other. Furthermore, I should say at the outset that the simulation results, when characterized by the mean across all the models, seem to accord with my intuition and to be plausible in magnitude. Perhaps economics really does have something useful to say.

The authors' framework is a five- to six-year simulation horizon, which they argue is long enough to show medium-term effects. One might ask whether there is any less arbitrary way to choose the time horizon. Since the authors make much of expectations and credibility, one could argue that political considerations dictate a four-year horizon corresponding to the date of the next U.S. election. Or one might ask, in economic terms, how long a period is necessary for, say, gross domestic product to return within x percent of its baseline level after some initial shock. In any event, I merely note that there is no particular significance to the time horizon chosen by the authors.

Simulations display the effect of policy changes relative to a baseline reference path. I should like to have seen more discussion of the baseline path in different models. When expectations are forward-looking, the entire future is considered, and unrealistic paths are eliminated. But many models incorporate backward-looking expectations. A fair model comparison then requires that baseline paths indeed be sustainable. For example, they should not imply governmental or external insolvency shortly after the time horizon actually adopted. Further discussion of these issues would have been illuminating.

I turn next to the presentation of results. The authors show the results of 20 model runs, but they confine most of their discussion to 12 particular models, eliminating those they judged outliers or inappropriate in some way. Whilst I am happy not to accord equal weight to all models, it would be nice to know whether, and if so in which respect, the omitted models systematically differ from those included.

Results across models are presented in terms of means and standard deviations for each variable. This certainly provides succinct summary statistics, but one should also ask to whom these results are to be sold. The problem arises because we disagree about the "correct" model, and different models yield (slightly) different answers. However, if the purpose of the analysis is to convince particular policymakers in particular countries, the prior beliefs of the policymakers may be important in the credence attached to different model results.

Turning to the reported results, the authors show that monetary policy tends to have only small effects on competitiveness and on the real economy, whereas fiscal policy has much larger spillover effects for other countries. If this result is as robust as the authors claim, it is of some importance for international policy coordination. I do wonder how robust the result about monetary policy can be: Whatever became of exchange rate overshooting when monetary policy is altered? Part of the answer is that many (but not all) of the models considered use backward-looking expectations, and part of the answer is simply that the fiscal shocks are larger in magnitude than the monetary shocks considered.

A U.S. fiscal contraction leads to a significant output loss in the short term in the United States, and this spills over into lower output and prices in the Federal Republic of Germany and Japan. Clearly, these results overstate the likely output cost to the United States; in practice, policy in Germany and Japan would surely respond with some expansionary measures, which the analysis does not acknowledge.

A similar mitigation is likely because of induced changes in the U.S. policy mix. With lower output and prices, any optimizing monetary authority would surely respond with some relaxation of monetary conditions in the United States. The recent literature on policy coordination has tended to de-emphasize optimal policy in favor of simpler, robust rules that are less sensitive to model-specific properties. But that does not mean that monetary and fiscal policy must be independent of one another.

Continuing the optimistic theme that the U.S. output cost of fiscal correction need not be too high, the authors show that when expectations are forward-looking, future interest rate and exchange rate reductions are brought forward, further lessening the recessionary impact of fiscal contraction.

Finally, I turn to the five specific fiscal packages the authors consider:

cuts in spending, higher income tax rates, higher sales taxes, higher corporate taxes, and cuts in transfer payments. All have similar initial impact effects but thereafter the packages with higher corporate or sales taxes perform less well than the others. Higher corporate taxes affect the supply side via their impact on investment. Higher sales taxes add to prices and inflation. Here, the higher sales tax is largely operating as a *monetary* contraction, confronting higher prices with an unchanged path for the money stock. Again this demonstrates the significance of the policy mix.

One last remark. I am not sure output should be the main criterion by which to assess alternative policy packages. The composition of output may also matter a lot. If a financial revolution has led to a consumer boom as households unlock previous borrowing constraints, there may be a case for favoring packages that raise income taxes or otherwise smooth the consumption response.

3

Policy Analysis with a Multicountry Model

*John B. Taylor**

I. Introduction

This paper summarizes the results of an empirical study of alternative international monetary arrangements using a multicountry econometric model. The focus of the research is on monetary policy in the Group of Seven countries: Canada, France, the Federal Republic of Germany, Italy, Japan, the United Kingdom, and the United States. The general econometric approach used is usually referred to as "rational expectations econometric policy evaluation." The hallmark of this approach is fitting a structural model with rational expectations to real world data, with the effect of different monetary policy rules on the performance of the economy determined by stochastic simulations of the estimated model (for simple models the effect can be calculated analytically).[1]

The issues examined using this approach are controversial and continue to be discussed and debated by leading international economists and policy-makers.[2] It is perhaps surprising, therefore, that many of the policy implica-

*This research was supported by a grant from the National Science Foundation at the National Bureau of Economic Research and by the Center for Economic Policy Research at Stanford University. I am grateful to Peter Klenow and Paul Lau for comments and research assistance, and to Paul Masson for comments on an earlier draft.

[1] This approach was used for the evaluation of domestic monetary policy rules for the United States in Taylor (1979) with a small one-country econometric model. The simulation results described in this paper are drawn from unpublished research contained in Taylor (1988d) using a multicountry econometric model. The two-country theoretical model that underlies the empirical multicountry model used for the simulations is described in Carlozzi and Taylor (1985) and Taylor (1985). An early version of the multicountry model is published in Taylor (1988a). The current version is published in Taylor (1988b) or Taylor (1988c).

[2] See, for example, McKinnon (1988), Dornbusch (1988), and Williamson (1988).

tions of the results of the research appear to be unambiguous and robust. The results suggest, for example, that with the current international economic structure it would be a mistake for Germany, Japan, and the United States to attempt to focus their monetary policies on fixing the U.S. dollar/Japanese yen or the dollar/deutsche mark exchange rates. A strongly preferred option *for internal as well as external stability* would be for each of these countries to orient their monetary policies toward domestic price level targets (or perhaps towards domestic nominal gross national product [GNP] targets in which real output also plays a role). One of the reasons for the lack of ambiguity in this study, compared with other studies of exchange rate regimes, may be that I use empirical measures of demand and supply elasticities and empirical estimates of the sizes of the shocks to the demand and supply curves. Thus, the advantage that one international monetary arrangement has for dealing effectively with one type of shock is assessed and measured up against the advantage that another arrangement has for dealing with other types of shocks. This assessment suggests that a more flexible exchange rate arrangement among Germany, Japan, and the United States measures up quite well, as compared with a fixed exchange rate system.

In discussing these econometric results, it is important to clarify their underlying economic rationale. This paper, therefore, attempts to contrast my findings with those of other researchers who have argued the case for a return to a fixed exchange rate system among the United States, Japan, and the European bloc of currencies. I consider, for example, the arguments of McKinnon (1988) and Krugman (1988). I believe many of the arguments made in favor of one international monetary arrangement or another are implicitly considered in empirical multicountry frameworks, such as the one used here. However, the explicit reason why a monetary policy that focuses away from domestic targets toward an exchange rate target seems to lead to a less than optimal performance has either been downplayed or not mentioned in many recent discussions.

The outline of this paper follows the research strategy used for the policy evaluation. In the interest of brevity and clarity, I report results for only three of the seven major industrial countries: Germany, Japan, and the United States. After summarizing the model in Section II, I examine the question of the exchange rate regime in Section III. As already mentioned, I find that policy rules that focus on fixing the exchange rates among Germany, Japan, and the United States perform poorly. I therefore focus the remaining part of the investigation on policies with more flexible exchange rates. Flexible exchange rate policies in which the central banks adjust their interest rate differential in response to movements of the exchange rates away from a long-run purchasing power parity target turn out to work better than a fixed exchange rate. However, for the United States, such policies do not work as well as a domestically oriented policy, and in Germany and Japan, such a policy does not dominate a price or GNP rule. I then go on to consider rules that focus explicitly on domestic price and output stability. In Section IV, I examine whether the choice of parameters of such rules has much effect on economic performance in other countries. Finally, in Section V, I consider the choice between price rules, nominal GNP rules, and mixed rules. Although the monetary policy rules in Sections IV and V do not incorporate exchange rates explicitly, they are evaluated partly in terms of the stability in the behavior of exchange rates. In general, I find that monetary policy rules that focus on domestic price and output stability generate surprisingly stable exchange rate behavior.

II. Key Features of the Multicountry Model

The seven-country model used for the policy experiments consists of 98 stochastic equations and a number of identities. The parameters of the model are estimated using quarterly data for the period from the first quarter of 1971 through the fourth quarter of 1986. On an equations-per-country basis this is not a large model relative to other models used for monetary and exchange rate policy, and the structure of the model should thus be fairly easy to understand. There is no reason to view this type of model as a "black-box" that only the builders of the model and no one else can understand intuitively. For example, the financial programming model that has been used on an operational basis by International Monetary Fund staff in analysis of developing economies' exchange rates and monetary policy is about the same size as each of the country submodels in terms of number of equations.[3] Moreover, most of the assumptions of the model—perfect financial capital mobility, sticky wages and prices, rational expectations, consumption smoothing, and slowly adjusting import prices and import demands—have been discussed widely during the last ten years. However, because of the assumption of rational and of forward-looking expectations in wage setting, consumption, investment, and portfolio decisions, the model is technically difficult to work with and solve, and this may hinder a more practical understanding of its properties.

To explain how the model works, I find it helpful to stress several key assumptions.[4] In my view these assumptions all have sound economic rationales although they continue to be the subject of research and debate.

(1) *Nominal wages and prices (measured in domestic currencies) are sticky.*The specific model of nominal wage determination is the staggered contracts model that I used in Taylor (1979) and elsewhere. Staggered wage-

---

[3] See Edwards (1988) for a recent discussion of models used by the IMF in policy analysis for developing economies.

[4] It is beyond the scope of this paper to describe all the equations in detail. The equations of the model used in the simulations are published in Taylor (1988b). A two-country analytical model with the same general structure is described in Carlozzi and Taylor (1985) and Taylor (1985). This two-country model is useful for understanding the workings of the multicountry model.

setting equations are estimated for each of the seven countries separately and the properties of these equations differ from country to country. For example, wages adjust most quickly in Japan and most slowly in the United States. A significant fraction of wage setting is synchronized in Japan, but full staggering of wage decisions occurs in the other countries. Prices are set as a markup over wage costs and imported input costs; the markup is not fixed in that prices adjust slowly to changes in costs. Import prices and export prices adjust with a lag to domestic prices and to world prices denominated in domestic currency units. Because of these lags (and because of imperfect competition and imperfect mobility of real goods and services discussed below), purchasing power parity does not hold in the short run in this model. The lags and the short-run elasticities in these equations differ from country to country, but throughout the model, long-run homogeneity conditions are imposed. Hence, all real variables are unaffected in the long run, after prices and wages have fully adjusted by a permanent change in the money supply.

(2) *Aggregate demand determines production in the short run; if the model were not continually shocked, production would eventually return to an exogenously growing level of "potential" output.* With wages and prices sticky in the short run, changes in monetary policy affect real money balances and aggregate demand and thereby affect real output and employment. Aggregate demand is disaggregated into consumption (durables, nondurables, and services), investment (residential and nonresidential), net exports, and government purchases. Both consumption and investment demand are determined according to forward-looking models in which consumers attempt to forecast future income, firms attempt to forecast future sales, and both reduce spending when the real interest rate rises. Export and import demand respond both to relative prices and to income. In all countries, net exports are significantly affected by relative prices and by changes in income. In all components of private demand (consumption, investment, net exports), there are lagged responses to the relevant variables, but these lags are longer for imports and exports than for the other components.

(3) *Government purchases are considered to be exogenous in the policy simulations, as are all components of fiscal policy; the primary operating instrument of monetary policy is the short-run interest rate.* Throughout this research, each country is assumed to have only one effective instrument of macroeconomic policy: the short-term money market rate, which is adjusted according to the behavior of prices, output, or exchange rates. Focusing on monetary policy and treating fiscal policy as exogenous appears to be a reasonable assumption, given current political realities. We seem to have enough trouble getting the level of fiscal policy right without worrying about countercyclical or exchange rate management as a goal of fiscal policy. Focusing on the interest rate rather than on the money supply also appears to be a more realistic characterization of monetary policy and automatically deals

with velocity shocks.[5]

(4) *Financial capital is mobile across countries, and within each country bond markets are efficient; however, time varying "risk premiums" exist both in foreign exchange markets and in domestic bond markets.* It is assumed that interest rate differentials between countries are equal to the expected rate of depreciation between the two currencies plus a random term that may reflect a risk premium or some other factor affecting exchange rates.[6] The risk premiums are estimated during the sample period and in the policy simulations are treated as exogenous random variables (first order autoregressions) with the same properties as in the sample period. Similarly, the long-term interest rate in each country is assumed to be equal to the expected average of future short-term rates plus a term that reflects a risk premium. This risk premium term is treated as an exogenous, serially uncorrelated random variable.

(5) *Expectations are assumed to be rational.* This assumption seems appropriate for examining more long-run issues such as the choice of an international monetary regime, which one would hope would remain in place for a relatively long period of time. Rational expectations does not, however, mean perfect foresight in these policy experiments. As described below, all equations of the model have stochastic shocks that cannot be anticipated. Hence, forecasts of the future are not perfect. Errors can sometimes be quite large. All we assume is that over the long run, the underforecasts and the overforecasts average out to zero.

(6) *The behavioral equations of the model are subject to continual disturbances, and the average size and correlation of these disturbances is similar to that observed during 1971–86.* This stochastic part of the model is essential to the policy evaluation. The policy question is how different types of policies affect the performance of the economy when hit by exogenous disturbances. Such disturbances are a fact of life: velocity shocks, international portfolio preference shocks, supply shocks, investment shocks, and so forth, can occur in all countries and are probably correlated across countries. Is one policy better than another in ironing out shocks, or does the policy tend to amplify (or cause) such shocks? In this research, the equations are "shocked" in two different ways:

- using a random number generator the equations are shocked with disturbances that have a normal probability distribution with a covariance matrix equal to that estimated for the structural residuals during the sample period, and
- the equations are shocked with exactly the same shocks that were estimated to have occurred during the sample period.

---

[5] Indeterminacy of the price level is avoided as long as the interest rate responds to prices as it does for all policy rules considered in this research.

[6] It should be clear that "risk premium" is not the only interpretation of this term. Miller and Williamson (1988) refer to a similar term as a "fad."

The properties of the variance-covariance matrix indicate that there is a significant amount of correlation between the shocks to the different equations (particularly the exchange rate equations and the import price equations) and that the size of the disturbances differs from country to country.[7] Hence, using the full variance-covariance matrix seems necessary. One disadvantage with this approach is that it implicitly assumes that future disturbances will be similar to those in the past. This disadvantage, however, exists with any empirical analysis based on actual data and can be dealt with by sensitivity analysis, that is, by changing the disturbances slightly and observing whether the results change. For example, if one suspected that the shocks to the exchange rate equations (the "risk premium terms") might be reduced significantly if exchange rates were fixed, the simulations could be conducted with and without the risk premium shocks. This approach is followed in the results reported below.

Several technical issues relating to the stochastic shocks are important. First, the shocks were estimated during the sample period by solving the model dynamically, using data through each sample point and using these simulations to substitute out for each expectations variable in each equation. Econometrically speaking, these constitute the structural disturbances to each equation. Second, because the sample size (which equals the number of estimated structural residuals to each equation) is less than the dimensions of the covariance matrix, the estimated covariance matrix is actually singular. Although certain algorithms, in particular the Cholesky decomposition (Faddeeva, 1959, pp. 81–84) for decomposing the matrix for the random number generator, cannot therefore be used, it is possible to make such a decomposition and draw the random numbers in the standard way. Nevertheless, it should be noted that the normal distribution generated randomly is singular. Finally, when actually drawing the shocks to each equation, in each time period it is assumed that the expectation of future shocks is zero (their unconditional mean). These shocks, however, prove not to be zero when the future periods of the simulation occur.

III. Choice of an Exchange Rate Regime

In order to evaluate the performance of a fixed exchange rate regime in comparison with a flexible-rate regime, I first specify the particular type of monetary policy rule used in each regime. Under both regimes the central banks are assumed to adjust their short-term interest rate in response to economic conditions.

---

[7] It is beyond the scope of this paper to describe the details of the variance-covariance matrix of the structural disturbances (that is, the relative size of the standard deviation of each shock and the correlation between the shocks). These are discussed in Taylor (1988d).

For the flexible exchange rate regime, the central bank in each country raises the short-term interest rate (the federal funds rate in the case of the U.S. Federal Reserve, the call money rate in the case of the Deutsche Bundesbank and the Bank of Japan) if the domestic price level (the GNP deflator) rises above a given target. Each central bank lowers the short-term interest rate if the price level falls below a given target. (The price targets need not be constant, and in these simulations some trend in the target price is permitted, although the results do not depend on the path for the target price level.) This adjustment of the nominal interest rate is relative to the expected rate of inflation, which is to be the forecasted rate of inflation from the model. Effectively, therefore, the central bank raises the real interest rate in response to deviations from target of the price level. For the first set of results, the response coefficient is assumed to be 1.6; that is, the interest rate is raised by 1.6 percentage points when the GNP deflator rises above the central bank's target by 1 percent. (Recall that this is a quarterly model so that the response rule for each of the central banks refers to quarterly averages.)

For the fixed exchange rate regime, the central banks cannot adjust their interest rates independently. Because of the perfect capital mobility assumption, sterilized intervention by the central banks has no effect on the exchange rate. Hence, in order to keep exchange rates fixed, the central banks must keep their interest rate differentials fixed. In other words, the short-term interest rates in each country must move in tandem, and effectively there is only one interest rate policy for all the central banks. This "world" interest rate policy is also assumed to be a "price rule" in which the interest rates in all short-term markets are moved up and down together depending on the behavior of an average of the price levels in the different countries. In particular, all interest rates are moved up by 1.6 percentage points if a weighted average of prices in the seven countries moves up by 1 percent. We start with weights of 0.3 for the United States, 0.2 for Germany, 0.3 for Japan, and 0.05 for the other four countries. (The high weight for Japan is chosen to ensure relatively good performance in Japan in this first case; alternative weighting schemes are discussed below.) As in the flexible exchange rate regime, the interest rate adjustments are made relative to a forecast of inflation (in terms of the same weighted average of individual country prices) and are, therefore, effectively real interest rate rules.

Table 1 shows estimates of economic performance under the two exchange rate regimes. Each regime is assumed to be in operation for ten years (40 quarters), from the first quarter of 1987 through the fourth quarter of 1996. Each regime is subjected to the same set of stochastic disturbances, except that there are no "risk premium" shocks to the exchange rate equations in the case of fixed exchange rates while such shocks are assumed to remain in the case of flexible exchange rates. This differentiation is an attempt to model the potential for a credible fixed exchange rate system to eliminate volatile shifts in risk premiums between countries. Given these shocks, the main difference be-

Table 1. Two Exchange Rate Systems: Ten Stochastic Simulations and Their Effects on Major Variables

	United States	Germany	Japan
Real GNP			
Fixed	3.5	6.0	8.0
Flexible	2.1	2.8	4.6
GNP Deflator			
Fixed	2.8	4.2	9.1
Flexible	1.3	1.8	4.0
Nominal GNP			
Fixed	5.6	8.7	11.5
Flexible	2.5	3.1	3.9
Short-Term Interest Rates			
Fixed	2.1	2.1	2.1
Flexible	1.9	2.2	4.4
Money (M1)			
Fixed	9.6	11.2	10.9
Flexible	9.2	5.1	6.5
Velocity			
Fixed	10.0	6.6	6.6
Flexible	9.1	5.9	7.4
Dollar Exchange Rates			
Fixed		0	0
Flexible		23.3	19.7
Real Investment			
Fixed	15.6	22.8	22.0
Flexible	10.0	13.0	13.3
Real Exports			
Fixed	6.5	9.3	10.5
Flexible	6.3	9.7	11.3
Real Imports			
Fixed	8.4	10.8	7.9
Flexible	5.5	5.2	7.8
Real Net Exports[1]			
Fixed	1.3	3.2	2.6
Flexible	1.0	2.7	2.7

[1] As a ratio to real GNP.

Note: Each entry shows the standard deviation of the percentage deviation of the variable from the baseline. The policy rule has interest rates responding to prices with a reaction coefficient of 1.6. The weights for each country in the fixed exchange rate case are 0.3 for the United States, 0.2 for Germany, 0.3 for Japan, and 0.05 for the other countries.

tween the macroeconomic performance under the two regimes is that the
policy rule is different. In Table 1 these disturbances are drawn from a random
number generator as described above. Each 40-quarter period is run 10 times,
and the data in Table 1 represent the average performance over these 10 runs.
In each case the number in the table is a measure of economic stability; it is the
standard deviation over the 40 quarters of the percentage deviation of the
variable from a given baseline. High values of these numbers represent a poor
performance.[8]

The most striking feature of Table 1 is that the flexible exchange rate
system seems to work better than the fixed exchange rate system according to
almost all measures of internal economic stability. The volatility of both real
output and the aggregate price level is less under flexible exchange rates in all
three countries. The volatility of nominal GNP is at least twice as high under
the fixed as under the flexible exchange rate system. The individual components of real GNP, especially investment and consumption, also have a
smaller variance under the flexible exchange rate system.

Note that the volatility of net exports is slightly reduced under the flexible
exchange rate system in Germany and the United States, but slightly higher in
Japan. (An examination of real imports and exports individually reveals an
improvement in import stability and a slight reduction in export stability for
these countries.) These results suggest that the exchange rate is playing some
role in helping to achieve stability in the external accounts in Germany and the
United States, but the effect is fairly small, or even nonexistent, in Japan. In
fact, exchange rates are far more volatile under the flexible exchange rate
system; much of this volatility comes from the risk premium shocks. Hence, it
is not surprising that the greater flexibility of exchange rates since the early
1970s has not reduced external instability as much as some had hoped.[9]
According to these calculations, one should not expect to see a great improvement on the external side. But, on the other hand, external instability should
not worsen under flexible exchange rates. Furthermore, there are large gains
associated with the reduction in internal instability. On balance, therefore, the
flexible exchange rate system works better.

Why Does the More Flexible Rate System Work Better?

There are almost 100 different shocks that cause the economy to fluctuate
in the stochastic simulation of the multicountry model. This makes it difficult
to explain, intuitively, why the flexible exchange rate system works better.

---

[8] This measure would better be described as the root mean square percentage difference of the
variable from the baseline. In other words, if there is a non-zero mean in the difference, its square
is included in the size of the measures in Table 1. Because the shocks have a zero mean, this
difference will be negligible over many stochastic draws.

[9] Krugman's (1988) rejection of the flexible exchange rate system is based largely on the
absence of improvement in external instability.

Open-economy macroeconomic theory suggests that there are advantages and disadvantages to flexible exchange rates. On the one hand, the flexibility of the exchange rate affords the central bank more independence to use monetary policy to stabilize prices and output when the economy is shocked out of equilibrium. Because the structure of different economies varies, the appropriate response of the central banks to shocks may differ. On the other hand, large swings in the exchange rates, which owe either to demand disturbances or to speculative activity in the financial markets, can cause instability in exports and thereby increase both internal and external volatility.

For the set of disturbances considered in these simulations, the gain from monetary independence outweighs the loss associated with exchange rate volatility. The net gain would be even larger if the risk premium shocks remain under the fixed exchange rate system or are smaller under the flexible exchange rate system. But why is the gain from monetary independence so large? And why is the loss associated with exchange rate volatility so small?

The importance of monetary independence is best understood by comparing the policy rule for the central banks under the two exchange rate systems. Consider the Bank of Japan. Under the flexible exchange rate system, the policy rule for the Bank of Japan depends only on the Japanese domestic price level. When the rate of inflation rises in Japan, the Bank of Japan promptly raises the call money interest rate. This interest rate rise reduces investment spending and slows down the growth of aggregate demand, thereby reducing inflationary pressures. When exchange rates are fixed, however, the Bank of Japan cannot raise the call money rate without a coordinated rise in interest rates by the U.S. Federal Reserve and the Deutsche Bundesbank. The policy rule under fixed rates allows for some rise in interest rates because the rise in prices in Japan raises the average of world prices. However, the increase is necessarily smaller than if the Bank of Japan had operated independently. For this model, the ability of the central banks to move independently proves to be important for internal stability. The requirement that the Bank of Japan wait for the U.S. Federal Reserve and the Deutsche Bundesbank to see a rise in world inflation means that the response in Japan is too little and too late. The rise in inflation is not cut off quickly enough, and this apparently leads to a large swing in inflation and an even larger recession later on.

Theoretically, one might argue that fixed exchange rates would serve as guides for domestic prices and money wages, and that with a fixed exchange rate system the kinds of swings in inflation described above would not occur. McKinnon (1988), for example, argues that "with exchange rates known to be fixed into the indefinite future, international commodity arbitrage and mutual monetary adjustment would insure convergence to the same rate of commodity price inflation (preferably zero) in all three countries. Tradeable goods prices (PPIs) would then be aligned close to purchasing power parity and relative growth in national money wage claims would eventually reflect differences in productivity growth. . . ." In my view, this theoretical effect is allowed for in the multicountry model; goods prices are influenced by exchange rates, and the model's long-run homogeneity properties will eventually force nominal wages to reflect productivity growth. The forward-looking behavior of the model allows expectations of future stability of exchange rates to have a particularly strong effect on current prices and wages. But, empirically, the effect is not strong enough. The inertia of domestic wages and prices in these large countries cannot be influenced sufficiently by exchange rates to permit the central banks to postpone or mitigate strong monetary policy reactions when needed (because they are tied to an international monetary policy rule).

Finally, consider the exchange rate fluctuations themselves. The calculations show that these fluctuations are large yet they do not have a large destabilizing effect on net exports. Net exports are even more stable in Germany and the United States under flexible exchange rates. Judging from the parameters of the model, the explanation for this phenomenon is that import prices adjust very slowly to fluctuations in exchange rates and that import demand adjusts slowly to changes in import prices. The small elasticities indicate that the fluctuations in the exchange rates do less damage to the real economy than if the elasticities were large. The low elasticities reflect the actual data for the Group of Seven countries during the period of flexible exchange rates, including the behavior of imports and import prices after the sharp fall in the U.S. dollar in early 1985. Much has been written about why these elasticities appear to be so small; hysteresis in trade and pricing to market are clearly part of the explanation, and the empirically estimated import equations and import price equations in the multicountry model are empirical approximations of these theoretical arguments.

It is interesting that Krugman (1988) focuses on the small effects of exchange rate changes as one reason to move back to a system of fixed exchange rates. The intuitive argument I make is exactly the opposite: according to the model used here, the smaller elasticities are one of the reasons that the fluctuations in the exchange rate are not a cause of external instability. The shorter-term fluctuations in the exchange rate, which are due mostly to shifts in risk premiums, have only small effects on import prices and on import demands. On the other hand, it appears that the longer-run changes in the exchange rate do affect trade flows and can thus achieve some external adjustment. Krugman's (1988) discussion focuses entirely on the problem that flexible exchange rates do not do much for external stability. He therefore rejects the flexible exchange rate system. However, the important gains to internal stability from exchange rate flexibility stressed here must also be taken into account in evaluating the international monetary system.

Nevertheless, the fluctuations in nominal exchange rates shown in Table 1 should not be taken lightly. The arguments made by McKinnon (1988) that such fluctuations can lead to protectionist actions are clearly correct. Two caveats are relevant, however. First, although it is not clear in Table 1, the fluctuations in the exchange rates in the simulations are short term (say, within a year) and are due largely to the risk premium shocks. To the extent that the fluctuations are short term, they might be effectively hedged even with the relatively short-horizon futures and forward markets in foreign exchange. This possibility for hedging is not included in the model and could reduce the real effects of the exchange rate fluctuations even further. Second, there are reasons to believe that the exchange rate fluctuations would be less than shown in Table 1. The policy rule under the flexible exchange rate system treats domestic price stability in each country as an important goal. To the extent that such a rule is credible, the expectation of domestic price stability in each country would lead to expectations of more exchange rate stability. If so, the size and volatility of the risk premiums would clearly be reduced, perhaps to levels far below the last 15 years that are implicit in the stochastic simulations in Table 1.

How Robust Are the Results?

The discussion of the results thus far has focused on a particular policy rule (one with a specific reaction coefficient) and a particular method of calculation (stochastic simulation with a random number generator). Are the results robust to alternative policy rules and to alternative methods of calculation?

Table 2 shows the effects of the two exchange rate regimes on real GNP, the GNP deflator, and the exchange rate when the shocks are the actual structural residuals over 40 quarters of the sample period: the first quarter of 1975 through the fourth quarter of 1984. In other words, it is assumed from these simulations that the shocks to the economy during the period from the first quarter of 1987 through the last quarter of 1996 are identical, and in the same order as the shocks that hit the economy during the late 1970s and early 1980s. Unlike the random number generator, the shocks drawn in this way are not normally distributed; they have a somewhat smaller variance because the effects around the period of the first oil crisis are omitted.

In addition, an alternative weighting scheme for the interest rate reaction function in the case of fixed exchange rates is examined in Table 2. The weight for the Japanese price is raised to 0.5, the weight for the U.S. price is reduced to 0.2, and the weight for the German price is lowered to 0.1.

The results are qualitatively similar to those in Table 1. The variance of the price level and real GNP is less under the fixed exchange rate regime, especially in Germany and Japan, compared with Table 1, but in most cases, the flexible exchange rate regime still shows a better macroeconomic performance. The higher weight for Japan helps Japanese performance but hinders the German and U.S. performance. With a high weight for Japan, the Japanese fixed exchange rate performance can actually beat the flexible exchange rate, but this is at the expense of deterioration of performance in Germany and the United States. The effect of changing the weights on the average price in the

Table 2. Two Exchange Rate Systems: Actual Structural Shocks and the Effect of Changing Weights on the Fixed Exchange Rate Rule

	United States	Germany	Japan
Real GNP			
Fixed (JA = 0.5)	4.1	5.7	3.3
Fixed (JA = 0.3)	4.1	5.4	4.2
Flexible	2.2	3.2	3.4
GNP Deflator			
Fixed (JA = 0.5)	3.4	4.1	1.5
Fixed (JA = 0.3)	3.2	3.8	3.3
Flexible	1.3	1.8	2.6
Dollar Exchange Rate			
Fixed (JA = 0.5)		0	0
Fixed (JA = 0.3)		0	0
Flexible		12.7	11.5

Note: Each entry represents the standard deviation of the percentage deviation from the baseline. The policy rule has interest rates reacting to prices with a reaction coefficient of 1.6. The weights for each country in the fixed rate case are either 0.5 for Japan, 0.2 for the United States, and 0.1 for Germany, or 0.3 for Japan, 0.3 for the United States, and 0.2 for Germany as shown (0.05 for the other countries).

policy rule confirms the intuition stated above about the importance of monetary independence.

The volatility of exchange rates under the flexible exchange rate regime is considerably less for these shocks than for the shocks in Table 1. This is because the risk premium shocks are smaller. This volatility does not appear excessive. Some proposals for target zones for exchange rates (see Miller and Williamson, 1988) have bands that are not much smaller than plus or minus one of these standard deviations.

Table 3 considers two alternative policy rules using the same set of actual structural residuals. In the case examined in Table 1, the reaction coefficient was 1.6. In Table 3, the reaction coefficient is either 1.0 or 2.5. Again, the interest rate reacts to deviations of the price level from some target in these simulations. In these simulations the weight for the Japanese price is 0.3 when exchange rates are fixed.

The results are qualitatively similar to the previous results. Regardless of the reaction coefficient, the macroeconomic performance under flexible exchange rates dominates fixed exchange rates. The change in the reaction coefficient does affect the size of the fluctuations in most cases, but the variances are always smaller with flexible exchange rates.

The results with two other policy rules are also noteworthy. *First,* if the central banks follow money supply rules, rather than interest rate rules, the

Table 3. Two Exchange Rate Regimes: Actual Structural Shocks and the Effect of Changing a Reaction Coefficient

	United States	Germany	Japan
Real GNP	*(reaction coefficient equals 1.0)*		
Fixed	4.4	5.3	4.8
Flexible	2.4	3.3	3.4
GNP Deflator			
Fixed	3.4	3.7	5.1
Flexible	1.4	2.2	3.4
Real GNP	*(reaction coefficient equals 2.5)*		
Fixed	3.9	5.3	4.7
Flexible	2.0	3.3	3.8
GNP Deflator			
Fixed	3.2	3.9	3.0
Flexible	1.1	1.6	2.2

Note: Each entry represents the standard deviation of the percentage deviation from the baseline. The policy rule has interest rates reacting to prices with a reaction coefficient of either 1.0 or 2.5 as shown. The weights for each country under the fixed rate regime are 0.3 for Japan, 0.2 for Germany, and 0.3 for the United States.

relative ranking of fixed and flexible exchange rates remains. This type of policy rule was considered at the preliminary stage of this investigation (see Taylor, 1986). Under the flexible exchange rate system, each central bank followed a constant growth rate rule for the money supply. Under the fixed exchange rate system, the central banks coordinated their monetary policies to generate a constant growth rate for the world money supply (a weighted average of the money supplies in the Group of Seven countries) according to an earlier proposal of Ronald McKinnon. It was generally found that the fixed rate system performed relatively poorly. However, both systems performed worse than with the interest rate rules discussed thus far in this paper. The large velocity shocks with fixed money growth translated into huge interest rate fluctuations, which tended to be destabilizing in either regime. For this reason, I focused my research on policy rules that automatically offset velocity shocks, as with the interest rate rules described above.

Second, the poor results for fixed exchange rates suggest that I also investigate a "leaning against the wind" policy in which the central banks do not commit to fix exchange rates exactly (or within a narrow band), but instead raise interest rates to counteract exchange-rate movements. To investigate this policy, I simulated the model with an interest rate rule in which the differential interest rate between the United States and Japan or between the United States and Germany was adjusted to move the exchange rate toward a given target.

This is similar to the proposal outlined by McKinnon (1988): "To keep the potentially volatile exchange rates within their prescribed bands, the three central banks must control *relative* short-term interest rates. . . ." The problem with this type of rule, however, is that shocks to exchange rates will tend to cause large changes in interest rate differentials. For example, if I simulate such a rule with the exchange rate equations shocked by the same set of shocks as in the flexible exchange rate cases described above, the volatility of interest rates is large (three or four times higher than the pure price rules for the United States and Germany) and does not lead to a better macroeconomic performance. For this type of policy, it does not seem reasonable to set the exchange rate risk premium shocks to zero because some fluctuations in exchange rates would occur. But in the absence of this, an exchange rate smoothing rule will generate large swings in interest rates and the reduction in exchange rate volatility will be small (about 25 percent).

Given the results described here, it would appear best not to focus monetary policy on the exchange rate. In the next two sections I examine a broader policy question: can central banks improve economic performance by choosing a policy rule other than the price rule considered thus far? In answering this question, I will maintain the flexible exchange rate regime and focus the monetary policy rule on domestic indicators.

IV. The Effects of a Monetary Policy Rule on Economic Performance Abroad

The search for better policy rules in the Group of Seven countries would be computationally, if not politically, easier if the choice of a policy rule in one country had little or no effect on economic performance in the other. If so, we could search across policy rules in each country individually and not simultaneously consider reaction functions in other countries.

Table 4 considers this issue. It shows the effect on price and output stability in each country when the policy rule in another country is changed. The policy rules examined in Table 4 are nominal GNP rules. The interest rate is increased or decreased according to whether nominal GNP is above or below a target. Of course, a nominal GNP rule differs from a price rule in that real output appears in the reaction function along with the GNP deflator and with the same coefficient.

The nominal GNP rules in Table 4 have reaction coefficients of either 1.5 or somewhat higher. For example, in the top part of Table 4, Germany and Japan have reaction coefficients of 1.5, and the United States has either 1.5 or 2.5. In the bottom part of Table 4, the United States and Germany have reaction coefficients of 1.5, and Japan has one of either 1.5 or 1.8. The table, therefore, shows what happens to the other countries when either the United States or Japan changes its policy rules. What is most striking about Table 4 is that a change in the policy rule within these ranges has a small impact

Table 4. Effect of U.S. and Japanese Policy Rule Changes on Economic Performance Abroad: Actual Structural Residuals

U.S. Policy Parameter	United States	Germany	Japan
Real GNP			
1.5	1.7	1.7	3.8
2.5	1.5	1.7	3.8
GNP Deflator			
1.5	1.3	2.1	6.1
2.5	1.2	2.1	6.1
Japanese Policy Parameter	United States	Germany	Japan
Real GNP			
1.5	1.7	1.7	3.8
1.8	1.7	1.7	3.3
GNP Deflator			
1.5	1.3	2.1	6.1
1.8	1.3	2.1	5.2

Note: Each entry represents the standard deviation of the percentage deviation from the baseline. The policy rule calls for interest rates reacting to nominal GNP with a reaction coefficient of 1.5 in the United States, Germany, and Japan with higher coefficients in either the United States or Japan, as shown. (The response coefficient is 0.5 in France and the United Kingdom, and 1.5 in Canada and Italy.)

abroad.[10] For example, raising the Japanese reaction coefficient to 1.8 from 1.5 reduces both output and price variability in Japan but has virtually no effect on either Germany or the United States. Even changing the U.S. policy rule has little effect on Germany and Japan.[11]

These results suggest that there is not much need to coordinate the choice or design of monetary policy rules among countries. Of course, it is important for each central bank to communicate with other central banks about what policy rule—at least approximately—is guiding policy.

The robustness of this result is not nearly as well established as the exchange rate results described in Section 1. The evidence presented here pertains to nominal GNP rules only. Similar results are found when we vary the reaction coefficients of price rules, but the effect of more drastic changes —such as changing the functional form of the rule—has yet to be examined.

---

[10] A similar result was found in the two-country simulation model of Carlozzi and Taylor (1985). However, stronger cross-country effects were found using a different approach in Taylor (1985).

[11] There is a small effect, but it only shows up in the third significant figure and is rounded off in Table 4.

V. Improvements in Macroeconomic Performance

The results discussed above indicate that, for flexible exchange rate systems, nominal GNP rules that weigh output deviations, as well as price deviations, in the central banks' reaction function frequently perform better than price rules. Compare Tables 3 and 4. For Germany and the United States, macroeconomic stability is improved when these countries use nominal GNP rules rather than price rules. The improvement in real output stability is especially large. Although a similar improvement is not observed for Japan, this finding suggests that by examining a wider array of policy reaction functions we could find improvements in macroeconomic stability.

In principle, the optimal policy objective is to find policy rules for the central bank, out of a general class, that minimize the loss in terms of both internal and external stability.[12] Computationally, such a general search is not yet possible with a nonlinear rational expectations model of the size used for this research. It is still expensive to compute extensive stochastic simulations. For this reason, I take a less ambitious approach.

Rather than optimize across a general class of policies, I examine a more limited class in which both price and real output appear in the interest rate reaction function for each central bank. However, the weights on output and the price level need not be the same. This is a more mixed class of rules than either price rules (where all the weight is on the price level) or nominal GNP rules (where the weight is the same for both price and output).

A summary of the results of this type of research is presented in Table 5. I focus on the stability of real GNP and the price level. The results show that it is possible to improve on either the price rule or the nominal GNP rule in Germany and the United States. Compared with the nominal GNP rule, a mixed rule seems to work better in the United States, but a heavy weight on the price level deviations still seems to work better in Japan. The mixed rule reduces output variability in Japan, but price variability increases somewhat, compared with the price rules. For these simulations the shocks are equal to the actual structural disturbances, and the weight on the price level is higher than the weight on real output (2.5 and 0.8, respectively).

A general conclusion from these results is that placing some weight on real output in the interest rate reaction function is likely to be better than a pure price rule. In addition, a mixed rule is likely to work better than a nominal GNP rule. Finally, all of these rules seem to result in exchange rate fluctuations that are not excessive, even though the exchange rate equations are being shocked by time-varying risk premiums. Although these policies focus the

---

[12] This is the approach used in Taylor (1979) and Taylor (1985), where formal dynamic optimization methods are employed to find optimal rules for monetary policy in simple linear models.

Table 5. Improvements in Economic Performance with a More Flexible Rule

	United States	Germany	Japan
Real GNP			
Price Rule	2.2	3.2	3.4
Nominal GNP Rule	1.7	1.7	3.8
Mixed Rule	1.7	2.2	3.2
GNP Deflator			
Price Rule	1.3	1.9	2.7
Nominal GNP Rule	1.3	2.1	6.1
Mixed Rule	1.1	1.8	3.2
Dollar Exchange Rate			
Price Rule		12.7	11.5
Nominal GNP Rule		12.7	12.0
Mixed Rule		12.6	11.4

Note: Each entry represents the standard deviation of the percentage deviation from the baseline. The policy rule calls for interest rates to react to both price and output with different elasticities. For the mixed rule, the elasticity for price is 2.0, and the elasticity for output is 0.8 in each country, except the United States where the weight is 2.5 on price and 0.8 on output. For both the price rule and for the nominal GNP rule, the elasticity is 1.5, except in France and the United Kingdom where it is 0.5.

reaction functions on domestic indicators, they have the potential for achieving a surprising amount of exchange rate stability.

VI. Concluding Remarks

The objective of this paper has been to report findings based on the use of a multicountry model for monetary policy evaluation. Unlike much recent policy evaluation with multicountry models, this research focuses on the performance of alternative reaction functions for the monetary authorities, rather than on the effects of one-time changes in the instruments of policy. Evaluating how different reaction functions stand up in the face of exogenous shocks to the economy appears to be a more realistic way to approach many policy problems, certainly questions about the design of the international monetary system.

Some of the results discussed above are more robust than others. The most robust finding, in my view, is that an agreement to fix exchange rates between Germany, Japan, and the United States has serious problems with respect to internal macroeconomic stability and achieves little, if anything, with respect to external stability (that is, the stability of net exports).

An important subject for future research might be to check the robustness of these results in a way that a single group of researchers cannot do by trying the same types of experiments in other multicountry econometric models with rational expectations. The models of Helliwell and others (1988) and Masson and others (1988), as well as a new model being developed at the U.S. Federal Reserve, would be excellent models on which to base a consideration of these policy issues. A comparison of the stochastic simulation results across such models would be a helpful way to assess the reliability of such results for practical monetary policy work.

References

Carlozzi, Nicholas, and John B. Taylor, "International Capital Mobility and the Coordination on Monetary Rules," in *Exchange Rate Management Under Uncertainty*, ed. by Jagdeep S. Bhandari (Cambridge, Massachusetts: MIT Press, 1985).

Dornbusch, Rudiger, "Doubts About the McKinnon Standard," *Journal of Economic Perspectives* (Nashville, Tennessee), Vol. 2, No. 1 (1988), pp. 105–12.

Edwards, Sebastian, "The International Monetary Fund and the Developing Countries: A Critical Evaluation," Carnegie-Rochester Conference Series on Public Policy (Amsterdam and New York: North-Holland, 1988).

Faddeeva, V.N., *Computational Methods of Linear Algebra* (New York: Dover Publications, 1959).

Helliwell, John F., and others, "Intermod 1.1: A G-7 Version of the IMF's Multimod," Working Group on International Macroeconomics, Department of Finance, Canada, 1988.

Krugman, Paul R., "Exchange Rate Instability," Robbins Lecture, London School of Economics (Cambridge, Massachusetts: MIT Press, January 1988).

McKibbin, Warwick, and Jeffrey Sachs, "Comparing the Global Performance of Alternative Exchange Rate Regimes," *Journal of International Money and Finance*, Vol. 7, No. 4 (Guildford, England: Butterworth Scientific Ltd., 1988), pp. 387–410.

McKinnon, Ronald I., "Monetary and Exchange Rate Policies for International Financial Stability," *Journal of Economic Perspectives* (Nashville, Tennessee), Vol. 2, No. 1 (1988), pp. 83–103.

Masson, Paul R., and others, "MULTIMOD: A Multi-Region Econometric Model," International Monetary Fund, *Staff Studies for the World Economic Outlook* (Washington: IMF, July 1988), pp. 50–104.

Miller, Marcus H., and John Williamson, "The International Monetary System: An Analysis of Alternative Regimes," Centre for Economic Policy Research Discussion Paper No. 266 (London: CEPR, 1988).

Taylor, John B., "Estimation and Control of a Macroeconomic Model with Rational Expectations," *Econometrica* (Evanston, Illinois), Vol. 47 (1979), pp. 1267–87.

————, "International Coordination in the Design of Macroeconomic Policy Rules," *International Economic Review*, Vol. 25 (Philadelphia, Pennsylvania: Wharton School of Finance and Commerce, 1985).

————," An Econometric Evaluation of International Monetary Policy Rules: Fixed versus Flexible Exchange Rates," unpublished paper presented at November 1986 Centre for Economic Policy Research conference on policy coordination (London: CEPR, 1986).

———— (1988a), "The Treatment of Expectations in Large Multicountry Econometric Models," in *Empirical Macroeconomics for Interdependent Economies,* ed. by Ralph Bryant and others (Washington: The Brookings Institution, 1988).

———— (1988b), "Japanese Monetary Policy and the Current Account Under Alternative International Monetary Regimes," *Monetary and Economic Studies,* Bank of Japan, Vol. 6, No. 1 (May 1988), pp. 1–36.

———— (1988c), "The U.S. Trade Deficit, Saving-Investment Imbalance and Macroeconomic Policy: 1982–87," in *The U.S. Trade Deficit: Causes, Consequences, and Cures*, 12th Annual Economic Policy Conference Proceedings, Federal Reserve Bank of St. Louis (Boston: Kluwer Academic Publishing, 1988).

———— (1988d), "International Monetary Policy Rules: An Econometric Evaluation," unpublished manuscript, 1988.

Williamson, John, "On McKinnon's Monetary Rule," *Journal of Economic Perspectives* (Nashville, Tennessee: 1988), Vol. 2, No. 1, pp. 113–19.

Comments

Manfred J. M. Neumann

John Taylor investigates two major issues of international monetary policy design:
- Which exchange rate system is more conducive to macroeconomic stability, fixed rates or floating rates?
- Given a clean float, which type of rule for monetary policy is more likely to promote domestic macroeconomic stability: a pure price rule, a nominal gross national product rule, or a rule that assigns different weights to output and the price level?

Answers to these questions are derived through stochastic simulations of a Group of Seven country model estimated over the period 1971–86. Each country has the same theoretical structure: a standard IS-LM specification augmented by staggered wage and price setting. Rational expectations and long-run homogeneity conditions are imposed. The country models are linked through trade flows and perfect bond substitutability. Standard deviations of the percentage deviations of real gross national product (GNP), and of the GNP deflator, from predetermined baseline paths serve as criteria of macroeconomic performance. As a rule, both measures of stability move in the same direction when the policy rule is changed.

Taylor's main results may be easily summarized: first, over various policy reaction rules coordination of monetary policies under fixed exchange rates yields poor results in terms of achievable output and price level stability for each of the three major countries considered: the United States, the Federal Republic of Germany, and Japan. Flexible exchange rates combined with independent policy responses to stochastic fluctuations at home appear to constitute a superior policy regime. Second, of all policy rules examined, a real interest rate reaction function—with differential responses to real output and the domestic price level—works the best.

These are important empirical results that will have to be taken into account by economists who promote target zones for the Japanese yen-U.S. dollar and the deutsche mark-dollar exchange rates, if not a return to a system of fixed exchange rates.

Taylor's nonsupportive results are all the more important as they are based on a stylized but plausible structure of the Group of Seven economies. Moreover, the simulations are not conditioned by arbitrary assumptions about the structure of stochastic disturbances; rather they are shaped by the properties of the variance-covariance matrix that Taylor has estimated with actual data from the 1970s and 1980s.

Must we be surprised about Taylor's observation that, in terms of macroeconomic stability, the flexible exchange rate system uniformly outperforms the alternative regime for various policy rules? I think this depends on what inferences we can draw from this observation about the underlying shock structure, and whether they fit our prior beliefs.

Since the early analysis by Poole (1970), we have learned how real output instability is affected by different types of disturbances, for alternative designs of monetary policy and different exchange rate regimes. In Table 1, I consider the exchange rate regimes—FLEX and FIX—and two policy rules—activist (AR) versus monetarist (MR). I also differentiate idealized states of nature, according to whether disturbances originate in the monetary or the real sector, and whether they are global or country-specific shocks. To simplify matters, I assume that all countries are of equal size and have the same structure. However, they may differ with respect to the type of exogenous disturbance that hits them.

Table 1. Output Stability Under Alternative Monetary Policy Rules and Exchange Rate Regimes

	Money demand shocks	Real sector shocks
Global shocks, identical across countries	AR > MR FLEX = FIX	AR > MR FLEX = FIX
Country-specific shocks, $\Sigma u_i = 0$	FLEX < FIX MR < AR	FLEX > FIX AR > MR

Note: AR and MR denote an activist policy rule and a monetarist rule, respectively; FLEX and FIX denote the alternative exchange rate system. Ranks are indicated by >.

Now suppose that in each period our model economies are hit by identical money demand disturbances, in the absence of real sector shocks. If each country follows a monetarist rule that keeps the domestic money stock unchanged, all prices and quantities will exhibit variance. Short-term interest rates will fluctuate in tandem but exchange rates will stay put. Of course, the monetary authorities can improve on the macroeconomic performance, at least in principle, by applying an activist rule—say Taylor's real interest rate reaction function—but this will leave the exchange rates unchanged, provided the authorities of each country choose the same accommodation parameter.

Virtually the same argument applies with respect to the effects on macroeconomic stability of global real sector disturbances. Note that we do not have to differentiate demand from supply disturbances as we are only interested in the relations between variances. Global real disturbances—whether transmitted to our model economies from the outside or originating simultaneously in all of them—will not affect bilateral exchange rates.

Next, consider country-specific disturbances that add up to zero over all countries. If the authorities are confronted with real sector shocks and choose flexible exchange rates, it is obvious that in principle, activist rules will dominate the monetarist rule. Alternatively, if the authorities choose fixed rates, they will be forced to move in tandem. Given country-specific real shocks, this is clearly detrimental to macroeconomic stability because none of the central banks retains the ability to respond optimally. In general, each central bank will be forced to react to a lesser degree than is desirable, and frequently it may happen that a central bank will have to act perversely, because the other countries' disturbances require adjustment in the wrong direction. The fixed exchange rate regime enforces the rapid and effective transmission across all countries of country-specific disturbances through the channel of collective policy behavior. This disadvantage is heightened, the lower the degree of spillover through international trade.

The final case shown in the accompanying table concerns country-specific money demand shocks. In the absence of real sector shocks, it is optimal to fix the world money stock and the exchange rates as well. This regime of collective monetarism dominates any other regime because, by assumption, the world money demand function stays put while shifting national money demands are automatically accommodated. With nonperfect information, the flexible rate regime cannot provide the same degree of stability. But note that this case for fixed exchange rates is a special one. It loses force once we abolish the restrictive assumption that the country-specific shocks sum up to zero over all countries. Then, collective activism may be organized to accommodate the sum of money demand shocks at the world level, but the stability performance of each country will suffer again from the tandem problems.

Evaluating Taylor's simulation results in the light of these considerations permits drawing the following inferences:

- Given that the choice of the exchange rate regime makes a significant difference for macroeconomic stability in all simulations, it follows that the estimated structure of disturbances is dominated by country-specific shocks rather than by global shocks.
- The result that national monetarism under flexible rates outperforms collective monetarism implies that direct currency substitution is not an empirically important phenomenon.
- The estimated stochastic structure is apparently dominated—in the sense of Poole—by country-specific real sector shocks rather than by money demand shocks. This follows from the observation that for all rules checked—activist and monetarist alike—flexible rates outperform fixed rates.

In my view, these inferences are not at odds with actual events since the early 1970s. Consequently, I conclude that Taylor's extensive evidence in favor of flexible rates cannot be easily dismissed. On the other hand, we must acknowledge the possibility that the simulations might be biased toward supporting flexible rates. After all, the data employed in the estimation of the underlying model belong to a period of flexible rates. In principle, therefore,

Taylor's simulations are vulnerable to the Lucas critique.

For example, consider the role of exchange rate risk. A number of studies document a significant negative effect of multilateral exchange risk on aggregate trade flows (Akhtar and Hilton, 1984; Kenen and Rodrik, 1986; and Cushman, 1986). It is not clear how Taylor's estimates of the export and import demand functions will change, if he takes exchange rate risk explicitly into account. But it seems unlikely that the exchange rate risk, as perceived by rational agents, is constant over time or identical under both exchange rate regimes. This suggests that the underlying baseline path cannot be the same for both regimes, and, probably more important, that the respective simulations for the two regimes should not employ the same set of disturbances to the trade equations. On this interpretation, Taylor's estimated residuals contain the innovations to perceived exchange rate risk, which will be smaller, if not absent, in a credible fixed rate regime.

These effects are, of course, likely to be of second order, and therefore will hardly affect Taylor's general result. But the proponents of fixed rates will certainly wish to argue that this regime is likely to induce a much closer integration of the economies involved. If this is correct, it follows that the low degree of international interaction implied by Taylor's model, as well as by other large-scale multicountry models, is a property of the recent flexible rate period, which puts the simulations for fixed rates at a disadvantage. Taylor himself points to the impressively small effects of exchange rate variability on trade variability in the simulations cited in his Table 1. Upon comparing the flexible rate simulations in his Tables 1 and 2, one finds that even a reduction by 50 percent in Taylor's measure of exchange rate variability does not make a big difference to output variability. If this is a property of the real world, it is good news. But clearly the robustness of the result needs checking in future research.

Given the low degree of real international spillover, it was to be expected, under a flexible rate regime, that the change of a policy rule in one country would have a minor impact on macroeconomic stability in the other. However, Taylor's respective simulations, shown in Table 4, indicate zero effects. I think that even a member of what Cooper (1988) calls the "German School" would hesitate to believe that. So something must be wrong.

Finally, let me comment on Taylor's preferred activist rules, which require the authorities to manipulate the real rate of interest in response to the domestic price level, real output, or nominal GNP. In principle, such rules are capable of delivering a more stable macroeconomic performance than monetarist rules can provide. In practice, however, the performance of Taylor's activist rules will be worsened by the existence of statistical reporting lags and forecast error variance. I think it would be interesting to learn by how much the performance advantage of activist rules over monetarist rules shrinks, if Taylor allows for a plausible forecast error variance with respect to the anticipated rate of inflation in his reaction functions for the real rate of interest.

To sum up, I think that Taylor's paper makes an important contribution in providing the necessary empirical underpinning to our understanding of why flexible exchange rates and decentralized policymaking may be preferable.

References

Akhtar, Akbar M., and Spencer Hilton, "Exchange Rate Uncertainty and International Trade: Some Conceptual Issues and New Estimates for Germany and the United States," Research Paper No. 8403, Federal Reserve Bank of New York (New York, 1984).

Cooper, Richard N., "International Economic Cooperation: Is It Desirable? Is It Likely?" unpublished, Harvard University, 1988.

Cushman, David O., "Has Exchange Risk Depressed International Trade? The Impact of Third-Country Exchange Risk," *Journal of International Money and Finance*, Vol. 5 (Guildford, England: Butterworth Scientific Ltd., 1986), pp. 361–79.

Kenen, Peter B., and Dani Rodrik, "Measuring and Analyzing the Effects of Short-Term Volatility in Real Exchange Rates," *Review of Economics and Statistics*, Vol. 58 (Amsterdam: North-Holland, 1986), pp. 311–15.

Poole, William, "Optimal Choice of Monetary Policy Instruments in a Simple Stochastic Macro Model," *Quarterly Journal of Economics*, Vol. 84 (Cambridge, Massachusetts: 1970), pp. 197–216.

Ralph Tryon

I would like to start by reminding you all that I am, or have been, associated with modeling projects at the International Monetary Fund and the U.S. Federal Reserve, which are closely related to John Taylor's work, so that anything I say about his paper might alternatively be regarded as either self-serving or disingenuous. Obviously, I think what is termed "rational expectations" econometric modeling is both interesting and fruitful. I like John Taylor's work a lot; his paper is another in a series of important contributions to this line of empirical research. Having made that caveat, I will take up my duties as discussant with enthusiasm!

This paper is simple and straightforward almost to a fault. I think Taylor adopts this style to try to spell out and drive home a simple empirical result. That result is that if monetary policy in the Group of Three industrial countries is targeted on nominal exchange rates, the variability of output and prices will be higher than if monetary policy is targeted on prices, nominal output, or the nominal money supply. Taylor evidently thinks the question is virtually open and shut, that the results presented here are conclusive, and that it is therefore appropriate to draw firm policy implications from this empirical work. The obvious question for the discussant of this paper is then, should we accept this conclusion? We can almost take for granted the technical competence of this paper, but is the *interpretation* of the results really so compelling as Taylor suggests? My view is that it is not, in view of some of the conceptual problems involved, and because of some of the conflicting results presented in other papers at this conference. Nonetheless, I think this paper makes a solid and useful contribution to the analysis of policy rules.

The Lucas Critique (Again)

The methodology used in this paper has two important, innovative features. One is that in the multicountry econometric model used, private agents correctly anticipate the future consequences of government policy actions and can therefore modify their behavior accordingly. (In other words, Taylor's model does not permit agents to be systematically "fooled" by the authorities.) The other feature is that alternative regimes are evaluated by their effect on the variability of ultimate targets using empirical estimates of the actual variance (and, especially, the *covariance*) of shocks to the economy, rather than simply by their ability to improve on historical outcomes. On both counts I think this paper is a significant advance over earlier papers that have used econometric models to evaluate the choice of an exchange rate regime.

Nonetheless, I am not wholly comfortable with the approach used by Taylor, as well as those used by McKibbin and Sachs (Chapter 4 in this volume) and by my colleagues at the Fund. There is a major obstacle to using *any* econometric model (as that term is usually understood) to evaluate regime choice; that is, of course, the much-invoked Lucas critique. In general, the parameters of an econometric model do not remain unchanged in the face of a policy regime change, even if, as in this case, agents are assumed to correctly anticipate outcomes for certain endogenous variables. Taylor acknowledges this difficulty in a somewhat oblique way in discussing the possibility that the distribution of the disturbances to the model will be different "in the future," but I do not think he addresses the issue as directly as he might.

In my view, this is not just a pedantic objection. Taylor quite properly considers the possibility that the distribution of the deviations from open interest parity shocks depends on the exchange rate regime, as it surely does. He comes up with two alternatives (no change, and the distribution collapsing to zero), which, while they do not bound the problem in any formal way, do appear to be sensible ways to examine the sensitivity of the simulations outcome to exchange rate expectations. But the open parity equation is not the only way in which exchange rate expectations enter the model. The possibility that the parameters in conventional trade equations depend on the volatility of the nominal exchange rate has been extensively studied recently, and it seems to me quite likely that these parameters in Taylor's model would be significantly affected by anything as dramatic as a return to fixed exchange rates. (In principle, of course, that is a testable hypothesis. Given that we actually have data for this particular type of regime switch, models can be estimated that explicitly incorporate the exchange rate regime in behavioral equations.

Indeed, some of the older, and otherwise less intellectually respectable, econometric models did just this.)

I think that another difficulty arises in the treatment of uncertainty in this model. Taylor's model, and its cousins, are not really designed to explore how the economy responds to *uncertainty*; if anything, the key idea is to incorporate agents' *knowledge*, not their uncertainty. Certainty equivalence is imposed on the model both in estimation and simulation; the stochastic disturbances, which here assume structural status, are initially viewed, it seems to me, merely as something to be purged from the model in order to reveal underlying behavior. In this world agents are indifferent to risk, there are no explicit costs of volatility, and governments do not attempt to offset shocks. I think that use of such a framework to analyze government policies that do try to offset stochastic shocks is essentially to admit that there are important phenomena missing from the original model. (The same sort of argument also leads me to question the basis for performing "risk premium" shocks with this class of model.)

Some Comments on the Modeling

In spite of all this, I do like the paper a lot. I have two technical points to raise. The first is based on the observation that the variance of, say, real gross national product (GNP) that Taylor calculates for a particular rule is taken across both time and the number of replications. That is, 10 replications of a simulation 40 quarters long gives 400 observations of the deviation of GNP from its baseline—the variance of GNP for a given rule is calculated using all 400 observations. This measure of variability combines the current shock and the policy response to it with the lagged effects of previous shocks in a way that blurs the distinction between the two. (Furthermore, the first few observations in each simulation would obviously be less affected by previous shocks, giving them different properties.)

Two alternatives come to mind. One is simply to simulate the first period 400 times (with each simulation extending 40 periods into the future, but with shocks only occurring in the first period). This way the dynamic response of the economy under a particular rule could be studied explicitly, and one could consider objective functions for the authorities with explicit weights on current and future effects of policy actions. Alternatively, one might allow a single simulation run for 400 periods into the future, applying a new shock in each period. This procedure would provide the best estimate of the steady state variance of target variables, but would obscure the dynamic effects of policy actions. A third alternative is simply to drop the first few periods from the calculation of the variance and see whether the results are affected significantly.

A second observation is that the price target rules used in Taylor's paper give a surprisingly large weight to Japan. This is presumably because wages are less sticky in Taylor's Japanese model than in the other countries, but this assumption does give the results a somewhat ad hoc flavor. I personally would prefer to see results for a rule based on a GNP-weighted average price. Similarly, the feedback coefficients in most of the rules apparently represent a certain amount of trial and error in the effort to find stable rules. To my taste this slightly weakens the force of the comparisons made because one always wonders what would happen with a larger or smaller coefficient here or there. The difficulty is that there is no algorithm for determining which rules are compared. (Taylor does report a number of sensitivity tests, which do go some way toward alleviating this concern.)

I did not find in Taylor's paper a description of how monetary policy in the other European Monetary System (EMS) countries was specified for these simulations. It might be interesting to see whether the result that exchange rate targeting is inferior for the Group of Three countries holds within the EMS as well, where there is perhaps a stronger presumption of the gains from fixed exchange rates.

Comparison with Other Models

Taylor's results are striking in that they are highly robust, at least within the framework of this model. Variations in the parameters of the rules, changes in the target variables, different assumptions about the volatility of exchange rate shocks—none of these seems to affect the basic result. It is puzzling, therefore, that two other papers (those of McKibbin and Sachs and of Frenkel, Goldstein, and Masson, Chapters 4 and 5 of this volume) using similar, although not identical, methods, do not confirm Taylor's result. I do not want to steal the thunder of either authors or discussants, so let me just take note of some points to look for in the later discussion. First of all, there is a common basis for comparison in the case of nominal income targeting versus fixed nominal exchange rates, results for which are reported by all three papers. The superiority of nominal income targeting reported by Taylor does not appear at all in the paper by Frenkel, Goldstein, and Masson, who run virtually the same experiments with a very similar model (see their Table 2). McKibbin and Sachs report only the response to individual shocks so that their results are less directly comparable; my reading of their results, however, is that nominal income and nominal exchange rate targeting perform roughly the same over a range of different shocks.

There are some differences in methodology among these papers, which may account for the different results. Both MULTIMOD and the McKibbin-Sachs Global models are annual, while Taylor's is quarterly—this surely means that the stochastic behavior of the underlying shocks is quite different. Would it be possible for Taylor to report the variance of annual average data for his model? Frenkel and others use a different method for calculating the residuals of their model, using auxiliary time series regressions to generate observations for the expected endogenous variables. Taylor, on the other hand, uses model simulations to create these forecasts; my own view is that Taylor's method is preferable. There are some differences in model structure: Taylor's model disaggregates consumption and investment, while MULTI-MOD has a more complete rest-of-world specification and accounts more completely for asset stocks. The McKibbin-Sachs model, of course, is calibrated to the data, while Taylor's and MULTIMOD are estimated.

While any one of these factors might in principle account for the different results, my own view (which is nothing more than a guess at this point) is that the differences are due simply to different parameter values in each model. Furthermore, I am a little surprised that Taylor's result is so robust to alternative formulations within his own model. To my naturally skeptical mind, this suggests that there may be some inherent structural property of this model that attaches a strong penalty to fixed exchange rates. The trade equations would seem to me to be obvious candidates.

4

Implications of Policy Rules for the World Economy

Warwick J. McKibbin and Jeffrey D. Sachs*

I. Introduction

The global economy is currently faced with continued trade imbalances, volatile asset prices, and persistent debt problems in many developing countries, problems that raise two major macroeconomic policy issues. The first and most pressing is the need to adjust global macroeconomic policies to help reduce current trade imbalances. The second issue, which is of a longer-term nature, is whether there exists a global regime, or set of "rules of the game," for macroeconomic policy interactions among countries that would avoid the macroeconomic problems the world is currently facing.

This paper provides a rigorous analysis of these issues—using a global model—and offers some preliminary answers. We use the MSG2 (McKibbin-Sachs Global) model of the world economy. We outline the model's main features and show that it does reasonably well in explaining the 1980s, using only changes in actual and anticipated monetary and fiscal policies in the world economy, cessation of lending to developing countries, and oil pricing behavior of the Organization of Petroleum Exporting Countries (OPEC). We use the model to analyze various scenarios for adjustments in the world economy from 1989 on, and argue that fiscal adjustment in the United States will help resolve the current imbalances without necessarily leading to a slowdown in global economic activity.

The second part of the paper, which is more forward looking, addresses the issue of alternative global monetary systems. Recently, theoretical and

---

* The authors thank Victor Argy, David Currie, Hans Genberg, Paul Masson, Patrick Minford, and Dirk Morris for comments and helpful discussion, and Graham Elliott and Tim Long for technical assistance. Financial support from the Ford Foundation and The Brookings Institution is gratefully acknowledged. The views expressed are those of the authors and should not be attributed to any of these institutions.

applied economists have begun to analyze alternative monetary regimes in a model-based framework. This seems inevitable given the complexity of the issue of multicountry interactions. Studies by McKibbin and Sachs (1986, 1988), Currie and Wren-Lewis (1988), Edison, Miller and Williamson(1987), Williamson and Miller (1987), and Taylor (1988) have attempted to provide some empirical magnitudes of the costs associated with different regimes under different shocks. McKibbin and Sachs (1988) have raised the question of the strategic behavior that countries follow when the rules of the game are imposed only on monetary policies, rather than also on fiscal policies. Williamson and Miller also address the importance of dealing with fiscal policy in designing a sustainable global system in their "blueprint" proposal, which attempts to place some restrictions on fiscal policies in different countries. We concur in the belief that fiscal policies cannot be ignored in designing a sustainable monetary regime.

A major implication of all of these studies is that the question of the most appropriate global regime is ambiguous. All regimes have a comparative advantage in handling particular types of shocks, and all elicit their own form of strategic behavior. The acceptance of the most appropriate regime, therefore relies on assessing not only how well it performs in the face of certain shocks, but also how badly it performs in the face of shocks that it is not designed for. These are ultimately empirical issues, which are investigated in Section V of this paper. We explore the operating characteristics and potential performance of many of the alternative regimes that have been proposed. This research updates the findings of earlier studies by McKibbin and Sachs (1986 and 1988a), but using a model with a much richer specification. We also consider more recent proposals, such as the modified McKinnon proposal and the Williamson and Miller blueprint proposal.

II. The MSG2 Model

The MSG2 model is in a constant state of development. Earlier studies[1] have used different versions of the model, although many of the key properties of the model remain little changed. The major differences between these other versions and the one used here are highlighted below. McKibbin and Sachs (1988) provide a complete derivation of the current model.

Theoretical Structure

The MSG2 model can be described as a dynamic general equilibrium model of a multiregion world economy. In the present paper the regions

---

[1] See Sachs and McKibbin (1985), McKibbin and Sachs (1986), Sachs (1985), McKibbin and Sachs (1988a), McKibbin, Roubini, and Sachs (1988), McKibbin (1988), and Bryant and others (1988).

modeled are the Federal Republic of Germany, Japan, the United States, the rest of the European Monetary System (denoted REMS), the rest of the Organization for Economic Cooperation and Development economies (denoted ROECD), the non-oil developing countries, and the oil exporting countries (consisting of countries as defined in the IMF *World Economic Outlook*, hereafter denoted OPEC). The model is of moderate size (about three dozen behavioral equations per industrial region). It is distinctive relative to most other global models in that it solves for a full intertemporal equilibrium in which agents have rational expectations of future variables.[2] In theoretical conception, therefore, the model is close in design to intertemporal dynamic models of fiscal policy in Lipton and Sachs (1983) and in Frenkel and Razin (1988). Those studies, like the present model, examine fiscal policy in an intertemporal perfect-foresight environment, giving considerable attention to intertemporal optimization and intertemporal budget constraints.

The MSG2 model rests on the assumption that, where possible, economic agents maximize intertemporal objective functions. This precept is similar to the class of models known as Computable General Equilibrium (CGE) models,[3] except that the concepts of time and dynamics are of fundamental importance in the MSG2 model. The various rigidities apparent in macroeconomic data are taken into account by allowing for deviations from fully optimizing behavior. As with any modeling project that purports to describe reality, the trade-off between theoretical rigor and empirical regularities seems inevitable.

The model has a mix of Keynesian and Classical properties by virtue of the assumption of slow adjustment of nominal wages in the labor markets of the United States, Germany, the REMS, and the ROECD. (Japan is treated somewhat differently, as described below.)

The model is solved in a linearized form, to facilitate policy optimization exercises, and especially to use linear-quadratic dynamic game theory and dynamic programming solution techniques.[4] We have experimented with the full nonlinear model and found that the properties of this model correspond closely to those of the linearized model, particularly over the initial years of any shocks. The global stability of the linearized model can be readily confirmed by an analysis of the model's eigenvalues.

In fitting the model to macroeconomic data, we adopt a mix of standard CGE calibration techniques and econometric time series results. The question

---

[2] The use of the rational expectations assumption in international models has become increasingly popular. For example, see Masson and others (1988) for description of the new MULTIMOD model, Minford and others (1986) for the Liverpool Model, and Taylor (1988).

[3] Such models are the basis of the work by Dixon and others (1982), Whalley (1985), and Deardorff and Stern (1986).

[4] In general, quantity variables are linearized around their levels relative to potential gross domestic product (GDP), while price variables are linearized in log form. See McKibbin (1987) for a detailed outline of the solution technique.

of calibrating the model is discussed further in McKibbin and Sachs (1988b).

The model has several attractive features. First, all stock-flow relationships are carefully observed: Budget deficits cumulate into stocks of public debt; current account deficits cumulate into net foreign investment positions; and physical investment cumulates into the capital stock. The underlying growth of Harrod-neutral productivity plus labor force growth is assumed to be 3 percent per region. Given the long-run properties of the model, the world economy settles down to the 3 percent steady-state growth path following any set of initial disturbances.

A second attractive feature is that asset markets are efficient in the sense that asset prices are determined by a combination of intertemporal arbitrage conditions and rational expectations. By virtue of the rational expectations assumption and the partly forward-looking behavior of households and firms, the model can be used to examine the effects of anticipated future policy changes, such as the sequence of future budget deficit cuts called for by the Gramm-Rudman-Hollings legislation in the United States. Indeed, one of the difficulties of using the MSG2 model is that every simulation requires that the "entire" future sequence of anticipated policies be specified. In practice, 40-year paths of policy variables, or endogenous policy rules, must be specified.

A third attractive feature of the MSG2 model is the specification of the supply side. There are several noteworthy points here. First, factor input decisions are partly based on intertemporal profit maximization by firms. Labor and intermediate inputs are selected to maximize short-run profits given a stock of capital that is fixed in each period. The capital stock is adjusted according to a "Tobin's q" model of investment, derived along the lines in Hayashi (1982). Tobin's q is the shadow value of capital, and it evolves according to a rational expectations forecast of future post-tax profitability.

Another point of interest regarding the supply side is the specification of the wage-price dynamics in each of the industrial regions. Extensive macroeconomic research has demonstrated important differences in the wage-price processes in the United States, Europe, and Japan, and these differences are incorporated in the model. In particular, the United States and the ROECD (including Canada and Australia) are characterized by nominal wage rigidities arising from long-term nominal wage contracts. In Japan, on the contrary, nominal wages are assumed to be renegotiated on an annual, synchronized cycle, with nominal wages selected for the following year to clear the labor market on average. In the ROECD, nominal wages are assumed to be more forward looking than in the United States, although real wages adjust slowly to clear the labor market. In Germany and the REMS we assume a form of "hysteresis," where a rise in unemployment leads to a rise in the natural rate of unemployment that persists for a substantial period of time.

Further enhancements, which do not appear in earlier published versions of the model, include further disaggregation—such as separate modeling of

Germany and the EMS bloc, independently of the residual ROECD bloc of countries. We also incorporate the slow pass-through of exchange rate changes into import prices, especially in the U.S. economy. Consumption in each industrialized region is now partly determined by permanent income or wealth (30 percent of total) and partly determined by current disposable income (70 percent). This follows the work of Hayashi (1979) and Campbell and Mankiw (1987).

Simulation Properties

To illustrate the properties of the model, we consider three simulations. The first is a permanent fiscal expansion in the United States and the other two are a permanent increase in the level of the U.S. money supply and a permanent increase in the rate of growth of U.S. money. A more detailed analysis of the properties of this model is undertaken in McKibbin and Sachs (1988b), which includes the important distinction among permanent, temporary, and anticipated shocks that must be made in a model that incorporates rational expectations behavior.

Fiscal Policy Transmission

In this section we examine the effects of a fiscal expansion in the United States. In implementing a change in fiscal policy, it is important that tax and spending policies in any country be consistent with the intertemporal budget constraint facing each government. The actual policy change is a permanent 1 percent of gross national product (GNP) increase in the level of government expenditure, with taxes only rising owing to endogenous changes in tax receipts resulting from changes in economic activity. Over time, taxes on labor income are also assumed to rise to cover the increasing interest burden of a rising stock of public debt. The overall fiscal deficit remains permanently higher, although the primary fiscal spending (defined as spending net of interest repayments minus total taxes) eventually moves into surplus to prevent the explosive growth of government debt.

Table 1 contains the results for the case of a 1 percent of GNP increase in real government expenditure in the United States. All variables are expressed as deviations from an initial baseline. GDP is recorded as a percentage deviation from the initial baseline (for example, 0.56 percent of GDP in year 1). Consumption, investment, exports, imports, and the trade balance are all reported as deviations from baseline in percent of potential GNP. Thus, in year 1, private consumption rises relative to the baseline by 0.2 of 1 percent of U.S. potential GNP. Labor demand (that is, total manhours in the economy) is reported as a percentage deviation from the baseline (for example, a rise of 0.7 percent in year 1). Inflation and interest rates are reported as deviations in percentage points relative to the baseline (rather than as deviations as a percent of their baseline values). Thus, inflation in year 1 is seen to fall by 0.11

**Table 1. Permanent 1 Percent GDP Increase in
U.S. Government Spending**
(Deviation from baseline)

	Year	1	2	3	4	5
		United States				
GDP	%Y	0.56	0.43	0.30	0.17	0.06
Private consumption	%Y	0.20	0.16	0.10	0.02	−0.05
Private investment	%Y	−0.09	−0.12	−0.15	−0.19	−0.23
Govt. consumption	%Y	1.00	1.00	1.00	1.00	1.00
Exports	%Y	−0.26	−0.27	−0.28	−0.29	−0.30
Imports	%Y	0.29	0.35	0.36	0.36	0.36
Trade balance	%Y	−0.39	−0.35	−0.34	−0.33	−0.33
Budget deficit	%Y	0.79	0.83	0.86	0.90	0.94
Labor demand	%	0.70	0.61	0.46	0.30	0.15
Inflation	D	−0.11	0.03	0.10	0.14	0.15
Short interest rate	D	1.17	1.11	1.10	1.14	1.21
Long interest rate	D	1.31	1.32	1.34	1.35	1.37
Short real interest rate	D	1.11	0.99	0.96	0.99	1.06
Long real interest rate	D	1.14	1.14	1.15	1.16	1.17
Money	%	−0.00	−0.00	−0.00	−0.00	−0.00
		Japan				
GDP	%Y	0.18	0.01	−0.01	−0.03	−0.05
Private consumption	%Y	−0.09	−0.15	−0.16	−0.17	−0.18
Private investment	%Y	−0.18	−0.26	−0.28	−0.29	−0.31
Govt. consumption	%Y	0.00	0.00	0.00	0.00	0.00
Exports	%Y	0.28	0.25	0.25	0.24	0.24
Imports	%Y	−0.16	−0.16	−0.18	−0.19	−0.20
Trade balance	%Y	0.43	0.32	0.28	0.27	0.26
Budget deficit	%Y	−0.03	0.03	0.03	0.04	0.05
Labor demand	%	0.26	−0.00	−0.00	−0.00	−0.00
Inflation	D	0.27	0.43	0.11	0.08	0.07
Short interest rate	D	0.44	0.89	1.02	1.10	1.16
Long interest rate	D	1.13	1.19	1.21	1.23	1.24
Short real interest rate	D	−0.00	0.79	0.94	1.03	1.10
Long real interest rate	D	0.99	1.04	1.05	1.05	1.05
Money	%	0.00	0.00	0.00	0.00	0.00
Exchange rate (dollar/yen)	%	−4.99	−4.26	−4.05	−3.96	−3.92
Real exchange rate	%	−4.85	−3.75	−3.55	−3.54	−3.58
		Germany, Fed. Rep. of				
GDP	%Y	0.21	0.13	0.02	−0.07	−0.14
Private consumption	%Y	−0.00	−0.04	−0.08	−0.11	−0.13
Private investment	%Y	−0.16	−0.20	−0.25	−0.28	−0.31
Govt. consumption	%Y	0.00	0.00	0.00	0.00	0.00
Exports	%Y	0.21	0.16	0.11	0.07	0.03
Imports	%Y	−0.16	−0.20	−0.23	−0.25	−0.27
Real trade balance	%Y	0.37	0.30	0.25	0.22	0.19
Budget deficit	%Y	−0.05	−0.02	0.02	0.04	0.07
Labor demand	%	0.34	0.21	0.06	−0.06	−0.14
Inflation	D	0.26	0.25	0.19	0.14	0.12
Short interest rate	D	0.56	0.81	0.94	1.02	1.10
Long interest rate	D	1.11	1.16	1.18	1.20	1.22
Short real interest rate	D	0.32	0.62	0.79	0.90	0.99

Table 1 (concluded).

	Year	1	2	3	4	5
Long real interest rate	D	0.97	1.00	1.02	1.03	1.04
Money	%	0.00	0.00	0.00	0.00	0.00
Exchange rate (dollar/DM)	%	−4.45	−3.83	−3.54	−3.37	−3.25
Real exchange rate	%	−4.29	−3.51	−3.15	−2.98	−2.90
REMS						
GDP	%Y	0.29	0.18	0.06	−0.03	−0.10
Private consumption	%Y	0.03	−0.03	−0.08	−0.11	−0.13
Private investment	%Y	−0.15	−0.21	−0.25	−0.29	−0.31
Govt. consumption	%Y	0.00	0.00	0.00	0.00	0.00
Exports	%Y	0.18	0.13	0.07	0.02	−0.01
Imports	%Y	−0.24	−0.29	−0.32	−0.35	−0.36
Trade balance	%Y	0.36	0.30	0.25	0.22	0.20
Budget deficit	%Y	−0.05	−0.01	0.02	0.05	0.08
Labor demand	%	0.36	0.18	0.01	−0.10	−0.18
Inflation	D	0.31	0.27	0.20	0.15	0.12
Short interest rate	D	0.56	0.81	0.94	1.02	1.10
Long interest rate	D	1.11	1.16	1.18	1.20	1.22
Short real interest rate	D	0.30	0.61	0.79	0.90	0.99
Long real interest rate	D	0.97	1.00	1.02	1.03	1.04
Money	%	0.03	0.02	0.02	0.02	0.03
Exchange rate (dollar/ EMS)	%	−4.45	−3.83	−3.54	−3.37	−3.25
Real exchange rate	%	−4.28	−3.47	−3.10	−2.93	−2.84
ROECD						
GDP	%Y	0.17	0.09	−0.01	−0.09	−0.15
Private consumption	%Y	−0.06	−0.07	−0.09	−0.11	−0.12
Private investment	%Y	−0.16	−0.20	−0.24	−0.27	−0.30
Govt. consumption	%Y	0.00	0.00	0.00	0.00	0.00
Exports	%Y	0.22	0.19	0.15	0.11	0.08
Imports	%Y	−0.16	−0.17	−0.18	−0.19	−0.20
Trade balance	%Y	0.40	0.31	0.26	0.24	0.22
Budget deficit	%Y	−0.04	−0.02	0.01	0.03	0.05
Labor demand	%	0.30	0.19	0.05	−0.05	−0.11
Inflation	D	0.24	0.22	0.17	0.13	0.10
Short interest rate	D	0.50	0.78	0.92	1.01	1.09
Long interest rate	D	1.11	1.16	1.19	1.22	1.23
Short real interest rate	D	0.26	0.59	0.78	0.91	1.01
Long real interest rate	D	0.98	1.02	1.04	1.05	1.06
Money	%	0.00	0.00	0.00	0.00	0.00
Exchange rate (dollar/ ROE)	%	−4.03	−3.35	−3.03	−2.84	−2.71
Real exchange rate	%	−3.91	−3.06	−2.67	−2.50	−2.42
Developing Countries						
Trade balance	%GNP	0.10	0.15	0.17	0.18	0.20
Terms of trade	%	−2.83	−2.26	−2.10	−2.06	−2.06
Oil Exporting Countries						
Trade balance	%GNP	−0.17	−0.15	−0.12	−0.11	−0.10
Terms of trade	%	−3.34	−2.76	−2.57	−2.54	−2.55

Note: %Y = deviation from baseline as percent of GDP; D = deviation from baseline; % = percent deviation from baseline.

percentage points in year 1, primarily because of the stronger currency, while short-term interest rates increase by 1.17 percentage points (that is, 117 basis points). The four U.S. bilateral exchange rates are reported as a percentage change from baseline values. Note that a negative value for the exchange rates indicates an appreciation of the U.S. dollar.

Now, consider the simulation results for the U.S. fiscal expansion. The Mundell-Fleming model tells us that we should expect that a bond-financed fiscal expansion in the presence of perfect substitutability of home and foreign financial assets should result in a rise in domestic income and an appreciation of the dollar exchange rate. Indeed, GNP rises by 0.56 percentage points in the first year, while the dollar appreciates by 5.0 percent vis-à-vis the Japanese yen, 4.5 percent vis-à-vis the deutsche mark and the REMS currency, and 4.0 percent vis-à-vis the ROECD currency. The rise in output and the appreciation of the dollar produces a large trade deficit in the United States, equivalent to 0.39 percent of GNP in the first year of the fiscal expansion. Note that there is some crowding out of private investment in the United States. The share market falls because the higher real interest rate overwhelms the effect of higher output on the valuation of future profitability. Investment of forward-looking firms falls but that of firms investing out of current profits rises. The former effect dominates. There are also two opposite effects on consumption; the forward-looking component falls, owing to higher long-term real interest rates, while the component driven by current disposable income rises.

The Mundell-Fleming model teaches that the transmission effect of a U.S. fiscal policy expansion on foreign output is ambiguous, for the reasons already alluded to. On the one hand, world interest rates rise, which tends to depress foreign income. On the other hand, U.S. demand for foreign products increases, which tends to raise foreign income through a spurt in exports. As described in Bruno and Sachs (1985, Chapter 6) and in Oudiz and Sachs (1987), the transmission is more likely to be negative if foreign wages and prices rise rapidly in response to the depreciation of the foreign currencies vis-à-vis the dollar following the U.S. fiscal action. If foreign wages and prices are fixed, the U.S. fiscal expansion will tend to be positively transmitted.

As Table 1 shows, the effect of the permanent fiscal expansion is a positive transmission to each region in the first two years. The positive transmission to Japan is quickly reversed after the first year because of the rapid adjustment of the Japanese labor market. In contrast, wages adjust slowly in Europe. As the table shows, the negative effects on foreign consumption and investment resulting from higher interest rates begin to dominate the expansionary effects of greater exports to the United States. Note that inflation is increased throughout the world following the U.S. fiscal expansion. Most of the inflationary effect outside the United States arises because foreign currencies depreciate against the dollar following the U.S. fiscal expansion.

Monetary Policy Transmission

In this section we examine the consequences of a sustained monetary expansion implemented in two alternative ways. The first assumes a permanent increase in the level of money balances, or a temporary cut in nominal interest rates, and the second assumes a permanent increase in the rate of growth of money.

As with fiscal policy, the international transmission of monetary policy has a theoretically ambiguous sign. A domestic monetary expansion tends to depreciate the home exchange rate and to reduce world real interest rates. The exchange rate depreciation shifts demand away from other countries and toward the home country, while the reduction in world real interest rates tends to raise demand in the rest of the world. In the simple Mundell-Fleming model—in which output prices and nominal wages are fixed in the other countries—the exchange rate effect dominates, so that foreign output falls when the home country increases the money supply. Home monetary expansion is then beggar-thy-neighbor. In more elaborate models with wage price dynamics, either the exchange rate channel or the interest rate channel might dominate.

Monetary policy is also ambiguous with respect to the effect on domestic trade and current account balances. An expanded domestic money supply improves international competitiveness by depreciating the home exchange rate. Assuming that the standard Marshall-Lerner conditions hold (as they do in the MSG2 model), this effect tends to improve the trade and current account balances. On the other hand, the fall in interest rates tends to raise investment demand and to lower savings, thereby worsening the trade and current account balances. The overall effect is ambiguous.

Finally, note the magnitude of the effect of a monetary expansion on the nominal exchange rate. It is well known from the Dornbusch (1976) model that the exchange rate will depreciate in response to a permanent, once-and-for-all increase in the money supply, but that the size of the depreciation on impact may exceed ("overshoot") or fall below ("undershoot") the long-run change in the nominal rate, which just equals the proportionate change in the money stock. If the effect of the exchange rate on domestic demand is large (through the effect on the trade balance), if the effect of domestic demand on money demand is large (through the income elasticity of demand for money), and if the exchange rate depreciation causes a rapid rise in domestic prices, then home nominal interest rates will tend to rise after the money expansion, and the home exchange rate will tend to undershoot its long-run change. If on the other hand, one or all of these three channels is weak, domestic nominal interest rates will tend to fall after the money expansion, and the exchange rate will tend to overshoot its long-run change.

Let us now examine these effects in the MSG2 model. As seen in Table 2, a 1 percent U.S. monetary expansion raises U.S. output by 0.42 percent in the

Table 2. Permanent 1 Percent Increase in
Level of U.S. Money Balances
(Deviation from baseline)

Year		1	2	3	4	5
United States						
GDP	%Y	0.42	0.27	0.15	0.07	0.02
Private consumption	%Y	0.22	0.14	0.08	0.04	0.01
Private investment	%Y	0.15	0.09	0.05	0.02	0.00
Govt. consumption	%Y	0.00	0.00	0.00	0.00	0.00
Exports	%Y	0.06	0.03	0.02	0.01	0.00
Imports	%Y	0.01	− 0.00	− 0.00	− 0.00	− 0.00
Trade balance	%Y	0.03	0.01	0.00	0.00	− 0.00
Budget deficit	%Y	− 0.13	− 0.08	− 0.05	− 0.02	− 0.01
Labor demand	%	0.72	0.41	0.20	0.07	− 0.02
Inflation	D	0.33	0.25	0.18	0.13	0.08
Short interest rate	D	− 0.46	− 0.29	− 0.17	− 0.08	− 0.02
Long interest rate	D	− 0.07	− 0.03	− 0.01	0.00	0.00
Short real interest rate	D	− 0.72	− 0.48	− 0.30	− 0.16	− 0.07
Long real interest rate	D	− 0.07	− 0.03	− 0.01	0.00	0.01
Money	%	1.00	1.00	1.00	1.00	1.00
Japan						
GDP	%Y	− 0.05	− 0.00	− 0.00	− 0.00	0.00
Private consumption	%Y	− 0.01	0.00	− 0.00	− 0.00	− 0.00
Private investment	%Y	0.00	0.01	0.01	0.00	− 0.00
Govt. consumption	%Y	0.00	0.00	0.00	0.00	0.00
Exports	%Y	− 0.02	− 0.00	0.00	0.00	0.01
Imports	%Y	0.03	0.02	0.01	0.01	0.00
Trade balance	%Y	− 0.05	− 0.01	0.00	0.01	0.01
Budget deficit	%Y	0.01	− 0.00	− 0.00	− 0.00	− 0.00
Labor demand	%	− 0.07	0.00	0.00	0.00	0.00
Inflation	D	− 0.06	− 0.05	0.04	0.04	0.03
Short interest rate	D	− 0.12	− 0.16	− 0.10	− 0.05	− 0.01
Long interest rate	D	− 0.02	− 0.01	0.00	0.01	0.01
Short real interest rate	D	− 0.06	− 0.20	− 0.14	− 0.07	− 0.02
Long real interest rate	D	− 0.01	− 0.01	0.00	0.01	0.01
Money	%	− 0.00	− 0.00	− 0.00	− 0.00	− 0.00
Exchange rate (dollar/yen)	%	1.50	1.16	1.03	0.96	0.93
Real exchange rate	%	1.15	0.49	0.21	0.05	− 0.04
Germany, Fed. Rep. of						
GDP	%Y	− 0.08	− 0.04	0.00	0.01	0.01
Private consumption	%Y	− 0.05	− 0.03	− 0.02	− 0.01	− 0.00
Private investment	%Y	0.00	0.01	0.01	0.00	0.00
Govt. consumption	%Y	0.00	0.00	0.00	0.00	0.00
Exports	%Y	− 0.02	− 0.01	0.01	0.01	0.01
Imports	%Y	0.01	0.01	0.01	0.00	0.00
Real trade balance	%Y	− 0.04	− 0.01	0.01	0.01	0.01
Budget deficit	%Y	0.02	0.01	0.00	− 0.00	− 0.00
Labor demand	%	− 0.12	− 0.05	− 0.00	0.01	0.01
Inflation	D	− 0.06	− 0.03	0.01	0.03	0.03
Short interest rate	D	− 0.20	− 0.19	− 0.13	− 0.07	− 0.02
Long interest rate	D	− 0.03	− 0.02	− 0.00	0.01	0.01
Short real interest rate	D	− 0.17	− 0.19	− 0.15	− 0.10	− 0.05

Table 2 (concluded).

	Year	1	2	3	4	5
Long real interest rate	D	−0.02	−0.01	−0.00	0.00	0.01
Money	%	−0.00	−0.00	−0.00	−0.00	−0.00
Exchange rate (dollar/DM)	%	1.35	1.09	0.98	0.94	0.93
Real exchange rate	%	0.99	0.44	0.15	0.01	−0.06
REMS						
GDP	%Y	−0.11	−0.05	−0.01	0.00	0.00
Private consumption	%Y	−0.10	−0.06	−0.04	−0.02	−0.01
Private investment	%Y	−0.00	0.00	0.01	0.00	−0.00
Govt. consumption	%Y	0.00	0.00	0.00	0.00	0.00
Exports	%Y	−0.02	0.00	0.01	0.02	0.01
Imports	%Y	−0.00	−0.00	−0.00	−0.00	−0.01
Trade balance	%Y	−0.02	0.00	0.02	0.02	0.02
Budget deficit	%Y	0.03	0.01	0.00	−0.00	−0.00
Labor demand	%	−0.16	−0.07	−0.01	0.01	0.01
Inflation	D	−0.07	−0.03	0.01	0.03	0.03
Short interest rate	D	−0.20	−0.19	−0.13	−0.07	−0.02
Long interest rate	D	−0.03	−0.02	−0.00	0.01	0.01
Short real interest rate	D	−0.17	−0.20	−0.16	−0.10	−0.05
Long real interest rate	D	−0.02	−0.01	−0.00	0.00	0.01
Money	%	−0.04	−0.03	−0.02	−0.01	−0.01
Exchange rate (dollar/ EMS)	%	1.35	1.09	0.98	0.94	0.93
Real exchange rate	%	0.97	0.43	0.14	0.00	−0.06
ROECD						
GDP	%Y	−0.06	−0.02	0.00	0.01	0.01
Private consumption	%Y	0.00	−0.00	0.00	−0.00	−0.00
Private investment	%Y	0.00	0.01	0.01	0.01	−0.00
Govt. consumption	%Y	0.00	0.00	0.00	0.00	0.00
Exports	%Y	−0.03	−0.01	0.00	0.01	0.01
Imports	%Y	0.04	0.02	0.01	0.00	−0.00
Trade balance	%Y	−0.07	−0.02	0.00	0.01	0.01
Budget deficit	%Y	0.02	0.01	−0.00	−0.00	−0.00
Labor demand	%	−0.10	−0.03	0.01	0.02	0.01
Inflation	D	−0.09	−0.02	0.02	0.03	0.03
Short interest rate	D	−0.17	−0.18	−0.13	−0.07	−0.03
Long interest rate	D	−0.03	−0.02	−0.00	0.01	0.01
Short real interest rate	D	−0.13	−0.19	−0.16	−0.11	−0.05
Long real interest rate	D	−0.02	−0.01	−0.00	0.00	0.01
Money	%	−0.00	−0.00	−0.00	−0.00	−0.00
Exchange rate (dollar/ ROE)	%	1.38	1.09	0.98	0.94	0.93
Real exchange rate	%	1.02	0.43	0.14	0.00	−0.06
Developing Countries						
Trade balance	%U	−0.08	−0.06	−0.04	−0.03	−0.01
Terms of trade	%	0.70	0.30	0.12	0.02	−0.03
Oil Exporting Countries						
Trade balance	%U	0.09	0.05	0.02	0.00	−0.01
Terms of trade	%	0.90	0.43	0.19	0.05	−0.02

Note: %Y = deviation from baseline as percent of GDP; D = deviation from baseline; % = percentage deviation from baseline; %U = deviation from baseline as percent of U.S. GNP.

first year and causes the exchange rate to depreciate by 1.5 percent, over-shooting its long-run level of 1 percent. Previous studies using this model find almost no overshooting. The reason for the current result is the assumption that import prices in the United States do not adjust fully to exchange rate changes in the short run. This is in line with the empirical results of Baldwin and Krugman (1987) and Mann (1987). U.S. inflation increases by 0.33 percent—which is far more inflation per unit of demand stimulus than for fiscal policy—because of the opposite direction of effect on the exchange rate (that is, for fiscal policy, the dollar appreciates, tending to reduce inflation; while for monetary policy, the dollar depreciates, tending to increase infla-tion). Remarkably, there is almost no international transmission of U.S. monetary policy to the output of the other countries. Moreover, the U.S. trade balance remains virtually unchanged.

Consider the effects on the direction of trade flows. The United States sells more to the rest of the world and buys more from the rest of the world. The other regions divert their own export sales to the U.S. market from the non-U.S. market. Total imports in the rest of the world remain unchanged, but their composition changes in the direction of a higher share of imports from the United States. Total exports in the rest of the world also remain virtually unchanged, but shift to supply the growing U.S. market, and away from third, non-U.S. markets.

The same pattern of proportionate depreciation of the exchange rate—with no effect on the trade balance of the expanding country or the outputs of the foreign countries—holds for a monetary expansion in the other OECD regions. This general conclusion is key because it means that floating ex-change rates effectively insulate the output of countries from monetary poli-cies abroad. The United States would benefit little on the output side from discount rate cuts in Europe and Japan.

Table 3 presents the results for a permanent 1 percent increase in the rate of U.S. money growth. Again, the policy raises real output as wages take time to adjust to the higher underlying inflation rate. The nominal exchange rate depreciates by 3.09 percent in the first year, but quickly converges to the steady-state depreciation rate of 1 percent a year. Nominal interest rates rise in this case because the expected price movements more than offset the short-term liquidity effect of the monetary expansion. Inflation eventually settles to 1 percent above the baseline. The transmission of the policy change is again small, although in this case it is now more negatively transmitted to the rest of the world. Monetary policy is neutral in the long run.

III. Tracking 1979 to 1988

In this section we use the model to explain the movements in a number of key macroeconomic variables from 1979 to 1988. The exercise of cumulating the multipliers from a rational expectations model to assess the tracking ability

Table 3. Permanent 1 Percent Increase in the Rate of Growth of U.S. Money
(Deviation from baseline)

	Year	1	2	3	4	5
		United States				
GDP	%Y	0.75	0.80	0.73	0.62	0.49
Private consumption	%Y	0.36	0.39	0.36	0.31	0.26
Private investment	%Y	0.26	0.27	0.25	0.21	0.16
Govt. consumption	%Y	0.00	0.00	0.00	0.00	0.00
Exports	%Y	0.12	0.12	0.11	0.09	0.08
Imports	%Y	−0.01	−0.02	−0.01	−0.00	0.00
Trade balance	%Y	0.08	0.07	0.06	0.05	0.04
Budget deficit	%Y	−0.23	−0.24	−0.22	−0.19	−0.15
Labor demand	%	1.32	1.32	1.15	0.93	0.69
Inflation	D	0.64	0.91	1.06	1.14	1.17
Short interest rate	D	0.53	0.44	0.45	0.52	0.62
Long interest rate	D	0.47	0.47	0.47	0.47	0.47
Short real interest rate	D	−0.37	−0.64	−0.70	−0.66	−0.56
Long real interest rate	D	−0.14	−0.13	−0.10	−0.07	−0.04
Money	%	1.00	2.00	3.00	4.00	5.00
		Japan				
GDP	%Y	−0.07	−0.01	−0.01	−0.00	0.00
Private consumption	%Y	0.03	0.04	0.03	0.03	0.03
Private investment	%Y	0.03	0.05	0.05	0.04	0.03
Govt. consumption	%Y	0.00	0.00	0.00	0.00	0.00
Exports	%Y	−0.06	−0.03	−0.02	−0.01	−0.00
Imports	%Y	0.07	0.07	0.06	0.06	0.05
Trade balance	%Y	−0.14	−0.09	−0.07	−0.05	−0.03
Budget deficit	%Y	0.01	−0.01	−0.01	−0.01	−0.01
Labor demand	%	−0.09	0.00	0.00	0.00	0.00
Inflation	D	−0.11	−0.17	−0.01	0.03	0.05
Short interest rate	D	−0.16	−0.36	−0.37	−0.32	−0.25
Long interest rate	D	−0.07	−0.06	−0.04	−0.01	0.02
Short real interest rate	D	0.02	−0.35	−0.40	−0.37	−0.30
Long real interest rate	D	−0.03	−0.03	−0.02	0.00	0.02
Money	%	−0.00	−0.00	−0.00	−0.00	−0.00
Exchange rate (dollar/yen)	%	3.09	3.78	4.58	5.40	6.24
Real exchange rate	%	2.45	2.06	1.77	1.47	1.18
		Germany, Fed. Rep. of				
GDP	%Y	−0.07	−0.07	−0.02	0.02	0.05
Private consumption	%Y	−0.01	−0.02	−0.01	0.00	0.01
Private investment	%Y	0.03	0.04	0.04	0.04	0.04
Govt. consumption	%Y	0.00	0.00	0.00	0.00	0.00
Exports	%Y	−0.05	−0.03	−0.00	0.02	0.04
Imports	%Y	0.05	0.05	0.05	0.05	0.04
Real trade balance	%Y	−0.12	−0.09	−0.05	−0.03	−0.01
Budget deficit	%Y	0.01	0.01	−0.00	−0.01	−0.02
Labor demand	%	−0.11	−0.11	−0.04	0.03	0.06
Inflation	D	−0.09	−0.10	−0.06	−0.01	0.02
Short interest rate	D	−0.19	−0.35	−0.38	−0.35	−0.29
Long interest rate	D	−0.08	−0.07	−0.05	−0.02	0.00
Short real interest rate	D	−0.09	−0.28	−0.36	−0.36	−0.32

Table 3 (concluded).

	Year	1	2	3	4	5
Long real interest rate	D	−0.04	−0.04	−0.03	−0.01	0.01
Money	%	−0.00	−0.00	−0.00	−0.00	−0.00
Exchange rate (dollar/DM)	%	2.84	3.57	4.35	5.18	6.05
Real exchange rate	%	2.20	1.92	1.57	1.23	0.93
REMS						
GDP	%Y	−0.12	−0.11	−0.06	−0.01	0.02
Private consumption	%Y	−0.03	−0.06	−0.05	−0.04	−0.03
Private investment	%Y	0.03	0.03	0.04	0.04	0.04
Govt. consumption	%Y	0.00	0.00	0.00	0.00	0.00
Exports	%Y	−0.04	−0.02	0.01	0.04	0.05
Imports	%Y	0.08	0.07	0.06	0.05	0.03
Trade balance	%Y	−0.12	−0.08	−0.04	−0.01	0.01
Budget deficit	%Y	0.02	0.02	0.01	−0.01	−0.01
Labor demand	%	−0.14	−0.13	−0.06	0.00	0.04
Inflation	D	−0.10	−0.11	−0.07	−0.01	0.02
Short interest rate	D	−0.19	−0.35	−0.38	−0.35	−0.29
Long interest rate	D	−0.08	−0.07	−0.05	−0.02	0.00
Short real interest rate	D	−0.08	−0.27	−0.36	−0.37	−0.33
Long real interest rate	D	−0.04	−0.04	−0.03	−0.01	0.01
Money	%	−0.02	−0.04	−0.05	−0.05	−0.05
Exchange rate (dollar/ EMS)	%	2.84	3.57	4.35	5.18	6.05
Real exchange rate	%	2.19	1.90	1.54	1.20	0.90
ROECD						
GDP	%Y	−0.06	−0.04	0.01	0.05	0.06
Private consumption	%Y	0.05	0.04	0.05	0.05	0.04
Private investment	%Y	0.03	0.04	0.05	0.05	0.04
Govt. consumption	%Y	0.00	0.00	0.00	0.00	0.00
Exports	%Y	−0.05	−0.03	−0.01	0.02	0.03
Imports	%Y	0.09	0.09	0.08	0.07	0.05
Trade balance	%Y	−0.15	−0.11	−0.08	−0.05	−0.04
Budget deficit	%Y	0.01	0.01	−0.01	−0.02	−0.02
Labor demand	%	−0.10	−0.06	0.01	0.06	0.07
Inflation	D	−0.13	−0.11	−0.06	−0.00	0.04
Short interest rate	D	−0.17	−0.34	−0.39	−0.36	−0.30
Long interest rate	D	−0.08	−0.07	−0.05	−0.03	0.00
Short real interest rate	D	−0.05	−0.27	−0.37	−0.38	−0.35
Long real interest rate	D	−0.04	−0.04	−0.03	−0.01	0.01
Money	%	−0.00	−0.00	−0.00	−0.00	−0.00
Exchange rate (dollar/ OEC)	%	2.84	3.55	4.32	5.16	6.04
Real exchange rate	%	2.19	1.88	1.51	1.18	0.91
Developing Countries						
Trade balance	%U	−0.03	−0.08	−0.10	−0.10	−0.09
Total		1.64	1.40	1.17	0.95	0.76
Oil Exporting Countries						
Trade balance	%U	0.08	0.10	0.08	0.06	0.04
Total		1.84	1.66	1.42	1.17	0.93

Note: %Y = deviation from baseline as percent of GDP; D = deviation from baseline; % = percent deviation from baseline; % U = deviation from baseline as percent of U.S. GNP.

of a model can be misleading.[5] The correct tracking exercise is far more complex, since in every period we must be careful to specify the expected future paths of all exogenous variables in the model. Revisions to expectations play a crucial role in determining the volatility of asset prices. In addition, we cannot use the actual outcomes of key variables (such as future fiscal deficits) because these do not necessarily reflect the ex-ante expectations held several years earlier. McKibbin (1988) shows that OECD forecasts of fiscal deficits at several crucial points (for example, the 1982 forecast for 1983) have differed considerably from the actual outcomes. If these were the generally accepted forecasts at the time, we would have expected some large changes in asset prices following the revisions in 1983.

The procedure followed here can be found in McKibbin (1988). It involves solving the model in 1979 given assumed paths for all future exogenous variables and then moving forward to the next year and re-solving the model forward, incorporating any realizations of actual variables as well as revisions to expectations of future exogenous variables. In the MSG2 model, few exogenous variables need to be specified, which makes this tracking exercise feasible; these variables include fiscal and monetary policy in each region, OPEC oil prices, and the availability of loans from the industrial countries to the non-oil developing countries. To tie down the fiscal policy expectations, we use the fiscal deficit forecasts for one year ahead as found in the *OECD Economic Outlook* (December quarter) each year. To obtain the entire future path of fiscal policy, we extrapolate this into the future assuming either no change from the forecast or using information of policy announcements such as Gramm-Rudman-Hollings in 1985. For OPEC oil prices we use the actual outcomes and forecasts in the *OECD Economic Outlook* and for developing country lending constraints we use the current account data in the IMF *World Economic Outlook*, assuming that the current account in any year is expected to continue. Monetary policy in each country is then arbitrarily geared toward approximately attaining the realized output gap in each year, as well as attempting to reach observed short-term and long-term nominal interest rates (working partly on inflationary expectations). There is a timing problem with this exercise. If policy changes toward the end of a calendar year, asset prices will likely change quickly, whereas the quantity effect of the shock will not show up until the following year. This must be taken into account in interpreting the tracking performance. McKibbin (1988) provides further details on the technique and the data sources. (The policy changes and shocks used to generate the baseline are illustrated in Table 6 and are discussed later.)

We focus on the results for the Group of Three countries of Germany, Japan, and the United States in this paper, although we must incorporate the policy changes in the rest of the world for the tracking exercise. The macro-

---

[5] It is nonetheless attempted and sometimes misinterpreted; for example, see Islam (1988).

economic experience of these countries is summarized in Table 4, which contains the outcomes, on an annual basis, of the output gap, inflation, short- and long-term nominal interest rates, trade balances, fiscal deficits, and real and nominal exchange rates. The key features of the past decade are clearly the large appreciation of the U.S. dollar relative to both the deutsche mark and the yen from 1981 until 1985, and the subsequent depreciation until 1988. This occurred in conjunction with substantial swings toward fiscal deficits in the United States and fiscal surpluses in Germany and Japan, and with the emergence of a large trade deficit in the United States and surpluses in Germany and Japan.

The results of the tracking exercise are given in Table 5. In calculating Table 5 we assume that without any policy changes from 1978—and with all nominal variables growing at their 1978 values—the real economy would change little and the divergence in relative nominal growth rates would show up only in changes in nominal exchange rates. We then solve the model forward for 40 years beginning in 1979, incorporating any policy changes and changes in expectations into the 1979 simulation. The deviation from base that we found was then added back to the assumed baseline from 1978. This procedure is repeated for each subsequent year until 1988. The first year of each simulation is that reported in Table 5. The expected path of the world economy and the path reported in Table 5 are not equal ex-post because new information is revealed in each year of the simulation.

The fiscal policy changes, shocks, and their expectations are shown in Table 6. The assumed path for money growth is not reported to avoid confusion. The exogenous policy variable called money is generated such that the short-term nominal interest rate and the longer-run inflationary expectations reflected in long nominal interest rates approximate those found in the data. The money growth that results from the model is not the observed money growth, but rather money growth inclusive of any exogenous velocity shifts. A better indicator of a change in monetary policy is given by the short and long nominal interest rates.

The key shocks that occurred begin with the rise in OPEC oil prices in 1979–80. This leads to an inflationary impulse that is met with a global tightening of monetary policy in 1981, especially in the United States. This policy appreciates the dollar and leads to a global slowdown in real growth. In addition, the gradual depreciation of the yen from 1979 is associated with Japanese fiscal tightness. The accelerated depreciation of the yen and deutsche mark from 1982–83 is due to the U.S. fiscal expansion announced in 1981 and implemented in 1982.[6] The deutsche mark continues to depreciate until 1985,

---

[6] See Morris (1988) for a study that tracks the real appreciation of the U.S. dollar and subsequent turnaround in 1985 using only fiscal policy changes in a small, empirical IS-LM model. That study relies on a sequence of temporary fiscal surprises to generate the results, whereas we assume the 1982–83 U.S. fiscal expansion was perceived to lead to a permanently larger fiscal deficit.

Table 4. Macroeconomic Experience of the Group of Three

	1978	1979	1980	1981	1982	1983	1984	1985	1986	1987
United States										
GNP growth	5.3	2.5	-0.2	1.9	-2.5	3.6	6.8	3.0	2.9	2.9
Output gap (trend = 2.5)	0.0	0.0	-2.7	-3.3	-8.3	-7.2	-2.9	-2.4	-2.0	-1.6
Inflation	7.7	11.2	13.5	10.4	6.1	3.2	4.3	3.5	1.9	3.7
Long nominal interest rate	8.4	9.5	11.5	14.0	13.0	11.1	12.5	10.6	7.7	8.4
Short nominal interest rate	7.2	10.1	11.6	14.1	10.7	8.6	9.6	7.5	6.0	5.8
Trade balance[1]	-1.3	-1.0	-0.9	-0.9	-1.4	-2.1	-3.3	-3.5	-3.9	-3.8
Fiscal deficit[1]	0.0	-0.6	1.3	1.0	3.5	3.8	2.8	3.3	3.5	2.4
Japan										
GNP growth	5.2	5.3	4.3	3.7	3.1	3.2	5.1	4.9	2.4	4.2
Output gap (trend = 4.2)	-1.1	0.0	0.1	-0.4	-1.5	-2.5	-1.6	-0.9	-2.7	-2.7
Inflation	3.8	3.6	8.0	4.9	2.7	0.9	2.2	2.1	0.4	-0.2
Long nominal interest rate	6.4	7.7	9.2	8.7	8.1	7.4	6.8	6.3	4.9	4.2
Short nominal interest rate	4.3	5.9	10.9	7.4	6.9	6.4	6.1	6.5	4.8	3.5
Trade balance[1]	1.9	-0.6	-1.1	1.0	0.7	1.8	2.7	3.4	4.2	3.4
Fiscal deficit[2]	5.5	4.8	4.4	3.8	3.4	3.5	2.1	0.8	0.9	1.2
Real exchange rate[2]	0.0	-9.1	-16.3	-19.0	-31.4	-30.2	-31.9	-33.3	-6.3	5.9
Nominal exchange rate[2]	0.0	-4.0	-7.2	-4.6	-15.5	-11.4	-11.4	-11.8	24.9	31.3
Germany, Fed. Rep. of										
GNP growth	3.3	4.0	1.5	0.0	-1.0	1.9	3.3	2.0	2.5	1.7
Output gap (trend = 2.5)	-1.5	0.0	-1.0	-3.5	-7.0	-7.6	-6.8	-7.3	-7.3	-8.1
Inflation	2.7	4.2	5.4	6.3	5.3	3.3	2.4	2.2	-0.2	0.2
Long nominal interest rate	6.4	7.4	8.5	10.4	9.0	7.9	7.8	6.9	5.9	5.8
Short nominal interest rate	3.7	5.6	7.8	10.6	8.0	5.6	5.6	5.0	3.9	3.3
Trade balance[1]	3.2	1.6	0.6	1.8	3.2	2.5	3.1	4.0	5.8	5.8
Fiscal deficit[1]	2.4	2.7	2.9	3.7	3.2	2.5	1.9	1.1	1.2	1.7
Real exchange rate[2]	0.0	4.8	1.6	-22.4	-29.2	-33.1	-41.0	-43.5	-23.1	-7.8
Nominal exchange rate[2]	0.0	9.6	10.5	-11.1	-17.2	-21.3	-29.4	-31.8	-7.5	10.5

Note: Nominal exchange rates in terms of U.S. dollars per domestic currency; real exchange rates in terms of GDP deflators; exchange rates are expressed as percentage change from 1978.

Source: OECD Economic Outlook (various issues).

[1] Percent of GDP.   [2] Average of period.

Table 5. Tracking Results
(Levels of variables)

	1979	1980	1981	1982	1983	1984	1985	1986	1987	1988	1989	1990	1991
United States													
Output gap	-0.3	-1.9	-3.5	-9.0	-9.1	-8.2	-6.4	-0.5	0.0	0.3	0.6	0.4	0.1
Inflation	9.0	10.8	11.7	6.6	4.7	2.9	2.8	4.2	5.6	6.4	7.3	7.9	8.3
Long interest rate	10.2	13.2	14.3	12.4	11.1	9.6	8.6	8.6	9.4	9.5	9.7	10.0	10.2
Short interest rate	9.3	12.9	12.5	10.3	10.2	9.7	7.0	9.5	6.9	5.4	5.5	6.0	6.7
Trade balance	-0.6	-1.2	-1.2	-3.0	-3.6	-3.8	-3.9	-3.3	-3.1	-3.0	-2.8	-2.7	-2.6
Budget deficit	-1.7	-0.3	0.2	2.8	3.5	3.7	3.5	2.5	2.1	1.7	1.6	1.7	1.8
Japan													
Output gap	-1.1	-1.1	-4.0	-2.4	-1.8	-1.1	-1.0	-0.8	-1.8	-0.6	-0.8	-0.9	-1.0
Inflation	4.9	7.2	5.9	3.0	3.0	1.2	1.5	-1.2	-3.6	-0.8	2.2	2.7	3.5
Long interest rate	7.5	9.5	9.8	9.3	7.4	5.8	4.7	3.7	6.3	6.5	6.8	7.2	7.6
Short interest rate	7.9	11.9	8.7	7.0	6.3	5.4	3.1	3.2	5.5	2.9	3.0	3.8	6.1
Trade balance	1.1	2.3	2.7	3.4	3.0	3.2	3.6	2.6	2.0	2.0	1.9	1.8	1.6
Budget deficit	4.3	4.2	3.8	3.5	3.3	2.3	1.4	1.2	1.8	1.8	2.1	2.5	2.8
Real exchange rate	-0.1	-14.0	-14.6	-37.8	-39.1	-41.9	-43.5	-25.7	-18.8	-20.2	-18.3	-16.6	-14.7
Germany, Fed. Rep. of													
Output gap	-0.7	-1.9	-2.7	-2.7	-3.1	-4.9	-6.5	-5.9	-7.1	-6.2	-5.1	-4.2	-3.9
Inflation	3.9	5.1	5.6	6.5	6.6	5.0	3.1	1.2	0.1	0.8	1.8	2.7	3.1
Long interest rate	8.1	10.3	11.4	11.4	9.9	8.1	6.6	5.5	6.7	6.7	6.8	7.0	7.1
Short interest rate	7.4	8.9	8.7	9.7	10.4	9.5	6.8	7.3	5.6	3.6	3.3	4.2	1.4
Trade balance	2.3	2.4	2.4	4.0	4.4	5.2	4.3	3.3	3.1	3.2	3.3	3.1	3.3
Budget deficit	2.8	3.3	3.5	2.6	1.9	0.5	1.0	1.2	1.6	1.7	1.7	1.8	1.7
Real exchange rate	-1.0	-4.8	-4.6	-30.4	-33.9	-34.8	-27.6	-13.9	-10.4	-11.8	-12.8	-13.2	-13.9

REMS

Output gap	0.1	-1.4	-2.6	-0.6	-0.9	-1.8	-4.6	-4.1	-4.9	-3.9	-2.9	-2.1	-1.5
Inflation	5.7	7.1	7.6	9.1	8.9	7.2	4.1	1.6	1.0	2.0	3.0	3.9	4.5
Short interest rate	8.6	10.1	9.5	9.9	11.3	4.3	3.0	5.1	11.3	10.1	8.8	7.5	5.3
Trade balance	1.6	1.3	1.4	0.6	0.3	0.5	0.9	0.9	1.0	1.3	1.5	1.6	1.6
Budget deficit	4.0	4.5	4.9	6.6	5.4	4.8	4.7	4.5	4.8	4.4	4.1	3.9	3.7
Real exchange rate	-0.7	-3.8	-3.0	-27.3	-29.7	-29.9	-23.4	-11.0	-8.2	-10.2	-11.5	-12.2	-13.1

ROECD

Output gap	-0.8	-2.2	-4.2	-4.8	-5.0	-5.9	-6.9	-5.0	-4.1	-3.0	-2.1	-1.5	-1.3
Inflation	7.6	10.1	10.0	11.0	11.1	9.0	7.1	4.6	4.7	5.1	6.0	6.7	7.2
Long interest rate	7.7	9.8	11.0	11.9	10.5	8.8	7.1	5.8	6.5	6.5	6.6	6.7	6.8
Short interest rate	6.2	7.0	7.6	9.9	10.9	11.3	8.1	7.5	5.0	3.5	3.1	3.5	4.1
Trade balance	-2.0	-1.4	-1.9	1.0	0.4	-0.1	-0.5	-1.1	-1.4	-1.5	-1.4	-1.2	-1.2
Budget deficit	3.1	3.6	4.2	3.0	2.8	2.6	2.2	2.1	2.2	1.9	1.6	1.4	1.4
Real exchange rate	-0.2	-4.7	-1.6	-27.8	-29.2	-27.6	-22.5	-11.8	-10.3	-11.5	-12.8	-13.4	-13.8

Table 6. Exogenous Policy Changes and Shocks
(Five-year expectations)

		1979	1980	1981	1982	1983
U.S. budget deficit	%Y	−1.7	−1.7	−1.7	−1.6	−1.6
Japanese budget deficit	%Y	4.5	4.5	4.5	4.5	4.6
German budget deficit	%Y	3.8	3.8	3.7	3.7	3.7
OPEC oil prices	%	26.7	28.5	30.5	32.5	34.5
Loans to developing countries	%Y	0.0	0.0	0.0	0.0	0.0

		1980	1981	1982	1983	1984
U.S. budget deficit	%Y	−0.3	−0.1	0.1	0.2	0.3
Japanese budget deficit	%Y	4.4	4.0	3.1	3.1	3.1
German budget deficit	%Y	3.3	3.3	3.4	3.5	3.6
OPEC oil prices	%	67.1	71.1	74.4	77.3	80.7
Loans to developing countries	%Y	0.0	0.0	0.0	0.0	0.0

		1981	1982	1983	1984	1985
U.S. budget deficit	%Y	0.3	0.5	0.7	0.8	0.9
Japanese budget deficit	%Y	4.0	3.8	3.8	3.8	3.9
German budget deficit	%Y	3.5	3.7	3.8	3.9	4.0
OPEC oil prices	%	91.9	95.9	99.9	103.5	107.0
Loans to developing countries	%Y	0.0	0.0	0.0	0.0	0.0

		1982	1983	1984	1985	1986
U.S. budget deficit	%Y	2.8	3.5	3.9	4.1	4.3
Japanese budget deficit	%Y	3.7	3.8	3.9	3.9	4.0
German budget deficit	%Y	2.6	2.6	2.6	2.9	3.1
OPEC oil prices	%	72.4	72.7	70.6	68.1	65.7
Loans to developing countries	%Y	0.0	0.0	0.0	0.0	0.0

		1983	1984	1985	1986	1987
U.S. budget deficit	%Y	3.5	3.9	4.2	4.4	4.3
Japanese budget deficit	%Y	3.5	3.7	3.7	3.7	3.7
German budget deficit	%Y	1.9	1.9	1.9	2.1	2.2
OPEC oil prices	%	67.5	66.4	63.7	61.3	59.2
Loans to developing countries	%Y	1.0	1.0	1.0	1.0	1.0

		1984	1985	1986	1987	1988
U.S. budget deficit	%Y	3.7	3.9	4.0	3.9	3.7
Japanese budget deficit	%Y	2.5	2.7	2.7	2.7	2.7
German budget deficit	%Y	0.5	0.9	1.0	1.1	1.2
OPEC oil prices	%	49.3	47.3	44.5	42.2	39.6
Loans to developing countries	%Y	1.0	1.0	1.0	1.0	1.0

Table 6 (*concluded*).

		1986	1987	1988	1989	1990
U.S. budget deficit	%Y	3.5	3.7	3.6	3.5	3.4
Japanese budget deficit	%Y	1.6	1.8	1.7	1.7	1.7
German budget deficit	%Y	1.0	1.2	1.3	1.3	1.3
OPEC oil prices	%	41.1	38.7	36.3	33.7	31.1
Loans to developing countries	%Y	1.0	1.0	1.0	1.0	1.0
		1986	1987	1988	1989	1990
U.S. budget deficit	%Y	2.5	2.0	1.6	1.6	1.6
Japanese budget deficit	%Y	1.4	1.5	1.7	2.0	2.3
German budget deficit	%Y	1.2	1.3	1.2	1.1	0.9
OPEC oil prices	%	7.9	6.6	5.9	5.7	6.2
Loans to developing countries	%Y	1.0	1.0	1.0	1.0	1.0
		1987	1988	1989	1990	1991
U.S. budget deficit	%Y	2.1	1.7	1.6	1.7	1.8
Japanese budget deficit	%Y	1.9	2.0	2.3	2.7	3.0
German budget deficit	%Y	1.6	1.7	1.7	1.8	1.7
OPEC oil prices	%	8.6	7.0	6.9	7.6	8.4
Loans to developing countries	%Y	1.0	1.0	1.0	1.0	1.0

Note: %Y = deviation from baseline as percent of GDP; % = percent deviation from baseline.

owing to the fiscal consolidation in Germany from 1983 on. The U.S. trade balance deteriorates, partly the result of the strong dollar crowding out net exports but also because of the cessation of loans to developing countries.

The turnaround in the dollar from 1985 on is associated with a belief in partial fiscal adjustment in the United States associated with the Gramm-Rudman-Hollings legislation, as well as a loosening of monetary policy in the United States and monetary tightening in Germany and Japan. The dollar continues to fall during 1986 and 1987 because of expected U.S. monetary loosening, U.S. fiscal adjustment, and small announced fiscal expansions in Germany and Japan. This depreciation is halted in 1988, owing to a reassessment of the U.S. fiscal position. Inflation does not pick up significantly in the United States because of the fall in oil prices.

Several of the key points illustrated in Table 5 are that the model misses some turning points—that the strong U.S. economy in 1984 does not show up in the model until 1985. In addition, the model has the U.S. economy growing faster than experienced (as far as current data estimates are concerned, but these have been revised upward since constructing Table 4). By 1985 the model captures the change in real exchange rates and trade imbalances very well. The adjustments from 1986 to 1988 are not as clear. The U.S. trade deficit improves faster than experienced during 1986 and 1987, but actually worsens by 1989. The Japanese real exchange rate depreciates in 1986 and 1987, but settles to a level that is about 10 percent above that experienced during this period.

IV. Appropriate Policies to Relieve Current Imbalances

To assess the current position of the Group of Three economies and possible action to reduce the U.S. trade deficit, we use the model to generate 1986 (the year of calibration of the data) and solve forward one year at a time to generate a path to 1993.

The technique for generating the baseline essentially involves adding constants to key behavioral equations such as investment, consumption, and money demand. The values of these constants are calculated so that when the model is solved for 1986—conditional on all future expected exogenous variables—the jumping variables (that is, Tobin's q, human wealth, and so forth) in the model are equal to the assumed values in the data set for 1986. The same technique could be applied to generating a baseline from 1979. This will be the focus of future work.

Note that Table 7 presents the levels of variables rather than deviations from some level. All quantity variables are expressed as a percent of GNP. Exchange rates are shown in terms of percentage changes from 1986.

These results show a world economy that grows quickly in 1987, owing to expansionary monetary policy—particularly in the United States. The output gap in the United States falls to 0.55 percent from 3 percent, implying a real growth rate of about 5.4 percent in 1987. The growth rate then levels out at 2.9 percent in 1988 and drops below 3 percent out to 1993, a result of rising real interest rates. The U.S. fiscal deficit is assumed to remain at about 2.3 percent of GNP over the horizon of the simulation, resulting in little improvement in the U.S. trade deficit. Inflation continues to rise throughout the period. The U.S. real exchange rate depreciates sharply in 1987, by 20.4 percent relative to the yen. Note that the exchange rates are shown as a percentage change from an index based in 1986. The outcome for the U.S.-Japanese bilateral real exchange rate in 1988 is a 16.5 percent depreciation relative to 1986, but this constitutes a 4 percent appreciation relative to 1987.

The Japanese economy slows down from 1988, owing primarily to rising real world interest rates and a slowing U.S. economy. The German economy grows consistently above trend from 1988 on, which gradually reduces the larger initial output gap.

Tables 8 through 10 give the deviations from this baseline of alternative policy scenarios announced in 1989. In Table 8 we show a gradual U.S. fiscal contraction sufficient to almost balance the budget in 1993. This package consists of a 1 percent cut in government expenditures in 1989 and then a 0.5 percent cumulative cut from 1990 to 1993. The announcement of the credible package lowers long-term real interest rates by 3.6 percent. This stimulates demand in the first year of the announcement, but over time the negative output effects of a declining government sector slows the U.S. economy. Note that the rest of the world does not necessarily suffer a slowdown from the U.S. fiscal reduction because of the positive effects of lower world real interest rates. The real exchange rate depreciates by 9.2 percent on the announcement of a credible fiscal package in 1989; it gradually depreciates so that by 1993 the real exchange rate is 13 percent below its level in 1988. Also notice that the gradual fiscal contraction improves the U.S. trade balance by 0.93 percent of GNP by 1991. This shows that a cut in the U.S. fiscal deficit to 0.5 percent of GNP by 1993 is not sufficient to remove the U.S. trade deficit. Fiscal adjustment in the rest of the world would aid in this process, but it would not necessarily be a good idea since a shuffling of world fiscal deficits would still constitute a drain on world savings. These results suggest that calls for a fiscal expansion in the rest of the world should not only be based on the need to offset a world economic slowdown.

Tables 9 and 10 give results for the same U.S. fiscal cut, but with U.S. monetary policy stabilizing U.S. unemployment in Table 9, and with this—as well as German and Japanese policy stabilizing inflation—in Table 10. The U.S. policy response is a monetary contraction in 1989, followed by a sustained monetary expansion from 1990 on. By 1991 we see that the monetary policy response slightly enhances the trade balance improvement, but at the expense of higher inflation than under the scenario of no U.S. monetary response.

V. Performance of Alternative Global Regimes

This section uses the MSG2 model to analyze the performance of different regimes in the face of seven shocks to the world economy. These shocks include shocks to OPEC oil prices, and real demand and money demand in the Group of Three countries. We calculate the stochastic steady-state variance of a range of variables, conditional on the assumption that the shocks are independent and have unit variance. An alternative procedure would be to use an estimated variance-covariance matrix of shocks from an estimated model, as used by Taylor (1988) and Frenkel and others (this volume). We do not undertake this exercise but examine each shock separately

Table 7. Model Baseline from 1986 to 1992
(Levels of variables)

	1986	1987	1988	1989	1990	1991	1992
United States							
Output gap	-3.00	-0.55	-0.65	-0.82	-1.14	-1.47	-1.77
Trade balance[1]	-3.64	-2.91	-2.96	-3.01	-3.00	-2.97	-2.91
Trade balance[2]	-151.77	-121.23	-123.53	-129.02	-132.65	-135.06	-136.61
Budget deficit[1]	3.50	2.10	1.96	2.03	2.13	2.23	2.33
Inflation	2.00	4.71	4.87	5.23	5.33	5.37	5.37
Short interest rate	7.00	7.89	7.12	7.04	7.03	7.09	7.17
Japan							
Output gap	-2.00	-1.64	-1.11	-1.83	-1.80	-1.78	-1.76
Trade balance[1]	4.84	2.96	3.31	3.18	3.20	3.20	3.20
Trade balance[2]	94.77	57.97	64.84	64.19	66.50	68.49	70.49
Budget deficit[1]	0.90	1.63	1.47	1.67	1.66	1.65	1.64
Inflation	0.50	-0.28	-0.02	2.08	1.27	1.42	1.51
Short interest rate	4.50	5.36	3.64	3.67	3.38	3.31	3.37
Real exchange rate[3]	0.00	20.43	16.50	16.99	16.32	16.03	15.95
Germany, Fed. Rep. of							
Output gap	-10.00	-9.90	-8.98	-8.55	-8.11	-7.70	-7.33
Trade balance[1]	6.22	4.91	4.27	4.38	4.42	4.43	4.42
Trade balance[2]	55.35	43.68	38.04	40.11	41.74	43.10	44.31
Budget deficit[1]	1.10	1.51	2.18	2.05	1.91	1.78	1.67
Inflation	-0.00	-0.34	-0.27	0.09	0.33	0.50	0.60
Short interest rate	4.00	4.24	4.09	3.20	2.75	2.52	2.40
Real exchange rate[3]	0.00	13.30	12.24	10.16	8.98	8.36	8.15

REMS

Output gap	−10.00	−10.85	−10.81	−10.28	−9.96	−9.75	−9.60
Trade balance[1]	−1.09	−1.89	−1.54	−1.26	−1.08	−0.97	−0.89
Trade balance[2]	−17.54	−30.25	−24.64	−20.73	−18.44	−16.99	−16.02
Budget deficit[1]	4.00	4.16	4.18	4.04	3.95	3.88	3.83
Inflation	−0.00	−0.71	−0.77	−0.05	0.34	0.56	0.69
Short interest rate	4.00	4.24	4.09	3.20	2.75	2.52	2.40
Real exchange rate[3]	0.00	13.00	11.22	8.90	7.70	7.16	7.05

ROECD

Output gap	−6.00	−5.92	−6.14	−5.94	−5.66	−5.39	−5.18
Trade balance[1]	0.18	−0.57	−0.54	−0.69	−0.83	−0.98	−1.15
Trade balance[2]	3.58	−11.09	−10.43	−13.83	−17.11	−20.84	−25.26
Budget deficit[1]	4.00	3.96	4.03	3.96	3.87	3.79	3.72
Inflation	4.00	3.81	3.37	3.37	3.47	3.58	3.65
Short interest rate	8.00	8.10	6.70	6.01	5.61	5.38	5.24
Real exchange rate[3]	−0.00	11.71	10.36	9.00	8.17	7.82	7.86

[1]Percent of GDP.
[2]Billion U.S. dollars in constant 1986 prices.
[3]Percent change in an index based in 1986.

Table 8. Response to Announced Gradual U.S. Fiscal Contraction
(Deviation from baseline)

		1989	1990	1991	1992	1993
United States						
GDP	%Y	0.67	− 0.20	− 0.91	− 1.47	− 1.88
Private consumption	%Y	0.26	− 0.17	− 0.48	− 0.67	− 0.72
Private investment	%Y	0.40	0.31	0.28	0.32	0.39
Government consumption	%Y	− 0.80	− 1.60	− 2.40	− 3.20	− 4.00
Exports	%Y	0.48	0.59	0.73	0.87	1.03
Imports	%Y	− 0.33	− 0.68	− 0.96	− 1.20	− 1.42
Trade balance	%Y	0.55	0.73	0.93	1.13	1.32
Budget deficit	%Y	− 0.97	− 1.46	− 2.00	− 2.60	− 3.25
Inflation	D	1.17	0.85	0.34	− 0.30	− 1.08
Short nominal interest rate	D	2.43	1.92	0.92	− 0.86	− 3.64
Long nominal interest rate	D	− 3.58	− 4.06	− 4.54	− 4.98	− 5.31
Japan						
GDP	%Y	0.27	0.00	0.04	0.08	0.14
Trade balance	%Y	− 0.80	− 0.92	− 1.02	− 1.11	− 1.12
Inflation	D	− 0.15	− 0.17	− 0.62	− 0.82	− 1.17
Exchange rate (dollar/yen)	%	10.08	11.72	13.42	14.98	15.89
Real exchange rate	%	9.17	10.00	10.91	12.10	13.06
Germany, Fed. Rep. of						
GDP	%Y	0.30	0.20	0.22	0.24	0.17
Trade balance	%Y	− 0.75	− 0.85	− 0.95	− 1.02	− 1.00
Inflation	D	0.09	− 0.30	− 0.49	− 0.69	− 0.96
Exchange rate (dollar/DM)	%	9.09	10.67	12.29	13.56	14.04
Real exchange rate	%	8.23	8.85	9.82	10.86	11.59
REMS						
GDP	%Y	0.21	0.16	0.19	0.19	0.05
Trade balance	%Y	− 0.86	− 0.98	− 1.08	− 1.14	− 1.04
Inflation	D	− 0.19	− 0.35	− 0.52	− 0.73	− 1.02
Exchange rate (dollar/EMS)	%	9.09	10.67	12.29	13.56	14.04
Real exchange rate	%	8.24	8.82	9.76	10.77	11.44
ROECD						
GDP	%Y	0.43	0.24	0.16	0.11	0.02
Trade balance	%Y	− 0.61	− 0.73	− 0.85	− 0.97	− 1.05
Inflation	D	0.08	− 0.15	− 0.37	− 0.62	− 0.93
Exchange rate (dollar/OEC)	%	7.84	9.22	10.61	11.69	12.05
Real exchange rate	%	7.07	7.64	8.48	9.38	10.02
Developing Countries						
Trade balance	%U	0.34	0.30	0.21	0.04	− 0.44
Terms of trade	%	6.04	6.36	6.92	7.54	7.80
Oil Exporting Countries						
Trade balance	%U	− 0.02	− 0.01	− 0.00	0.07	0.32
Terms of trade	%	6.17	6.58	7.32	8.27	9.31

Note: %Y = deviation from baseline as percent of GDP; D = deviation from baseline; % = percent deviation from baseline; %U = deviation from baseline as percent of U.S. GNP.

Table 9. Response to Announced Gradual U.S. Fiscal Contraction with U.S. Monetary Policy Stabilizing Employment
(Deviation from baseline)

		1989	1990	1991	1992	1993
United States						
GDP	%Y	−0.18	−0.21	−0.20	−0.16	−0.09
Private consumption	%Y	−0.26	−0.26	−0.19	−0.05	0.24
Private investment	%Y	0.09	0.32	0.57	0.83	1.06
Government consumption	%Y	−0.80	−1.60	−2.40	−3.20	−4.00
Exports	%Y	0.40	0.63	0.86	1.07	1.27
Imports	%Y	−0.38	−0.70	−0.97	−1.19	−1.34
Trade balance	%Y	0.53	0.79	1.04	1.26	1.45
Budget deficit	%Y	−0.70	−1.45	−2.22	−3.00	−3.81
Inflation	D	0.55	1.13	1.57	1.90	2.04
Short nominal interest rate	D	5.89	5.42	4.45	2.35	−3.75
Long nominal interest rate	D	−3.05	−3.76	−4.49	−5.20	−5.80
Japan						
GDP	%Y	0.43	0.01	0.04	0.08	0.14
Trade balance	%Y	−0.76	−1.05	−1.21	−1.33	−1.30
Inflation	D	−0.01	−0.15	−0.92	−1.16	−1.42
Exchange rate (dollar/yen)	%	7.64	12.34	17.21	22.39	27.12
Real exchange rate	%	7.44	11.15	13.76	16.08	17.49
Germany, Fed. Rep. of						
GDP	%Y	0.58	0.32	0.23	0.20	0.04
Real trade balance	%Y	−0.74	−0.98	−1.14	−1.24	−1.13
Inflation	D	−0.09	−0.30	−0.65	−0.95	−1.31
Exchange rate (dollar/DM)	%	7.03	11.34	15.92	20.58	24.60
Real exchange rate	%	6.93	10.06	12.65	14.65	15.45
REMS						
GDP	%Y	0.62	0.33	0.20	0.11	−0.20
Trade balance	%Y	−0.96	−1.19	−1.34	−1.38	−1.08
Inflation	D	0.01	−0.35	−0.72	−1.03	−1.42
Exchange rate (dollar/EMS)	%	7.03	11.34	15.92	20.58	24.60
Real exchange rate	%	7.00	10.09	12.62	14.55	15.20
ROECD						
GDP	%Y	0.68	0.33	0.18	0.11	0.01
Trade balance	%Y	−0.50	−0.82	−1.05	−1.22	−1.30
Inflation	D	0.31	−0.20	−0.60	−0.95	−1.30
Exchange rate (dollar/OEC)	%	5.56	9.78	14.18	18.70	22.68
Real exchange rate	%	5.55	8.75	11.23	13.10	13.88
Developing Countries						
Trade balance	%U	0.70	0.60	0.40	0.06	−0.81
Terms of trade	%	5.25	7.41	9.09	10.37	10.56
Oil Exporting Countries						
Trade balance	%U	−0.34	−0.21	−0.06	0.15	0.68
Terms of trade	%	4.69	7.24	9.41	11.35	12.91

Note: %Y = deviation from baseline as percent of GDP; D = deviation from baseline; % = percent deviation from baseline; %U = deviation from baseline as percent of U.S. GNP.

**Table 10. Response to Announced Gradual U.S. Fiscal Contraction with
U.S. Monetary Policy Stabilizing Employment and Japanese and German
Monetary Policy Targeting Inflation**
(Deviation from baseline)

		1989	1990	1991	1992	1993
United States						
GDP	%Y	−0.18	−0.19	−0.16	−0.11	−0.03
Private consumption	%Y	−0.25	−0.24	−0.16	−0.00	−0.30
Private investment	%Y	0.11	0.35	0.61	0.87	1.10
Government consumption	%Y	−0.80	−1.60	−2.40	−3.20	−4.00
Exports	%Y	0.38	0.61	0.84	1.05	1.26
Imports	%Y	−0.38	−0.69	−0.95	−1.17	−1.31
Trade balance	%Y	0.51	0.77	1.00	1.22	1.42
Budget deficit	%Y	−0.70	−1.46	−2.23	−3.02	−3.83
Inflation	D	0.54	1.09	1.50	1.78	1.89
Short nominal interest rate	D	5.95	5.38	4.31	1.98	−4.08
Long nominal interest rate	D	−3.14	−3.87	−4.61	−5.31	−5.89
Japan						
GDP	%Y	0.44	0.02	0.04	0.09	0.15
Trade balance	%Y	−0.77	−1.07	−1.22	−1.32	−1.25
Inflation	D	0.00	−0.00	−0.00	0.00	0.00
Exchange rate (dollar/yen)	%	7.52	12.04	15.70	19.39	22.59
Real exchange rate	%	7.33	11.05	13.45	15.56	17.02
Germany, Fed. Rep. of						
GDP	%Y	0.49	0.57	0.77	1.02	1.15
Real trade balance	%Y	−0.81	−0.95	−1.05	−1.11	−0.83
Budget deficit	%Y	−0.20	−0.24	−0.32	−0.41	−0.45
Labor demand	%	0.81	0.89	1.14	1.43	1.51
Inflation	D	−0.00	−0.00	0.00	−0.00	−0.00
Exchange rate (dollar/DM)	%	7.32	10.50	13.72	16.85	18.65
Real exchange rate	%	7.16	9.45	11.37	12.87	12.85
REMS						
GDP	%Y	0.51	0.57	0.72	0.87	0.88
Trade balance	%Y	−1.02	−1.14	−1.22	−1.21	−0.79
Inflation	D	−0.10	−0.02	−0.02	−0.05	−0.04
Exchange rate (dollar/EMS)	%	7.32	10.50	13.72	16.85	18.65
Real exchange rate	%	7.21	9.46	11.35	12.79	12.68
ROECD						
GDP	%Y	0.76	0.35	0.20	0.15	0.05
Trade balance	%Y	−0.49	−0.86	−1.11	−1.30	−1.38
Inflation	D	0.40	−0.26	−0.72	−1.09	−1.49
Exchange rate (dollar/ OEC)	%	5.39	9.47	13.71	18.08	21.84
Real exchange rate	%	5.42	8.53	10.83	12.54	13.10
Developing Countries						
Trade balance	%GNP	0.76	0.65	0.43	0.06	−0.92
Terms of trade	%	5.28	7.17	8.60	9.66	9.60

Table 10 (concluded).

		1989	1990	1991	1992	1993
Oil Exporting Countries						
Trade balance	%GNP	−0.36	−0.22	−0.07	0.16	0.70
Terms of trade	%	4.64	6.92	8.84	10.58	12.01

Note: %Y = deviation from baseline as percent of GDP; D = deviation from baseline; % = percent deviation from baseline.

assuming no covariation between shocks. The technique is outlined in McKibbin and Sachs (1986).

The Regimes

A regime in this paper is defined as a set of rules for monetary and fiscal policies in the Group of Three economies of Germany, Japan, and the United States. The rules can be general—such as a feedback rule linking monetary and fiscal policies to all observed variables in the economy based on the full optimization of a control problem—or a specific restriction on this rule, such as targeting exchange rates or nominal income.[7]

The regimes we consider include closed economy rules in a world of floating exchange rates, and rules that take into account interdependence in the world economy by requiring some form of coordination of policies among countries. When rules only specify restrictions on the use of monetary policies, we make two alternative assumptions about fiscal policy: either it does not change or it is chosen by each country noncooperatively to reach objectives of inflation, unemployment, and fiscal deficits within the restriction imposed by the monetary regime.

The regimes considered in this paper are listed in Table 11. They are grouped according to those that allow exchange rates to fluctuate and those that impose a fixed exchange rate. In discussing these regimes, it is important to note that where both monetary and fiscal policies are specified, they are usually assigned by the proponents to particular targets. We do not deal with the assignment problem directly in this paper, but merely specify the set of targets and the set of instruments and allow the algorithm used to solve the model to calculate the optimal assignment. In general, it is unlikely that in this assignment all the responsibility for one target would fall on one instrument.

The technicalities of our solution can be found in McKibbin and Sachs (1986). It is worth briefly mentioning the form the solution takes. The general problem facing policymakers is assumed to be the choice of policy instruments to minimize a loss function that is quadratic in the targets, subject to the

---

[7] Argy (1988) provides a useful survey of many of the regimes examined in this paper.

Table 11. Alternative Regimes
(Based on Group of Three countries)

Floating exchange rates
1) constant money growth rules in each country;
2) monetary policy chosen to target nominal income in each country;
3) monetary policy chosen noncooperatively based on ultimate targets in each country;
4) monetary policy chosen cooperatively based on ultimate targets in each country;

Fixed nominal exchange rates
5) McKinnon Rule I, in which n-1 countries target nominal exchange rates and the nth country targets the Group of Three money stock;
6) McKinnon Rule II, in which n-1 countries target nominal exchange rates and the nth country targets the average price level of the Group of Three;
7) McKinnon Rule III, in which n-1 countries target nominal exchange rates and the nth country targets the total nominal income of the Group of Three;
8) blueprint proposal, in which monetary and fiscal policies are chosen to fix real exchange rates in the Group of Three, target total Group of Three nominal income, and target nominal income in the Group of Three.

Note: In each regime where fiscal policy is not specified, we assume a) that it is unchanged given a shock, and b) that it adjusts within the constraints imposed by the monetary regime to minimize the variance of a set of ultimate targets that we specify for each country.

structure of the economy. The formal problem is presented in Appendix I. When calculating the path for policy we express it as a feedback rule on the observed state variables and exogenous variables in the economy. The rules calculated this way are complicated functions that are unlikely to be followed in practice. It is, therefore, useful to assess the performance of simple rules based on one or two variables.

The first regime we consider is a world of floating exchange rates with each country following the Friedman (1959) rule of targeting monetary aggregates. In the second regime we again assume that each economy targets nominal GNP (see Taylor, 1985), taking as given the policies of other countries. In the third regime, we calculate the optimal time-consistent monetary policy rule for the Group of Three economies, assuming that each country targets a set of ultimate objectives, taking as given the policies of other countries. The result is the Nash equilibrium of a dynamic game among the three countries, which we label "noncooperation." The ultimate objectives are assumed to vary across countries. In each country we arbitrarily assume that inflation and fiscal deficits are targets, but we also include unemployment in the United States. The relative weights are inflation (0.6), fiscal deficit (0.2), and unemployment (0.4 in the United States, zero elsewhere).

The fourth regime is our way of formalizing a cooperative policy rule. In this case we set up the same problem as faced by the individual countries in the noncooperative regime, except we assume that a global planner undertakes the optimization problem to find a monetary rule for each country. In case (a), cooperation is confined to monetary policy, while in case (b) both monetary and fiscal policies are considered. The rule we find is the optimal, cooperative, time-consistent policy rule conditional on the objective functions we have specified for each country. Although these objective functions are quite arbitrary, this regime does give us a standard for comparing the other regimes.

The fifth regime is McKinnon's original (1984) proposal for n-1 countries to target nominal exchange rates and the nth country to target the world money stock. This regime would be expected to work well for negatively correlated shifts in portfolio preferences—as it was originally designed for. The constraint on nominal exchange rates would force countries that experienced a shift away from their currencies to contract monetary policy and the countries with the increased demand to expand monetary policy. The result would be an automatic rebalancing of portfolios without any spillover into goods markets. McKinnon (1988) has subsequently revised this rule to accommodate shifts in global velocity by advocating a world traded good price as the global target; this is called McKinnon Rule II in this paper. McKinnon Rule III is a natural extension of this regime with the global target defined as world nominal income.

The blueprint proposal put forward by Williamson and Miller (1987) assigns monetary policy in n-1 countries to targeting real effective exchange rates within a target zone.[8] The nth country should then target world nominal demand. Fiscal policies in each country are assigned to own nominal demand. The fiscal policy assignment is included in an attempt to tie down the steady-state price level. At first glance there appear to be more instruments than targets since world nominal demand is merely the sum of each individual country's nominal demand. In solving for the rule, we found this only to be a problem when world nominal demand was calculated using a base period exchange rate. When world nominal demand was defined appropriately using current exchange rates, the use of the nominal exchange rate was sufficient to break down the linear dependence of targets. We also assumed that the targeting of nominal demand and real exchange rates was undertaken cooperatively and so avoided any asymmetries from allocating countries to particular targets.

Implications of Regimes for Key Variables

The asymptotic operating characteristics of the eight regimes—including alternative assumptions about fiscal policy (when this is not specified by the regime)—are set out in Tables 12 to 18. The results presented in each table are

---

[8] We cannot at this stage incorporate a target zone in our modeling framework, although the approach of Krugman (1988) may be a future possibility.

Table 12. Asymptotic Standard Deviation of Variables (x 100)
(Shock: oil price shock with unit variance)

Monetary regime Fiscal regime	Friedman rule a	nominal income a	noncooperative a	noncooperative b	cooperative a	cooperative b	McKinnon I a	McKinnon I b	McKinnon II a	McKinnon II b	McKinnon III a	McKinnon III b	blueprint
United States													
Output	3.05	3.81	5.21	4.20	5.11	4.12	3.11	4.79	7.87	6.62	3.82	2.76	3.51
Inflation	4.55	3.89	2.53	2.01	2.57	1.93	4.54	2.63	0.50	0.37	3.79	4.20	2.05
Current account	0.27	0.45	0.83	1.58	0.81	1.21	0.29	0.95	1.31	3.46	0.46	0.87	34.41
Budget deficit	0.95	1.19	1.62	2.60	1.59	1.98	0.97	1.75	2.45	5.35	1.19	1.80	61.10
Japan													
Output	1.12	2.16	4.99	7.45	4.70	8.76	1.09	6.64	5.62	5.78	1.91	6.55	1.55
Inflation	3.64	2.93	0.20	0.00	0.41	0.00	3.49	0.08	1.13	0.58	3.12	0.10	2.19
Current account	0.23	0.22	0.19	0.75	0.18	0.87	0.23	0.23	0.26	0.85	0.23	0.53	9.37
Budget deficit	0.35	0.68	1.58	0.00	1.49	1.22	0.34	0.67	1.78	2.95	0.61	0.71	40.49
Exchange rate	2.45	2.78	10.37	10.77	10.70	16.72	0.00	0.00	0.00	0.00	0.00	0.00	3.82
Real exchange rate	4.67	4.82	4.94	10.90	4.38	17.63	4.85	6.09	3.99	1.51	4.81	4.51	0.00
Germany, Fed. Rep. of													
Output	3.63	2.86	3.12	3.52	2.95	3.59	3.72	5.38	2.91	3.22	3.16	4.76	21.76
Inflation	3.06	1.95	0.12	0.00	0.41	0.11	3.41	0.85	0.75	0.89	2.71	0.66	8.96
Current account	0.43	0.67	1.20	1.99	1.16	1.74	0.40	1.82	1.57	3.94	0.61	2.15	103.55
Budget deficit	1.14	0.90	0.98	0.00	0.93	0.48	1.17	2.04	0.92	1.89	0.99	1.57	138.37
Exchange rate	2.77	3.85	11.59	7.12	9.81	6.95	0.00	0.00	0.00	0.00	0.00	0.00	18.51
Real exchange rate	4.55	3.68	4.92	1.88	4.60	2.32	4.91	5.37	2.46	2.92	4.27	4.89	0.00
ROECD													
Output	2.34	2.39	2.71	2.49	2.65	2.11	2.33	3.60	3.05	6.12	2.35	2.37	32.56
Inflation	4.20	5.16	7.09	6.97	6.93	5.37	4.10	1.79	8.16	13.54	4.86	4.71	47.68
Current account	0.27	0.55	1.08	1.33	1.04	0.78	0.26	1.04	1.55	3.53	0.46	0.66	46.99
Budget deficit	0.73	0.74	0.84	0.78	0.83	0.66	0.73	1.12	0.95	1.91	0.73	0.74	10.15
Exchange rate	2.87	1.45	11.02	12.31	11.25	10.27	2.83	4.13	13.44	25.97	2.06	3.98	244.03
Real exchange rate	2.72	2.67	5.78	8.70	5.68	6.47	2.44	4.96	10.09	20.79	2.73	3.37	188.40

Note: Fiscal policy assumptions are that regime a is exogenous fiscal policy and regime b is noncooperative fiscal policy (except for the optimal cooperative regime, which assumes cooperative fiscal policy).

Table 13. Asymptotic Standard Deviation of Variables (x 100)
(Shock: U.S. money demand shock with unit variance)

Monetary regime	Friedman rule	nominal income	noncooperative		cooperative		McKinnon I		McKinnon II		McKinnon III		blueprint
Fiscal regime	a	a	a	b	a	b	a	b	a	b	a	b	
United States													
Output	25.13	0.20	0.23	0.19	0.23	0.19	16.31	1.90	0.41	0.17	0.24	0.10	0.00
Inflation	21.93	0.21	0.13	0.11	0.13	0.11	11.56	2.36	0.13	0.04	0.06	0.13	0.00
Current account	5.15	0.39	0.37	0.31	0.37	0.33	3.28	8.04	0.33	0.32	0.36	0.37	0.00
Budget deficit	7.83	0.06	0.07	0.14	0.07	0.11	5.08	11.33	0.13	0.14	0.07	0.07	0.60
Japan													
Output	2.35	0.04	0.09	0.11	0.10	0.04	12.99	2.16	0.38	0.05	0.52	0.09	0.00
Inflation	5.04	0.09	0.00	0.00	0.01	0.00	11.89	0.76	0.30	0.04	0.53	0.04	0.00
Current account	1.08	0.12	0.12	0.11	0.12	0.11	0.50	1.60	0.12	0.07	0.12	0.08	0.00
Budget deficit	0.74	0.01	0.03	0.00	0.03	0.07	4.11	5.83	0.12	0.21	0.17	0.27	0.00
Exchange rate	79.63	2.17	1.79	1.67	1.77	1.35	0.00	0.00	0.00	0.00	0.00	0.00	0.00
Real exchange rate	62.69	2.04	1.61	1.52	1.58	1.15	6.92	4.91	0.46	0.15	0.40	0.20	0.00
Germany, Fed. Rep. of													
Output	9.82	0.11	0.08	0.11	0.08	0.11	11.62	6.13	0.23	0.20	0.34	0.24	0.00
Inflation	6.53	0.11	0.00	0.00	0.01	0.01	8.44	2.45	0.21	0.09	0.32	0.11	0.00
Current account	3.12	0.32	0.28	0.23	0.28	0.24	3.56	6.13	0.27	0.24	0.32	0.29	0.00
Budget deficit	3.09	0.04	0.03	0.00	0.02	0.03	3.66	5.90	0.07	0.20	0.11	0.28	0.00
Exchange rate	69.97	1.01	1.37	1.11	1.32	1.06	0.00	0.00	0.00	0.00	0.00	0.00	0.00
Real exchange rate	53.62	0.94	1.05	0.83	1.03	0.79	13.46	3.31	0.63	0.25	0.71	0.28	0.00
ROECD													
Output	5.82	0.55	0.51	0.45	0.51	0.50	6.12	14.21	0.48	0.54	0.55	0.66	0.00
Inflation	7.91	0.73	0.65	0.56	0.65	0.66	11.91	20.77	0.67	0.77	0.81	0.96	0.00
Current account	4.16	0.34	0.31	0.26	0.31	0.30	4.17	8.34	0.29	0.32	0.34	0.38	0.00
Budget deficit	1.81	0.17	0.16	0.14	0.16	0.16	1.91	4.43	0.15	0.17	0.17	0.21	0.00
Exchange rate	73.45	2.67	2.56	2.17	2.57	2.33	41.37	53.95	1.80	1.99	2.28	2.49	0.00
Real exchange rate	57.11	2.29	2.14	1.80	2.14	1.93	30.38	45.57	1.64	1.71	1.97	2.09	0.00

Note: Fiscal policy assumptions are that regime a is exogenous fiscal policy and regime b is noncooperative fiscal policy (except for the optimal cooperative regime, which assumes cooperative fiscal policy).

Table 14: Asymptotic Standard Deviation of Variables (× 100)
(Shock: U.S. real demand shock with unit variance)

Monetary regime / Fiscal regime	Friedman rule a	nominal income a	noncooperative a	b	cooperative a	b	McKinnon I a	b	McKinnon II a	b	McKinnon III a	b	blueprint
United States													
Output	136.41	33.27	38.70	32.23	38.14	31.63	155.59	14.89	69.15	28.15	39.67	17.01	0.00
Inflation	57.94	35.18	21.74	18.92	22.14	18.18	81.42	7.53	21.03	5.98	9.71	20.93	0.00
Current account	42.85	64.42	60.91	51.57	61.01	55.53	39.11	4.12	54.42	53.16	60.76	61.93	0.00
Budget deficit	42.51	10.37	12.06	24.03	11.88	18.34	48.48	95.09	21.55	24.09	12.36	10.96	100.18
Japan													
Output	42.62	6.36	14.52	17.72	16.68	6.07	7.85	0.85	62.73	9.09	87.04	15.21	0.00
Inflation	39.08	15.46	0.57	0.00	1.16	0.01	10.48	0.28	49.58	6.76	88.53	6.45	0.00
Current account	18.37	19.84	20.51	18.35	20.48	17.68	17.57	1.91	19.52	12.36	19.93	13.19	0.00
Budget deficit	13.50	2.01	4.60	0.00	5.28	11.01	2.49	2.57	19.86	34.46	27.56	44.65	0.00
Exchange rate	186.90	361.66	297.62	277.94	295.32	224.43	0.00	0.00	0.00	0.00	0.01	0.00	0.00
Real exchange rate	214.09	340.08	267.96	253.96	262.69	191.72	99.36	15.83	76.28	24.69	66.89	33.23	0.00
Germany, Fed. Rep. of													
Output	72.75	18.80	13.85	18.01	12.51	19.12	30.22	4.79	38.08	33.05	57.38	39.89	0.00
Inflation	43.02	18.68	0.53	0.00	2.43	1.03	16.52	0.88	34.79	15.36	53.03	19.08	0.00
Current account	27.89	52.50	46.47	37.82	46.77	40.28	28.82	3.87	45.19	40.00	53.12	47.53	0.00
Budget deficit	22.91	5.92	4.36	0.00	3.94	4.46	9.52	2.33	12.00	33.12	18.07	46.16	0.00
Exchange rate	147.37	168.85	228.15	185.72	220.39	177.39	0.00	0.00	0.00	0.00	0.00	0.00	0.00
Real exchange rate	170.57	156.01	174.40	138.12	171.55	131.14	75.63	18.63	105.00	41.76	118.24	47.09	0.00
ROECD													
Output	53.26	91.51	84.54	74.20	84.94	83.78	52.38	5.07	80.52	90.14	91.79	110.29	0.00
Inflation	46.19	121.30	107.95	94.07	108.96	109.64	53.08	4.87	111.52	128.32	135.08	160.18	0.00
Current account	29.33	56.12	51.53	44.15	51.76	49.36	28.74	3.20	48.88	52.89	56.34	63.93	0.00
Budget deficit	16.59	28.51	26.34	23.12	26.47	26.10	16.32	1.58	25.09	28.09	28.60	34.36	0.00
Exchange rate	152.54	445.06	426.20	361.63	428.31	388.56	83.45	13.03	299.74	332.02	380.11	415.24	0.00
Real exchange rate	175.50	381.99	355.89	300.00	356.30	322.26	124.36	18.07	272.64	284.21	328.35	348.55	0.00

Note: Fiscal policy assumptions are that regime a is exogenous fiscal policy and regime b is noncooperative fiscal policy (except for the optimal cooperative regime, which assumes cooperative fiscal policy).

Table 15. Asymptotic Standard Deviation of Variables (x 100)
(Shock: Japanese money demand shock with unit variance)

Monetary regime Fiscal regime	Friedman rule a	nominal income a	noncooperative a	b	cooperative a	b	McKinnon I a	b	McKinnon II a	b	McKinnon III a	b	blueprint
United States													
Output	1.02	0.09	0.10	0.10	0.10	0.10	8.21	0.90	0.42	0.08	0.26	0.04	0.00
Inflation	1.79	0.12	0.06	0.07	0.06	0.07	5.70	1.13	0.27	0.05	0.14	0.02	0.00
Current account	0.24	0.02	0.01	0.05	0.01	0.04	1.45	3.78	0.07	0.07	0.04	0.01	0.00
Budget deficit	0.32	0.03	0.03	0.09	0.03	0.07	2.56	5.61	0.13	0.12	0.08	0.01	0.00
Japan													
Output	22.18	0.19	0.52	0.75	0.52	0.70	4.87	1.15	1.05	0.24	1.16	0.17	0.00
Inflation	25.71	0.48	0.02	0.00	0.02	0.00	4.68	0.28	0.62	0.10	0.80	0.08	0.00
Current account	0.63	0.09	0.09	0.12	0.09	0.12	0.14	0.73	0.10	0.04	0.10	0.03	0.00
Budget deficit	7.02	0.06	0.16	0.00	0.17	0.04	1.54	2.17	0.33	0.51	0.37	0.57	0.60
Exchange rate	92.59	4.62	3.09	4.04	3.07	3.82	0.00	0.00	0.00	0.00	0.00	0.00	0.00
Real exchange rate	75.47	4.39	3.16	4.16	3.14	3.92	3.76	2.21	0.79	0.33	0.74	0.26	0.00
Germany, Fed. Rep. of													
Output	2.11	0.15	0.10	0.18	0.10	0.18	5.54	2.92	0.19	0.11	0.10	0.03	0.00
Inflation	1.82	0.13	0.00	0.00	0.01	0.00	4.00	1.15	0.16	0.03	0.08	0.01	0.00
Current account	0.54	0.02	0.04	0.10	0.04	0.10	1.65	2.89	0.13	0.07	0.09	0.02	0.00
Budget deficit	0.66	0.05	0.03	0.00	0.03	0.02	1.75	2.78	0.06	0.07	0.03	0.01	0.00
Exchange rate	1.84	0.13	0.30	0.20	0.26	0.19	0.00	0.00	0.00	0.00	0.00	0.00	0.00
Real exchange rate	2.81	0.20	0.18	0.07	0.18	0.06	6.37	1.56	0.26	0.08	0.15	0.03	0.00
ROECD													
Output	1.06	0.09	0.11	0.17	0.11	0.13	2.86	6.68	0.21	0.14	0.16	0.02	0.00
Inflation	1.87	0.19	0.23	0.34	0.23	0.29	5.63	9.77	0.38	0.21	0.27	0.03	0.00
Current account	0.06	0.04	0.06	0.10	0.06	0.08	1.95	3.93	0.13	0.09	0.09	0.01	0.00
Budget deficit	0.33	0.03	0.03	0.05	0.03	0.04	0.89	2.08	0.07	0.04	0.05	0.01	0.00
Exchange rate	0.95	0.14	0.31	0.58	0.31	0.49	19.56	25.40	1.05	0.60	0.67	0.09	0.00
Real exchange rate	0.90	0.12	0.17	0.42	0.17	0.34	14.22	21.44	0.78	0.47	0.49	0.06	0.00

Note: Fiscal policy assumptions are that regime a is exogenous fiscal policy and regime b is noncooperative fiscal policy (except for the optimal cooperative regime, which assumes cooperative fiscal policy).

Table 16. Asymptotic Standard Deviation of Variables (x 100)

(Shock: Japanese real demand shock with unit variance)

Monetary regime	Friedman rule	nominal income	noncooperative		cooperative		McKinnon I		McKinnon II		McKinnon III		blueprint
Fiscal regime	a	a	a	b	a	b	a	b	a	b	a	b	
United States													
Output	10.86	15.72	16.30	17.03	16.25	16.67	20.19	2.53	70.40	13.06	42.66	6.70	0.00
Inflation	18.22	19.79	10.51	11.97	10.52	11.54	6.80	0.14	45.06	8.63	23.34	2.95	0.00
Current account	2.37	2.73	1.83	8.43	1.81	6.47	2.73	1.10	12.29	11.57	6.90	0.84	0.00
Budget deficit	3.39	4.90	5.08	15.39	5.06	11.78	6.29	3.52	21.94	19.56	13.29	1.87	0.00
Japan													
Output	155.34	31.50	85.90	125.15	86.90	117.39	210.94	25.99	175.09	40.01	194.13	28.78	0.00
Inflation	79.01	80.25	3.43	0.00	2.61	0.00	151.49	12.56	104.25	16.57	132.61	13.66	0.00
Current account	16.86	14.65	15.83	20.04	15.82	19.17	17.75	4.88	17.16	6.75	17.39	5.76	0.00
Budget deficit	49.19	9.98	27.20	0.00	27.52	7.27	66.80	95.75	55.44	84.41	61.47	94.88	100.18
Exchange rate	300.25	769.23	514.58	673.58	511.15	635.86	0.00	0.00	0.00	0.00	0.00	0.00	0.00
Real exchange rate	354.62	730.96	526.20	693.49	523.08	654.16	119.88	34.34	132.04	55.06	123.84	42.48	0.00
Germany, Fed. Rep. of													
Output	20.21	25.20	17.24	30.45	17.06	30.79	3.88	6.19	31.87	18.01	16.04	5.41	0.00
Inflation	16.89	22.44	0.66	0.00	1.34	0.65	2.33	0.81	26.08	5.60	12.68	0.87	0.00
Current account	3.29	3.35	7.02	17.25	6.96	15.85	10.16	4.22	21.33	12.27	14.89	3.46	0.00
Budget deficit	6.37	7.94	5.43	0.00	5.37	2.86	1.22	2.00	10.04	11.96	5.05	2.10	0.00
Exchange rate	11.33	22.47	49.62	32.84	43.21	31.86	0.00	0.00	0.00	0.00	0.00	0.00	0.00
Real exchange rate	22.89	32.58	29.25	11.50	29.40	10.31	10.98	3.03	42.62	13.28	24.48	5.55	0.00
ROECD													
Output	9.97	14.51	18.06	28.09	17.92	22.47	18.71	2.82	35.43	22.81	26.35	3.00	0.00
Inflation	16.85	31.79	38.13	57.11	37.90	47.99	28.62	4.16	63.41	34.98	44.18	5.17	0.00
Current account	4.29	6.09	9.34	16.37	9.32	13.14	10.20	2.84	21.67	14.82	15.40	2.45	0.00
Budget deficit	3.11	4.52	5.63	8.75	5.58	7.00	5.83	0.88	11.04	7.11	8.21	0.93	0.00
Exchange rate	11.90	23.29	51.07	96.35	51.95	81.76	57.83	13.57	174.38	99.64	111.31	15.45	0.00
Real exchange rate	10.72	20.26	27.76	69.84	27.65	56.23	41.98	9.27	129.90	77.05	81.46	10.53	0.00

Note: Fiscal policy assumptions are that regime a is exogenous fiscal policy and regime b is noncooperative fiscal policy (except for the optimal cooperative regime, which assumes cooperative fiscal policy).

Table 17. Asymptotic Standard Deviation of Variables (x 100)

(Shock: German money demand shock with unit variance)

Monetary regime Fiscal regime	Friedman rule a	nominal income a	noncooperative a	noncooperative b	cooperative a	cooperative b	McKinnon I a	McKinnon I b	McKinnon II a	McKinnon II b	McKinnon III a	McKinnon III b	blueprint
United States													
Output	2.84	0.06	0.05	0.05	0.05	0.05	3.68	0.41	0.11	0.07	0.04	0.02	0.00
Inflation	2.50	0.08	0.03	0.03	0.03	0.03	2.56	0.51	0.06	0.05	0.01	0.00	0.00
Current account	0.88	0.03	0.02	0.03	0.02	0.02	0.65	1.71	0.02	0.06	0.01	0.00	0.00
Budget deficit	0.89	0.02	0.02	0.04	0.02	0.03	1.15	2.55	0.33	0.10	0.01	0.01	0.00
Japan													
Output	3.18	0.05	0.07	0.12	0.06	0.14	2.78	0.46	0.07	0.02	0.02	0.01	0.00
Inflation	1.34	0.10	0.00	0.00	0.00	0.00	2.53	0.16	0.06	0.01	0.01	0.00	0.00
Current account	1.38	0.03	0.01	0.02	0.01	0.03	0.10	0.35	0.02	0.03	0.02	0.02	0.00
Budget deficit	1.01	0.02	0.02	0.00	0.02	0.02	0.88	1.25	0.02	0.06	0.01	0.01	0.00
Exchange rate	4.31	0.23	0.07	0.24	0.07	0.33	0.00	0.00	0.00	0.00	0.00	0.00	0.00
Real exchange rate	5.53	0.23	0.02	0.26	0.03	0.35	1.55	1.07	0.06	0.06	0.05	0.01	0.00
Germany, Fed. Rep. of													
Output	36.73	0.47	0.40	0.54	0.40	0.53	1.79	1.31	0.76	0.49	0.81	0.47	0.00
Inflation	26.64	0.39	0.02	0.00	0.02	0.00	1.43	0.35	0.34	0.17	0.38	0.18	0.00
Current account	3.57	0.18	0.23	0.29	0.23	0.29	0.43	1.09	0.27	0.19	0.29	0.22	0.00
Budget deficit	11.57	0.15	0.13	0.00	0.13	0.01	0.56	0.86	0.24	0.36	0.25	0.43	0.60
Exchange rate	93.06	2.58	1.33	1.58	1.31	1.57	0.00	0.00	0.00	0.00	0.00	0.00	0.00
Real exchange rate	88.35	2.56	1.44	1.74	1.42	1.72	2.62	0.73	0.67	0.35	0.68	0.31	0.00
ROECD													
Output	5.51	0.23	0.17	0.22	0.17	0.21	1.33	3.07	0.13	0.16	0.10	0.04	0.00
Inflation	12.32	0.41	0.26	0.33	0.26	0.31	2.55	4.46	0.14	0.21	0.09	0.03	0.00
Current account	3.29	0.12	0.09	0.12	0.09	0.11	0.89	1.80	0.06	0.09	0.05	0.03	0.00
Budget deficit	1.72	0.07	0.05	0.07	0.05	0.07	0.41	0.96	0.04	0.05	0.03	0.01	0.00
Exchange rate	19.40	0.42	0.13	0.09	0.12	0.13	8.71	11.50	0.23	0.49	0.11	0.03	0.00
Real exchange rate	18.09	0.47	0.23	0.22	0.23	0.24	6.33	9.70	0.22	0.39	0.15	0.08	0.00

Note: Fiscal policy assumptions are that regime a is exogenous fiscal policy and regime b is noncooperative fiscal policy (except for the optimal cooperative regime, which assumes cooperative fiscal policy).

Table 18. Asymptotic Standard Deviation of Variables (x 100)
(Shock: German real demand shock with unit variance)

Monetary regime Fiscal regime	Friedman rule a	nominal income a	noncooperative a	b	cooperative a	b	McKinnon I a	b	McKinnon II a	b	McKinnon III a	b	blueprint
United States													
Output	4.52	10.23	8.73	8.38	8.43	8.22	5.61	2.29	18.33	10.97	7.42	3.87	0.00
Inflation	10.42	13.36	4.56	4.62	4.68	4.44	2.64	0.88	10.39	7.96	1.96	0.78	0.00
Current account	2.46	4.81	2.95	4.91	2.89	4.10	1.08	0.65	3.46	10.74	1.50	0.71	0.00
Budget deficit	1.41	3.19	2.72	6.11	2.63	4.50	1.75	1.75	5.71	17.08	2.31	1.17	0.00
Japan													
Output	1.01	8.71	10.98	20.31	10.64	23.39	2.40	2.24	11.80	2.50	2.98	2.07	0.00
Inflation	8.20	16.03	0.43	0.00	0.52	0.00	2.11	0.14	9.43	1.96	1.33	0.15	0.00
Current account	2.00	4.18	2.24	4.17	2.13	4.38	3.57	2.89	3.80	4.24	3.62	2.65	0.00
Budget deficit	0.32	2.76	3.48	0.00	3.37	2.88	0.76	1.12	3.74	9.97	0.94	1.02	0.00
Exchange rate	6.36	38.15	10.99	39.32	11.55	54.67	0.00	0.00	0.00	0.00	0.00	0.00	0.00
Real exchange rate	10.19	38.70	4.01	42.73	4.19	58.91	9.50	2.98	9.20	9.33	9.16	1.32	0.00
Germany, Fed. Rep. of													
Output	85.23	78.38	66.27	89.30	66.69	86.09	137.49	78.30	127.10	82.18	134.84	78.46	0.00
Inflation	18.87	65.09	2.53	0.00	3.00	0.24	65.95	29.95	57.39	28.14	64.00	29.93	0.00
Current account	43.34	30.02	39.00	48.43	39.04	49.00	48.86	36.87	45.71	31.02	48.15	37.24	0.00
Budget deficit	26.85	24.69	20.88	0.00	21.01	1.18	43.31	71.36	40.04	59.71	42.47	71.17	100.18
Exchange rate	164.74	430.19	221.96	263.41	217.82	261.14	0.00	0.00	0.00	0.00	0.00	0.00	0.00
Real exchange rate	191.83	425.94	240.52	289.64	237.42	287.17	115.39	49.74	110.92	58.18	113.98	51.66	0.00
ROECD													
Output	21.77	38.31	28.07	37.43	27.95	34.93	15.74	6.61	20.94	26.85	16.95	6.59	0.00
Inflation	28.86	68.41	43.38	55.78	42.99	51.78	12.89	5.36	23.43	35.29	15.32	5.49	0.00
Current account	10.20	20.59	14.45	19.31	14.32	17.91	6.69	4.88	10.21	15.41	7.51	4.74	0.00
Budget deficit	6.78	11.94	8.75	11.66	8.71	10.88	4.90	2.06	6.53	8.37	5.28	2.05	0.00
Exchange rate	37.19	70.03	21.49	15.81	20.83	20.90	18.81	5.77	38.55	81.16	18.04	5.73	0.00
Real exchange rate	42.34	78.20	38.84	37.13	38.11	40.60	26.08	12.71	36.24	64.21	25.58	14.05	0.00

Note: Fiscal policy assumptions are that regime a is exogenous fiscal policy and regime b is noncooperative fiscal policy (except for the optimal cooperative regime, which assumes cooperative fiscal policy).

the asymptotic standard errors of a range of variables in response to a particular shock drawn from a distribution with unit variance. Note that each result has been multiplied by a factor of 100 for convenience of presentation. Each column contains the results for a particular regime under a given shock. Specific details on each regime are summarized in Table 11. To understand the tables, note that the steady-state standard deviation of U.S. output under an OPEC price shock of unit variance when all countries float and target money is 0.0305 (that is, 3.05 after adjusting by the scaling factor of 100).

Several points emerge from these tables, and from the exercise in general. *First*, each set of policy rules converged and each was stable, except for the blueprint proposal. The rules calculated for the blueprint regime converged reasonably well to stable coefficients, linking the instruments to the state and exogenous variables in the system. In the MSG2 model we can check for the stability of the model by calculating the eigenvalues of the system after substituting in the rules for the control variables. In the case of the blueprint regime, there were two unstable eigenvalues of exactly 1.02 detected. The 0.02 component is the difference between the real rate of interest and the steady-state growth rate in the model. This suggests that several of the asset accumulation equations are gradually exploding at this constant rate. The interpretation of this problem is that the attempt to target real exchange rates leads to instrument instability; the specific problem is with the fiscal deficit. In a model such as the MSG2 model, where intertemporal budget constraints are carefully observed, any policy rule will imply a path for real asset prices as well as a long-run equilibrium solution. Targeting real exchange rates at an unchanging level along the solution path, as well as at an unchanged equilibrium value, is not consistent for some shocks. Another way of looking at this problem is that fiscal policy can directly offset a real shock in the goods market through changes in aggregate demand. However, over time the changes in debt resulting from the spending changes will ultimately require a change in relative asset prices, including the real exchange rate.

This suggests that we need to know the equilibrium real exchange rate at which to target. Does the target zone for real exchange rates explicit in the blueprint proposal (but which we ignore) resolve this problem? Unfortunately, not necessarily. It depends very much on the relation between the equilibrium real exchange rate and the initial real exchange rate, as well as on the nature of the transition path between the two. If the target zone did not encompass the equilibrium exchange rate—or even if it encompassed it but the transition path led to a real exchange rate traversing the bands—the policy response at the band would be sufficient to cause the same instability as we found with a rigid target for the real exchange rate. The information requirement of the blueprint in setting up the bands seems rather extreme. It appears to us that allowing the real exchange rate to adjust avoids the instability and long-run sustainability problems associated with this regime. This will be a focus of future work with the model.

Note that we still calculate steady-state variances for variables under the blueprint proposal, even when some variables will have infinite variance. This is because we are interested in seeing where the instability manifests itself. The technique for calculating steady-state variance can be approximated by imposing a shock on the model and calculating the infinite sum of squared deviations of each variable. The results for the blueprint in the table are calculated by using this approximation for 20 years following the shock so that we can explore the impact of the fundamental instability. As can be seen, the instability takes a long time to emerge for real shocks, but it eventually shows up in the deficit numbers. The regime is indeed capable of offsetting the country-specific real shocks, but it leads to instrument instability. In terms of monetary shocks, the regime also performs extremely well and without the instability problems associated with the real shocks. This is because the shock in the money markets can be completely offset by monetary policy without any fiscal policy implications. Finally, note that for the oil price shock the instability of the blueprint shows up most vividly. In this case the real exchange rates among the Group of Three need to adjust owing to the asymmetry in the countries. The result of attempting to offset this is large fluctuations in fiscal deficits and in current account balances.

Following are the key results of our tabular analyses:

- Cooperation with only monetary policy and with both monetary and fiscal policy is not always welfare-improving since we are imposing time consistency in the optimizing regimes.
- Nominal-income rules dominate comparable money targeting rules (although this is not clear for the oil price shock).
- McKinnon I works well for an OPEC shock, but badly for money demand shocks that are independent in different countries; this deficiency is improved in McKinnon II and McKinnon III.
- Apart from long-run instability, which has already been discussed, the blueprint works very well for all country-specific shocks, but not for the oil price shock.

Not surprisingly, no regime seems to dominate under the full range of shocks considered.

VI. Conclusions

This paper has used the MSG2 model to analyze some of the major issues of macroeconomic policy in the world economy. The model is shown to be capable of tracking many of the large swings in asset prices during the 1980s, although it does overestimate the improvement in the U.S. trade balance in

1986 and 1987 and underestimates the extent of real depreciation of the U.S. dollar since 1985. The model is used to explore the implications of U.S. fiscal policy adjustment from 1989 on. We show that a large U.S. fiscal contraction phased in over a number of years need not lead to a global recession, because the large fall in real, long-term world interest rates resulting from the credible policy announcement can stimulate demand sufficiently to offset the direct demand reduction associated with lower government spending. Indeed, one could argue that the expectation in 1988 that U.S. fiscal policy would adjust owing to mechanical deficit-reduction legislation is the reason behind the current worldwide investment boom.

The paper then examined the medium-term issue of alternative rules for the world economy. The Williamson and Miller (1987) blueprint proposal is found to have a long-run stability problem, at least in the way we implement it in the model. The problem is due to the targeting of real exchange rates at a fixed level. To be fair to the blueprint authors, they do argue for a moving target and indeed recommend a target zone rather than a fixed rate. Nonetheless, our results suggest that the targeted rate has important implications for the sustainability of the rule. The apparent contradiction of these results, compared with Currie and Wren-Lewis (1988) and Edison, Miller, and Williamson (1987), owes possibly to the strict adherence to all intertemporal budget constraints in the MSG2 model—which imposes certain paths for debt accumulation and relative price adjustment—not considered in the models used in these other two studies.

Further analysis of these issues using a range of global models is necessary. We intend to pursue in more detail the problems with the blueprint proposal in future work.

Appendix I
Policy Rules

The problem facing the policymaker in each country is assumed to be the choice of a path for policy (U) to minimize an expected loss function of a set of targets (τ), given the world economy represented by the MSG2 model. This can be written as:

$$\underset{U_s}{\text{Min}} \; E_t \left\{ \sum_{s=t}^{\infty} \delta_s \, \tau_s' \Omega \tau_s \right\},$$

subject to

$$X_{t+1} = \alpha_1 X_t + \alpha_2 e_t + \alpha_3 U_t + \alpha_4 E_t + \alpha_5 \epsilon_t$$
$$_t e_{t+1} = \beta_1 X_t + \beta_2 e_t + \beta_3 U_t + \beta_4 E_t + \beta_5 \epsilon_t$$
$$\tau_t = \gamma_1 X_t + \gamma_2 e_t + \gamma_3 U_t + \gamma_4 E_t + \gamma_5 \epsilon_t \, ,$$

where U = a vector of control variables;
τ = a vector of targets;
X = a vector of state variables (e.g., asset stocks, wages);
e = a vector of jumping variables (e.g., asset prices, etc.)
   where $_t e_{t+1}$ is the rational expectation of e_{t+1} conditional on information in period t;
E = a vector of exogenous variables; and
ϵ = a vector of stochastic shocks.

The optimal time-consistent policy rules we calculate (see McKibbin (1987)) are written in the form:

$$U_t = \Gamma_1 X_t + \Gamma_2 E_t + \Gamma_3 \epsilon_t + \Gamma_{4t} \, ,$$

where the vector Γ_{4t} is a cumulation of all expected future values of exogenous variables and shocks.

The alternative rules used in this paper can be written in this form with different restrictions imposed on the Γ matrices.

References

Argy, Victor, "Monetary-Fiscal, Exchange Rate Policy Rules: A Survey," Working Paper 8854B, Macquarie University Centre for Studies in Money, Banking and Finance (Sydney, Australia, 1988).

Baldwin, Robert, and Paul Krugman, "The Persistence of the U.S. Trade Deficit," *Brookings Papers on Economic Activity* (Washington: The Brookings Institution, 1987), pp. 1–43.

Bruno, Michael, and Jeffrey Sachs, *Economics of Worldwide Stagflation*, Harvard University Press (Boston, Massachusetts, 1985).

Bryant, Ralph, and others, eds., *Empirical Macroeconomics for Interdependent Economies* (Washington: The Brookings Institution, 1988).

Campbell, John, and N. Gregory Mankiw, "Permanent Income, Current Income and Consumption," National Bureau of Economic Research Working Paper 2436 (Cambridge, Massachusetts: NBER, 1987), pp. 1–43.

Currie, David, and Simon Wren-Lewis, "Evaluating the Extended Target Zone Proposal for the G3," Centre for Economic Policy Research Discussion Paper 221 (London: CEPR, 1988), pp. 1–33.

Deardorff, Alan, and Robert Stern, *The Michigan Model of World Production and Trade* (Cambridge, Massachusetts: MIT Press, 1986).

Dixon, Peter, and others, *ORANI: A Multisectoral Model of the Australian Economy* (Amsterdam: North-Holland, 1982).

Dornbusch, Rudiger, "Expectations and Exchange Rate Dynamics," *Journal of Political Economy*, Vol. 84 (Chicago: 1976), pp. 1161–76.

Edison, Hali, Marcus Miller, and John Williamson, "On Evaluating and Extending the Target Zone Proposal," *Journal of Policy Modeling* (New York: Spring 1987), pp. 199–224.

Frenkel, Jacob, and Assaf Razin, *Fiscal Policies in the World Economy* (Cambridge, Massachusetts: MIT Press, 1988).

Frenkel, Jacob, Morris Goldstein, and Paul Masson, "Simulating the Effects of Some Simple Coordinated Versus Uncoordinated Policy Rules," this volume.

Friedman, Milton, *A Program for Monetary Stability* (New York: Fordham University Press, 1959).

Hayashi, Fumio, "Tobin's Marginal q and Average q: A Neoclassical Interpretation," *Econometrica*, No. 50 (Evanston, Illinois: 1979), pp. 213–24.

————, "The Permanent Income Hypothesis: Estimation and Testing by Instrumental Variables," *Journal of Political Economy*, Vol. 90 (Chicago: 1982), pp. 895–916.

Islam, Shafiq, "The Dollar and the Policy Performance, Confidence Mix," *Essays in International Finance,* No. 170 (Princeton, New Jersey: Princeton University Press, 1988).

Krugman, Paul, "Target Zones and Exchange Rate Dynamics," National Bureau of Economic Research Working Paper 2481 (Cambridge, Massachusetts: NBER, 1988).

Lipton, David, and Jeffrey Sachs, "Accumulation and Growth in a Two-Country Model," *Journal of International Economics*, Vol. 15 (Amsterdam: 1983), pp. 135–59.

Mann, Catherine, "After the Fall: The Declining Dollar and Import Prices," mimeographed (Washington: Federal Reserve Board, 1987).

Masson, Paul, and others, "MULTIMOD—A Multi-Region Econometric Model," Part II, *Staff Studies for the World Economic Outlook* (Washington: International Monetary Fund, 1988).

McKibbin, Warwick, "Numerical Solution of Rational Expectations Models, With and Without Strategic Behaviour," Research Discussion Paper 8706, Reserve Bank of Australia (Australia: 1987), pp. 1–20.

————, "The World Economy from 1979 to 1988: Results from the MSG2 Model," presented to the Bicentennial Economics Congress (Canberra, Australia: August 30, 1988).

————, Nouriel Roubini, and Jeffrey Sachs, "Resolving Global Imbalances: A

Simulation Approach," in *U.S.-Canadian Trade and Investment Relations With Japan*, ed. by J. Stern (Chicago: University of Chicago Press, 1988).

McKibbin, Warwick, and Jeffrey Sachs (1988a), "Coordination of Monetary and Fiscal Policies in the Industrial Economies," in *International Aspects of Fiscal Policies*, ed. by Jacob Frenkel (Chicago: University of Chicago Press, 1988).

_____ (1988b), "The MSG2 Model of the World Economy," mimeographed, forthcoming National Bureau of Economic Research Working Paper (Cambridge, Massachusetts: NBER, 1988).

_____, "Comparing the Global Performance of Alternative Exchange Arrangements," National Bureau of Economic Research Working Paper 2000 (Cambridge, Massachusetts: NBER, September 1986); forthcoming in *Journal of International Money and Finance* (Guildford, England: Butterworth Scientific Ltd.).

McKinnon, Ronald, "An International Standard for Monetary Stabilization," *Policy Analyses in International Economics*, Vol. 8 (Washington: Institute for International Economics, 1984).

_____, "Monetary and Exchange Rate Policies for International Financial Stability: A Proposal," *Journal of Economic Perspectives*, Vol. 2 (Nashville, Tennessee: 1988), pp. 83–103.

Minford, Patrick, Philip Agenor, and Eric Nowell, "A New Classical Econometric Model of the World Economy," *Economic Modelling*, Vol. 3 (London: July 1986), pp. 154–74.

Morris, Dirk, *Government Debt in International Financial Markets* (London: Frances-Pinter, 1988).

Oudiz, Gilles, and Jeffrey Sachs, "Macroeconomic Policy Coordination Among the Industrial Economies," *Brookings Papers on Economic Activity* (Washington: The Brookings Institution, 1984), pp. 1–75.

Sachs, Jeffrey, "The Dollar and The Policy Mix: 1985," *Brookings Papers on Economic Activity* (Washington: The Brookings Institution, 1985), pp. 117–97.

_____, and Warwick McKibbin, "Macroeconomic Policies in the OECD and LDC External Adjustment," National Bureau of Economic Research Working Paper 1534 (Cambridge, Massachusetts: NBER, 1985).

Taylor, John B., "International Coordination in the Design of Macroeconomic Policy Rules," *European Economic Review* (Amsterdam), Vol. 28, 1985, pp. 53–81.

_____, "What Would Nominal GNP Targeting Do to the Business Cycle," in *Understanding Business Cycles*, ed. by Karl Brunner, *Carnegie-Rochester Conference Series on Public Policy* (Amsterdam: North-Holland, 1985), pp. 61–84.

_____, "Should the International Monetary System Be Based on Fixed or Flexible Exchange Rates?" mimeographed, Chapter 7 of *International Monetary Policy Rules: An Econometric Evaluation*, 1988.

Whalley, John, *Trade Liberalization Among the Major World Trading Areas* (Cambridge, Massachusetts: MIT Press, 1985).

Williamson, John, and Marcus Miller, *Targets and Indicators: A Blueprint for the International Coordination of Economic Policy*, Institute of International Economics, Vol. 5 (Washington: IIE, 1987).

Comments

Patrick Minford

This is an interesting and impressive paper, both in its technical depth and in the broad sweep of ideas it examines empirically. While retaining the basic New Keynesian postulate of substantial nominal wage rigidity, the authors have otherwise integrated all the structural paraphernalia of intertemporal optimization by firms and consumers—by contrast with the usual approach of estimated consumption, investment, and other functions (or "Euler" equations). To obtain parameter estimates, they use "relevant existing studies" so that the model is not estimated but calibrated. It is solved in a linearized form by an algorithm for finding the saddlepath. McKibbin and Sachs give us a tracking exercise—to check the calibration, simulate some alternative world fiscal and monetary policies, and finally review—by simulation analysis of responses to shocks—virtually all of the suggestions on record for reformed global regimes.

It is a massive undertaking and one cannot but admire such intellectual energy (physical too, no doubt, given the problems of coordinating an Australo-American duo). Not surprisingly—given the ambitious scale of the enterprise—I have a number of criticisms to make, first of the model and second, of the simulation results. Ultimately, I fear that in its present form this model (McKibbin-Sachs Global or MSG) does not provide very helpful answers.

In spite of all the sophisticated intertemporal aspects, the model's key properties derive from its wage equations with their massive nominal rigidity. Apart from Japan, which is attributed with perfect wage flexibility, every country's wage increases are a weighted average of current and the previous year's actual inflation, with a small response to unemployment's deviation from a natural rate; given that inflation is itself determined by wage increases, this imparts a long distributed lag to nominal wage-price inflation, rather like that found in adaptive expectations Phillips curves. For good measure—with the effect of further reducing the tendency of real wages to return to long-run equilibrium—a "hysteresis" effect is added to all of the European Monetary System (EMS) countries' natural unemployment rates, whereby the natural rate rises for a time in response to the actual rate.

There is an intellectual incongruity in finding these rigidities attached, like self-inflicted wounds, to agents of otherwise sophisticated rationality; rather as if one found an old steam turbine in the engine room of the ultra-chic Queen Elizabeth 2.

But the evidence for these properties too is, at least from the empirical work I have done and seen, extremely thin. In Europe it is hard to find, in rational expectations wage equations, much effect of inflation surprises. In the United Kingdom and in Italy, in particular, there is virtually no discernible effect, no doubt because effective indexing has become widespread with these countries' high-inflation experience. Even in the Federal Republic of Germany, the coefficient does not reach 0.5. For the United States the coefficient is also not large. Of course this does not preclude finding wage changes related to price and lagged price changes in equations unconstrained by rational expectations; but given the serial correlation in monetary growth together with the dynamics of transmission, this is quite consistent with the results just mentioned. For rational expectations modelers to reject this evidence of encompassing is odd indeed.

As for hysteresis, the model falls between two stools. There is plenty of evidence of real factors (for example, benefit systems, union powers, and labor market restrictions) raising the natural rates of unemployment in Europe. But these will not conveniently disappear after a lag as the MSG model has it. Given the higher natural rate, there is evidence that European unemployment and real wages adjust more slowly than in the United States, but this appears to reflect the optimal strategies of intertemporally maximizing unions—not a source of hysteresis as usually defined, but then the term has come to acquire a Humpty-Dumpty-like versatility of meaning.

The tracking exercise, as Messrs. Warwick and McKibbin admit, is really a misnomer. The model's errors are not defined here because there is no counterfactual baseline. Instead, we are given the model's responses to cumulative shocks from an initial year. This is interesting because it indicates that the model does have a potential for capturing stylized features of the period, such as large U.S. dollar swings and trade deficits. Constructing a baseline is a major task that would involve estimating time-series processes for the exogenous variables (and perhaps error processes for endogenous equation errors) and simulating the model forward in a rolling fashion to generate overlapping forecasts. I look forward to seeing this at a later date.

The simulations of fiscal and monetary policies produce the hoary old chestnut that the way to set the world right today is to have a U.S. fiscal contraction plus a U.S. and/or a Group of Three monetary accommodation. I would be more willing to believe this if money were not so incredibly powerful in this model, even when fully anticipated, because of the nominal rigidity already discussed; for example, U.S. money contracts in 1989 and then expands, thereby averting a U.S. recession in the early 1990s.

The evaluation of regimes is the main focus of the McKibbin-Sachs paper. There is a tangle over instability in the blueprint proposal; but this occurs because the authors assign fiscal policy to the real exchange rate, thus violating the government's capacity to meet its long-term budget constraint. But that simply rules out this particular interpretation of the blueprint, one that its authors seemed in any case puzzled by.

Otherwise, the regimes all show extraordinarily high variances for at least one major set of countries in the face of at least one set of shocks. A brief look at Tables 12–18 in the paper will confirm that no part of the world can be in favor of any of these regimes, because, for at least one of the shocks, their economies are badly destabilized. The only exception is the United States, which can possibly make do with regimes 3(a), 5(b), 7(b), and 8 (using their notation). This suggests that if the MSG2 model is correct, there can be no agreement on a reformed system, leaving the floating rate as the default (no-agreement) regime.

I expect lovers of coordination, whether Keynesian or not, will not accept this conclusion of a model from the New Keynesian stable. Interestingly, however, it tallies with Taylor's finding from a similar exercise, also in a New Keynesian model with much nominal rigidity, that a floating rate regime is more stable than a fixed rate one.

I too am not inclined to use these results against the coordination case, suspicious as I am of it. For I suspect that what we are seeing here is what happens when global rules with nominal rigidity built into them encounter a model with substantial nominal rigidity and otherwise globally optimizing agents. It is a case of an irresistible force meeting an immovable object.

David A. Currie

This paper by Warwick McKibbin and Jeffrey Sachs covers an enormous range. It describes the properties of the current version of the McKibbin-Sachs Global (MSG2) model, and it discusses how well this model explains the behavior of the world economy during the past decade. The paper examines alternative scenarios for adjusting current account imbalances among the Group of Three countries. It concludes by evaluating eight different regimes that have been proposed as possible candidates for the reform of the international monetary system. Given the range, it is inevitable that the issues are handled with less precision and detail than we might expect. But the compensating benefit is that the paper brings together a substantial body of work in a convenient form, written with considerable insight.

In structuring my discussion, I shall follow the order of the paper, first discussing the properties of the MSG2 model, moving on to issues of historical tracking. I will then consider alternative world scenarios through to 1993, and conclude with an examination of the authors' evaluation of alternative blueprints.

The main features of the MSG2 model have been well described in a number of places, including Bryant and others (1988). As John Taylor's model, it has rational, or model-consistent, expectations, but it is distinguished from Taylor's model in including a full specification of stock-flow relationships and accounting identities. These two features combine to give the MSG2 model its distinctive properties: long, drawn-out asset dynamics that exert a powerful influence on the present through expectations. (These features are not evident from the simulations reported in the paper, since these are cut off after five years.) Some may question—and rightly so—whether such persistent dynamics are a feature of the real world. But I do not see this as a weakness of the MSG2 model. The long, drawn-out dynamics result from the rather inflexible behavior of policymakers, who make once-and-for-all cuts in taxes with no subsequent adjustment of fiscal or monetary policy. Open loop policy simulations of this kind are illuminating, but I am uncomfortable with the combination of intelligent private-sector behavior and stupid, inflexible public policy. These simulations tell us little about how the economy will behave when policymakers strive intelligently to reach certain macroeconomic objectives.

Other features of the model are highly relevant to the issue of macroeconomic interdependence in the international economy. The MSG2 model, for example, exhibits rather small spillover effects among the Group of Three from monetary policy, but quite large spillovers associated with fiscal policy. Floating exchange rates appear to be quite effective in the MSG2 model in insulating output and prices in the rest of the world from monetary policy changes in the United States. But this is not true of fiscal policy. Particularly interesting is that these fiscal spillovers arise primarily through the effect of changes in real interest rates on capital accumulation and the supply side. The general argument for policy coordination rests on adverse spillover effects, implying that uncoordinated policymaking generates undesirable outcomes. These MSG2 model results suggest that we should place rather less emphasis on the monetary policy games and demand spillovers emphasized by Oudiz and Sachs (1984) and others, and more on fiscal policy and supply-side spillovers. It may also suggest that current international policy coordination is heading in the wrong direction, emphasizing as it does coordination among central banks over monetary policy rather than fiscal policy.

For these MSG2 model results to be persuasive, one needs to know how well the model represents reality. On this, the MSG2 model suffers from a serious deficiency, namely, that it is calibrated rather than estimated econometrically. Being in the business of using econometric models for regular forecasting and policy analysis, I find myself inclined to give greater weight to econometrically estimated models than to calibrated ones. But McKibbin and Sachs correctly throw down a challenge to the international modeling groups to test how far their models are able to track the historical past. Although the Brookings comparison of the international models (Bryant and others, 1988) has proved to be enormously useful, it provides only a comparison of model properties and does nothing to help distinguish between those models that track the past well and those that do not. Historical tracking exercises using the international models are rare but would provide useful information. They would also allow us to determine whether, as one would expect a priori, econometrically estimated models outperform calibrated models.

Tracking exercises using models with rational expectations are fraught with difficulties, for reasons noted by McKibbin and Sachs. Thus, the results reported in the paper do not represent a proper replication of the tracking performance of the MSG2 model. They are, nonetheless, of interest, and give an indication of how well the model can replicate the past. I like especially the careful analysis of the importance of revisions to the expected values of the exogenous variables in explaining the movement of asset prices, particularly the U.S. dollar. I would have welcomed evidence on the model's capacity to track current account imbalances, both because of their importance in the 1980s and because of the role of current accounts in driving asset accumulation in the MSG2 model. The model seems to replicate essential features of the 1980s, but its tracking of inflation is somewhat erratic, seriously overpredicting the fall in Japanese inflation in 1983 and systematically underpredicting U.S. inflation during 1980–87.

The section concerned with global scenarios and the correction of current account imbalances examines the consequences, in the MSG2 model, of a gradual fiscal contraction in the United States. This generates a small improvement in the U.S. trade balance and a mild recession in the United States. The Federal Republic of Germany and Japan experience lower inflation, because their exchange rates appreciate, but with no output loss since lower real interest rates boost capital accumulation. McKibbin and Sachs comment on the rather small adjustment of the U.S. current account that results from the fiscal action. They suggest that a matching fiscal expansion in the rest of the world is not appropriate because of the need to raise world savings and lower world real interest rates. But it would have been interesting to have seen the effects of a monetary expansion in Japan and Germany that left their inflation rates largely unchanged in the face of U.S. fiscal expansion. As indicated by the results shown in Table 3 of the paper, it seems at least possible that this would have only a limited impact on the United States, but could offset recession in the rest of the world without raising world interest rates. Unfortunately, we are given insufficient information to be sure on this point.

Finally, let me turn to the evaluation by McKibbin and Sachs of alternative blueprints, or regimes, for the international economy. I had the most difficulty with this section of the paper. This is because it is so abbreviated that important and substantive points are not covered. But it is also because points of substance are at issue.

McKibbin and Sachs seek to evaluate a range of blueprints by examining their consequences for long-run stochastic behavior, or, in technical terms, by looking at asymptotic variances. For most of the regimes, there are sufficient instruments to hit the targets exactly, so that no explicit optimization is required. For the two regimes represented by optimal rules—both cooperative and noncooperative—an explicit loss function is minimized. However, the resulting loss is not reported, even though various statements (for example, that cooperation pays) are made that rest on an explicit welfare comparison. It would have aided interpretation enormously had the resulting loss been reported for all the regimes. The arbitrary character of the loss function could then be allowed for by standard sensitivity analysis, testing the robustness of the conclusions in the face of variation in the parameters of the loss function. In the absence of this, one must struggle to impose one's own judgment on the reported vectors of asymptotic variances.

The paper summarizes fairly the main conclusions of the analysis. These are as follows: First, cooperation pays so that the Rogoff (1985) result does not hold. Second, noncooperation may be dominated by fixed rules, such as the Friedman k% rule. Third, nominal income targeting is superior to monetary targeting. Fourth, in broad terms the best regime is the so-called McKinnon III scheme, whereby monetary and fiscal policy are jointly used to target fixed nominal exchange rates and world nominal income. Fifth, that the extended target zone proposal advanced by Williamson and Miller exhibits long-run instability, although its short-run properties are quite good. To these I would add a sixth conclusion: that the flexible use of fiscal policy is helpful, except where there is an absence of cooperation among governments. This reemphasizes the point I made earlier about the MSG2 model: The presence of appreciable supply-side spillovers from fiscal policy puts a premium on cooperation over fiscal policy.

There are, however, a series of questions that I have about these results.

First, regimes 6–8 do not involve monetary targeting, and should therefore exhibit no fluctuations in the face of money velocity shocks. An essential feature of all these regimes is that they should automatically accommodate velocity shocks. Yet, in the reported results, this does not happen. This occurs presumably because the money supply—not the interest rate—is used as the instrument, but this is an error of specification.

Second, regimes usually regarded as symmetrical, such as the McKinnon or the Williamson-Miller proposals, have been set up in an asymmetrical manner. This may be seen from the fact that U.S. velocity shocks affect the system, while Japanese or German velocity disturbances do not. It is not clear how much this affects the results, but it is clearly a cause for concern.

Third, it is rather dangerous to design policy rules that use instruments to hit targets exactly, as McKibbin and Sachs do, even if there are enough instruments relative to targets. The reason is that while such rules are typically highly activist, they are not robust in the face of parameter or model uncertainty, and they may well generate instrument instability. (The paper by Frenkel, Goldstein, and Masson illustrates precisely this danger.) One should be concerned about this, either by attaching costs to instrument variation or, better still, by explicitly designing policy rules that are robust. This will, of course, mean that targets are hit less accurately, but also that the rules are somewhat less activist, surely a desirable feature in a world of uncertainty. The Williamson-Miller blueprint recognizes this explicitly. It incorporates wide bands that allow "coarse tuning"—rather than fine-tuning—of exchange rate objectives. It also envisages simple policy rules that incorporate both proportional and integral feedback elements. If designed well, such rules should be robust and should not generate instrument instability. Let me therefore enter a plea that we do not overlook elementary control theory when undertaking the ambitious task of evaluating blueprints for the world economy.

Finally, let me turn to the conclusion that McKibbin and Sachs draw concerning the Williamson-Miller extended target zone blueprint. The authors find this policy scheme to be unstable, exhibiting large asymptotic variances in the long run. I have already discussed one possible reason for this—that concerned with the potential instabilities arising from instrument instability— and I have indicated why this should not be a problem. But the principal problem of instability results from cumulatively unstable processes of asset accumulation arising through the external accounts of countries. This occurs particularly with the Williamson-Miller scheme since it is the only regime that seeks to target a set of real asset prices, corresponding to perceived real equilibrium exchange rates (FEERs). If real equilibrium exchange rates are persistently misjudged, the result will be sustained external disequilibrium, and the external net wealth position will rise or fall without limit.

It is clearly possible that governments will misjudge the FEERs, so that for periods of time they will be targeting inappropriate exchange rates (although the width of the proposed bands will limit the consequences of such errors). But it is not plausible that they will persistently and systematically misjudge FEERs for all time. Yet this is what McKibbin and Sachs assume in their evaluation of the extended target zone blueprint. This is what generates the problems of long-run instability that the scheme is said to exhibit. Granted, it is right not to ascribe to governments great insight or speed of response, but this is going to the other extreme. For it assumes that governments will go on targeting their chosen FEERs, ignoring the mounting evidence from a destabilizing current account position that they have made a mistake. For these reasons, I think that we should discount the reported results of the Williamson-Miller blueprint and wait for a more sensibly specified evaluation.

References

Bryant, Ralph, and others, *Empirical Macroeconomics for Interdependent Economies,* The Brookings Institution, Washington, 1988.

Oudiz, Gilles, and Jeffrey Sachs, "Macroeconomic Policy Coordination Among the Industrial Economies," *Brookings Papers on Economic Activity* (Washington: The Brookings Institution, 1984), pp. 1–75.

Rogoff, Kenneth, "Can International Monetary Cooperation Be Counterproductive?" *Journal of International Economics,* Vol. 18 (Amsterdam: 1985), pp. 199–217.

5

Simulating the Effects of Some Simple Coordinated Versus Uncoordinated Policy Rules

Jacob A. Frenkel, Morris Goldstein, and Paul R. Masson*

I. Introduction

Ever since the introduction of generalized floating of exchange rates in 1973, there have been proposals for various policy rules intended to improve the functioning of the international monetary system. Two popular ones are McKinnon's proposal (McKinnon, 1984) for targeting the world money supply and Williamson's proposals for target zones for the exchange rates of major currencies (Williamson, 1985, and Williamson and Miller, 1987). There are many related strands to the literature on policy choice, particularly as regards the exchange rate regime. This includes the early literature on optimum currency areas (Mundell, 1961; McKinnon, 1963; and Kenen, 1969), more recent discussions of the optimal degree of exchange rate flexibility (Frenkel and Aizenman, 1982; Boyer 1978; and Henderson 1979), papers on the theme of rules versus discretion (Fischer, 1988), comparisons of optimal uncoordinated versus optimal coordinated policies in simple macroeconomic models (Buiter and Marston, 1985), and the literature on assignment of instruments to targets and on the policy mix (Tinbergen, 1952; Mundell, 1962, 1971; and Sachs, 1985).[1]

---

* The authors have benefited from conversations with Hali Edison, Warwick McKibbin, and John Taylor, and are grateful to a number of their colleagues, especially Ralph Tryon, for comments on an earlier draft, and also to Stanley Fischer and Jeffrey Shafer for comments made at the conference. Holger Wolf assisted with initial model simulations and Toh Kuan with charts. The views expressed in the paper are the authors' alone and do not represent those of the International Monetary Fund.

[1] For more recent discussion of the assignment problem in the context of floating rates, see Genberg and Swoboda (1987) and Boughton (1988).

The theoretical literature has succeeded in isolating the elements that are most important in influencing the attractiveness of various policy regimes—ranging from the nature of shocks (real versus monetary) to the structural characteristics of economies (the degree of wage indexation, capital mobility, openness, and so forth) and to the elements of the objective function (stabilizing real output, consumption, and so forth); but the evaluation of different policy rules is ultimately an *empirical* question. To date, there have been relatively few examples of the use of empirical models to evaluate different policy rules.[2] This reflects both some skepticism about the reliability of the models themselves, and a recognition of the serious methodological problems involved in simulating different policy regimes in standard models.[3] In this connection, early applications of optimal control theory to empirical macroeconomic models were more successful in isolating implausible features of the models than in yielding insights into policy design (Chow, 1980). Fully optimal rules (or optimal time-consistent rules) also have the disadvantage of being complex and model-dependent, making their implementation less likely.[4] Methodological problems relating to regime changes have been most clearly identified by Lucas (1976), who makes the point that the behavior of the private sector will be affected by changes in governments' policy rules. In particular, a change in the policy regime can change the way the private sector forms *expectations* of important variables.

Recent applications of empirical models to simple international policy rules include Edison (1987), Currie and Wren-Lewis (1987, 1988a, 1988b), Taylor (1985a, 1986), McKibbin and Sachs (1985, 1988), and Frenkel, Goldstein, and Masson (1989). The first two sets of papers use models—namely, the U.S. Federal Reserve's Multicountry Model (MCM) and the Global Economic Model (GEM) of the U.K. National Institute of Economic and Social Research—in which expectations are of the adaptive, backward-looking variety. In these models, changes in policy regime have no direct effect on private sector behavior; instead, their effects operate through changes in market prices and in aggregate demand. In contrast, Taylor's model and the

---

[2] Some early work, by Fischer and Cooper (1973) and Cooper and Fischer (1974), considered monetary and fiscal policy choice in the MPS model (developed at the Massachusetts Institute of Technology, the University of Pennsylvania, and the Federal Reserve System) and in the St. Louis model.

[3] Friedman (1953) argued early on that, given the imperfections of models, the fine-tuning associated with optimal policies could in the real world destabilize the economy. In addition, there is the issue of the time consistency of the resulting policies; see Kydland and Prescott (1977). Because a path for policies that is optimal at t may not be optimal at $t+1$, private agents may not believe that the policies announced at t will actually be carried out. The issue of credibility can be treated in the context of repeated games between the government and the private sector; see, for instance, Barro and Gordon (1983).

[4] Hence the search for simple, robust rules that perform well in all models; see Currie and Levine (1985).

McKibbin-Sachs Global (MSG) model, and our own work, use models that have forward-looking expectations that are consistent with the solution to the model in future periods. In these models, a change in policy rule will change the relationship between expectations and other endogenous variables.

This paper will evaluate some simple rules for aggregate monetary and fiscal policies using a multi-region econometric macroeconomic model (MULTIMOD) developed in the Research Department of the Fund. Unlike the MSG model, whose parameters are calibrated to plausible values and to base period levels for variables, MULTIMOD is estimated using annual data beginning in the mid-1960s.[5] MULTIMOD also includes all of the industrial countries, either separately or aggregated with others, and the developing countries; it is thus a closed, global system, unlike the MCM or the Taylor model. Given these features, MULTIMOD is likely to be a useful tool for policy analysis of international monetary arrangements, though we would not suggest that the answers it gives should be considered definitive. In the light of the discussion above, it is clearly important to examine the *robustness* of rules across different, plausible models.

In this paper, MULTIMOD will be used to compare several simple policy rules. We have classified these policy rules into two categories. One set, which we call *uncoordinated policies*, envisages monetary policy being aimed at either the monetary base or nominal gross national product (GNP). The second set, which we have labeled *coordinated* policies, envisages monetary policy being used to target either a real or a nominal exchange rate; coordinated policies also encompass some more ambitious rules that use both monetary and fiscal policies to target both an external variable (either the real exchange rate or the current account balance) and a domestic variable (nominal domestic demand). Policy coordination has been variously defined in the literature; it has been viewed as " . . . a significant modification of national policies in recognition of international economic interdependence" (Wallich, 1984, p. 85), and as " . . . agreements between countries to adjust their policies in the light of shared objectives or to implement policies jointly" (Horne and Masson, 1988, p. 261). The rationale for regarding the second set of policies as "coordinated" derives from the well-known "n-1 problem," which implies that targets for external variables cannot be set independently. Therefore, targets for nominal or real exchange rates or for current account balances would have to result from some coordination process. Note, however, that the coordination considered here is limited in scope, and should not in particular be confused with joint utility maximization, which is the subject of much of the coordination literature.[6]

Before proceeding to the model simulations, it is useful to consider

---

[5] MULTIMOD is described in Masson and others (1988).

[6] See the papers in Buiter and Marston (1985).

several methodological issues that have, in our view, received insufficient attention.

The *first* one relates to the distinction between a policy rule and a path for some target variable. In Edison, Miller, and Williamson (1987) and Currie and Wren-Lewis (1987, 1988a, and 1988b), a model is simulated over a given historical period with a different policy rule from the one that was actually in place; in this way, the modeler can "rerun history." In practice, this involves replacing the policy reaction function in the model with a new policy rule. However, the *effect* of this new rule depends both on the target that is imposed for that variable relative to its historical path, *and* on the shocks in the historical data. The effect of the new rule will thus depend on two sets of factors whose effects cannot be disentangled by examining the final outcomes alone. Ex post, it is easy to find a target path that, when simulated with a new policy rule, would have given a better result on the basis of some objective function. But the relevance for policy of such simulation results is dubious. A preferable procedure is to distinguish the effect of the choice of values for the target variable(s) from the structural part of the new rule—that is, the response of policy instruments to shocks. In the simulations that follow, the target path is chosen to be the baseline path, and the behavior of each rule in response to shocks is studied explicitly.

The *second* issue concerns the desirability of stochastic simulations versus historical ones. Edison and others (1987) and Currie and Wren-Lewis (1987, 1988a, and 1988b)—because they examine a particular historical period—evaluate their policy rules only on the basis of a short sample of drawings for the errors in behavioral equations. The evaluation is, therefore, specific to a particular historical experience.[7] A more robust procedure is to take many drawings from the joint distribution describing the errors. In what follows, we do simulations both with the historical shocks and with shocks drawn from their estimated distribution. The results should help to indicate which rules perform well in a variety of circumstances.

The *third* issue is the importance of isolating the influence of shocks to endogenous variables from expectations errors. The latter are properly endogenous and depend on the policy rule. In the simulations that follow, drawings are made from the joint distribution describing innovations to structural residuals, while expectations errors depend on the particular rule that is assumed for policy.[8]

---

[7] Currie and Wren-Lewis (1987) are conscious of this limitation; in order to examine the sensitivity of their results, they look at the behavior in 1985–86 of rules with parameters chosen to optimize the 1975–84 period.

[8] There are, however, at least two cases in which the distribution describing structural residuals might also be affected by the policy rule. First, the errors may contain speculative bubbles that may be more or less important under different rules. For instance, there may be

The next section of this paper discusses the appropriate methodology for simulating and evaluating alternative policy rules in a model with forward-looking expectations. Section III describes the rationale of each of the policy rules, as well as the precise form that each rule takes in the simulation exercise. Section IV presents the results—first for the single-shock simulations, and then for the full stochastic simulations. Finally, Section V draws some conclusions and outlines a few possible extensions for future work. The detailed procedures used in simulating MULTIMOD outlined are in two appendices.

II. Simulation Methodology

On first thought, it might seem that if one had a "structural" model—in the sense of Lucas and Sargent (1979)—it would then be straightforward to evaluate different policy rules. One might simply simulate the model over the historical period of interest, changing the structure of the model through the substitution of one policy reaction function for another. Simulated values could then be compared with the historical data, and outcomes could be evaluated using some implicit or explicit criterion function. The policy producing the best results could then be argued to be the appropriate guide for policymakers.

This is the procedure essentially followed by Edison, Miller, and Williamson (1987) and by Currie and Wren-Lewis (1987, 1988a, and 1988b). The former paper argues, for instance, that target zones—based on the fundamental equilibrium exchange rates calculated by Williamson (1985)—would have led to "better" macroeconomic outcomes than observed historically since generalized floating. Currie and Wren-Lewis calculate optimal feedback coefficients for various policy rules, and then evaluate the counter-factual if these rules had been in effect in the period since generalized floating. They conclude that, compared with actual history, the Williamson-Miller (1987) blueprint rule would have led to a substantial pareto-welfare improvement.

Such results are hard to interpret, for several reasons. One pitfall, suggested earlier, is that the models may not be "structural" after all; in that case, the change in policy will not leave unchanged the behavior captured in the rest of the model. In this situation, the model could not be used correctly for policy evaluation—as argued strongly by Lucas (1976) and by Lucas and Sargent (1979). In particular, if the model generates expectations in a mechanistic fashion, the model will not allow expectations to reflect the change in policy as it should.

---

bandwagon effects in exchange rates. Second, if the variances of say, exchange rates and interest rates, change, then unless agents are risk neutral, their demands for assets and goods will change. To the extent that the model does not capture these features, they will be reflected in equation residuals that will not be invariant to the policy regime.

Even if a model is structural, it may be difficult to judge the implication of replaying history for future policy. Typically, the model is first constrained to track history exactly by including the appropriate residuals in each behavioral equation; next, the policy reaction function that relates a policy instrument to one or more intermediate or final target variables is modified or replaced. The following step is the key one: specifying values for the target variables. If historical values are specified as the target values, the model will reproduce the historical data exactly; on the other hand, if different values are given, and if deviations from these targets appear in the criterion function, then (almost necessarily) the "new" policy rule will be judged superior because it tries to resist deviations from the targets. In any case, the evaluation of rules will be specific to one historical episode, and to one set of drawings from the residuals.

Moreover, the reasons *why* a target variable departs from its desired level are not identified in such historical simulations. The deviations from target are the result of a combination of elements: innovations to structural equations, expectations errors, changes in other policy variables, and shocks to exogenous (nonmodeled) variables. The evaluation of rules should depend on the relative importance of these elements.

In an earlier paper[9] we followed the same procedures as Edison and others (1987) and Currie and Wren-Lewis (1987, 1988a, and 1988b): alternative policy rules were simulated by altering the reaction functions for various policy instruments, by imposing target paths that were consistent with those advocated by the proponents of specific rules, and by keeping other exogenous variables at their historical values. Given the forward-looking nature of expectations in MULTIMOD, there was a problem with this methodology: by giving agents knowledge of the future values of exogenous variables, the simulation did not tell us how the economy would respond to shocks. This limited the inferences one could draw from such experiments about the respective policy rules.

There is an alternative procedure that should permit a clearer interpretation of simulation results: it is *not* tied to a particular historical episode, and it can identify the source of deviations from targets. If the model is assumed to be an accurate representation of reality, it is possible to identify the innovations to structural residuals in the historical data. This procedure, which is followed in the simulations of MULTIMOD described below, poses the following well-defined question: how would the economy perform under different policy rules, given that innovations to structural residuals are drawn from the same distribution? The procedure abstracts from other special elements that may affect the historical data. It also abstracts from the choice of the target value, since the target is just set equal to the value of the variable in

---

[9] See Frenkel, Goldstein, and Masson (1989).

the baseline solution to which the shocks are applied.[10] In short, this procedure provides a more straightforward way to evaluate how a given feedback rule responds to shocks.

In the simulation exercises discussed in Section IV, policy rules are compared by focusing on differences in root mean square (RMS) errors for major macroeconomic variables (real output, prices, current account balances, and exchange rates) relative to an arbitrary baseline. The shocks to the major behavioral relationships in the model are consistent with the estimated covariance matrix. A wide variety of shocks is considered. On the industrial-country side, shocks are applied to the equations for each country's consumption (oil and non-oil), investment, commodity imports, manufacturing export and import volumes and prices, non-oil output prices, and money demand. Shifts in portfolio preferences are also assumed to arise, and to explain deviations from uncovered interest parity; the distribution of these shocks is also made consistent with historical data. Finally, shocks to residuals in equations for developing-country exports of manufactures and their supply of commodities are also generated. The serial correlation properties of the errors and the covariance matrix of the innovations are discussed in Appendix II.

As an alternative to performing stochastic simulations, Taylor (1985a) and McKibbin and Sachs (1985,1988) calculate asymptotic variances of endogenous variables that result from shocks to the errors in the model's equations. While convenient, this procedure is applicable only to linear models. Although MULTIMOD is probably sufficiently linear for coefficients to be little changed from period to period (and, hence, expectations for the following period can be formed by setting residuals to zero), over the extended horizon that we consider (1988–2044), asset stock accumulations are a potentially important source of non-linearity. Therefore, we have chosen not to linearize the model but rather to use the more computer-intensive technique of stochastic simulations.

III. Alternative Policy Rules

The policy rules that we consider in this paper fall into three groups. The first group is characterized by *un*coordinated monetary policies and freely flexible exchange rates. The rules that are compared are money targeting and nominal GNP targeting. The second group encompasses two rules that use monetary policy to limit the flexibility of exchange rates. The first rule is a Bretton-Woods-like regime of nominal exchange rate parities; the second rule

---

[10] The choice of target levels may depend on other considerations—for instance distortions that may raise measured unemployment or inflation—but they are not well captured by macroeconomic models. Moreover, the use of baseline values or targets presupposes a degree of knowledge on the part of the policymaker, concerning such things as the level of capacity output or the equilibrium real exchange rate, which may not, in fact, exist.

is a target zone plan that targets a real effective exchange rate. Whereas the first two groups of rules have assumed that fiscal policy is exogenous, the third group contains rules that use *both* monetary and fiscal policy to hit domestic and external variables.

Uncoordinated Rules: Money Versus Nominal Income Targeting

During the 1970s, many central banks moved from a more discretionary monetary policy to explicit targets for monetary aggregates. *Money targeting* was seen as a way of avoiding destabilizing fine-tuning, and of counteracting the alleged bias of central banks to aim for more-than-full employment. In a well-known article, Poole (1970) showed that in the face of shocks to the investment-saving (IS) curve, stabilizing the nominal money supply stabilizes output. In contrast, if shocks are primarily to money demand, the appropriate policy is to accommodate them and to stabilize interest rates.

The widespread evidence that money demand had shifted in the early 1980s as a result of financial innovations and of deregulation led to disenchantment with monetary targeting. Concern for the inflationary consequences of pegging interest rates led to a search for another nominal indicator that could serve as an intermediate target. Tobin (1980) argued that nominal GNP had several advantages over monetary aggregates: it was less sensitive to the shocks facing money demand, and it was not affected by the positive relationship between velocity and the nominal interest rate. The latter feature of money demand could lead to a *fall*, rather than a rise, in *real* interest rates in the face of an inflationary shock. The disadvantage of nominal GNP targeting, however, is that hitting a preset nominal GNP path exactly implies a linear, one-for-one trade-off between changes in the price level and output (Fischer, 1988, p. 17).

Moreover, although both monetary and nominal GNP targeting are susceptible to *instrument instability* (Holbrook, 1972), the problem is thought to be most severe for nominal GNP targeting. Consider the case where the short-term interest rate is the instrument for hitting a target for nominal GNP. The lags in the effects of interest rates on real activity and prices are likely to be "long and variable," and contemporaneous effects, to be small. An attempt, therefore, to achieve a given target in the current period will require the central bank to respond to shocks with large movements in interest rates. In subsequent periods, these interest rate movements will have much larger effects on nominal income. In the absence of further shocks, interest rates will therefore have to move in the *opposite* direction, possibly by more than their initial change. The bottom line is that the potential clearly exists for undesirably large—even explosive—movements of policy instruments.

The following algebraic example may make the basic point more concrete. Suppose that nominal income, Y, responds to the interest rate, R, according to the following reduced-form relationship:

$$Y = -aR - bR_{-1} + u, \tag{1}$$

where a and $b > 0$ and u includes the effects of all other exogenous variables and shocks. Forcing nominal income to track *exactly* some target path, $\bar{Y}$, would imply the following reaction function for monetary policy:

$$R = (u - \bar{Y})/a - (b/a)R_{-1}. \tag{2}$$

If the contemporaneous effect of interest rates is smaller than the lagged effect, so b/a is greater than unity, this reaction function implies an unstable, oscillatory pattern for R in response to a shock to Y. Even if $b/a < 1$, there is still overshooting of interest rates; that is, in response to a permanent positive shock, δ, the interest rate moves more on impact (dR_0) than in the long run $(d\bar{R})$:

$$d\bar{R} = \delta/(a+b) < dR_0 = \delta/a. \tag{3}$$

In order to avoid both instrument instability and overshooting, the central bank could choose not to achieve its target period by period. Instead, it could adjust the interest rate gradually to the level consistent in the long run with the nominal income target; for instance,

$$\Delta R = \alpha(\bar{R} - R_{-1}), \tag{4}$$

where $0 < \alpha < 1$. Alternatively, it could simply resist moments of nominal income away from its target:

$$\Delta R = \beta(Y - \bar{Y}), \tag{5}$$

where $0 < \beta < \infty$. The interest-rate rule in equation (4) is guaranteed to produce a *smooth* adjustment in response to a shock to u; substitution for $\bar{R}$ in (4) yields:

$$R = \alpha(u - \bar{Y})/(a+b) + (1-\alpha)R_{-1}. \tag{6}$$

In contrast, depending on the value assigned to β, the interest-rate rule in equation (5) may also involve problems of instability or oscillation. Substitution for Y in (5) yields:

$$R = \beta(u - \bar{Y})/(1+\beta a) + [(1-\beta b)/(1+\beta a)]R_{-1}. \tag{7}$$

The coefficient on lagged R has to be greater than -1 to rule out instability; this will be true if and only if

$$\beta b < \beta a + 2. \tag{8}$$

To rule out oscillations, we require the stronger condition that the coefficient on lagged R be greater than zero; this is the case if

$$\beta b < 1. \tag{9}$$

In complicated models it is not, however, straightforward to calculate the appropriate values of the feedback parameters. In implementing various policy rules, we have therefore proceeded by trial and error to establish reaction functions of form (4) or (5) that: (i) permit the tightest control over target variables; and (ii) do not simultaneously produce either large swings in instruments or dynamic instability more generally. When interest rates were used to target nominal GNP, or the real exchange rate, or domestic demand, the feedback parameters had in particular to be carefully set.[11]

Simple Coordinated Rules: Real and Nominal Exchange Rate Targets

Target zones for real effective exchange rates, to be defended through changes in monetary policies, have been proposed by Williamson (1985) in order to limit exchange rate misalignments and associated current account imbalances:

> The basic focus of exchange rate management should be on estimating an appro-priate value for the exchange rate and seeking to limit deviations from that value beyond a reasonable range (p. 47). . . . While other techniques, like sterilized intervention, may be able to give limited assistance, a serious commitment to exchange rate management leaves no realistic alternative to a willingness to direct monetary policy at least in part toward an exchange rate target (p. 56).

We use a similar monetary reaction to the one employed by Edison, Miller, and Williamson (1987) to simulate target zones, but augment it with a term that resists movements away from a target for the aggregate nominal GNP of industrial countries.[12] In the absence of such a term, or of some other way of providing a nominal anchor to the system, real exchange rate targeting does not have any mechanism for ensuring price stability (see Adams and Gros, 1986).

---

[11] Concern for instrument instability also influenced the way money targeting is specified in the model. The standard version of MULTIMOD includes a reaction function that makes changes in interest rates a function of the gap between the long-run demand for base money and its target. This specification is admittedly a stylized representation of monetary policy, but it has the advantage of being simple and transparent.

[12] Such a mechanism forms part of Williamson and Miller's (1987) "extended target zone scheme"—discussed in detail below.

Coordinated Monetary and Fiscal Policy Rules:
The Williamson-Miller "Blueprint" and Reversed Assignment

Williamson and Miller (1987) have proposed a "blueprint" for international monetary reform. The proposal goes beyond the original target zone proposal by supplementing the rule for monetary policies with a fiscal policy rule that uses government spending to target domestic demand in each of the major industrial countries. In addition, to avoid inflationary or deflationary pressures and to provide a nominal anchor for the price level, they have proposed that the average level of interest rates be shifted up or down depending on whether industrial-country nominal income exceeds, or falls short of, a target for nominal demand.

Some have argued, however, that Williamson and Miller have the answer to the assignment problem upside-down. Specifically, Genberg and Swoboda (1987), and Boughton (1988) reason that if the concern of external balance is to limit the magnitudes of current account surpluses and deficits, then monetary policy should not be assigned to external balance because it has only small and ambiguous effects on the current account. The intuition here is that a monetary expansion will stimulate demand (which will tend to worsen the current account), but also depreciate the currency (which will tend to improve it). The *net* effect could be either positive or negative. In contrast, the expenditure-reducing and expenditure-switching effects of fiscal policy reinforce each other: a fiscal contraction will decrease spending on foreign goods (improving the current account), and will also—at least for countries facing perfect capital mobility—be associated with currency depreciation (which likewise strengthens the current account).

Following the principle of effective market classification, which says that each policy instrument should be assigned to the target on which it has the largest effect, a "reversed assignment" would pair fiscal policy with the current account and monetary policy with domestic demand growth. According to its supporters, this revised assignment would limit external imbalances, while at the same time leave scope for domestic stabilization and anti-inflation policy.[13]

IV. Simulation Results

We first consider the behavior of each of the rules in response to *individual* shocks (that is, shocks to *individual* residuals). Each shock is

---

[13] The literature on the assignment of instruments to targets will not be surveyed here; it is well known that, depending on the slopes of excess demand schedules, a particular assignment may be stable, while another may be unstable. For instance, Kenen (1985, p. 654) shows that in a very open economy with a marginal propensity to import larger than its marginal propensity to save, the conventional assignment of exchange rate policy to external balance and expenditure policy to internal balance will be unstable.

assumed to be unanticipated when it occurs, and to be an innovation that applies to a single period. Although temporary, such shocks will nevertheless have persistent effects because errors in the model are serially correlated and because the various structural equations of the model contain dynamic effects.[14] Expectations are assumed to be formed in the model in a way that properly takes into account the subsequent dynamics; that is, once the shock has occurred, perfect foresight is assumed to prevail.

The results from single shocks do not, of course, allow a complete evaluation of policy rules.[15] Nevertheless, single-shock exercises can be useful because they allow a characterization of *when* particular rules are likely to perform better than others.

As suggested earlier, we follow the single-shock simulations with some *stochastic* simulations when errors are consistent with their estimated distribution. One advantage of these stochastic simulations is that the variances of the shocks reflect their relative importance. A formal ranking of the policy rules would require an explicit objective function that specifies the weights assigned to output fluctuations, inflation, and to other objectives. We do not provide such a ranking; rather, we suggest some strengths and weaknesses of each of the rules.

The Form of the Reaction Functions

As a prelude to the simulation results, it is necessary to specify exactly how we have implemented the various policy rules in MULTIMOD. In brief, we imposed reaction functions for the short-term interest rate, assumed to be the instrument for monetary policy, and for real government spending on goods and services, assumed to be the fiscal policy instrument.[16] Details of the feedback rules are given in Appendix I.

The form of the policy rules requires some explanation, as there is inevitably some element of arbitrariness in their specification. In general, we have attempted to follow as closely as possible the intentions of the advocates

---

[14] Error properties are discussed in Appendix II. The standard version of the model (Masson and others (1988)) ignores this feature. Two other modifications to the standard model were made for the purposes of the simulations reported in this paper: the stock of debt owed by developing countries was made exogenous, and tax rates in industrial countries were made more responsive to government debt accumulation.

[15] Poole (1970); see Henderson (1979) for a treatment of the open economy case.

[16] Equivalently, the monetary policy instrument could be considered the domestic component of the monetary base; however, this variable does not appear explicitly in the model. An additional fiscal instrument—a tax rate—is already endogenous to the model, and is assumed to change in order to assure the government's long-run solvency. Tax rates in the model depend positively on deviations in both the government debt-to-GNP and the deficit-to-GNP ratios from their baseline values, with coefficients chosen to stabilize the debt ratio without causing oscillations. (See Masson and others (1988).) Different parameter values for this reaction function could also affect the properties of the policy rules considered for interest rates and government spending.

of these policy rules. The final form chosen has the result of experimentation that identified inadequacies with alternative specifications or with feedback parameters.[17]

Rule 1. *Money targeting* used the same specification as in the standard version of MULTIMOD. The exact achievement of a money target would produce large swings in short-term interest rates. For that reason, the model includes an equation in which interest rates equate the long-run demand for money—conditional on observed GNP—with the money stock target.

Rule 2. *Nominal GNP targeting* was specified in terms of a target for the *level* of nominal income, rather than its rate of change, because of the potential instability from targeting the latter discussed in Taylor (1985b). Some experimentation with feedback coefficients led to a value that yields a flatter aggregate demand schedule (in real output, price space) under nominal income targeting than under money targeting, again as discussed in Taylor (1985b).

Rule 3. *Fixed nominal exchange rates* were implemented by putting a large feedback coefficient on the deviation of the actual from the targeted nominal rate in the equation for short-term interest rates. Variations of exchange rates are thereby kept within narrow margins. It should be stressed that there is an asymmetry in the implementation of this rule as between the United States and other industrial countries. The latter are assumed to subordinate their monetary policies to maintaining U.S. dollar parities, while the United States is assumed to target monetary aggregates independently of exchange rate considerations, thereby providing a nominal anchor for the system.

Rule 4. *Target zones* follow as closely as possible the guidelines described in Williamson and Miller (1987) and simulated earlier (using the MCM model) by Edison, Miller, and Williamson (1987). We experimented with various values of the feedback coefficients to achieve the closest control over the targets without producing explosive behavior in the model. As in Edison and others, there is nothing that ensures that the real exchange rate will not depart from the zone (if shocks are large enough). As described in Williamson and Miller (1987), a target for the level of world nominal income serves as the nominal anchor for prices. Note, however, that it is the level, not the rate of

---

[17] For some parameter values, target zones, nominal income, blueprint, and reversed assignment simulations became explosive and could not be made to converge. However, it is possible that other combinations of parameters could have been simulated. For instance, under reversed assignment a tighter control of domestic demand could have been achieved if current account targeting had been made less precise. In the light of the discussion in Kenen (1985), it is also possible that the assignment of targets to instruments should depend on the degree of openness of each economy, in order to avoid instability; such hybrid systems have not been explored here, however.

change, of world nominal income that appears in our equation;[18] the latter is subject to the criticisms made by Taylor (1985b) for domestic targeting and did, in practice, produce problems of nonconvergence in MULTIMOD. The feedback coefficient on world nominal income implies that a 10 percent deviation from the baseline raises world interest rates by 1 percentage point.

Rule 5. The *extended target zones, or "blueprint" proposal,* contains a policy reaction function for government spending as well as the target zone assignment of monetary policy to the real exchange rate. The equation that makes endogenous fiscal expenditures is a feedback rule that aims to close a gap between domestic absorption and its target value.[19] This rule does not hit domestic absorption exactly, but with the feedback coefficient that is imposed, deviations from absorption targets are typically small.

Rule 6. In implementing *reversed assignment,* we have specified that the short-term interest rate responds to the proportional gap between nominal absorption and its target, while government spending responds strongly to the gap between the current account (as a ratio to GNP) and its target. Instrument instability does not seem to be a problem in the latter case; indeed, in principle, the feedback coefficient could be infinite, forcing deviations of current balances from targets to zero. However, the conclusions derived from the simulations are unlikely to be sensitive to the small deviations from current account targets that result from our specification. If anything, our simulations probably give too much weight to current account targets and not enough to nominal demand targets; closer control of the latter might have been possible otherwise.

Simulations of Individual Shocks

Four individual shocks are considered:
- an aggregate *demand shock* in the United States; a positive innovation in consumption equal to 1 percent.
- an aggregate *supply shock* in the United States; in particular, the residual in the equation for the rate of change in the non-oil GNP deflator is increased by 2 percent.
- a *shift in demand* toward U.S. goods, equal to 10 percent of U.S. exports.
- a *portfolio preference shift* out of U.S. dollar assets, leading to an increase in the required rate of return on dollar assets of 10 percentage points.

---

[18] Williamson and Miller (1987) do not specify the form that this term should take.

[19] The reason that absorption, and not GNP, is targeted by fiscal policy is that external imbalances in the form of current account surpluses and deficits should be lessened by such a rule, supplementing the role of the real exchange rate.

Each of the rules is simulated subject to each of the four shocks, one at a time. The results are portrayed in Charts 1 to 4.[20]

The *aggregate demand shock*, namely a 1 percent increase in U.S. consumption,[21] has quite different effects under the different policy rules (see Chart 1). Absent any policy changes, such a shock will increase output and put upward pressure on prices, as well as appreciate the real exchange rate and lead to a rise in the current account deficit. It also generates positive spillover effects for the output of other countries. Since nominal GNP rises, as does the demand for money, both uncoordinated rules cause interest rates to increase; given the relative steepness of the aggregate demand curves, output and price increases are more moderate under nominal income targeting than under monetary targeting.

Under target zones, the real appreciation of the U.S. dollar leads to a smaller rise in interest rates in the United States than in other industrial countries. However, by limiting the interest rate increases in the United States in response to a demand increase, this rule builds in inflationary pressures, which persist longer than for other rules. Fixed nominal exchange rates yield a similar outcome. In contrast, the extra degree of freedom accorded by fiscal policy in both the blueprint and the reversed assignment rules allows the aggregate demand shock to be almost completely offset by lower government spending. As a result, the output, price, and real exchange rate effects are the smallest under these two rules. A comparison of the blueprint with the reversed assignment rule illustrates the relative effectiveness of monetary and fiscal policies. Government spending cuts can easily offset the effects of increased consumption on absorption, allowing the blueprint rule virtually to neutralize the shock. In contrast, control of nominal absorption through the interest rate is not as powerful, at least for values of feedback coefficients that do not produce large swings in interest rates or other variables.

The negative *aggregate supply shock* (or cost-push inflation shock) likewise yields a variety of responses (see Chart 2). This shock has persistent effects because of considerable stickiness in the inflation process.[22] In response to this "stagflationary" shock, nominal GNP targeting leads to a greater response of interest rates, and, hence, to greater short-run output losses but smaller increases in prices, than does money targeting. Which of the two is preferable depends on the trade-off between the two objectives of output and

---

[20] The money, nominal income, target zone, and blueprint results are the same as those presented in Frenkel, Goldstein, and Masson (1989). In addition, there are two new rules: fixed rates and reversed assignment.

[21] The error in this equation has a serial correlation coefficient equal to 0.148, so that roughly 15 percent of the shock persists into the second year, 2 percent into the third year, etc. See Appendix II, Table 1.

[22] The error in the equation for the rate of change in the non-oil output deflator is negatively serially correlated, however (see Appendix II, Table 1).

Chart 1. Shock to U.S. Consumption
(Deviations of U.S. variables from baseline)

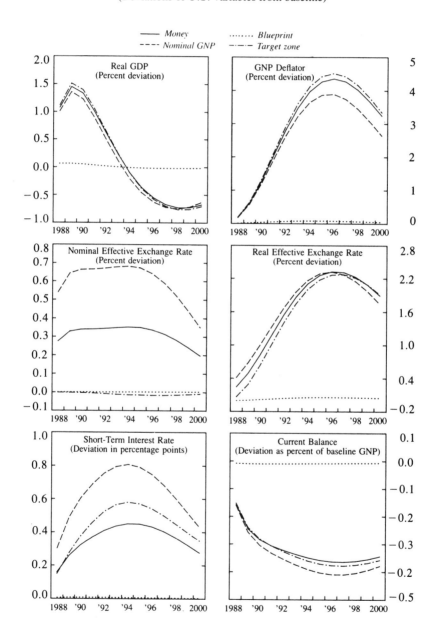

Chart 2. U.S. Aggregate Supply Shock

(Deviations of U.S. variables from baseline)

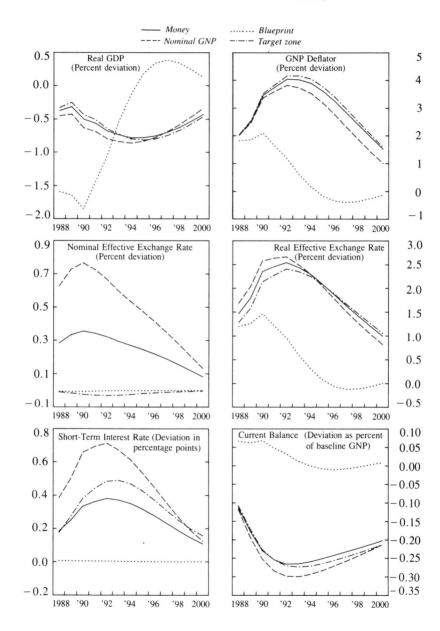

price level stability, as well as on the discount rate that captures intertemporal trade-offs.[23] Given the small effects on exchange rates under all rules, fixed rates produce results similar to uncoordinated money targeting.

The responses under target zones and blueprint rules are another story. Using monetary policy to counteract the real appreciation of the U.S. dollar requires *lower,* not higher, U.S. nominal interest rates. However, for both the target zones and blueprint rules there is an additional term that tends to raise interest rates in all countries if world nominal income grows too fast, which is the case here. The end result with target zones is that U.S. interest rates rise, but by somewhat less than interest rates in other industrial countries. Price level increases continue longer—and are larger in the medium term—than for any other policy rule. In addition, interest rates have to continue increasing for six years in response to a purely transitory supply shock because of the inertia in the inflation process.

In contrast, interest rates have to rise much less under the blueprint rule because government spending contracts, helping to limit the real appreciation of the dollar. The contraction of government spending is required because the increase in U.S. prices yields an improvement in the terms of trade, which raises real disposable income and stimulates consumption. Although the net effect on output is negative in the short run, output is actually higher after seven years, by which time prices have returned to their baseline levels. An aggregate supply shock clearly causes a dilemma for target zones because one instrument, monetary policy, has to wear *two* hats: resisting inflationary pressures and limiting appreciation of the real exchange rate (in the country experiencing the shock).[24] The reversed assignment rule behaves much like the blueprint; both result in relatively small effects on the current balance.

Chart 3 illustrates the effects of an *expenditure-switching shock* that correspond to a shift toward U.S. goods and away from other countries' goods. The positive shock to U.S. exports of 10 percent shows up in lower exports of other countries in proportions that correspond to their shares in world trade.[25] The U.S. current account improves by some 0.6–0.7 percent of GNP in the first period under all rules except reversed assignment, under which the current account change is smaller. Under all policy rules, U.S. real output rises initially, and price increases are small. Neither real exchange rates

---

[23] As shown in Buiter and Miller (1982), if the model has a natural rate property, the cumulative output losses resulting from different disinflation policies are the same, when discounting is ignored.

[24] If there is no feedback of inflation on monetary policy—such as through world nominal income—then the target zone rule cannot be simulated, given the absence of a nominal anchor.

[25] The shock is distributed using the weights that serve to allocate the world trade discrepancy in MULTIMOD. As a result, the shock to the United States is also reduced by the U.S. share, so that U.S. exports rise on impact by about 8.6 percent, not the full 10 percent.

Chart 3. Shock to U.S. Exports
(Deviations of U.S. variables from baseline)

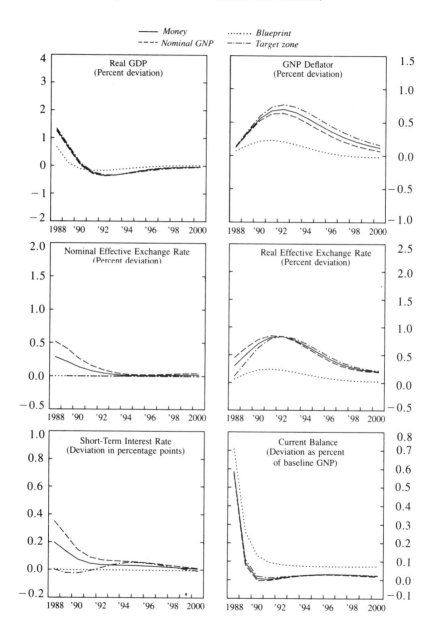

nor industrial-country nominal GNP change much, so there is little effect on interest rates under either fixed rates, target zones, or the blueprint. In contrast, under the reversed assignment rule, the increase in the U.S. current balance leads to *increased* U.S. government spending, adding to the stimulus to U.S. output; conversely, government spending declines in other countries. Higher U.S. nominal GNP has to be resisted by higher U.S. interest rates, so that shifts in preferences between countries' goods lead to a shift in the monetary and fiscal mix under reversed assignment—to a combination of tighter monetary and looser fiscal policy in the country facing the increase in its exports, and conversely for those facing lower exports. The contrast between this rule and the others has been heightened by the large feedback coefficient on the current balance; attempts to exert tight control over the current account lead to large swings in other variables under reversed assignment.

The *exchange rate shock* (see Chart 4) puts downward pressure on the dollar relative to the Japanese yen, to the deutsche mark, and to other industrial country currencies. The initiating factor is assumed to be a 10 percent increase in the required return on dollar assets.[26] Output effects are largest under reversed assignment and under the two uncoordinated rules (money and nominal GNP targeting)—and are smallest under the blueprint rule and fixed rates. The exchange rate always overshoots except under fixed rates, with the U.S. nominal effective exchange rate depreciating by about 15 percent in the first year. Under target zones, despite an initial increase of 6 percentage points in the short-term interest rate, the real effective exchange rate still depreciates considerably. Moreover, the behavior of the GNP deflator suggests that target zones can generate price level instability—a point we return to below in the context of stochastic simulations. Under reversed assignment, government spending *rises* because of the improvement in the U.S. current account; again, this tends to induce large movements in output.

A *money demand shock* was also examined. The results are not plotted because they are simple to describe. It is only in the case of money targeting that the money shock has any significant effect on policy settings and on other endogenous variables (there is a small effect of the money shock on consumption because money is a component of net wealth, but the magnitude is negligible). Under money targeting, the positive innovation to money demand leads to temporarily higher short-term interest rates, and as a consequence, to lower economic activity for a time. Other policy rules ignore the money demand shock and maintain policy instruments unchanged, allowing macroeconomic variables to remain at their equilibrium levels. This points up the

---

[26] As in the historical data, the risk premium shocks are quite persistent (owing perhaps to speculative bubbles as well as to shifts in portfolio preferences), with serial correlation coefficients equal to 0.43 for shocks to interest parity between the United States and Japan, and 0.75 between the United States and the Federal Republic of Germany.

Chart 4. Shock to Value of U.S. Dollar
(Deviations of U.S. variables from baseline)

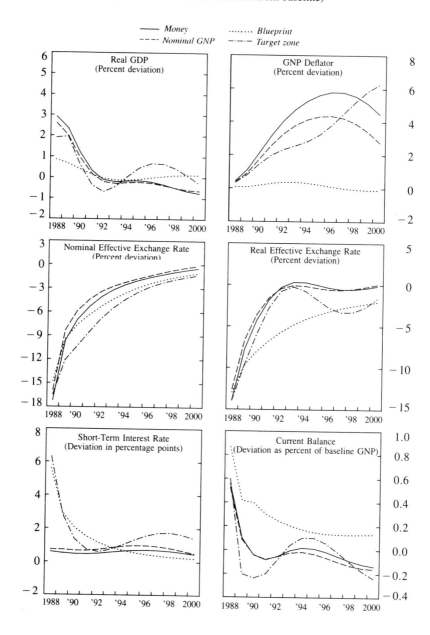

superiority of these rules in the face of money demand shocks, an argument that has long been emphasized by advocates of nominal GNP targeting (Tobin, 1980).

Stochastic Simulations

Simulations of individual shocks, although instructive, do not lend themselves to easy generalizations because no rule dominates the others for all kinds of shocks. It is clear that monetary policy rules (assumed to be credible, and fully understood by the private sector) are relatively ineffective, especially in affecting real variables. Rules using fiscal policy, therefore, have distinct advantages in offsetting shocks, although the assumed flexibility for fiscal policy may be unrealistic. In addition, the proper assignment of monetary and fiscal policies to internal or external balance depends on the nature of shocks.

We now turn to simulations where the variances of the shocks reflect their relative importance. Moreover, instead of applying shocks for one period only, we apply shocks in successive periods. By looking at a sufficient number of years, the model should provide useful information about the variances of endogenous variables under the alternative policy rules.

The simulations are performed on the assumption that expectations are formed rationally. The shocks (by definition) are unanticipated at the time they occur. In this context, rational expectations of variables in future periods are formed taking the expected value of those shocks—namely, zero.[27] In each period, however, a drawing is made from the covariance matrix describing the shocks. The *realized* values of endogenous variables are affected by the shocks, and generally will differ from the expectations for those variables formed in previous periods.

The stochastic simulations involve multiple simulations. It is necessary to iterate repeatedly in order to force expectations to be consistent with the model's solution conditional on information available at time t and with end-point values at a terminal date far in the future; it is also necessary to redo the process each time a new drawing of shocks is made.

In the first set of stochastic simulations (for which root mean square deviations from baseline are presented in Table 1), we use a drawing for the shocks that corresponds to residuals in the model's behavioral equations for 1974–85. These shocks are applied to a baseline for the period 1988–99; the model is simulated over another 20 years in order to minimize the effect of the terminal conditions on the period of interest (Appendix II gives more details on how the simulations were done). As with the single shocks exercise, the implicit objective is to minimize deviations of target variables from the baseline, so that shocks have as little disruptive effect as possible. We do

---

[27] The model has to be linear for this to be fully consistent with rationality.

not make a judgment about how target variables should be weighted in the objective function; however, we presume that macroeconomic performance

Table 1. Root Mean Square Deviations from Baseline for Various Policy Rules, Historical Shocks

			Policy Rule				
	Money targeting	Nominal GNP targeting	Fixed rate (1)	(2)	Target zone	Blueprint	Reversed assign- ment
United States							
Real GDP[1]	3.6	3.2	3.0	2.8	2.7	1.4	7.9
Inflation	3.0	2.3	3.4	3.0	1.7	0.8	3.2
Current balance[2]	0.7	0.7	0.6	0.6	0.4	0.5	0.2
Real effective exchange rate[1]	9.1	8.3	5.6	4.3	7.3	4.9	9.1
Nominal effective exchange rate[1]	7.2	8.1	0.3	0.1	7.0	5.8	5.8
Nominal interest rate	1.4	1.2	1.5	1.4	2.8	1.8	1.7
Japan							
Real GDP[1]	3.8	3.2	4.0	4.1	3.7	1.6	5.2
Inflation	5.8	4.8	4.8	4.3	4.1	1.7	3.9
Current balance[2]	0.6	0.6	0.5	0.5	0.5	0.8	0.2
Real effective exchange rate[1]	8.9	8.2	3.8	3.8	6.9	5.5	5.9
Nominal effective exchange rate[1]	11.9	9.8	0.5	0.1	11.8	10.1	11.8
Nominal interest rate	1.5	2.3	4.4	1.3	2.5	1.3	2.3
Germany, Fed. Rep. of							
Real GDP[1]	4.4	4.3	3.4	3.1	6.9	2.9	4.2
Inflation	3.7	3.0	4.9	4.2	2.9	2.4	2.2
Current balance[2]	1.4	1.4	1.0	1.0	0.1	2.2	0.6
Real effective exchange rate[1]	8.2	7.6	2.1	2.2	10.4	7.4	8.0
Nominal effective exchange rate[1]	11.9	8.5	0.4	0.0	16.3	14.2	11.8
Nominal interest rate	2.7	1.8	5.9	1.4	3.3	1.1	1.1
Developing Countries							
Real GDP[1]	3.4	3.4	3.2	1.3	2.1	1.6	1.5
Terms of trade[1]	5.5	5.1	5.6	5.1	4.5	2.5	3.7

[1] Root mean square percent errors.
[2] As a percent of GNP.

would be evaluated using some subset of the variables presented in Table 1.[28] Several conclusions emerge from the examination of the results.

First, it appears that nominal GNP targeting produces smaller errors in response to typical shocks than money targeting. As noted earlier, nominal GNP targeting has a clear advantage over money targeting when there are shocks to velocity, that is, to the demand for money. For other kinds of shocks, the comparison between the two rules derives from small differences in the elasticity with respect to nominal income and in the speed with which the interest rate reacts to shocks. For the historical shocks considered here, the stabilization properties of the nominal income rule clearly dominated those of base money targeting.

Second, the two rules that ignore domestic variables in setting monetary policy in favor of targeting an exchange rate measure—while keeping fiscal expenditures exogenous—show mixed results: they have some success in reducing the variability of gross domestic product (GDP) for the United States and for developing countries, but yield no clear advantage for Germany and Japan.

Note also that the behavior of macroeconomic variables is quite different under fixed nominal exchange rates (see Table 1, column (1)) than under target zones. Recall that fixed rates are implemented here through changes in monetary policies of non-U.S. industrial countries. The United States is assumed to target the monetary base, as under monetary targeting. As a result, the variability of nominal interest rates is considerably higher abroad than in the United States. The fixity of nominal exchange rates is also associated with more variability of inflation in all industrial countries.

Some might argue that stochastic simulations of fixed exchange rates using historical shocks overstate the need for movements in interest rates. Since the period 1974–85 was characterized by flexible exchange rates, a credible announcement of a set of nominal exchange rate targets could be seen as reducing shifts between currencies. Moreover, our earlier single-shock simulations suggested that target zones could be unstable under exchange rate shocks; responses to such shocks could be unfavorably biasing the results against target zones. In order to examine this question, we also ran some simulations under which shocks to interest parity conditions were absent. These results—shown in Table 1, column (2) under fixed rates—exhibit only slightly less variability. Our results do not appear to be strongly affected by

---

[28] It could be argued that the sole criterion should be the discounted present value of consumption, and the variances of variables would matter only insofar as they reduced the output available for consumption. The model as currently specified does not incorporate such effects, making it necessary to evaluate rules on the basis of their effectiveness in reducing the variability of key variables. Of course, the absence in the model of links between second and first moments of variables makes it subject to Lucas critique problems.

changes in speculative behavior in currency markets that might be associated with the exchange rate regime.

The target zones rule, in contrast to fixed nominal rates, posits a *symmetric* assignment of monetary policies to real effective exchange rates. As hinted at earlier, the achievement of narrow target zones is difficult in the model, and root mean square deviations from baseline for real exchange rates are quite high; on the other hand, real GDP, at least in the United States, and inflation, generally, are quite stable. The policy reaction functions for target zones used here are based on Edison, Miller, and Williamson (1987); our results suggest, however, that a more complicated rule for setting interest rates—perhaps using proportional, integral, and derivative control terms—would be more appropriate.[29] Such rules may also be more robust to model misspecification. At the same time, we would argue that the fact that a simple rule does not perform well suggests some skepticism about the practicality of real exchange rate targeting, given the uncertainty associated with the precise dynamics of the economy.

Third, the blueprint rule produces considerably lower error variance for most variables,[30] but does so with the benefit of an additional policy instrument—namely, real government spending. Somewhat surprisingly, the reversed assignment rule does not succeed in stabilizing either real GDP (except for developing countries) or real effective exchange rates.[31] Although current account targets are achieved under reversed assignment, they may not be the preferred measure of external balance because shocks that change the terms of trade will change the valuation of trade flows for given trade volumes. Stabilizing the current balance will, therefore, not be sufficient to neutralize the domestic demand effects of external shocks.

Our historical shocks reflect a small sample—only 12 observations. As discussed above, it does not seem appropriate to evaluate policy rules on the basis of one historical episode. Our second set of stochastic simulations, therefore, draws shocks for 61 residuals over 40 years from the distribution describing the historical shocks. The simulations were then performed as described above, one year at a time. Table 2 presents the RMS deviations from baseline for the various policy rules.

---

[29] Such specifications have been used by Currie and Wren-Lewis (1987, 1988a, 1988b), among others.

[30] Although not for nominal effective exchange rates in Japan and Germany. Nominal effective exchange rates use Multilateral Exchange Rate Model (MERM) weights, and include only industrial country currencies, while *real* effective exchange rates are calculated using relative manufacturing export prices weighted according to export shares; developing countries are included in this calculation.

[31] Currie and Wren-Lewis (1988a) also find that such a rule performs less well than the blueprint assignment.

Table 2. Root Mean Square Deviations from Baseline for Various Policy Rules, Generated Shocks, 1988-2027

	Policy Rule					
	Money targeting	Nominal GNP targeting	Fixed rate	Blueprint (1)	(2)	Reversed assignment
United States						
Real GDP[1]	5.1	5.4	5.0	1.9	3.2	4.4
Inflation	3.7	3.3	3.4	1.2	1.3	2.3
Current balance[2]	0.9	1.2	0.8	1.2	0.9	0.2
Real effective exchange rate[1]	11.6	12.8	11.8	6.3	5.7	7.6
Nominal effective exchange rate[1]	8.1	8.5	0.4	10.3	8.8	5.1
Nominal interest rate	2.0	4.0	1.6	1.4	1.7	1.7
Japan						
Real GDP[1]	5.2	6.0	5.8	2.9	5.9	4.4
Inflation	5.3	4.9	4.9	2.4	2.7	3.6
Current balance[2]	4.9	2.5	1.5	1.9	1.8	0.4
Real effective exchange rate[2]	7.8	10.1	5.7	5.0	5.0	6.8
Nominal effective exchange rate[2]	11.3	17.2	0.4	9.2	9.4	8.2
Nominal interest rate	2.3	2.8	3.7	0.9	1.1	2.0
Germany, Fed. Rep. of						
Real GDP[1]	5.1	4.5	3.8	3.5	4.4	4.8
Inflation	4.8	4.1	3.9	2.4	2.2	2.9
Current balance[2]	3.9	1.6	2.4	3.5	3.2	0.4
Real effective exchange rate[1]	8.4	6.6	6.1	7.4	6.4	9.8
Nominal effective exchange rate[1]	14.2	11.9	0.5	15.9	14.0	11.8
Nominal interest rate	2.8	3.0	6.3	1.5	1.3	2.2
Developing Countries						
Real GDP[1]	2.4	3.7	2.1	2.3	2.5	2.0
Terms of trade[1]	4.9	6.4	3.9	2.8	2.8	3.1

[1] Root mean square percent errors.
[2] As a percent of GDP.

Table 2 features several qualitative differences relative to the historical shocks shown in Table 1:

First, the ranking of money and nominal GNP targeting is changed. The reason seems to lie in the timing of shocks to developing country supplies of commodities and manufactured exports. In the historical simulations, these shocks occur mainly at the *end* of the simulation period; they have persistent effects, but since the RMS deviations are calculated only over the 12 years of the shocks, some of those effects are not captured. In contrast, the generated shocks distribute those effects more evenly over the simulation, and nominal GNP targeting, with its steeper aggregate demand curve, performs more poorly than money targeting.

Second, fixed rates in Table 2 no longer dominate the two uncoordinated rules with respect to real GDP in Japan, nor for the real effective exchange rate of the dollar. Unless a considerable premium is placed on *nominal* exchange rate stability, there seems little to choose among the first three rules—money and nominal GNP targets, and fixed rates. Unfortunately, the target zone proposal could not be simulated here; with the feedback parameters specified in Edison, Miller, and Williamson (1987), the target-zone rule suffers from dynamic instability that eventually prevents MULTIMOD from converging to a solution. The problem is worsened by the longer simulation period, as real shocks push the short-run equilibrium real exchange rate further away from its long-run equilibrium value.[32]

Third, the blueprint rule (see Table 2, column (1)) again seems to yield, for most variables, lower RMS deviations than the other rules. Its superiority with respect to reversed assignment, however, is less marked than in Table 1. As discussed above, both of these rules assume that real government spending can be flexibly used in the current period to respond to deviations from targets—be it nominal domestic demand (blueprint) or the current balance (reversed assignment). A more realistic assumption, in our view, would be for fiscal spending to respond with a *lag* of one year to deviations from targets. Taking account of this inflexibility would mean that lower (higher) growth in nominal domestic demand under the blueprint rule would lead to higher (lower) government spending in the *following* year. In our first attempt to make this constraint operational, we used the same feedback coefficients as in column (1); however, this produced dynamic instability. The results presented in column (2) use a feedback of nominal domestic demand on to government spending that is half of the contemporaneous effect: 0.5, instead of unity. Interestingly enough, the RMS deviations for this variant of the blueprint rule are now closer to those for the other rules.[33] It is a topic for further research to

---

[32] Of course, given the assumption that agents know those values, policymakers could (in the model) have moving targets for exchange rates, trying only to offset current shocks, and not the lagged effects of past shocks. Such an experiment—which would in effect involve starting each period's simulation at baseline values—was not performed, however.

[33] Except for current account balances. It seems that because of J-curves, the lagged response of government spending actually does better in offsetting the current account effect of most shocks.

examine the constrained use of fiscal policy to achieve other targets—for instance, under the reversed assignment rule.

V. Summary and Conclusions

A theme running through the results from the individual-shock simulations is the relative ineffectiveness of monetary policy under rational expectations, despite the existence of price stickiness in MULTIMOD. One implication is that target zones that rely on a monetary policy instrument alone do not seem capable of maintaining real effective exchange rates within bands of even 10 percent on either side of the target. Conversely, fiscal policy—in particular, variations in government spending—appears to be quite powerful in influencing output, real exchange rates, and current accounts. But there is an important catch: fiscal policy may simply not have the flexibility assumed for it in the blueprint and reversed assignment rules. It may be constrained by other objectives—budget deficits[34] or the desire to reduce the importance of government in the economy—and be the product of a lengthy political process. Fiscal policy may, therefore, not be able to react immediately to shocks.

Simulations of individual shocks also illustrate the point emphasized in much of the theoretical literature that the performance of simple policy rules varies with the nature of the shocks facing the economy. Rules that perform "best" for some shocks may perform least well for others. In some cases it is clear which rule(s) dominate; for example, if money demand shocks are prevalent, the targeting of monetary aggregates will produce inferior results. However, in the real world there is a *variety* of shocks; any evaluation of rules must take into account their relative variances and the covariances among them. The stochastic simulations reported above attempt to meet that requirement. When all is said and done, our results lead us to be cautious in drawing strong conclusions about the dominance of one rule or another. This caution is rooted in several features of our results.

To begin with, we found that some rules that on the surface appear quite straightforward could not in fact be simulated easily. In particular, we found that *dynamic instability* was a serious problem when monetary policy was used to achieve close control over either nominal GNP or real exchange rates. Although we have isolated rules that are stable in MULTIMOD, our experience suggests that rules may not be robust across models, and, hence, may in practice cause instability problems.

In a similar vein, we discovered that the *intuition of some simple models*

---

[34] Indeed, tax policy in MULTIMOD is varied in order to prevent the unbounded accumulation of debt; however, simulated effects on budget deficits in the short-to-medium run are still substantial.

did not tell the whole story. In particular, the notion that fiscal policy should be assigned to an external target—the current account—because of its stronger effect on that target needs to be weighed against its apparent tendency to generate greater fluctuations in other macroeconomic variables. Terms of trade effects, J-curve dynamics, and asset accumulations may make the outcome more complex than suggested by the simple models.

A third factor—and in our view, a crucial one—concerns the need to model the *constraints* on the use of policy instruments, particularly on *fiscal* policy. While we have done some exploratory work on this, our results suggest that rules that rely on a fiscal instrument are substantially affected by lags in its operation. This consideration suggests that fiscal policy should be assigned to variables that move slowly and for which short-term control is not necessary.

Differences in *model specification* also need to be taken into account in evaluating simulation results. In models such as MULTIMOD, where the formation of expectations is affected by the policy rule, the effects of a regime change are complex and are highly sensitive to the precise way in which private-sector behavior—and the policies themselves—are modeled. Indeed, this sensitivity of the results makes us skeptical of claims that model simulations—at this stage in our knowledge—can provide an unambiguous ranking of policy rules.

Last but not least, we want to stress that simulation results for simple coordinated and uncoordinated policy rules should *not* be used to draw inferences about the effects of judgmental (discretionary) coordinated policies, including the ongoing coordination exercise among the largest industrial countries. In this connection, the differences between the effects of coordinated policy rules and judgmental coordinated policies may be as large as those between uncoordinated policy rules and coordinated policy rules. A key challenge for future researchers in this area is to learn about the effects of judgmental policies—even though they do not lend themselves easily to simulation exercises.

Appendix I
Reaction Functions

The precise forms ascribed to the various policy rules discussed in the body of the paper are given by the following equations. Lower case variables are in logs; upper case variables are in levels.

Variables were defined as follows: M is the monetary base (m its logarithm, and m^d is the log of long-run money demand); u is a money demand disturbance (in logs); Y is nominal GNP; WY is the U.S. dollar value (at current exchange rates) of aggregate nominal income of industrial countries taken together; Q is real GNP; P is the GNP deflator; A is nominal domestic absorption; G is real government expenditure on goods and services; B is the balance on current account; C is competitiveness (the relative price of domestic to foreign output); E is the nominal exchange rate (U.S. dollars per local currency); and R is the short-term interest rate. A b superscript indicates baseline values, which are also assumed to be the target values of the relevant variables. Implicitly then, the simulations start from a position of equilibrium, which is disturbed by the shocks being considered; the goal of each of the rules should be to return the economy as quickly and smoothly as possible to the initial equilibrium.

1) *Money Targeting:* $\qquad\qquad R = R^b + 13.5\,(m^d - m^b),$

where m^d is given by $\qquad\quad m^d = p + .970\,q + 5.15\,u.$

This interest-rate rule sets the long-run demand for money equal to its target (baseline) value, conditional on current values for prices, output, and the error in the demand for money. The short-run demand for money can be written (see Masson and others (1988), p. 60) as follows:

$$m = p + .1883\,q - .0070\,R - .0074\,R_{-1} + .8058\,(m - p)_{-1} + u,$$

where u is an error term. Therefore, the value of the interest rate that achieves $m = m^b$, once all lags have worked themselves out, is

$$R = -13.5\,(m^b - p) + 13.1\,q - 69.4\,u.$$

A rearrangement of this equation, on the assumption that the equation also holds in the baseline, yields rule 1.

2) *Nominal GNP Targeting:* $\quad R = R^b + 25\,(y - y^b).$

3) *Fixed Exchange Rates:*

     for the United States: $\qquad R = R^b + 13.5\,(m^d - m^b)$

     for other countries: $\qquad\quad R = R^b + 1000\,(e^b - e).$

4) *Target Zones:* $\qquad\qquad\quad R = R^b + [(c - c^b)/.1]^3 + 10\,(wy - wy^b).$

5) *Blueprint:* $\qquad\qquad\qquad\quad R = R^b + [(c - c^b)/.1]^3 + 10\,(wy - wy^b)$

$$(G - G^b)/Q^b = (A^b - A)/A^b.$$

6) *Reversed Assignment:* $\qquad R = -R^b + 25\,(a - a^b)$

$$(G - G^b)/Q^b = -10\,(B^b - B)/Y^b.$$

Appendix II

Procedures for Simulating MULTIMOD

For convenience, the model is written as a linear function of endogenous variables y, exogenous variables x, and errors u:[35]

$$y = A\, y(-1) + B\, x + C\, y^e + u. \tag{1}$$

Current endogenous variables depend on values for the previous period, $y(-1)$, as well as on expected values for the following period, $y^e = E(y(+1)|I)$, where I is information available in the current period. The vector of errors may include some that are identically zero, in particular, for equations that are identities. To perform the stochastic simulations, we need an estimate of the covariance matrix of the us. This is complicated by the fact that y^e is unobservable.

In MULTIMOD, equations with expectations variables were estimated using McCallum's (1976) instrumental variables method. Therefore, errors from the first stage regression should capture the expectations errors. Let us call these errors v, so that

$$y(+1) = y^e + v. \tag{2}$$

Substitution of (2) into (1) permits decomposition of the equation residuals into two parts: the structural residuals u and the expectations errors v:

$$y = A\, y(-1) + B\, x + C\, y(+1) + u - C\, v. \tag{3}$$

A slight problem arises because the y^e in (2) is not the same as what a model simulation would produce for the next period: the instrumental variable estimator does not impose the model's restrictions as a full information estimator would.[36] Therefore, the model would not exactly track historical values of y with the estimation residuals.

In practice, the forecasts for $y(+1)$ were not taken from the first stage of the instrumental variables estimation. For one thing, these were not easily recoverable. For another, expectations appear in some equations without estimated parameters, in particular in uncovered interest parity and bond rate arbitrage equations. Instead, time series equations were fit for the variables for which the model incorporates expectations; the forecasts from these equations —call them $yfit(+1)$—were substituted into equation (1) in place of y^e. The

---

[35] MULTIMOD is nonlinear, but coefficients that correspond to a linearized version, as in equation (1), vary little from one period to the next. Therefore, expected values of the endogenous variables are calculated by simulations that set residuals equal to zero.

[36] In practice, given MULTIMOD's size, a full information estimator would not be feasible.

structural residuals were calculated residually as

$$u = y - [A\,y(-1) + B\,x + C\,\mathit{yfit}(+1)].\tag{4}$$

A second problem concerns serial correlation of the residuals u. In principle, the process describing residual autocorrelation could be estimated jointly with the parameters in the equation. In practice, this was in most cases not done, mainly because the constraints imposed across equations did not allow separate autoregressions to be estimated for each country, and also because the interest parity equation was not estimated. There is, however, no reason to expect deviations from uncovered interest parity to be serially uncorrelated. Therefore, autoregressions of the following form (where L is the lag operator) were fit to the us calculated by equation (4):

$$A(L)\,u = a + b\,t + e.\tag{5}$$

The e vector then constitutes the innovation in the model. In simulation, the model constituted by equations (1) and (5) was solved together, given a drawing for the vector e of innovations. It should be noted that these shocks have persistent effects for two reasons: first, a shock in period t will affect u in the current period and in subsequent periods, via $A^{-1}(L)\,e$; and second, shocks have persistent effects because of the dynamics described in equation (1). Solution to the model in period t replaces y^e by the value calculated for $y(+1)$, given information available at t (call it $\mathit{yhat}(t, t+1)$), which itself depends on $x(+1)$ as well as $y(+2)$ (which in turn is replaced by its model solution, $\mathit{yhat}(t, t+2)$, and so forth). Some terminal condition is imposed on $y(+T)$. The effects in future periods are thus assumed to be correctly anticipated; however, future *shocks* are, of course, not anticipated before they occur. This implies that the forward-looking simulations have to be redone for each time period in which a new shock is applied, so that, for instance, $\mathit{yhat}(t+1, t+2)$ $\neq \mathit{yhat}(t, t+2) \neq y(t+2)$. This greatly increases the number of simulations relative to the number needed for deterministic simulations.

To be specific, residuals calculated for the period 1974–85 were used to estimate the parameters of equation (5) and the 61×61 covariance matrix describing the e vector. In practice a first-order autoregression plus a time trend was estimated for each of the residuals u. Table 3 gives the results of these regressions, as well as the standard errors of the residuals e. The residuals e were then correlated, giving a covariance matrix V. Because of the small number of observations, V is singular. Rather than imposing a diagonal structure on the V matrix (since some of the correlations are substantial), a small number was added to the diagonal, creating a non-singular approximation V^* to the V matrix:

$$V^* = V + .000001\ \mathrm{I}.$$

Table 3. Estimated Autoregressions and Standard Error of Innovations, 1974–85

$$u = \alpha + \rho u_{-1} + \beta t + e$$

(Coefficient standard error in parentheses)

Residual	ρ	σ_e	Residual	ρ	σ_e
us_c	.148 (.321)	.013	gr_rl	.655 (.253)	.110
us_coil	.519 (.257)	.022	gr_pgnp	−.074 (.364)	.008
us_k	.265 (.334)	.004	gr_pxm	−.045 (.379)	.016
us_xm	.289 (.318)	.031	gr_ycap	.655 (.205)	.010
us_im	−.087 (.336)	.051	gr_er	.745 (.250)	.059
us_icom	−.412 (.277)	.040	li_c	.444 (.296)	.010
us_m	.159 (.273)	.019	li_coil	−.123 (.322)	.019
us_rl	.131 (.335)	.056	li_k	−.154 (.573)	.008
us_pgnp	−.546 (.280)	.012	li_xm	.084 (.323)	.026
us_pxm	.103 (.351)	.025	li_im	−.177 (.323)	.056
us_ycap	.706 (.229)	.006	li_icom	−.485 (.302)	.032
ja_c	.128 (.312)	.021	li_m	.006 (.267)	.030
ja_coil	.126 (.338)	.038	li_rl	.251 (.311)	.063
ja_k	.685 (.299)	.006	li_pgnp	−.543 (.291)	.028
ja_xm	.494 (.292)	.043	li_pxm	−.010 (.316)	.021
ja_im	.176 (.279)	.096	li_ycap	.592 (.124)	.006
ja_icom	.172 (.323)	.063	li_er	.038 (.357)	.031
ja_m	−.087 (.159)	.025	si_c	.352 (.318)	.012
ja_rl	.430 (.280)	.090	si_coil	−.010 (.332)	.028
ja_pgnp	−.008 (.312)	.021	si_k	−.375 (.252)	.004
ja_pxm	−.294 (.319)	.035	si_xm	−.043 (.352)	.016
ja_ycap	.628 (.112)	.006	si_im	.016 (.325)	.031
ja_er	.428 (.294)	.041	si_icom	.124 (.324)	.031
gr_c	.100 (.333)	.009	si_m	−.166 (.308)	.032
gr_coil	.012 (.355)	.007	si_rl	.104 (.207)	.035
gr_k	.161 (.392)	.002	si_pgnp	−.416 (.304)	.011
gr_xm	−.054 (.362)	.018	si_pxm	−.013 (.463)	.039
gr_im	.161 (.318)	.029	si_ycap	.868 (.142)	.010
gr_icom	−.365 (.309)	.031	si_er	.830 (.272)	.058
gr_m	.052 (.169)	.036	dc_xcom	.097 (.322)	.032
			rw_xm	.361 (.253)	.054

The stochastic simulations were run by making repeated drawings from a random number generator, giving standard normal variates z, where

$$E(z) = 0$$

$$E(z' z) = I.$$

A Cholesky decomposition was performed on the matrix V^*, yielding a matrix L such that $L L' = V^*$.

The generated shocks z were premultiplied by L, yielding shocks e^* with the same properties as the es, that is, with estimated covariance V^*:

$$e^* = L\,z,$$

so that

$$E(e^*\,e^{*\prime}) = E(L\,z\,z'L') = L\,L' = V^*.$$

Values for the es were generated for the period 1988–2027, and the calculated es were added to equation (5) in order to calculate the residuals u. The model was first calibrated to track a smooth baseline. For each year from 1988 to 2027, a drawing was made for the es; using inherited $y(-1)$, which depends on past es, the model is solved forward to the terminal date, which in each case was taken to be 2044. No shocks were applied to the years 2028–44; a sufficient period at the end was included so that the simulations over the period of interest, 1988–2027, would not be much affected by the terminal conditions on the expectations variables.

A project for subsequent work would be to include forecasting equations for the exogenous variables as well as for the residuals, and to shock innovations in those equations as well.

References

Adams, Charles, and Daniel Gros, "The Consequences of Real Exchange Rate Rules for Inflation: Some Illustrative Examples," *Staff Papers*, International Monetary Fund (Washington), Vol. 33 (September 1986), pp. 439–76.

Barro, Robert J., and David B. Gordon, "Rules, Discretion and Reputation in a Model of Monetary Policy," *Journal of Monetary Economics* (Amsterdam), Vol. 12 (July 1983), pp. 101–21.

Boughton, James M., "Policy Assignment Strategies with Somewhat Flexible Exchange Rates," International Monetary Fund Working Paper No. 40 (Washington: IMF, May 1988).

Boyer, Russell, "Optimal Foreign Exchange Market Intervention," *Journal of Political Economy* (Chicago), Vol. 86 (December 1978), pp. 1045–55.

Buiter, Willem, and Richard Marston, *International Economic Policy Coordination* (New York: Cambridge University Press, 1985).

Buiter, Willem, and Marcus H. Miller, "Real Exchange Rate Overshooting and the Output Cost of Bringing Down Inflation," *European Economic Review* (Amsterdam), Vol. 18 (May/June 1982), pp. 85–123.

Chow, Gregory C., "Comparison of Econometric Models by Optimal Control Techniques," in *Evaluation of Econometric Models*, ed. by J. Kmenta and J. B. Ramsey (New York: Academic Press, 1980).

Cooper, J. Phillip, and Stanley Fischer, "Monetary and Fiscal Policy in the Fully Stochastic St. Louis Model," *Journal of Money, Credit and Banking* (Columbus, Ohio: February 1974), pp. 1–22.

Currie, David A., and Paul Levine, "Simple Macroeconomic Policy Rules in an Open Economy," *Economic Journal* (London), Vol. 85 (1985), pp. 60–70.

Currie, David A., and Simon Wren-Lewis, "Conflict and Cooperation in International Macroeconomic Policymaking: The Past Decade and Future Prospects" (unpublished; Washington, International Monetary Fund, December 1987).

———— (1988a), "A Comparison of Alternative Regimes for International Macropolicy Coordination," London Business School Discussion Paper No. 07-88 (London: 1988).

———— (1988b), "Evaluating the Extended Target Zone Proposal for the G-3," Centre for Economic Policy Research Discussion Paper No. 221 (London: CEPR, 1988).

Edison, Hali J., Marcus H. Miller, and John Williamson, "On Evaluating and Extending the Target Zone Proposal," *Journal of Policy Modelling* (New York), No. 1 (Spring 1987).

Fischer, Stanley, "Rules versus Discretion in Monetary Policy," National Bureau of Economic Research Working Paper No. 2518 (Cambridge, Massachusetts: NBER, February 1988).

————, and J. Phillip Cooper, "Stabilization Policy and Lags," *Journal of Political Economy* (Chicago), Vol. 81 (July/August 1973), pp. 847–77.

Frenkel, Jacob A., and Joshua Aizenman, "Aspects of the Optimal Management of Exchange Rates," *Journal of International Economics* (Amsterdam), Vol. 13, (November 1982), pp. 231–56.

Frenkel, Jacob A., Morris Goldstein, and Paul Masson, "The Rationale for, and Effects of, International Economic Policy Coordination," in *Policy Coordination and Exchange Rates*, ed. by William Branson, Jacob Frenkel, and Morris Goldstein (Chicago: National Bureau of Economic Research and University of Chicago Press, forthcoming, 1989).

Friedman, Milton, "The Effect of Full Employment Policy on Economic Stability: A Formal Analysis," in *Essays in Positive Economics* (Chicago: University of Chicago Press, 1953).

Genberg, Hans, and Alexander Swoboda, "The Current Account and the Policy Mix under Flexible Exchange Rates," International Monetary Fund Working Paper No. 70 (Washington: IMF, October 1987).

Henderson, Dale, "Financial Policies in Open Economies," *American Economic Review* (Nashville, Tennessee), Vol. 69 (May 1979), pp. 232–39.

Holbrook, Robert S., "Optimal Economic Policy and the Problem of Instrument Instability," *American Economic Review*, (Nashville, Tennessee), Vol. 62 (March 1972), pp. 57–65.

Horne, Jocelyn, and Paul R. Masson, "Scope and Limits of International Economic Cooperation and Policy Coordination," *Staff Papers*, International Monetary Fund

(Washington), Vol. 35 (June 1988), pp. 259–96.

Kenen, Peter B., "Macroeconomic Theory and Policy: How the Closed Economy Was Opened," in *Handbook in International Economics*, ed. by Ronald W. Jones and Peter B. Kenen, Vol. 2 (Amsterdam: North-Holland, 1985), pp. 625–77.

_____, "The Theory of Optimum Currency Areas: An Eclectic View," in *Monetary Problems of the International Economy*, ed. by Robert A. Mundell and Alexander K. Swoboda (Chicago: University of Chicago Press, 1969), pp. 41–60.

Kydland, Finn E., and Edward C. Prescott, "Rules Rather than Discretion: The Inconsistency of Optimal Plans," *Journal of Political Economy* (Chicago), Vol. 85 (June 1977), pp. 473–92.

Lucas, Robert, "Econometric Policy Evaluation: A Critique," in *The Phillips Curve and Labor Markets*, ed. by Karl Brunner and Allan H. Meltzer, Carnegie-Rochester Conference Series on Public Policy, Vol. 1 (Amsterdam: North-Holland, 1976), pp. 19–46.

_____, and Thomas Sargent, "After Keynesian Macroeconomics," *Federal Reserve Bank of Minneapolis Quarterly Review*, Vol. 3 (Spring 1979), pp. 1–16.

McCallum, Bennett T., "Rational Expectations and the Estimation of Econometric Models: An Alternative Procedure," *International Economic Review* (Philadelphia), Vol. 17 (1976), pp. 484–90.

McKibbin, Warwick, and Jeffrey Sachs, "Comparing the Global Performance of Alternative Exchange Arrangements," National Bureau of Economic Research Working Paper No. 2024 (Cambridge, Massachusetts: NBER, September 1985).

_____, "Coordination of Monetary and Fiscal Policies in the OECD," in *International Aspects of Fiscal Policies*, ed. by Jacob Frenkel (Chicago: University of Chicago Press, 1988).

McKinnon, Ronald I., "Optimum Currency Areas," *American Economic Review* (Nashville, Tennessee), Vol. 53 (September 1963), pp. 717–25.

_____, *An International Standard for Monetary Stabilization*, Policy Analyses in International Economics, No. 8 (Washington: Institute for International Economics, March 1984).

Masson, Paul R., and others, "MULTIMOD: A Multi-Region Econometric Model," International Monetary Fund, *Staff Studies for the World Economic Outlook* (Washington: IMF, July 1988).

Mundell, Robert A., "A Theory of Optimum Currency Areas," *American Economic Review* (Nashville, Tennessee), Vol. 51 (November 1961), pp. 609–17.

_____, "The Appropriate Use of Monetary and Fiscal Policy for Internal and External Stability," *Staff Papers*, International Monetary Fund (Washington), Vol. 9 (March 1962).

_____, *The Dollar and the Policy Mix*, Essays in International Finance No. 85 (Princeton, New Jersey: Princeton University Press, May 1971).

Poole, William, "Optimal Choice of Monetary Policy Instruments in a Simple Stochastic Macro Model," *Quarterly Journal of Economics* (New York), Vol. 84 (May 1970), pp. 197–216.

Sachs, Jeffrey, "The Dollar and the Policy Mix: 1985," *Brookings Papers on Economic Activity*, Vol. 1 (Washington: The Brookings Institution, 1985), pp. 117–97.

Taylor, John, "An Econometric Evaluation of International Monetary Policy Rules: Fixed versus Flexible Exchange Rates," (mimeographed; California: Stanford University, October 1986).

_____ (1985a), "International Coordination in the Design of Macroeconomic Policy Rules," *European Economic Review* (Amsterdam), Vol. 28 (June–July 1985), pp. 53–81.

_____ (1985b), "What Would Nominal GNP Targeting Do to the Business Cycle?" in *Understanding Monetary Regimes*, ed. by Karl Brunner and Allan H. Meltzer, Carnegie-Rochester Conference Series on Public Policy, Vol. 22 (Amsterdam: North-Holland, 1985), pp. 61–84.

Tinbergen, Jan, *On the Theory of Economic Policy* (Amsterdam: North-Holland, 1952).

Tobin, James, "Stabilization Policy Ten Years After," *Brookings Papers on Economic Activity* (Washington: The Brookings Institution, 1980), pp. 19–71.

Wallich, Henry C., "Institutional Cooperation in the World Economy," in *The World Economic System: Performance and Prospects*, ed. by Jacob Frenkel and Michael Mussa (Dover, Massachusetts: Auburn House, 1984), pp. 85–99.

Williamson, John, *The Exchange Rate System*, Institute for International Economics, Policy Analyses in International Economics No. 5, 2nd ed. (Washington: IIE, 1985).

_____, and Marcus H. Miller, *Targets and Indicators: A Blueprint for the International Coordination of Economic Policy*, Institute for International Economics, Policy Analyses in International Economics No. 22 (Washington: IIE, 1987).

Comments

Jeffrey R. Shafer*

Since the first empirical macroeconomic models appeared about 50 years ago, their development and use have been driven by the search for answers to two questions:
1) What are better and worse ways of conducting monetary and fiscal policies so as to stabilize output and prices?
2) How will economies evolve in the future?
This conference is directed at the first question, considered in a multinational context, and the papers prepared for it provide a good picture of how far computing power and analytical developments have brought us in using large models to derive practical insights into the design of policies.

In some respects we have come a long way. The models have become more carefully considered with respect to their theoretical underpinnings. We now have a family of multinational models within which to examine international interactions. And the techniques for simulating policy alternatives have undergone considerable development. In some respects, however, there is less reason for satisfaction. In particular, skepticism is still warranted as to how well the models capture the dynamic processes of national economies and their interactions. This question is not on the agenda of the conference, but uncertainty about a model must be borne in mind when interpreting results. In addition, the research presented in these papers still falls short of incorporating all that economic theory has to say about policy choice. It therefore seems most fruitful at this stage to focus on the methodological issues rather than on the specific results.

The paper by Frenkel, Goldstein, and Masson provides a good basis for considering where advances in economic analysis and computing power have brought us. It has been carefully thought out methodologically, starting from the state of the art and breaking new ground. It also provides a good perspective on the practical lessons from this line of work. The authors are humble about this; they say they are "skeptical of claims that model simulations—at this stage in our knowledge—can provide an unambiguous ranking of policy rules." This is a fair warning, but it is not as nihilistic as it sounds. Recognizing more clearly the limits of our knowledge about the effects of policies is an important step in the research program, and it has immediate practical implications for policymaking. Moreover, this conclusion ought not

---

* The views expressed are those of the author and do not necessarily reflect those of the Organization for Economic Cooperation and Development or its member governments.

be permitted to obscure the important attributes of sound policies that emerge from their analysis.

I will comment first on the simulation methodology used in the paper and its relevance for policy. I will then offer some observations about the simulation results. Finally, I will suggest how an expansion of computing capacity by another order of magnitude might be used by those engaged in large model research, and where further empirical work appears most critical to advance the debate over alternative policy approaches.

Simulation Methodology

Two features of the simulation methodology used in this paper, taken together, mark an important advance in the use of empirical macroeconomic models for policy analysis. One is the implementation of forward-looking expectations; the second is the use of Monte-Carlo methods of stochastic simulation under alternative policy rules. Forward-looking expectations have been a trendy way to dress up empirical macroeconomic models for several years. So long as the simulation approach was to subject the model to one-time shocks—either unanticipated or anticipated as from a certain date—their inclusion in models seemed a step away from realism in policy analysis. It is rare, if ever, that a policy change can be characterized as breaking clearly with the past, and as immediately transparent and fully credible as to its implementation over the indefinite future. Rational economic agents would rarely, if ever, assign zero probability to a policy in one period and a probability of one the next. It also strains realism to assume that economic agents would immediately and precisely trace through the implications of an unanticipated shock. Their knowledge of fundamental economic relationships, like that of model builders, is too imprecise for this. Thus, while single-shock simulations under perfect foresight provide insight into the properties of a model (and are so used by Frenkel, Goldstein, and Masson), they are a poor guide as to the actual effects of policies.

The simulation strategy of Frenkel and others poses the question: How would linked economies perform under alternative policy rules, if a given rule were adopted and maintained indefinitely, and if the structure of economies and the distribution of disturbances were those observed in the past? This is an interesting and potentially fruitful line of investigation. It requires a Monte-Carlo approach to dynamic simulation; in this I agree with the authors' judgment concerning the inadequacy of simulations limited to historical disturbances. And it represents a domain of research where forward-looking expectations come into their own in making a fundamental contribution. Since the time-series behavior of variables on which economic agents form expectations depends on the policy rule (as well as on the fundamental structure of the model and the distribution of disturbances), the way in which past data are translated into expectations will differ from rule to rule. Thus, representations of expectations as functions of past observations of variables—which may serve passably well for forecasting purposes and for assessing the effects of judgmental policy actions within an unchanged policy strategy—could not be expected to apply in a different policy regime. For addressing systematic policy issues, the two central features of the simulation methodology—forward-looking expectations and the use of Monte-Carlo methods—reinforce one another.

The Monte-Carlo approach also puts the focus of the investigation of systemic questions where it should be—on the robustness of policies. The authors conclude, on the basis of their single-shock experiments, that no one regime is ideal for all shocks. The practical import of this well-known theoretical proposition is that policies should perform well over the range of disturbances to which the system is likely to be subjected. It is sound practice to eschew policies that are optimal in the most likely event, but which would do poorly under other conditions, in favor of those that have flatter payoff functions over the domain of possible outcomes.

Policy Implications of the Results

The authors are properly modest about the operational policy conclusions to be drawn from their work to date. Rankings in the performance of various rules depend on the weight given to containing fluctuations of different variables; they are likely to be quite sensitive to the particular specification and parameter values of the model, which exhibits some questionable behavior, and to the specific form of the rule used for simulation. Indeed, the authors found the latter to be the case where alternatives were investigated. Nevertheless, the simulation exercise provides reminders of two important policy lessons: one explicit and one implicit.

First, two policy instruments are generally better than one. Thus, policy rules that involve both fiscal and monetary policy instruments tend to do better than those that involve monetary policy alone. This is a well-established proposition, but it is all too often overlooked. Indeed, the tendency to burden monetary policies with the full job of macroeconomic stabilization appears once more to be on the rise. Using both macroeconomic instruments wisely does not necessarily imply extremely active manipulation of either of them. And, as the authors point out, fiscal policy may not be manageable on a timely enough basis to contribute as much to stabilization as the simulations would suggest. Nevertheless, the choice of the rule governing budgetary setting matters for macroeconomic performance in all but limiting-case models.

Second, satisfying certain a priori requirements for policies seems much more important than the choice among those that satisfy them. All of the results reported in Table 2 of the paper are for policy rules that are stable over the medium to long run in the context of the authors' model. While this may seem to be a trivial consideration, it is by no means clear that it carries the weight that it deserves in policy debates. One indication of this is the inability to simulate the target zone rule, which fails to pin down national inflation rates in the long run. This flaw in the target zone proposal, one not shared by its "blueprint" offspring, would manifest itself in long-run simulations of most modern linked macromodels. Yet the target zone proposal is seriously discussed as a practical policy option.

Experience supports the importance of long-run sustainability as a criterion for policies. Monetary policies justly came under fire in the 1970s for myopic neglect of longer-run implications. The costs of similar neglect of the sustainability criterion for fiscal policies have been felt in the 1980s and are still with us. The long-run simulations required to impose forward-looking expectations serve to sort out sustainable from unsustainable policies in the context of a particular model. This is an additional strength of the approach. That one may be left with little to choose among the policies that can be implemented in such simulations may be to miss the most important point—many bad policies fall by the wayside.

Future Work

The search for robust policies, which motivates the work of Frenkel and others, should, in my view, be a principal objective of macroeconomic policy research. Such a focus is warranted by uncertainty about models and future disturbances in them. The paper takes account of the latter, but not the former, by incorporating additive disturbances to the structural equations of the model. Taking account of model uncertainty can fundamentally alter optimal policy strategies, as was first pointed out by William Brainard.[1] As far as I am aware, the implications of his theoretical insights have not been investigated systematically in the context of dynamic, empirical macroeconomic models.

We know that parameter values are imprecise estimates, with sample distributions conditional on the specification available from the estimation process. The time may be approaching when it will be feasible to do Monte-Carlo experiments incorporating drawings of parameter values from estimated variance-covariance matrices, as well as drawings of additive disturbances. This would provide a richer treatment of uncertainty in examining the properties of alternative policy rules, although it would not resolve the problems posed by uncertainty about model structure. Conjecturing on the basis of Brainard's simple, static examples, I would expect that allowing for parameter uncertainty would reinforce the case for using all available instruments, but to do so in a less activist manner than suggested by research until now. Explora-

---

[1] See William Brainard's "Uncertainty and the Effectiveness of Policy," *American Economic Review, Papers and Proceedings*, May 1967, pp. 411–25.

tion of this question deserves priority in the program of model-based research on policy regimes.

One area where empirical work is especially needed to strengthen the basis for policy evaluations of the sort undertaken by Frenkel and others is that of identifying the sources of noise in expectationally important variables. The authors explore the performance of a fixed exchange rate regime under the assumption that disturbances to demand across currencies would disappear in such a regime. In doing so, they give a nod to the possibility that the magnitude of observed shifts of demand between currencies during the period of floating exchange rates is greater than could be accounted for by fundamental disturbances. One rationale for this is that expectations of a time series could have a noise component, the magnitude of which was positively related to the volatility of the series. The experience with the European Monetary System (EMS) suggests there may be something to this excess noise hypothesis. There is evidence that exchange rate volatility among the currencies adhering to these exchange rate arrangements has been sharply reduced without a commensurate increase in monetary volatility, which would have been required had the volatility of asset demands across countries not receded.[2]

Hence, there are reasons to suspect that under a policy rule in which exchange rates are permitted to float freely, the amplitude of fluctuations could be magnified by shifts in demand arising from noisy expectations. If expectations were subject to such noise, measuring the performance of a policy rule partly in terms of the volatility of exchange rates, as the authors do, would be justified, although the authors do not explicitly give this rationale. Otherwise, it is difficult to motivate exchange rate stability as an objective of policy in its own right, independent of its effects on output and price stability. (The external balance would seem to be another macroeconomic variable with a weak claim to a place in the objective function of policymakers, independent of its relevance for the behavior of other variables.)

The question of whether a link exists between the weight given to stabilization of expectationally important variables (such as the exchange rate) and the magnitude of disturbances in the macroeconomy would seem to be fundamental. This question needs to be considered before drawing more specific operational policy conclusions from the research pursued in the paper by Frenkel and others, and in a number of other papers presented at this conference. It is key to the issue of whether exchange rate stabilization enhances the overall stability of internationally independent economies, or whether it merely alters the intensity with which truly exogenous disturbances are manifested in different variables.

---

[2] See Tomasso Padoa Schioppa's "Policy Cooperation and the EMS Experience," and my comments on it in *International Economic Policy Coordination,* by Willem H. Buiter and Richard C. Marston (New York: Cambridge University Press, 1985).

Stanley Fischer

In this interesting and exploratory paper, Jacob Frenkel, Morris Goldstein, and Paul Masson focus on matters of both substance and technique. By emphasizing not only results, the authors implicitly and appropriately treat MULTIMOD as mainly a useful framework for thinking about policy issues. Before turning to the methodological issues, I briefly examine the substantive results, which, because there are many, are somewhat difficult to summarize.

Results

The distinction made by the authors between coordinated and uncoordinated rules is that under the former, governments have exchange rate targets. In all cases, rules are coordinated in the sense that governments in each country follow the *same* rule, except that when the exchange rate is targeted, the United States gets to be the nth country. Thus, there are no results on the effects of a lack of coordination in the sense that countries fail even to pursue the same monetary and/or fiscal rules.

Another feature to note is that monetary policy is always implemented through feedback rules on nominal interest rates. The monetary rule is essentially an interest rate rule that avoids nominal indeterminacy by aiming to return the money stock to a targeted long-run level.

The strongest general finding of the paper is that monetary policy, as implemented through interest rate feedback rules, can do very little to stabilize the economy. This result does not follow from the rational expectations feature of MULTIMOD, which does allow for some nominal price stickiness. It may be that the use of an annual model limits the effectiveness of monetary policy, since the degree of price stickiness found in annual data probably gives little leverage to monetary policy.

The blueprint or fiscal policy augmented policy rule of Williamson-Miller—in which monetary policy responds to the current account and fiscal policy is used to control nominal gross national product (GNP)—does have significant stabilizing effects[1]. Surprisingly, the Williamson-Miller policy assignment appears to perform better than the reverse assignment in which fiscal policy is aimed at the current account and monetary policy at a nominal GNP target. This result may occur because the feedback parameters used in simulating the original assignment are taken from earlier work by Edison and Williamson-Miller, presumably based on extensive experimentation; it is quite possible that further experimentation with the reverse assignment would lead to improved results.

---

[1]The authors note that the fiscal policy involves changes in government spending together with changes in tax rates that enable the government to meet its long-run budget constraint.

Examining Table 2 in the paper by Frenkel and others, note that the blueprint rule (1) produces the lowest variability in real GNP for each of the Group of Three countries, and is almost best for the developing countries. It also does well in reducing the variability of the inflation rate. However, for good reasons, the authors play down this result. Their skepticism stems from the implementation lags of fiscal policy; they suggest that fiscal policy should be allowed to react only with a one-year lag, a change that leaves the blueprint superior to all other rules only for the United States. While the inclusion of the one-year lag increases the realism of the results, even that may be too optimistic, for fiscal policy in recent years has been extraordinarily immobile —except in the immediate aftermath of the 1987 stock market crash.

Methodological Issues

All policy analysis uses models—although not all are explicit. Real-world policy decisions are made using models, most of them implicit. The authors of this paper, and of the others in this volume, are to be commended for not being paralyzed by the Lucas econometric policy evaluation bogey-man. The Lucas policy evaluation critique could always be invoked to challenge simulations of the type undertaken here, for it is quite possible that the supposedly structural equations of MULTIMOD would change if policy changed. But once expectations have been made rational, it is hard to see why the profession should hold off doing serious policy work using econometric models.

A priori arguments of the type that led Lucas, in his famous 1976 paper, to conclude that steady money growth was the optimal policy cannot be used to settle either that issue or the issue of optimal exchange rate rules. (Indeed there is much evidence, namely the behavior of money demand in the 1980s, to suggest that the Lucas monetary policy would have produced worse economic outcomes than the discretionary monetary policies that were followed.) Advocates of floating exchange rates used a priori arguments to make their case; events have been sufficiently different from those advertised that it is more than legitimate to attempt to move on to a serious evaluation of alternatives.

The usefulness of the exercise is enhanced by the simplicity of the feedback rules. Because it is essential to explain policy to the policymakers who have to live by the consequences, policy rules have to be reasonably simple, as the rules in this paper are.

The authors are to be commended too for undertaking stochastic simulations rather than confining themselves to a rerun of history. The stochastic simulations in effect provide a way of calculating the asymptotic variances that could be calculated directly in a linear model.

It would, however, be useful to know just how important the non-linearities in the present model are, for it may be possible to calculate optimal feedback policies in a linearized version of the model. The search procedure over policy parameters in the present paper is highly informal and, perhaps, unorganized and a more systematic approach would be desirable.

Examination of the charts raises the question of whether the full dynamics of the model have been allowed to work themselves out. The charts certainly do suggest very slow dynamics; nor is it obvious in all cases that the oscillations are damped.

The authors present a useful description of the problem of instrument instability which clearly plagues their simulations. Instrument instability is a problem because of doubts about model specification: if the model was correct the consequences of instrument instability would be reflected in economic performance. Since the model is never correct, instrument instability should be precluded. It can be handled in a maximizing model by putting costs on the variability of instruments, which is another reason it would be desirable for the authors to try to find even an approximate optimizing procedure for choosing their feedback rules.

The authors conclude by raising the question of how to model discretion. The issues may be similar to those of modeling a good chess player, although the rules of the game of chess can be modeled better than the economy. I used to believe that one could model discretion by sitting a policymaker down with a model and observing his actions. This is probably not right. One possibility suggested by the findings of this and other papers that different rules perform better in different circumstances is that discretion may be a switching rule—and such rules can be specified.

Finally, what are we to make of this paper's lack of clear results? The results are obviously early, but the authors are on the right track in using simple rules. They should probably go further in examining the results of their simulations, and they should venture to use formal optimality criteria. The most important next steps are to model similar rules in other models: the case for using a particular rule will be most convincing if it works well for many different views of the detailed working of the economy—and if the reason it works well can be explained to both professionals and policymakers.

6

The Stabilizing Properties of Target Zones

Marcus Miller, Paul Weller, and John Williamson*

I. Introduction

Exchange rate targeting is an integral element of the "blueprint proposals" for policy coordination developed previously by two of the authors of this paper (Williamson and Miller, 1987). The proposals called for adopting, as intermediate targets, a set of mutually consistent *exchange rate trajectories* calculated to reconcile internal and external balance in the medium term. Sterilized intervention and international differences in interest rates would be used to maintain exchange rates within relatively wide zones around the exchange rate targets.

To the "target zones" (previously advocated in Williamson, 1985), the blueprint added another set of intermediate targets, namely, *growth rates of domestic demand*, calculated to support the gradual elimination of any inherited inflation and the gradual restoration of internal and external balance. The average world level of interest rates and fiscal policy would be used to manage the growth of demand.

These proposals have two important purposes: to secure the international consistency of macroeconomic policies, and to impose a measure of discipline on governments. These general objectives seem to have a certain appeal to academic economists, although the second one has not been embraced by governments or central bankers (Pöhl, 1987). But matters are considerably different so far as *exchange rate targeting* is concerned. The Group of Seven governments have adopted this with enthusiasm: Although their rhetoric has supported efforts to construct a set of indicators to secure comprehensive policy coordination, their main practical efforts were directed toward eliminating U.S. dollar overvaluation, and then to preventing a dollar overshoot. In

*We are grateful to Olivier Blanchard, Bill Branson, Willem Buiter, and Brad De Long for their comments.

contrast, most academics regard exchange rate targeting as an intellectual error whose only justification is that it may secure some coordination of fiscal and monetary policies, which affect the exchange rate. But, according to this view, it would be better to focus directly on the policy coordination and to forget about the exchange rate targeting.

This paper is directed at those academics skeptical of the value of exchange rate targeting, rather than at the officials doubtful of the virtues of policy discipline. This does not imply that we believe that disciplining markets is a more important objective than disciplining governments. Indeed, the blueprint is directed at achieving both; we focus on only one objective in this paper, however, in keeping with the principle of division of labor.

The paper is organized as follows: we first define the issue and subsequently analyze the impact of imposing a target zone in three different models: the standard Dornbusch model, with "Blanchard bubbles" incorporated; a similar model with "noise" in the fundamentals; and a model where traders are divided into "sophisticated" investors who look at fundamentals and "noise traders" (or chartists) who do not. We then summarize our conclusions.

II. The Issue

We believe that academic hostility to exchange rate targeting arises largely because the models used to analyze macroeconomic policy have treated exchange rates as an accurate reflection of economic fundamentals—a reflection marred at most only by serially uncorrelated errors. However, the significance of economic fundamentals in determining exchange rates was thrown into question by Meese and Rogoff (1983), whose empirical research was conducted before the dollar rose to the extraordinary heights that triggered the turnaround in U.S. policy in 1985, and, subsequently, by Frankel and Froot (1986). Moreover, the accumulating evidence of excess volatility and serially correlated errors in financial markets in general—not to mention the stock market crash of 1987—has called into question the efficient markets paradigm. In particular, it has been suggested that the failure of market efficiency may be due to the presence of "noise traders," who both increase market volatility and make systematic errors about the underlying asset values (see, for example, De Long and others, 1987; and Campbell and Kyle, 1988). Sophisticated investors, or "smart money," must allow for the behavior of such noise traders, as well as economic fundamentals, in forecasting market performance. So, too, should policymakers.

A prime example of the importance of assuming that exchange rates accurately reflect fundamentals arises in the debate on the ability of a target-zone system to limit misalignments. This debate was initiated by Edison, Miller, and Williamson (1987); they performed historical simulations using the U.S. Federal Reserve's Multicountry Model (MCM), designed to test the ability of a target zone system to limit exchange rate misalignments during

1976–85. They concluded that the feedback rule from exchange rate misalignments to short-term interest rates, by which they represented target zones, "does indeed succeed in appreciably diminishing the magnitude of misalignments." Subsequent historical simulations on the Global Econometric Model (GEM), reported by Currie and Wren-Lewis (1988), also concluded that target zones could have had a modest, but significant, effect in limiting misalignments.

In contrast, the historical simulations reported by Frenkel, Goldstein, and Masson (1988) show target zones or the blueprint having almost no ability to influence exchange rates, even though Frenkel, Goldstein, and Masson attempted to stay close to the spirit of the original proposals and adopted the same feedback rule from exchange rate misalignments to the short-term interest rate as that used by Edison, Miller, and Williamson. Real effective exchange rates simply could not be kept within target zones even as wide as ±10 percent, because this would have required driving interest rates negative. They attributed the small impact of short-term interest rates on exchange rates to their use of MULTIMOD, in which exchange rates are anchored by perfect foresight. The relative success of Edison, Miller, and Williamson and Currie and Wren-Lewis in limiting exchange rate misalignments by using monetary policy is attributed to the failure of the MCM or GEM models to incorporate forward-looking expectations; their findings are thus dismissed as subject to the Lucas Critique.

Ironically, Edison, Miller, and Williamson had argued that monetary policy's modest ability to influence the real exchange rate, illustrated in their simulations, probably *understated* the power of monetary policy for three reasons. First, the feedback rule used was fairly weak: interest rates could have been adjusted more than they were. Second, the model made no allowance for intervention. And third, "it neglects the impact that exchange rate targeting might have had in focusing market expectations and thus limiting misalignments caused by speculative bubbles."

This paper elaborates on the third argument. It shows how broadening the conventional rational-expectations/efficient-market models to allow for market inefficiencies strengthens the case for focusing policy on exchange rates *per se*, rather than simply on the economic fundamentals that should affect them. It demonstrates that forward-looking expectations do not preclude the use of monetary policy (including the announcement of targets and intervention, as well as interest rates) to manage the exchange rate. On the contrary, credible exchange rate targeting could be expected, in the models we present, to limit misalignments more effectively than suggested by perfect-foresight simulations of models estimated over the period of free floating.

The models we use to make these points doubtless lack some descriptive accuracy. They are used because they provide a convenient way of demonstrating that the claims of Frenkel, Goldstein, and Masson depend on the absence of market inefficiencies such as those incorporated in these particular models. Rejection of our conclusions requires not so much a demonstration that these particular representations of market inefficiency fail to describe some period of history, as a proof that markets are efficient.

We use three models of market inefficiency to make our point. The first of these is the Blanchard (1979) model of a rational bubble. A Blanchard bubble is characterized by a progressively faster deviation of the asset price from its equilibrium trajectory; investors know that the bubble must ultimately burst and the price collapse back to equilibrium, but they are tempted nonetheless to continue holding the asset in the hope that the price will rise yet further—sufficiently fast to compensate them for the risk of its collapse—before the collapse occurs. We show in the next section that, if all market participants believe that the authorities will prevent the exchange rate from moving outside a specified target zone through sterilized intervention, this must cause the bubble to burst when it hits the edge of the zone. But if collapse were certain at that time, it must occur earlier because the possibility of a capital gain in the previous period is zero. Extending the argument back, it can be shown that a credible target zone will prevent a Blanchard bubble from ever starting.

The second model adds the existence of "noise" to the fundamentals. This produces Krugman's (1987) "bias in the band," where the presence of a band and the credible promise of action at its margins tends to push the exchange rate toward the middle of the band even before the intervention or policy action.

The third model introduces "fads," defined as autoregressive deviations of an asset price from the equilibrium trajectory associated with "fundamentals." The high U.S. dollar of 1981–86 might, for example, be regarded as partly the consequence of the bullish views of a group of unsophisticated investors. Our analysis shows how a target zone could help to reinforce the influence of informed speculators in limiting the ability of such unsophisticated investors to push rates away from equilibrium. Once again, an analysis of the type conducted by Frenkel, Goldstein, and Masson, which assumes that all speculators are well-informed—even without guidance from the public sector—will underestimate the stabilizing power of a target zone.

III. Blanchard Bubbles and Currency Bands
in a Dornbusch Model

To examine the impact of credible currency bands on the behavior of the exchange rate in a setting with rational expectations, we use the log-linear model of Dornbusch (1976). The equations are given in Appendix I (which also lists the symbols used), but, as they are doubtless familiar, they are not discussed in detail in the text. Surely, the absence of inflation expectations in the Dornbusch model enhances the power of interest rate policy to affect the real exchange rate, relative to MULTIMOD, for example; by how much is an interesting question for investigation. But, as we argue below, to end bubbles, *direct foreign exchange market intervention* is probably more important in checking the exchange rate than are the effects of monetary policy on interest rates.

In the discussion that follows, we indicate the effect of including Blanchard bubbles on the usual phase diagram, before turning to the impact of currency bands. We then repeat the procedure, in circumstances where fundamentals are themselves subject to stochastic shocks.

The Deterministic Case

As Appendix I shows, the formal model consists of four linear equations determining four variables. The first two equations are not dynamic; they are the LM and IS curves, which determine output and interest rates, conditional on current values for the price level and the exchange rate. The evolution of the latter over time are characterized, respectively, by a Phillips relation and the "no-profitable-arbitrage condition"—that any anticipated changes in the exchange rate be matched by the international interest differential. (Foreign interest rates are assumed constant, as is the domestic money stock, except at the edge of a currency band; see below.)

The essential feature of this model is the contrast between the dynamic behavior of the domestic price level and that of the exchange rate. The domestic price level, p (in logs), is a "sticky" variable that changes relatively slowly over time, influenced by movements in current production above or below the noninflationary level. By contrast, the nominal exchange rate, x (in logs), is a "forward-looking" variable in no way influenced by its previous value. As indicated formally in Appendix I, its current value is the long-run equilibrium value, "discounted" by the international interest differential. (Here, the exchange rate is defined as the foreign currency value of the home currency. Thus, a future interest differential that is, on average, in favor of the domestic economy will be associated with an appreciation of the currency above equilibrium.)

As there are only two dynamic processes involved, the system of four equations can be reduced to a couple of simultaneous, linear differential equations in the variables, p and x, with a two-dimensional phase diagram that possesses a "saddlepoint" structure. These saddlepoint dynamics are indicated by the solid lines in Chart 1. There SS indicates the unique *stable* path leading to equilibrium (defined to be at the origin); UU indicates the *unstable* path leading from equilibrium; and other paths that satisfy the equations of the model are shown to be diverging progressively away from SS toward UU as time proceeds.

Faced with this multiplicity of solutions, it is typically assumed in such saddlepoint models that, for any historically given value for the predetermined variable (here, the price level), the forward-looking variable (here, the ex-

Chart 1. Blanchard's Rational Bubbles in a Dornbusch Model

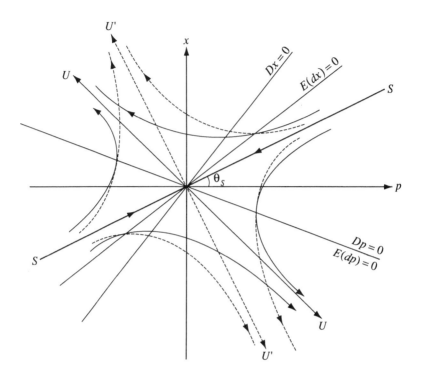

change rate) adjusts precisely so as to position the system on the stable adjustment path, SS. All other paths are ruled out because, while they satisfy the necessary arbitrage condition, they require the exchange rate to diverge ever further from equilibrium as time passes.

However, in the context of models with such forward-looking asset prices, Blanchard (1979) has proposed an alternative class of rational expectations solutions, which exhibit "bubble" instability but do not entail the exchange rate following a divergent path forever. A Blanchard bubble always has a positive probability of "bursting," and when it does, the exchange rate reverts to the stable manifold and the system moves progressively toward equilibrium. It is essential that such bubbles end with probability one—which Blanchard assures by assuming that the bursting is governed by a Poisson process. [1] In what follows we describe the nature of these rational bubble paths

---

[1] A number of attempts have been made to test for the existence of bubbles in asset markets (see, for example, Blanchard and Watson, 1982; Flood and Hodrick, 1986; West, 1988; and Smith, 1987), with mixed results. Controversy also surrounds the question of whether bubbles are

in the Dornbusch model; we then show that a currency band can effectively "kill off" all such deviant behavior.

The characteristic feature of these bubble paths is, of course, the risk of a jump in the exchange rate when the bubble bursts. (If the speculation has been in favor of the domestic currency, this will imply a downwards collapse; if the speculation has been adverse, the foreign currency collapses, giving a jump appreciation to the home currency.) To take account of this, the usual arbitrage condition needs to be modified as the expected movement of the rate along a bubble path must now equal the international interest differential *together with a term that can be thought of as the cost of buying insurance against a crash* (see equation (7) in Appendix I). [2]

The effect that this modification has on the phase diagram, Chart 1, is easy to see. First, there is no change to the stable path, SS, itself. But the other trajectories are affected. Specifically, the dotted lines in the chart represent bubbles that have to diverge faster from the stable manifold than do the deterministic paths, as necessary to compensate for the possibility of a collapse. The unstable manifold of the original system, UU, is rotated to $U'U'$: by the same logic, a steadily exploding Blanchard bubble also requires a faster appreciation in the exchange rate to compensate for the ever-present likelihood of collapse. [3]

Of course, for all these bubble paths, when the bubble eventually bursts, the system reverts to the stable path of adjustment to equilibrium. But, as the exchange rate movements may nevertheless wreak considerable havoc on the way, it would be reassuring to know whether or not a form of market intervention exists that could identify the errant paths and end them. In fact, as we shall argue, the imposition of a fully credible currency band has an even stronger impact: no such bubbles ever emerge.

The reasoning is straightforward. If all market participants believe that, when the exchange rate hits the edge of the band, the authorities will defend the rate by sudden intervention (designed to produce a jump in the rate), this

---

truly consistent with rationality. Tirole (1982) argues that if agents have infinite horizons, rational bubbles cannot occur (but, see Gilles and Leroy, 1987). But in a deterministic, overlapping-generations model, such bubbles are possible (Tirole, 1985).

[2] The arbitrage equation is an approximation, which, in discrete time, takes the form $(1 - \pi) x_{t+1} + \pi \theta_s p_{t+1} - x_t = i_t^* - i_t$. On the left-hand side is the expected "capital gain." (The logarithmic transformation preserves symmetry between domestic and foreign currencies and is a means of avoiding the "Siegel paradox," where strict arbitrage conditions for the two currencies are inconsistent.) We are grateful to Willem Buiter for pointing out an error in our original formulation.

[3] The presence of negative bubbles in the diagram requires comment, since a number of writers have made the simple point that a non-negativity constraint upon prices must rule out a negative bubble. Since we work with logarithmic transformations of variables, our model has no such constraint. However, the approximation used in the reformulated arbitrage equation clearly becomes less satisfactory as variables diverge progressively further from their equilibrium values.

must cause the bubble to burst. But this is inconsistent with the existence of a bubble in the first place: If all know that collapse is certain to occur at time t, all will wish to sell the currency at $t - \epsilon$. But then collapse will occur at $t - \epsilon$. Repeating this argument we find that collapse must occur at time zero, that is, all such bubbles are "strangled at birth."

The effect of imposing a fully credible currency band in a Dornbusch model containing Blanchard bubbles is consequently easy to show, as the infinite range of possibilities suggested by the paths depicted in Chart 1 is reduced to the single stable trajectory in Chart 2. Between L and U the system lies on the stable path itself. When the price level is above the limit p_U, the exchange rate lies on the upper edge of the currency band and is held there by a suitable adjustment in monetary policy designed to set the interest differential to zero; but there remains a downward pressure that ensures stable convergence toward SS. (Similar arguments apply along the bottom edge.)

An important distinction needs to be drawn between the monetary policy intended to hold an equilibrium path at the edge of the band and that designed to deter bubbles. The latter, consisting, as argued above, of sudden intervention in the exchange market, is analogous to a so-called "punishment strategy" in game theory; it possesses the same characteristic that in equilibrium, if the strategy is fully credible, is never observed.[4] The former, by contrast, is

Chart 2. A Currency Band in a Deterministic Setting

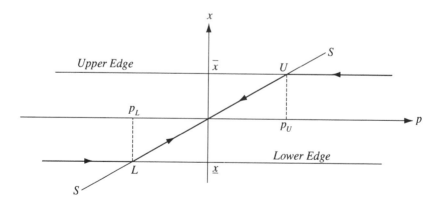

---

[4] Well-organized, coordinated intervention has clearly delivered on occasion the necessary "punishment." Witness the following quotation from Peter Norman in the *Financial Times* (January 10, 1989):

"After frantic speculative activity in 1987, currency markets treated the stabilisation efforts of the [Group of Seven] with notably more respect last year, after being caught in a costly central bank "bear trap" early in January. At that time, sudden, coordinated intervention to prop up the dollar when it had been oversold forced commercial banks to cover open positions at considerable cost."

observed if, for whatever reason, the price level lies outside the range $[p_L, p_U]$. (For further discussion of the monetary policy changes required at the edges of the band see Miller and Weller, 1989.)

It seems natural to ask how the price level might be driven outside the range $[p_L, p_U]$. One answer is as a result of changes in exogenous influences (such as foreign prices or the money stock); another possibility is stochastic disturbances to the price level. But, as Krugman (1987) points out, in a stochastic context currency bands should surely affect the behavior of the rate inside the currency band itself.

The next section, therefore, discusses how imposing currency bands causes a "bending" of the stable trajectory inside the band when inflation is continually subjected to random shocks. We also indicate how Blanchard bubbles would affect these stochastic solutions and discuss the stabilizing effects of credible currency bands.

Shocks to the Fundamentals

Allow stochastic disturbances to be introduced in the form of serially uncorrelated shocks to the Phillips curve. Then, even in the absence of bubbles, the arbitrage equation must be written in expected value terms. (See Appendix I, for further discussion of noise in fundamentals.)

Finding the solutions to such a system is a matter of some technical difficulty (see Appendix III), but the details need not detain us here. Suffice it to say that, even without the presence of bubbles, the solutions to the resulting stochastic system now include an *infinity* of paths connected to the equilibrium at the origin (in addition to the two paths SS and UU already encountered). These solutions are shown graphically in Chart 3.

What would happen if Blanchard bubbles were added to this stochastic system? Given our earlier analysis, it is easy to show (see Appendix I) that once again the bubbles modify the arbitrage condition and, while leaving SS unchanged, they would distort the trajectories as necessary to cover the risk of a collapse, rotating the UU path clockwise toward the vertical axis as before. (These paths could be shown as dotted trajectories in Chart 3, but have been omitted for the sake of clarity.)

Those features of rational bubbles that are alleged to be implausible disappear in our stochastic model. These paths are considerably more well-behaved in that they can spend periods of time converging *toward* equilibrium in the presence of favorable shocks to fundamentals. Many paths will stay close to the "free-float" path for long periods of time, so that when they burst the discontinuity in the exchange rate will not be large. So far, we are unaware of any attempts to test for the existence of this type of bubble.

The reason for the more regular behavior of such bubbles in a stochastic framework is clear enough. When a system is subject to random shocks, which (as a consequence of feedback effects) generate a tendency to return to

Chart 3. Stochastic Solutions Passing Through the Origin

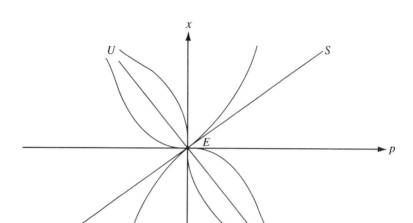

equilibrium, this acts in part to offset the divergent influence of the bubble. Nevertheless, the appearance of such bubbles would indicate an undesirable degree of instability.

Can we say what the effect of imposing a fully credible currency band would be? An argument similar to that used in the deterministic model suggests that no such bubble is sustainable. The unique exchange rate path is given by the S-shaped curve tangential to the top and bottom of the band, as shown in Chart 4. This is the solution first identified by Krugman (1987) in a model that assumed fundamentals followed a random walk.

The benefits stemming from the imposition of a target zone are now twofold. Not only does it do away with bubbles, it also generates what Krugman has labeled "the bias in the band," the bending of the exchange rate path away from the stable manifold toward the middle of the band; this produces what he refers to as a "honeymoon effect," where the existence of a credible band postpones, perhaps quite significantly, the need for intervention to hold the rate at the edge of the band.

IV. Target Zones and Currency Fads

It is increasingly evident that a number of phenomena, such as "excess volatility" in equity markets and the predictability of "excess returns," cannot

Chart 4. Krugman's "Bias in the Band"

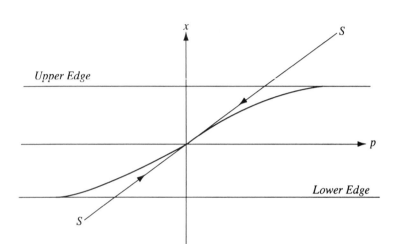

be satisfactorily explained within the framework of the efficient markets paradigm. This has led to empirical and theoretical work designed to document and explain such phenomena.

At a theoretical level, a standard criticism leveled at any appeal to irrational behavior in asset markets is that any such behavior would be taken advantage of by sophisticated agents in the market; that this would lead to irrational agents incurring losses; and that, as a consequence, they would exit the market. In other words, a powerful selection mechanism would tend to promote market efficiency by eliminating naive investors.

This argument, however, has recently been challenged. De Long and others (1987) show that it is possible to have a situation in which sophisticated and "irrational" groups coexist in a market, and that in equilibrium the irrational group earns a higher expected return. This occurs because the misperceptions of the irrational group increase the noise in the market and sophisticated investors rationally adjust to this by requiring a higher yield on the risky asset. In certain circumstances—particularly if the unsophisticated group is, on average, "bullish"—it is possible to show that the irrational investors end up holding a portfolio earning a higher expected return than the sophisticated group. They are, of course, paying a price for this higher return in the form of a higher variance. But the force of the "natural selection" argument is considerably weakened. (The case, as De Long and others point out, is not conclusive, because it may be important to avoid a high probability of low wealth—a probability that increases for the unsophisticated group.)[5]

On the empirical side, Poterba and Summers (1987) have argued that standard tests of market efficiency have low power in detecting autoregressive "fads." Campbell and Kyle (1988) have tested a general equilibrium model of asset prices, which includes such fads, and find that one possible explanation for the data is that noise trading increased price volatility in U.S. stocks during 1871–1976. De Bondt and Thaler (1985, 1987) present evidence to suggest that a trading strategy of buying stocks that have recently performed poorly, and going short in those that have done well, can earn excess returns (see also Lehmann, 1987).

Since the autoregressive fads associated with noise trading can explain not only excess volatility but also prolonged periods of excess returns, and since there is some econometric support for these departures from efficient markets, we now consider the effect of including such fads in a model of exchange rate determination.

Already, Miller and Williamson (1988) have taken a first step by including a colored noise term in the arbitrage equation of a Dornbusch-style model—with the natural result that the exchange rate could deviate substantially (and for a prolonged time) from the level implied by fundamentals. We did not, however, consider how imposing wide target zones might affect the stochastic solutions discussed there—not because it was unimportant, but simply because at the time we could not see how to analyze this nonlinear stochastic problem. (We essentially assumed that the edges of the target zone coincided!) As risk neutrality was postulated, this fad suffered from the criticism that risk-neutral speculators would have been able to make profits in betting against it. Thanks largely to the work of Paul Krugman we can now tackle the problem of imposing wide bands; and, by introducing risk aversion, we can avoid the criticism just discussed. (Also, to simplify the problem, we suppress all shocks other than those propagating the fad, and take domestic prices as fixed.) The formal specification is given in Appendix II. Here, we outline the key features and then proceed diagrammatically.

In addition to the effect of (properly discounted) fundamentals, the exchange rate, x (in logs), is now assumed to be disturbed by an autoregressive "fad," denoted n (in logs) for "noise traders." This fad is expected to revert to zero (with an autoregressive coefficient of $-\psi$), but it is constantly renewed by uncorrelated shocks with mean zero and variance σ. The expected change in the exchange rate anticipated by the rational investors ("smart money") must take account both of the stochastic elements involved in the fad process (since they are assumed to be risk averse) and of the expected change in the fad itself.

---

[5] De Long and others (1988) prove some results on the long-run survival of noise traders taking this factor into account, but they have to assume that noise traders have no effect on prices.

The arbitrage condition relevant to the exchange rate now requires that the expected change in the rate should equal the international interest differential (as before), but now *corrected* by a risk term (assumed to be a scalar multiple of σ) and *augmented* by a term giving the expected decline of the fad (see equation (13) in Appendix II).

The model to be analyzed consists of four equations. The first two are, as before, the *IS* and *LM* curves for the goods and money market; the third is the arbitrage condition governing the expected change in the exchange rate, modified as just described. But, as the price level is assumed to be fixed, there is no Phillips curve: instead the fourth equation is a dynamic description of how the fad evolves. Once again, the system can be reduced to a couple of (stochastic) differential equations (see equation (17) in Appendix II). Since the noise process is taken to be autonomous, the diagram showing the stable and unstable paths, *SS* and *UU*, is rather simpler than for the Dornbusch model (where the evolution of the price level was endogenous). This can be seen in Chart 5, where the exchange rate appears on the vertical axis, as before; but it is the fad, *n* (rather than *p*) that appears on the horizontal axis.

The independence of the noise process from the rest of the economy means that the unstable path, *UU*, now coincides with the vertical axis. As for the stable path, *SS*, it has a positive slope that is flatter than the 45° line. Both of these lines must pass through the point *E*, which lies below the deterministic equilibrium shown as the point $x = 0$ on the vertical axis. (The reason the log of the exchange rate must be less than zero, even when the fad is actually zero, is that risk is still present; this means that the domestic interest rate must be higher than the foreign interest rate and this is achieved by a "devaluation" to *E*, where $x = \bar{x} < 0$.)

In the absence of target zones, the system is assumed to be stochastically "diffused" along the stable path, so the exchange rate will have an asymptotic normal distribution centered on *E* (formally, $N(\bar{x}, \sigma^2/2\psi)$). Note that for points to the right of the asymptotic expected value *E* in Chart 5, the bullishness of noise traders has lifted the currency above equilibrium. But as the high exchange rate moves the economy into a recession, it cuts the domestic interest rate and, hence, the asset value of the domestic currency.[6] Consequently, in the model, the effect of the bullish psychology of noise traders is partly offset by the calculations of rational investors.

In contrast to what we observe in the fully rational model, therefore, it is possible for the currency to be strong despite the expected interest differential being in favor of the *foreign* currency. Sophisticated investors depress the currency below the level it would have been driven to by noise trading alone.

---

[6] It is true that in the mid-1980s interest rates in the United States were high by historical standards, but they were not high enough to explain the strength of the U.S. dollar; see, for example, Krugman (1985).

Chart 5. Noise Traders, Smart Money, and the Exchange Rate

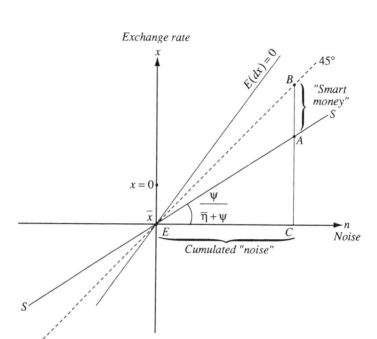

At point A, for example, the effect of the noise traders on the value of the currency is given by the horizontal distance CE, which is, of course, the same as the vertical distance BC measured from the 45° line. Hence, the implied contribution of rational investors (smart money) must be the negative quantity AB—which corresponds to the (negative) risk-adjusted interest differential at point A, scaled by $1/\psi$.

Despite this damping factor, the activities of the noise traders can take the exchange rate anywhere along the line SS. And such meandering will have real consequences in a model where the exchange rate represents the relative price of traded goods (since own-goods prices are fixed in domestic currency)—real effects that have, by construction, nothing to do with the fundamentals that have been held constant.

In such a situation, it is reasonable to suppose that the authorities will be eager to limit the resulting distortions to trade. Specifically, let us assume that the monetary authorities are determined—by intervening in the exchange market, by changing interest rates, or by whatever other means—to try to stop any growth of bullish sentiment in the currency beyond a certain point and take the appropriate action (of opposite sign) if and when bearish sentiment has developed to the same extent. And let us assume that these actions will indeed be effective; and that the smart money knows this.

What we have described is an example of the *regulation* of a stochastic process. The relationship between the exchange rate and the noise process is characterized, as before, by a solution to the *fundamental differential equation* (see Appendix III), together with the appropriate boundary conditions. The shape of all solutions symmetric about the origin is shown in Chart 6. Note that, because the noise process is autonomous, they have a simpler pattern than in the Dornbusch example, simply bending away from the line *SS*, with no points of inflection anywhere but at the origin. In the figure, the upper bound on the fad is imposed at *C*, and the lower bound at *C'*. The appropriate boundary conditions for a problem of this kind are derived by Dixit (1988). They consist of the requirement that the solution trajectories have a slope of zero at the points where the process is checked or "regulated."[7]

Chart 6. Bounded Noise and Target Zones

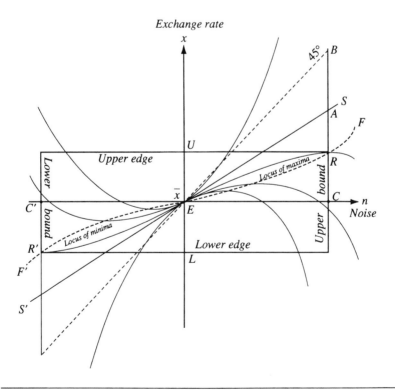

---

[7] Dixit's results are derived for a regulated Brownian motion process, but are also applicable to the autoregressive process in our model.

By constructing the locus of points (the dashed line FF') where the solution paths reach a maximum or minimum, we can work out how the exchange rate will behave for any given bounds on the fad. In the figure, the upper and lower limits at C and C' (which act as reflecting barriers) will have the effect of restricting the range of variation of the *exchange rate* to the interval $[L, U]$. Within this range the system will lie on the solid line $R'ER$, buffeted now this way, now that, by the vagaries of market sentiment.

It is important to emphasize that the range for the currency is *derived* from the limits imposed upon the noise process. In this respect, the analysis is different from the case of the stochastic Dornbusch model, where the currency band was directly imposed, and the driving process was free to wander unchecked. Note that these limits on the gross amount of noise, if feasible and credible, increase the "stabilizing" effect of smart money. At C, for example, this has increased from BA to BR (where the extra effect, the bending of the trajectory, arises because the occurrence of a rebound from C raises the possibility for sophisticated investors to make arbitrage profits if the trajectory is not stationary at C).

What this means for target zones in this simple model can be appreciated by considering a zone with upper and lower edges at L and U (as shown), where these limits are to be defended by taking whatever action is necessary to stop the fad growing—here the only thing that can take the rate further away. The bands are narrower than the limits that are set for the cumulated noise (CC'), for reasons we have just considered. But, since the outcome is to limit the sentiment of noise traders and not to prick a speculative bubble, the rate can wander about inside the range LU, tending toward the middle (the asymptotic equilibrium value), but being gently reflected from ceiling and floor as and when these are reached.

V. Summary and Conclusions

Recent analysis of financial markets suggests that policies specifically focused on those markets might be an effective way to check "noise" not associated with economic fundamentals. As a contribution to this debate, we have studied the stabilizing properties of currency bands or target zones when the foreign exchange market suffers from two stylized forms of inefficiency— "rational bubbles" and autoregressive "fads" attributable to noise traders. We assumed that the authorities choose the bands or zones "correctly," in the sense that the equilibrium rate is encompassed within the zone.

As for Blanchard bubbles, we have shown the deterrent effect of credible bands to apply both in an (otherwise) deterministic context and also when shocks disturbed the fundamentals. In the latter case, however, currency bands have an additional stabilizing effect. Paul Krugman has labeled this the "bias in the band."

As the end of the dollar's dizzy rise in 1985 came not with a crash but with a prolonged decline, we also examined how a target zone might operate in the context of an autoregressive fad caused by noise traders. Assuming that policy could not prevent swings in sentiment from emerging—but that it could limit the gross size of such fads—results on such regulated stochastic processes suggest that the same sort of "beneficial bias" would emerge because the monetary authorities' willingness to do this would encourage the smart money to play a stabilizing role.

An exercise such as this raises many questions; one is how robust the findings reported by the researchers at the International Monetary Fund are to such simple changes in the stochastic specification as we have examined here. If exchange rates are importantly influenced by market inefficiencies—of the stylized forms examined in this paper or of more general forms—this must cast some doubt on their conclusions about the inability of monetary policy to manage exchange rates. For if, as we believe to be the case, their simulations of target zones leave unchanged the residuals observed in the historical data base[8]—residuals that may include bubbles, fads, and forecasts that are sensitive to the exchange regime in force—then they are not immune to the Lucas critique!

---

[8] Note that, in a later paper (this volume), Frenkel, Goldstein, and Masson do report some simulations "for which shocks to interest parity conditions were assumed to be absent, that is, the residuals are suppressed." On the basis of these, indeed, they deny that their results are "strongly affected by changes in speculative behavior in currency markets that might be associated with the exchange rate regime." But the simulations they report are for a regime of *fixed* exchange rates, and not for target zones.

Appendix I

The Deterministic Case

The equations of the Dornbusch model used here are as follows:

$$m - p = \kappa y - \lambda i \tag{1}$$

$$y = -\gamma i - \eta (x + p - p^*) \tag{2}$$

$$Dp = \phi y \qquad \text{or} \qquad p = \phi \int_{-\infty}^{t} y(s)\, ds \tag{3}$$

$$Dx = i^* - i \qquad \text{or} \qquad x = \int_{t}^{\infty} (i^* - i(s))\, ds + \bar{x} \tag{4}$$

The symbols used above are defined as follows:

m = the log of the domestic money stock,
p = the log of the price of domestic final product,
y = the log of the level of domestic final production, measured from its noninflationary level,
x = the log of the exchange rate, defined as the foreign currency price of domestic currency,
i = (instantaneous) domestic nominal interest rate,
$*$ denotes a variable in the "rest of the world," and
D denotes differentiation with respect to time, $Dx = dx/dt$.
(A bar above a variable denotes its long-run equilibrium value.)

The system described in equations (1)–(4) may be succinctly summarized as two simultaneous differential equations:

$$\begin{bmatrix} Dp \\ Dx \end{bmatrix} = A \begin{bmatrix} p \\ x \end{bmatrix}, \tag{5}$$

where p and x are now measured as deviations from long-run equilibrium. The matrix A takes the form

$$A = \frac{1}{\Delta} \begin{bmatrix} -\phi(\gamma + \lambda\eta) & -\phi\lambda\eta \\ \kappa\eta - 1 & \kappa\eta \end{bmatrix},$$

where $\Delta = \kappa\gamma + \lambda$.

Since the system displays saddlepoint dynamics, a unique stable path converges to equilibrium. This is the linear path associated with the (negative) stable root (ρ_s), so

$$x = \theta_s\, p \;, \tag{6}$$

where $\theta_s = \dfrac{1 \; - \; \kappa\eta}{\kappa\eta \; - \; \rho_s\Delta}$.

To introduce Blanchard bubbles it is simplest to assume that the bubbles have a constant "death" probability π. We can then rewrite (5) as:

$$\left[\begin{array}{c} Dp \\ Dx + \pi(\theta_s\, p - x) \end{array} \right] = A \left[\begin{array}{c} p \\ x \end{array} \right] , \tag{7}$$

where the arbitrage equation is modified to take into account the fact that interest rates must adjust to compensate asset holders for the possibility that the bubble will burst. The term π ($x - \theta_s\, p$) may be thought of as the cost of buying insurance against a collapse onto the stable manifold.

We compare the dynamics of the system with and without such bubbles in Chart 1, see text.

Noise in the Fundamentals

We modify the original model by adding a white noise disturbance term to the Phillips curve equation (3):

$$dp = \phi y\, dt + \sigma\, dz \;, \tag{8}$$

and modifying the arbitrage equation:

$$E(dx) = (i^* - i)dt \;, \tag{9}$$

assuming risk neutrality for simplicity. The nature of the solutions to this system, illustrated in Chart 3, is analyzed in detail in Miller and Weller (1988, 1989). A brief outline of the solution procedure is presented below in Appendix III.

In the absence of specified boundary conditions, we assume that the system follows a "free float" along the stable manifold of the deterministic system. Now introduce the possibility that Blanchard bubbles may appear. We rewrite (9) as

$$E(dx) + \pi\, (\theta_s\, p - x)dt = (i^* - i)dt. \tag{9'}$$

How this affects the solutions illustrated in Chart 3 is discussed in the text.

Appendix II

Let the (log of the) exchange rate be treated as the sum of two components—the integral of expected future (risk-adjusted) interest differentials plus a "noise" term reflecting the psychology of noise traders (see Poterba and Summers, 1987; and Campbell and Kyle, 1988). Assuming that the noise component is autoregressive, we may write

$$x = E_t \int_t^\infty (i(s) - i^* - \alpha\sigma)\, ds + n , \tag{10}$$

where

$$dn = - \psi n dt + \sigma dz , \tag{11}$$

and

$n =$ the colored noise component,
$\psi =$ the autoregressive coefficient,
$\sigma =$ the instantaneous variance parameter of the noise,
$z =$ a unit variance Brownian motion process, and
$\alpha =$ a risk-aversion parameter.

As time evolves, (10) implies that,

$$dx = (i^* - i + \alpha\sigma)dt + dn. \tag{12}$$

Note that dx and dn involve white noise terms. By taking their expected values we get the desired arbitrage condition.

$$E(dx) - E(dn) = (i^* - i + \alpha\sigma)dt. \tag{13}$$

Now suppose that the foreign interest rate is determined exogenously but the domestic rate is determined by the interaction of the domestic money and good markets, that is, by equations (1) and (2). In order to simplify the exposition, we now take the price index to be constant. If the money supply is also constant, then setting $p = m = p^* = 0$ for convenience, we find from (1) and (2) that

$$i = \frac{-\eta x}{\kappa^{-1} \lambda + \gamma} \equiv - \bar{\eta}x \tag{14}$$

that is, the interest rate falls when the high exchange rate depresses the economy. By substituting this into equation (13), and combining this with the colored noise equation (11), we obtain the simple two-equation model to be analyzed, namely,

$$dn = -\psi n dt + \sigma dz \tag{15}$$

$$E(dx) = (i^* - i + \alpha\sigma)dt + E(dn)$$
$$= (i^* + \alpha\sigma)dt + \bar{\eta}x dt - \psi n dt. \tag{16}$$

The asymptotic expected value of the noise is zero by construction; but the risk associated with the noise means that domestic rates must stand above foreign rates (by $\alpha\sigma$) even when $E(dx) = E(dn) = 0$. As a consequence (assuming symmetric boundary conditions), the mean level of the exchange rate is negative, specifically $\bar{x} = -(i^* + \alpha\sigma)/\bar{\eta}$, where $\bar{\eta}$ is defined in (14) above.

By redefining the variable x as a deviation from equilibrium, the system can be written in homogeneous matrix fashion, as

$$\begin{bmatrix} dn \\ E(dx) \end{bmatrix} = \begin{bmatrix} -\psi & 0 \\ -\psi & \bar{\eta} \end{bmatrix} \begin{bmatrix} n \\ x \end{bmatrix} dt + \begin{bmatrix} \sigma \\ 0 \end{bmatrix} dz . \tag{17}$$

Formally this is rather similar to the stochastic Dornbusch model used earlier in the paper. But because the first equation now describes an autonomous noise process (rather than the endogenous adjustment of prices as in the Dornbusch example), there is no feedback coefficient in the top right-hand corner of the matrix. This simplifies the analysis, as may be seen with reference to Chart 5, see text.

Appendix III

Solving the Stochastic Model

The model can be written in a form analogous to (5), as

$$\begin{bmatrix} dp \\ Edx \end{bmatrix} = A \begin{bmatrix} pdt \\ xdt \end{bmatrix} + \begin{bmatrix} \sigma dz \\ 0 \end{bmatrix} . \tag{18}$$

We postulate first a *deterministic* functional relationship between x and p; thus:

$$x = f(p) . \tag{19}$$

Applying Ito's Lemma, we write

$$dx = f'(p)dp + \frac{\sigma^2}{2} f''(p)dt \ . \tag{20}$$

Taking expectations, and noting from (18) and (19) that

$$Edp = (a_{11} p + a_{12} f(p))dt \ , \tag{21}$$

we find that

$$Edx = (a_{11} p + a_{12} f(p)) f'(p)dt + \frac{\sigma^2}{2} f''(p)dt \ . \tag{22}$$

But from (18),

$$Edx = (a_{21} p + a_{22} f(p))dt \ . \tag{23}$$

Equating (22) and (23), we obtain the *fundamental differential equation*

$$\frac{\sigma^2}{2} f'' + (a_{11} p + a_{12} f)f' - (a_{21} p + a_{22} f) = 0, \tag{24}$$

whose solutions characterize the equilibrium relationships between x and p.

If we impose the initial condition $f(0) = 0$, we obtain solutions that satisfy the symmetry condition $f(x) = -f(-x)$. These are the appropriate ones to examine in the presence of symmetric boundary conditions.

The *fundamental differential equation* has no general closed form solutions, but we have derived a complete qualitative characterization of the symmetric solutions (see Miller and Weller, 1988 and 1989).

References

Blanchard, Olivier J., "Speculative Bubbles, Crashes and Rational Expectations," *Economics Letters* (Amsterdam: North-Holland, 1979), pp. 387–89.

_____, and Mark Watson, "Bubbles, Rational Expectations and Financial Markets," National Bureau of Economic Research Working Paper No. 945 (Boston, Massachusetts: NBER, 1982).

Campbell, John Y., and Albert S. Kyle, "Smart Money, Noise Trading, and Stock Price Behavior," National Bureau of Economic Research Technical Working Paper No. 71 (Boston, Massachusetts: NBER, 1988).

Currie, David, and Simon Wren-Lewis, "Evaluating the Extended Target Zone Proposal for the G3," Centre for Economic Policy Research Discussion Paper No. 221 (London: CEPR, 1988).

De Bondt, Werner F. M., and Richard Thaler, "Does the Stock Market Overreact?" *Journal of Finance*, 40 (New York: 1985), pp. 793–808.

———, "Further Evidence on Investor Overreaction and Stock Market Seasonality," *Journal of Finance*, 42 (New York: 1987), pp. 557–81.

De Long, J. Bradford, and others, "The Economic Consequences of Noise Traders," National Bureau of Economic Research Working Paper No. 2395 (Boston, Massachusetts: NBER, 1987).

———, "The Survival of Noise Traders in Financial Markets," National Bureau of Economic Research Working Paper No. 2715 (Boston, Massachusetts: NBER, 1988).

Dixit, Avinash, "A Simplified Exposition of Some Results Concerning Regulated Brownian Motion" (mimeographed; Princeton University, 1988).

Dornbusch, Rudiger, "Expectations and Exchange Rate Dynamics," *Journal of Political Economy*, Vol. 84 (Chicago, Illinois: University of Chicago Press, December 1976), pp. 1161–76.

Edison, Hali J., Marcus Miller, and John Williamson, "On Evaluating and Extending the Target Zone Proposal," *Journal of Policy Modelling*, Vol. 9 (New York: 1987), pp. 199–224.

Flood, Robert P., and Robert J. Hodrick, "Asset Price Volatility, Bubbles and Process Switching," *Journal of Finance*, Vol. 41 (New York: 1986), pp. 831–42.

Frankel, Jeffrey A., and Kenneth A. Froot, "The Dollar as an Irrational Speculative Bubble: A Tale of Fundamentalists and Chartists," *The Marcus Wallenberg Papers on International Finance*, Vol. 1 (1986), pp. 27–55.

Frenkel, Jacob A., Morris Goldstein, and Paul R. Masson, "International Economic Policy Coordination: Rationale, Mechanisms, and Effects" (mimeographed; Washington: International Monetary Fund Research Department, 1988).

Gilles, Christian, and Stephen F. Leroy, "Bubbles and Charges" (mimeographed; Santa Barbara, California: University of California, 1987).

Krugman, Paul, "Is the Strong Dollar Sustainable?", National Bureau of Economic Research Working Paper No. 1644 (Boston, Massachusetts: NBER, 1985).

———, "The Bias in the Band: Exchange Rate Expectations under a Broad-Band Exchange Rate Regime," presented at Conference on the European Monetary System (mimeographed; Cambridge, Massachusetts: NBER, December 1987).

———, *Exchange Rate Instability* (Cambridge, Massachusetts: MIT Press, 1989).

Lehmann, Bruce, "Fads, Martingales and Market Efficiency," National Bureau of Economic Research Working Paper No. 2533 (Boston, Massachusetts: NBER, 1987).

Meese, Richard, and Kenneth Rogoff, "Empirical Exchange Rate Models of the 1970s: Do They Fit Out of Sample?" *Journal of International Economics*, Vol. 14 (Amsterdam: February 1983), pp. 3–24.

Miller, Marcus, and Paul Weller, "Solving Stochastic Saddlepoint Systems: A Qualitative Treatment with Economic Applications," Warwick Economic Research Paper No. 309 (Coventry, England: University of Warwick, 1988).

————, "A Qualitative Analysis of Stochastic Saddlepaths and its Application to Exchange Rate Regimes" (mimeographed; University of Warwick, 1989).

Miller, Marcus, and John Williamson, "The International Monetary System: An Analysis of Alternative Regimes," *European Economic Review* (Amsterdam: 1988), pp. 1031–48.

Pöhl, Karl-Otto, "You Can't Robotize Policymaking," *The International Economy*, Vol. 1 (Washington: October–November 1987).

Poterba, James M., and Lawrence H. Summers, "Mean Reversion in Stock Returns: Evidence and Implications" (mimeographed; Harvard University, 1987).

Smith, Gregor W., "Apparent Bubbles and Misspecified Fundamentals," Queens University Institute for Economic Research Working Paper No. 692, 1987.

Tirole, Jean, "On the Possibility of Speculation under Rational Expectations," *Econometrica* (Evanston, Illinois: 1982), pp. 1163–81.

————, "Asset Bubbles and Overlapping Generations," *Econometrica* (Evanston, Illinois: 1985), pp. 1071–1100.

West, Kenneth D., "Bubbles, Fads and Stock Price Volatility Tests: A Partial Evaluation," National Bureau of Economic Research Working Paper No. 2574 (Boston, Massachusetts: NBER, 1988).

Williamson, John, *The Exchange Rate System* (Washington: Institute for International Economics, 2nd ed., 1985).

————, and Marcus Miller, *Targets and Indicators: A Blueprint for the International Coordination of Economic Policy* (Washington: Institute for International Economics, 1987).

Comments

Michael Mussa

Marcus Miller, Paul Weller, and John Williamson build a case for a system of exchange rate target zones by analyzing the capacity of such a system to correct possible inefficiencies in foreign exchange markets. Specifically, they consider the virtues of target zones in dealing with "Blanchard bubbles," "noise" in economic fundamentals, and "fads" in the behavior of exchange rates. The authors' analysis of these points is an interesting and worthwhile application of recently developed models of asset pricing and techniques for analyzing stochastic dynamic models. However, in my view, their technical analysis of possible inefficiencies in foreign exchange markets fails to provide a convincing case for a system of target zones.

As the authors emphasize, their analysis of market inefficiencies develops only one of several important arguments for a system of target zones. Disciplining governments to pursue appropriate and mutually consistent economic policies is also an important potential virtue of a system of target zones. However, the key point of the paper is to show " . . . how broadening the conventional rational expectations-efficient market models to allow for market inefficiencies serves to strengthen the case for focusing policy on exchange rates per se, rather than simply on the economic fundamentals that should affect them."

This point is centrally important. In the academic literature, it has long been recognized that exchange rates might play important roles as either objectives or indicators for the conduct of economic policy, without rigid commitment to a system of fixed exchange rates or target zones. In policy discussions, greater consistency and better coordination of economic policies are often perceived to enhance exchange rate stability, without necessarily adopting specific zones for permissible exchange rate movements. Thus, the Miller, Weller, and Williamson paper is significant not simply for providing one possible rationale for target zones, but for providing a key rationale that distinguishes target zones from more general efforts at exchange rate management.

Clearly, as Miller, Weller, and Williamson argue, models that assume that foreign exchange markets are always efficient cannot provide a valid basis for assessing the relevance of target zones in correcting problems arising from market inefficiencies. Also, I agree with the authors that it may not be a fatal defect that their models " . . . doubtless lack something in terms of descriptive accuracy." However, the authors go too far in their bold assertion that, "rejection of our conclusions requires not a demonstration that [our] particular representations of market inefficiency fail to describe some period in history, but proof of the proposition that markets are efficient."

272

Many of the usual arguments in favor of a system of fixed exchange rates (a system of narrow target zones) do not rely on the presence of inefficiencies in foreign exchange markets. In particular, I believe that a system of floating exchange rates among the various states of the United States would have important disadvantages even if foreign exchange markets linking different state currencies were "efficient" in the narrow sense of financial market efficiency. Conversely, evidence of possible inefficiencies in foreign exchange markets does not establish that a system of target zones would be the safest and most effective means of correcting these inefficiencies. To make their case in support of a system of target zones, Miller, Weller, and Williamson need to establish two important points: (1) that the types of inefficiencies considered in their theoretical analysis are relevant to the real world; and (2) that a system of target zones is the safest and most effective means of dealing with these inefficiencies. On both of these points, I have significant reservations.

Blanchard Bubbles and Rational Maniacs

Blanchard bubbles are a special case of "rational speculative bubbles" that potentially arise in almost all dynamic asset pricing models. In this general class of models, the dynamic system has at least one positive characteristic root, r, which functions as the "discount rate" in the particular solution of the model that expresses the dependence of the current asset price on the expected path of future fundamental determinants of the asset price. The general solution of the model involves this particular solution, together with an infinite number of solutions of the homogeneous form of the dynamic system. For a discrete time linear model with this general structure, the general solution for the price of the asset at time s, $P(s)$, expected on the basis of information available at time t, has the following form:

$$E[P(s);t] = E[F(s);t] + E[B(s);t], \tag{1}$$

where $F(s)$ is a discounted sum of economic fundamentals beginning at time s, and where $E[B(s);t]$ is the "rational speculative bubble" which has the form,

$$E[B(s);t] = C(t)(1 + r)^{(s-t)}, \tag{2}$$

with $C(t)$ equal to some arbitrary constant.

The key point about the rational speculative bubble is that for any $C(t)$, except $C(t) = 0$, the term $E[B(s);t]$ in the expression for $E[P(s);t]$ explodes exponentially to plus or minus infinity. This exponential explosion in the asset price occurs regardless of the expected behavior of the economic fundamentals. In Blanchard's specific formulation, the rational speculative bubble collapses in any given period with some probability, k, and survives to the next period with probability $1 - k$. The probability that the bubble collapses, however, is offset by more rapid growth when it survives. Thus, even though Blanchard bubbles are expected to collapse, they are also expected to grow at an exponential rate. Expected growth dominates expected collapse in the sense that equation (2) describes the expected evolution of a Blanchard bubble. The mathematical solution of the Dornbusch model of exchange rate dynamics analyzed by Miller, Weller, and Williamson (and the solutions of many other models of exchange rate determination) admit the possibility of rational speculative bubbles. Formally, such bubbles can be excluded by assuming, explicitly or implicitly, that $C(t) = 0$ for all t. The authors argue that such an assumption is unwarranted, that in the real world, rational speculative bubbles may "wreak considerable havoc" on the economic system.

If exchange rates are influenced by rational speculative bubbles, the authors argue this problem can be corrected by target zones. With a target zone, market participants will know that a bubble cannot grow indefinitely. Hence, no bubble could satisfy equation (2). The mathematics of the model of exchange rate dynamics demands that if no bubble can satisfy equation (2), then no rational speculative bubble can ever exist. Thus, an effective target zone rules out all rational speculative bubbles. Three points should be made in response to this argument for target zones.

First, it is a logical implication of the existence of rational speculative bubbles affecting exchange rates that there is no reliable means to prevent them by enforcing a target zone. A rational speculative bubble lives a life of its own, independent of economic fundamentals. Altering economic fundamentals will change the actual and expected path of the exchange rate by altering the part of the solution of the exchange rate that reflects economic fundamentals. But, this does not affect the expected path of the rational speculative bubble. Evidence that coordinated intervention can "punish" exchange rate speculators (cited in a footnote by Miller, Weller, and Williamson) is relevant for some forms of exchange rate speculation, but not for rational speculative bubbles. If one adopts the mathematical logic that allows for the existence of such bubbles, there is no reason to believe that coordinated intervention or any other policy action can affect the evolution of a rational speculative bubble.

Second, if a target zone for exchange rates could effectively exclude rational speculative bubbles, any target zone will do equally well. This is because the mathematics of rational speculative bubbles requires that for a bubble ever to exist, it must be expected to keep growing forever. Even a very broad target zone for exchange rates—one, for example, that limits movements in the logarithm of the exchange rate to plus or minus one hundred trillion percent—would be fully effective in ruling out rational speculative bubbles. Relatively narrow target zones have absolutely no advantage over very broad target zones in dealing with rational speculative bubbles. Indeed, the mathematics of rational speculative bubbles implies that any finite bound on any finite (expected) derivative of the exchange rate is sufficient to rule out such bubbles. Thus, even if rational speculative bubbles are a problem that could be corrected by some economic policy, this provides a case only for extremely broad limits on possible exchange rate movements and not for recently proposed systems of target zones.

Third, the notion that exchange rates and other asset prices may be influenced by rational speculative bubbles amounts to assuming that economic agents are "rational maniacs." Economic agents understand, fully and correctly, the dynamic system governing the behavior of the exchange rate. They calculate, without error, the influence that economic fundamentals should have on the behavior of exchange rates. In this respect, they are completely rational. However, in determining the current exchange rate, these agents add an arbitrary constant to the value they know to be implied by economic fundamentals. There is no good reason why they should add such a constant, other than that the general solution of the dynamic system governing the exchange rate admits such a possibility. Nevertheless, the introduction of this arbitrary constant, together with the requirements of "rationality," compels these agents to expect that the exchange rate will follow an exponentially explosive path, regardless of the behavior of economic fundamentals. Of all of the possible means of modeling divergences of the behavior of asset prices from the implications of rationality and efficiency, this combination of rationality and insanity impresses me as particularly bizarre.

Noise and Fads

These objections to rational speculative bubbles do not apply, in general, to other methods of modeling divergences from rationality and efficiency in the behavior of exchange rates and other asset prices. The debate over the empirical evidence in support of "excess volatility" and other anomalies in the behavior of asset prices is far from conclusive. However, there certainly is not overwhelming evidence that exchange rates and other asset prices respond only to rational evaluations of economic fundamentals.

In my view, models that allow for the coexistence of "noise" traders, who may be subject to fads, and "sophisticated" traders, who understand economic fundamentals, provide a promising approach to analyzing divergences from rationality and efficiency in the behavior of asset prices. The authors' application of such models to analyze the effects of target zones for exchange rates is both interesting and worthwhile. As their analysis shows, a hard and announced target zone for the exchange rate (around the value implied by economic fundamentals) will tend to stabilize the behavior of the exchange rate within the zone as well as keep the exchange rate from diverging beyond the bounds of the zone.

This analytical result, however, does not provide a conclusive case in favor of target zones, even if the noise trader versus sophisticated trader model is the correct model of exchange rates. To pursue a target zone policy, the government must have a reasonably good idea of the equilibrium value of the exchange rate implied by economic fundamentals; it must also be prepared to back this assessment with actions that have some capacity to affect the exchange rate. However, any policy of exchange rate management that has these characteristics, not just a policy of target zones, will presumably have some important effect in stabilizing exchange rates. Indeed, it is probably not necessary for the government's policy to be explicitly directed at influencing the exchange rate, provided that sophisticated traders recognize the significance of the government's policy for the behavior of the exchange rate. Knowledge of the government's policy will strengthen the hand of sophisticated traders, relative to noise traders, in determining the behavior of the exchange rate. If it is anticipated that the government will resist wide divergences of the exchange rate from equilibrium, the behavior of the exchange rate will be affected even when it is nearer to equilibrium. In this critical respect, there is nothing special about a policy of target zones.

Target Zones and the Experience of the 1980s

Finally, in assessing arguments in favor of a system of target zones for exchange rates, the experience of the 1980s is relevant. The major development that continues to underlie much of the dissatisfaction with the floating exchange rate system was the roughly 50 percent real appreciation of the U.S. dollar between the summer of 1980 and early 1985. Much of this real appreciation is widely viewed as a movement of the dollar away from the value that would have been consistent with balance of payments equilibrium in the medium and longer term. John Williamson has been a leading and effective proponent of this view. Under his proposals for target zones, the last 25 percent to 30 percent of the real appreciation of the dollar in the early 1980s would have been actively and effectively resisted. Indeed, any system of target zones that has practical significance would presumably have implied aggressive resistance to the appreciation of the dollar from late 1982 through early 1985. The issue that needs to be addressed is whether it would have been feasible and desirable to resist much of the appreciation of the dollar during the early 1980s, given the prevailing economic conditions.

In my view, much of the appreciation of the dollar between the summer of 1980 and late 1982 owes to the tightening of U.S. monetary policy, the reduction in the U.S. inflation rate, and the restoration of confidence in the future conduct of U.S. monetary policy. The appreciation of the dollar during this period also clearly helped reduce the U.S. inflation rate. At best, it is highly questionable whether economic policy should have resisted appreciation of the dollar from the summer of 1980 until late 1982. Surely, continuation of an expansionary U.S. monetary policy and a high U.S. inflation rate in an effort to keep the dollar from appreciating would have been a serious error.

The factors responsible for dollar appreciation between late 1982 and early 1985 are difficult to identify with confidence and precision. Presumably, the vigorous rebound of the U.S. economy from the 1981–82 recession (a 9 percent annual growth rate of real domestic demand for the first six quarters of recovery) was an important influence. Weak recoveries in other industrial countries and political uncertainties in Europe also probably contributed to dollar appreciation. Noise trading, fads, bandwagon effects, and other divergences from rationality may have played a significant role as well.

Whatever its cause, the dollar appreciation during 1983–84 helped contain U.S. inflation and to spread some of the force of U.S. demand growth to the rest of the world economy. In my view, these important favorable effects of further dollar appreciation during this critical period outweigh the continuing balance of payments problems that have also been a heritage of dollar appreciation. This assessment is buttressed by the success in reducing the foreign exchange value of the dollar since early 1985, without suffering the harmful consequences of a "hard landing." An effective system of target zones would presumably have prevented most of the dollar's appreciation from late 1982 through early 1985, obviating the need for much of the corresponding depreciation from early 1985 through 1986. However, it is far from clear that avoiding these exchange rate movements would have improved the overall performance of the world economy.

Moreover, there is the critical question of how government policy would have effectively resisted dollar appreciation during 1983–84. A better mix of U.S. monetary and fiscal policy might have moderated upward pressures on the dollar, without sacrificing much of the progress in reducing U.S. inflation. A less cheerful official U.S. attitude toward dollar appreciation during 1984, perhaps backed by exchange market intervention, might also have reduced the extent of dollar appreciation. However, a meaningful system of target zones cannot rely on such halfway measures. To be effective, such a system must be perceived to be supported by serious and substantive government policies—most important, by monetary policy.

In August 1982, U.S. monetary policy shifted to a much easier stance in order to promote economic recovery, and it remained quite easy through early 1984. In view of the rapid recovery of the U.S. economy from late 1982 through mid-1984, it is difficult to argue that U.S. monetary policy should have been more expansionary, even if this would have reduced pressures for dollar appreciation. In fact, by April 1984, the U.S. Federal Reserve had become sufficiently concerned with the increase in inflationary forces within the U.S. economy that it tightened monetary policy for about six months. This tightening was probably an important element contributing to the dollar's appreciation during 1984. Given the cost of bringing down inflation during the recession of 1981–82, it is understandable that the Federal Reserve wished to preserve its victory over inflation, even at the expense of a further movement of the dollar away from its medium-term equilibrium value. In the circumstances of 1984, it is extremely difficult to make the case that U.S. monetary policy should have been directed at preserving a target zone for the dollar, rather than at the more fundamental task of sustaining noninflationary economic growth.

James M. Boughton *

The paper by Messrs. Miller, Weller, and Williamson is the latest in an important and impressive series in which John Williamson and others have developed, promoted, clarified, and extended the idea of target zones for exchange rates. The paper's essential line of argument may be summarized as follows:

- speculative noise ("bubbles and fads") is an important cause of misalignments of real exchange rates among the large industrial countries;
- misalignments, irrespective of their source, are costly for the real economy because they alter relative prices of traded goods; and
- target zones, enforced by monetary policies, are an effective means of limiting misalignments.

The following remarks address these three points in turn.

The Importance of Speculative Noise

How important is destabilizing speculation—trading that is unrelated to economic fundamentals—in altering exchange rates for key currencies? The short answer to this question is that we do not know. There are two empirical arguments in favor of the view of Miller and others. The first is that exchange rate models based on "fundamentals" do not explain much. It is not true, however, that such models have been proved to be useless; nor does it follow that their low explanatory power demonstrates that *persistent* noise has been important. My own model, for example, explains about 10 percent of the monthly variation in exchange rates (both within- and post-sample)—addressing primarily the longer-run swings.[1] If speculative noise is limited to the higher frequencies and if it dissipates within a few months, it will have few if any real economic effects.[2]

The second argument in favor of a dominant role for speculative noise is that recent survey data suggest that expectations about the exchange rate are dominated by bandwagon effects. Here again, however, the evidence is consistent more with a short-run problem than with a persistent one. The paper by Frankel and Froot cited by Miller and others, for example, finds that the importance of bandwagon effects in the survey data diminishes substantially as the forecast horizon is lengthened beyond one month. At 6– to 12–month

---

*I am grateful to Marcus Miller and John Williamson for a number of clarifying discussions, and to Jacob Frenkel and Paul Masson for comments on an earlier draft.

[1] This point is demonstrated in Figure 3 in Boughton (1988).

[2] For a review of evidence on the limited importance of high-frequency exchange rate volatility on trade flows, see International Monetary Fund (1984).

horizons, expectations are stabilizing and largely reflect fundamental forces. This relationship does not imply that bandwagon effects have not been persistent, but it suggests that such a conclusion would require the persistence of short-run expectations. That is, only when speculative behavior is strongly dominated by short horizons—with longer-run expectations not being acted upon—will bandwagon effects persist over meaningfully long periods.

Aside from the apparent predominance of short-run behavior in speculative noise, one can argue that destabilizing speculation may itself have been generated by policy instability. In another paper, Frankel and Froot (1986) showed that the survey data are consistent with the view that the appreciation of the U.S. dollar in the early 1980s was initially explained by economic fundamentals, as manifested by real interest differentials. Later, as the appreciation persisted, portfolio managers appear to have begun giving less weight to fundamentals and more to bandwagon effects. But suppose that the initial shift in fundamentals—in large measure a response to the adoption of a more expansionary fiscal policy in the United States—had not occurred? Would traders have started the dollar on a "bubble path" all by themselves, or was the policy shift a prerequisite? We do not know, but it is difficult to think of a case in which a key-currency exchange rate has experienced a major swing without a precipitating large policy move.

Consequences of Misalignments

One of the fundamental conclusions of empirical studies of internationally linked macromodels is that the real economic consequences of large swings in exchange rates largely depend on the source of the shock (Boughton and others, 1986; Frenkel and others, this volume). The fact that real exchange rate swings are also swings in relative traded goods prices obviously does not imply that they are always to be avoided. It is instructive in this context to compare two cases in which the U.S. dollar is subjected to an incipient appreciation, one where the disturbance is speculative pressure and the other where the disturbance is a fiscal expansion.

For the first case, assume that currency traders bid up the value of the dollar (with no change in current policies) simply because they come to believe that its value will rise. In the absence of a policy reaction, the traded goods sector in the United States will be squeezed by a loss in competitiveness. With target zones, a temporary monetary expansion will drive the dollar back down; even better, as Miller and others demonstrate, the *threat* of such action may prevent the pressures from arising in the first place. As long as the monetary expansion is temporary, there will be no remaining problem.

In the second case, assume that the dollar's appreciation is initially driven by a policy of fiscal expansion in the United States. In this case, the proposed remedy—monetary accommodation—will *not* offset the economic consequences of the incipient appreciation, because the underlying fiscal problem will remain and because the required monetary expansion will be permanent rather than temporary. Furthermore, the effects of monetary policy on the current account balance are far weaker than those of fiscal policy (for a given effect on the exchange rate); indeed, the sign of the effect of monetary expansion on the current account is ambiguous. For this reason, the external deficit—along with the reduction in the national saving rate—will remain even if the real exchange rate does not appreciate. Hence, the success of target zones in solving real economic problems is contingent not only on knowing the source of the disturbance, but also on being able to correct any underlying disturbances.

This example implies that the enforcement of target zones—or of any other approach to policy coordination—depends in the long run on the appropriate use of both monetary and fiscal policies to maintain overall economic equilibrium. (This point was emphasized by Williamson and Miller in their "blueprint" but is kept in the background in the present paper.) But how does the appropriate fiscal policy get determined? Appeals to "fiscal responsibility" do not suffice: there is no rationale, from a purely fiscal perspective, to think that a balanced budget is any better than an unbalanced budget, or that governments will be persuaded by such appeals.[3] The Williamson Miller blueprint determines fiscal policy through a combination of domestic demand growth targets and estimation of sustainable underlying capital flows; I have argued elsewhere (Boughton, 1989) in favor of using current account targets more directly to determine internationally consistent net saving and, hence, fiscal balances. These differences aside, the main point is that international payments flows are linked inexorably to the determinants of net saving positions, including fiscal policies; they are not linked inexorably to exchange rates.

The introduction to the paper by Miller and others defends target zones against an anonymous academic opponent who believes that the only justification for them is to "secure some coordination in fiscal and monetary policies." Unfortunately, the rest of the paper does not support that defense, and the only fair conclusion is that the academic is correct. Target zones may often be a valuable item in the policymaker's tool kit, but only when they help to attain the right monetary and fiscal policies. As long as macroeconomic policies are inappropriate, target zones will not help.

The Role of Target Zones

What is the role of target zones for exchange rates, given that most speculative noise is probably short term in nature, and given that it remains necessary to get the right macroeconomic policies in any case? I would argue

---

[3] Long-run macroeconomic stability is usually taken to require a stable ratio of debt to output, but there is a wide range of paths for fiscal balances consistent with that requirement. From a political perspective, of course, appeals for balanced budgets may help to constrain expenditure or monetary growth, or both.

that target zones, aside from whatever role they may have in promoting the right underlying policies, are primarily an aid to short-run management of the economy. That is, target zones are helpful in situations where policymakers are seeking primarily to curb speculative disturbances, but they are not helpful in obtaining longer-run economic stability.

The reason that reliance on target zones may be less helpful for longer-run problems is that such policies may reverse the role that should be played by fiscal policy. As McKibbin and Sachs note in their paper (in this volume), the assignment of monetary policy to a real target, with fiscal policy used as a nominal anchor, is bound to fail in the long run unless one gets the target right in the first place or imposes something approximating a closed-loop feedback rule for adjusting it. But at that level of sophistication, as Friedman (1975) established, there is no convincing reason for using intermediate targets (such as exchange rates) in formulating monetary policy.

A reasonable alternative for a policy assignment strategy focused on longer-run objectives is to use monetary policy to provide a stable nominal anchor by aiming it at nominal income or domestic demand growth, with fiscal policy aimed at limiting—or at least not promoting—current account imbalances over the medium term. Such a strategy would have three principal advantages over schemes based predominantly on target zones. *First*, it avoids the suggestion that fiscal policy has the flexibility to enable it to be used to stabilize domestic demand growth. *Second*, as long as fiscal policy is aimed at preventing the emergence of internationally inconsistent national saving rates, one is practically assured that the unsustainable growth of government debt will also be avoided. In other words, the internationalization of fiscal policy objectives may, as a practical matter, provide an effective means of tying down the fiscal balance in the longer run. *Third*, by focusing both monetary and fiscal policies on longer-run targets over which they have a strong and direct influence, one avoids the confusion and the potential instability associated with trying to fine-tune economies on the basis of weak and temporary linkages operating through intermediate targets.

References

Boughton, James M., "Exchange Rates and the Term Structure of Interest Rates," *Staff Papers*, International Monetary Fund, Vol. 35 (Washington: March 1988), pp. pp. 36–62.

————, "Policy Assignment Strategies with Somewhat Flexible Exchange Rates," in Barry Eichengreen, Marcus Miller, and Richard Portes, eds., *Blueprints for Exchange Rate Management* (forthcoming; Cambridge, England: Cambridge University Press, 1989).

Boughton, James M., and others, "Effects of Exchange Rate Changes in Industrial Countries," *Staff Studies for the World Economic Outlook*, International Monetary Fund (Washington: July 1986), pp. 115–49.

Frankel, Jeffrey A., and Kenneth A. Froot, "The Dollar as an Irrational Speculative Bubble: A Tale of Fundamentalists and Chartists," *The Marcus Wallenberg Papers on International Finance, 1* (1986), pp. 27–55.

Friedman, Benjamin M., "Targets, Instruments, and Indicators of Monetary Policy," *Journal of Monetary Economics*, Vol. 1 (Amsterdam: October 1975), pp. 443–73.

International Monetary Fund, "Exchange Rate Volatility and World Trade," IMF Occasional Paper No. 28 (Washington: International Monetary Fund, July 1984).

7

The Exchange Rate Question in Europe

*Francesco Giavazzi**

Europe today stands at a monetary cross-roads. The only way to establish a unified financial market is to kill the sporadic and unsettling speculation over currency prices that ravages European markets and permits discounts and premia to develop on currency futures. The exchange rate should be taken out of both national and international politics within Europe (Mundell, 1973).

I. Introduction

The choice of the exchange rate regime is a central issue in Europe today. The European Monetary System (EMS) has performed surprisingly well during the past nine years. It has forced inflation convergence beginning from large inflation differentials, and it has survived unprecedented swings in the value of the U.S. dollar.[1] To a great extent, however, the success of the EMS must be ascribed to the presence of exchange controls that severely limit the possibility of speculative attacks against central banks' reserves. The possibility of fighting speculative attacks by imposing exchange controls has often enabled central banks to postpone parity realignments. This has been a key element in forcing inflation convergence, because the discipline that the EMS imposes upon its high-inflation members requires that the interval between successive currency realignments be sufficiently long. If high-inflation countries could realign as soon as higher-than-average inflation (combined with

* I thank Luigi Spaventa for discussions and Daniel Gros and Richard Portes for comments on an earlier draft. Many of the ideas discussed in this paper have been developed in a joint research project with Alberto Giovannini on the European Monetary System (see Giavazzi and Giovannini, 1989). This paper is part of the CEPR program in international macroeconomics; financial support from the Ford and Alfred P. Sloan Foundations is gratefully acknowledged.

[1] On the role of the EMS in European disinflation see Collins (1988) and Giavazzi and Giovannini (1989c, Chapter 4). On the asymmetric response of European currencies to dollar fluctuations, see Giavazzi and Giovannini (1986).

rigidity of the nominal exchange rate) begins hurting competitiveness, the system would be indistinguishable from a crawling peg: all discipline gains would vanish.[2] Exchange controls have also allowed central banks to avoid realignment during periods of "crisis" in the system, for example, when the dollar falls.

In order to survive, the EMS has thus become addicted to a mechanism that precludes further financial integration. This is a major problem since item number one on the European policy agenda is the full integration of financial markets. Will the EMS survive the removal of exchange controls? This is a controversial issue; theoretical analyses suggest that a system of fixed but adjustable parities cannot survive in the absence of a mechanism that limits the volume of speculative attacks.[3] The recent experiences of liberalization have had mixed outcomes. No sooner had the Italian monetary authorities removed controls on "leads and lags" (in May 1987) than they were faced with a severe speculative attack. Because of the level and maturity structure of the Italian public debt, the authorities could not accept a rise in domestic interest rates large enough to stop the capital outflow.[4] The Bank of Italy was thus forced to decide between giving in and accepting a realignment that it viewed as unwarranted by "fundamentals," or reintroducing administrative controls. Financial liberalization was temporarily suspended. The French experience has been more successful, notwithstanding a few attacks on the French franc. There are two likely explanations for this. The first is that France does not have a public debt problem, so that the French authorities have been more prepared than the Italian to let domestic interest rates bear the burden of adjustment. The other possible explanation is that foreign lending in domestic currency is still controlled, so that the volume of funds that can be mobilized to stage an attack is limited.

If full financial integration remains the primary political objective in Europe, and if the current system of fixed but adjustable parities cannot survive full financial liberalization, the choice is between allowing greater exchange rate flexibility, or giving up realignments altogether, moving toward a system of credible and, thus, irrevocably fixed rates—that is, a monetary union.[5]

As documented by Mundell, a time-honored tradition of debate and analysis of monetary unification exists in Europe. The high point of this

---

[2] On the disciplinary role of the EMS see Melitz (1988) and Giavazzi and Pagano (1988b).

[3] See, for example, Wyplosz (1986), Driffill (1988), and Obstfeld (1988).

[4] Giavazzi and Pagano (1988a) discuss the link between the maturity of public debt and the sustainability of fixed exchange rates with perfect capital mobility.

[5] The decision to lift capital controls fits Cooper's description of an integration strategy: "Integration as a process involves establishing a situation that is not in long-run equilibrium: partial integration creates new problems that, in turn, call for further integrative measures" (Cooper, 1976).

tradition is the 1975 *All Saints' Day Manifesto*.[6] The rationale behind the proposal to create a European monetary union rests on the comparison of classical arguments for and against optimal currency areas. Among the advantages of a common currency, the manifesto included the informational advantages of using a common numeraire, the efficiency of a single money as a unit of account and store of value, lower transaction costs in international trade, and the elimination of exchange rate risk. The proposal recognized that the social cost of monetary unification would arise from Europe's deep regional diversity. It therefore suggested that the institution of a common currency be accompanied by a series of supply-side policies, fiscal reforms, and transitory income transfers designed to eliminate the causes of regional imbalances and to alleviate the costs of sectoral shocks in the transition.

This paper reviews the arguments for and against monetary unification in Europe. One motivation for such an assessment has been discussed above: irrevocably fixed exchange rates may be necessary for liberalizing European financial markets. Another motivation is that the emphasis in the theoretical discussion of exchange rate regimes has shifted since the early 1970s. The effects of strategic interactions among countries—which was rarely discussed in the early 1970s—is a central issue in present-day analysis of exchange rate regimes. The way we think about inflation has also changed. In the early 1970s, one of the arguments against irrevocably fixed exchange rates was that they might force countries to accept undesirable positions along a stable long-run trade-off between inflation and unemployment. Today, we tend to think of the long-run level of inflation as determined by the "credibility" of the monetary authorities: the choice of the exchange rate regime modifies the constraints faced by the monetary authorities and may thus modify the equilibrium inflation rate. Another important aspect is the "public-finance" role of inflation. Since the early 1970s, many European countries are highly concerned about budget deficits and public debt levels. In some countries where debt levels are higher, money creation remains an important source of government revenue. The possibility that currency unification may substantially reduce the revenue from seigniorage, and thus destabilize the budget, constitutes an important argument against monetary union.

The paper adds these analytical items to the cost-benefit analysis of a

---

[6] "All Saints' Day Manifesto for European Monetary Union," by G. Basevi and others, *The Economist*, November 1, 1975. The manifesto recommended that European central banks issue a parallel currency, "Europa," against national currencies. Europa's exchange rate would be determined so that the new currency would maintain a constant purchasing power in terms of a European basket of goods. The purpose of this parallel currency was to substitute national currencies with a single money of stable value. Currency substitution would have taken place spontaneously in the market, because Europa would have offered a more stable store of value and unit of account. This tradition has recently been revived in the papers collected in De Cecco and Giovannini (1989).

monetary union. Section II discusses the benefits from irrevocably fixed exchange rates in light of the literature on international strategic interactions. Section III addresses the effects of the exchange rate regime on the equilibrium level of inflation. Section IV discusses the role of inflation in public finance and the effects of financial integration. And Section V summarizes the main conclusions of the paper.

II. Policy Interactions, Structural Asymmetries, and the Optimality of Fixed Exchange Rates

The analysis of international policy interactions has added new insights to the comparison of exchange rate regimes by studying the worldwide efficiency losses that arise from "beggar-thy-neighbor" policies.[7] Under flexible exchange rates, a noncooperative equilibrium is inefficient because each country perceives that it faces a more favorable output-price-level trade-off than it actually does. Each country sets its monetary policy taking its partners' monetary policy as given: therefore, it believes that a change in its money stock can affect the exchange rate. If the exchange rate feeds back into domestic prices through aggregate supply channels (imported materials' prices or wage indexation rules), each central bank believes that by engineering a real appreciation it can reduce the price level at a comparatively small cost in output terms. Following a worldwide negative supply shock, for example, each country has an incentive to over-contract money, but, if countries are identical, in equilibrium the exchange rate does not move; the outcome is a lower level of output than could be obtained if countries had recognized the spillover effects of domestic monetary policy.

The inefficiency associated with noncooperative equilibria carries through to alternative exchange rate regimes. Consider for example a two-country world in which one country (the nth country) sets monetary policy for the entire region, while the other country retains the power to affect the bilateral exchange rate.[8] In such a regime the two countries perceive different output-price-level trade-offs. The nth country faces the region-wide output-price-level trade-off, and does not attempt to run a beggar-thy-neighbor policy; its asymmetric position at the center of the international monetary system removes the inefficiency associated with the strategic interaction. The country that retains control of the exchange rate, on the contrary, will still have an incentive to improve its output-inflation trade-off by affecting the

---

[7] The literature originates from Hamada (1974). Recent developments are discussed in Bean (1985), Buiter and Marston (1985), Fischer (1989), and Currie, Holtham, and Hughes Hallet (this volume).

[8] Policy interactions under managed exchange rates are studied in Giavazzi and Giovannini (1989b).

exchange rate. The equilibrium keeps being characterized by a worldwide efficiency loss, but losses from the lack of international cooperation are not equally shared by all countries. The country that controls the exchange rate can generate domestic price deflation by changing the exchange rate at the expense of the foreign country; following a supply shock it is thus better off than the nth country.

The analysis of noncooperative equilibria points to the superiority of permanently and credibly fixed exchange rates in a world of identical countries and identical world shocks. Fixed rates would reproduce the outcome of a command world economy, where the inefficiencies stemming from countries' incentives to run beggar-thy-neighbor policies are ruled out by construction. However, when countries' macroeconomic structures differ—or when identical countries are hit by asymmetric shocks—exchange rate changes may be the easiest instrument to use for redistributing the effects of external shocks. Thus, the analysis of international policy interactions points to an important trade-off that underlies the choice of the exchange rate regime. On the one hand, the theoretical appeal of fixed exchange rates is that they eliminate the incentive to use inefficient beggar-thy-neighbor policies. On the other hand, in the absence of significant international factor mobility and of fiscal redistributions, adjustable parities can be efficient in the short run at evening out country-specific imbalances, but they can also be used for selfish purposes, at everybody's loss.

In Giavazzi and Giovannini (1987), we illustrate the suboptimality of fixed exchange rates when realignments can be used effectively to counteract external shocks. We show, for example, that in the presence of cross-country asymmetries in the intermediate input-wage-price transmission mechanism, common external shocks are transmitted unevenly to different countries: under these circumstances, exchange rate realignments—to the extent that they have some real effect—are part of the optimal (centralized) response to the common external shocks. What is the empirical importance in Europe of asymmetries in the intermediate input-wage-price transmission mechanism? Giavazzi and Giovannini (1987) also present some evidence. Using input-output tables for five European countries, we estimate the aggregate and sectoral response of domestic prices to a change in the world price of materials. These estimates are interesting in two respects: they permit us to assess the cost of keeping exchange rates fixed in the face of common external shocks and structural asymmetries; and they provide a structure for the computation of the optimal (centralized) setting of intra-European exchange rates and monetary policy in the face of external shocks. The results demonstrate the empirical importance of asymmetric transmissions of price disturbances.

III. Inflation and the Exchange Rate Regime

The analysis of international strategic interactions discussed in Section II *assumes* that monetary policy can affect real variables, at least in the short run.

In doing so, it overlooks the strategic interaction between central banks and the private sector that takes place within each country, and that may undermine the effectiveness of monetary policy. This issue is addressed in this section.

The observation (originally owing to Kydland and Prescott, 1977, and Calvo, 1978, and later developed by Barro and Gordon, 1983) that optimal plans may be time-inconsistent has brought the credibility and reputation of monetary authorities to the center of the analysis of inflation.[9] The basic point is that in the presence of nominal wage contracts, monetary authorities face an output-inflation trade-off that is not the equilibrium one. Since nominal wages are fixed for the time of the contract, monetary authorities have the *power* to affect real wages through unanticipated inflation. If the equilibrium level of output is below the social optimum (for example, because of distortions or externalities), monetary authorities will also have an *incentive* to affect real wages. Because their power and incentives are public knowledge, they are rationally discounted by wage-setters in forming their forecasts of inflation, so that the equilibrium will have two properties: monetary authorities do not succeed in their attempt to affect real variables (this is why the trade-off they perceive is not the equilibrium one); and the expected, and actual, rate of inflation is higher than the inflation rate that would prevail if the central bank could credibly tie its hands.

Two ideas have been proposed to improve upon the inefficiency of time-consistent equilibria. The first is to modify the preferences of policymakers: this is Rogoff's (1985a) idea to appoint "conservative" central bankers, that is, officials whose relative dislike for inflation exceeds that of the general society. An alternative is to modify the constraints, rather than the preferences of policymakers. In an open economy, the exchange rate regime modifies the constraints faced by the monetary authorities, and may thus modify the equilibrium inflation rate.[10] Consider two identical countries characterized by a domestic inflation inefficiency arising from the time-consistency problem discussed above. Under flexible exchange rates, the two central banks have an incentive to try to engineer a real exchange rate appreciation to disinflate. Each has an incentive to tighten monetary policy to appreciate its currency, thus reducing domestic inflation. This is the deflationary bias of flexible exchange rates discussed in Section II. As noted by Rogoff (1985b), the presence of an externality at the international level also affects the outcome of the game that takes place between wage-setters and the central bank within each country; the deflationary bias that arises from the incentive to

---

[9] The problem of time-consistency in an international setting is addressed in Currie and Levine (1986), McKibbin and Sachs (1986), van der Ploeg (1987), Canzoneri and Henderson (1987), and others.

[10] Another possibility is to sustain more efficient equilibria through reputational mechanisms. See, for example, Backus and Driffill (1985).

run a beggar-thy-neighbor policy internationally partly offsets the domestic inflation inefficiency. What we have is a typical second-best situation in which fixed exchange rates, by eliminating the externality associated with the flexible exchange rate equilibrium, may produce an inferior outcome.

Are there any conditions under which fixed exchange rates could still help alleviate a domestic inflationary bias? Consider a fixed exchange rate regime that works asymmetrically: one central bank sets monetary policy for the entire region; the other gives up monetary autonomy and passively pegs the exchange rate. The result is that both countries will end up with the inflation rate that would prevail in the center country (the one that sets monetary policy for the entire region) if it were a closed economy. If the center country is less inflation-prone than its partner, the latter can gain by credibly pegging. There are thus three conditions that must be satisfied for fixed exchange rates to be able to correct a domestic inflation inefficiency. *First*, the fixed exchange rate regime must work asymmetrically: monetary policy for the entire region must be independently set by the least inflation-prone country; the other countries must passively accommodate, thus effectively losing monetary sovereignty. *Second*, the "credibility-gap" between the center country and its partners must be large relative to the incentive that central banks have to affect the exchange rate. *Third*, the commitment to peg the exchange rate must be credible; this is in contrast to the authorities' inability to precommit to a monetary rule under flexible exchange rates.[11]

IV. Inflation, Public Finance, and Fixed Exchange Rates

If inflation were only a source of inefficiency, a regime of irrevocably fixed exchange rates would be effective at reducing the degree of inefficiency, provided that it worked asymmetrically. The approach taken in Section III, however, completely overlooks the public finance role of inflation. The ability of governments to generate revenue through money creation is important to the design of optimal monetary policy. Countries turn to the inflation tax not only when it becomes their last resort, but also in more normal times, as an alternative to increasing the distortions induced by the tax system; or as a way around the rigidities of the fiscal-decision process; or simply to circumvent the difficulties of collecting taxes. Differences in fiscal structures may therefore justify differences in the "optimal" revenue from money creation. An important argument against irrevocably fixed exchange rates is thus the difficulty of agreeing on the optimal inflation rate for all countries involved.[12]

The basic facts are summarized in Table 1. The data show that in those

---

[11] The credibility of exchange rate targets is discussed in Giavazzi and Giovannini (1989c, Chapter 4).

[12] Dornbusch (1988a,b) identifies the public finance role of inflation as an important element in choosing an exchange rate regime for Europe.

European countries where tax revenues are lower, the Treasury tends to finance a larger share of the budget through loans by the central bank. I have emphasized the fiscal asymmetry across Europe by leaving a gap between the South and the North. Money financing amounts to 4–5 percent of gross domestic product (GDP) in Portugal, 2–3 percent in Greece, and 2 percent in Italy; Spain has experienced a sharp turnaround in recent years, with money financing falling from 1.5 percent of GDP to zero. In the north of Europe, money financing accounts for a negligible share of GDP—less than ½ of 1 percent.

The evidence presented in Table 1 suggests that in the south of Europe it should be possible to reduce money financing by raising tax revenues to the European Economic Community (EEC) average. In some southern European countries, however, low tax revenues reflect the structure of the economy, and it is not clear that they could be raised quickly. Low tax revenues often reflect a narrow tax base, rather than lower-than-average tax rates. In discussing the Greek economy, for example, the Organization for Economic Cooperation and Development (OECD) writes: "There is [in Greece] a relatively heavy tax burden on incomes and transactions that are easily taxable (wages and salaries, purchases of cars and some consumer durables, real estate and inheritance transactions). Tax evasion and avoidance are partly responsible, but the most

Table 1. The Fiscal Asymmetry
(Percent of GDP)

	Monetary Financing of the Budget		Tax Revenue	
	1976–87	1984–87	1976–86	1984–86
Portugal	5.3	4.5	29.6	32.0
Greece	3.0	2.1	30.9	35.6
Italy (a)	2.1	2.2	31.2	35.3
Italy (b)	1.8	1.8	n.a.	n.a.
Spain	1.5	-0.5	25.4	29.5
Ireland	0.5	0.7	35.8	39.5
France	0.4	0.2	41.8	44.4
Belgium	0.1	0.4	44.5	46.1
Germany, Fed. Rep. of	0.0	0.0	37.6	37.6
Netherlands	0.06	0.0	45.1	45.2
Denmark	0.6	-3.4	45.4	49.0
United Kingdom	-0.4	-0.3	36.4	38.5

Note: Monetary financing is the change in the central bank's claim on the government. Money financing for Italy is computed as a share of GDP according to the old national income accounts and the new national income accounts. Tax revenues refer to total tax revenues, including taxes on personal and corporation income, employers' and employees' social security contributions, property taxes, consumption taxes, and excises.

Source: IMF, *International Financial Statistics*; OECD, *Revenue Statistics of OECD Member Countries*.

important factor is the structure of the economy characterized by a large share of agriculture in GDP (18%), and of self-employment in the non-agricultural labor force (33%)" (OECD, *Economic Survey of Greece*, 1987, p. 42). The case of Portugal is similar: "Low tax yield is attributable to the narrowness of the tax-base, which is not unrelated to the high marginal tax-rates" (OECD, *Economic Survey of Portugal*, 1986, p.19). In Greece and Portugal, raising taxes to reduce money financing may not be possible without adding distortions to the tax system.

The fiscal asymmetry documented in Table 1 raises two questions: (1) Do optimal taxation arguments justify differences in the degree of money financing across Europe? and (2) What are the implications of money financing for the conduct of monetary policy and thus for the ability of the central bank to peg the nominal exchange rate? The two questions are closely linked.

Consider a central bank that decides to join a monetary system where exchange rates are fixed and interest rates are set independently by a center country. A primary source of concern for such a central bank is the extent to which the treasury may turn to it in order to finance the budget. If capital mobility is high, an increase in domestic credit will induce an outflow of foreign exchange reserves and may force the central bank to give up the exchange rate target. These central bank concerns reflect the more general point (illustrated, for example, in Helpman and Razin, 1987)[13] that an asymmetric fixed exchange rate regime not only implies a loss of monetary sovereignty, but also imposes a constraint on fiscal policy: the menu of taxes and money financing must be consistent with the exchange rate target.

Inflation and Public Finance

In a world in which governments could finance public expenditure through nondistortionary taxes, the optimal inflation rate would simply be the negative of the real interest rate. At that level of inflation the nominal interest rate is zero, and the cost of carrying over real money balances equals the social opportunity cost of supplying money—namely, zero. Unfortunately, governments must resort to distortionary taxes in order to finance public expenditure. It has long been recognized that because taxes are distortionary, it may be optimal to tax money balances to the point where the marginal welfare cost of raising revenue through the inflation tax equals the marginal welfare cost of raising revenue through other forms of taxation. Phelps (1973) first pointed this out. The result, however, is by no means uncontroversial. One way to think about it is to consider the tax rate on money as a determinant of the relative price of cash and credit goods. If tax rates are set optimally, it is unclear that the tax rate on money should be positive—that is, that money-

---

[13] See also Cumby and van Wijnbergen (1987) and Giavazzi and Giovannini (1989b).

using goods should be taxed more heavily than credit- or barter-using goods.[14] However, if the main existing taxes are on some of the factor inputs, especially labor, then it may be desirable to tax all inputs, including monetary services.[15]

Another important argument (suggested, for example, by Barro, 1988) is that a positive tax rate on money allows the government to tax some black market activities where final output escapes taxation. The argument can be illustrated considering the optimal mix of money and tax financing for a government whose goal is to minimize the expected present value of social losses. Consider the government's intertemporal budget constraint:

$$\dot{b} = (r-n)b + (g - \tau) - \frac{\dot{C}}{py}, \tag{1}$$

where b is the public debt, as a share of national income; r is the real rate of interest; n is the growth rate of income; g is the ratio of government expenditure to income; and τ the average tax rate. $\dot{C}/(py)$ represents credit to the government by the central bank, also as a share of GDP. Suppose that velocity is constant, so that the demand for money (currency and bank deposits), M, can be described by the quantity equation:

$$\frac{M}{py} = k, \tag{2}$$

where k is a constant. Banking regulations and the structure of the financial system determine the relation between M and high-powered money, H. We simply describe it as:

$$H = g(\rho)M, \qquad\qquad \text{with } g'>0, \tag{3}$$

where ρ is the reserve requirement ratio. For any given level of M, an increase in required reserves raises H. Substituting from equation (3) for M in equation (2), differentiating, and neglecting central bank intervention in the foreign exchange market, we obtain:

$$\frac{\dot{C}}{py} = g(\rho) \, k \, (\pi+n), \tag{4}$$

---

[14] This argument is made in Lucas (1986); see also Drazen (1979) and Kimbrough (1986).

[15] Feldstein's (1976) distinction between "tax design" (tax laws being written *de novo* on a clean sheet of paper), and "tax reform" (taking as a starting point the existing tax system and the fact that actual changes are slow and piecemeal) is relevant on this point.

where π is the inflation rate, and therefore:

$$\dot{b} = (r-n)b + (g - \tau) - g(\rho) k (\pi+n). \tag{1'}$$

From equation (1') we see that different combinations of π, τ, and ρ can be used to finance any given level of government expenditure and to service the existing stock of debt, so as to keep the debt-to-income ratio constant.

What is the optimal combination of π, τ and ρ? Assume that the deadweight losses incurred by taxation and the social costs of inflation are linear in output.[16] The government's objective is:

$$\min_{\pi_t, \tau_t} \int_0^\infty e^{-rt} [f(\tau_t) + h(\pi_t)] \, y \, dt, \tag{5}$$

where the functions $f(\times)$ and $h(\times)$ (with f', h', f'', and h'' all positive) describe the social losses per unit of output associated with the two forms of raising revenue. The government minimizes equation (5) subject to (1') and to a transversality condition that rules out indefinite accumulation of public debt. The ratio of the two static first-order conditions of the optimal taxation program is:[17]

$$\frac{h'[(\pi)]}{f'[(\tau)]} = \frac{g(\rho)ky}{y} = g(\rho)k. \tag{6}$$

The ratio of the marginal social cost of inflation to the marginal deadweight loss of taxation is equal to the ratio of the two tax bases: y for taxation and $g(\rho)ky = (H/p)y$ for inflation. For given tax bases, equation (6) implies—as is well known—that the two tax rates are positively related. For instance if permanent expenditure rises, both tax rates have to increase.[18]

Equation (6) has important implications for the design of an optimal tax program. Consider first the case of tax evasion. In the presence of an underground economy where transactions are settled in cash and escape taxation, the two real income terms that appear in the numerator and denomi-

---

[16] As Fama (1980) and others have argued, reserve requirements have something in common with a tax on interest on bank deposits; the deadweight loss they give rise to should thus also be included in equation (5). Romer (1985) shows, however, that such a proposition is not necessarily true. In what follows, I overlook the possible distortions associated with reserve requirements.

[17] The intertemporal first-order conditions of this problem describe the "tax smoothing" property of optimal fiscal policy, as discussed in Barro (1979).

[18] This, of course, depends on the assumption of increasing marginal costs. Pagano (1988) discusses the solution of the optimal tax problem when inflation and tax rates may affect the level of output.

nator of the right-hand side of equation (6) measure quite different phenomena, and their ratio is proportional to the relative size of the underground economy. For a given velocity of high-powered money, the marginal cost of inflation relative to taxation should be higher in countries where the phenomenon of tax evasion is more widespread. The intuition runs as follows: the larger the tax base, the larger the revenue raised with a given tax rate. Since distortions depend only on tax rates, a larger tax base optimally justifies a larger distortion. Whether this also implies that the ratio of π to τ should be higher in countries where tax evasion is relatively more pervasive depends on the form of the f and h functions; it would be true if, for example, $[h(\pi)+f(\tau)]$ were homogeneous.

Consider next the effect of an increase in the social cost of inflation. In equation (6), when the ratio of the two marginal costs rises, so should the ratio of the two tax bases. An optimal response to an upward shift in h' is thus an increase in the base of the inflation tax. This can be accomplished by raising reserve requirements.[19] An increase in reserve requirements is indeed often observed at the outset of a disinflation. Charts 1 and 2 document the increase

Chart 1. Bank Reserve Ratios
(Percent of bank deposits)

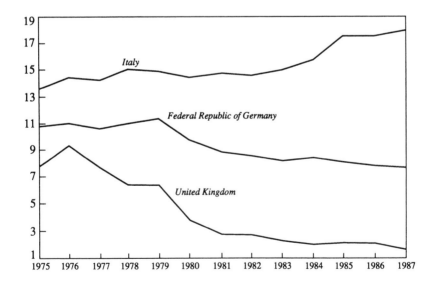

---

[19] I assume that an increase in reserve requirements raises the monetary base. If the demand for deposits is sensitive to the interest rate on deposits, an increase in reserve requirements could lower the monetary base (see for instance Calvo and Fernandez (1983)). For a recent review of the literature on seigniorage and reserve requirements, see Spaventa (1989).

Chart 2. Bank Reserve Ratios
(Percent of bank deposits)

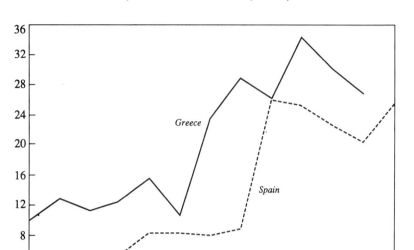

in reserve requirements in Italy, Greece, and Spain in the early 1980s.[20] When Italy joined the EMS, marginal reserve requirements were raised in a few years from 15.75 percent to 25 percent.[21] In Spain average reserve requirements were below 10 percent until 1982; they then jumped to 25 percent in 1983. In Greece average reserve requirements were also raised from 12 to almost 30 percent in the early 1980s.

In each country the timing of the increase in reserve requirements corresponds to a policy shift aimed at stabilizing the price level. As discussed in Section III, a disinflation is often associated with a change in the preferences of the monetary authorities—be it the appointment of a "conservative" central banker or the decision to peg the exchange rate to a low-inflation country. Both cases can be described as an increase in the relative cost of inflation in the authorities' objective function.

Monetary Financing and the Conduct of Monetary Policy

The view that central banks in southern Europe may have used (perhaps even "optimally") reserve requirements to widen the inflation tax base in the

---

[20] The figures plot total reserves (including free reserves) at the end of the period, as a percentage of bank deposits, as available from the International Monetary Fund's *International Financial Statistics*. More recent data on reserve requirements are reported in Table 3.

[21] For an analysis of the Italian experience see Bruni and others (1988).

Table 2. Base Money, Currency, and Bank Reserves
(Percent of GDP)

	Monetary Base		Currency		Bank Reserves	
	1981	1987	1981	1987	1981	1987
Portugal	25.3	15.7	12.9	8.8	12.4	6.9
Greece	22.6	25.5	12.9	10.1	9.7	15.4
Italy	15.1	15.2	6.3	5.5	8.8	9.7
Spain	13.6	22.6	7.8	7.7	5.8	14.9
Ireland	9.9	8.7	6.5	5.6	3.4	3.1
France	6.0	5.6	5.1	4.3	0.9	1.3
Belgium	10.6	8.1	10.1	7.7	0.5	0.4
Germany, Fed. Rep. of	9.8	10.4	5.5	6.2	4.3	4.2
Netherlands	6.6	8.1	6.3	7.6	0.3	0.5
Denmark	3.7	3.5	3.5	3.0	0.3	0.5
United Kingdom	5.1	4.2	4.2	3.4	0.9	0.8

Source: IMF, *International Financial Statistics*; Bank of Portugal, *Quarterly Bulletin.*

Table 3. Reserve Requirements of Commercial Banks
(Percent of demand deposits in banks, mid-1988)

Italy	25.0
Spain	18.0
Portugal	15.0
Ireland	1.0
Greece	7.5
Germany, Fed. Rep. of	6.6–12.1
France	5.0
United Kingdom	0.5
Belgium	0.0
Netherlands	0.0
Denmark	0.0

Note: In Spain, Italy, and Greece required reserves are remunerated to some degree. In Italy 25 percent is the marginal rate; the average rate is 20 percent.

Source: J. P. Morgan, *World Financial Markets*, No. 5, 1988.

presence of a falling inflation tax rate is attractive. Table 2 shows that the increase in reserve requirements in each of the four countries (Italy, Greece, Spain, and Portugal) in the early 1980s was not (at least fully) offset by a fall in bank deposits, and it thus produced an increase in the ratio of base money to GDP.

This view, however, encounters two difficulties. The first is that bank reserves in these countries pay some interest—5.5 percent, for example, in Italy. The implicit tax rate thus falls along with the fall in inflation and in nominal interest rates. Table 4 shows the implicit tax rate and the correspond-

Table 4. Italy: The Tax on Bank Reserves

	Reserves (percent of bank deposits)	Interest Rate Wedge	Implicit Tax Rate	Tax Revenue (percent of GDP)
1976–81	14.9	13.5	1.75	1.35
1982–85	17.6	14.7	2.19	1.15
1986–87	20.1	9.1	1.55	0.40

Note: The interest rate wedge is the difference between the lending rate and the interest rate paid on reserves. The implicit tax rate is the product of the wedge times the reserve ratio.

Source: Pagano (1988).

ing tax revenues in the case of Italy. In the late 1970s and early 1980s—when the difference between the lending rate and the interest rate paid on bank reserves was above 10 percent—the yearly tax revenue exceeded 1 percent of GDP; in 1986–87, when the interest rate wedge became much smaller, the revenue fell to less than ½ of 1 percent of GDP.[22]

The second difficulty is that central banks provide different motivations for their decision to raise reserve requirements. According to the Bank of Italy, for instance, "an increase in the reserve coefficient was necessary in order to reduce the value of the bank multiplier and dampen the impact of disturbances originating from central bank lending to the Treasury" (Bank of Italy, *La Mobilizzazione della Riserva Obbligatoria: Motivazioni e Implicazioni* (October 1988, p.7)). These motivations suggest that it is important to draw a distinction between treasury access to the central bank and money creation. The important question is not whether the central bank is obliged to lend to the Treasury, but whether, given that obligation, it is still in a position to conduct a monetary policy, and whether the ability to use reserve requirements provides an additional instrument.[23]

Changes in reserve requirements affect the multiplier and can be used to control the money supply. Thus, from equation (3):

$$dM = - H(g'/g)d\rho + (1/g)dH, \tag{7}$$

where $(1/g)$ is the multiplier: an increase in ρ reduces the multiplier. Equation

---

[22] In Spain, also, the interest rate on bank reserves is a fraction of the market rate. Gros (1988) also points to the role of the interest paid on bank reserves.

[23] This point has recently been made by Connolly and Kroger (1988) in connection with the EMS. Distinguishing between the Treasury and the central bank may, however, be misleading in situations where the Treasury is able to shift expenditure to the central bank. In Turkey, for instance, a substantial part of the interest payments on the government's foreign debt is handled directly by the central bank without being recorded in the government's budget. See van Wijnbergen and others (1988).

(7) shows the two effects of a change in reserve requirements. An increase in ρ—as in Spain and Italy from the late 1970s to the mid-1980s—allows the central bank to "sterilize" its lending to the Treasury (this is the first term in equation (7)). At higher values of the reserve coefficient, the variance of the money supply is lower for any given variance of credit creation by the Treasury (this is the second term in the equation). Reserve requirements can thus shelter the central bank from the effects of its obligation to lend to the Treasury. However, since ρ is bounded, reserve requirements cannot be used indefinitely. Over time, as ρ stabilizes, the only effect is a reduced variance of the money supply.

The possibility of using bank reserves to sterilize central bank lending to the Treasury can be seen even more clearly, rewriting equation (7) in the following form:

$$dM/M - dp/p = (C/H)dC/C - [(R/H)(dp/p - \bar{r})$$
$$+ (Cu/H)dp/p + \eta \, d\rho/\rho], \tag{7$'$}$$

where I have assumed that a fixed rate of interest $\bar{r}$ is paid on bank reserves. C denotes, as above, central bank lending to the Treasury; R and Cu the two components of the monetary base (bank reserves and currency, respectively); dp/p the inflation rate; and η the elasticity of the multiplier with respect to a change in the reserve coefficient. The first two terms in the square brackets are the seigniorage on currency and bank reserves, respectively; the last term measures the effect of a change in reserve requirements.

Consider first a steady state with constant reserve requirements and with $\bar{r}$ = 0. From equation (7$'$) $(C/H)dC/C = dM/M = dp/p$: Treasury borrowing from the central bank determines the rate of money growth (overlooking the effects of central bank intervention in the foreign exchange market), itself equal to the rate of inflation. Consider now a change in monetary regime, for example a disinflation driven by a reduction in the growth rate of money.[24] If the Treasury does not adjust the amount it borrows from the central bank, the latter has only two options: sterilization through an open market operation, or adjustment of the term in the square brackets on the right-hand side of equation (7$'$); this can be done by changing reserve requirements.

The central bank may decide not to run an open market operation for two reasons. First, if the financial system is not well developed, there may be no market; this was the case in Italy in the mid-1970s when reserve requirements were first increased. Second, the central bank may want to avoid accompanying the shift in the monetary regime with a buildup of public debt.

---

[24] Alternatively equation (7$'$) could be used to study the shift toward a fixed exchange rate regime run by a "low-inflation" country. With fixed exchange rates and high capital mobility, money demand is exogenous, and the excess of central bank lending to the Treasury over the growth rate of money demand results in a loss of foreign exchange reserves.

There is, however, a limit to the use of reserve requirements as a substitute for open market operations. Eventually the increase in ρ will have to stop; moreover, if central banks pay a fixed interest rate on reserves—as in Italy—when inflation falls so does the seigniorage attached to bank reserves.[25] For some time, however, the use of reserve requirements allows the central bank to run a monetary policy consistent with the new monetary regime even *before* the menu of taxes and money financing has been set consistently with the new regime, and without putting additional pressure on public debt. If the central bank can set reserve requirements, a reduction in the degree of money financing is no longer a *precondition* for the shift in monetary regime.

This has clearly been Italy's experience since the start of the EMS. In the mid-1980s—from 1983 to 1985—when the reserve ratio was growing at 1 percent a year and the interest rate paid on bank reserves was 6 percentage points below the inflation rate, the Bank of Italy was able to sterilize through bank reserves two thirds of its total lending to the Treasury, equal on average to 2 percent of GDP a year. Another one third was sterilized through the increase in demand for currency (the middle term in equation $(7')$).

Inflation, Fixed Exchange Rates, and Financial Liberalization

The bottom line of the previous two sections is that in countries where money financing is a relatively important source of revenue, a shift to a less expansionary monetary regime implies a choice between higher taxes now and higher taxes in the future, and if it is "now," between different types of taxes. If the tax base is relatively small, and (at least in the short run) tax revenues can only be increased by raising marginal tax rates, it may be optimal not to shift at once the entire burden of the fiscal correction on explicit taxes. An increase in reserve requirements can avoid building up a debt problem in the transition.

The analysis of the role of bank reserves has important implications for the plans to create a unified market for financial services in Europe. If reserve requirements work like a tax on the interest paid on bank deposits, banks subject to relatively higher reserve requirements would tend to go out of business; it would be difficult to keep different reserve requirements in an integrated financial market.

In countries such as Greece and Portugal—where inflation is still relatively high—it may be unwise to erase reserve requirements as a policy instrument and, at the same time, suggest a shift in monetary regime. On the contrary, in such countries as Italy, where the shift in monetary regime has already occurred, and where the possibility of using bank reserves as a buffer

---

[25] If reserves pay no interest, the tax on bank deposits will eventually reduce the role of banks as financial intermediaries and, thus, also the revenue attached to bank reserves. The experience of the southern European countries shows that this may be a long process provided that foreign banks may not operate in the domestic market subject to their home reserve requirements.

in the transition appears to have been exhausted, the setting of reserve requirements at the European average would, at this point, have only minor effects, subtracting no more than ½ of 1 percent of GDP from the budget.

In the case of Italy, however, a long transition—ten years from the start of the EMS—seems not to have been sufficient for the adjustment in fiscal policy required by the new monetary regime. As the safety nets provided by exchange controls and reserve requirements have become less effective, debt has begun to accumulate. This brings us back to the question of the optimality of common inflation rates throughout Europe discussed at the beginning of this section.

V. Summary and Conclusions

This paper has analyzed some of the merits and difficulties of a transition toward fixed exchange rates in Europe. The motivation for the analysis was the observation that the "shock of 1992" will come from the integration of financial markets since financial integration is inconsistent with the current system of fixed but adjustable parities. The paper's main points can be summarized as follows:

- The analysis of international policy interactions points to an important trade-off that underlies the choice of the exchange rate regime. On the one hand, the theoretical appeal of fixed exchange rates is that they eliminate the incentive to use beggar-thy-neighbor policies. On the other hand, while in the absence of significant international labor mobility and of fiscal redistributions, adjustable parities can be efficient in the short run at evening out country-specific imbalances, they can also be used for selfish purposes—to the detriment of everyone.
- For fixed exchange rates to be able to correct the inflationary bias of the more inflation-prone countries in Europe, the exchange rate regime must work asymmetrically. Monetary policy for the entire region must be set independently by the least inflation-prone country; the other countries must passively accommodate, thus effectively giving up monetary sovereignty. This point has important implications for the organization of a European central bank.
- The analysis of the public finance role of inflation and the evidence on fiscal asymmetries point to the risks of a change in monetary regime in countries characterized by a relatively small tax base and a relatively large ratio of money financing to tax revenues.

References

Backus, David, and John Driffill, "Inflation and Reputation," *American Economic Review*, Vol. 75 (Nashville, Tennessee), 1985, pp. 530–38.

Barro, Robert J., "Interest Rate Smoothing," National Bureau of Economic Research Working Paper No. 2581 (Cambridge, Massachusetts: NBER, 1988), pp. 1–51.

————, "On the Determination of Public Debt," *Journal of Political Economy*, Vol. 87 (Chicago: University of Chicago Press, October 1979), pp. 940–71.

————, and David Gordon, "Rules, Discretion, and Reputation in a Model of Monetary Policy," *Journal of Monetary Economics*, Vol. 12 (Amsterdam: North-Holland, July 1983), pp. 101–21.

Bean, Charles, "Macroeconomic Policy Coordination: Theory and Evidence," *Recherches Economiques de Louvain*, Vol. 51, No. 3/4 (Louvain: Université Catholique, 1985).

Bruni, Penati, and A. Porta, "Financial Regulation, Implicit Taxes and Fiscal Adjustment in Italy," mimeographed (Milan: Bocconi University, 1988).

Buiter, Willem H., and Richard C. Marston, eds., *International Economic Policy Coordination* (Cambridge, United Kingdom: Cambridge University Press, 1985).

Calvo, Guillermo A., "On the Time Consistency of Optimal Policy in a Monetary Economy," *Econometrica*, Vol. 46, No. 6 (Chicago: University of Chicago Press, 1978), pp. 1411–28.

————, and R. Fernandez, "Competitive Banks and the Inflation Tax," *Economics Letters*, Vol. 12 (Amsterdam: North-Holland, 1983), pp. 313–17.

Canzoneri, Matthew B., and Dale W. Henderson, "Is Sovereign Policymaking Bad?" Carnegie-Rochester Conference Series on Public Policy (Rochester, New York: 1988), pp. 93–140.

Collins, S., "Inflation and the EMS," in *The European Monetary System*, ed. by Francesco Giavazzi and others (Cambridge, United Kingdom: Cambridge University Press, 1988).

Connolly, B., and J. Kroger, "Financing of Budget Deficits and Monetary Integration," mimeographed (Brussels: European Economic Community, 1988).

Cooper, Richard, "Worldwide versus Regional Integration," in *Economic Integration,* ed. by Fritz Machlup (London: Macmillan, 1976).

Cumby, Robert, and Sweder van Wijnbergen, "Fiscal Deficits, the Crawling Peg and Speculative Attacks on the Central Bank: an Empirical Analysis of Argentina," National Bureau of Economic Research Working Paper No. 2376 (Cambridge, Massachusetts: NBER, September 1987).

Currie, David, and Paul Levine, "Credibility and Time Consistency in a Stochastic World," Centre for Economic Policy Research Discussion Paper No. 94 (London: CEPR, 1986), pp. 1–32.

Currie, David, Gerald Holtham, and Andrew Hughes Hallett, "The Theory and Practice of International Economic Policy Coordination: Does Coordination Pay?" this volume.

De Cecco, M. and Alberto Giovannini, *A European Central Bank?* (Cambridge,

United Kingdom: Cambridge University Press, 1989).

Dornbusch, Rudiger (1988a), "The EMS, the Dollar and the Yen," in *The European Monetary System*, ed. by Francesco Giavazzi and others (Cambridge, United Kingdom: Cambridge University Press, 1988).

———— (1988b), "Money and Finance in European Integration," mimeographed (Cambridge, Massachusetts: MIT, 1988).

Drazen, Allan, "The Optimal Inflation Tax Revisited," *Journal of Monetary Economics*, Vol. 5 (Amsterdam: North-Holland, 1979), pp. 231–48.

Driffill, J., "The Sustainability and Stability of the EMS with Perfect Capital Mobility," in *The European Monetary System*, ed. by Francesco Giavazzi and others (Cambridge, United Kingdom: Cambridge University Press, 1988).

Fama, Eugene, "Banking in the Theory of Finance," *Journal of Monetary Economics*, Vol. 6 (Amsterdam: North-Holland, 1980), pp. 39–57.

Feldstein, Martin S., "On the Theory of Tax Reform," *Journal of Public Economics*, Vol. 6 (Amsterdam: North-Holland, 1976), pp. 7–104.

Fischer, Stanley, "International Macroeconomic Policy Coordination," National Bureau of Economic Research Working Paper No. 2244 (Cambridge, Massachusetts: NBER, 1987), pp. 1–56.

Giavazzi, Francesco, and Alberto Giovannini, "The EMS and the Dollar," in *Economic Policy: A European Forum*, Vol. 1 (United Kingdom: April 1986), pp. 455–74.

————, "Exchange Rates and Prices in Europe," *Weltwirtschaftliches Archiv*, Vol. 4 (Tübingen: December 1987), pp. 592–605.

———— (1989a), "Can the EMS Be Exported? Lessons from Ten Years of Monetary Policy Coordination in Europe," Centre for Economic Policy Research Discussion Paper No. 285 (London: CEPR, 1989).

———— (1989b), "Monetary Policy Interactions Under Managed Exchange Rates," *Economica* (London, forthcoming, 1989).

———— (1989c), *Limiting Exchange Rate Flexibility: The European Monetary System* (Cambridge, Massachusetts: MIT Press, 1989).

Giavazzi, Francesco, and Marco Pagano (1988a), "Confidence Crises and Public Debt Management," Centre for Economic Policy Research Discussion Paper (London: CEPR, 1988).

———— (1988b), "The Advantage of Tying One's Hands: EMS Discipline and Central Bank Credibility," *European Economic Review*, Vol. 32, No. 5 (Amsterdam: 1988), pp. 1055–82.

Gros, Daniel, "Seigniorage in the EC: The Implications for the EMS and Financial Market Integration," mimeographed, Center for European Policy Studies, Brussels, 1988.

Hamada, Koichi G., "Alternative Exchange Rate Systems and the Interdependence of Monetary Policies," in *National Monetary Policies and International Financial Systems*, ed. by R. Z. Aliber (Chicago: Chicago University Press, 1974).

Helpman, Elhanan, and Assaf Razin, "Exchange Rate Management," *American Eco-*

nomic Review (Nashville, Tennessee: March 1987), pp. 107–23.

Kimbrough, K. P. "Inflation, Employment, and Welfare in the Presence of Transaction Costs," *Journal of Money, Credit and Banking*, Vol. 18, No. 2 (Columbus, Ohio: Ohio State University Press, 1986), pp. 127–40.

Kydland, Finn E., and Edward C. Prescott, "Rules Rather than Discretion: The Inconsistency of Optimal Plans," *Journal of Political Economy*, Vol. 85, No. 3 (Chicago: University of Chicago Press, 1977).

Lucas, Robert, "Principles of Fiscal and Monetary Policy," *Journal of Monetary Economics*, Vol. 17 (Amsterdam: North-Holland, 1986) pp. 117–34.

Mankiw, Gregory N., "The Optimal Collection of Seigniorage," *Journal of Monetary Economics*, Vol. 20 (Amsterdam: North-Holland, 1989), pp. 327–41.

McKibbin, Warwick, and Jeffrey Sachs, "Comparing the Global Performance of Alternative Exchange Arrangements," National Bureau of Economic Research Working Paper No. 2024 (Cambridge, Massachusetts: NBER, 1986), pp. 1–62.

Melitz, Jacques, "Germany, Discipline and Cooperation in the EMS," in *The European Monetary System*, ed. by Francesco Giavazzi and others (Cambridge, United Kingdom: Cambridge University Press, 1988).

Mundell, Robert A., "A Plan for a European Currency," in *The Economics of Common Currencies*, ed. by H. G. Johnson and Alexander Swoboda (London: Allen & Unwin, 1973).

Obstfeld, Maurice, "Competitiveness, Realignment and Speculation: The Role of Financial Markets," in *The European Monetary System*, ed. by Francesco Giavazzi and others (Cambridge, United Kingdom: Cambridge University Press, 1988).

Pagano, Marco, "Monetary Policy, Capital Controls and Seigniorage in an Open Economy: Discussion of a Paper by A. Drazen," in De Cecco and Giovannini (1989).

Phelps, Edmond S., "Inflation in the Theory of Public Finance," *Swedish Journal of Economics*, Vol. 75 (1973), pp. 67–82.

Ploeg, Frederick van der, "International Policy Coordination in Interdependent Monetary Economies," *Journal of International Economics*, Vol. 19 (Amsterdam: North-Holland, 1989).

Rogoff, Kenneth (1985a), "The Optimal Degree of Commitment to an Intermediate Monetary Target," *Quarterly Journal of Economics*, Vol. 100, No. 4 (Cambridge, Massachusetts: 1985), pp. 1169–90.

————— (1985b), "Can International Monetary Cooperation be Counterproductive?" *Journal of International Economics*, Vol. 18 (Amsterdam: North-Holland, 1985), pp. 199–217.

Romer, David, "Financial Intermediation, Reserve Requirements and Inside Money: A General Equilibrium Analysis," *Journal of Monetary Economics*, Vol. 16 (Amsterdam: North-Holland, 1985), pp. 175–94.

Spaventa, Luigi, "Seigniorage: Old and New Policy Issues," *European Economic Review* (Amsterdam, forthcoming, 1989).

van Wijnbergen, Sweder, and others, "Inflation, External Debt and Financial Reform," mimeographed (Washington: World Bank, 1988).

Wyplosz, Charles, "Capital Controls and Balance of Payments Crises," *Journal of International Money and Finance* (Guildford, United Kingdom: Butterworth Scientific Ltd., June 1986), pp. 167–79.

Comments

Francesco Giavazzi's paper correctly alerts us to the problems facing the current, and potentially expanded, European Community (EC) as a result of the combination of "Europe 1992" in the financial markets and the exchange rate arrangements of the European Monetary System (EMS). The paper observes that the combination means the end of the EMS regime of fixed but adjustable parities, and a choice between more continuously adjustable rates and immutably fixed rates with, eventually, a common currency. The open financial markets of 1992 will spawn intense speculative pressure around realignments. This will lead to strong political pressure for either fixed rates or, potentially, for the abandonment of the arrangements. The benefits of fixed rates with open capital markets—eliminating the dimension of exchange risk from business decisions—will ultimately lead to a decision for immutably fixed rates in the EC. This will require approximate inflation convergence among the member states, and, eventually, a common currency to rule out the potential for parity adjustments.

In his discussion of the public finance view of inflation, Giavazzi points out that inflation convergence means that some of the more inflation-prone southern European countries will have to give up the inflation tax. Previous reliance on this tax suggests that, for these countries, raising the tax revenue from alternative sources is costly, so that the necessary tax reform will take time. As a transitional measure, Giavazzi suggests an increase in reserve requirements, to increase the base for the inflation tax as the rate is reduced. One problem with this proposal is that it would increase the spread between deposit and lending rates in the banking systems involved, just when they are feeling the competitive pressure from 1992. These banking systems are already at a competitive disadvantage owing to their lack of development, and in some cases, to backlogs of nonperforming loans. And, I argue below, it may be important for the governments involved to preserve some degree of local intermediation. This is therefore the one point of disagreement I have with the paper.

I would like to discuss briefly three problems with the convergence to fixed rates implied by the combination of Europe 1992 and the EMS:

- Whether the member states' current account balances with each other are anywhere near equilibrium as the process begins.
- The means of adjustment to relative, real disturbances among the member states.
- The preservation of local capital markets, alluded to above.

Projections of the Organization for Economic Cooperation and Development (OECD) and the International Monetary Fund for 1989 show a large

305

surplus on the current account in the Federal Republic of Germany and its neighbors, Belgium, the Netherlands, and Switzerland (plus heroic Ireland, out on the periphery). Their combined surplus is about $55 billion, with about $45 billion accounted for by Germany. But OECD Europe is approximately in balance. The deficits are distributed among the EC members that do not participate in the exchange rate arrangements (that is, the United Kingdom and Spain) and among non-EC members. How should this pattern of imbalances be interpreted? If we assume that Germany is integrated with the members in the exchange rate arrangements, an appreciation of that group against the rest of the EC and non-EC Europe is needed before exchange rates become fixed. The needed appreciation would be smaller if we assumed the entire EC as an integrated unit, with the German surplus automatically available to finance the deficits of other members. If we assume that all of Europe is integrated, with the European Free Trade Association (EFTA) members joining the EC to benefit from 1992, the surplus vanishes and a change in the U.S. dollar-Japanese yen rate is then needed. Thus, the seriousness of the imbalances within Europe depends on how integrated Europe is at present.

The second problem is the lack of policy instruments for adjustment in the event of relative, real disturbances among the member countries. The exchange rate arrangements combined with Europe 1992 mean that aggregate monetary policy in the member states will be aimed solely at stabilizing the exchange rate; the members will have to give up autonomous monetary policy. This is true even for any EC members that opt for a "soft currency" option and peg their real exchange rate to the EMS grid. Their monetary policy will be fully occupied, moving the nominal exchange rate along the path required to fix the real rate. This leaves fiscal policy and migration as the only instruments of adjustment. Without an integrated fiscal system at the EC level, the EC would lack an automatic fiscal redistribution mechanism in the case of relative real disturbances. As Kenen (1969) points out, the United States has automatic transfers among states through the federal tax and transfer system. This provides income support with temporary relative, real disturbances such as an oil price shock that has opposite effects on income in, for example, Texas and Massachusetts. Without any analogous system, the EC may find adjustment to such shocks more costly than does the United States.

The last problem is the potential need to preserve local financial intermediaries. Recent theoretical work on financial intermediation has stressed that asymmetric and costly information is the reason for the existence of local intermediaries such as banks. Banks deal with the problem of asymmetric information by developing the capacity to monitor local borrowers. The fixed cost of such an investment gives banks local market power by deterring entry. It also makes it unprofitable for nonlocal intermediaries or international lenders to lend to local borrowers because they know they are at an informational disadvantage. Small local businesses thus come to depend on local banks as their source of financing. There is empirical evidence that this form of local intermediation is important even in the relatively unified U.S. market. Fazzari and others (1988) find that firms with less than $100 million in assets obtain over 75 percent of their debt financing from banks. Only the largest firms have access to the bond market.

Thus, with costly and asymmetrical information about small borrowers, these borrowers will have to rely on local sources of funds. If the competitive winds of Europe 1992 lead to the disappearance or absorption of local intermediaries by larger units, this lending pattern may be disrupted, at least temporarily. This could result in a drying up of financing sources for small, local firms, and potential bankruptcies, while new informational arrangements are made. National monetary authorities will have an interest in preserving the health of the structure of local intermediation as their markets are opened by 1992.

References

Fazzari, Steven M., R. Glenn Hubbard, and Bruce C. Petersen, "Financing Constraints and Corporate Investment," *Brookings Papers on Economic Activity:1* (Washington, The Brookings Institution, 1988), pp. 141–95.

Kenen, Peter B., "The Theory of Optimal Currency Areas: An Eclectic View," in *Monetary Problems of the International Economy*, ed. by Robert A. Mundell and Alexander K. Swoboda (Chicago: University of Chicago Press, 1969), pp. 41–60.

Mario Draghi

The policy prescriptions presented in Professor Giavazzi's paper are based on the following assumptions:

• The current situation in Europe is characterized by perfect capital mobility, independent monetary policies, and fixed but adjustable exchange rate parities. These requirements are mutually inconsistent, and since integration of capital markets is primary on the European agenda, either exchange rates and/or independent monetary policies will have to yield.

• Fully independent monetary policies would not be compatible with a system of fixed exchange rates, and would make suboptimal a system of flexible rates. For different reasons, a system of centralized parities with adjustable pegs would also not be desirable. If reality is as described above, the clear winner would be a system of permanently fixed exchange rates and centralized monetary policy.

• The current European system functions like a national economy without intraregional transfers or internal labor mobility. Both are excluded from the analysis since as yet there seems to be no clear mechanism providing for transfers, and labor mobility is likely to be low in the early stages of the union. As such, the system, deprived of regional corrective measures, is particularly exposed to structural asymmetries of which the fiscal ones are most important.

- Giavazzi warns countries with more fragile fiscal systems that, in joining the monetary union, they will lose the seigniorage that is now an important part of their tax revenue, and they should therefore reform their fiscal systems. However, this process may take a long time, and, in order to avoid a buildup of debt during this transition, they should increase their seigniorage tax base; they could do so by raising the reserve requirements of their commercial banks.

I would now like to touch briefly on some of Giavazzi's perceptions of the current reality, and then devote most of my comments to his main policy prescription.

First, I am not sure I would agree with the characterization of the current situation. I see one country running its own monetary policy without too much regard for the rest of the area, and, in spite of this, being closely followed by the other partners. In other words, monetary policies are not independent. The leading country is also the less inflation-prone country. Therefore, although the others control the exchange rate, they are prevented from running a beggar-thy-neighbor policy. To use Giavazzi's example, faced with a negative supply shock, they cannot appreciate their exchange rates to engineer a disinflation, since they would quickly run into a trade deficit, a loss of reserves, and, ultimately, exchange rate readjustment. To the extent that monetary policies are not independent of the leading country, the current system can survive even in a situation of perfect capital mobility. Obviously the system remains—as any other arrangement with quasi-fixed exchange rates—exposed to structural asymmetries. The periodic changes in exchange rates would reflect such asymmetries, as well as occasional and short-lived attempts to run independent monetary policies by one or another state in the region. In other words, the present system, perhaps slightly modified in a way to make speculation more expensive, is not doomed to failure.

This brings me to Giavazzi's other point: that a system of flexible exchange rates and independent monetary policies has an inborn deflationary bias. His analysis constructs a case where central banks, in reacting to a negative supply shock, would take each other's monetary policy as given, and would believe it possible to appreciate the exchange rate and reduce the price level at a "comparatively smaller cost in terms of output." Each country would have the incentive to overcontract, but the exchange rate would not move and the "outcome is a lower level of output." The problem I have with this analysis is that countries are assumed to be identical and, therefore, their trade surplus is always zero. In this case, focusing only on strategic interactions between the two players constrains the choice of the exchange rate system. As soon as we allow countries to differ—in the intensity with which the negative supply shock affects their economies, in their capacity to export, and in the availability of external financing—we have a variety of outcomes of which the deflationary bias is only a special case. More generally, the suboptimality of a flexible exchange rate system described in the paper derives from the assumptions that countries are identical and that they take each other's monetary policies as given. Since the first assumption is not true and there is no incentive to behave as if the second were, we should focus our attention on the properties of a system—which I consider more realistic in today's Europe—based on one monetary policy of the leading country and cooperatively managed exchange rates.

But suppose we move to a permanently fixed exchange rate system where monetary policy is run by the less inflation-prone country. Here the credibility of the monetary authorities is the greatest, but so is the exposure to the problems caused by structural differences, particularly in the fiscal area. It is clear that with monetary union, substantial fiscal divergences will not be sustainable. For countries with low tax bases and high public deficits, the political cost of fiscal adjustment may simply be too high, and they could easily end up having high levels of public debt. Giavazzi suggests that these countries—I assume before entering the union—should increase their reserve requirements, so as to increase the tax base of seigniorage. This policy prescription is arguable from several standpoints. Commercial banks would react to this measure by increasing their lending rates and lowering their borrowing rates. Under perfect capital mobility, there would be a simultaneous capital outflow and an increase in private borrowing abroad substituting private for public debt, and partly defeating one of the original intentions of the policy prescription. Even disregarding the consequences that such a measure could have on the country's current account—which in the case of some developing countries have not been negligible—it is not at all clear that the tax base of seigniorage will be larger after the increase in reserve requirements. It would depend on the degree of substitutability between the domestic and foreign currencies. Perhaps this prescription might work better under a regime of strict capital controls, which, however, would be considered as a step back from any monetary union. But even in a closed economy, the extent to which a rise in the banks' reserve requirement enlarges the seigniorage tax base crucially depends on the interest elasticity of demand deposits. The analysis in the paper is carried through assuming a constant velocity of circulation: if one allows it to respond to the rate of inflation, it can be shown that the ratio of the two tax bases in equation (6) of the paper is a decreasing function of the interest elasticity of money demand. The higher this elasticity, the lower the seigniorage tax vis-à-vis the revenue base of the other taxes.

The possibility that some of the taxes, other than seigniorage, may be partly indexed to inflation is one institutional aspect that should also be taken into account in some countries. Obviously, in this case an increase in the social cost of inflation—as would be caused by joining a monetary union led by the less inflation-prone country—will not necessarily elicit, as an optimal response, an increase in the base of the seigniorage tax relative to other taxes.

Finally, the case against using increases in reserve requirements as a tool for financing fiscal deficits is especially compelling when the transition toward a monetary union concerns countries with banking systems made fragile by many years of tight protectionist regimes. In such circumstances, this or any other similar measure—such as constraining commercial banks to hold large amounts of government bonds at lower-than-market rates—would further weaken these financial systems at a time when they need all their resources to restructure themselves so as to face the oncoming market unification.

In summary, I would offer the following points:

- The current European Monetary System, perhaps with some slight modification of the band's width, does not appear to be dying under the strains of destabilizing speculation, and its present condition is not by itself sufficient to justify a movement toward monetary union. This is mainly a political decision with costs and benefits that go far beyond the issue of the exchange rate. In any case, to the extent that perfectly fixed exchange rates will further expose the structural differences among countries, progress toward monetary union must go hand in hand with fiscal harmonization, with the construction of a mechanism providing for intraregional transfers and with rules governing the issuance of public debt by member states.

- If this is done, I do not see the need for an increase in reserve requirements, although temporary, or for any other equivalent measure. If the government deficit is unsustainable with the tax structure prevailing before joining the union, it should be corrected immediately, and the sooner the better. If it is made unsustainable by joining the union—for instance, because of the loss of tax seigniorage—then intraregional transfers should be negotiated and obtained by the joining member; otherwise, entrance should be delayed until the tax structure of the joining member is credibly harmonized, in the sense that membership in the union will not by itself be a cause of debt accumulation.

8

The European Monetary Union: An Agnostic Evaluation

*Daniel Cohen and Charles Wyplosz**

I. Introduction

E urope will wear new clothes in 1993. The Single Act will have removed most, if not all, remaining trade barriers. As early as 1990, capital movements should, in principle, be free among most European Community countries.[1] A natural further step, it is argued by the EC Commission, is monetary integration. The expected result is a degree of economic integration similar to that achieved at the national level, with considerable returns to scale rewarding such a bold move.

From a political point of view, the prospect of a European Monetary Union (EMU) is, paradoxically, remote. Indeed, it may be surprising that the concept of free trade is unanimously agreed upon, despite its likely distributive implications, while monetary integration, which is supposedly neutral in the long run, encounters so much resistance.

The debate about the EMU revolves mainly around two issues. Opponents object to the loss of a national policy instrument, which is a tool for stabilization and offers revenues from seigniorage. Supporters, on the other hand, argue that the benefits from policy coordination warrant the sacrifice of some freedom, monetary policy being a prime candidate. We reject both arguments for the following reasons:

- seigniorage is a second order effect except, perhaps, during the transition, and
- policy coordination is not optimally achieved through monetary integration.

---

* This paper is part of the Centre for Economic Policy Research program in international macroeconomics. Financial support from the Ford Foundation, the Alfred P. Sloan Foundation, and CEPR is gratefully acknowledged. We thank Veronique Brunhes and Katrina Maxwell for research assistance, and Richard Portes for useful suggestions.

[1] Spain, Portugal, and Greece have been allowed to extend this deadline to 1992.

In Section II, we assess the nonstrategic aspects of monetary integration. In particular, we show that revenues from seigniorage are small and of the same order of magnitude as seigniorage revenues that could be raised with the European currency unit (ECU) from the rest of the world. The strategic argument—the policy coordination gains from monetary integration—is assessed within the framework of a formal model, which we present in Section III. The model shows that the EMU would leave unresolved a key issue of policy integration, namely, how to determine collectively the trade balance of the zone vis-à-vis the rest of the world. We show that this externality arises even though each country follows its own intertemporal budget constraint. Yet, it is unfair to gauge the EMU against the background of a first-best scheme, which, we argue, faces considerable credibility problems. The proper yardstick should be the likely alternatives. Section IV compares the EMU with the European Monetary System (EMS), and Section V concludes on an agnostic note.

II. Nonstrategic Aspects

Seigniorage

According to Dornbusch (1988), Giavazzi and Pagano (1988), and Drazen (1989), some countries simply cannot afford to join an EMU. These countries are those whose money base is relatively large and whose public debt is high—and the servicing of which entails, now and for the long run, significant tax pressure. Optimal taxation suggests that the tax pressure should be carefully spread out. With a large and relatively inelastic money base, giving up seigniorage would worsen the inefficiency of taxation. A worst case scenario includes the inability of servicing the debt in the absence of seigniorage and the threat of government insolvency.

There is some question about whether the money base should be taxed at all. Assuming this problem away, the strength of the argument is largely empirical. Table 1 provides some evidence. Seigniorage revenues in 1987 are shown in column 2 as a proportion of gross domestic product (GDP) Y:

$$\frac{\dot{H}}{Y} = \mu.h,$$

where $\mu = \dot{H}/H$ is the growth rate of the money base H and $h = H/Y$ is the tax base shown in the first column. By 1987, with monetary policies generally held in check over concern for inflation, seigniorage revenues typically amount to less than 1 percent of GDP. In many countries, however, seigniorage has sometimes provided far more significant revenues: column 3 shows the maximum amount recorded in each country since 1960. This maximum level ranges from 1.2 in the Netherlands to 11.4 percent in Spain. Such levels, however, are not sustainable over any significant period. They are the out-

Table 1. Seigniorage
(Percent of GDP)

| | | | | Seigniorage | |
| | | | | Steady-State Theoretical | |
	Tax Base (1987) (1)	Actual (1987) (2)	Maximum (Year) (3)	Zero inflation (4)	5 percent inflation (5)
Belgium	8.0	0.2	1.8 (1972)	0.6	1.0
Denmark	3.4	0.5[1]	4.6 (1985)	0.4	0.6
France	6.2	0.4	3.1 (1972)	0.8	1.1
Germany, Fed. Rep. of	9.9	0.8	1.8 (1970)	0.5	1.0
Ireland	10.2	0.3	4.3 (1968)	1.6	2.1
Italy	15.2	1.2	6.7 (1975)	3.1	3.9
Netherlands	8.1	0.7	1.2 (1964)	0.3	0.7
Spain	19.8[2]	1.5[2]	11.4 (1983)	2.5	3.5
United Kingdom	3.5	0.1	2.3 (1973)	0.5	0.7

Source: IMF, *International Financial Statistics.*
[1] Average 1979–87.
[2] 1986.

come of a surprise inflation, an issue we return to in the next section. Sustainable seigniorage is closer to the numbers shown in column 4, where μ is set equal to the average real GDP growth rate recorded over the EMS period 1979–87. This would be a steady state situation should the income elasticity be unity and inflation nil. As income elasticity is typically less than unity, the numbers in column 4 overestimate seigniorage revenues under zero inflation. Column 5 shows the case where inflation is set at 5 percent a year. These numbers become meaningful only for Ireland, Italy, and Spain—owing to the size of their money base; they are also likely to be so in Portugal and Greece. Furthermore, at the global level seigniorage will still be extracted; there is thus room for at least some compensation.

The only cases of concern are those of the three large money base countries. For Ireland and Italy, which have high public debts, it may have been rational for the authorities to maintain a large taxable money base. Spain's situation is more likely explained by its relative backwardness, now quickly fading away. In any case, a clear implication of the EC Single Act is that by 1992 competitive pressures will dent the existing regulations that have led to such large money bases. While the EMU is not, as we argue in Section III, implied by the Single Act, a convergence toward low money bases is inevitable; this removes the first argument against the EMU (except, of course, during the transition period).

The Possibility of a Surprise Inflation

Having asserted that seigniorage is not a major source of steady government revenue, we certainly do not wish to argue for sustained high inflation rates. However, for countries with high public debts—Belgium, Ireland, and Italy—the inflation-surprise option may be difficult to give up. After all, there are numerous historical examples of how high public debts have been significantly eroded through inflation; an interesting case is that of the United Kingdom as described by Buiter (1985).

There are, however, two important provisions. First, inflation must come as a surprise so that nominal interest rates do not compensate fully for its effect. Therefore, if the public debt is indexed, or if its maturity is short, the benefits of inflation are very limited. Given the costs of an eventual disinflation, the incentive for a surprise inflation may then be most limited.

Table 2, borrowed from Giavazzi and Pagano (1988), provides evidence for the EC countries. Interestingly, only the non-EMS member countries (Spain, Greece, and Portugal) have a high proportion of short-term debt. For

Table 2. Maturity of Public Debts

	Short-Term Debt (percent total debt)	Average Maturity (years)
Belgium	21.8	3.6
Denmark	14.5	3.6
Germany, Fed. Rep. of	1.8	—
Greece	92.5	—
Spain	60.8	1.5
France	45.3	4.0
Ireland	6.5	4.3–8.8
Italy	30.3	3.5
Netherlands	9.1	5.9
Portugal	62.5	—
United Kingdom	30.3	8.2–9.1

Source: Giavazzi and Pagano (1988).
Note: Short-term debt is Treasury bills and other short-term debt, that is, less than one-year maturity.

the other countries—including highly indebted Belgium, Ireland, and Italy—the average maturity is 3.5 years or more. For the indebted EMS members, the option of an inflation surprise exists and may not be relinquished lightly. For these countries to join the EMU, it may be necessary either to offer some relief mechanism,[2] or to have them devalue their debts one way or another.

The second reinforcing provision is the Sargent-Wallace (1981) argument. If the foreseen path of government deficits violates its budget constraint, the public should rationally anticipate the possibility of an eventual pick-up in money growth and inflation. Under such circumstances, inflation accelerates immediately. It may well be the case that, today, the disciplinary effect of the EMS reassures the public in high-debt countries that monetization on a large scale is ruled out. Clearly, the EMU would mightily reinforce this effect. We return to this issue in the broader context of the discipline argument in Section IV.

Exchange Market Interventions

A benefit from the EMU is that exchange market interventions within the EMS would become unnecessary. Data provided by Mastropasqua and others (1988), however, show that a large majority of EMS member countries carry out exchange interventions in U.S. dollars. While part of these interventions were no doubt related to intra-EMS parities, it is quite obvious that the EMU will not free European monetary authorities from intervening in the exchange markets. The expected savings are therefore limited.

In neoclassical models designed to compare exchange rate regimes, Helpman (1981) and Frenkel and Razin (1987) have shown that the main difference between flexible and fixed exchange rate regimes is the need, in the latter case, for central banks to face the opportunity cost of holding foreign exchange. An upper bound of these costs is presented in Table 3, where the reserve holdings of central banks are assumed to be held in noninterest bearing dollars. Multiplying these amounts by the yield on U.S. dollar government bonds provides the upper bound. This is a greatly exaggerated cost for two main reasons. First, as is argued above, EMU central banks would still intervene in dollars, and this has represented at least 50 percent of their interventions so far. Second, most reserves are yielding market-related interest payments, so that the opportunity cost is a fraction of the one shown. The upper bounds shown in Table 3 clearly dispel the notion that such considerations are of any practical interest.

World Portfolio Diversification

In many respects, we still operate in a world dominated by the Bretton Woods era. The U.S. dollar remains the most common means of exchange for

---

[2] It is interesting to remember that when the Reichsbank was created in Germany in 1876, the Reich took over the debts of the newly unified member states (see Holtfrerich, 1989).

Table 3. Maximum Opportunity Costs of Exchange Reserves
(Percent of GDP)

Belgium	Denmark	France	Germany, Fed. Rep. of	Ireland	Italy	Netherlands	Spain	United Kingdom
0.7	0.6	0.9	0.7	1.3	1.1	1.1	0.6	0.4

Source: IMF, *International Financial Statistics*.
Note: Computed as $i(R/Y)$, where i is the yield on long-term U. S. government bonds, R the foreign exchange reserves of the monetary authorities, and Y the GDP.

international trade and the most widely held reserve currency. While a number of explanations have been advanced (such as the sophistication of U.S. financial markets or the unwillingness of other countries to allow their currencies to become widely held internationally), the current state of affairs is most probably due to the size of the U.S. and the dollar-related markets.[3] In this view, the lack of competing currencies is largely due to the fact that countries like Japan, the Federal Republic of Germany, or Switzerland are much smaller than the United States. The creation of the EMU will make available such a competing currency. Assuming that world portfolios react by giving, say, equal weights to the dollar and the ECU, ceteris paribus, what effects can be expected?

The first effect is a once-and-for-all increase in the demand for ECU-denominated assets. As a result, their price should rise or their yield decrease permanently. In other words, either the ECU will appreciate in effective terms, or the real interest rate will decrease, or a combination of both will occur. This much is understood. What is impossible to know is the size of these effects. Because we are concerned with a serious change in regime, estimates based on past data are likely to be misleading.

The second effect concerns seigniorage at the world level. If, as is reasonable to assume, world holdings of ECU-denominated assets will grow along with world wealth, demand for such assets will be continuing. As far as interest-yielding assets are concerned, this is nothing but an implication of the portfolio rebalancing effect of the previous paragraph. A flow demand remains for noninterest bearing assets, namely ECU currency. How big could this be? A simple "back-of-the-envelope" calculation goes as follows: Suppose world trade is 10 percent of world gross national product (GNP) and half of it is mediated in ECUs. If the GDP of the European Community is one third of world GDP and world GNP grows at 5 percent a year, we find that the demand for ECUs generated by world trade would equal 0.75 percent of the GNP of

---

[3] Eichengreen (1987) relates explicitly the ability of a country to act as a "hegemon" to its size and ability to affect prices and quantities worldwide. The theoretical basis for the size effect is spelled out in Mundell (1968).

the European Community. Even allowing for a large margin of error, this calculation yields two interesting insights. First, the value of this "external" seigniorage, while large in absolute value, is quite limited relative to GDP and tax revenues. Second, this estimate is strikingly similar to the "internal" seigniorage available to most EC countries as discussed earlier. Those who fear a loss of internal seigniorage, should the EMU lead to zero inflation rates, should be reassured that external seigniorage might offset such revenue shortfalls.

III. Strategic Considerations

Exchange Rates as a Public Good

The nonstrategic aspects of the previous section clearly fail to shift the advantage against or in favor of the EMU. Could strategic considerations be decisive? The literature on policy coordination (Hamada, 1985; Sachs, 1983; and Canzoneri and Henderson, 1988) has shown that the real exchange rate between two countries is like a public good that may be delivered inefficiently when the countries do not act cooperatively. For example, in the presence of a common adverse supply shock, each country has an incentive to have its currency appreciate relative to the other. The outcome is likely to be inefficient unless both countries cooperate and recognize that they cannot both appreciate. The inefficiency that results from the lack of cooperation will be greater the more closely integrated the two countries are since integration increases the (wrongly) perceived benefit from exchange rate manipulation.

Recent work on the quantitative importance of cooperation (Oudiz and Sachs, 1984; Bryant and others, 1988) is not conclusive. Yet, if gains from coordination between the United States, Europe, and Japan are indeed limited, this is most likely because of the limited trade interaction among these zones. Within Europe, in contrast, trade interaction is much more intense: each EC country is relatively open whereas the EC as a whole is as closed as the United States or Japan. The Single Act will accentuate this feature and make European cooperation more important. Drawing on the traditional literature on policy coordination, the desirability of a monetary union may appear to hinge on the symmetry or asymmetry of the shocks affecting the EC countries. Indeed, when the shocks are asymmetric, a monetary union is not likely to be an optimal response to the extent that it forces a joint monetary policy on countries that face different problems. However, in most models, a monetary union is fully desirable when the shocks affecting the economies are symmetric. Indeed, a common central bank will set a collectively chosen monetary policy and avoid beggar-thy-neighbor competition on exchange rates.

The traditional literature on policy coordination, however, usually postulates a two-country world economy in which the only inefficiency that arises stems from the determination of *the* exchange rate linking the two currencies. Such frameworks are ill-suited to the problems facing Europe, for which the joint determination of the ECU vis-à-vis the U.S. dollar or the Japanese yen will appear to be a crucial task of a European central bank. To assess the implication of this question, we suggest a simple analytical framework in which fiscal policies are set independently in each country, while monetary integration (possibly) achieves a socially desirable European inflation rate. We shall see that the relevant characteristic of the stochastic shocks affecting the European economy is not only whether the shocks are symmetric or asymmetric, but whether they are *permanent* or *transitory*. The logic is as follows: Because Europe is not well integrated in world markets, its overall trade balance determines its (joint) real exchange rate vis-à-vis the rest of the world. Europe's external trade balance is in the nature of a public good, and the provision of this public good may be inefficient when countries act noncooperatively. This will indeed be the case when shocks are transitory, because governments can be expected to smooth out the effects of transitory shocks by adopting measures that affect national saving and, therefore, the trade balance.

Trade Balance as a Public Good

The concept of the trade balance as a public good can be illustrated by considering a world composed of two zones and three countries. The first zone, which we call Europe, consists of two countries, France and the Federal Republic of Germany, which are perfectly integrated in both goods and financial markets. We assume, for simplicity, that only one good is produced in each country and that the law of one price prevails.

The other zone is composed of only one country, the United States. While Europe and the United States are perfectly well-integrated financially— with the interest parity condition holding—the goods markets are not perfectly integrated across the two zones so that the law of one price is not satisfied. Limited arbitrage in goods exists, however, so that trade flows between the two zones reflect the price discrepancy. This price discrepancy and the associated trade flows are the potential source of inefficiency that coordination must solve and which, we shall show, monetary integration fails to internalize.

We present, in the Appendix, a simple three-country model designed to show the role of the trade balance externality. By assuming that France and Germany have the same real exchange rate vis-à-vis the United States, we eliminate the familiar exchange rate externality. On the other side, the common real exchange rate determines Europe's trade balance with the United States, given the imperfect degree of goods market integration. Thus, when France and Germany are identical, each country's trade balance is equivalent to one half of Europe's trade balance (shown in Chart 1 as the TT schedule).

The externality arises because one country, France, does not necessarily perceive the relationship between its own trade balance and the (common) real exchange rate that way. Suppose that France raises domestic spending through

Chart 1. The Trade Balance Externality

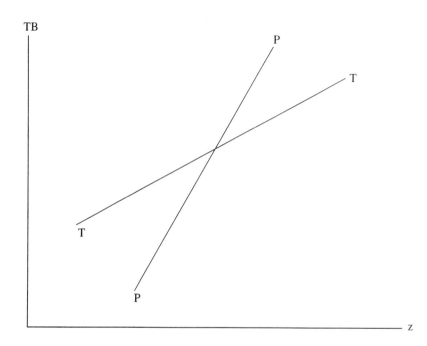

an expansionary fiscal policy move. If it assumes that Germany remains passive, France foresees a one-to-one relationship between its own trade balance and Europe's trade balance. An example of how such a misperception arises is when one country, say France, assumes that the other country, Germany, keeps its inflation and spending unchanged in the face of a joint real depreciation. France overestimates the responsiveness of its own trade balance to a real depreciation on two counts. First, if Germany's trade balance is taken as given, France expects that the full effect of the depreciation on Europe's trade balance will be reflected, one-for-one, in its own trade balance. Second, France recognizes that Germany's trade balance will worsen, given inflation and demand, because German output falls in response to the increase in imported (American) materials. Given the overall European trade balance, Germany's deficit implies a further surplus for France.

The overestimated trade balance responsiveness is shown in Chart 1 as the PP schedule. The comparison between the TT and PP schedules illustrates the trade balance externality. If each country attempts to enact independently optimal monetary and fiscal policies with the perception that they move along PP, they discover, ex-post, that they are along TT at a collectively inefficient position. This generic externality may well have important implications. It certainly suggests a reassessment of the nature of an EMU.

In our simple framework (see Appendix), fiscal and monetary policies allow each government to control inflation and domestic spending in an effort to stabilize these variables as well as output. While we allow for a misperception about the trade balance responsiveness to real exchange rate changes, we explicitly account for each country's intertemporal constraint via the trade account. This constraint leads to a clear separation between permanent and temporary disturbances.

Consider, for example, a permanent adverse output shock. The trade balance constraint imposes a corresponding fall in demand: any (long-run) optimizing government responds by accepting immediately the permanent fall in demand. Consequently, the trade balance remains in equilibrium, and the trade balance externality is irrelevant (except during an interim period where the shock is asymmetric and there is some degree of nominal rigidity). As a result, when each country chooses its optimal policies in isolation, the outcome is the socially optimal solution (SOS), and the real exchange rate is entirely driven by the need to maintain a balanced trade account in both France and Germany.

A transitory shock, on the contrary, elicits a policy response designed to smooth out spending. To simplify, consider a supply shock that is of sufficiently short duration that the present value of current and future outputs remains roughly unchanged. The optimal policy response, therefore, is to maintain spending roughly unchanged. This is achieved through a trade account imbalance. Thus, for each country, there exists an optimal trade deficit and an optimal rate of real exchange rate appreciation. When the country is hit by an adverse supply shock, it will try to engineer an appreciation of the real exchange rate so as to import from abroad and to sustain the inflationary impact of the shock. Conversely, when hit by a favorable supply shock, the country will produce more than it spends and seek to bring about a depreciation of the real exchange rate.

The inefficiency of the resulting equilibrium is best understood if we consider France and Germany hit by a transitory asymmetric shock of equal magnitude. Each country, optimally, keeps spending unchanged. As output increases in one country by the same amount as it decreases in the other, Europe's trade balance remains in equilibrium and the common real exchange rate remains unchanged. However, it is in each country's interest to attempt to cushion the supply shock through a change in output, and in doing so, each country overreacts. For example, the country hit with an adverse shock will want to bring about a trade deficit to borrow abroad and thus it will seek an appreciation of its real exchange rate. The appreciation, if achieved, would worsen the favorably hit country's trade balance, precisely as it wishes to run a surplus to cushion its own temporary positive shock. The country hit with a favorable shock then counteracts, prompting a round of inefficient conflicts over the zone's trade balance and real exchange rate.

The same inefficiency would occur in the case of a symmetric shock, albeit to a lesser extent. The reason is that both countries wish to go in the same direction (for example, a trade deficit in response to an identical, joint adverse shock). Yet, each individual country would like the other to absorb more of a drop in output to achieve the desired exchange rate appreciation. As a result, insufficient action is taken relative to the SOS.

Monetary Integration

An asymmetric shock cannot be appropriately dealt with by a monetary union. Indeed, the socially optimal response in such a case must involve an asymmetric inflation rate in each country, which a monetary union cannot deliver.

Neither is a transitory symmetric shock efficiently dealt with by a monetary union. Indeed, in a monetary union only the inflation rate is set effectively. Each country is left to determine which trade balance it wants to achieve. Consequently, the trade balance of the zone itself, hence the *real* exchange rate of Europe vis-à-vis the rest of the world, is not determined efficiently. In a monetary union—at least in the noncooperative one addressed in the previous section—each government fails to realize that its *own* response to a (symmetric) shock will be accompanied by an exactly identical response by the other country.

To summarize, it is not enough to determine whether shocks are symmetric or asymmetric in order to conclude that a monetary union is efficient or not. We have suggested adding another distinction to this typology and to check whether the shocks that affect Europe are more transitory or permanent in nature. Only permanent shocks fail to trigger the inefficiency of determining the EMU trade balance.

IV. Empirical Investigation

The costs of deviating from the SOS that the EMU—or any other noncooperative set of policies—would impose are related to the stochastic nature of the disturbances. We have found that temporary shocks matter more than permanent ones,[4] and that asymmetric shocks run more against the rationality of the EMU than symmetric ones. Thus, the worst case of the EMU would be a preponderance of temporary asymmetric disturbances. Indeed, it is transitory shocks that should lead to trade imbalances—where the externality arises— and it is with asymmetric shocks that common inflation rates are likely to be dominated by the SOS.

In order to gauge the empirical relevance of these arguments, we attempt to detect in the recent experience the nature of the disturbances. In line with the model, we focus on the two largest countries that would be part of the EMU,

---

[4] More precisely, what matters in permanent shocks is the transition period.

France and Germany. All variables of interest are transformed into sums and differences.[5] Sums describe the aggregate "European" economy and reveal symmetric shocks; differences reveal the asymmetric disturbances. Our task is to extract from each composite its permanent and temporary components.

There is now substantial research on how to decompose nonstationary time series into permanent and temporary fluctuations. The key issue is whether the permanent component is allowed to be stochastic. Nonstochastic, permanent components may be captured by regression on a linear trend—and, possibly, higher degrees of the trend. Stochastic permanent trends require filtering techniques as presented in Beveridge and Nelson (1981), Nelson and Plosser (1982), Prescott (1986), or Blanchard and Quah (1988). Stochastic trends normally follow more closely the original series than nonstochastic trends so that they allocate a much larger share of fluctuations to the permanent components.[6]

In principle, there is little basis for choosing one method over the other. We do not delve deeper into this issue as our objective is not to separate out trend and temporary components. Our objective is rather to *compare* the relative proportion of the temporary component for "Europe"—the sum of France and Germany—thus capturing the symmetric shocks, and for the difference between France and Germany—thus identifying the asymmetric shocks. For this reason, quite agnostically we adopt a variety of methods: a linear trend, a quadratic trend, and the stochastic trend method proposed by Beveridge and Nelson (1981). All data are used in level form. The stochastic trend is allowed to follow a random walk with a nonstochastic drift and random disturbances. Table 4 presents the ratio of the standard deviation of the temporary component to the standard deviation of the original series. A high ratio, therefore, indicates a preponderance of temporary fluctuations.

We consider three variables for France and Germany: real GDP, the real wage, and the price level. We also consider separately the French and German current accounts as a proportion of their respective GDPs. For the whole sample period (the first quarter of 1965 through the fourth quarter of 1987), Table 4 suggests that symmetric shocks are much larger than asymmetric shocks, at least as measured by the standard deviation. Further, symmetric shocks tend to be more permanent than transitory, while the reverse characterizes asymmetric shocks. It is interesting to compare these results with those shown in Table 5. In Table 5, France and Germany are aggregated to make up "Europe," and the sums and differences are applied to "Europe" and the United States. In contrast with the intra-European results, it is no longer true that symmetric shocks prevail over asymmetric shocks, and there is no overwhelming association between asymmetric and temporary disturbances.

---

[5] Such models are used in Oudiz (1985), Begg and Wyplosz (1987), among others, to study policy coordination.

[6] Recently, Clark (1987) proposed a maximum likelihood estimator, which provides a result strikingly similar to the linear trend for the (log of) U.S. gross national product.

Table 4. Decomposition in Permanent and Temporary Components: France and Germany
(Ratio of standard deviations of temporary component to the standard deviation of the original series, in percent)
Period = 1965 QI to 1987 QIV

Variable:	Real GDP		GDP Deflator		Real Wages		Current Account/GDP	
	Sum	Difference	Sum	Difference	Sum	Difference	France	Germany
Standard deviation of original variable	0.252	0.056	0.864	0.271	0.335	0.031	0.234	0.306
Ratio (percent) with:								
— linear trend	34.9	43.2	8.2	29.5	31.6	99.0	99.4	94.6
— quadratic trend	19.0	32.6	8.2	15.5	11.1	65.0	93.0	92.2
— stochastic trend	7.5	27.6	1.3	4.1	NA	43.9	71.9	50.6

Source: IMF, *International Financial Statistics*.
Data definition: GDP: sum is sum of logs of French and German GDPs in constant FF; difference is log of ratio of French over German GDP. Other variables: sum (difference) is sum (difference) of logs of the original variables.

Table 5. Decomposition in Permanent and Temporary Components:
United States and "Europe"
(Ratio of standard deviations of temporary component to the standard deviation
of the original series in percent)
Period = 1965 QI to 1987 QIV

Variable:	Real GDP		GDP Deflator		Real Wages	
	Sum	Difference	Sum	Difference	Sum	Difference
Standard deviation of original variable	0.203	0.213	1.291	0.438	0.316	0.357
Ratio (percent) with:						
— linear trend	33.0	92.9	8.8	8.2	36.9	27.8
— quadratic trend	26.6	70.7	8.8	7.9	14.8	10.4
— stochastic trend	7.0	20.5	1.1	2.4	NA	NA

Source: IMF, *International Financial Statistics*.
Note: Data definition: GDP: "Europe" is the sum variable of Table 4, that is, France and the Federal Republic of Germany taken together. Given this, the data are defined as for Table 4: GDP: sum is log of sum of U.S. and "European" GDPs in constant U.S. dollars; difference is log of ratio of U.S. over "European" GDP. Other variables: sum (difference) is sum (difference) of logs of the original variables.

The results support the view that monetary integration makes more sense between France and Germany than between "Europe" and the United States. They do not imply, however, wholehearted support for the EMU in view of our model because symmetric shocks, while compatible with the equalization of inflation rates, still generate a trade balance externality that puts full coordination at a premium.

V. EMU Versus EMS

Doubts About the Feasibility of an SOS

While the EMU does not deliver the first best collective outcome for Europe, two questions must be answered before arriving at a conclusion about the desirability of monetary integration. First, is the superior socially optimal solution feasible? And, second, if the SOS is not feasible, which of the feasible alternatives are preferable? In particular, how does the EMU compare with the EMS, either in its current form or suitably modified?

The SOS achieves, in our model, an agreement on a real exchange rate vis-à-vis the rest of the world. For this to be achieved, each member country must set its own trade balance in accordance with the trade balance of the whole zone so that the joint real exchange rate agreed upon is indeed enforced. The requirements in terms of credibility appear formidable. The SOS member countries must commit a combination of both monetary and fiscal policies to this task. Such precise fiscal policy coordination is not likely to be politically feasible and credible among sovereign states. There is not much evidence in the EMS experience to show that it has moved in this direction. This stands in sharp contrast with the case of the United States, often considered an example for the EMU to follow. The relative proportion of federal and state budgets effectively solves this difficulty. This may be the key reason that political unification always precedes monetary integration.

Has the EMS Been Effective?

In the previous section we do not model the EMS. Two particular characteristics would be required to do so. First, the EMS stabilizes real exchange rates, and since we assume the law of one price, we cannot consider this aspect here. Second, the EMS has important credibility effects both for inflation and for the balance of trade. Our model focuses on the balance of trade and would need to be amended to account for the inflation aspect.

What is puzzling is the wide agreement among most policymakers and researchers (Giavazzi and Giovannini, 1989; and Mélitz, 1987) that the EMS has been functioning as a deutsche mark zone. The reason, it is argued (Giavazzi and Pagano, 1988), is that the other central banks have borrowed from the Deutsche Bundesbank credibility regarding their tolerance to inflation.[7] Evidence about the deutsche mark zone hypothesis is not overwhelming. Giavazzi and Giovannini (1989) show that forward premia on the French franc/deutsche mark and lira/deutsche mark rates are entirely mirrored by the French franc or lira offshore interest rates, not at all the deutsche mark rate. Yet, as noted by De Grauwe (1989), domestic French and Italian interest rates are not any more responsive to the premia than the German rate. It is altogether irrelevant that capital controls provide the means to avoid a policy conflict. Euro-interest rates have no effect on the domestic economy and are, therefore, of no help in assessing the outcome of the game; neither do they help predict what will happen once controls are removed and the rules of the game are modified.

In our view, the evidence needs to be confirmed by a somewhat more formal treatment of the data. One way is to perform vector autoregressions (VAR) on base money growth figures as well as on one-month (domestic) interest rates. Table 6 shows the results of tests of significance using four lags (similar results were obtained using six lags). There is some evidence that Germany's monetary instruments influence the other countries. Yet Italy and France are seen to exert some influence on Germany. The German monetary instruments significantly affect money growth, or interest rates, or both, in all other countries. At the same time, the German variables are affected by the French and Italian instruments. These VAR estimates can be used to simulate

---

[7] Wyplosz (1988) suggests that any fixed and adjustable exchange rate system has a tendency to regress to the least inflationary monetary policy stance.

Table 6. Vector Autoregression: Tests of Significance of Explanatory Variables, 1981 QIII to 1987 QIII

Dependent Variable		United States	Germany, Fed. Rep. of	Explanatory Variable France	United Kingdom	Italy	Netherlands
United States	money		0.14	0.49	0.12	0.29	0.79
	int. rate		0.02*	0.35	0.77	0.97	0.15
Germany, Fed. Rep. of	money	0.05*		0.03*	0.29	0.08*	0.12
	int.rate	0.02*		0.01*	0.26	0.69	0.17
France	money	0.40	0.55		0.06*	0.26	0.79
	int.rate	0.00*	0.00*		0.01*	0.06*	0.00*
United Kingdom	money	0.77	0.03*	0.28		0.07*	0.06*
	int.rate	0.93	0.95	0.94		0.08*	0.75
Italy	money	0.58	0.03*	0.08*	0.11		0.22
	int.rate	0.50	0.13	0.69	0.67		0.12
Netherlands	money	0.40	0.06*	0.12	0.19	0.86	
	int.rate	0.12	0.09*	0.17	0.44	0.58	

Note: Entries show the significance level for the corresponding F-statistic. Asterisks have been added when the level is less than 10 percent to allow for easier reading.

the effects of a unit interest rate disturbance arising in each country on the other country's own interest rates. In doing so, we have to arbitrarily set the order in which these disturbances affect each country. The results presented, in Table 7, correspond to the order indicated there. Reported are the sources of interest rate variability two and ten months after the initial impulse. Clearly again, the results attribute a more powerful influence to Germany than to other countries, but France, Italy, and the Netherlands also appear to transmit their interest rate innovations.

Similar results are obtained with the money base figures.[8] We do not pretend that these results establish a meaningful causality link. They are proposed to suggest that the unidirectional influence of Germany is not based on clear-cut evidence. There is room to suspect that strategic behavior is at work within the EMS. This is of course compatible with an SOS, more so than if the EMS were to operate effectively as a deutsche mark zone.

For the EMS to be a socially optimal solution, however, it must have successfully solved the credibility problem described in Section IV. In order to approach this issue, we have attempted to measure the "interest premium" separating out French and German interest rates. The interest premium ψ_t is defined as:

$$\psi_t = i_t - i^*_t - {}_t e_{t+1} + e_t,$$

where i_t and i^*_t are the French and German interest rates; e_t the French franc/deutsche mark exchange rate; and ${}_t e_{t+1}$ its expected value in the next period. This interest premium includes the usual risk premium and a peso-type premium, given that for most of the sample period, e_t has been limited to move within the narrow band of the EMS. Following Hansen and Hodrick (1983), we estimate ${}_t e_{t+1}$ by regressing e_t on four of its lags and on once-lagged values of its possible determinants, updating the regression each quarter. The determinants are taken here as the differences between France and Germany's consumer price inflation rates, current accounts, and budget deficits. Then ${}_t e_{t+1}$ is generated by using the regression on variables known as of time t. The interest premium is calculated as in (1) and is shown in Chart 2. Credibility should have led to a reduction in the interest premium. Separating the sample at the time of the creation of the EMS (in the first quarter of 1979), we find no clear evidence of a reduced premium: Its average and standard errors are 3.8 and 3.3, respectively, for the period from the first quarter of 1975 to the first quarter of 1979, and 3.2 and 3.1 for the period from the second quarter of 1979 to the second quarter of 1987. If anything, Chart 2 shows a strong "Mitterrand effect."

---

[8] De Grauwe (1989), using Granger causality tests on interest rates, is able to reject more often the hypothesis that Germany's monetary policy leads to similar policies in the other countries.

Table 7. Decomposition of Variance

Dependent Variable: Interest Rate in	Horizon	Independent Variables: Interest Rate Disturbances in					
		Germany, Fed. Rep. of	France	Italy	Netherlands	United Kingdom	United States
Germany, Fed. Rep. of	2	87.9	1.5	0.8	0.2	1.1	8.5
	10	59.6	8.0	3.0	3.8	2.8	22.8
France	2	3.4	71.7	0.0	3.7	12.2	9.1
	10	33.7	18.2	0.1	32.7	9.6	4.8
Italy	2	2.0	5.6	92.0	0.2	0.1	0.1
	10	18.2	11.9	50.5	15.3	2.8	1.2
Netherlands	2	15.0	1.8	1.9	74.1	0.0	7.3
	10	38.6	3.8	3.0	35.7	1.2	17.7
United Kingdom	2	0.1	0.5	8.0	17.9	73.5	0.0
	10	5.8	1.7	12.5	22.1	56.4	1.4
United States	2	1.6	10.7	0.9	0.8	0.9	85.0
	10	26.4	10.9	2.9	11.2	6.2	42.4

**Chart 2. Interest Premium: France over the Federal Republic
of Germany**
(Percent)

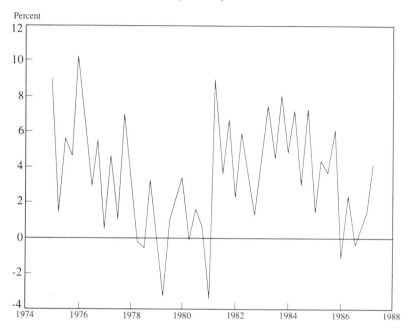

Still, it is interesting to check whether the sources of the interest premium
have changed since the creation of the EMS. To investigate this, we have
regressed the premium on its own lag and on innovations of the determinants
used to compute the interest premium. The innovation for each variable is
interpreted as the risk premium. For each quarter, we regress the variable on
its first four lags and on the other determinants of the premium lagged, once.
Updating once, we generate a forecast and take as the innovation the difference between the actual variable and the forecast. The results, shown in
Table 8, indicate that until the first quarter of 1979, the interest premium is
influenced by monetary (inflation) innovations; after the second quarter of
1979, it is influenced by fiscal policy innovations. The first obvious interpretation is that the EMS has helped establish the credibility of the French monetary
authorities. It provides some empirical support to the view that the EMU—
seen as the ultimate result of the EMS's evolution—will reduce real interest
rates in the traditionally inflation-prone countries.

There is, however, another, more novel, interpretation of the results
presented in Table 8, which conforms more directly with the theoretical
framework of this paper. We note that the *private* current account innovations
do not appear to contribute significantly to the interest rate risk premium.
Along with the significant influence of the budget deficit, it suggests that what

Table 8. Determinants of the Interest Premium
Dependent Variable: ψ_t

	Constant	ψ_{t-1}	Innovations in Differences of			$\bar{R}^2$	DW
			Inflation rates	Current accounts	Budget deficits		
1975 QII-1979QI	3.11	0.30	3.48	−2.97	0.15	0.31	2.38
	(2.80)	(1.32)	(2.08)	(−1.59)	(1.32)		
1979 QII-1987QII	2.31	0.23	−0.69	0.09	0.11	0.22	1.88
	(3.34)	(1.45)	(−0.72)	(0.21)	(3.33)		

¹Source: Organization for Economic Cooperation and Development.

Note: The interest premium is defined as in (1), and $\hat{e}_{t+1} = \sum\limits_{i=0}^{3} \hat{a}_i e_{t-1} + \Sigma \hat{b}_j x_{jt}$, where $x_t = [\pi_t - \pi^*{}_t, CA_t - CA^*{}_t, BD_t - BD^*{}_t]$. The estimates $\hat{a}_i$ and $\hat{b}_j$ are updated each quarter with the regression $e_t = \sum\limits_{i=1}^{4} a_i e_{t-1} + \Sigma b x_{j,t-1} + u_t$. Similarly, the innovations for, e.g., x_{jt} are $\hat{\epsilon}_{j,t+1} = \hat{x}_{j,t+1} - x_{j,t+1}$, where $\hat{x}_{j,t+1} = \sum\limits_{i=0}^{3} \hat{a}_i x_{j,t-i} + \sum\limits_{k \neq j} \hat{b}_k x_{k}, t$, and where $\hat{a}_i$ and $\hat{b}_k$ are updated each quarter with the regression $x_{j,t} = \sum\limits_{i=1}^{4} a x_{j,t-1} + \sum\limits_{k \neq j} b_k x_{k,t-1} + v_t$. The current account and budget deficit figures for Germany are converted in French francs. The interest rates are money market three-month rates.

matters is the *public* current account. Within our analytical framework, it means that the EMS has not succeeded in internalizing the (public) trade balance. As we showed, this is a feature also to be expected from the EMU: Indeed, this is the reason why the EMU cannot be a socially optimal solution.

VI. Conclusions

The theoretical arguments presented in Section III point to a potentially important shortcoming of the EMU, namely that uncoordinated fiscal policies fail to recognize the balance of trade externality. We interpret the empirical evidence as suggesting that the EMS has not been successful in dealing with this externality. On the surface, one would be tempted to look for other criteria to guide the choice between the two competing systems. This would be unwarranted. A shift from the EMS to the EMU would lead to an identical, riskless interest rate everywhere in Europe. Each agent, public or private, would face the same riskless rate and would pay a premium according to its own riskiness. In contrast, the EMS, as we have seen, imposes on all agents in a given country an interest premium related to the public sector's borrowing, but not to the private current account. On these grounds, the EMU should be favored over the EMS.

In theory, a system of sophisticated contingent rules will always dominate a one-money-for-Europe system. The superiority of such a system, however, is established only relative to the inefficiencies that arise in the absence of policy coordination. Much recent work has focused on the inflation externality associated with the setting of exchange rates. For this externality, a deutsche-mark-dominated zone exhibits some desirable features. We have suggested the existence of another externality, the collective determination of the zone's balance of trade. No doubt, other reasons can be found that require particular sets of contingent rules. Under current political conditions, at least, such sophisticated coordination is far too ambitious.

The current debate on the EMU is prompted by the Single Act, due to take effect in 1992. We have argued that the EMU is not implied by the full integration of goods and financial markets. On the other hand, this integration will undoubtedly require an adaptation of the existing rules of the game. The issue is not, we believe, a formal and exhaustive evaluation of the merits of monetary integration, but a comparison with the merits of a possible reform of the EMS. The EMS has achieved some progress in monetary policy coordination and discipline. But on this criterion, the EMU is bound to do better and to free the private sector from the interest premium associated with public finances. Both the EMS and the EMU are likely to fail to enforce the extent of fiscal policy coordination required for a proper internalization by each country of Europe's overall trade balance constraint.

Consequently, the EMU must not be judged in comparison with an abstract, socially optimal system, but relative to the other feasible alternatives.

This is reminiscent of Guesnerie's (1977) survey on second best taxation, which concludes that it is preferable, in practice, to improve an existing system rather than to attempt to design a grandiose, optimal system. The key consideration may be whether the extreme simplicity of the EMU is an advantage or a drawback.

Appendix

The Model Behind the Analysis

Exchange Rates and Trade

Let $e_{1,t}$ be the (log) of the French franc rate per U.S. dollar, and $e_{2,t}$ the deutsche mark rate. The logs of the price levels in France and Germany are, respectively, p_t and p^*_t. The law of one price implies:

$$p_t = (e_{1,t} - e_{2,t}) + p^*_t. \tag{2}$$

The common European real exchange rate vis-à-vis the United States is:

$$z_t = e_{1,t} - p_t = e_{2,t} - p^*_t. \tag{3}$$

Whenever a divergence from the law of one price occurs between Europe and the United States, that is when $z_t \neq 0$, arbitrage takes place, but on a limited scale, leading to a European-wide trade imbalance (in volume):

$$\overline{TB}_t = hz_t. \tag{4}$$

In what follows, we assume that transatlantic shipping of goods is undertaken by U.S. traders.

Supply of Goods

Price and wages are determined in the spirit of Taylor's staggered mechanism. Wage contracts are set for two periods, half of them being reviewed each period so as to keep unchanged the expected (average) real wage:

$$w_t = (p_t + {}_tp_{t+1})/2, \tag{5}$$

where ${}_tp_{t+1}$ is period t's rational expectation of period $t+1$'s price level.

Prices, in turn, are set as a markup over average wages, the markup itself being an increasing function of output Q_t and a decreasing function of United States' competitiveness, z_t:

$$p_t = (w_t + w_{t-1})/2 + (a/2)z_t + (b/2)Q_t + \epsilon_t/2, \tag{6}$$

where ϵ_t is a stochastic shock, which we will allow to be either permanent or transitory.

If $\pi_t = p_t - p_{t-1}$ is the inflation rate, (5) and (6) yield:

$$\pi_t = (_{t-1}\pi_t + {}_t\pi_{t+1})/2 + az_t + bQ_t + \epsilon_t. \tag{7}$$

Equation (7), an expectations-augmented Phillips curve, will be interpreted as a supply curve.

Demand

For simplicity, we let aggregate demand, A_t, be a government's instrument, which we interpret as fiscal policy. As will become clear, demand management is used only as a transitory instrument so that the model is consistent with a Barro-Ricardo equivalence imposed on a government's finances.

The other policy instrument is money, m_t. We postulate a much simplified money demand function:

$$m_t = p_t. \tag{8}$$

In other words, the authorities can set directly the inflation rate, π_t.

Policy Objectives

The government uses its two instruments, A_t and π_t, to minimize the following loss function:

$$L = 1/2 \sum_{t=0}^{\infty} \beta^t [\phi_o (A_t - \bar{A})^2 + \phi_1 (Q_t - \bar{Q})^2 + \phi_2\pi_t^2], \tag{9}$$

where $\beta = 1/(1+r)$ is the time-discounting factor. We assume that r is equal to the real U.S. interest rate and applies to all countries, given the complete integration of world financial markets.

All variables should be seen as deviations from their steady state equilibrium level. The loss function, (9), indicates that the authorities favor a zero inflation rate, but wish to achieve spending and production levels $(\bar{A} > 0, \bar{Q} > 0)$ above their feasible long-run levels.

Goods are sold abroad at their domestic price since we assume no transport costs in Europe and that transatlantic shipping of goods is undertaken by the U.S. traders. Under this condition, the value in U.S. dollars of the country's trade balance is:

$$V_t = (Q_t - A_t) e - z_t,$$

which is linearized as

$$V_t = (Q_t - A_t) (1 - z_t).$$

Assuming zero initial net debt, the budget constraint is written as

$$\sum_{t=0}^{\infty} \beta^t (Q_t - A_t) (1 - z_t) = 0. \tag{10}$$

The above equations describe one European country, say France. The other European country, Germany, is assumed to be exactly identical so that the same equations apply, with German variables being asterisked. In solving for the optimal government program, we look for the time-consistent policy, that is, we assume that governments are expected to choose the best policy available each period.[9]

The Trade Balance Externality

When each country optimizes individually, it must make an assumption about the other's trade balance. In a Nash feedback equilibrium, France, for example, assumes that the Federal Republic of Germany sets A^*_t and M^*_t as a given function of ϵ_t and ϵ^*_t. Then, given (7), it expects:

$$Q^*_t = - (a/b)z_t + f(\epsilon_t, \epsilon^*_t), \tag{11}$$

and

$$TB^*_t = - (a/b)z_t + g(\epsilon_t, \epsilon^*_t). \tag{12}$$

Given (4), this implies that the trade balance constraint perceived by France is:

$$Q_t - A_t = (a/b + h)z_t - g(\epsilon_t, \epsilon^*_t). \tag{13}$$

This is where the externality appears. A European social planner would, instead, optimize, using (4), and, with full symmetry, would set: $TB_t = TB^*_t = (h/2)z_t$. Thus, the perceived effect of z_t on TB_t is different.

---

[9] See Cohen (1989a) for a similar structure where the time-inconsistent solution is considered.

References

Begg, David, and Charles Wyplosz, "Why the EMS? Dynamic Games and the Equilibrium Policy," in Ralph Bryant and Richard Portes, *Global Macroeconomics* (London: Macmillan, 1987).

Beveridge, Stephen, and Charles Nelson, "A New Approach to Decomposition of Economic Time Series into Permanent and Transitory Components with Particular Attention to Measurement of the 'Business Cycle'," *Journal of Monetary Economics*, Vol. 7, No. 2 (Amsterdam: North-Holland, 1981), pp. 151–74.

Blanchard, Olivier, and Danny Quah, "The Dynamic Effects of Aggregate Demand and Supply Disturbances" (unpublished, Cambridge, Massachusetts: Massachusetts Institute of Technology, October 1988).

Bryant, Ralph, and others, eds., *Empirical Macroeconomics for Interdependent Economies* (Washington: The Brookings Institution, 1988).

Buiter, Willem, "A Guide to Public Sector Debt and Deficits," *Economic Policy No. 1* (Cambridge, United Kingdom: Cambridge University Press, 1985).

Canzoneri, Matthew, and Dale Henderson, "Non-Cooperative Policies in an Interdependent World," unpublished, 1988.

Clark, Peter, "The Cyclical Component of U. S. Economic Activity," *Quarterly Journal of Economics*, Vol. 102 (Cambridge, Massachusetts: 1987), pp. 797–814.

Cohen, Daniel (1989a), "Monetary and Fiscal Policy in Open Economy with or without Coordination," *European Economic Review*, Papers and Proceedings (Amsterdam: 1989).

————— (1989b), "The European Central Bank," in *A European Central Bank?*, ed. by M. De Cecco and Alberto Giovannini (Cambridge, United Kingdom: Cambridge University Press, 1989).

—————, and Philippe Michel, "How Should Control Theory Be Used to Calculate a Time-Consistent Government Policy?" *Review of Economic Studies,* Vol. 55 (Edinburgh: 1988), pp. 263–74.

De Grauwe, Paul, "Is the European Monetary System a DM Zone?" Centre for Economic Policy Research Discussion Paper (London: CEPR, 1989).

Dornbusch, Rudiger, "The EMS, the Dollar, and the Yen," in *The European Monetary System*, ed. by Francesco Giavazzi, S. Micossi, and Marcus Miller (Cambridge, United Kingdom: Cambridge University Press, 1988).

Drazen, Allan, "Inflation Tax Revenue in Open Economies," in *A European Central Bank?*, ed. by M. De Cecco and Alberto Giovannini (Cambridge, United Kingdom: Cambridge University Press, 1989).

Eichengreen, Barry, "Hegemonic Stability Theories of the International Monetary System," Centre for Economic Policy Research Discussion Paper No. 193 (London: CEPR, July 1987), pp. 1–76.

Frenkel, Jacob, and Assaf Razin, *Fiscal Policies and the World Economy* (Cambridge, Massachusetts: MIT Press, 1987).

Giavazzi, Francesco, and Alberto Giovannini, *Limiting Exchange Rate Flexibility: The European Monetary System* (Cambridge, Massachusetts: MIT Press, 1989).

Giavazzi, Francesco, and Marco Pagano, "The Advantage of Tying One's Hands: EMS Discipline and Central Bank Credibility," *European Economic Review*, Vol. 32 (Amsterdam: 1988), pp. 1055–75.

Guesnerie, Roger, "On the Direction of Tax Reform," *Journal of Public Economics*, Vol. 7 (Amsterdam: North-Holland, 1977), pp. 179–202.

Hamada, Koichi, *The Political Economy of International Monetary Independence* (Cambridge, Massachusetts: MIT Press, 1985).

Hansen, Lars, and Robert Hodrick, "Risk Averse Speculation in the Forward Foreign Exchange Market: An Econometric Analysis of Linear Models," in *Exchange Rates and International Macroeconomics*, ed. by Jacob Frenkel (Chicago: University of Chicago Press, 1983).

Helpman, Elhanan, "An Exploration in the Theory of Exchange Rate Regimes," *Journal of Political Economy*, Vol. 89 (Chicago: University of Chicago Press, 1981), pp. 865–90.

Holtfrerich, Carl, "Monetary Cooperation and the Central Bank Question in the German Unification Process During the Nineteenth Century," in *A European Central Bank?*, ed. by M. De Cecco and Alberto Giovannini (Cambridge, United Kingdom: Cambridge University Press, 1989).

MacDougall Report, *Rapport du groupe de réflexion sur le rôle des finances publiques et l'intégration européenne* (Brussels: European Economic Community, 1977).

Mastropasqua, Carlo, Stefano Micossi, and Remo Rinaldi, "Intervention, Sterilization and Monetary Policy in EMS Countries (1979–1987)," in *The European Monetary System*, ed. by Francesco Giavazzi, S. Micossi, and Marcus Miller (Cambridge, United Kingdom: Cambridge University Press, 1988).

Mélitz, Jacques, "Discipline monétaire, République Fédérale Allemande, et le Système Monétaire Européen," *Annales d'Economie et Statistique* 8 (Paris: 1987), pp. 58–88.

Mundell, Robert, *International Economics* (London: Macmillan, 1968).

Nelson, Charles, and Charles Plosser, "Trends and Random Walks in Economic Time Series," *Journal of Monetary Economics*, Vol. 10 (Amsterdam: North-Holland, 1982), pp. 139–62.

Oudiz, Gilles, "European Policy Coordination: an Evaluation," *Recherches Economiques de Louvain*, 51 (Louvain: Université Catholique, 1985), pp. 301–39.

————, and Jeffrey Sachs, "Macroeconomic Policy Coordination Among the Industrial Economies," *Brookings Papers on Economic Activity* (Washington: The Brookings Institution, 1984), pp. 1–64.

Prescott, Edward, "Theory Ahead of Business Cycle Measurement," *Quarterly Review*, Federal Reserve Bank of Minneapolis (Minneapolis, Minnesota, Fall 1986), pp. 9–22.

Rogoff, Kenneth, "The Optimal Degree of Commitment to an Intermediate Target," *Quarterly Journal of Economics* (Cambridge, Massachusetts: 1985), pp. 1169–89.

Sachs, Jeffrey, "International Policy Coordination in a Dynamic Macroeconomic Model," National Bureau of Economic Research Working Paper No. 1166 (Cambridge, Massachusetts: NBER, July 1983), pp. 1–25.

Sargent, Thomas, and Neil Wallace, "Some Unpleasant Monetarist Arithmetics," *Quarterly Review*, Federal Reserve Bank of Minneapolis (Minneapolis, Minnesota, 1981).

Wyplosz, Charles, "Asymmetry in the EMS: Intentional or Systemic?" Institut Européen d'Administration des Affaires, Working Paper No. 88/41 (Fontainebleau, France: August 1988).

Comments

Massimo Russo

The Cohen-Wyplosz paper comes elegantly to an agnostic view of the European Monetary Union (EMU). This is because monetary union per se does not necessarily lead to a collective optimal outcome, which is the strategic consideration of the paper. Let me deal with this issue first, since I think it is the most important.

The model used by the authors shows that, given the high degree of integration of their economies, European countries would greatly benefit from cooperation on *both* monetary and fiscal policies in dealing with outside disturbances. Given wage and price rigidities, when confronted with temporary shocks only cooperative behavior would permit Europe to internalize the trade balance externalities, that is, to arrive at a *commonly determined* optimal real exchange rate.

How could the EMU, or for that matter the European Monetary System (EMS), automatically ensure such an optimal outcome? By irrevocably fixing nominal exchange rates, a monetary union would enforce a common rate of inflation; this is found to be an obstacle to optimal adjustment, if asymmetric shocks affect the EMU. Even in the presence of symmetric shocks—which do not have different effects on inflation rates—the model shows that there would still be a need for cooperatively set fiscal policies in order to achieve the optimal real exchange rate of the zone. There is nothing in the EMU that would ensure such cooperative behavior; so why bother? By permitting nominal exchange rates to adjust, albeit infrequently, within the area, the EMS allows for greater flexibility in relative prices than the EMU; it also permits different inflation rates to coexist, at least in the short run. Therefore, why not improve on the former without being blinded by the mirage of an EMU?

Under the new cloth of strategic modeling, we find the perennial discussion on rules versus discretion. Why impose rules, when discretionary and enlightened cooperation provides the best results? To be fair, the authors themselves accept that such continuous and close cooperation among sovereign nations is not a realistic possibility. That is why the EMS members found it useful to impose some rules in the first place. Ten years of experience have shown that these rules have been successful in bringing about a much greater degree of monetary cooperation. Suffice it to compare the divergent policies and inflation performances of the early years with the decisions of Basle and Nyborg in the fall of 1987 and their subsequent applications. No similar progress has been made on fiscal policy. It is well recognized by all (and especially by the monetary authorities in the EMS countries) that not even the

338

more stringent monetary rules of the EMU—relative to the EMS—would ensure coordination of fiscal policies. On the contrary, as the authors point out, the EMS imposes a tighter constraint on fiscal policy, since the interest rate on the public debt contains both a solvency and an exchange risk premium; the latter would disappear in the EMU.

The results of the model greatly depend on two crucial assumptions:

- that monetary policy, including a common European monetary policy, cannot affect the real exchange rate of the zone and is only used to minimize the common inflation rate; and
- that the law of one price would make it impossible for movements in relative prices within the EMU to play any role as shock absorbers.

Given the large weight of the EMU in the world economy (and, indeed, the greatly increased role foreseen elsewhere in the paper for the ECU as a result of the EMU), why couldn't a common monetary policy affect—at least on a temporary basis—the real exchange rate of the common currency and thus the evolution of the trade balance of the EMU? Does purchasing-power-parity (PPP) always hold between the U.S. dollar, the Japanese yen, and the ECU? Equation (3) of the model says no.

On the second and more difficult point, isn't the role of relative price changes within the EMU underestimated? Arbitrage mechanisms do not affect the prices of nontraded goods, which may thus exhibit substantial intra-regional variations. Such variations can persist for long periods of time even in a monetary union, as is evident from experience in the United States where, say, housing price behavior in Texas may systematically diverge from that in New York. Proponents of the EMU usually go to great lengths to stress the need for complementing monetary unification with measures that promote greater flexibility of relative prices, including wages.

There is a fundamental bias against the EMU in the paper because it is defined as implying only a common currency or, more specifically, a common monetary policy. The EMU, in other words, is a much more constraining EMS with, by assumption, the role of monetary policy limited to setting the common inflation rate, with no effect on the real exchange rate of the zone. Interest rates are given to the EMU by the much larger financial markets of the United States (assuming they remain so). If and when the EMU materializes, it will be the outcome of much deeper political and economic integration within Europe, which would have to allow for flexible intercountry adjustments. The need for such adjustments is well recognized, as evidenced by the ongoing discussions concerning the harmonization of indirect taxes, levies on income from capital, and of company taxation. The decision to double transfers through the European Community budget is another example. This point is likely to be made clearly in the forthcoming report of the Expert Group on European Monetary Union, chaired by Jacques Delors.

On the nonstrategic issues, I would tend to agree with the authors that seigniorage is a second order effect. To their arguments I would add that the

elimination of an exchange risk premium in the interest rate on the *stock* of the
public debt could compensate to a large extent for the net loss of national
seigniorage resulting from the EMU.

The Cohen-Wyplosz paper represents a useful step in the study of the
EMU. It identifies some important issues, but it also disregards others. Of
particular significance are the effects of a common monetary policy on the real
exchange rate of the EMU, the role of intraregional variations in prices and
wages, and the potential of transfer mechanisms in smoothing the impact of
intra-EMU imbalances. All these issues deserve further study. To create a
common currency area among 12 (or more) European countries is indeed a
formidable task. Maybe a "variable speed" Europe is a model worth considering in the path to the EMU.

Alberto Giovannini

An article in the winter 1988 issue of a U.S. airline magazine described—in
the style of such magazines, which sometimes portray Europe as a collection of
museums rather than an area of real economic significance—the 1992 European
unification project. The amusing aspect of this project, according to the author of
that article, was that Europeans intended to achieve economic integration with
different currencies. Could you imagine, the author asked, running a business in
the United States if the state of Massachusetts had a different currency from New
York and all the other members of the Union?

The agnostic conclusion on the issue of monetary unification in Europe
offered by Charles Wyplosz and Daniel Cohen is particularly unsettling since
it reveals a wide gap between the thinking of "practical people" and economists. The former are convinced that in a single market, different currencies
cannot coexist since they would complicate the day-to-day running of businesses. Economists, by contrast, are not sure. This lack of a clear view on this
crucial issue is due, in part, to the state of monetary theory: We are unable to
quantify, in a reliable way, the costs of different currencies for the same
reasons that we aren't sure why people use cash to settle their transactions.

Cohen and Wyplosz conclude, following many researchers before them,
that the liberalization of European capital markets will require a change of
European Monetary System (EMS) rules. They call for "feasible alternatives,"
but they do not tell us what they might be.

Their theoretical model is used to study the costs of a monetary union
between two countries in the face of different shocks. Their conclusion, much
in the spirit of Mundell's "optimal currency area" arguments, is that a
monetary unification is less desirable when shocks affecting the two countries
are asymmetric, than when they hit the two countries symmetrically. They
also find that temporary shocks can best be adjusted to with exchange rate
changes; hence, temporary shocks can be damaging in a monetary union.

The theoretical model raises an important empirical question: What is the nature of the shocks affecting European economies? Cohen and Wyplosz study France and the Federal Republic of Germany, and ask whether real gross domestic product, the real wage, and the price level in these two countries were affected by symmetric or asymmetric shocks, and whether these shocks were permanent or transitory. To answer these questions, they compute sums and differences (over the two countries) of those three variables, and they extract, from each of the composite series, permanent and temporary components. To extract such components they apply three methods: a linear trend, a quadratic trend, and a stochastic trend. The sums of the series are used to identify "aggregate" shocks, while their differences are used to identify "asymmetric" shocks.

I question this method. A decomposition of the output, wage, and price level series is not a decomposition of the shocks affecting output, wages, and prices. Indeed, in their model these three variables are endogenous. Hence, their statistical analysis only serves to determine the time-series properties of the endogenous variables, not the properties of exogenous shocks. The paper by Blanchard and Quah cited by the authors is a good example of the difficulty of identifying exogenous shocks in a macromodel.[1]

In the last part of the paper, Cohen and Wyplosz question the now-conventional wisdom that the EMS has worked asymmetrically. Once again, I have problems with the empirical methods they employ to illustrate their point. They estimate a vector autoregression (VAR) that includes money growth rates and interest rates in France, Germany, and Italy. They look at the decomposition of the variance of the variables in the system, using the moving-average representation implicit in the VAR, and orthogonalizing the disturbances in individual equations. It is well known, however, that the matrix that achieves the orthogonalization of the disturbances produces a linear transformation of the variables in the system. Hence, for example, the German money growth rate in the orthogonalized system becomes a linear combination of the money growth rate in Germany and all the other variables. For this reason, variance decompositions do not tell us what the authors claim.

The authors also perform Granger causality tests to determine whether German monetary policy influenced monetary policies in the other two countries. We know well, however, that these types of causality tests cannot detect the types of phenomena that the authors try to uncover. To illustrate this point, consider an extreme and unrealistic example where the Deutsche Bundesbank optimally controls all interest rates in Europe, including French and Italian

---

[1] Even by spelling out a number of identifying conditions in their multivariate analysis, Blanchard and Quah do not achieve an uncontroversial definition of exogenous shocks; they need to assume, for example, that demand shocks are always stationary. It is well known, however, that many taste shocks (such as changes in impatience), as well as many shocks in fiscal policy, are permanent.

rates. In that case German monetary variables *would not* "Granger cause" French and Italian variables.[2] Hence, the interpretation of the evidence from the VARs is extremely difficult and does not necessarily go along with the authors' claims.

Cohen and Wyplosz have provided an interesting and original paper. I sympathize with their uneasiness on the question of monetary unification, but I am not convinced by the empirical evidence they provide. Defining the boundaries of an optimal currency area remains one of the most challenging questions for theoretical and empirical research in international economics.

---

[2] This occurs because, in equilibrium, the Deutsche Bundesbank would have exploited all systematic correlations between its own instruments and the targets.

9

The Role of International Institutions in Surveillance and Policy Coordination

Andrew Crockett*

I. Introduction

Since 1985, when the recent intensification of policy coordination among the major industrial countries began, the world economy has performed relatively well. Economic expansion has been maintained, while inflation has stayed low. The dollar has been brought down from the unsustainably high level it had reached in early 1985. Progress has been made in reducing fiscal and current account imbalances. And financial hiccoughs (such as the 1987 stock market crash and periodic bouts of foreign exchange market turbulence) have been contained without lasting adverse consequences. While there are a number of less satisfactory aspects of the situation—notably the lack of progress in improving the economic performance and creditworthiness of heavily indebted developing countries—the industrialized economies have on the whole come through the 1985–88 period much better than most economists had expected.

Policy coordination[1] has been credited, by its authors, with an important role in this success.[2] Moreover, it has been suggested that the *mechanisms* of policy coordination could be developed to constitute, in effect, the reform of the international monetary system that has been called for in a number of quarters.[3] For this reason, it is important to discuss how coordination

---

* The views expressed are those of the author and do not necessarily reflect those of the International Monetary Fund.

[1] The term "policy coordination" is used because of its familiarity in current debate. However, "coordination" implies joint policymaking of a more detailed and far-reaching kind than is actually practiced or contemplated by the countries concerned. "Policy cooperation" would probably better describe the process.

[2] See, for example, the Toronto Economic Declaration, para. 6, June 21, 1988.

[3] U.S. Treasury Secretary James A. Baker III appeared to suggest this in his Paris speech of May 20, 1988.

is implemented, and how the analytical and procedural foundations of the process can be strengthened. This leads to the question of the institutional framework within which coordination takes place and how it needs to evolve. These issues, rather than the analysis of the economic effects of coordination, are the main focus of this paper.[4]

In examining how surveillance and policy coordination have developed, it is important to recognize that policy cooperation among the major industrial countries did not begin with the Plaza Agreement of September 1985.[5] It was a recurring theme in the last decade and a half of the Bretton Woods period, induced in part by the greater payments instability that followed the restoration of convertibility by the European countries.[6] It was also an important theme in the 1970s, as policymakers attempted to develop guidelines to help the floating exchange rate regime function in a way that was compatible with efficient adjustment and with reasonable exchange rate stability. Indeed, it was only in the early 1980s that a continuous dialogue on policy cooperation was considered dispensable (and then only by some). One objective of this paper is to revisit earlier attempts to institutionalize cooperation, to see what lessons they hold for the current situation.

Following the introduction, the next section of this paper poses the question, "Why coordination?" Would it not be possible to design an international monetary system in which countries pursued their own national agenda, and the systemic "hidden hand" ensured compatibility with the general welfare? This question has been addressed in a number of papers;[7] it is nevertheless helpful to understand clearly the circumstances under which systematic policy coordination is required. Against this background, the next section takes a look at two earlier attempts to institutionalize cooperation and compares them with the developments of the past three or four years. These two earlier episodes are the establishment and early history of Working Party 3 of the Organization for Economic Cooperation and Development (OECD), and the development in the mid-1970s of principles for the guidance of exchange rate policies in the Fund. The paper concludes by exploring future prospects. It considers whether policy coordination could in fact evolve in the direction of systemic reform and what developments in the analytical and procedural elements of existing arrangements would help attain this goal.

---

[4] Theoretical and empirical papers analyzing the channels of international economic interactions are to be found in Bryant and others (1988).

[5] Wallich (1984) contains a description of the institutional arrangements for international economic cooperation.

[6] Going back further, the history of the 1920s and 1930s is replete with meetings and conferences aimed at shoring up the international monetary system. Indeed, it was the ultimate failure of these attempts that reinforced the determination of the allied countries, in planning postwar arrangements, to create international institutions as a focus for cooperative effort.

[7] See, for example, Frenkel, Goldstein, and Masson (1988), and Corden (1983).

II. Why Coordination?

Policy coordination has been defined by Wallich as "a significant modification of national policies in recognition of international economic interdependence."[8] The mere existence of economic interdependence, however, does not make coordination necessary. After all, individual economic agents within a national economy are highly interdependent but do not need to consciously "coordinate" their decisions. The coordination function is performed by the hidden hand of atomistic markets.

It is now well recognized that decentralized decisions can be rendered inefficient for two reasons. The first is the existence of externalities, or "spillover" effects, whereby part of the costs or benefits of decisions made by one economic agent accrue to other agents. The second is the existence of a public good—such as economic stability—which will tend to be undersupplied in the absence of collective decisionmaking. National economies have developed mechanisms to deal with the problems of externalities and public goods. Externalities can be internalized through taxes and subsidies, or controlled through regulation. Public goods can be supplied by a public agency—for example, a central bank charged with the responsibility to maintain price stability.

At the international level, however, it can be argued that comparable institutional mechanisms do not exist: While international agreements exist in some spheres (such as the General Agreement on Tariffs and Trade), they are generally insufficient to deal fully with the problem of externalities. And there is not yet any analogue at the international level to the role of the central bank domestically.

In order to deal with international spillover effects and to make proper provision for "international public goods," instruments have to be developed to regulate international economic relations. Still, such instruments do not necessarily have to be based on judgmental policy coordination. Indeed, most of the history of attempts to strengthen the international monetary system has involved a search for rules to guide individual country policymaking, thereby avoiding (or at least limiting) the need for discretionary coordination.

Since the exchange rate is the most important and obvious point of contact between economies, the exchange rate system has been the focus of most attempts to develop rules. The polar cases are, of course, a regime of fixed exchange rates and one of free floating. Under the former, participating countries are obliged to intervene in exchange markets to prevent exchange movements; under the latter, they are obliged not to.

A satisfactory monetary system, however, cannot be defined only in terms of rules governing the exchange rate. The instruments that are used to keep exchange rates fixed under a par value system have implications both for

---

[8] Wallich (1984), p. 85.

partner countries' welfare and systemic stability. Thus, simply fixing exchange rates does not deal adequately with either the problem of externalities or that of public goods. Similarly with floating rates, merely refraining from exchange market intervention is inadequate to take proper account of international economic interactions.

While exchange rate rules clearly require additional mechanisms to ensure policy compatibility, this need not necessarily be achieved through discretionary policy coordination. An alternative approach is to supplement the exchange rate rules with additional rules or guidelines that govern policy responses in particular circumstances. In deciding the "rules versus discretion" frontier, a trade-off operates. Well-defined rules and obligations limit the uncertainty surrounding policy responses and reduce the need for potentially difficult coordination decisions; by the same token, rules make it harder to adapt policy responses to the requirements of particular cases. Full reliance on discretion, on the other hand, permits policy decisions to be made on a case-by-case basis, with proper allowance for circumstances; however, in the absence of guidelines, it may become more difficult to reach such decisions and to give the desired degree of guidance to agents in private markets.

In practice, as the remainder of this paper will attempt to show, earlier approaches to coordination have sought to develop guidelines (which might be termed "presumptive rules") to illustrate how policies may be expected to respond in typical situations. These guidelines constitute the "analytic environment" in which coordination takes place—they *suggest* policy responses, but they do not *compel* them. Coordination efforts since 1985 have been more modest in this respect. While procedures for discussions have been developed, and a list of analytical "indicators" specified, much less has been said about how developments in various indicators might be related to policy responses. The final section of this paper offers some reflections about whether current efforts at policy coordination could usefully evolve in the direction of more explicit guidelines.

III. Approaches to Policy Coordination

The existence of sovereign nation states means that, whatever the nature of international monetary arrangements, considerable discretion will remain to policy authorities. Moreover, the way in which this discretion is exercised will have important effects on trading partners and, where major countries are concerned, on the international monetary system at large. This recognition has led to a variety of attempts to strengthen both the institutional structure and the analytical underpinning for international economic cooperation.

In this section, three of these attempts are analyzed: the first is the establishment of Working Party 3 of the OECD in 1961, and the subsequent efforts to develop principles to guide the working of the adjustment process; the second is the negotiations on the Fund document, "Surveillance Over

Exchange Rate Policies," adopted following the move to floating exchange rates and the second amendment to the Fund's Articles of Agreement; and the third is the more recent development of procedures for policy coordination, particularly among the Group of Seven countries.

Working Party 3 and the Bretton Woods Adjustment Process

The Articles of Agreement of the Fund, as agreed at Bretton Woods, clearly envisaged that cooperation would be a continuous feature of the monetary system. The first purpose of the Fund is stated to be: "To promote international monetary cooperation through a permanent institution which provides the machinery for consultation and collaboration on international monetary problems."

Nevertheless, the cooperation envisaged in 1944 was not exactly the cooperation that proved to be necessary as the Bretton Woods system evolved. When the Fund was created, it was generally assumed that a workable distinction could be drawn between "external" and "internal" policies. The Fund's task was expected to be to monitor external policies—in particular exchange rate policies and payments restrictions—and to prevent competitive devaluation or other beggar-thy-neighbor policies. The danger of competitive devaluation was regarded as significant because it was feared that "secular stagnation" would lead countries to use export promotion as a means of supporting domestic employment. In the event, aggregate demand proved much more robust than expected, and competitive devaluation was not a major problem in the postwar period. A more troublesome matter was the balance of payments adjustment process. The need for cooperation in the management of the adjustment process does not appear to have been explicitly envisaged by the founders of Bretton Woods.[9]

A growing awareness of this lacuna, together with a recognition that policy choices by individual countries had important spillover effects on their trading partners, led to the creation in 1961 of Working Party 3 of the Economic Policy Committee of the OECD. The OECD had been established in 1960 as the successor institution to the Organization for European Economic Cooperation, which had played a central role in the implementation of the Marshall Plan. The OECD has 24 member countries (essentially the advanced industrial countries) and promotes cooperation in a wide range of areas, extending well beyond macroeconomic policies and balance of payments adjustment. Still, macroeconomic policies are a key focus of both the annual ministerial meetings and the semiannual meetings of the Economic Policy Committee (EPC). Working Party 3 was established in order to permit a more continuous dialogue on the balance of payments adjustment process, in a

---

[9] Solomon (1984), p. 19.

more manageable forum.[10] Its purpose was (and remains) "the promotion of better international payments equilibrium," and its terms of reference state that its members "will analyze the effect on international payments of monetary, fiscal, and other policy measures, and will consult together on policy measures, both national and international, as they relate to international payments equilibrium."

The Working Party quickly established the practice of holding meetings every six to eight weeks.[11] Its work was underpinned by detailed analyses and projections provided by the OECD Secretariat, which was prepared in the light of regular meetings of forecasters from national capitals. Working Party 3 soon became the key forum in which senior policymakers discussed global economic prospects, as well as policy requirements in situations that seemed to pose a balance of payments adjustment problem. Nevertheless, it became apparent that a forum alone was not sufficient to guide the process of cooperation. A firmer analytical basis for the Working Party's deliberations was needed. In particular, guidance was required concerning the circumstances in which exchange rate adjustment (which the Fund's Articles of Agreement permitted only in cases of "fundamental disequilibrium") could be used. In mid-1964, the ministers of the Group of Ten (which had been formed earlier to provide additional liquidity to the Fund) called, in effect, for policy guidelines to be established.[12]

The result was the report on "The Balance of Payments Adjustment Process," released by the OECD in August 1966. This report did not question the desirability of maintaining fixed par values as the basis for the international monetary system. However, it recognized that automatic adjustment mechanisms, though important, might not be adequate to restore external equilibrium in a sufficiently timely way. In effect, the report sought to complement the rules of the Bretton Woods system in two ways: first, by establishing an

---

[10] The members of the Working Party are the deputy ministers and deputy central bank governors (or equivalent) from Belgium/Netherlands, Canada, France, the Federal Republic of Germany, Italy, Japan, Sweden, Switzerland, the United Kingdom, and the United States. Observers from other international institutions, as well as the OECD Secretariat, also participate.

[11] Meetings of Working Party 3 are held approximately three times a year.

[12] Ministerial Statement of the Group of Ten, August 1964. In the Deputies' annex to this statement, a survey was requested of the "measures and instruments" by which:

". . . Member countries, individually and collectively, and compatibly with the pursuit of their essential internal objectives, could in the future preserve a better balance of payments equilibrium and achieve a faster and more effective adjustment of imbalance."

The survey was to include studies of ". . . how measures in the field of fiscal, trade and incomes and other policies can be used by both surplus and deficit countries in combination with monetary policy, to achieve internal and external objectives, particularly where there is a possibility of conflict between the two . . ." and to "explore whether standards can be formulated on the contribution of monetary and related policies to balance of payments equilibrium against which the performance of countries could be appraised."

analytical framework in which policy guidelines could be drawn up; and second, by developing procedures that would allow these policy guidelines to be implemented (and, if necessary, adapted) in specific circumstances.

The report was an important milestone in acknowledging the role of international institutions in policy coordination. It implicitly recognized that this role had to go beyond monitoring compliance with a set of agreed international obligations. A mechanism was needed both to develop policy guidelines and to provide procedures for consultation. Initially, the focus in Working Party 3 was on the adjustment obligations of individual countries; coordination, in the strict sense of the term, was a subsidiary part of the process. As time passed, however, it became increasingly apparent that international economic interactions had to be addressed more explicitly.[13]

The need for consultation procedures and policy guidelines is the fundamental justification for assigning a central role to an international institution (in this case the OECD) with a staff that is independent of national capitals. An international institution can constitute the forum for regular meetings of national policymakers, while its staff can provide a common data set as a basis for discussions.[14] Moreover, when criteria are developed to facilitate a dialogue on policy consistency, there is an important role for disinterested analysis from a source that is clearly impartial.

The procedures developed by Working Party 3 involved four main elements:

- an exchange of information on balance of payments aims, to help produce ex ante consistency in countries' policies;
- a review of short-term balance of payments forecasts, to consider whether actual developments are taking countries toward, or away from, a desired situation;
- an early warning system, to identify emerging imbalances or inconsistencies; and
- an analysis ("confrontation" was the term originally used by the Working Party) of national policies, in order to reach judgments on their appropriateness and mutual consistency.

The guidelines proposed in the Working Party 3 Report had both a *diagnostic* and a *prescriptive* aspect. The principle on which they were based was the need to reconcile internal and external balance. Internal balance could be defined as the simultaneous achievement of full employment and reasonable price stability. External balance could be defined as a current account position that (in the absence of restrictions) was exactly balanced by "normal" capital flows.

To diagnose emerging payments problem, the 1966 Report proposed the

---

[13] This is developed in Solomon (1982).

[14] The provision of a common data set is by no means a trivial contribution. Since national projections are often made at different dates, on the basis of different underlying assumptions, discussions on the basis of national estimates and projections can easily bog down on data.

use of indicators. Interestingly, the indicators suggested were much the same as those identified in the declaration of the Tokyo Summit of industrial countries some 20 years later. They are grouped in the 1966 Report into three categories: (1) indicators of external balance, such as trade and current account positions and nonmonetary capital flows; (2) indicators of domestic balance, such as the growth of demand and output, unemployment, and inflation; and (3) indicators of fiscal and monetary policies. The "early warning" system proposed in the Report envisaged using forecasts of the indicator variables to assess whether a departure from internal or external equilibrium seemed likely to emerge.

Policy cooperation, however, involves more than the diagnosis of emerging imbalances. It implies a willingness to reach agreement on remedial measures, if necessary in a concerted manner. While such agreements can, in principle, be reached on an ad hoc basis, they are more likely to come about if the parties concerned have a common understanding of how their objectives and policies interact.[15] The purpose of the 1966 Report is to promote such an understanding, and specifically "to explore whether standards can be formulated on the contribution of monetary and related policies to balance of payments equilibrium, against which the performance of countries could be appraised." The Report envisages that imbalances can usually be attributed to one or more of three main factors: inappropriate levels of domestic demand, inappropriate international competitiveness, and excessive capital flows. It attempts to identify the policy response that is called for in each case.

The most straightforward case arises when an external imbalance is attributable to inappropriate levels of domestic demand. In such a situation, the requirements of internal and external imbalance point in the same direction: demand restraint is called for in deficit countries and demand stimulus in surplus countries. Given the "Keynesian consensus" of the 1960s, it was also relatively easy to define the instruments by which stimulus and restraint would be applied; monetary and fiscal policies were considered effective short-term tools of demand management.

The Report also reveals a broad consensus on how to respond to situations where difficulties are created by excessive capital flows. A shift in policies toward a tighter monetary/easier fiscal mix is seen as appropriate to counter capital outflows, with the reverse shift in policy mix to deal with excessive inflows. (Note that these recommendations imply considerably more confidence in the authorities' ability to influence economic conditions through short-term policy adaptations than exists today.)

A more complex policy problem arises when external disequilibrium is caused by price competitiveness factors. This is where the tricky problem of defining the concept of "fundamental disequilibrium" enters in. The guidelines

---

[15] This point is made with particular force by Cooper (1984).

of the 1966 Report imply a slightly asymmetric response, depending on whether the problem is too little competitiveness or too much. Where a country is excessively competitive, it is recognized that the international community can hardly encourage that country to stimulate domestic inflation to reduce its payments surplus; revaluation is therefore seen as a potentially preferable alternative. Where the problem is inadequate competitiveness, the Report suggests that countries should seek to bring down inflation by means other than the exchange rate (including incomes policies and policies to increase productivity) and to use devaluation only if the alternative is "a prolonged period of stagnant demand."

How closely were countries expected to follow the policy recommendations in the Working Party 3 Report? The Report's guidelines were said to have provided "a set of presumptions" about policies, although it was also recognized "they can be . . . no more than a highly simplified framework," and that "every balance of payments problem can have its own particular characteristics." Thus, while policy guidelines were seen as useful in fleshing out the obligations that countries assumed under the rules of the international monetary system, they still needed to be complemented by more-or-less continuous cooperation in the light of evolving economic circumstances. A key element of the process was, therefore, the regular meetings of the Working Party at which policymakers analyzed the circumstances of specific cases. Policymakers could discuss emerging problems at successive stages of their development. They could request analysis from their international secretariat, and they were usually able to reach broad analytical agreement on the source of imbalances.

The guidelines set out in the Working Party 3 Report were the basis for policy cooperation in other forums as well. In the late 1950s and 1960s, the Fund became more active in supporting members' programs of economic adjustment. In the 1966–71 period, for example, the Fund approved 142 stand-by arrangements in the upper credit tranches with 42 member countries, 4 of which were developed countries. With the accumulation of experience, a methodology was developed for identifying the sources of countries' payments imbalances and proposing an appropriate set of remedial measures. In principle, this methodology was symmetrical, and was applied symmetrically in the Fund's regular consultations. Still, the influence of the international community on a country's policies is obviously greater when the country needs financial support than when it doesn't.

Surveillance Under Floating Exchange Rates

Cooperation in the management of the adjustment process helped alleviate the strains that emerged in the par value system in the 1960s.[16] Eventually,

---

[16] Solomon (1982) provides a detailed account of international responses to payments difficulties in the 1960s. See also de Vries (1976).

however, the combination of divergences in international competitiveness and growing capital mobility was too much to be contained by the informal policy cooperation established in Working Party 3 and the consultation procedures of the Fund. Fixed exchange rates broke down in 1971, and the attempt to re-establish them was abandoned in 1973.

When it became clear that the international monetary system would be based for the foreseeable future on floating exchange rates, attention shifted to how to harness cooperative mechanisms to make such a system work most effectively. Once again, cooperation could be seen as taking place on three levels:

- agreement on a set of rules to be embodied in the Fund's Articles of Agreement;
- development of guidelines on how policies should respond in typical situations; and
- establishment of institutional procedures for monitoring and evaluating policies on a continuing basis.

The first level of cooperation was provided by the agreement reached by the Fund's Interim Committee (of the Board of Governors on the International Monetary System) at its January 1976 Jamaica meeting, on a new Article IV of the Fund's charter. Article IV governs exchange rate obligations, and under the original Articles of Agreement it had prescribed par value obligations. The new Article IV essentially placed two obligations on countries: one to pursue "stable" domestic policies, and the other to avoid exchange rate "manipulation."

It was recognized, of course, that the general language of Article IV was a framework for policy guidance, rather than a blueprint. Article IV therefore called on the Fund to develop "specific principles" to guide members' exchange rate policies and then to exercise "firm surveillance" over the way they were implemented. (In terms of the three levels of cooperation outlined above, agreement on principles to guide policies would constitute the second level, and the development of surveillance procedures would constitute the third.)

While the move from fixed to flexible exchange rates involved important changes in the policy instruments that would bear the burden of adjustment, this did not imply major changes in the economic "model" (or view of underlying economic processes) used by policymakers. Indeed, in a number of important respects, the new Article IV was based on a view of how the adjustment process worked that was quite similar to that underlying the Working Party 3 Report.[17] *First*, it was believed that a meaningful analytic distinction was possible between "domestic" and "external" (or exchange rate)

---

[17] Crockett and Goldstein (1987), Chapter II.

policies. The main source of concern from the standpoint of the international community was that countries would use "external policies" to manipulate exchange rates and hamper the efficient working of the adjustment process. *Second*, current account positions were expected to move in a reasonably predictable manner as a result of changes in competitiveness and shifts in relative cyclical positions. As a practical matter, the most important factor giving rise to trend changes in current account positions seemed likely to be differential inflation rates. *Third*, there was thought to be a pattern of "normal" capital flows that was fairly stable over time. Thus, exchange rate pressures were likely to arise mainly from shifts in current account positions, possibly magnified by "speculative" capital flows. The overall implication of these views was that stable domestic policies (in particular, a low and stable rate of inflation), together with a hands-off policy toward the exchange rate, would produce a stable and resilient international monetary system.[18]

Given this view of the world, the first task of cooperation was to find a way of distinguishing between external developments that constituted "manipulation" of the exchange rate (and were therefore to be avoided), and developments that reflected the normal operation of adjustment processes (and should therefore be allowed). The Fund's Executive Board spent much of late 1976 and early 1977 wrestling with this issue. Early drafts by the Fund staff attempted to specify preferred policy responses in different types of situations. In the end, however, it was realized that specific guidance was unlikely to be feasible, in part because it was almost impossible to make a useful distinction between exchange rate and other policies.[19] Moreover, the "Keynesian consensus" on the effects of macroeconomic policies had largely eroded by the late 1970s.

The policy guidelines themselves, therefore, do little more than reiterate the injunction against manipulation contained in the underlying Article. An attempt is made, however, to provide an illustrative list of circumstances that might raise doubts about the appropriateness of an exchange rate policy. This list includes predictable examples (such as prolonged one-way exchange market intervention, the use of payments restrictions, and heavy official financing of payments deficits and surpluses). In addition, in order to ensure that countries that did not intervene in exchange markets could also be subject to surveillance, the final item in the list is "behavior of the exchange rate that appears to be unrelated to underlying economic and financial condi-

---

[18] The IMF Articles permitted countries to peg their exchange rates (other than to gold), which would require that countries pick the "right" rate. But it was also envisaged that the absence of manipulation would, with stable domestic policies, result in a stable and appropriate exchange rate.

[19] de Vries (1985), Vol. 2, Chapter 43.

tions. . . ."[20] Observers at the time recognized, however, that, even with these illustrations, the "exchange rate principles" were not a sufficient basis to guide individual countries' policy formulation.[21]

In the absence of a strong "second level" of cooperation, in the form of policy guidelines, it was envisaged that additional weight would be placed on the third component of cooperation—the development of international procedures for consultation. These various procedures, generically called "surveillance," were expected to produce a body of case law that would help identify the kinds of policies that would be appropriate in particular circumstances. This approach to surveillance places a particularly heavy responsibility on the international institution charged with its implementation. In the absence of clear guidance on what were considered inappropriate policies, the Fund itself would have to provide the analysis and rationale for potentially sensitive judgments about members' policies. Four elements of the surveillance procedures that were adopted are worthy of mention:

First, the periodic Executive Board discussions of the World Economic Outlook (WEO) were made more systematic and more regular.[22] The WEO analysis made a conscious attempt to review the interactions of policies and performance, and to assess the appropriateness of exchange rate trends.[23]

Second, the regular consultations with member countries were placed under the umbrella of Article IV (previously they had been under either Article VIII or Article XIV, both of which dealt with the exchange and trade system). As a result, the consultations became wider in scope and incorporated an appraisal of whether members' policies were consistent with the rather vaguely worded obligations of Article IV.

Third, a process of special consultations was established whereby a spotlight could be focused on the policies of an individual country when these policies raised questions. (This innovation was of limited success, however. During the first ten years of the provision's existence, only two countries were examined; neither examination was under the formal provisions for special consultations and neither country was censored.)

Fourth, an "information notice system" was established to bring to the attention of the Fund's Executive Board any sizable change in exchange rates occurring between periodic consultations, and to provide some analysis of the change that had occurred.

While these procedural arrangements were all useful, they were clearly not sufficient to deal with the kinds of problems that emerged. The inadequacy

---

[20] International Monetary Fund, *Selected Decisions*, 13th issue, Decision No. 5392-(77/63) (Washington: International Monetary Fund, April 30, 1987), p. 12.

[21] Artus and Crockett (1978).

[22] de Vries (1985), Vol. 2, Chapter 40.

[23] For description of the Fund staff's approach to exchange rate analysis, see *Issues in the Assessment of the Exchange Rates of Industrial Countries*, IMF Occasional Paper No. 29 (1984).

of existing surveillance mechanisms was demonstrated by the two most striking developments of the first half of the 1980s: the onset of the debt crisis in 1982; and the overvaluation of the U.S. dollar, which reached its peak in early 1985. These developments undermined the premises on which floating exchange rates had been accepted up to that point. In the first place, it became apparent that the avoidance of deliberate exchange rate manipulation was not sufficient to prevent the emergence of inappropriate exchange rates. Second, events showed that Fund surveillance, in the absence of stronger international agreement on the policy responsibilities of individual countries, was not sufficient to maintain an appropriate and stable pattern of exchange rates.

The recognition that changes (in emphasis, if not in basic substance) were needed came in 1985. In that year the dollar had reached a level that, by common consent, could not be regarded as indefinitely sustainable. In the same year the reports of the Group of Ten and the Group of Twenty-Four on strengthening the working of the monetary system were released.[24] The Group of Ten report did not call for major changes in the system. Nevertheless, like the more critical Group of Twenty-Four report, it recognized shortcomings in the working of surveillance. The report notes that ". . . the system has not adequately promoted sound and consistent policies. . . . Large movements in real exchange rates may lead to patterns of international transactions that are unlikely to be sustainable. . . ." To strengthen surveillance, the report proposed a number of initiatives to strengthen the influence of "peer pressure" among countries. Therefore, 1985 can be regarded as the beginning of the current efforts to strengthen the institutional and analytical basis for policy coordination.

Strengthening Policy Coordination: 1985 Onward

The strengthening of arrangements for policy coordination since 1985 has been proceeding along two separate but related tracks. One is the Group of Seven track, the mileposts of which are the periodic communiqués issued after summit meetings or Group of Seven ministerial meetings. The second is the Fund track, involving the entire membership of the Fund and carried on, with the assistance of Fund management and staff, in the Fund's Executive Board and in the twice-yearly Interim Committee meetings. Bridges between the two tracks are evidenced by the fact that the members of the Group of Seven are also active in surveillance discussions in the Fund, as well as through the participation of the Fund's Managing Director in Group of Seven meetings.

The current Group of Seven coordination arrangements are the latest stage in a rather lengthy evolution of the process of policy cooperation among the largest countries. Meetings of the ministers and governors of the Group of Five countries began in the mid-1970s. These meetings provided a forum for

---

[24] Group of Ten (1985). Group of Twenty-Four (1985).

discussing the world economic situation and policy requirements, even though specific policy commitments were not sought, and no communiqués were usually issued after the meetings. A procedural step forward was taken in 1982, following the Versailles Summit, when the Managing Director of the Fund began to participate in the surveillance discussions of the Group of Five, and submitted statistical and analytical material as input to the discussion. A further step was taken in 1986 when a Fund staff representative began to participate in certain meetings of Group of Five deputies. Lastly, the extension of the Group of Five to Group of Seven occurred in 1987.[25]

The beginning of the current attempt to use regular meetings of policy-makers to promote a more structured form of policy coordination can be said to have begun with the Plaza meeting of September 1985. The immediate objective of that meeting was a rather limited one: to help ease protectionist pressures in the United States by demonstrating that policymakers were prepared to act to reduce the extent of the dollar's overvaluation.[26] Nevertheless, the apparent success of the Plaza initiative, coupled with the recognition that exchange rates could not be viewed in isolation from domestic policies, created an environment in which further initiatives were likely to be welcomed. The subsequent evolution can be seen as a series of stages, each involving a combination of procedural and analytical innovations.

The Tokyo Summit

The Tokyo Economic Declaration of June 1986 stated that policy coordination was to be continuous rather than episodic. Procedurally, a new Group of Seven finance ministers was created with a mandate to work together closely in the periods between annual summit meetings. Analytically, the key advance at the Tokyo Summit was the role given to economic indicators.[27] The summit communiqué "request[ed] the seven Finance Ministers to review their individual economic objectives and forecasts collectively at least once a year, using the indicators specified below, with a particular view to examining their mutual compatibility."

---

[25] The Group of Seven met before 1987, and the Group of Five continued to meet after 1987; still, 1987 is the year in which seven became the size of the group in which most surveillance discussions took place.

[26] Funabashi (1988), p. 15.

[27] Indicators had been referred to in the April 1986 Interim Committee communiqué, a month before the Tokyo Summit: "To improve the multilateral setting for surveillance . . . an approach worth exploring further was the formulation of a set of objective indicators related to policy actions and economic performance, having regard to a medium-term framework." (Lest this approach be thought to imply triggers for policy changes, the following sentence is deliberately cautious: "Such indicators *might help* to identify a need for *discussion* of countries' policies.") (Emphasis added.)

The role of the Fund in this process was explicitly recognized in the paragraph that referred to the indicators. The relevant sentence reads as follows: "[the Heads of State or Government] reaffirm the undertaking at the 1982 Versailles Summit to cooperate with the IMF in strengthening multilateral surveillance, particularly among the countries whose currencies constitute the SDR, and request that, in conducting such surveillance and in conjunction with the Managing Director of the IMF, their individual economic forecasts should be reviewed, taking into account indicators such as GNP growth rates, inflation rates, interest rates, unemployment rates, fiscal deficit ratios, current account and trade balances, monetary growth rates, reserves, and exchange rates."[28]

By the time of the Tokyo Summit, therefore, the Fund had been asked to assist in developing an approach to multilateral surveillance using indicators, although it had not received much guidance on how indicators should be analyzed in practice. To help advance the discussion, the Fund staff prepared an analytical paper on the use of indicators.[29] This paper was discussed by the Fund's Executive Board in mid-1986, and the approach it described was applied in the World Economic Outlook analysis prepared in September 1986.

The approach employed made use of two familiar economic concepts: the "sustainability" of financial imbalances (domestic or internal); and the national income identity that equates the current account of the balance of payments with the domestic savings-investment balance. The Fund staff's analytical paper noted that the indicators proposed in the Tokyo Declaration could be subdivided into three categories: performance variables, policy variables, and intermediate variables. The paper traced the transmission mechanisms through which policy variables had their impact on intermediate variables and then influenced economic performance. A "tension" would be created if the medium-term consequences of a continuation of current policies led to a potentially "unsustainable" result. Whether or not a given trend should be regarded as "unsustainable" was recognized as involving a significant degree of judgment. However, if the prospective evolution of the balance of payments—given current levels of competitiveness and prospective growth rates—was inconsistent with a desired evolution of domestic savings and investment, then questions about sustainability would clearly arise.

The Louvre Accord and the Venice Summit

The use of indicators by the Group of Seven and the Interim Committee was an important first step. But, of course, such indicators had always been

---

[28] Tokyo Economic Declaration. Reproduced in Funabashi (1988).

[29] An amended version of this paper was published as Chapter III of IMF Occasional Paper No. 50 (1987).

used. To push the process forward required some consensus on how policies would be adapted in the light of evidence provided by the indicators. This was clearly more difficult, especially given the important disagreements that existed concerning the channels of transmission of economic influences among countries. Cooper has put the matter thus: "even if countries have compatible objectives and similar circumstances . . . they may disagree on the structure of the economy and hence on the relationship of means to ends."[30]

In order to make effective use of indicators, one or more of several approaches could be followed. One would be to attempt to fill in some of the "empty boxes" of the analytical framework. Another might be agreement on "standards" by which developments in various indicators might be appraised. Still another would be to institutionalize procedures for dealing with unsatisfactory developments.

The April 1987 meeting of the Interim Committee advanced the coordination process by proposing "that actual policies should be looked at against an evolution of economic variables that could be considered desirable and sustainable." At about the same time, the Group of Seven countries also took an important procedural step. They agreed on a format for submitting their individual short-term forecasts and medium-term projections for collective review. The idea was that these projections should be looked at early in each year to ensure that they met the "sustainability and desirability" criterion. If they did, developments in a number of "interim indicators" would be monitored later in the year to ensure that economic performance was keeping to the intended track. (What was to be done in case projections were "undesirable" or "unsustainable" was not clearly spelled out.)

An agreement that prospective economic trends should be "sustainable and desirable" is not much of an agreement unless some further content can be given to the relevant concepts. The Fund's staff attempted to do this in its WEO analysis in September 1987. It was recognized that concepts such as "sustainability" and "desirability" could not be defined with any precision; nevertheless, some rules of thumb were offered. For example, the analysis suggested that domestic demand should grow somewhat more rapidly than potential output in countries with payments surpluses, while domestic demand should grow more slowly than potential output in countries with external deficits and relatively high rates of resource utilization. (The analysis also offered estimates of potential output growth in the major countries.) It further suggested that fiscal policies should aim at a stable budgetary position in which the fiscal deficit would not "crowd out" productive private investments. The speed with which a desired medium-term budgetary position was restored would depend on such elements as the balance of payments position and the

---

[30] Cooper (1985), pp. 1228–29.

strength of domestic demand. Monetary policy should aim at a low and stable rate of inflation. And as far as the balance of payments was concerned, the WEO analysis suggested that a rapid buildup of a large net external liability or asset position was considered to introduce an undesirable potential for instability in exchange markets.

Generalizations like these do not define "desirable and sustainable" policies in a quantitative way. Nevertheless, they can help identify the direction in which policies need to move and thus provide a focus for policy discussions in specific circumstances.

A further development in 1987 was the use by the Group of Seven of aggregate indicators. Aggregate indicators can shed light on changes in the economic performance of the seven countries as a group. As such, they serve two purposes: first, to help assess the implications for the rest of the world of developments in the major countries; and second, to help decide which country's policies should be changed when convergence is required. To take a simple example, in the face of undesirable exchange rate pressure, a monetary policy tightening by a weak currency country would be indicated when inflation was a collective problem, whereas policy easing by a strong-currency country might be indicated when inflation was under control and the general problem was one of weak growth in demand. Commodity price movements were proposed in September 1987, as an additional variable to be considered in Group of Seven surveillance discussions,[31] to provide an aggregate indicator of potential inflation pressures.

Current Status

Within the Group of Seven, the basic procedural framework for mutual surveillance and policy coordination appeared to be fairly well established at the end of 1988. Early in each year, the Fund staff collects each country's forecasts (for the short term) and "objectives" (for the medium term) for a set of key variables related to: (a) domestic demand and output; (b) inflation; (c) trade and current account balances; and (d) fiscal and monetary policies. If updated and comprehensive national projections cannot be made available, the Fund staff itself constructs national projections on the basis of partial information and informal discussions with the authorities.

National authorities' figures and comparable Fund staff estimates are then made available at a meeting of the Group of Seven, at the level of deputies from finance ministries. A Fund staff representative participates in this meeting to explain issues related to the projections and to help assess the consistency of prospective trends. The meeting of deputies is intended to identify the

---

[31] This proposal was made in the speeches of U.S. Treasury Secretary James Baker and British Chancellor of the Exchequer Nigel Lawson to the 1987 International Monetary Fund Annual Meetings.

key issues that need to be considered at a subsequent meeting of ministers and governors. This latter meeting usually takes place at the time of the spring meeting of the Interim Committee (normally in early April). At this meeting, participants aim to agree on an acceptable and mutually consistent set of medium-term objectives, as well as on short-term projections for key indicators that are consistent with this medium-term outlook. The Managing Director of the Fund participates in the part of the meeting dealing with surveillance issues.

The next set of meetings take place in the autumn, prior to, and at the time of, the Fund's annual meetings. At these meetings, actual developments during the current year are compared with those envisaged six months earlier. In addition, the Fund staff presents its revised set of projections for the short and medium term and assesses whether new policy issues have arisen on the basis of developments during the course of the year.

This complete exercise was first undertaken in 1988. Since developments during 1988 had in most respects been more favorable than expected earlier in the year, little need for "remedial action" (in the words of the 1986 Tokyo Declaration) was indicated. It remains to be seen, therefore, how indicators will be used in circumstances when actual economic developments diverge unfavorably from expectations.

Surveillance by the Fund can be seen as complementing and extending the Group of Seven process. The Fund staff's WEO analysis is reviewed each spring and autumn by the Executive Board and the Interim Committee. The conclusions of these reviews are reflected in the summing up by the Managing Director of the Executive Board discussion and in the communiqué of the Interim Committee. Such conclusions then form the background against which Article IV consultations with individual countries take place. In this way, policy discussions with individual countries can take international economic interactions properly into account and can focus on policy changes needed to promote a satisfactory and mutually compatible outcome.

IV. Policy Coordination and International Monetary Reform

Given the apparent success of cooperative efforts in recent years, the question arises of whether more needs to be done to institutionalize the process. Beyond this, is it possible, as U.S. Treasury Secretary James Baker III suggested in his Paris speech of May 1988,[32] to use a step-by-step process of strengthening coordination to, in effect, bring about systemic monetary reform?

It has been argued in earlier sections of this paper that effective international policy cooperation requires three elements: first, a framework of rules

---

[32] Baker (1988).

and obligations; second, a set of generally agreed guidelines by which the rules can be interpreted; and third, a process of multilateral surveillance whereby countries can meet regularly to discuss the evolving economic situation and agree on remedies for emerging imbalances. (The first two elements, it should be noted, do not involve coordination in the sense of joint policymaking. They do, however, require cooperation in the development of rules and guidelines to govern policymaking by individual countries. The third element may or may not involve coordination in setting policy, depending on the nature and strength of policy interactions.)

As far as the first element of cooperation is concerned, the framework of rules is provided by the Second Amendment to the Fund's Articles of Agreement which, as noted earlier, requires countries to pursue domestic economic stability and to avoid exchange rate manipulation. As far as the third element is concerned, much progress has been made in establishing a workable process for continuous monitoring of the international economic situation, as well as of the evolution of the monetary system more generally. The seven major industrial countries meet regularly and have agreed on the statistical basis for their discussions. Parallel discussion of international economic developments also takes place in other forums, most notably in the Executive Board and the Interim Committee of the IMF, and in various organs of the OECD, as well as in other institutions such as the European Economic Community, the Bank for International Settlements, and the General Agreement on Tariffs and Trade.

It is in the second element of coordination—the development of policy guidelines—that the least progress appears to have been made. Certain aspects of guidelines are implicitly agreed. For example, it is recognized that a middle ground should be sought between placing too much of the adjustment burden on domestic policies (as under the Bretton Woods system) and too much on exchange rate movements (as in the early years of floating rates).[33] It is also accepted that monetary, fiscal, and structural policies should be placed in a medium-term framework, with relatively more emphasis on internationally consistent medium-term goals, and relatively less emphasis on short-term demand management. Lastly, there is agreement that adjustment obligations should be symmetrical—not through automatic rules but through an analytical structure that addresses equivalently positive and negative imbalances. However, although there is much consultation about exchange rates, there is still no comprehensive analytical framework for appraising exchange rate developments and for establishing policy responsibilities in particular circumstances.

Thus far, the absence of formal guidelines has not been an impediment to the effective implementation of coordination. The major countries have had a fairly consistent view of the nature of the problems facing the world economy

---

[33] U.S. Treasury Department. Report to the Congress on International Economic and Exchange Rate Policy (October 1988).

and the kinds of policies needed to deal with them. Specifically, in the post-Plaza period, it was recognized that three major requirements needed to be pursued simultaneously:

- a reduction in the U.S. budget deficit;
- a strengthening of domestic demand in other major countries; and
- an orderly depreciation of the U.S. dollar.

This degree of consensus may not always exist, however. Moreover, it is a consensus that has so far paid little attention to the role of countries outside the Group of Seven (other than through urging smaller surplus countries, especially those in East Asia, to try to cut their surpluses).

The implication of the foregoing is that more could usefully be done to develop the existing process of coordination so that it can constitute a basis for systemic reform. One possible line of evolution would be to develop an analytical framework that would provide clearer guidance to countries concerning their responsibilities in the adjustment process. Another approach (not mutually exclusive) would be the development of standards for appraising developments in key indicators. This appears to be the thinking of the U.S. authorities, as indicated by Secretary Baker in his May 1988 Paris speech:

We should refine the means of assessing whether an economy is deviating from an appropriate path suggesting the need for consultation and possible actions. This might involve consideration of "monitoring zones" for key indicators such as growth, trade balances, and so forth.

If such a proposal were to be adopted, it would presumably involve two stages, each of which would entail an important role for the international institutions. The first stage would be to agree on criteria by which an "appropriate path" for an economy could be defined. The second would be to propose monitoring zones on the basis of whatever path was established.

These are complicated issues that will require intensive staff work and cover matters in which individual national interests may diverge. The role of an international institution will be to provide an agreed data base, an impartial source of analysis, and the necessary staff resources to prepare supporting material on a continuous basis. Moreover, linkage of the coordination process that takes place among the Group of Seven (which, owing to market sensitivities, may have to remain restricted)[34] to the broad international collaboration on the functioning of the world economy requires an institution that is comprehensive enough in membership to bring together both the larger and the smaller countries. Thus, if policy coordination is to continue evolving toward being a systematic process—as opposed to an episodic function—it seems inevitable that the role of the Fund will have to remain central.

---

[34] Solomon (1984) discusses some of the reasons why certain types of policymaking can take place only in a restricted form.

References

Artis, Michael J., and Sylvia Ostry, *International Economic Policy Coordination,* Chatham House Papers, No. 30 (London: Royal Institute of International Affairs, 1986).

Artus, Jacques R., and Andrew Crockett, *Floating Exchange Rates and the Need for Surveillance,* Essays in International Finance, No. 127 (Princeton, New Jersey: International Finance Section, Princeton University, May 1978).

Baker, James A. III, "Economic Policy Coordination and International Monetary Reform," Speech to Council on Foreign Relations (Paris, May 20, 1988).

Bryant, Ralph C., and others, eds., *Empirical Macroeconomics for Interdependent Economies* (Washington: The Brookings Institution, 1988).

Cooper, Richard N., "Economic Interdependence and Coordination of Economic Policies," in *Handbook of International Economics,* Vol. 2, ed. by Ronald W. Jones and Peter B. Kenen (Amsterdam: North-Holland, 1984).

Corden, W. Max, "The Logic of the International Monetary Non-System," in *Reflections on a Troubled World Economy,* ed. by Fritz Machlup and others (London: Macmillan, 1983).

————, "Fiscal Policies, Current Accounts, and Real Exchange Rates: In Search of a Logic of International Policy Coordination," *Weltwirtschaftliches Archiv,* Vol. 3 (1986), pp. 423–38.

Crockett, Andrew, and Morris Goldstein, "Strengthening the International Monetary System: Exchange Rates, Surveillance, and Objective Indicators," IMF Occasional Paper No. 50 (Washington: International Monetary Fund, February 1987).

de Vries, Margaret G., *The International Monetary Fund, 1966–1971: The System Under Stress* (Washington: International Monetary Fund, 1976).

————, *The International Monetary Fund 1972–1978: Cooperation on Trial* (Washington: International Monetary Fund, 1985).

Frenkel, Jacob A., Morris Goldstein, and Paul R. Masson, "International Economic Policy Coordination: Rationale, Mechanisms and Effects," Paper presented at National Bureau of Economic Research conference on "International Policy Coordination and Exchange Rate Fluctuations" (Kiawah Island, South Carolina, October 27–29, 1988).

Funabashi, Yoichi, "Managing the Dollar: From the Plaza to the Louvre" (Washington: Institute for International Economics, 1988).

Group of Ten, "The Functioning of the International Monetary System," Report of the Deputies of the Group of Ten, June 1985 (reproduced as Appendix I of IMF Occasional Paper No. 50, International Monetary Fund, Washington, 1987).

Group of Twenty-Four, "The Functioning and Improvement of the International Monetary System," Report of the Deputies of the Group of Twenty-Four, August 1983 (reproduced as Appendix II of IMF Occasional Paper No. 50, International Monetary Fund, Washington, 1987).

Horne, Jocelyn, and Paul R. Masson, "Scope and Limits of International Economic Cooperation and Policy Coordination," *Staff Papers,* International Monetary Fund (Washington), Vol. 35 (June 1988).

International Monetary Fund, *Issues in the Assessment of the Exchange Rates of*

Industrial Countries, IMF Occasional Paper No. 29 (Washington: International Monetary Fund, 1984).

Organization for Economic Cooperation and Development, "The Balance of Payments Adjustment Process," A Report by Working Party No. 3 of the Economic Policy Committee of the OECD (Paris: Organization for Economic Cooperation and Development, August 1966).

Solomon, Robert, *The International Monetary System, 1945–81*, 2nd ed. (New York: Harper and Row, 1982).

————, "Forums for Intergovernmental Consultations About Macro-Economic Policies," Brookings Discussion Papers in International Economics (Washington: The Brookings Institution, 1984).

Toronto Economic Declaration, June 21, 1988, *New York Times,* June 22, 1988.

Wallich, Henry C., "Institutional Cooperation in the World Economy," in *The World Economic System: Performance and Prospects*, ed. by Jacob A. Frenkel and Michael Mussa (Dover, Massachusetts: Auburn House, 1984).

Comments

Sylvia Ostry

Andrew Crockett's excellent and timely paper provides a most useful contribution to the growing literature on international economic coordination by focusing on an area that has scarcely been explored, that is, the role of the international institutions.

He delineates three elements of coordination:

- agreement on rules;
- guidelines for implementing rules; and
- procedures for monitoring and evaluating, or surveillance, to use the generic term.

It is with respect to the latter two, that is, guidelines and surveillance, that he assigns the institutional role. He also raises the question—which, of course, remains unanswered and unanswerable at the present time—of whether the evolution of the Group of Five and Group of Seven process since the Plaza Agreement, and especially since the Tokyo Summit, could result in a change in regime.

The economists' rationale for international coordination rests on the theory of policy optimization, assuming the existence of international externalities and of "international public goods." Taking this as given, Crockett alludes to, but does not stress, the impediments to the further evolution of the Group of Seven process in the direction of a change in regime. Indeed, if I read him correctly he is rather optimistic in his brief assessment of future developments, saying that "the major countries have had a fairly consistent view of the nature of the problems facing the world economy and the kinds of policies needed to deal with them."

Hence, future evolution toward systemic reform, especially with respect to the development of policy guidelines, *could* perhaps be facilitated by more institutional input: "an agreed data base, an impartial source of analysis, and the necessary staff resources to prepare supporting material on a continuous basis."

One hopes that this rather sanguine assessment of recent history—from Plaza to Toronto—will prove correct. But the impediments to coordination should not be underestimated. Crockett quotes Richard Cooper's statement about the lack of a consensus model. To this I would add model uncertainty (the two are linked, of course). But much more important in my view are differences in views among countries about economic behavior and the workings of the international economy. These differences are not precise or technical, but reflect deep-seated historical and cultural views as well as institutional arrangements. The "disarray among economists" (to use Cooper's term) can provide a useful rationalization to buttress, rather than reconcile, these differing views. Equally important are differences in policy targets among countries, which, again, are often based on historical, institutional, and cultural factors. These impediments to systemic change are less likely to yield to the analytical data improvements that are the terrain of institutional contribution, but require political decisions by the countries themselves. In fact, these political decisions are now confined to only a few countries—the United States, Japan, and the Federal Republic of Germany—reflecting the multipolar world that has emerged from the earlier postwar period of hegemonic dominance.

From this vantage point the risks involved in the present evolutionary process take on a different meaning. The issue is put most clearly by Charles Kindleberger's hypothesis that international public goods will tend to be underproduced in the absence of world leadership. That hypothesis as yet remains untested.

Furthermore, recent experience has shown that differences of opinion or judgment among countries are far more acute in the realm of fiscal, rather than monetary, policy. As I said in October 1986 at the symposium marking the 25th anniversary of the Organization for Economic Cooperation and Development, the highest priority in facilitating the further evolution of coordination in the direction of a new "pragmatic consensus" should be to improve "the analytic and information base in the field of fiscal impact." Two years of further evolution of the Group of Seven process has given me no reason to change my opinion.

At the time I also stressed the need to place a higher priority in the surveillance process on microeconomic or structural policies—both domestic and international—thereby broadening the scope of coordination beyond its traditional macroeconomic framework. A little-noted, but highly significant, outcome of the Toronto Summit (in addition to the endorsement of a new aggregate indicator on commodity prices) was the statement by Group of Seven Heads of State and Government at the Toronto Summit that "international cooperation involves more than coordination of macroeconomic policies. . . . We shall strive to integrate structural policies into our economic coordination process."

Finally, Crockett's survey of developments in the role of international institutions in coordination entirely omits the field of international trade and the General Agreement on Tariffs and Trade (GATT). This is hardly surprising in historical terms but, perhaps in the light of recent developments, deserves some discussion.

It is worthwhile noting that the trigger for the present process of international coordination was, in fact, mounting disquiet about protectionism in the United States. The Plaza Agreement was timed as a backdrop to a strategic speech on trade policy by U.S. President Ronald Reagan, rather than profound concern about Nash and Pareto. What did Lord Keynes say about the need for economists to be humble?

This example of *pragmatic* linkage between the international monetary system and the multilateral trade system could, of course, be greatly amplified by detailed analysis of the present and future development of the international economy. Despite welcome progress in global adjustment, a significant and continuing adjustment process lies ahead. One may debate the order of magnitude, the time path, or the precise policy mix, but what is unarguable is that the elimination or substantial reduction of the U.S. current account deficit will involve a sizable deterioration in the current account positions of other countries. This will entail a greatly heightened risk of protectionist pressures emanating from resistance to the painful process of structural change. The GATT at present is—to put it quite simply—ill-equipped to counter such pressures. Furthermore, these risks are likely to be particularly acute in Europe as the global process will coincide with another major force for structural change, that is, the completion of the internal market and, possibly as well, renewed strains within the European Monetary System (EMS) in light of the growing disparity in the external payments positions of European Community countries. If world growth is to be sustained, the improvement of the policy coordination process must include not only macroeconomic and microeconomic policies, but also trade policy and, therefore, the GATT, the third leg of the postwar triad of institutions.

The present Uruguay Round of multilateral trade negotiations (for which a mid-term ministerial review took place in Montreal in December 1988) is unique in many respects, but in the context of today's discussion a significant feature is the stress on systemic issues—the strengthening of the GATT as a contract and, for the first time since the Havana Conference, a proposal to add an institutional face to the "interim agreement." The acronym for the latter negotiating group is "FOGS," or functioning of the GATT system.

The FOGS proposal includes:
- the establishment of a regular trade policy surveillance mechanism to be applied with different frequency to countries of differing weight in the world trading system;
- regular ministerial meetings; and
- delineation of ways and means to improve coordination between the GATT and the two international financial institutions.

The significance of the FOGS proposal is best highlighted by using Crockett's three-level taxonomy. In the GATT, all three levels are absent. There are no *policy* rules and, therefore, no guidelines for policy implementation and no policy surveillance. The GATT is a contract, and the rules of the GATT relate to the contractual obligations of contracting parties, not to the policies of those countries. The FOGS proposal, in effect, places all the weight of systemic reform on the surveillance mechanism. This situation resembles that described in Crockett's paper of the stage of building coordination in the international monetary field after the move to flexible exchange rates in the mid-1970s. But the situation with respect to the GATT is more difficult if only because it lacks most of the characteristics of an institution, especially an adequate capacity for strong and continuing analytical and informational contributions.

Nonetheless, the adoption of the FOGS proposal would certainly be a welcome step in the right direction. However, at the December 1988 ministerial meeting in Montreal, because the European Community and the United States failed to reach agreement on agricultural reform, the areas in which agreement was reached—including FOGS—were put "on hold" pending a meeting of officials in the first week of April 1989. The international public good of the multilateral trading system as a whole was thus put "on hold." The next test of the Kindleberger hypothesis will take place in April in Geneva.

Jacques J. Polak

The Revival of Policy Coordination

Policy coordination was given a new lease on life when in 1985 the United States reverted to a more traditional attitude on exchange rates from free floating to a managed float—and hence, inevitably, on monetary cooperation as well. A managed float requires close contact among the main participants on critical issues of management: when and where to intervene, by how much, by whom, at whose risk. Intimately connected with this range of issues are the participants' monetary policy positions, which will have to be such as to produce interest rate differentials consonant with the agreed understandings on exchange rates (whatever their degree of precision). One would expect from past experience that potential creditors in intervention arrangements will seek assurances that the underlying payments imbalances were being addressed—whether out of concern for the system or worry about the assets they were acquiring. Thus, in situations of severe imbalance, exchange rate management must be backstopped by understandings among the parties involved on fiscal and balance of payments policies of the deficit countries and, if the latter are in a strong enough bargaining position, of the surplus countries as well.

Although exchange rate management for the major currencies has implications for all countries in the system, it must be conducted by a small group of countries with five or seven being a plausible number. The particular version of exchange rate management applied to date has also required a high degree of secrecy.

This, in broad strokes, is the arrangement that has evolved within the Group of Seven over the last three years. It has so far produced a soft landing for the U.S. dollar, in a context of satisfactory growth. The practice of close monetary consultation that has been re-established as part of the process proved particularly valuable when the U.S. Federal Reserve had to deal with the liquidity crisis that followed from the October 1987 stock market crash; it is good to know that such close consultation will occur in the event of future shocks.

The bare bones of the arrangement have been fleshed out with procedures for mutual surveillance in which the Managing Director and the staff of the IMF play a certain role. All this is well described—I believe for the first time—in Crockett's paper. I also welcome the paper's use of plain words to describe some of the relevant concepts. Thus "coordination" is, correctly, translated as "joint policymaking"[1] and "indicators" are de-glamorized to "the statistical basis for [the Group of Seven] discussions."

Some, such as U.S. Treasury Secretary James Baker in his May 1988 speech in Paris, see these new arrangements as the nascent reformed monetary system. Crockett does not go that far. In particular, he notes the absence in these arrangements of an analytical framework to guide countries about their responsibilities in the adjustment process. Without such guidelines, the success of coordination is not assured; "consensus [on what needs to be done] may not always exist." I would not share Crockett's judgment that up to now the lack of agreed guidelines "has not been an impediment to the effective implementation of coordination." The fact that countries have strung together in their communiqués what were mostly their individual wish lists for action does not constitute joint policymaking. Nor would I consider the Louvre Accord, which was an attempt to stabilize exchange rates at what was clearly the wrong level, as an example of effective coordination.

The statistical and analytical exercises in which the Group of Seven are engaged may prove useful in helping policymakers in each of the countries better understand the mechanism that steers (and sometimes fails to steer) the economies of the six others. If valuable techniques—such as—for monitoring surface, they may be applicable to the Fund's own surveillance of all its members. But the process as such, limited as it is to about half a dozen countries, cannot become the new international monetary system. Any international system must be applicable to all countries. While broadly based institutions, such as the Fund and the Organization for Economic Cooperation and Development (OECD), have every reason to welcome collaborative group

---

[1] Wallich's often cited definition of coordination (Crockett, this volume) as "a significant modification of national policies in recognition of international economic interdependence" has obvious operational difficulties. This definition assumes that countries first formalize policies without recognition of action by others and then modify these policies. If coordination works well, the process of policymaking would not contain such a two-step procedure and "modification" could not be pinpointed. For a discussion of the concepts of cooperation and policy coordination, see Horne and Masson (1988).

arrangements, such as those among the European Community (EC) and the Group of Seven countries, they cannot contract out chunks of their surveillance tasks to any such groups. Specifically, failure to adjust by a major country remains an issue of prime concern to the Fund and to the OECD, even if such failure can be attributed to a breakdown of the bargaining process within the Group of Seven.

In this context let me dispose rapidly of two notions (both fortunately, absent from Crockett's paper) that relate the Group of Seven to the world. One is that these are, broadly speaking, the countries that matter in the system. As I already mentioned, that proposition is not widely off the mark as far as exchange rate management is concerned, although the Group of Ten (including Switzerland) would come closer. It is nowhere near the truth as far as world payments imbalances are concerned. Perhaps the best piece of evidence on this score is found in the October 1988 U.S. Treasury Department's Report to the Congress required under the Omnibus Trade Act. The report devotes a total of nine lines to the developments in the United Kingdom, France, Italy, and Canada and seven pages to four other "economies" (two of which are not even countries): South Korea, Singapore, Taiwan Province of China, and Hong Kong. The second notion is that the Group of Seven watch over the interests of the rest of the world thanks to the presence of (a) the Fund's Managing Director in some of their meetings, and (b) a global price index, including gold and oil, in their indicator kit. No comment seems required.

In his final paragraphs, Crockett hints at some ideas of how the Group of Seven process of coordination could develop into a basis for systemic reform. One of these would be "to develop an analytical framework that would provide clearer guidance to countries concerning their responsibilities in the adjustment process." The other: "The development of standards for appraising developments in key indicators." The second approach is, rather obviously, contained in the first: an "appropriate path" (the term is U.S. Treasury Secretary Baker's) for an economy is obviously one that is compatible with its performance under the adjustment process.

Surely, there is little new in these suggestions. The Fund and the OECD have written on these subjects throughout their history. They also practice what they preach. In its annual consultations with member countries the Fund does not hesitate to appraise whether countries observe their responsibilities under the adjustment process. There are, no doubt, imperfections and uncertainties in the practices underlying these exercises. In particular, the demarcation line between sustainable (and perhaps desirable) and unsustainable (and for that reason alone undesirable) payments imbalances is sometimes difficult to place. International organizations can do much to bring greater clarity to this issue, the more so since individual countries may have biased views on the correct label to be put on other countries' imbalances. But further work should build on current practice, with its recognized strengths and weaknesses, rather than set out to re-invent the wheel. The balance of my presentation develops the subject of Crockett's paper from this historic angle.

Decentralized Adjustment in the IMF and the OECD

The achievement of the Fund's purposes (including "the expansion and balanced growth of international trade") requires that countries pursue policies aimed at internal and external balance. Internal balance refers to the achievement, over the medium term, of "full" employment growth. External balance is defined as a surplus or deficit on current account that is not in excess of what the country can finance over the medium term.

During most of the postwar period, it could readily be assumed that countries would, in their own interest, pursue what they considered the maximum sustainable rate of growth, so that internal balance need not be considered as a matter of international concern other than that it constituted an accepted constraint on policies to deal with external imbalance. But this has not always been the case. The "scarce currency" provisions in the Articles of Agreement of the Fund were intended to provide an international corrective against the risk that the United States might be unwilling or unable to reverse a sharp decline in domestic demand and thus, through a persistently low level of imports, make the dollar scarce to other countries. The United Nations Charter includes a full employment pledge (Article 55) and in its early years the UN tried actively to implement that pledge. In the period of stagflation and reduced growth of the last 15 years, international organizations such as the OECD and the Fund have again become concerned about whether countries were not underperforming on the domestic side of their adjustment obligations.

This was much less a matter of concern in the intervening years. When Working Party No. 3 of the Economic Policy Committee of the OECD issued its report on the *Balance of Payments Adjustment Process* in 1966,[2] it took as its premise that "each country seeks to achieve a number of economic and social objectives, including full employment and a satisfactory rate of growth . . . . " (para. 9).

The assumption that internal balance could be assumed to be taken care of focused countries' responsibilities to the international monetary system on the balance of payments adjustment action that they could be expected to take and to describe the substance of collaboration on international monetary problems as action by all countries in accordance with the internationally agreed rules of the *adjustment process*.

An attempt to make these rules explicit, with policy prescriptions lined up in accordance with the diagnosed cause of the disequilibrium that required

---

[2] The report was commissioned by the Ministers and Governors of the Group of Ten as a complement to the study by their deputies on international liquidity.

reversal, was made in the Working Party No. 3 report just referred to. The same general approach was contained in the 1974 report of the Committee on Reform of the International Monetary System (Committee of 20).[3] That report states that, as part of "reformed world monetary order": "There will be a better working of the adjustment process in which adequate methods to assure timely and effective balance of payments adjustment by both surplus and deficit countries will be assisted by improved international consultation in the Fund . . . ." (p. 8).

Much of the effort of the Committee of 20 was directed toward making it more difficult for deficit countries to finance deficits by incurring liabilities, thus avoiding adjustment. Universal "asset settlement" was proposed to ensure the impact of deficits on countries' reserves, and thus to force adjustment action on deficit countries. Reserve indicators were proposed to signal the need for adjustment on the part of both surplus and deficit countries, and these signals were to have been reinforced by means of sanctions set off when the reserve indicators pointed to large and persistent disequilibria.

It should be noted that both reports envisaged that imbalances would be corrected in a "decentralized" or "atomistic" manner. Each country that experienced an imbalance that was large in terms of its trade or reserves would act to bring that imbalance down. If all countries followed that rule, all imbalances in the system would be reduced to a harmless level. While new shocks would, of course, continue to bring about new disequilibria, general adherence to the rule would keep the total degree of imbalance in the system within acceptable bounds.[4]

As the Committee of 20 report notes, the decentralized approach to the adjustment process that it favors fits naturally into the Fund's existing consultation procedure. In these consultations, the economic situation of countries is considered one at a time, and recommendations for adjustment are formulated for those countries that show evidence of persistent international imbalances.

Subject to certain qualifications, this decentralized approach, functioning within the framework of a number of agreed rules, did not need to rely on

---

[3] Crockett does not refer to the 1972–74 reform exercise. While that exercise had only few memorable successes, it did produce an earlier attempt by the United States to push surplus countries into adjustment action by the use of indicators (on that occasion, reserve indicators).

[4] A formal requirement for this proposition to be true is that individual adjustment actions taken sequentially by countries lead to a convergence of all balances toward zero. This seems highly plausible if all adjustment action proceeds through demand management, provided overshooting by excessive adjustment is avoided as countries are aware of each others' adjustment actions. It is not quite so obvious in those cases where adjustment is sought by exchange rate or other action in terms of relative prices. Here it is quite possible for country P to achieve a desired overall improvement which consists of a larger improvement against Q, offset by a deterioration against R. If Q now devalues to correct its larger imbalance, will the adjustment process still converge? The question bothered us in the early days of the Fund, but an analysis conducted at the time produced reasonably convincing evidence that even for adjustment by exchange rate policy the atomistic approach would provide convergent results (Polak and Liu, 1954).

explicit coordination for the effective functioning of the system. There are a few references in the Working Party No. 3 report to the benefits of international policy coordination (paras. 50, 64, 65, and 71), but the main tenor of its approach is that if each country takes care of its own payments imbalances in the right way, the needs of the system will be met. The Committee of 20 report also lacks a discussion of policy coordination as such; countries undertake only that, in choosing among different ways to adjust, they "will take into account repercussions on other countries as well as internal considerations" (p. 8). Under an alternative definition of coordination, one could say that seen from the present perspective, the Bretton Woods era was "one of significant policy coordination," but achieved not by *ad hoc* action but "through countries adjusting their policies in response to the discipline imposed by the rules, and accepting the right of international institutions to comment on and criticize their policies" (Group of 30, 1988, p. 8).

Decentralized versus Coordinated Adjustment

There are some particularly attractive features to the process of decentralized decision making, which stand out in contrast to some of the difficulties presented by collective decision making on adjustment.

First, the decentralized approach answers the question of which country should take action and how much. (It does not answer the question of what action should be taken; the OECD Working Party No. 3 report attempts to define the policy prescription on the basis of the cause of the disequilibrium; the Committee of 20 report, less ambitiously, simply leaves the choice to the country.) Each country with a substantial unsustainable external disequilibrium should take action sufficient to reduce its disequilibrium to manageable proportions.

Second, the decentralized approach is likely to put the adjustment burden to a large extent on the country where the disequilibrium originates. Although this point is not touched upon in either of the reports on adjustment referred to, it is their implied message and it constitutes an important political argument in support of that approach. If, starting from a position of world payments equilibrium, country A expands credit too much, thus bringing about a large current account deficit, payments surpluses in countries B to Z will, of course, sum to the same amount. But the individual surpluses will be relatively small in proportion to the trade flows of these countries, unless A accounts for a very large share of world trade. Thus, in terms of its proportional disequilibrium (measures for example of a percentage of imports), A will show up as the prime candidate for adjustment. Similarly, if B allows its economy to slump into a deep depression, its large surplus will stand out against many relatively small deficits.

Compare these features of the decentralized approach to adjustment with those of a coordinated approach under which countries—in practice, the main industrial countries—consult in order to reach agreement on a set of policies to bring about the best possible performance of their economies. In principle— and this is the basis for its intuitive appeal—the latter approach can always produce results that are better (or at least not worse) than those achieved by decentralized action. This is because the collaborating countries have the option to agree on the actions that would follow from that approach if they consider it to be optimal, and on something else if they perceive a better course (Cooper, 1985, p. 1227). In that sense, policy coordination is a positive sum game. However, as Cooper has also pointed out, that game is likely to be played by the rules of a zero sum game, since that is what the distribution of the positive gain comes down to. There is no assurance that agreement on a positive sum solution will be reached, since some players may be unwilling to settle for a loss compared to the "fair share" of the collective gain that they had hoped to attain. In a real sense, under the coordinated approach, the better is the enemy of the good. Under the coordinated approach, there is no single answer as to who should do how much to remedy a given disequilibrium situation: any disequilibrium can be removed by an infinite number of combinations of actions by deficit and surplus countries. Countries that have sorted out internally the "best" balance among conflicting national objectives will attach a disutility to the adoption of another package of policies. In the probably rare cases where internal optima are unstable—i.e., where different parts of the same government pull with about equal strength toward different policy packages—coordination may lead to the attainment of an international optimum that is indeed better for all. The 1978 Bonn Summit is cited as the prime example of such a case.

In the context of our present analysis it is irrelevant that, with the benefit of hindsight, most observers in the Federal Republic of Germany consider that their country made a mistake in agreeing to the expansionary policy package in mid-1978; it is not unknown for countries to make policy mistakes even without the help of advice from abroad and one German participant has raised the question of whether Germany would not have followed the same course of action without the Summit (Tietmeyer, in Guth, 1988, p. 137). But it is a relevant comment on the functioning of international policymaking at its historic best that the Bonn deal took about two years to negotiate (Group of 30, 1988, p. 14).

In the absence of unstable national optima, "policy coordination" implies negotiation, or a power struggle, to determine which country accepts what share of the collective adjustment burden. In this process, which is essentially political since there is no single technical answer to this question, appeals to national and international public opinion have a role to play. As U.S. spokesmen have made clear, policy coordination is a game for ministers rather than their deputies, and while the Managing Director of the Fund and his staff have a useful role to play, their participation was not sought for the purpose of providing guidance on the desired outcome.

Recent experience—as well as the time consumed before the Bonn agreement was reached—makes it clear that the willingness of a group of countries to attempt policy coordination does not guarantee a coordinated policy outcome within a reasonable period of time. The indeterminacy of the approach puts a premium on "patience," the ability of one partner to wait for the other to move (Basevi, 1988). Since "unsustainable" situations can usually be sustained a little longer, the coordinated approach carries a built-in delay factor (Guth, 1988, p. 212). Any resulting postponement of adjustment is costly in any event; but the delay factor may prove extremely costly if on some occasion the game of "chicken" is carried on a little too long.

The risk of failure of the policy coordination approach has a bearing on the need for rules barring mutually destructive policies. Cooper has pointed out (1985, p. 1226) that if an atomistic adjustment process is to lead to a satisfactory development of the world economy, it needs to be constrained by rules that preclude countries resorting to certain undesirable policies. Thus something like the General Agreement on Tariffs and Trade (GATT) rules are necessary so that countries do not deal with trade imbalances by successive retaliatory rounds of tariffs or trade restrictions, leading to the mutual destruction of international trade. Similarly, an effective rule against competitive depreciation (appreciation) is necessary to avoid countries trying to push unemployment (inflation) on each other by successive rounds of exchange rate changes. The Bretton Woods system provided such a rule; it is doubtful whether in the absence of the provision for Fund approval of par value changes that was contained in the Fund's original Articles, the present Fund rules for surveillance can achieve the same end. A similar comment applies to the third competitive instrument in countries' economic tool chest: interest rates. Interest rate differentials are effective instruments to guide exchange rates and capital movements toward desired positions. But unless there is an understanding that this instrument will be used only in a manner to promote adjustment, and not to frustrate it, successive national actions can produce a world interest rate that is too high for an optimum level of world employment (or output) or too low for the achievement of an optimum degree of price stability.

A clear distinction needs thus to be made between a coordinated *approach* and a coordinated *outcome*. Perhaps, over time, the practice of the former may lead with increasing frequency to the latter. But if a coordinated outcome is to be ensured, countries will have to commit themselves beyond the coordinated approach, to an agreed form of collective decision making. I have the impression that the discussion on policy coordination in the Fund does not always pay sufficient attention to this distinction. While it recognizes the risks of misguided coordination, such as maintaining exchange rates at an inappropriate level, the Fund's work tends *to assume* that coordination will lead to "better" policies.

Thus (*pace* Cooper), the coordinated approach is as much in need of agreed limitations on the use of competitive policy instruments as is the decentralized approach, if sub-optimal outcomes are to be avoided. The theoretical literature on policy coordination abounds with examples in which countries have the option of adopting mutually destructive competitive policies as a means of driving their partners toward the acceptance of Pareto optimal solutions. To cite just one, Basevi (1988) suggests the need to equip countries with the freedom to act and react by means of high tariff rates in order to reach agreement on the stance of monetary policy. For such threats to be effective, they must be credible, and credible threats carry an uncertainty cost of their own. The threat of rampant protectionism was certainly present at the 1985 Plaza meeting and it is not difficult to discern some periods in the last three years when the United States relied on the threat of a further fall of the dollar as a negotiating tactic (Funabashi, 1988).

Arrangements aiming at policy coordination are no substitute for rules that put certain policy options out of bounds, whether coordination is successful or not. These rules need not be enshrined in the statutes of international organizations. Under the overly rigid but unwritten rule of the gold standard regime, the major players in the international monetary system could take for granted that exchange rate changes were not available—either to themselves or to their competitors—as an instrument of adjustment. In what has been called the present non-system, it might not be beyond the realm of the possible for central bankers to have a firm understanding about avoiding competitive interest rate escalation even in situations in which their finance ministers could not reach agreement on the coordination of fiscal or other policies.

The Limits of Decentralized Decision Making on Adjustment

The preceding discussion indicates that there is considerable scope in the system of surveillance by international institutions for decentralized adjustment and one-on-one (sometimes called, bilateral) surveillance. This is implicitly recognized in the Fund's technique of individual country consultations.

It can be said for almost all countries that their policies are overwhelmingly more important for their own economic health than for the impact they have on the world economy. In the Fund's annual consultations, much attention is paid to the importance for the rest of the world of the policies pursued by the United States, Japan, and Germany. But in the consultations with the other members of the Group of Seven (the United Kingdom, France, Italy, and Canada), the focus is entirely on the benefits (or otherwise) that each of these countries derives from its own policies. In none of these consultations does the Fund argue for a particular stance of macroeconomic policies as being desirable from a world point of view. (The Fund does make a point in consultations with these and other countries on two issues of importance to the rest of the world: protectionism and foreign aid.)

Similarly, in the par value era, the Fund was prepared (I believe, correctly) to deal with almost all proposals for par value changes on an individual basis. The 1949 devaluation of sterling and many other currencies should probably have been an exception, but the Fund hardly played a role in those currency adjustments. On the very different occasion of the devaluation of sterling in 1967, the Fund acted to prevent other countries' repeating the 1949 model of following sterling. Clearly, the major currency realignment of 1971 was one that needed to be treated on a multilateral basis.

The atomistic approach to adjustment would benefit as much as a coordinated approach from the widest availability to each member of knowledge of the policies—and, if possible, the policy intentions—of other members. While efforts at joint policymaking have a built-in information content, every effort should be made to extend that aspect of collaboration to the Fund membership as a whole. The Fund's regular consultations and its special contacts in connection with the World Economic Outlook (WEO) exercise provide the channels for this. While there is reason to keep the contents of negotiations among the Group of Seven secret, I would doubt that significantly more policy description transpires at the meetings of the Group of Seven deputies than during Fund consultations. Thus, there would not seem to be a systemic reason for Cooper's assumption that in the absence of systematic policy coordination countries need to be condemned to design their own policies without an adequate understanding of the policies of partner countries (Cooper, 1985, p. 2324).

There is one thing that a process of adjustment to imbalances does *not* ensure, namely, a satisfactory level of world activity. In general, adjustment by deficit countries will have a negative impact on world demand and adjustment by surplus countries, a positive impact. The prevailing state of the world economy should set the direction, positive or negative, in which the balance of the adjustment impacts of individual countries is slanted. There is no reason to expect the separate adjustment actions of individual countries to conform to this rule. In some contexts, policy coordination may rather easily provide the answer. Where differential monetary policies are used by a group of major countries, their actions should be based on a judgment of the direction in which interest rates in the world in general should move. In an inflationary context, deficit countries should raise their rates, perhaps acting alone or by more than the increases in the interest rates in surplus countries. By contrast, in a deflationary context, surplus countries should lower their rates—or lower them further than the decreases of the rates in deficit countries. The learning experience of the Group of Seven cooperation in monetary policy in the last two years suggests that action along these lines is effectively being developed among policymakers. When interest rates are not a major instrument of adjustment, it may be more difficult to achieve an appropriate balance of positive and negative adjustment effects by policy coordination; it may also be more difficult to define, or to agree on, an appropriate balance.

This raises a major challenge for international organizations: to guide the decentralized adjustment process, on which they have to rely even with an active Group of Seven, to the desired result in terms of aggregate demand.

This was always seen as one of the most important functions of the Fund's WEO exercises. The belief that a price index of primary commodities could by itself provide the needed guidance is a throwback to proposals for commodity currency arrangements of earlier decades. Only a careful analysis of the balance of expansionary and contractionary forces in the world economy can guide the Fund and its members as to where the main weight of adjustment should fall, and even then the result is likely to be far from perfect. In applying the inferences that can be drawn from the WEO to the situations of industrial countries (or, for that matter, to the correct guidance of coordinated policy-making in the Group of Seven), attention will in any event have to be paid to the needs of individual countries. It can never make sense to encourage a country with a debilitating deficit to postpone or mitigate its adjustment "for the good of the system" (Polak, 1984, p. 251).

It seems to me that, consciously or not, this issue of maintaining adequate noninflationary growth in the world economy underlies the concern about the "incompatibility of countries' economic objectives" that pervades the coordination literature. The particular risk envisaged is that the pursuit by countries of an incompatible set of current account targets[5] could propel the world economy into a depression (if the aims summed up to a collective surplus) or into an inflationary binge (if they summed up to a collective deficit).[6]

The answer to this concern is that the problem as posited does not exist and would not be amenable to a coordinated resolution if it did. Most countries simply do not have current account objectives that drive their economic policies. Insofar as governments have views on the current account at all,[7]

---

[5] An earlier concern, about incompatible *reserve* aims, is no longer relevant. There was reason for concern in the 1960s about the potential risk of deflation if countries attempted to achieve a secular increase in their international reserves that would in total exceed the growth in the supply of such reserves. This risk was averted by international action to increase, when necessary, the supply of reserves through the creation of SDRs, not by attempts to coordinate countries' demand for reserves to fit the available supply. Since the mid-1970s, the issue has to a large extent disappeared. With reserves consisting almost exclusively of reserve currencies, the demand for such currencies on the part of foreign official holders has become merely one element in the total demand for national money that central banks in the reserve currency countries have to take into account in setting monetary policy.

[6] The OECD in particular paid a great deal of attention to this issue in the 1960s. The Working Party No. 3 report devotes two sections to balance of payments aims and expresses interest in assessing "the mutual consistency of different countries' [balance of payments] aims and their overall implications for the allocation of world resources." Except with respect to the question of reserve aims, the interest in compatibility of aims shown in the report seems soon to have subsided, although it was revived after the first oil shock in the form of exercises to "allocate" the effects of that shock.

[7] If countries did attach great importance to their current account balances as guides to policy, they would be sure of having good statistics for them. The fact that in recent years the world's current account statistics summed up to a combined deficit of about $100 billion instead of the theoretical zero is proof in itself that the current account is not uppermost in governments' minds as they plan their economic policies.

these must be in terms of schedules, not of single points. If the preferred points on the schedule are reported as the targets *rebus sic stantibus*, any incompatibility among these points will be resolved as each country moves along its schedule. The savings/investment connection is particularly instructive in this context. Ask all firms and households about their savings and investment targets for next year and the figures you will collect will likely be incompatible. These ex ante positions will set in motion interest rates, incomes, and other variables to produce the inevitable ex post equality of saving and investment. National governments do not make it their business to reconcile private savings and investment targets; they are, however, concerned about the outcomes in terms of growth, inflation, and other variables. By the same token, international institutions need not concern themselves with the reconciliation of national savings-*minus*-investment targets or current account targets (Polak, 1977; Salop and Spitäller, 1980; and Corden, 1986).

It is a good thing that that is so. If current account targets needed to be reconciled, a meeting of, say, the Group of Seven would not get very far. In the last 15 years, large current account surpluses have accrued to some small countries, such as some of the Gulf oil exporters or even to territories such as Taiwan Province of China. Large current account deficits have been run by many developing countries, and, of course, by the United States. Had these figures constituted policy targets, any attempt at reconciliation would surely have failed. Fortunately, a market mechanism was available to perform the reconciliation task. Large surpluses, such as those of the oil exporters, produced matching deficits through the process of recycling. Large deficits, such as that of the United States, produced matching surpluses as high real interest rates raised saving and compressed investment throughout the world. It would not be difficult to think of more attractive outcomes for the world economy in the 1970s and the 1980s, but attempts at reconciliation of current account targets would not have been the way to achieve such outcomes.

References

Baker, James A., III, "Economic Policy Coordination and International Monetary Reform," Remarks to the Council on Foreign Relations (Paris, May 20, 1988).

Basevi, Giorgio, "International Monetary Cooperation under Tariff Threats," at a symposium on International Trade and Global Development (Erasmus University, Rotterdam, 1988).

Committee of Twenty, *International Monetary Reform* (Washington: International Monetary Fund, 1974).

Cooper, Richard N., "Economic Interdependence and Coordination of Economic Policies," in *Handbook of International Economics*, ed. by Ronald W. Jones and Peter B. Kenen, Vol. 2 (Amsterdam: 1985).

Corden, W. Max, *Inflation, Exchange Rates and the World Economy,* 3rd ed., Chapter 12 (Chicago: 1986).

Funabashi, Yoichi, *Managing the Dollar: From the Plaza to the Louvre,* Institute for

International Economics (Washington: IIE, 1988).

Group of Thirty, *International Macroeconomic Policy Coordination* (New York and London: 1988).

Guth, Wilfried (moderator), *Economic Policy Coordination* (Washington: International Monetary Fund, 1988).

Horne, Jocelyn, and Paul R. Masson, "Scope and Limits of International Economic Cooperation and Policy Coordination," *Staff Papers*, International Monetary Fund (Washington), Vol. 35 (June 1988), pp. 259–96.

OECD, Working Party No. 3 of the Economic Policy Committee, *The Balance of Payments Adjustment Process* (Paris: OECD, 1966).

Polak, Jacques J., "International Coordination of National Economic Policies," in *U.S.-European Monetary Relations*, ed. by Samuel I. Katz (Washington: 1977).

————, "The Role of the International Monetary Fund," in *The International Monetary System: Forty Years After Bretton Woods* (Federal Reserve Bank of Boston, 1984).

————, and T. C. Liu, "Stability of the Exchange Rate Mechanism in a Multi-Country System," *Econometrica*, Vol. 22 (1954), pp. 360–89.

Salop, Joanne, and Erich Spitäller, "Why Does the Current Account Matter?" *Staff Papers*, International Monetary Fund (Washington: March 1980), Vol. 27, pp. 101–34.

U.S. Treasury Department, *Report to the Congress on International Economic and Exchange Rate Policy*, prepared under the 1988 Omnibus Trade and Competitiveness Act (Washington: October 15, 1988).

10

Macroeconomic Interactions Between the North and South

*Anton Muscatelli and David Vines**

I. North-South Interactions

At present there is renewed interest in the macroeconomic linkages between the Organization for Economic Cooperation and Development (OECD) (what we often refer to as the "North") and the developing countries (often known as the "South"). This interest was initially a response to the developing country debt crisis, with its consequences not only for the developing world, but also for the stability of financial markets in the North.

It is now recognized that the problem lies far deeper. Recent studies of international interdependence and policy coordination among the Northern OECD countries (for example, Buiter and Marston, 1985, and Bryant and Portes, 1987) suffer from a missing link, namely, the Southern economies. The failure to model the behavior of the South may have distorted the results of these studies of the Northern economies.

This paper gives the preliminary findings of a large research project that we are undertaking to investigate these issues. Our ultimate aim is to construct a four-regional econometric model of the South (Latin America, Africa, the Asian newly industrializing economies, and other Asia) that incorporates these groups within a global econometric model, which itself distinguishes the Group of Seven countries and a number of other regions in the world economy. This enterprise involves large amounts of data, detailed economet-

---

*This paper forms part of a research project on North-South Macroeconomic Interactions, directed by David Currie and David Vines and carried out under the auspices of the Centre for Economic Policy Research (CEPR). Financial support from ESCOR and from the University of Glasgow is gratefully acknowledged. The paper partly draws on Currie and Vines (1988b). We are grateful to our colleague, Stan Hurn, for helpful comments on earlier drafts, and for technical assistance in preparing the paper. We also thank Paul Masson and Ralph Bryant for valuable comments on a previous draft.

ric investigation, and extensive computer simulations. But it also needs to be disciplined by a strong set of prior theoretical hypotheses about the nature of North-South interactions. This paper aims to discuss these hypotheses.

At an early stage of our work we decided to build two prototype simulation models to shed light on the nature of North-South interactions, and to aid econometric investigations. These prototypes are not "architectural drawings" of our larger model-building enterprise, but rather preliminary sketches. Our "Mark I" simulation model was described in Currie and others (1988). In what follows we present our "Mark II" (MkII) version. Our exposition uses this model to show how the projected parts of our investigation will be joined up. This model is not a rigorous or complete representation of reality.

The paper is organized as follows. Section II briefly reviews the key interdependencies between North and South. Section III describes the basic structure of the MkII model. Section IV discusses how we may model the South in practice. The two main questions addressed in this section are how our proposed empirical analysis of the South will draw upon the representation of the South in our purely theoretical MkII model, and, more generally, why modeling a region of the South is different from modeling an OECD country.

Section V discusses our proposed empirical modeling of global North-South interactions. Again our discussion is based on the MkII model. We focus on how our proposed analysis of North-South interactions will differ from existing models (for example, the OECD's INTERLINK model and the International Monetary Fund's MULTIMOD model).

Section VI presents two simulations carried out using the MkII model. These explore, in concrete terms, some of the key processes likely to be at work in our full empirical model. Section VII considers some of the key issues concerning strategic interactions and policy coordination on the agenda for future study. And Section VIII presents our conclusions.

II. Key Interdependencies Between North and South

This paper's focus is on the *global* macroeconomic interdependencies between North and South. (For a recent review of these interactions, see Currie, Muscatelli, and Vines, 1988, which summarizes earlier literature including thoughts on development, trade, and growth.) Our focus here is purely macroeconomic.

The linkages from North to South are well known: developing countries depend on OECD markets for exports, on OECD capital markets for finance, and on the import of OECD technology. The linkages from South to North are far less evident and are frequently regarded as having only a negligible impact on Northern economies. As noted earlier, this assumption may be incorrect, for two major reasons.

Interdependence Through Commodity Markets

The first major influence of the South upon the North operates through commodity markets: shortages of raw materials in the South may raise world commodity prices, and, conversely, surpluses may depress world commodity prices. This influence has both a demand-side and a supply-side aspect. On the demand side, any expansion in the OECD leads to commodity shortages and higher commodity prices. These boost the export revenue of Southern countries, loosen their balance of payments constraint, and enable them to import more from the North again.[1] Similarly, any contraction in the OECD is augmented by the effects of falling commodity prices on the demand of the South.

On the supply side, the linkages are more subtle. Clearly, in the short run, an expansion in the OECD will, by bidding up commodity prices, cause inflation in the North quite independently of what happens in Northern labor or output markets.[2] This we might call "supply-side interdependence." But it is only one aspect of that phenomenon. Supply-side interdependence has a longer-term aspect as well, related to capital accumulation. We particularly wish to highlight the effects of that link. This spillover effect works in the following manner: any failure to expand in the North will, by jeopardizing the export revenue of the South, force a reduction of domestic absorption there. Because consumption is difficult to squeeze (owing to, say, permanent income consumption smoothing, and/or wage bargaining and political pressures to defend incomes in the face of worsened terms of trade) the brunt of this reduction in absorption tends to fall on investment. The reduced investment then leads to lower productive capacity and, therefore, to lower Southern supply in the longer term (see Fritsch, 1988, on Brazil).[3] To the extent that this occurs in the primary commodity producing sector, the effect is to alter the balance between supply and demand in world commodity markets, raising commodity prices, causing inflation in the North, depressing profitability there, and retarding Northern investment. Hence, low investment in the South, arising from low export revenues, may impair medium-term growth prospects in the North.

Some observers are now concerned that this supply-side interdependence might prevent the OECD economies from maintaining their present growth

---

[1] Kanbur and Vines (1987) show formally how the rise in commodity prices augments the global Keynesian multiplier emanating from the demand expansion in the North. This is explored in more detail by Moutos and Vines (1989). See Khan and Knight (1986) for an analysis of import compression.

[2] In the simplest technical terms, dearer raw materials depress the real wage that the industrial sector in the North can pay to its workforce and so lessen the scope for activity in the North to be expanded without generating claims for real wages in excess of what the economy can afford. In effect, the NAIRU in the North comes to correspond to a lower level of activity. This feature is built into both the model described in this paper and that of Moutos and Vines (1989).

[3] This feature is also built into MULTIMOD (see Masson and others, 1988).

impetus even if other global economic problems, such as the U.S. current account deficit, can be resolved. The proposal by U.S. Treasury Secretary James Baker, for the use of a commodity price index as an indicator of inflationary potential, points to an awareness of this possible problem.[4]

Interdependence Through Capital Markets

The behavior of the South also affects the North through the operation of international capital markets. In cases where the South is not totally excluded from world capital markets, high Northern interest rates depress investment in the South. The effect is even more dramatic where the South faces a vertical supply curve of new loans. Profitable projects in such highly indebted Southern countries are likely to go unfinanced, because of the potential threat of default. Either lowering Northern interest rates or eliminating the "market failure" associated with the risk premium would enable investment to flow to the South again.

This channel of interdependence also operates through the process of capital accumulation. It too has a demand- and a supply-side aspect. In the short run, an increased flow of investment to the South increases the demand for capital goods produced in the North—with an expansionary effect on the OECD (see Moutos and Vines, 1989). But over the longer term, it will also increase the ability of the developing countries to supply more exports to the OECD countries. Both North and South would benefit from this longer-run effect, since markets could then achieve a more desirable global allocation of resources.

Arrangements such as debt-equity swaps have been proposed to alleviate the problem of default risk,[5] and Gilbert and Powell (1988) analyze other innovative ideas in this area. Changes in macroeconomic policies in the OECD countries could also help alleviate this problem—if they had the effect of either reducing interest rates or the probability of default (see Vos, 1988). Furthermore, policies in the South can affect default risk. These issues are discussed below.

III. A Simulation Model of North-South Interaction

Estimated empirical macroeconometric models that focus on North-South interaction already exist. These include those by Beenstock (1988); van

---

[4] Commodity prices turned down sharply in late 1988, following an even sharper rise in 1987 and early 1988 (see Boughton and Branson, 1988, and Holthan and Durand, 1987). But, at the time of writing, the outlook for metals still bears out the above remarks. (We thank Christopher Gilbert for this point.) See also Bruno and Sachs (1985), Beckerman and Jenkinson (1986), Giovanetti (1985), and Moutos and Vines (1989) for an analysis of the influence of commodity prices on the supply performance of the North.

[5] However, Bulow and Rogoff (1988) have recently questioned the usefulness for the South of such schemes as debt buy-backs and debt-equity swaps.

Wijnbergen (1985); Marquez and Pauly (1986), an application of which can be found in Hughes Hallett (1988); and the IMF's MULTIMOD model (see Masson and others, 1988). Vos (1988) is also developing a model. This section sketches out a nonestimated simulation model of North-South interaction. The model has a number of features in common with our Mark I model presented in Currie and others (1988). Simple simulation models of the type presented here may aid in understanding the complex interaction processes reviewed in Section II. Such an understanding is a useful preliminary to the construction and use of fully estimated econometric models, even though such models are necessarily oversimplified abstractions of the real world. They aid in understanding in two ways. First, simulations can reveal something about interactions (two simulations will be presented in Section VI). Second, they act as a framework in which to set qualitative discussions of model specification. (We will use our model in this way in Sections IV and V.)

A brief description of the structure of the MkII model now follows. A detailed listing of the equations of the model, and the parameter values used, is provided in Appendix I, to which we refer. The description focuses on differences of treatment between the South and the North (which will be addressed in Section IV) and on interactions between them (discussed in Section V).

Differences Between South and North

Crucially, the model assumes that the South and North specialize in production, with the South producing exclusively primary commodities and the North, industrial goods. Consumers in both regions are assumed to consume both Northern and Southern goods. In contrast, specialization in production implies that the North supplies capital goods to both regions. This specialization is a common assumption in the theoretical trade and development literature (see, for example, Lewis, 1954; Findlay, 1980 and 1984; Taylor, 1983; Riedel, 1984; Currie, Muscatelli, and Vines, 1988; and Molana and Vines, 1989). It is obviously a great oversimplification; we will remove it when we come to empirical work. It is, however, a useful assumption when seeking to identify key processes because, in reality, the South is *relatively* specialized in primary products.

The structures of the two regions are dissimilar in a number of other respects. We now turn to these structures, focusing on the asymmetries between regions. We begin with the North, which is called Region 1 (see equations A1.16 to A1.36).

Our treatment of the stylized North follows a mainstream OECD type of macromodel, with an IS-LM structure augmented by consideration of the supply-side and of asset-stock accumulation processes. Output is demand-determined in the short run (see equations A1.16 to A1.23), but is constrained by productive capacity in the long run. Wages and prices adjust sluggishly according to an expectations-augmented Phillips curve (see equation A1.26).

Also, investment leads to capital accumulation, which augments productive capacity; this, in turn, affects the evolution of wages (see equations A1.24 to A1.28) and will be reflected in the long-run properties of the model. The North is assumed to possess developed financial markets, with wealth held in the form of speculative holdings of primary commodities as well as money and government bonds (see A1.29 and A1.30). For simplicity, secondary markets for capital and Southern debt are not modeled; both of these are included in wealth at face value (see equation A1.34). Goods markets as well as asset markets incorporate wealth effects, and a government budget constraint is incorporated (see equation A1.35); this implies that in the long run the model achieves a full-stock equilibrium. Government spending and the money supply are treated as exogenous policy instruments for the North, but the tax rate is treated as endogenous (see equation A1.36), to ensure against an unstable accumulation of debt of the kind associated with Blinder and Solow (1973).

Forward-looking behavior in the treatment of the North is introduced by assuming that the Northern long-term interest rate (which determines Northern investment) is a forward-looking convolution of the Northern short-term interest rate. The model is solved under perfect foresight so that the expected long rate, R_{1t}^{Le} is always correctly forecast.

Our treatment of the stylized South (see equations A1.1 to A1.15) is different from that of the North. Here, we simply state these differences; they are discussed in detail in Section IV.

In the South (equations A1.1 to A1.15), output is supply-determined at all times (see equation A1.1). This implies that a change in the employment of labor (see A1.2) or a change in the capital stock (see equation A1.12) will have immediate effects on output. Given the claims on output by the private sector and the government (consumption, investment, and government expenditure), exports are assumed to be the residual (see equation A1.9). Financial markets are assumed to be "underdeveloped" in the South. In this model we implement this assumption in two ways. First, the government finances its deficit only by increasing the money stock (see equation A1.14). Second, the cost of capital (in equation A1.11) reflects the interest rate charged by the North on the South's debt. This "Southern" interest rate is equal to the Northern short-term interest rate plus a risk premium that depends positively on the South's debt-export ratio (see equation A1.32). Debt accumulation in the South is purely a result of deficits on current account, with the exchange rate between the two regions assumed to be fixed. This model, therefore, assumes that the South is not constrained in the amounts it can borrow, although the presence of a risk premium will clearly discourage it to increase its borrowing without limit. In this model we assume that debt accumulation is kept under control through changes in Southern government spending on imports (see equation A1.8).

Commodity prices are assumed to be forward-looking, owing to the speculative demands for primary commodities (see equation A1.30). The model is solved under perfect foresight, so that dq^e is always correctly forecast. Formally, commodity prices must find that level such that, given the expected future price, the outstanding stock of them (see equation A1.22) is willingly held. This introduces another important asymmetry between price-formation of Southern goods and that of Northern goods, as the latter evolve sluggishly. This issue has begun to be treated in the macroeconomics literature (see Frankel, 1986; Boughton and Branson, 1988; and Moutos and Vines, 1988a, 1988b, and 1988c).

Interactions Between North and South

The MkII model includes a number of channels of interdependence between the North and South, both on the demand and the supply side.

On the demand side, the usual positive spillover effects between the two regions result from the trade balance linkage (see equation A1.7 to A1.10, and A1.18 and A1.23). As far as the South is concerned, given the fact that output is supply-determined in the short run, a Northern demand expansion will be beneficial insofar as it raises the price of primary commodities and improves the South's terms of trade. Fiscal expansions in the North are likely to be less beneficial to the South compared with monetary expansions (even in the absence of supply-side effects) simply because higher interest rates tend to increase the South's debt burden (see equation A1.13). These demand-side spillover effects were already present in our earlier MkI model (see Currie and others, 1988). They are likely to dominate in the short run.

On the supply side, since we have included capital accumulation and a full treatment of stock-flow effects, a number of channels of interdependence are introduced. These are likely to be of some importance in the medium to long run, as we suggested in Section II. The following types of supply-side effects are present in the model.

First, changes in commodity markets will feed through into changes in aggregate supply. Cheaper commodities will encourage Northern supply (both by encouraging investment and by lowering the real product wage of labor at any level of output; see equations A1.21 and A1.25). But cheaper commodities will do exactly the opposite in the South (see equation A1.3). These global supply responses to lower commodity prices—which reduce relative commodity output—are important parts of the equilibration process in global commodity markets and are familiar to students of North-South growth models (see Findlay, 1980 and 1984; Currie, Muscatelli, and Vines, 1988; and Molana and Vines, 1989).

Second, increases in world interest rates will also feed into aggregate supply by reducing capital accumulation in both regions (see equations A1.11 and A1.19). This contributes an additional consequence for the South (of higher Northern interest rates) over and above the effects on debt service. The decline in productive capacity may lower the longer-term supply of commodities from the South to the North and may worsen the South's longer-term trade balance.

Third, Southern debt and export performance will have a secondary feedback effect on the South's ability to invest, and on its debt service burden, via the risk premium (see equations A1.13 and A1.33). This will tend to augment any effects of higher Northern interest rates, on both the South's debt service burden and on the South's investment, since higher interest rates will tend to cause the debt-to-export ratio to increase.

Limitations of the Model: Diversity in the South

The MkII model is clearly a highly oversimplified framework in which to analyze North-South interactions. The key question at the outset is whether some assumptions made in this prototype model depart from reality so much that they make the MkII model unhelpful as a preliminary step in analyzing issues of North-South interdependence.

First, the assumption of complete specialization is clearly a gross simplification. A large number of developing countries have, since the 1970s, seen their manufacturing sectors expand considerably. By ignoring the South's potential to compete in manufacturing (illustrated by the performance of the South-East Asian newly industrializing economies), we neglect the significant effects on the North of switches in the composition of Southern production, which is the basis for Beenstock's "transition thesis" (Beenstock, 1982). An empirical model must distinguish among different Southern regions, in this connection. Second, the assumption that the South relies exclusively on the North for capital goods involves a similar oversimplification. Again this will differ greatly within the South. A third important question relates to the way we have modeled financial markets in the South in the MkII model, and in particular the availability of foreign lending. Treatment of this will need to distinguish between newly industrializing economies and the heavily indebted regions.

These objections suggest the need to distinguish among different developing countries when building an empirical model. This is at present lacking in existing global econometric models, and in building our empirical model we seek to construct a multisectoral model of the South (see Sections IV and V). Thus, the aggregate "South" in the MkII model is only a caricature.[6]

The following three sections show that this model may nevertheless be a useful device for a preliminary analysis of the channels of interdependence between North and South.

---

[6] We originally attempted to modify the MkII model to allow Southern goods to be used in production, and to allow both regions to produce both goods. The results would not be drastically affected if we assumed that the South mainly produced commodities, and the North mainly produced industrial goods.

IV. Empirical Modeling of the South

This section considers three key issues that will arise in the empirical modeling of four regions of the South, and illustrates why the MkII model may provide a helpful starting point. It also shows how we may wish to deviate from a MkII-type model in our applied work.

The Financial Sector of the South

In general, the capital markets of developing countries are not as well-developed as those of OECD countries. As a result, the usual portfolio equilibrium model paradigm (see, for instance, Tobin, 1982) seems particularly inappropriate. On the other hand, the modeling of financial intermediation in the presence of credit constraints is still in its infancy (for example, see van Wijnbergen, 1985), and while the estimation of credit rationing models is undertaken in some macromodels of individual developing countries, the incorporation of a full model of the credit market is not likely to be successful on aggregated data for groups of developing countries.

Thus, it seems best to treat most of the developing country regions as what McKinnon has called "overdraft economies" (by way of contrast with the "portfolio-allocation economies" described by Tobin). In such economies the government budget deficit and the balance of payments surplus play a vital role in affecting the domestic money supply. Arguably, the main instrument of monetary policy in such economies is fiscal policy, which, in the absence of a well-developed market for government debt, has a direct effect on domestic credit expansion. In such economies, the transmission mechanism from the budget deficit and balance of payments surplus to the quantity of money and, thence, to aggregate demand is crucial: the link with the monetary approach to the balance of payments should also be apparent (see McCallum and Vines, 1981, and Khan and Knight, 1981).

The treatment of the financial sector of the South in the MkII model does follow closely the above description. (See, in particular, equations A1.5, A1.14, and A1.15.) We have already illustrated the balance of payments stock-flow dynamics that such a system implies in Currie and others (1988). Such a set-up enables one to go on and study the stock-flow interconnections among foreign savings, private savings, and government savings, which lie behind current "three-gap" analyses of the developing country debt problem.

At the empirical level, we propose to retain this basic framework. An alternative, richer study of interest-rate determination seems a hopeless task, since this involves analysis of the factors affecting the ratio of money holdings to the value of nonmonetary financial assets along traditional portfolio lines. Data are scarce for such aggregates in many developing countries, and regional aggregation across heterogeneous financial systems is likely to complicate matters further.

On the other hand, we intend to develop the monetary sector illustrated in the MkII model by examining how changes in the stock of high-powered money affect the total money stock. This involves a simple analysis of the bank lending process, which appears essential, as our preliminary investigations have shown an important role for financial wealth in influencing consumption.

Inflation in the South

Views differ as to the appropriate way to model inflation in a developing country. One view notes the simplicity of the financial sector just discussed, especially the close link between monetary expansion and aggregate demand. Supporters of this view also take output to be supply-constrained. These two things, it is often suggested, point toward a monetarist-new classical approach to inflation as the appropriate one. Such an account does not, however, square with the suggestion that the money stock is endogenous to both the government budget constraint and the balance of payments.

An alternative account is provided by the "structuralist" theories of inflation (see Cardoso, 1981, and Taylor, 1983). In some versions of such models output is also supply-constrained, and an inflationary gap is created between the level of aggregate demand and this supply-constrained output level. Inflation is treated as a mechanism that eliminates this inflationary gap. Such an approach tends to ignore monetary developments that are treated as passively accommodating, and places much stress on the effect of redistributions between profits and wages on aggregate demand and on inflationary pressures. However, this account also seems unsatisfactory. Although endogenous to the budget deficit and balance of payments surplus, the money stock can clearly not be treated as passively accommodating, and the resulting money creation may have a significant effect on consumption, aggregate demand, and inflation.

On the demand side our MkII model of the South represents in part a reconciliation and development of these two views: the joint endogeneity of money, aggregate demand, and inflationary pressure is modeled. Furthermore, inflation itself narrows the gap between demand and supply, by an inflation tax (higher prices lower the real value of the V_2 term in the consumption function, A1.5). But the MkII model does not incorporate the effects of income distribution on aggregate demand. (We may be able to incorporate distributional effects into our consumption function—but a shortage of data for developing countries on wages and profits and on the split of private-sector income into company and personal sectors makes this unlikely.)

On the supply side, we have chosen in the MkII model to depict a Southern region that is supply-constrained, and, further, one in which real wages are entirely fixed exogenously. Output and employment are determined by the intersection of the demand for, and supply of, primary commodities. Unemployment is a Lewis-type phenomenon. An increased demand for primary commodities will cause commodity prices and wages to rise; it will only increase output and employment if it raises relative commodity prices. In this sense, our treatment of the supply side is classical, with output effects deriving solely from changes in labor supply and the capital stock deriving purely from changes in the interest rate and the terms of trade.

But existing empirical evidence for Latin America (Vial, 1987, and Adams and Vial, 1987) suggests that output is certainly not kept perpetually at full capacity through instantaneous price flexibility.

In fact, this treatment in the MkII model is acceptable only because of the assumption that the South does not possess an industrial sector. In an empirical model, we would wish to examine the effects on inflation of output deviating from its capacity level. This will involve an empirical investigation of the wage-price determination process for the different Southern regions, which will go well beyond the structure of equations A1.3 and A1.4. There are likely to be many similarities in such an account with models of the Northern inflationary process. On the other hand, the models will also have a "Southern flavor" as we take account of the relationship between supply constraints and the inflationary process. A two-way relationship can be expected here, as supply constraints affect the inflationary gap, while the effects of inflation on both consumption and investment will have an impact on supply.[7]

Investment Behavior in the South

Existing evidence on the behavior of aggregate investment in the South is rather scarce. One difficulty is that the treatment of investment behavior is closely tied to the assumptions about the debt accumulation process (discussed in detail in Section V). In the MkII model we treat the private-sector investment decisions in the South as "unconstrained" (that is, not rationed because of any shortage of external finance) (see equation A1.12). This is because the South's debt accumulation is not quantity-constrained by Northern lenders. In the MkII model it is Southern government policy that plays an important part in ensuring that the debt accumulation process is contained (see equation A1.8).

A number of issues have to be taken into account in considering the empirical modeling of investment. First, one has to consider the extent to which the South's investment is likely to be independent of the country's external indebtedness. In practice, the presence of a balance-of-payments constraint implies a constraint on the availability of capital goods if the Southern region under scrutiny is dependent upon the North for these goods. Since the degree of indebtedness will vary among different groups of developing countries, it makes sense to adapt our empirical model of investment

---

[7] We should note here that, as in the MkII model, prices of many developing country commodity exports will be determined on world markets (and that speculative holdings of commodities play a part in the short-run determination of these commodity prices). We return to this point in Section V.

behavior to the region's condition. Second, data limitations (particularly on the cost of capital) make a detailed model of the investment decision difficult to implement, and any model that aggregates over different countries will need to sacrifice some theoretical rigor.

A useful starting point is the assumption that Southern investment follows an accelerator-type relationship and is also affected by profitability and domestic financial considerations.[8] In addition, the effect of external constraints on investment will depend on the degree of indebtedness of the particular developing country region. This treatment generalizes that in the MkII model, since that model considers the Northern interest rate as the most important financial determinant of investment (and includes only a "risk premium," instead of allowing for any actual external constraint). We would also expect forward-looking influences (of profitability, financial considerations, and of external constraints) to be important, unlike in the MkII model.

V. Modeling Global North-South Interactions

In this section, we explain aspects of our projected work on embedding our models of the four Southern regions within a full North-South econometric model. We focus on two key issues: the determination of commodity prices and the supply of funding from the North to the South. Again the MkII model is our starting point. As already noted, this model includes speculative holdings of commodity stocks, and assumes that the South faces an upward-sloping supply curve of funding (with the South always able to receive additional loans at the appropriate price, which includes a risk premium). These features govern, fundamentally, the properties of the prototype model,[9] and refinements and amendments of them have to be borne in mind when constructing an empirical model.

Speculative Holdings of Commodity Stocks

Best-practice estimates of primary commodity price equations now have primary commodity prices dependent on forward-looking expectations of interest rates, as a result of commodity stockholding (see Gilbert, 1988 and 1989, and Trivedi, 1989). Indeed, in estimating structural commodity price equations these effects may dominate in the short run over flow-demand effects of higher economic activity.[10] This effect is captured in equation A1.30 of our

---

[8] Note that there is a link here with our treatment of inflation, as inflation effects on profitability could be considered. This would reinforce the two-way aggregate demand-aggregate supply feedback effects discussed in Section IV.

[9] A useful contrast to our MkII model is provided by the simple theoretical North-South model of Moutos and Vines (1989), which extends an earlier basic analysis by Kanbur and Vines (1987). The Moutos-Vines model ignores the existence of speculative commodity stocks and of a risk premium; it also does not address capital accumulation.

[10] Such structural equations should be contrasted with the equations in MULTIMOD and INTERLINK discussed below.

MkII model, where the commodity price q adjusts so that the rate of return on commodities dq^e ensures that outstanding commodity stocks are willingly held. These stocks are equal to the excess of exports of the South over flow demands for them from the North (see equation A1.22).

At the empirical level we are now estimating four-equation rational-expectations structural models of primary commodity prices for four commodity groups. The four commodity groups are food, beverages, agricultural raw materials, and metals. The econometric work builds on the method of Gilbert (1989). The four structural equations are (i) a flow-supply curve, at the world level, depending upon relative prices; (ii) a flow-demand curve, again at the world level, depending on relative prices and OECD activity; (iii) the identity, an analogue to equation A1.22, which makes stock holdings absorb any imbalance between flow supply and flow demand; and (iv) a price equation, equivalent to a version of equation A1.30, which has been inverted so as to solve for q.

The inclusion of such commodity-price equations is likely to affect the properties of an empirical North-South model in the following ways as compared with models that do not incorporate stockholding effects.

First, significantly lower commodity prices will follow fiscal expansion, because of the effects of higher interest rates on commodity stockholding decisions. Second, the drop in commodity prices will be buffered following an increase in commodity supply. Third, commodity prices will "overshoot" following a monetary expansion (see Boughton and Branson, 1988; Moutos and Vines, 1988a, 1988b, and 1988c). The key empirical unknown to be determined for each of the four commodity markets is the equivalent of σ_2 in equation A1.30, namely, the elasticity of the demand for commodity stocks as a function of the expected rate of return on commodities.

The proposed treatment in our empirical model should be contrasted with the treatment of commodity prices in existing global macromodels. For example, in INTERLINK (see Holtham and Durand, 1987), commodity prices for each of the four commodity groups are a reduced form depending mainly on economic activity in the OECD, capturing the flow-demand effects. There are also interest-rate effects, implicitly capturing the effects of commodity stockholdings, but these are weak. In MULTIMOD (see Masson and others, 1988) commodity prices are simply solved for in simulation. There are no stockholding effects: the model solves for the level of commodity prices that equates flow supply for commodities to flow demand.

One great difficulty with our treatment should be noted. For each of the commodities, the flow supply and demand curves are a mixture of supplies and demands in developing countries, the OECD, and elsewhere. It will be a challenge to ensure even implicit consistency between these processes and macroeconomic developments in each region. In particular, the effects of capital accumulation in each of the Southern regions will need to be integrated with supply in each of the four commodity markets. One way to do this more fully would be to disaggregate by commodity market for all the macroeconomic models of each region. This is suggested by Gilbert and Hughes Hallett in work they have proposed, to be carried out under the auspices of the Centre for Economic Policy Research in London, but it is beyond the scope of our own investigations.

Debt Accumulation and Repayment in the South

The issue of debt accumulation and repayment has, for obvious reasons, received much attention in the recent literature. At the theoretical level, the main focus has been on strategic considerations underlying debt accumulation and debt rescheduling problems. Recent experience has revealed a remarkable reluctance for developing countries to default entirely on debt obligations. Various reasons have been advanced for this. Early analysis tended to focus on the South's desire to retain a good reputation and, hence, access to international capital markets (see Eaton and Gersovitz, 1981; Eaton and others, 1986; and Grossman and van Huyck, 1987). The argument here is that the penalties that a sovereign debtor incurs by defaulting are minimal, and, hence, that the only reason large loans were granted to the South in the first place was because of a reliance of lenders on a reputational equilibrium.

This approach has been challenged more recently by Bulow and Rogoff (1989a and 1989b). Two reasons underlie arguments against the relevance of reputation as a factor in international lending. First, it is arguable that there are, in fact, severe penalties unrelated to the loss of reputation; substantial damage may be incurred by countries abandoning any attempts to service their debt in terms of reduced access to short-term trade credit (see Cline, 1987).[11] Second, it is not clear in reputational models why developing countries should not purchase insurance contracts instead of relying on foreign borrowing. And existing historical evidence seems to indicate that past reputation seems to have little effect on future borrowing (see, Eichengreen, 1987, and Lindert and Morton, 1987). As an alternative to the reputational model, Bulow and Rogoff (1989b) suggest a bargaining approach to the recontracting of debt. This suggests that changing economic conditions in the 1980s caused developing countries to default on their original obligations. But it also suggests that their response has been governed by fear of reprisal; they have recontracted their repayments schedules, rather than entirely repudiating their debts. Nevertheless, as a consequence, they have been locked out of new lending. This is not as a result of any loss of reputation, but rather because any new lenders will be unable to obtain full service or repayment of their debt while obligations to existing creditors are only being met in part.

---

[11] The recent Bolivian and Peruvian experiences suggest that the availability of short-term trade credits to developing countries will be reduced in response to defaults on repayments.

At the empirical level, econometric evidence still remains rather scarce. This is not surprising since game-theoretic and bargaining models do not readily lend themselves to formal econometric modeling. In particular, there seems little point in estimating the demand and supply of lending to the South.[12] The most useful approach may involve a recognition that the South is either in a relatively unconstrained position in international capital markets (as in the case of the present highly indebted countries in the 1970s, or some of the newly industrializing economies in the 1980s), or in a constrained position (as in the case of the highly indebted countries in the 1980s).

When dealing with a country or region that is completely constrained in its foreign borrowing, the MkII model approach is inappropriate. However, the opposite assumption—where the South is completely constrained on its balance of payments position in every time period—is also extreme, as the Southern highly indebted countries still possess foreign exchange reserves that enable them to manage fluctuations in their balance of payments.

A useful point of departure for such countries, which avoids many of the pitfalls associated with the explicit modeling of structural behavioral equations for both borrowers and lenders, might be as follows. One could recognize that debtors who have defaulted on their original repayment obligations are currently receiving little or no new loans, but are actually repaying some of their debt (to avoid sanctions). These rescheduled repayments are not likely to be positively correlated with movements in Northern interest rates (Bulow and Rogoff, 1989b, suggest that there may be a *negative* correlation between interest rates and repayments[13]), but are likely to increase with the South's ability to pay. Debt repayments would then be explicitly modeled. A region with outstanding debts would only have access to long-term official borrowing (which is best treated as exogenous), to short-term trade credits, and to the use of its own reserves. No new private lending would take place. For such a debt-constrained Southern region, we may therefore expect the level of reserves to exert a strong, medium-term constraint on imports, and that should be modeled.

In the case of developing countries that are not in default on their original obligations, it makes more sense to focus on the process of debt accumulation broadly along the lines in the MkII model (see equation A1.13). One would model the determinants of the trade balance and the interest-rate cost of lending in the normal way, but there would be no need to model rescheduled interest payments, which would be at contracted interest rates. One could consider the factors affecting the determination of the interest-rate risk pre-

---

[12] In much the same way, it would seem inappropriate, in an industry dominated by oligopolistic elements that act strategically, to model pricing and output behavior via a simple supply and demand system.

[13] This occurs because with higher interest rates Northern lenders become more "impatient," as they have good alternative investment opportunities. This affects the bargaining solution (see Bulow and Rogoff, 1989b).

mium along the lines suggested in the literature on country risk (see Aizenman, 1989).[14] But once again we should expect the main factors affecting the interest rate to be closely related to the lender's perception of the borrower's ability to pay. (We might want, also, to make this forward-looking.)

Thus, for both constrained and unconstrained developing country regions, the elements influencing the South's *ability to pay* will play an important part in our empirical modeling exercise. The above theoretical considerations, of course, suggest that borrowers' preferences and their *willingness to pay* should also be important, as should be the lenders' ability to punish defaulters. Unfortunately, such elements are difficult to quantify, especially when aggregating across different developing countries. The modeling approach suggested here takes a "reduced form" approach to the modeling of debt accumulation and debt repayments (focusing on the determinants of the South's ability to repay its debts). In view of the strategic bargaining considerations underlying the problem of developing country borrowing, it appears to be the only feasible approach.

Our proposed approach, differing according to region, may be contrasted with the treatment in MULTIMOD. That model has only one aggregate developing country region, the supply of capital to which is constrained. The constraint is forward-looking: Northern lenders effectively look ahead to the effect on exports (via increased investment and aggregate supply) when determining any increased financing. In INTERLINK, there is no elaborate treatment of aggregate demand or debt in the South. A number of Southern regions exist, each of which simply spends, with a lag, any improvement in its current account. This implies that these regions are all debt-constrained to some degree, but the model does not investigate in detail the reasons for—or the workings of—that constraint.

VI. Two Illustrative Simulations of the MkII Model

We now examine the effects of simulating the MkII model. While our examination incorporates only some of the features discussed in Sections IV and V, we believe that the MkII model may be useful in describing some of the channels of North-South interdependence.

We consider the long-run effects and transition effects on some key variables of two exogenous shocks in the MkII model. The long-run multipliers of the shocks are presented in Table 1. The transition effects are shown in Charts 1 and 2.

An Aggregate Demand Shock in the North

The type of exogenous shock considered here is a 1 percent permanent increase in Northern government expenditure on Northern goods.

---

[14] For an attempt to model risk premia empirically, see Edwards (1986).

Table 1. Long-Run Multipliers
MkII Version of the North-South Model

Permanent 1 percent Increase in	Northern Aggregate Demand	Southern Aggregate Supply
Northern Output (Y_1)	0.025	0.149
Southern Output (Y_2)	−0.191	1.278
Southern Real Consumption ($C_2 - q^c$)	−0.232	1.816
Northern Prices (p)	0.626	0.749
Northern Consumer Prices (p^c)	0.602	0.475
Southern Prices (q)	0.462	−1.141
Northern Interest Rate (r_1)	0.426	0.549
Southern Interest Rate (r_2)	0.307	0.171
Nominal Debt (D)	−0.053	−0.038
Southern Government Spending (G_2^m)	19.024	22.033
Southern Money Supply (M_2)	0.352	0.183
Northern Capital Stock (K_1)	−0.060	0.040
Southern Capital Stock (K_2)	−0.376	−0.623

We first consider *long-run* effects (although the long run is very distant). The fact that higher government expenditure drives up interest rates sets up supply-side responses of the kind that we have been emphasizing. The Southern capital stock contracts markedly as does Southern output. The fall in Southern output is due in part to the higher interest rates (which have caused K_2 to contract), and in part to the fact that the terms of trade have turned against the South ((q/ep) has fallen). The contraction of Southern capital and output reduces Southern income, wealth (money supply), and real expenditures. The private sector undertakes all of the adjustment required by the fall in available output. In fact, Southern government spending on Northern imports is actually higher in the long run, as the Southern private sector more than keeps the debt accumulation process under control.

Why does the relative price of commodities fall in the long run in the MkII model? The reason is straightforward. The higher Northern government expenditure is on *Northern* goods. But the higher prices and interest rates crowd out expenditures on *both* goods. Lower relative commodity prices are thus inevitable for helping to remove the resulting excess supply of commodities. Lower relative commodity prices enable the North to expand marginally its output even though Northern capital falls slightly, because of the beneficial terms-of-trade, supply-side response referred to in Section III.

All this suggests that, in the long run, Reaganomics (that is, fiscal expansion) in the North can benefit the North and might inflict a loss of capital, output, income, and expenditure on the South. The North is able to obtain a supply-side advantage by inflicting a terms-of-trade loss on the South. Notice too that a higher risk premium faces the South. (Although the South's real debt falls, its debt-to-export ratio rises as the North's demand for the South's goods is crowded out.) This augments the adjustment that the South must carry out. The important thing to notice is the long-run supply effects on the South, in the presence of an endogenous supply response. Demand spillover effects operate so as to turn the terms of trade toward the North. Interest rate and negative capital accumulation supply-side effects reinforce the demand effect so as to depress Southern output further.

We now turn to the *transition* process. The terms of trade for the South remain depressed throughout the transition period (see Chart 1). Thus, Southern output falls because of two factors, namely, higher interest rates and lower terms of trade. Investment in both regions is also depressed by interest-rate effects, although Northern investment is initially stimulated by the higher output in the North. One of the main elements to note is that Southern debt does not display major fluctuations, and, in fact, declines marginally in the

Chart 1. MkII Model: Government Expenditure Shock in the North

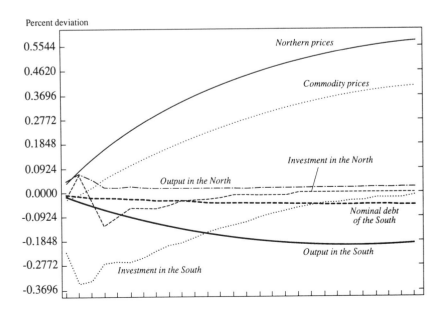

short run in nominal terms. This emphasizes one feature of this model that we have noted above, namely, that private expenditures in the South (particularly investment) decline sufficiently so as to keep debt accumulation under control. This particular outcome is, of course, sensitive to the parameterization of our model.

We note in passing that these results may overemphasize the damage that Reaganomics might do to the South. One could argue that a Northern fiscal expansion might benefit the South by improving its terms of trade enough to relieve its external balance position (even in the presence of higher interest rates on debt). The fact that this does not occur in our model depends on the particular balance of interest-rate and demand effects on commodity prices implied by our parameters, and also on the speed with which the increase in demand is crowded out in the North. Any such beneficial effect would then be especially strong if the South were debt-constrained. Such a beneficial effect is present in some models (for example, MULTIMOD, see Masson and others, 1988). In practice, we would only expect any adverse effects on the South to be significant under some conditions, and even then, probably only in the medium term. Ultimately, which effects dominate over which time horizon is a matter for sensitivity analysis and empirical scrutiny in future work.

An Aggregate Supply Shock in the South

Once again we first consider the long-run effects of this exogenous shock. As Table 1 shows, the 1 percent rise in Y_2 stimulates further increases in output. This is due to the "multiplier" effect operating through labor demand and the demand for capital (see Currie and others, 1988, footnote 3, and Appendix II). To some extent this effect is augmented by the fall in the risk premium and in r_2, which will *tend* to increase the South's capital stock. However, the South's capital stock actually falls, because the South's terms of trade have deteriorated sufficiently to offset this.

Thus, overall and in the long run, a Southern aggregate supply shock has mixed effects on the South in the MkII model: output and export availability increase. The unit price elasticity of demand for commodities imposed on the model limits the resulting fall in commodity prices. As a result, the Southern government is able to purchase more imports, and Southern real consumption also rises. But the South's capital decumulation has partially reversed the increase in output. Unlike some models where Southern output shocks are unambiguously "immiserizing" for the South (see Bhagwati, 1958; Molana and Vines, 1989; and Kanbur and Vines, 1987), in our prototype model the outcome can be partly beneficial, at least for the parameter values chosen in our simulations. Note that the North also benefits from the increase in Southern output, as the South is now less constrained in its balance of payments position and is able to import more from the North. This is one reason why Northern prices actually rise.

Chart 2. MkII Model: Aggregate Supply Shock in the South

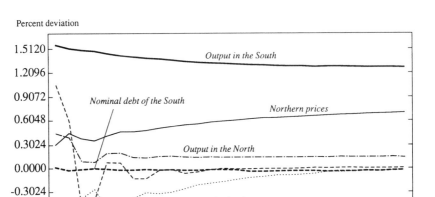

Percent deviation

In the transition (see Chart 2), we can clearly see how the terms-of-trade effects operate. Overall, Southern output benefits, but Southern investment tends to be depressed as Southern capital is run down. The increase in Northern output prompts the price rise in the North during the transition, overcoming the downward effect of lower nominal commodity prices.

VII. The Study of Strategic Interactions

Having examined some of the issues underlying our theoretical analysis of North-South interactions, and having considered the issues that will govern our empirical modeling, we now examine the issues of strategic interaction that follow from any discussion of international economic interdependence.

Our discussion so far has indicated that bi-directional "spillovers" between the South and the North may be important. In such cases, it is now well-known from the literature on North-North policy coordination that cooperative policies are helpful. These ensure that outcomes are mutually beneficial, which they will not be, in the absence of cooperation, when spillovers are large.[15] Such cooperation would give substance to the IMF concept of "adjustment with growth," whereby the South does adjust to the debt crisis, but is at the same time given sufficient extra lending to enable it to continue to grow during the adjustment period.

In Currie and others (1988), we examined the benefits that could accrue from policy cooperation between North and South. For simplicity, we concentrated our attention on nonreputational policies. Under these circumstances, it is well-known that policy coordination may not necessarily lead to an improvement in welfare (see Rogoff, 1985; Currie and Levine, 1987; Currie and others, 1987). However, with our earlier MkI model,[16] we demonstrated that policy coordination following an adverse current account shock for the South was beneficial for *total* welfare, but that the South suffered welfare losses. Thus, we concluded that cooperation could only be operational if the North made a side-payment to the South.

In the MkI model, the problem for the North, in the absence of cooperation, was that a deterioration in the South's current-account position did not force the South to adjust. The South pushed the burden of adjustment onto the North by forcing the North to inflate away the Southern debt. This is because the North was aware that a growing stock of Southern debt would lead to increased interest revenue in the North, which, by stimulating Northern spending, would cause inflation. The North sought to avoid the resulting inflationary instability; the only way it could do so was through expansionary monetary policy.

We now consider, in the abstract, whether the changes made in our MkII model are likely to alter these results.[17] In the new model, Southern output and consumption will be affected by capital accumulation. Thus, if the South is seeking to stabilize its real consumption, it may wish to avoid large changes in the capital stock. Given that capital accumulation in the South is heavily influenced by the presence of the risk premium and, moreover, given that debt accumulation affects the risk premium, it is likely that, in the absence of cooperation, following a current account shock, the South *will* have to adjust, in contrast to the results of Currie and others (1988). This "threat" from the North means that in the MkII model the South would be unable to escape the burden of adjustment.

---

[15] To some extent the presence or absence of reputation with regard to the private sector may be important in deciding whether cooperation is really beneficial (see Rogoff, 1985). In Currie and others (1988), we presented a model where, even in the absence of reputation, cooperation was found to be beneficial.

[16] The MkI model, in contrast to the MkII model, does not include investment behavior, capital accumulation, the Northern government budget constraint, and a risk premium on Southern debt.

[17] We have not yet conducted such policy coordination experiments at a formal level, even using the MkII model.

Other alternatives do exist, as suggested earlier. The South may continue to make payments on its debt, to avoid such sanctions as the denial of trade credit, but not enough to avoid partial default and exclusion from new lending. Two policy coordination questions then become as follows: (i) Under what circumstances will it be in the South's interest to make payments on its existing debt that are sufficient to induce the resumption of new lending? (ii) Under what circumstances will it be in the interests of the Northern lenders to write off enough of the existing debt to induce the voluntary resumption of new lending?

These are important questions. But the rudimentary nature of North-South models makes any formal response somewhat premature (Bryant, 1988). What makes the evaluation of such different cooperative policies difficult is the lack of *empirical* models of North-South interaction. Our proposed development of a multiregion North-South model should contribute to this debate, but a full analysis of strategic issues of the type common in the case of North-North models is probably still some way off in the future.

VIII. Conclusions

We have argued that an examination of North-South economic interactions is important for a proper understanding of the workings of the global economy. Our own work in this area has initially been restricted to an analysis of North-South spillover effects using small- and medium-size theoretical models. Arguably, this is a useful step prior to the construction of a full econometric model of the world economy.

Thus, in this paper we have used such a prototype model to identify some aspects of North-South interactions. We presented two simulations. The model also served as a framework for discussing how best to model the Southern regions, and how best to deal with two key issues in global interactions. We noted some key questions concerning policy coordination between North and South.

An overall theme is that the diversity of developing countries makes it inappropriate to aggregate all of them in a single region of a world econometric model. Our current work on a multiregional model of the South will attempt to provide a fuller, regionally disaggregated picture of the Southern "missing link" in the economic interdependence debate.

Appendix I
North-South Model, MkII

(a) *The South*

(i) *The Supply Side*

As in the case of MkI (see Currie and others, 1988) the production function for primary commodity output, Y_2, in the South is of a Cobb-Douglas type. But it now includes capital, K, explicitly as a variable factor, as well as labor, L. Nevertheless, it is not constant returns to scale because of the omission of the implicit fixed factor: land.

$$Y_2 = A_2 K_2^{\alpha 2} L_2^{\beta 2} + AS^s. \tag{A1.1}$$

Labor demand, L_2, is given by the usual marginal productivity condition, where q is the price of primary commodities, and W_2 is the Southern nominal wage:

$$L_2 = \beta_2 q Y_2 / W_2. \tag{A1.2}$$

The rate of change of wages, W_2, depends on past cost-of-living increases:

$$dW_2 = k_0 dq^c + k_1 dq^c_{t-1} + k_2 dq^c_{t-2}, \tag{A1.3}$$

where q^c is a cost-of-living index defined as:

$$q^c = q^{\pi 2}(ep)^{(1-\pi 2)}. \tag{A1.4}$$

(ii) *Demand*

Nominal consumption expenditure in the South, C_2, now depends on nominal income and on nominal Southern wealth, V_2 (where t_2 is the tax rate):

$$C_2 = \theta_1(1 - t_2)qY_2 + \theta_2 V_2. \tag{A1.5}$$

Notice that the coefficients on income and wealth do not sum to unity (since wealth is a stock and income a flow), but that there is a value of wealth such that all disposable income is consumed.

Total (nominal) consumption in the South is shared out between expenditure on home-produced primary commodities, C_2^h, and imports of manufactures, C_2^m, where the (nominal) shares spent on each good are independent of relative prices (e is the exchange rate, defined as the price of the North's currency in terms of the South's currency):

$$C_2^h = \pi_2 C_2 \tag{A1.6}$$

$$C_2^m = (1 - \pi_2)C_2/e. \tag{A1.7}$$

Southern government expenditure on Northern goods, G_2^m, follows a feedback rule on the South's real external debt, D/p, where p is the price of the Northern good:

$$G_2^m = \tau_0 - \tau_1(D_{t-1}/p) - \tau_2(D_{t-1} - D_{t-2})/p_{t-1} + G_2^{mx}. \tag{A1.8}$$

After the claims on Southern output by the private sector have been met, what is left is exported, X_2:

$$X_2 = Y_2 - C_2^h/q - G_2^h. \tag{A1.9}$$

Southern imports, Z_2, include Southern private consumption, public consumption, and private investment expenditure on Northern goods:

$$Z_2 = C_2^m/p + G_2^m + (K_2^m - K_{2,t-1}^m). \tag{A1.10}$$

(iii) *Asset Stocks*

The desired total capital stock in the South, K_2^*, is determined by the usual marginal productivity conditions, where r_2 is the interest rate paid on Southern debt:

$$K_2^* = \alpha_2 q Y_2/p(r_2 - dp). \tag{A1.11}$$

The actual capital stock, K_2, adjusts to its desired value according to a partial adjustment mechanism:

$$K_2 = w_2(K_2^* - K_{2,t-1}) + K_{2,t-1}. \tag{A1.12}$$

Debt, D, evolves according to the Southern trade deficit. If Southern exports exceed the sum of Southern imports and debt interest repayments, $r_2 D_{t-1}$, debt liabilities increase:

$$-eD + e_{t-1}D_{t-1} = qx_2 - epG_2^m - er_2D_{t-1} - eC_2^m + DEB. \tag{A1.13}$$

The Southern money supply, M_2, evolves according to the following government budget constraint:

$$M_2 - M_{2,t-1} + eD - e_{t-1}D_{t-1} = qG_2^h + epG_2^m + er_2D_{t-1} - t_2qY_2. \tag{A1.14}$$

Nominal wealth in the South, V_2, consists of money balances plus the value of the capital stock:

$$V_2 = M_2 + pK_2. \tag{A1.15}$$

(b) *The North*

(i) *Demand*

Northern nominal consumption, C_1, depends on current income (including interest income from external debt and bond holdings), and nominal wealth, V_1:

$$C_1 = \phi_1(1 - t_1)p(Y_1 + r_2 D_{t-1}/p^c + r_1 B_{t-1}/p^c) + \phi_2 V_1. \tag{A1.16}$$

Total Northern consumption is shared between home-produced manufactures, C_1^h, and imported primary goods, C_1^m, in an analogous fashion to Southern consumption:

$$C_1^h = \pi_1 C_1 \tag{A1.17}$$

$$C_1^m = (1 - \pi_1)eC_1. \tag{A1.18}$$

The desired capital stock in the North also depends on the usual profit-maximization condition, where R^L is the long-term interest rate:

$$K_1^* = \alpha_1 Y_1/R^L. \tag{A1.19}$$

As is the case for the South, the actual capital stock, K_1, adjusts to its desired value according to a partial adjustment scheme:

$$K_1 = w_1(K_1 - K_{1, t-1}) + K_{1, t-1}. \tag{A1.20}$$

The consumption price index in the North, p^c, is defined as follows:

$$p^c = p^{\pi 1}(q/e)^{(1 - \pi 1)}. \tag{A1.21}$$

Speculative stocks of primary commodities held in the North, S, are determined by the excess of exports over Northern consumption imports:

$$S - S_{t-1} = X_2 - C_1^m/q. \tag{A1.22}$$

Northern aggregate demand is given by the usual goods-market balance equation:

$$Y_1^d = C_1^h/p + (K_1 - K_{1,\,t-1}) + G_1 + Z_2 + AD^n. \qquad (A1.23)$$

Output of manufactures in the North is assumed always to be demand determined.

(ii) *The Supply Side*

Employment in the North, L_1^d, is demand determined, and may be found by inverting the production function, which is assumed to be Cobb-Douglas, as in the case of the South, but with constant returns to scale:

$$L_1^d = (Y_1^d(A_1K_1^{\alpha 1})^{-1})^{1/\beta 1}. \qquad (A1.24)$$

Labor supply, L_1^s, depends positively on the real wage:

$$L_1^s = L^s(W_1/p^c) + AS^n, L^{s\,'}(.) > 0. \qquad (A1.25)$$

The Northern nominal wage, W_1, adjusts to remove excess demand in the labor market following an expectations-augmented Phillips curve:

$$dW_1 = \pi_3(L_1^d - L_1^s) + dp^{ec}. \qquad (A1.26)$$

The price level for the Northern good, p, is determined according to the usual profit-maximization condition, given the output level and the nominal wage:

$$p = W_1L_1^d/\beta_1Y_1^d. \qquad (A1.27)$$

Consumer price expectations, p^{ec}, are formed according to the adaptive expectations hypothesis:

$$dp^{ec} - dp_{t-1}^{ec} = \delta\ (dp_{t-1}^c - dp_{t-1}^{ec}). \qquad (A1.28)$$

(iii) *Asset Demands, Interest Rates, and Asset Stocks*

The following equations show the demands for money, M_1, and (real) speculative commodity stocks, qS/p, in the North in terms of the Northern short-term interest rate, r_1, and the expected rate of change of primary commodity prices in Northern currency $(dq^e - de^e)$. Real wealth is also a determinant of the demand for commodity stocks and, therefore, implicitly, also of the demand for bonds.

$$M_1/p = \mu_0\ exp\{\mu_1r_1\}\ Y_1^{\mu 3} \qquad (A1.29)$$

$$qS/p = \sigma_0\ exp\{\sigma_1r_1 + \sigma_2(dq^e - de^e)\}Y_1^{\sigma 3}\ (V_1/p)^{\sigma 4}. \qquad (A1.30)$$

The real long-term interest rate in the North, R^L, is a forward-looking variable that is influenced by expectations of future short-term interest rates and inflation:

$$R_1^L = \Omega_1 R_{1,t+1}^{Le} + (1 - \Omega_1)(r_1 - dp).\tag{A1.31}$$

The interest rate charged on Southern external debt, r_2, is equal to the Northern short-term interest rate plus a risk premium, Φ:

$$r_2 = r_1 + \Phi.\tag{A1.32}$$

The risk premium, Φ, depends on the Southern debt-export ratio, plus an exogenous disturbance, Γ:

$$\Phi = \pi_4(D / (qX_2/e)) + \Gamma.\tag{A1.33}$$

Nominal wealth in the North, V_1, is defined as:

$$V_1 = M_1 + B_1 + qS/e + pK_1 + D\tag{A1.34}$$

where B is the stock of Northern government bonds. We incorporate the Northern government budget constraint, where it is assumed that budget deficits in the North are bond financed:

$$B_1 - B_{1,t-1} = G_1 - t_1 Y_1^d - (M_1 - M_{1,t-1}) + r_1 B_{t-1}.\tag{A1.35}$$

The Northern government is assumed to adjust the Northern marginal tax rate, t_1, according to a feedback rule on the bonds to nominal income ratio:

$$t_1 = \pi_5(B_{t-1}/p_{t-1}Y_{t-1}).\tag{A1.36}$$

(c) *Variable Definition and Parameters*
   All variables listed are expressed in levels. The model was linearized before the simulations were carried out. In some cases the subscripts "1" and "2" identify parameters as relating to the North and the South, respectively, as in the production function parameters α and B.

(i) *Exogenous Variables (Exogenous Shocks):*

   $e, G_2^h, G_1, M_{1,}f, AS^s, AS^n, AD^n, DEB, \Gamma, G_2^{mx}.$

(ii) *Parameter Values:*

   $\alpha_2 = 0.2 \quad \beta_2 = 0.5 \quad \theta_1 = 0.8 \quad \theta_2 = 0.032 \quad t_2 = 0.2$

$$\pi_2 = 0.75 \quad \tau_0 = 1 \quad \tau_1 = 0.7 \quad \tau_2 = 0.7 \quad \Omega_1 = 0.95 \quad k_0 = 1$$
$$k_1 = 0 \quad k_2 = 0 \quad w_2 = 0.1 \quad \pi_1 = 0.75 \quad \phi_1 = 0.8 \quad \phi_2 = 0.010$$
$$w_1 = 0.1 \quad \pi_3 = 0.5 \quad \alpha_1 = 0.2 \quad \beta_1 = 0.8 \quad \pi_4 = 0.5$$
$$\mu_1 = -1.5 \quad \mu_3 = 0.5 \quad \sigma_1 = -5 \quad \sigma_2 = 5 \quad \sigma_3 = 0.5 \quad \sigma_4 = 0.2$$
$$\delta = 0.5 \quad L^{s'}(.) = 0.5 \quad \pi_5 = 0.1$$

Notes:

The operator d is such that dx denotes the rate of change in x. All variable values are current-period unless otherwise denoted via time subscripts.

Appendix II

In this appendix we demonstrate that Southern output is determined by the terms of trade, and by the real interest rate charged to the South. We consider the South's production function (equation A1.1), its demand for labor (equation A1.2), and its demand for capital (equation A1.11), where all of these equations are expressed in logarithms for simplicity:

$$y_2 = \alpha_2 k_2 + \beta_2 l_2 \tag{A2.1}$$

$$l_2 = y_2 + q - w_2 \tag{A2.2}$$

$$k_2^* = q + y_2 - p - r_2. \tag{A2.3}$$

Furthermore, we recall that given that there is complete wage resistance, in the long run:

$$w_2 \approx q^c,$$

and, in long-run equilibrium, it also follows that $k_2 = k_2^*$.

From this, we know that:

$$l_2 = y_2 + q - q^c \tag{A2.4}$$

$$k_2 = q + y_2 - p - r_2. \tag{A2.5}$$

We can substitute these two expressions into (A2.1) to obtain the following expression for output after some manipulation:

$$(1 - \alpha_2 - \beta_2)y_2 = (q - p) + (q - q^c) - r_2. \tag{A2.6}$$

We may suppose for simplicity, and without loss of generality, that the following weights are applied to the definition of the price index q^c:

$$q^c = 0.5q + 0.5 (e + p). \tag{A2.7}$$

Substituting (A2.7) into (A2.6), we finally obtain:

$$y_2 = (q-p)/(1-\alpha_2-\beta_2) - r_2/(1-\alpha_2-\beta_2) + 0.5 (q-e-p)(1-\alpha_2-\beta_2).$$

This demonstrates the positive relationship between Southern output and the terms of trade, and the negative relationship between Y_2 and the interest rate charged to the South.

References

Adams, F. Gerard, and Joaquin Vial, "Comparison of LDC Macroeconomic Models," presented at American Economic Association meeting, Chicago, December 1987.

Aizenman, Joshua, "Country Risk, Incomplete Information, and Taxes on International Borrowing," *Economic Journal*, Vol. 99 (London: 1989), pp. 147–61.

Beckerman, Wilfred, and Tim Jenkinson, "What Stopped the Inflation? Unemployment or Commodity Prices?" *Economic Journal*, Vol. 96 (London: 1986), pp. 39–54.

Beenstock, Michael, *The World Economy in Transition* (London: Allen and Unwin, 1982).

————, "An Econometric Investigation of North-South Interdependence," in Currie and Vines (eds.) (1988a).

Bhagwati, Jhagdish, "Immiserizing Growth: A Geometrical Note," *Review of Economic Studies*, Vol. 25 (Edinburgh: 1958), pp. 201–205.

Blinder, Alan, and Robert Solow, "Does Fiscal Policy Matter?" *Journal of Public Economics*, Vol. 2 (Amsterdam: North-Holland, 1973), pp. 319–37.

Boughton, James, and William Branson, "Commodity Prices as Leading Indicators of Inflation," mimeographed (Washington: International Monetary Fund, August 1988).

Bruno, Michael, and Jeffrey Sachs, *Economics of Worldwide Stagflation* (Cambridge, Massachusetts: Harvard University Press, 1985).

Bryant, Ralph C., "Comment on Hughes Hallett," in Currie and Vines, eds. (1988a).

————, and Richard Portes, eds., *Global Macroeconomics: Policy Conflict and Cooperation* (London: Macmillan, 1987).

Buiter, Willem, and Richard C. Marston, eds., *International Economic Policy Coordination* (Cambridge, England: Cambridge University Press, 1985).

Bulow, Jeremy, and Kenneth Rogoff, "The Buyback Boondoggle," *Brookings Papers on Economic Activity*, No. 2 (Washington: The Brookings Institution, 1988).

———— (1989a), "Sovereign Debt: Is to Forgive to Forget?" *American Economic Review*, Vol. 79 (Nashville, Tennessee: March 1989).

———— (1989b), "A Constant Recontracting Model of Sovereign Debt," *Journal of Political Economy*, Vol. 97 (Chicago: February 1989).

Cardoso, Eliana, "Food Supply and Inflation," *Journal of Development Economics*, Vol. 8 (Amsterdam: 1981), pp. 269–84.

Cline, William, *Mobilizing Bank Lending to Debtor Countries* (Washington: Institute for International Economics, 1987).

Cohen, Daniel, and Jeffrey Sachs, "Growth and External Debt under Risk of Debt Repudiation," *European Economic Review*, Vol. 30 (Amsterdam: 1986), pp. 529–60.

Currie, David, and Paul Levine, "Credibility and Time-Consistency in a Stochastic World," Centre for Economic Policy Research Discussion Paper (London: CEPR, February 1986), pp. 1–32.

Currie, David, and David Vines, eds. (1988a), *Macroeconomic Interactions between North and South* (Cambridge, England: Cambridge University Press, 1988).

———— (1988b), "Southern Economics: The Missing Link in Studies of the Global Economy," oral presentation at Centre for Economic Policy Research, London, September 1988.

Currie, David, and others, "International Cooperation and Reputation in an Empirical Two-Bloc Model," in Ralph C. Bryant and Richard Portes, eds., *Global Macroeconomics: Policy Conflict and Cooperation* (London: Macmillan, 1987).

————, "North-South Interactions: A General-Equilibrium Framework for the Study of Strategic Issues," in Currie and Vines, eds. (1988a).

Currie, David, Anton Muscatelli, and David Vines, "Introduction," in Currie and Vines, eds. (1988a).

Eaton, Jonathan, and Mark Gersovitz, "Debt with Potential Repudiation: Theoretical and Empirical Analysis," *Review of Economic Studies*, Vol. 48 (Edinburgh: 1981), pp. 289–309.

Eaton, Jonathan, Mark Gersovitz, and Joseph Stiglitz, "The Pure Theory of Country Risk," *European Economic Review*, Vol. 30 (Amsterdam: 1986), pp. 481–513.

Edwards, Sebastian, "The Pricing of Bonds and Bank Loans in International Markets," *European Economic Review*, Vol. 30 (Amsterdam: 1986), pp. 565–89.

Eichengreen, Barry, "Till Debt Do Us Part: The U.S. Capital Market and Foreign Lending: 1920–1955," mimeographed (Berkeley: University of California, 1987).

Findlay, Ronald, "The Terms of Trade and Equilibrium Growth in the World Economy," *American Economic Review*, Vol. 70 (Nashville, Tennessee: 1980), pp. 291–99.

————, "Growth and Development in Trade Models," in R. W. Jones and P. B. Kenen, eds., *Handbook of International Economics*, I (Amsterdam: North-Holland, 1984).

Frankel, Jeffrey A., "Expectations and Commodity Price Dynamics: The Overshooting Model," *American Journal of Agricultural Economics* (St. Paul, Minnesota: 1986), pp. 344–48.

————, "The Implications of Conflicting Models for Coordination between Monetary and Fiscal Policymakers," in Bryant and others, eds., *Empirical Macroeco-*

nomics for Interdependent Economies (Washington: The Brookings Institution, 1988).

—————, and Katherine E. Rockett, "International Macroeconomic Policy Coordination when Policymakers Do Not Agree on the True Model," *American Economic Review*, Vol. 78 (Nashville, Tennessee: 1988), pp. 318–40.

Fritsch, Winston, "Brazil's Growth Prospects: Domestic Savings, External Finance and OECD Performance Interactions," in Currie and Vines, eds. (1988a).

Gilbert, Christopher, "The Dynamics of Commodity Stocks and Prices, and the Specification of Econometric Commodity Price Models" mimeographed (Oxford: Oxford University, 1988).

—————, "Expectation Formation in Equilibrium and Disequilibrium: Econometric Commodity Market Models," oral presentation at Centre for Economic Policy Research Conference on Primary Commodity Prices, London, March 1989.

—————, and Andrew Powell, "The Use of Commodity Contracts for the Management of Developing Country Commodity Risks," in Currie and Vines, eds. (1988a).

Giovanetti, Giorgia, "The International Transmission of Price Level and Output Disturbances between Raw Material Producer Countries and Industrial Countries: A Theoretical Analysis," *Economic Notes*, No. 1 (Siena, Italy: 1985), pp. 148–61.

Grossman, Herschel, and John B. van Huyck, "Sovereign Debt as a Contingent Claim: Excusable Default, Repudiation, and Reputation," mimeographed (Providence, Rhode Island: Brown University, 1987).

Holtham, Gerald, and Martine Durand, "OECD Economic Activity and Non-Oil Commodity Prices: Reduced Form Equations for Interlink," Organization for Economic Cooperation and Development Working Papers, No. 42 (Paris: OECD, June 1987).

Hughes Hallett, Andrew, "Commodities, Debt and North-South Co-operation: A Cautionary Tale from the Structuralist Camp," in Currie and Vines, eds. (1988a).

Kanbur, Ravi, and David Vines, "North-South Interaction and Commodity Control," *Journal of Development Economics* (Amsterdam: 1987), Vol. 23, pp. 371–87.

Khan, Mohsin, and Malcolm Knight, "Stabilisation Programmes in Developing Countries: A Formal Framework," International Monetary Fund *Staff Papers*, Vol. 28 (Washington: IMF, 1981), pp. 1–53.

—————, "Import Compression and Export Performance in Developing Countries," unpublished manuscript (Washington: International Monetary Fund, November 1986).

Lewis, W. Arthur, "Economic Development with Unlimited Supplies of Labour," *Manchester School of Economics and Social Studies*, Vol. 22 (Manchester, England: 1954), pp. 139–91.

Lindert, Peter H., and Peter J. Morton, "How Sovereign Debt Has Worked," mimeographed (Davis: University of California, 1987).

Marquez, Jaime, and Peter Pauly, "Cooperative Policies Among the North, South and OPEC," *Economic Modelling*, Vol. 3 (London: 1986), pp. 213–36.

Masson, Paul, and others, "MULTIMOD: A Multi-Region Econometric Model,"

International Monetary Fund *Staff Studies for the World Economic Outlook*, (Washington: IMF, July 1988), pp. 50–104.

McCallum, John, and David Vines, "Cambridge and Chicago on the Balance of Payments," *Economic Journal*, Vol. 91 (London: 1981), pp. 439–53.

Molana, Hassan, and David Vines, "North-South Growth and Terms of Trade, A Model along Kaldorian Lines," *Economic Journal* (London), forthcoming.

Moutos, Thomas, and David Vines (1988a), "Microeconomic and Macroeconomic Theories of Commodity Prices," forthcoming, *Journal of International Economic Studies*.

_____ (1988b), "A Prototype Macroeconomic Model with Integrated Financial and Commodity Markets," *Economic Notes*, No. 1 (Siena, Italy: 1988), pp. 51–65.

_____ (1988c), "Output, Inflation and Commodity Prices," Centre for Economic Policy Research, Discussion Paper (London: CEPR, 1988), pp. 1–32.

_____ , "The Simple Macroeconomics of North-South Interaction," *American Economic Review*, Vol. 79 (Nashville, Tennessee: 1989).

Ramanujam, P., and David Vines, "OECD Economic Activity, Interest Rates and Primary Commodity Prices: A Structural RE Model," mimeographed (Glasgow: University of Glasgow, 1988).

Riedel, James, "Trade as the Engine of Growth in Developing Countries, Revisited," *Economic Journal*, Vol. 94 (London: March 1984), pp. 56–73.

Rogoff, Kenneth, "Can International Monetary Cooperation be Counterproductive?" *Journal of International Economics* (Amsterdam: 1985), Vol. 18, pp. 199–217.

Taylor, Lance, "Structuralist Macroeconomics" (New York: Basic Books, 1983).

Tobin, James, "Money and Finance in the Macroeconomic Process," *Journal of Money, Credit and Banking*, Vol. 14 (Columbus, Ohio: 1982), pp. 171–204.

Trivedi, Pravin, "The Prices of Perennial Crops: The Role of Rational Expectations and Commodity Stocks," oral presentation at Centre for Economic Policy Research Conference on Primary Commodity Prices, London, March 1989.

van Wijnbergen, Sweder, "Interdependence Revisited: A Developing Countries Perspective on Macroeconomic Management and Trade Policy in the Industrial World," *Economic Policy*, Vol. 1 (London: 1985), pp. 81–114.

Vial, Joaquin, "Macroeconomic Models for Policy Analysis in Latin America," Working Paper, Corporación de Investigaciones Económicas para Latinoamerica (Santiago, Chile: 1987).

Vos, Rob, "Global Savings, Investment and Adjustment: On Micro- and Macroeconomic Foundations of North-South Financial Interdependence," in Currie and Vines, eds. (1988a).

Comments

Michael P. Dooley

The interesting paper by Anton Muscatelli and David Vines deals with several important aspects of North-South economic interaction. I will focus on one important aspect of that interaction: the credit-flow problem, which receives considerable emphasis in the paper.

When I and my colleagues at the International Monetary Fund approached this problem in designing a developing country sector for MULTI-MOD, we concluded that a useful model would need to incorporate certain features in order to model the flow of credit from the North to the South.

First, *the supply of credit should be based on some forward-looking assessment of the debtor's ability to repay.* If we look at the world right now, it is clear that, beyond relending of interest payments, very little net, new private credit is going to the heavily indebted developing countries. This suggests that a conventional supply curve for credit may be inappropriate. An alternative is the well-known rationing model in which, as interest rates rise above a given level, the debtor becomes insolvent.

We reasoned that looking down the road (many years down the road in a forward-looking model), it seemed useful to assume that if the amount required for debt service became too large as a percent of the debtor's exports or gross national product (GNP), payment would be doubtful. A country in that position would receive no net, new credit from commercial lenders.

The solvency criterion—I do not particularly like the word "solvency" because it means too many things to too many people—is that, at some point, the country hits a wall in terms of its net credit from the rest of the world—at least, net private credit from the rest of the world. And at that point, the country either has to amortize its foreign debt, which severely constrains its current account balance, or default, which would also probably force the non-interest current account to zero. The current account is then not determined by trade elasticities or activity in the rest of the world, but rather by the optimal rate of amortization for the insolvent debtor.

The second required feature of a model is *some linkage between this kind of a credit system and domestic economic activity within the debtor country.* This is also a new and difficult problem. How should investment be modeled in a developing country, and how should it be put into a simulation model?

We assume in MULTIMOD that domestic savings in developing countries are insufficient to support enough domestic investment to lower the rate of return domestically to the world (risk-free) rate of interest. Therefore, if we close the capital account, we have, by assumption, a relatively high rate of return in the domestic economy. For solvent developing countries, nonresident investors, then, determine the relevant part of the savings function and the

413

savings-investment equilibrium in the debtor country. Again, the supply of foreign savings depends on forward-looking expectations of export growth. Favorable changes in the world economy, a fall in real interest rates, a rise in the expected future exports of the country, or a number of other kinds of changes in the environment, will encourage capital inflows into solvent developing countries and allow some insolvent countries to graduate from the credit-constrained group into the non-credit-constrained group. Thus, investment is only undertaken if the present value of exports generated by the increases in output that it permits is sufficient to pay the world rate of interest.

An alternative approach, employed by Muscatelli and Vines, is to assume that lending from North to South carries a risk premium with no solvency constraint on that system. In principle, the two approaches could yield similar predictions, but the risk-premium approach may not be well-suited in cases where existing debt sells at a deep discount in secondary markets. Suppose, for example, that a debtor country was expected to make, about one half of its contractual-interest payments on existing debt. That would imply that the debt would sell at about 50 cents on the secondary market. It would also imply a marginal risk premium of roughly double the risk-free interest rate. A market rate of 10 percent would imply a risk premium of an additional 10 percent.

We could then say that foreign savings would be available to this country if it paid a 20 percent rate of return. But it seems unlikely that we would know enough about the investment decisions in this range of risk premia to have capital inflows be a function of that price.

The forward-looking, rationing approach seems to have an important implication for most of the experiments we have done. Since in order to change the flow of foreign savings to developing countries in MULTIMOD, debtor countries must graduate from one group to another (from credit constrained to nonconstrained) savings flows—although this is not a theoretical result—seem to be less sensitive to short-run or temporary changes in policy settings, as compared with models that use a more conventional specification.

In summary, one of the interesting and unresolved issues in modeling strategy is whether to focus on marginal capital flows to developing countries as conditioned by risk premia, or to develop an explicit rationing model and attempt to model solvency criteria.

Pierre Defraigne

Let me start my comments by welcoming the idea of providing the missing link of international interdependence and policy cooperation by addressing certain economies in a North-South model. I think that Anton Muscatelli and David Vines have made an important and promising contribution.

I would like to consider some specific issues raised by the paper. First of all, with regard to North-South interdependence, the model cites the interdependencies that operate through commodity and capital markets, and widens the scope to spillover effects via interest rates, risk premiums, and investment.

But, in my opinion, it overlooks two important developments. On the one hand, a growing proportion of internationally traded commodities come from the Northern economies, the Organization for Economic Cooperation and Development (OECD) countries, and the Soviet bloc. On the other hand, the developing countries—mainly the newly industrialized economies—export more and more manufactured goods. By 1982, manufactures accounted for 52 percent of all non-fuel exports of developing countries, with primary products accounting for only 48 percent; this compared with shares of 75 and 25 percent, respectively, in 1970.

What is important here is that a large part of the manufacturing export surge by the developing countries reflects increases in market shares, owing to their improved competitiveness. What matters here is not only the level of demand from the North, but its readiness to absorb competitive imports from the South—that is, the degree of openness of the North's economies. Here, trade policies are just as important as macroeconomic conditions.

Second, the Muscatelli and Vines paper singles out three requirements of cooperative global policies between the North and South: a favorable global environment, satisfactory adjustment policies in the developing world, and an appropriate net flow of financial resources to the South.

Many of us would probably agree that the domestic policies carried out by the developing countries are by far the strategic element in these countries' development. It seems to me that, for some major middle-income indebted countries, mere macroeconomic adjustment is not enough to resume growth. What those countries need is to move from policies that create and support domestic economic rents and inefficiencies toward deep structural reforms, ranging from market liberalization to breaking down trade barriers, slimming down public-sector industries, broadening and strengthening the tax system, and securing social and infrastructural services—as well as improving income and wealth distribution.

How can the North most effectively contribute to bringing about such changes? The International Monetary Fund and the World Bank, through conditionality attached to their support, have such reforms, but are there other channels through which the North could encourage and actually support trade liberalization in the developing countries?

For example—and here I am talking in my personal capacity and not as a European Community (EC) official—I wonder whether the major trading partners, instead of indulging in rigid attitudes and sometimes tactical posturing on agricultural issues in Montreal (at the December 1988 OECD ministerial meeting), should not get together to offer to the middle-income developing countries strategic trade-offs, specifically, a trade-off between their trade liberalization over a long period—departing from the special and preferential treatment granted by Part 4 of the General Agreement on Tariffs and Trade—in return for an effort by the industrial countries to bring down all the obstacles that make up the so-called gray area measures of the GATT so as to increase effective access to their markets.

An improved integration of the developing countries into the multilateral trading system would help them diversify their exports, which would make them less vulnerable to shocks coming from the global environment.

The reason I emphasize this microeconomic issue, rather than macro-economic relationships between North and South, is because I am deeply convinced that such qualitative progress would be crucial to the development of the developing world—especially for the middle-income countries. Such progress would be more effective—especially if combined with an effort by the developing countries to improve their domestic policies—than any demand pull from the North, which has been achieved for the last six years and is unlikely to go on indefinitely.

Now let me come to a third point, the agenda for the developing world. Here, it seems to me that the authors' objective of developing a model for the South—that is, Africa, Latin America, the newly industrialized economies, and other Asian countries—to be embedded within a global simulation model is, of course, an interesting one, and I welcome this recognition of the fundamental differences among developing countries. The concept of "the South" is clearly no longer an operational one for economic policy and management of interdependence.

But neither is the North homogeneous. The dominant economies—the United States, Japan, and the EC countries—differ widely with respect to economic performance, external vulnerability, long-term economic strategy, and domestic and external imbalances.

Moreover, lack of cooperation within the North may have dramatic consequences for the South, regardless of the degree of cooperation between North and South. A good example is, of course, the lack of effective coordination of fiscal policy among the major industrial countries, with the attendant adverse consequences for the South in terms of interest rates.

Thus, for a global cooperation model to be a fully operational input in decision-making processes, North and South ought to be disaggregated and the key channel of intra- and inter-group interdependence brought clearly into evidence. An additional problem to take into account is the direct interdependence that may exist between some sub-groups from the North and some from the South. For an example of such a bilateral sort of relationship, look at the current relationship in the Pacific area between Japan and its Asian neighbors, where we see Japanese financial surpluses and technology combining with cheap Asian labor to export an increasing flow of manufactured goods to the United States. Another example—although a very different one—would be the relationship between the European Community and Africa through the prefer-ential trade agreement with regard to access for African commodities and tropical products to the EC.

Participants*

Authors

Ralph C. Bryant
Senior Fellow, The Brookings Institution, Washington

Daniel Cohen
Professor of Economics, University of Nancy II, France

Andrew Crockett
Deputy Director, Research Department, International Monetary
Fund, Washington

David A. Currie
Professor of Economics and Director, Centre for Economic Forecasting,
London Business School, London

Jacob A. Frenkel
Economic Counsellor and Director, Research Department,
International Monetary Fund, Washington

Francesco Giavazzi
Professor of Economics, Universita degli Studi di Bologna, Italy

Morris Goldstein
Deputy Director, Research Department, International Monetary
Fund, Washington

John F. Helliwell
Professor of Economics, University of British Columbia, Canada

Gerald Holtham
Chief International Economist, Shearson Lehman Hutton, London

Peter Hooper
Assistant Director, Division of International Finance, Federal
Reserve Board, and Guest Scholar, The Brookings Institution, Washington

---

*Participants' titles indicated are those as of the time of the conference.

Andrew Hughes Hallett
Professor of Economics, University of Newcastle,
Newcastle upon Tyne, England

Paul R. Masson
Advisor, Research Department, International Monetary Fund, Washington

Warwick J. McKibbin
Head of Special Projects, Research Department, Reserve Bank of
Australia, Sydney, Australia

Marcus Miller
Professor of Economics, University of Warwick, Coventry, England

Anton Muscatelli
Professor of Economics, University of Glasgow, Glasgow, Scotland

Richard Portes
Director, Centre for Economic Policy Research, and Professor of
Economics, Birkbeck College, London.

Jeffrey D. Sachs
Professor of Economics, Harvard University, Massachusetts

John B. Taylor
Professor of Economics, Stanford University, California

David Vines
Professor of Economics, University of Glasgow, Glasgow, Scotland

Paul Weller
Professor of Economics, University of Warwick, Coventry, England

John Williamson
Senior Fellow, Institute for International Economics, Washington

Charles Wyplosz
Ecole des Hautes Etudes en Sciences Sociales, Fontainebleau,
France

Discussants
David Begg
Professor of Economics, Head of Economics Department, Birkbeck
College, London

James M. Boughton
Advisor, Research Department, International Monetary Fund, Washington

William Branson
Professor of International Economics, Princeton University,
New Jersey

Pierre Defraigne
Director of North-South Relations, Commission of the European
Communities, Brussels

Michael P. Dooley
Chief, External Adjustment Division, Research Department,
International Monetary Fund, Washington

Mario Draghi
Executive Director, World Bank, Washington

Stanley Fischer
Vice President, Development Economics, and Chief Economist,
World Bank, Washington

Jeffrey A. Frankel
Visiting Professor of Public Policy, Harvard University,
Massachusetts

Alberto Giovannini
Professor of Economics, Columbia University, New York

Haruhiko Kuroda
Personal Secretary to the Minister, Ministry of Finance, Japan

Patrick Minford
Edward Gonnor Professor of Applied Economics, University of
Liverpool, Liverpool, England

Michael Mussa
William H. Abbott Professor of International Business, University
of Chicago, Illinois

Manfred J. M. Neumann
Professor of Economics and Director, Institut für Stabilisierungs-
und Strukturpolitik, University of Bonn, Bonn

Sylvia Ostry
Ambassador, Multilateral Trade Negotiations, External Affairs, Canada

Jacques J. Polak
President and Director of Per Jacobsson Foundation, and former Executive Director, International Monetary Fund, Washington

Massimo Russo
Director, European Department, International Monetary Fund, Washington

Jeffrey R. Shafer
Deputy Director, General Economics Branch, Organization for Economic Cooperation and Development, Paris

Vito Tanzi
Director, Fiscal Affairs Department, International Monetary Fund, Washington

Ralph Tryon
Economist, Research Department, International Monetary Fund, Washington